PRINCIPLES OF EDUCATION

S.S. Chandra
Rajendra K. Sharma

ATLANTIC
PUBLISHERS & DISTRIBUTORS (P) LTD

Published by

ATLANTIC

PUBLISHERS & DISTRIBUTORS (P) LTD

7/22, Ansari Road, Darya Ganj, New Delhi-110002
Phones : +91-11-40775252, 40775214, 23273880, 23275880
Fax : +91-11-23285873
Web : www.atlanticbooks.com
E-mail : orders@atlanticbooks.com

Branch Office: Chennai
Phones : +91-44-48531784, 28291383
E-mail : chennai@atlanticbooks.com

Printed & bound in India by Atlantic Print Services

PREFACE

This is a comprehensive book covering Principles of Education, Philosophy of Education—Western and Indian and Sociology of Education. It is based on the syllabi of all the Indian universities for B.Ed. and M.Ed. courses.

The book has been written in an analytical style. Each topic has been treated in detail so as to provide a thorough understanding to the readers. The conclusions on controversial issues have been arrived at through a balanced and systematic approach. Subject matter has been drawn from several authentic sources—Western and Indian. Language has been kept as simple as possible. Examples have been drawn from the Indian context to facilitate understanding. We have left no stone unturned to make this book an authentic source on the subject.

The book with such a vast coverage will be highly useful to the students and teachers of Education. It will serve as a good reference source to those pursuing research in this field.

S.S. Chandra
Rajendra K. Sharma

Contents

PART II

1

EDUCATION: MEANING, TYPES AND FUNCTIONS

The word education has its origin in the Latin word 'educatum' composed of two terms 'E' and 'Duco'. E' implies a progress from inward to outward while 'Duco' means developing or progressing. In its most literal sense, therefore education means becoming developed or progressing from inside to outside. Education, thus, is the process of developing the inner abilities and powers of an individual. The term is also often connected with the Latin 'educere', meaning a propulsion from the internal to the external. This Latin term means to educate through a change brought about by practice or usage. In this manner, education implies some kind of change for the better in a person.

In general usage, the term education is used either in its narrow sense or in its more liberal connotation. A slight elaboration of these two senses is given here.

MEANING OF EDUCATION IN THE WEST

Educational thinking, like every other branch of knowledge, started in the philosophical deliberation of the ancient Greek philosophers. Thus the meaning of education in west is initially available in the works of Plato. It is interesting to note that thousands of years ago Plato gave a meaning to education which is even now followed in the West with slight changes here and there. Plato defined education as a life-long process starting, "from the first years of childhood and lasting to the very end of the life"[1] He used the term education in a very wide sense, "which makes a man eagerly pursue the ideal perfection of citizenship and teaches him how rightly to rule and how to obey."[2] Education not only provides knowledge and skills but also inculcates values, training of instincts, fostering right attitudes and habits. In *Republic*, Plato points out, that "true education, whatever that may be, will have the greatest tendency to civilise and humanise them in their relation to one another and to those who are under their protection."[3] This humanist definition of education propounded by Plato is still the most widely accepted meaning of education in the West. Education everywhere has been

1. Plato, *Protagoras*, Jewett, 325.
2. Plato, *The Laws*, Jowett, 644.
3. Plato, *The Republic*, Jowett, 416.

taken as a process of inculcating values. As Plato said, "Now I mean by education that training which is given by suitable habits to the first instincts of virtue in children."[4] These views of Plato have been universally accepted in West as well as in the East. Education has been defined differently by the idealists, the pragmatists, the naturalists and the realist philosophers. However, its meaning has been generally idealistic. Without some sort of idealism there can be no education worth the name. In the words of Robert R. Rusk. "We may accept that the aim of education is the enhancement or enrichment of personality, the differentiating feature of which is the embodiment of universal values." [5] The Western educational philosophers have generally agreed that the growth of the human child is the essence of education. In the words of A.G. Hughes. "The essence of discipline is, thus not forced subordination to the will of the hated tyrants, but submission to the example of admired superiors. "In the middle ages Comenius declared education to be a process w hereby an individual developed qualities relating to religion, knowledge and morality, and thereby established his claim to be called a human being. "The fundamental principles of education", according to Froebel, "instruction and teaching should be passive and protective not directive and interfering."[6] The principle of liberty has found most eloquent expression in the definition of education given by Rousseau when he said, "Let us obey the call of Nature. We shall see that her yoke is easy and that when we give heed to her voice we find the joy in the answer of a good conscience."[7] Others have laid emphasis upon the social meaning of education whereby it aims at making an individual fit in the society, it was in this sense that Aidous Huxley said, "A perfect education is one which trains up every human being to fit into the place he or she is to occupy in the social hierarchy, but without, in the process, destroying his or her individuality."[8]

All the foregoing definitions have stated that education is the process of development. It, therefore, becomes necessary to discover what is implied in this development. Although the ability to learn depends upon development, but development is not synonymous with education. Development means the gradual and continuous progress of mind and body. Through this development the child acquires the following elements:

1. Knowledge of the environment by which he is surrounded.
2. The necessary motor control to fulfil his individual needs.
3. Linguistic abilities to enable him to converse.
4. Some know ledge of individual and collective relationships.

The development of all these elements begins at home itself. The educator's task is to continue this process and to encourage it while the child is at school.

In fact this process of development continues right through an individual's life time. Consequently, it is accepted that education in its general sense continues

4. Plato, *The Laws*, Jowett, 653.
5. Robert R. Rusk, *The Philosophical Bases of Education*, p. 154.
6. Froebel's *Chief Educational Writings on Education*, Translated by Dr. Fletcher, p. 32.
7. Rousseau. J. *Emile*, p. 151.-
8. Huxley. A., *Proper Studies*, Chatto and Windus, London (1928). p. 136

throughout a man's natural span of life. Even the successful teacher or educator himself remains a student throughout his life. On the one hand, he teaches certain things to some people but at the same time he learns something from them. All successful educators experience that the development undergone by their thoughts, personalities and abilities would have been impossible otherwise. In much the same way, people other than the educators, teach and learn simultaneously.

MEANING OF EDUCATION IN INDIA

Turning to the Indian approach, it becomes necessary to include the spiritual aspect also because it is accepted as a part of the development by education. In fact, Indian thinkers have placed special emphasis upon this. Yajnavalkya opined that only that is education which gives a sterling character to an individual and renders him useful for the world. Shankaracharya said that education is that which leads to salvation. Even the more recent educationists have stressed the importance of the spiritual aspect. In the words of A.S. Altekar, "Education has always been regarded in India as a source of illumination and power which transforms and ennobles our nature by the progressive and harmonious development of our physical, mental, intellectual and spiritual powers and faculties."[9]

This spiritual tradition has been carried on by contemporary Indian philosophers of education in their integral approach, synthesis of idealism and pragmatism, rationalism and humanism, diversity in unity and harmony of the individual and society. It was due to this emphasis on the spiritual meaning of education that Vivekanand said, "Religion is the inner most core of education."[10] In the words of Sri Aurobindo, "The child's education ought to be an outbringing of all that is best, most powerful, most intimate and living in his nature, the mould into which the man's action and development ought to run is that of his innate quality and power. He must acquire new things but he will acquire I hem best, most wholly on the basis of his own developed type and inborn force."[11] M.K. Gandhi expressed the same idea when he defined education by saying, "By education I mean an all round drawing out of the best in child and man, body, mind and spirit. Literacy is not the end of education not even the beginning. It is one of the means whereby man and woman can be educated. Literacy in itself is no education."[12]

SYNTHETIC DEFINITION

It is clear from the above discussion of the meaning of education in West and India, ancient and modern that it may be synthesised since all these accept some common characteristics of education. The following points concerning the meaning of education emerge from a review of the meaning of education in the West and in India:

1. *A life-long process.* Education according to most of the philosophers continues from birth to death. As Madam Paul Richard pointed out, the education of man,

9. Altekar, A. S., *Education in Ancient India*, p. 8.
10. Vivekanand, *Collected Works*, Volume V, p. 161.
11. Sri Aurobindo, *Essays on the Gita*, Arya Publishing House, Cal. (1949), p. 319.
12. Gandhi, M. K., *Harijan*, 31 -7-37.

"should begin at his very birth and it is to continue the whole length of his life."[13]

2. *Unfolding.* Education is a gradual unfolding. In his allegory of the cave Plato observed that "the power and capacity of learning exists in the soul already, and just as the eye was unable to turn from darkness to light, without the whole body, so too, the instrument of knowledge can only, by the movement of the whole soul, be turned from the world of the becoming into that of being and learn by degrees to endure the sight ofbeing and of the brightest and best of being or in other words of the good."[14] It is in the same sense that Sri Aurobuido said, "The chief aim of education should be to help the growing soul to draw' out that in itself which is best and make it perfect for a noble use."[15]

3. *Based on child psychology.* Western thinkers unanimously agree that true education should be based on child psychology . This again has been accepted by Indian philosophers of education. According to Sri Aurobindo, "Nothing can be taught to the mind which is not already concealed as potential knowledge in the unfolding soul of the creature."[16] Educational theory must be based on sound psychology. As Sri Aurobindo points out, "The true basis of education is the study of the human mind, infant, adolescent and adult."[17]

4. *Individual as well as social.* True education is individual as well as social. Plato brought out a scheme of education according to each individual's capacities to serve the society. Philosophers in the West have everywhere laid emphasis upon individual as well as social aims of education. Contemporary Indian philosophers also exhibit this tendency. M K. Gandhi said, "I value individual freedom, but you must not forget that man is essentially a social being. He has risen to his present status by learning to adjust his individuality to the requirements of social progress."[18]

5. *Total development.* Thus education by general agreement is a total development, physical, mental and spiritual, individual as well as social. This total development is the meaning of self-realisation. This synthesis of the different aspects of man's development is characteristic of not only idealism but also naturalism, pragmatism and realism. It is again the meaning of perfection, acclaimed as the aim of education by so many thinkers. It is also what is known as complete education. It is again the humanist meaning of education since man is a complex being having several aspects of his personality all of which require full development. According to Sri Aurobindo, education should help the individual to grow, "into a fulness of physical and vital energy and utmost breadth, depth and height of his emotional, his intellectual and his spiritual being."[19] The total development

13. *Sri Aurobindo and the Mother on Education*, Aurobindo Ashram, Pondicherry (First edition 1972), p. 59.
14. Plato. *The Republic.* Jowett, p. 518.
15. Sri Aurobindo. *A System of National Education*, p. 5.
16. Sri Aurobindo, *The Synthesis of Yoga*. New York. 1950. p. 2.
17. Sri Aurobindo, *A System of National Education*, p. 1.
18. Gandhi. M. K., *Hahjan*, 27-5-39.
19. Sri Aurobindo. *Birth Centenary Library*. Vol. 15, 1971, p. 605.

lays equal emphasis upon physical as well as spiritual growth. Without physical culture mental training has been considered as one-sided. In the words of Aldous Huxley, "Where the body is maladjusted and under strain, the mind's relations, sensory, emotional, intellectual, conative, with external reality are likely to be unsatisfactory."[20] Education aims at an all round and total perfection of the individual and society. Hence, physical culture should form an important part of the educational process. As Sri Aurobindo puts it, "If seeking is for a total perfection of the being, the physical part of it cannot be left aside, for the body is the material basis, the body is the instrument which we have to use."[21] Similar quotations may be hunted from other philosophers of education in West and East. The total development involves character development, development of social virtues and individual skills. It includes all the various aims of education. It involves all the functions of education in human life such as development of natural abilities, character building, personality integration, preparation for adult life, control and sublimation of basic instincts, creation of useful citizens, development of a sense of community, progress of culture and civilization, social welfare, use of leisure and synthesis of national as well as international consciousness.

TYPES OF EDUCATION

Education is a comprehensive concept which comprehends the knowledge obtained through newspapers, magazines, radio, television and other means, in addition to the formal education provided in colleges. The average individual interprets the term in the sense of college education, which is obviously different from the education obtained from the other sources. Educationists have distinguished between the various types of education in order to remove this confusion. Briefly, education is of the following kinds:

1. *General education.* As is evident from the name itself, general education is the minimal education required by an individual to satisfy all his various needs. It aims at developing the general qualities of the child, so that its personality can develop and it can become capable of adjusting to its environment. It also enables him to earn his livelihood and to behave properly, in accordance with his age. It is generally believed that this general education continues upto the eighth class. All modern states make general education compulsory for all children, and in many cases it is provided free of charge.

2. *Specific education.* General education, which is outlined above, is a supplement to specific education, which, as is evident, trains the child to pursue some specific profession or job. The modern age is a period of specialization. As long as an individual cannot perform some particular task better than any other person, he will find it difficult to make a place for himself in society. It is for this reason that nowadays individuals are given vocational guidance in order to help them to take up professions for which their abilities are best suited. If the individual is given some specific education which concurs with his inherited capabilities, he stands the best chance of developing these qualities to the limit. General education

20. Huxley, A., *Ends and Means*, p. 220.
21. Sri Aurobindo. *The Supramental Manifestation*, Sri Aurobindo Ashram, Pondicherry (1952), p. 8.

is more liberal while specific education is comparatively narrow. It is not so closely connected with the development of the person's general personality and character. This is the task of general education. Specific education is spread over a long period of time and is often centred in specialized institutions such as medical colleges, engineering colleges, technical institutes, etc. In each case, the aim is to make the individual proficient in a particular skill, be it curing sick people, designing or repairing machines, growing crops, or anything else. Besides, specific education is also often more expensive than general education. Few people can afford the burden of sending their children to medical and engineering colleges. General education, on the other hand, is within the reach of almost all people. It also does not require the possession of special mental traits. Specific education, on the contrary, can be really profitable only if the individual possesses mental and physical qualities commensurate with that profession. Specific education plays a very important role in a nation's development because it provides specially trained personnel in every field who can serve society and enhance the welfare of the nation.

3. *Formal education.* In another classification, education is divided into the formal and the informal. The former comprehends education as it is provided in educational institutions according to a particular pattern. In the school, the educator educates the educands according to a specific programme aiming at particular goal. He follows a predetermined syllabus. In this formal kind of education, the time and place of teaching are fixed, and the educand has to arrive at that place and at that specific time to receive education. The length of such education is also fixed in terms of years. Both the kinds of education mentioned earlier can be included under the formal classification because both are often provided in schools The advantages of the formal kind of education lie in that it can be scientifically and consistently provided to a large number of children simultaneously. The objectives of this education are also determined beforehand. Although, of course, education in one form or the other continues as long as a person lives, education in its more common meaning starts at the age of four or five and continues to the age of twenty-five. During this period the individual passes through a succession of institutions of primary, secondary and advanced education in the form of schools, colleges and universities. At all these places of learning he receives formal education, provided on a pattern determined by syllabus which is itself framed with a view to achieving certain fixed targets. The fact that it can be provided to a large number of people is an advantage but also a drawback. Because of its completely formal nature, formal education often fails to touch certain aspects of one's personality and leaves it completely undeveloped. At times, it can also become so detached from reality that it hinders rather than helps the educand in satisfying his needs. This fact can be seen in the case of the contemporary pattern of formal education in India. It would not be inaccurate to state that, in India, the more formal education a person receives after a certain stage, the more useless he becomes in facing the problems of real life. His adjustment deteriorates instead of improving.

4. *Informal education.* Informal education complements the formal education outlined above, without which formal education remains incomplete. Education of this kind has no specific time or place at which it is provided. Even the educator is not fixed. All fixed syllabi, rules, formalities are absent from it. Education of this kind is the education one receives while playing in field, talking to family members in the house, roaming around somewhere, in fact, everywhere. This kind of education never comes to an end, and it teaches the individual more than he can ever learn through his formal education. A child learns many things when he comes in contact with new people. He discovers many new worlds when he goes to new places. This education that he receives cannot be evaluated as formal education can. Formal education can be evaluated by some specific techniques, and the quality and quantity of education imbibed by the educand can be known. But this is not true of informal education for there is no standard of measure in its case. It also does not provide the recipient with a certificate or a degree. Informal education is a gradual process, for people learn a few things after years of experience. But the things learnt in this manner prove to be more valuable than all the degrees accumulated through formal education. Formal education provides education on specific subjects while informal education is more general in nature.

5. *Direct Education.* In another classification, education is divided into the direct and indirect classes. Direct education is the equivalent of formal education and specific education. In this form of education, the educator and the educand are in direct contact whence education on a specific subject is disseminated. Its chief advantage lies in the material learnt by the educand more by the example of the educator's personality and character than by the formal material he seeks to impart. It is for this reason that direct education was very much in vogue in India in the past. The student lived with the teacher and learnt various skills and sciences. Direct education becomes difficult when the number of students becomes very large, or education itself becomes very mechanical and purely vocational. It then loses the advantage of the direct contact between the educator and the educand. If the pattern of direct education is to be maintained, then the number of teachers must be very large, for one teacher can establish rapport only with a small number of educands. Once the value of direct education was realized, educationists stressed the importance of limiting the size of a class.

6. *Indirect education.* Direct education was efficacious and practicable in the past when the population was not too large and life had not become as complex as it is today. With the present increase in population, it is no longer possible to provide direct education to all the people. In the past this kind of education was popular also because of the comparative primitive forms of communication. Such modern developments as the printing press, radio, television, etc., have made it possible to communicate the ideas of the greatest thinkers to those people who have never come into direct contact with the thinkers themselves. For this reason, in the present context, indirect education has come to acquire greater significance than direct education. Many universities have undertaken to conduct correspondence

courses, which are a fine example of indirect education. In this form of education, the subject of a lecture is printed and posted to the student. The student is required to answer certain questions sent along with the lecture. These answers are sent by him to the university where they are evaluated and returned to the student with the appropriate guidance: As this kind of indirect education offers a better and more practical adjustment to the circumstances of a very large number of individuals, it is becoming increasingly popular, particularly in the West. All the books that are written by the greatest thinkers and read by a vast audience are an excellent example of this indirect education. It cannot be denied that irrespective of the abilities of the educator, he cannot provide complete education to the educand without turning to books for assistance. For this reason the scope and field of indirect education is increasing steadily. In the last few years, teaching through the medium of radio and television is becoming more popular and reaching a higher level of sophistication. In India, the All India Radio regularly broadcasts lectures and programmes on musical education, cultural education and the like. By this many millions of individuals gain some kind of education.

7. *Individual education.* Education is also classified into the individual and the collective groups. Many of the modern educational psychologists have stressed the importance of individual differences between people and suggested that the educator should pay individual attention to each educand, remove his difficulties and, if necessary, modify the syllabi and the teaching programme to suit the specific abilities and traits of the educand. Scientifically considered, this advice is very good, and if arrangements can be made to provide individual education at this level, nothing could be better. Kindergarten, Montessori and Project methods, all of which are modern methods of child education, attempt to provide the highest degree of individual attention possible. But where education is to be provided to a very large number of individuals, it is the most expensive kind of education yet devised since one educator can pay attention to the specific needs of only a very small number of students. The experiment conducted by Rabindra Nath succeeded as an experiment, but if it is accepted as a pattern for large scale education, it would be completely impractical. That is why arrangements are made for collective education, although the value of individual education can be clearly visualized.

8. *Collective education.* Collective education is provided to a group of individuals collected at one place. Formal education is often also collective education. Keeping in mind the obvious advantages of individual education, efforts are made to restrict the size of the group of educands. The very meaning of education would be lost if the educator lost all contact with the educands, if they are in too large a number. This form of education is comparatively economical of time and money because one single educator can teach a large number of educands. In view of the present size of the population, and the possibilities of its growing further, collective education is the only practicable answer to the need for universal education.

9. *Conscious education.* Education is also divided into the conscious and the unconscious kind. The conscious kind of education is the education which is

provided with a full knowledge of the objectives to be achieved through it. College education is of this kind. It is intended to fulfil certain predetermined objectives. Conscious education is arranged for the child by his parents and by the state, but the child deliberately receives conscious education.

10. *Unconscious education.* An individual does not learn all the things he actually knows consciously. Many of the important facts that a child learns are absorbed unconsciously from his natural and social environment which surrounds him. This kind of education is informal and since it supplements the education received consciously, neither can be said to be more or less important than the other.

Of the various classifications listed above, the division into the formal and informal classes is the most common. All the other classifications are based on some specific approaches to education, although most of them resemble each other. For example, formal education is also collective education. This classification of education into different kinds has been made by different educationists according to their individual standpoint. A study of each one of these can help to throw much light on the vast field of education and on the various aspects of it. In every classification, both the kinds described, supplement each other because the process of education is many-sided and synthesizing. It takes place at all times and places, but it does not remain the same in every circumstance. It has a multiplicity of forms, means, quantity and quality. It is imbibed both consciously and unconsciously by the individual.

NATURE OF EDUCATION

Difference between Art and Science

Some people associate the term science with a specific body of knowledge and then distinguish between science and arts. But as Biesanz and Biesanz have remarked, the criterion of science is attitude or approach, not subject matter. Karl Pearson has rightly pointed out that the unity of all sciences lies in their methodology, not in the subject matter. Science differs from art in its methodology. The other characteristics of science, besides its special method of working, are its factuality, its universality, the validity of its laws, its search for causal relations and its attempt to make predictions based on these laws. It is possible to distinguish between science and arts on the basis of these features. The arts do not possess these qualities, and neither can it profess a similar approach. Science is a system of truths in which, through a definite language and terminology, a search is made for truth for its own sake. Despite the practical application of its principles and laws, science is a theoretical discipline. Science lies in knowledge, while art consists in skill rather than in knowledge. Criterion of art is the skill of the craftsman, while the criterion of a scientist's ability lies not in his skill but in his knowledge. Art raises any individual to a high pedestal, but science does not do this invariably. The aim of science is to know, that of art is to do. It cannot be denied that some practical sciences are nearer to the arts than to theoretical science, but they cannot be identified with the arts because of their distinctively scientific method of working. Art includes skill and practice in addition to knowledge. Art cannot be achieved without practice and repetition. The craftsman is better than other people in performing his own brand of skill.

It is evident from the above delineation that education can be called a science as well as an art. Skill in teaching cannot be derived merely from theoretical or verbal knowledge. It is only after long practice that an individual can acquire some skill. This skill is not derived from his knowledge but from the qualities of his personality and character and his ability in explaining new problems in ever changing situations in education. In this manner the educator is an artist but at the same time, he is also a scientist. He approaches all elements which enter the sphere of teaching scientifically. He observes them, and on the basis of his observation he arrives at some general principles which can help in making forecasts for future situations.

Classification of Sciences

In order to understand the scientific nature of education, it is desirable to understand a famous classification of the sciences. This classification divides the sciences into two categories — theoretical and applied. Theoretical sciences are concerned with the search for truth for its own sake, without paying any attention to its practical applications. On the other hand, the applied sciences pay particular attention to the application of scientific principles to human life. In actual fact, if this distinction is analysed, it will be seen that no science can be classed as either purely theoretical or purely applied. A theory or principle lacks body without any practical application, while action or application without theory is unfounded. For example, general psychology is the theoretical aspect of psychology whereas applied psychology is its practical aspect. In the same way, sociology has a branch known as applied sociology. Much the same thing can be seen in the case of all other sciences. In actual fact, it is improper to attempt a separation of the theoretical and the practical. The successful educator must concentrate not only on gaining theoretical knowledge of the various sciences but also on a practical application of his knowledge in educational circumstances. In the field of science, a theory has value only so far as it has some practical utility. In the words of Prof. Sidgwick, "The history of education is the battle ground and burial ground of impractical theories and one who studies it is soon taught to abate his constructive self-confidence, and to endeavour humbly to learn the lessons and harmonise the results of experience." No teacher can hope to become a successful teacher by learning the principles of teaching. As Raymont puts it, "Good teaching, like the efficient practice of any other art, is a function of many variables, of which the study of principles and methods is only one." It is evident from this that the art of teaching comprehends many things — such as practice — in addition to the knowledge of the theories and methods of teaching.

Education is a Science and an Art

In must be evident from the above discussion that education can neither be categorized as a science nor as an art. It is both a science and an art. It is as proper to use the term art of education as it is to use the term science of education. And even as a science, educational science is neither exclusively theoretical nor only practical because it has a theoretical as well as a practical aspect. In fact, it is more a practical and applied discipline than a theoretical one. Hence, in classifying sciences, we would place education in both the theoretical and the applied categories. It is a social science. But, at the same time, since it is also a study of the ideals of education, it is also a normative discipline. The art of education requires the objectivity of the physical sciences like biology, the social aspect of the social sciences like psychology and sociology, and value considerations of the normative sciences like ethics and logic. In addition, it also needs practice in the process of teaching under actual educational circumstances.

FUNCTIONS OF EDUCATION IN HUMAN LIFE

Whatever is acquired in human life is the result of formal or informal education. When the child is born, he has no knowledge of his surroundings. Gradually he comes to recognize his environment by using his sense organs and by coming in contact with other people. Many ideas and habits he learns merely by observing others. But in no civilized society is it believed possible for an individual to be fit for adult life if he does not have some degree of formal education. For this reason, one finds arrangements for education everywhere. Not only in civilized societies, but even in primitive societies the adults try to educate adolescents in the ways of adult life. Among the tribals of India, this social education of the young girls and boys takes place at the dormitories. To put it briefly, the individual's character, personality, culture, thinking, commonsense, skills, habits and even the other less significant things of life depend upon education. The importance of education in human life is thus evident. This importance is further clarified if we look at the following functions of education:

1. *Development of natural abilities.* When the child is born, he is already possessed of many kinds of natural abilities. As the body grows the mind also grows, but the innate abilities and qualities do not develop quite so naturally and without aid. It is often said that if the mind is not exercised its abilities cannot be developed. Hence, the first aim of education is to try to develop such abilities as power of imagination, of thinking, etc., by providing appropriate opportunities and stimuli. It is for this reason that, as a part of child education, one of the first steps is to put various kinds of instruments and apparata before the child so that he can learn to use his sense organs. This is called education of senses. The child is also made to improve his power of thinking by presenting many different kinds of problems. His imagination is allowed to develop through the medium of various arts and skills He is taught to concentrate by using many kinds of techniques to attract his attention. The various methods of learning are brought to his notice by letting him do different kinds of work. He is also taught to make adequate use of the different parts of his body by various games and sports. Such basic requirements of life as eating, sleeping, sitting and walking, moving around, are taught to the child by the family itself. All these activities are part of the child's early education.

2. *Character-building.* Psychologists contend that the foundation of the child's character is laid in the first few years of his life. The impressions about behaviour and conduct that fall upon the infant's mind are later exhibited in the form of his character. The importance of character is hardly a subject to be discussed. It is developed by education, mainly informal education. Putting it differently, the infant's character is built up not so much by lectures and lessons as by the examples presented to him in the family, school, neighbourhood, group, etc. Character is the organisation of various sentiments. The focus of this organisation is the sentiment of self-regard. And it is upto the teacher and the child's parents to develop this sentiment of self-regard in the child. Once this is developed, the child can then move further on the road to self-development. Education is of particular significance in the development of a moral character because the child is not naturally endowed with the power of distinguishing between the right and the wrong. The difference between right and wrong is taught by adults. Socialization is an important factor in the development of a moral character. This is aided by story-telling, setting good examples and providing education of social life. In fact, many educationists believe thatthe aim of education is to develop a moral character. As Herbart has expressed it, the development of a good moral character amounts to education.

3. *Development of personality.* The patterns of behaviour that a child chooses in his adjustment with the individuals and objects in his environment depend upon his personality. It is the development of personality which leads to a development of individuality, which is an inevitable characteristic of an educated individual. The informal development of the personality takes place through his family, neighbourhood, the conditions of work, etc., but educationists believe that one important objective of education is to develop personality. Hence, the child is given opportunities of performing different kinds of work so that his personality may develop. Games play an important role in personality development. Child's personality achieves integration and strength in facing the many kinds of problems which make up a game. The social aspect of his personality is developed in the communal life of the school. Social customs, traditions, the forms of social control, cultural element, etc., also play an important part in developing the personality. It is for this reason that distinct differences can be seen in the personalities of individuals belonging to different cultures and societies. The first and most permanent influence upon the child's personality development is of the family. Such things as his order of birth in the family, his place among his brothers and sisters, the social and economic status of the family, the parents' behaviour towards the child, the mutual behaviour of the parents themselves, their profession etc., influence his personality. It is said that parental education plays a large part in building the personality of great men. Apart from this, the child's personality is influenced by many kinds of literature such as biographies of great men, stories, novels, essays, etc. It is believed that it is the duty of the teacher to prevent his wards from developing bad habits and also to see if the wards are developing balanced personalities. The teacher can take the assistance

of the psychologist and also of the parents in ensuring a healthy development of personality. If the child does not develop a balanced personality, it can be said that his education is incomplete.

4. *Preparation for adult life.* Livelihood is believed to be the aim of education. Economic factors controlling life in the present day world have become so complex that no one who is not properly educated can hope to successfully earn his living. In the past, most people pursued agriculture, which does not demand such a high degree of specialization. For them education was not so essential. But the recent developments in science and the increasing specialization of all professions has made it impossible for one individual to perform any job without previous training and education. As a general rule, highly paid jobs require specialized training of a very high calibre. The ability to earn enough is not the only factor to be considered in the preparation for adult life. Earning money is one of the aspects of adult life, another is marriage and children. Once this stage is reached, the individual has to face all the attendant responsibilities. Education aims at training the individual to earn his livelihood, to marry, to bring forth children, to fulfil his duties towards other individuals and society in general. In fact, if the child is helped to develop a balanced personality and a good character, there can be no better preparation for adult life. If education can perform this task, then men and women become highly responsible and useful citizens.

5. *Control and sublimation of basic instincts.* Every living being is born into the world possessed of certain basic instincts. There may be difference of opinion about the instincts that the child is born with, but there can be no doubt about the presence of some instincts. The child's mind is not a blank tablet on which anything can be written. Psychologists have demonstrated that not only does the human infant possess some instincts, but also that there are individual differences in respect of these instincts. If a human being lives alone, he can give expression to his instincts in any manner that he likes. But human beings live in groups, and hence it becomes necessary for them to control some instincts and to change the mode of expression of other instincts in such a manner that they do not injure other people. Besides, there are certain instincts which can be fulfilled only with the co-operation of another human being. Sex is one such instinct. Since, from the moral standpoint, the individuality and the humanity of every individual must be respected, it becomes necessary for people to control their instincts in all forms of communal life, such as marriage. Civilized life would become impossible if such instincts as aggressiveness and sex were not sublimated. Education helps in the control, sublimation and change of instincts. Various kinds of arts are used as a medium of sublimation. Education in social life helps the child to learn how to control his instincts. The same end is served through the system of reward and punishment found in the family, college or society at large. Rules of administration and the means of social control also help in this work.

6. *Creation of useful citizens.* Although many thinkers have dreamt of a society without government, in actual fact no such society exists. Individuals who have been deprived of their citizenship or have never been granted this, make all kinds

of efforts to get the citizenship of one nation or another. If they cannot obtain it, they have to face all kinds of difficulties. Hence, the relationship between the individual and the state is universal. In this relationship, the status of the individual is called the status of citizenship. Hence, it is desirable that the individual should be trained in behaving as a citizen so that he can fulfil his duties to the state. In the present age, this function of education is emphasized very much because most states themselves are responsible for providing education. In democratic systems, the public also plays a hand in guiding the educational system. But in communist countries, the state has complete control of the educational system. Despite this, it is believed that education must provide capable citizens, because in the absence of such citizens the adjustment between the individual and the state would suffer. The thinkers of ancient Greece believed that this is the most important function of education. Now-a-days almost all thinkers agree that true democracy in any country is possible only when almost all its citizens are properly educated. Education in responsible citizenship is also given through the medium of political parties, radio, television, newspapers, magazines, etc.

7. *Development of a sense of community.* The statement that man is a social animal means no more than that he lives in society. It does not imply that the human child is possessed of social qualities at birth. These social qualities are acquired and taught. One major objective of education, therefore, is the teaching of social qualities and development of a sense of community. This community feeling urges the child to co-operate with his fellows, to make sacrifices if they become necessary, to rise above the considerations of caste and creed and develop a sense of oneness with the nation, etc. The development of this feeling depends upon opportunities provided in family life, play groups and schools and colleges. For this reason educational institutions pay particular attention to this. The student is given the opportunity of collectively running the administration, of organising extracurricular programmes, of devising constructive programmes which help in developing this sense of community. This feelingis the basis of national unity. The efforts being made in India to-day to evolve an emotional unity are in fact efforts to develop this feeling of community.

8. *Protection and increase of culture and civilization.* As compared to other animals, man has progressed more because human society has succeeded in protecting its knowledge and in conveying it to future generations. This has been done through the medium of culture and civilization. A child born in the present time does not think of everything from the beginning. His thinking and modes of behaviour are determined by customs, traditions and social institutions, which are repositories of the experience and thinking of his ancestors. For this reason, societies which have a more ancient culture show signs of greater organisation, systematization and greater stability. Hence, it is now universally accepted that culture and civilization should be protected and allowed to grow through new developments. This is mainly achieved through education. The child receives the social heritage in the form of education. Then, through education the child develops his own knowledge, character and personality thus becoming capable of

contributing to the literary, cultural and social life of his society. In this manner he helps to maintain his own culture and to add to it. Developments in the arts, literature, the sciences, etc., are all the efforts of educated people. Their efforts are collected in the form of books and objects in libraries, museums, etc., and thus passed on as social heritage to the coming generations. For this reason many contemporary thinkers in India have suggested that teaching of Indian culture should be made compulsory in all universities.

9. *Encouragement to social welfare.* Both formal and informal education helps the individual to evolve a critical attitude which helps him to analyse everything presented to him. If he finds any faults in it, he exercises his mind to find some ways of removing the faults. In this manner education has been the basis of all social welfare programmes. When English education was introduced in India, it brought along with it the Western tendencies of individualism, rationalism, etc. As a consequence all educated people in the country were impelled to re-examine ancient Indian traditions and institutions. This led to the development of such institutions as the Brahmo Samaj, Arya Samaj, Prarlhana Samaj, Theosophical Society etc. Each one aimed at social welfare. And the inspiration for each of these institutions came from highly educated individuals. Education thus leads to a continuous analysis of the various constituents of society, its institutions, modes of social control, etc., and inspires efforts to make improvements where they are needed.

10. *National development.* The overall development of all national groups is essential for the development and progress of human society, but this is not possible without universal education. It is for this reason that the U.N.O. is making efforts to provide education to the backward countries. In every country, efforts are made to develop a sense of belonging among its citizens, the sense of nationality. It helps to induce the individual to do his best for the nation. Besides, almost every nation has its own plan of national education which seeks to fulfil the aims of that nation.

11. *Use of leisure.* One of the main aims of education is to teach an individual to make the best use of leisure. Using leisure time in educational activities is itself useful. On the other hand, education itself guides the individual to utilize his leisure time properly. Educated people can use their leisure time effectively by devoting themselves to magazines, arts, etc. Even the standard of their normal conversation, discussions, etc., is higher than that of the uneducated person. Education helps to develop various kinds of interests so that leisure itself does not become a burden.

12. *Increasing consciousness of other cultures.* In countries in which many different cultural groups co-exist, education helps to increase consciousness of these other cultures and of cultural exchange. This helps individuals to understand each other, thus increasing national unity. There are many different cultures in the world today. As long as education cannot create a feeling of cooperation and of mutual love, the ideal of a unified world cannot be realized.

16. *Improving emotional unity.* At the present time, many disintegrating forces such as regionalism, casteism, communalism, linguism, etc., are working towards

a complete disintegration of the country. If the nation is to be saved from complete fragmentation, it is necessary to generate a sense of emotional unity in all men and women. Then individuals can be expected to feel that they are members of the same nation and to behave in the interests of the nation. Education can help to create this emotional unity. Many educationists have given valuable suggestions for achieving this.

14. *Developing an international feeling.* As a result of the unprecedented improvements in the means of transport and communications, people of different nations are constantly coming into contact with each other. All kinds of people are also realizing the importance of internationalism, after having witnessed the havoc caused by the two recent world wars. All contemporary educationists in India, including Sri Aurobindo, Rabindra Nath, Vivekanand, have stressed the importance of creating this feeling of internationalism in all educands. In the present context, therefore, one of the main tasks of education is to generate this sense in the student community.

From the foregoing description of the functions of education in human life, it is evident that the functions of education are the same as its objectives. To put it differently, the objectives which have been assigned to education by various thinkers are the tasks it has to do. It need hardly be stressed that the functions of education change when ideals governing it undergo changes. Nevertheless, the fundamental elements of human life are the same today as they were in Plato's and Aristotle's times. Hence, such aims of education as character building, development of personality, social welfare, proper use of leisure, protection of culture and civilization, development of community feeling, creating able citizens, preparation for adult life, development of innate qualities, etc., are permanent objectives which will remain the same in future also.

FUNCTIONS OF EDUCATION IN NATIONAL LIFE

The functions of education in national life differ somewhat from its functions in normal life because human life is possible even without a nation. Primitive societies still do not possess any kind of nation. Nations are found in more civilized societies. Before examining the role of education in national life, it is necessary to discover the nature of a nation. Nation is a group of human beings which lives in a country delimited by geographical boundaries. This group is possessed of a desire to be bound by common traditions, common interests, similar political ambitions and political unity. The important aspects of national life can be understood from this description. For national life to be possible, it is essential that its members should have common traditions, interests, sentiments and political ambitions, and an emotional unity. Education aims at creating and maintaining all these various elements, and thus it contributes to national life. The following points are to be considered in this connection:

1. *Maintaining communal interests and traditions.* The main objective in applying a uniform system of education to an entire nation is that a similarity of interests and traditions may be generated among the people. For India, this is of even

greater importance, because the nation is composed of many different cultural and linguistic groups. Education achieves this similarity and identity through its prescribed syllabi and various kinds of extra-curricular programmes.

2. *Similarity of political ambitions.* If different groups within a single nation are found to possess various and contradictory political ambitions, it becomes difficult to maintain that nation's independence and unity. One chief objective of education, thus, is to propagate similar political ambitions among all classes and groups of people. In India, young men and women who received English education studied the history of Western nations and concluded that India must also win its freedom. Once this political awakening spread among the educated classes and led to similarity of political ambitions, national movements took shape and the demand for a free India was put forward. In the more recent context, education should aim at creating a desire for complete and comprehensive development of the nation so that people may rise above their own narrow interests and work in the interests of the nation as a whole.

3. *Diffusion of emotional unity.* It is obvious that one task of education is to diffuse a feeling of emotional unity in the younger generation so that all its members may feel identified with the nation and be inspired to work for its improvement. Such forces of disintegration as communalism, casteism, linguism, regionalism, etc., can be countered only when emotional unity is increased. For this the educational programme should insist on the teaching of the same history, same cultural heritage, etc. Sense of community is an essential part of nationalism and the foundations of sense of belonging to a community are laid in schools. Hence, efforts should be made to create such an atmosphere in schools that the students may have a sense of belonging, not of alienation.

4. *Development of a national language.* Although the development of many different languages and the common use of them does not hinder national unity in any way, the absence of a single common language hinders it considerably since language is the medium through which thoughts and emotions are expressed. Just as thoughts and language are intimately connected, nationalism and language are also intimately related to each other. Hence, one objective of education is the development of a national language. In India, the Constitution has laid down Hindi as the national language and it has been accepted in principle that this language must be spread over the entire country. But it is regrettable that the work of giving this status to Hindi is not progressing as fast as is desirable. If greater efforts are not made in this direction, it may create a danger to national unity in the country. Hence, it is desirable that the teaching of Hindi should be compulsory at all stages of education.

5. *Respect to all religions.* India is a secular state in that it grants equal status and importance to every religion, and refuses to discriminate between citizens on the basis of their religious beliefs. But despite this provision of the Constitution, the poison of communalism is found in greater abundance in the country, and it has been impossible to remove it despite the greatest efforts. One way of achieving this is to indoctrinate the children through education that every religion deserves

equal respect and that one's own religion is not necessarily the best. Education must seek to eliminate all such prejudices. Hence, in a country like India, one task of education is to generate respect for all religions.

6. *Training for leadership.* Proper development in any sphere can be achieved only if there is adequate leadership. A country can progress only if it has able leaders in the social, economic, political, literary, cultural, artistic, industrial and moral fields. Education can provide such leaders. Hence, one of the objectives of education is to bring forth leaders in various spheres and to train them to perform their tasks efficiently. This can be done by encouraging student participation in various kinds of extra-curricular programmes in the college so that the student's capabilities can find expression. This also helps to train him in leadership.

7. *Fulfilling the need for skilled workers.* In addition to leaders, every sphere needs the dedication and cooperation of skilled and efficient workers. Such workers are required not only in industry and commerce, but also in the social and political spheres. This need can be fulfilled by education. During the process of education it is possible to discover the sphere for which a particular individual is best suited. Once this has been found out, he can then be trained in his particular profession.

8. *Consciousness of duties.* If a nation is to progress, it is essential that its citizens should be aware of their duties and responsibilities. Education can spread this awareness among the people. In schools the students are told of their responsibilities as members of the nations. This awareness of their duties is created in them, and they are also taught how they can fulfil these duties. This role of education is of the greatest importance in democratic states.

9. *Evolution of a national feeling.* The strength of national feeling in an individual is judged by the extent to which he can subjugate his personal and narrow class interests in favour of the wider national interest and the extent to which he is prepared to work for the national interests. For this it is essential that the individual should be conscious of his duties to the nation as well as capable of rising above narrow interests of regionalism, communalism, casteism, etc. Both these can be made possible through education. National feeling is generated among the students in the colleges through various extra-curricular programmes and syllabi. Butin fact the informal modes of education, such as family, newspapers, magazines, radio, television, etc., play an important role in generating a national feeling. National education programmes should pay particular attention to these and to the creation of a national literature.

It is evident from the work of education in national life that the members of the nation should be educated in such a way, through the teaching of national history, the national language, different kinds of programmes, etc., that a national sentiment should be created in them. They should begin to consider national interests as higher than any other interest, and they should be prepared to make any sacrifice for the nation. It is education which provides efficient leadership in the various spheres of national endeavour, and it is education which maintains the nation's heritage and hands it over to the future generations.

2

FORMAL, INFORMAL AND NON-FORMAL EDUCATION

FORMAL EDUCATION

In another classification, education is divided into the formal and the informal. The formal comprehends education as it is provided in educational institutions according to a particular pattern. In the school, the educator educates the educands according to a specific programme aiming at a particular goal. He follows a predetermined syllabus. In this formal kind of education the time and place of teaching are fixed, and the educand has to arrive at that place and at that specific time to receive education. The length of such education is also fixed in terms of years. Both the kinds of education mentioned earlier can be included under the formal classification because both are often provided in schools. The advantages of the formal kind of education lie in that it can be scientifically and consistently provided to a large number of children simultaneously. The objectives of this education are also determined beforehand. Although, of course, education in one form or the other continues as long as a person lives, education in its more common meaning starts at the age of four or five and continues to the age of twenty-five. During this period the individual passes through a succession of institutions of primary, secondary and advanced education in the form of schools, colleges and universities. At all these places of learning he receives formal education, provided on a pattern determined by syllabus which is itself framed with a view to achieving certain targets. The fact that it can be provided to a large number of people is an advantage but also a drawback. Because of its completely formal nature, formal education often fails to touch certain aspects of one's personality and leaves it completely undeveloped. At times, it can also become so detached from reality that it hinders rather than helps the educand in satisfying his needs. This fact can be seen in the case of the contemporary pattern of formal education in India. It would not be inaccurate to state that, in India, the more formal education a person receives after a certain stage, the more useless he becomes in facing the problems of real life. His adjustment deteriorates instead of improving.

INFORMAL EDUCATION

Informal education complements the formal education. Education of this kind has no specific time or place at which it is provided. Even the educator is not fixed. All fixed syllabi, rules, formalities are absent from it. Education of this kind is the education one receives while playing in field, talking to family members in the house, roaming around somewhere, in fact, everywhere. This kind of education never comes to an end, and it teaches the individual more than he can ever learn through his formal education. A child learns many things when he comes in contact with new people. He discovers many new worlds when he goes to new places. This education that he receives cannot be evaluated as formal education can. Formal education can be evaluated by some specific techniques, and the quality and quantity of education imbibed by the educand can be known. But this is not true of informal education for there is no standard or measure in its case. It also does not provide the recipient with a certificate or a degree. Informal education is a gradual process, for people learn a few things after years of experience. But the things learnt in this manner prove to be more valuable than all the degrees accumulated through formal education. Formal education is on specific subjects while informal education is more general in nature.

NON-FORMAL EDUCATION

In July 1979, the Central Board of Secondary Education, New Delhi, started the Open School — the first of its kind in the country. It is an institution set up to bring the flexibility and openness in the educational system and to extend educational opportunities to the weaker and disadvantaged sections of the society. The main objectives of the Open School are the following:

1. To offer a parallel non-formal system as an alternative to formal schooling.
2. To provide the opportunity of education to out-of-school learners, school drop-outs, working adults, housewives and learners from disadvantaged sections of society living in remote areas of the country.
3. To offer bridge/preparatory courses for enabling learners to take up secondary level courses.
4. To offer Secondary, Senior Secondary, Technical, Vocational and life enrichment courses through distance teaching methods.
5. To promote an open distance-learning system of education through research, publication and information dissemination.

This is an example of non-formal education

Non-formal Education is an arrangement wherein flexibility is the key word. Such a system is an open one with regard to various aspects of education, *i.e.*, admissions, curriculum, place of instruction, mode of instruction and the time and duration of instruction. Various examples of such a system are the Open School and Open University, Open Learning and the Correspondence Courses.

Definition of Non-Formal Education

Non-formal education includes adult education, continuing education and on the job-education, etc. Philip Coombs talked about it in 1968. However, until 1970 it had not been defined. Non-formal education is a new concept for an ancient phenomenon. Some of its definitions are as follows:

1. *Coombs and Ahmed (1974).* "Any organized, systematic, educational activity carried on outside the framework of the formal system to provide selected types of learning to particular sub-groups in the population, adults as well as children."
2. *La Bella.* Non-formal education refers to "organized out-of-school educational programmes designed to provide specific learning experiences for specific target population."
3. *Illich and Freire.* Non-formal education is anti-formal education.
4. *Mott Lal Sharma.* "In brief one could say that non-formal education is an active, critical, dialectical educational programme which aims at helping people to learn, to help themselves, to place them in consciously critical confrontation with their problems. To develop integrated authentic human beings who can contribute to the development of the society is the aim of Non-formal education. In this not only the individuals but also the total system learns, adding up to a true learning society."

Nature of Non-Formal Education

Non-formal education is the "missing ingredient" in accelerated social and economic development schemes that do not work. Therefore, it has its own valid claim to reality. It is deliberate, planned, staffed, financially supported like formal education. It is functional, unrestricted as to time and place and in general responsive to needs like formal education. It is much more responsive to needs and change. Thus, it is a more effective tool for rural development. It unlocks the doors of development plans. According to Malcom A. Adiseshiah, "Non-formal education should be marketable and vocationalised. It should lay emphasis on the self-learning pattern." According to H.S.S. Lawrence, "Non-formal education system was not rival to the formal educational system but it was complementary to the latter. The common ingredients in both should be identified and an integrated system evolved."

Non-formal Education and Adult Education

Explaining the difference between non-formal and adult education Anil Bordia writes, 'The New Non-formal Education Plan differs from previous adult education programmes in that it provides for adequate administrative and resource support and emphasizes need-based curricula and teaching and learning materials; but it is unique in emphasizing evaluation at all stages on a continuing basis. All training programmes and teaching and learning materials are to be pretested and also subjected to impact studies."

Origin of Non-formal Education

After the World War II, in the post-colonial period new nations, one after another, scrambled for expanded and improved formal education. By the late sixties, there was a growing uneasiness that expansion in the facilities in formal education was not the whole answer. The traditional two-fold categorisation of education into formal and informal education leaves a big gap. Studies by Philip Coombs and others revealed that as societies developed, a third kind of education emerged which could be labelled as non-formal education. Thus, non-formal education accounts for much of the highly functional, developmental and short term related needs of a rapidly changing society.

Advantages of Non-formal Education

To sum up, Non-formal education is needed on account of the following advantages:

1. Universaliztion of primary education.
2. Eradication of adult illiteracy.
3. Meeting the omissions of formal education.
4. Meeting the enormous and imperative challenges of democratic set-up.
5. Enabling the pupils to learn and earn.
6. Enabling those students to study who had to discontinue formal education owing to pecuniary and other circumstances.
7. Enabling the students in geographically remote areas to get education because the formal education cannot be within their easy reach.
8. Enabling individuals to refresh and update their knowledge.
9. Rectifying the educational imbalance between those who live in villages and those who live in towns.
10. Providing educational facilities to socially and economically neglected sectors of society.

Objectives of Non-formal Education

Following are the three sets of objectives of Non-formal education:

1. The immediate objective is the removal of illiteracy.
2. The middle-range objective is the application of 'new' knowledge to resolve economic, cultural and social problems.
3. The long-range objective is to provide for life-long education.

Types of Non-formal Education Programmes

1. Adult Functional Literacy Programmes.
2. Correspondence Courses.
3. Open School Studies.

4. Satellite Instructional Television Programme.
5. Programme for drop-outs in the age-group 6—14.

Persons Benefited by Non-formal Education

Non-formal education is particularly useful for the following categories of persons:

1. *People of all ages.* Those who never had the opportunity to follow any formal education programme.
2. *Students.* Those who are not in a position to complete primary, middle or secondary school.
3. *Learners.* Learners of different stages of education who feel the need for deeper and more comprehensive knowledge in a subject of particular interest.
4. *Labourers.* Both in urban and rural areas, young workers, small farmers, landless labourers, small entrepreneurs, etc., who need up-to-date knowledge related to their job particularly related to latest technological improvements.
5. *Educated unemployed.* Unemployed educated persons of various age groups whose non-relevant education needs to be made relevant in order to increase their chances of employment.
6. *Graduates, perfessionals, intellectuals.* Those who need a refreshment or orientation to make themselves up-to-date in their knowledge.
7. *Other Persons.* Those who require programmes for personal satisfaction like recreation, leisure time activities, cultural or artistic programmes, etc.

AGENCIES OF NON-FORMAL EDUCATION

The various agencies for organizing programmes for non-formal education are as follows:

1. Institutions for formal education.
2. Special agencies for non-formal education such as Nehru Yuvak Kendras, training centres in factories, public libraries, centres of correspondence education, etc.
3. Voluntary non-government organizations like clubs and societies.
4. Radio and television.

Non-formal education is one of the modes of education, others are formal and informal. Therefore, non-formal education ought to be perceived and designed in co-ordination with formal and informal systems. It will prove an insufficient and an ineffective mechanism for solving the complex problems or for achieving concrete goals if organized in isolation. Again, it must not be limited to the imparting of basic skills only. It must be designed as an integrated system in the context of the total socio-economic environment. To make it effective in modern societal context, a more integrated community based programme of innovation and change is needed to which various forms of education may contribute. This requires filling the gaps between the learning systems and the community needs.

Formal *Vs.* Non-Formal Education

Formal Education	*Non-formal Education*
1. Limited to a period taught.	1. Life-long and not limited to any period of being taught.
2. Generally not integrated with work.	2. Integrated with work.
3. Has fixed points of entry and exit.	3. Has flexible points of entry, exit, re-entry and re-exit. In fact, it continues throughout the life span of the individual.
4. Has fixed points curriculum.	4. Has a diversified and varied curriculum.
5. In it the 'giver' dominates and the 'receiver' is rather passive.	5. A process of sharing, exploring, analysing and judging together.
6. Geared to knowledge acquisition.	6. A process of enabling the individual to understand his needs, the environmental situations and mutual relationships.
7. Fosters an uncritical obedience.	7. An open-end process of education which develops self-reliant awareness.
8. Works within a fixed social frame,	8. Anticipates and prepares for change.
9. Associated with traditional schooling, schooling confined to a school or a college, etc.	9. Not confined to any educational set-up.
10. Rigid withregard to various aspects of education, *i.e.,* admissions, curriculum, place of instruction, mode of instruction, the time and duration of instruction.	10. Very flexible in regard to various aspects of education.

One should try to avert the danger of education being isolated from the subject-matter of life-experience. Hence one of the weightiest problems with which the philosophy of education has to cope with is the method of keeping a proper balance between the informal, the formal and non-formal, the incidental and the international modes of education. It may be remembered that one should try to incorporate the virtue of informal education as far as he can and also to keep away the dangers of too much formal education.

3

AIMS AND OBJECTS OF EDUCATION

The aims of education are determined by human life. Putting it differently, the aims of education are formulated after deciding the kind of life we want human beings to lead. In addition to this, the aims of education are also determined by the kind of life human beings live. It can thus be said that the aims of education are based upon human nature. Since the basic form of human nature has remained unchanged over many centuries, the aims of education have also remained the same while humanity has passed through many centuries. For example, the human being is constituted not only of the reason and intellect, but also of emotions and the body. Any system of education which seeks to fulfil its aims must provide for the development of all these aspects. In view of the complex social and economic structure of human society, every adult human being is faced with the necessity of earning his bread and of fulfilling his various needs. In view of this permanent necessity of human life, one of the aims of education has always been to equip the individual to earn his livelihood. Man has to fight with nature to ensure his own existence, and in this process he needs his physical abilities and powers. For this reason children are taught to maintain their health, not only in civilized societies but even in the most primitive ones. Education is also made to conform to the changing environment of a particular social group so that its later generations may be able to adjust better. For this reason one finds distinct differences in the pattern of education in societies living near the coast and societies living inland.

AIMS OF EDUCATION IN HUMAN LIFE

It is evident from the above description that the aims of education are intimately connected with human life. The following points can be made in this connection:

1. *Livelihood.* As has been already pointed out, livelihood is essential for human life everywhere. Hence, one of the main aims of education is to train men and women according to their abilities so that they can earn their own livelihood.

2. *Development of personality.* A balanced development of personality is essential for the individual's private and social life, for without this he can neither satisfy all his needs nor lead a successful life. Consequently, all modern educationists unanimously agree that education must aim at the complete development of human personality.

3. *Intellectual development.* Man is distinct among all living beings because of his intelligence. It is on the basis of his intelligence that he has become superior to all other forms of life. Through his intelligence he developed the sciences and by using them he has gained mastery over nature. It will, therefore, be quite in order to state that all his future progress depends to an extent upon his intellectual development. This, too, has become one of the major aims of education.

4. *Physical development.* In the struggle for survival, man needs a healthy and strong body, for without it, he cannot either live or satisfy his requirements. Hence, education must also aim at developing the individual's body,

5. *Moral development.* Ethical and moral values are considered the most important in human life. Character is the most valuable thing an individual can possess. Success in human life in every sphere, be it the family, the neighbourhood, society at large, depends very much upon the possession of moral qualities and upon obedience of moral laws. The importance of moral values is even more evident in the modern world due to the unprecedented improvement in the means of transport and communications and the remarkable power of destruction possessed by modern weapons. In the absence of ethical values there would be little to prevent the world from being destroyed in catastrophic wars. For this reason, moral and ethical development has also become an important object of education.

6. *Aesthetic development.* As other living beings are, man is not satisfied merely by maintaining his existence. He seeks to raise his life above the level of survival, and the things he needs for his requirements must not only be useful but also attractive and aesthetically satisfying. Cultural development includes development of the sensibilities, awareness of the aesthetically satisfying in art and literature. Education also seeks to develop the aesthetic sensibility.

7. *Social development.* Most of man's life is spent in a social environment, and in order to accommodate to this environment, the individual requires many social qualities. Education tries to develop these social qualities to facilitate the child's social adjustment.

8. *Cultural development.* When human beings are to be distinguished from other living beings, they are said to be cultured. Culture is man's prerogative, since it is not found among other animals. It is culture which maintains a man's relationship with his ancestors and ensures his own connections with the succeeding generations. He gets it as his social heritage and passes it on. Cultural development is also an important aspect of education.

9. *Spiritual development.* Another distinctive feature of human life is the presence of the spiritual element. It is for this reason that Indian religious texts state that human life is granted to the soul after it has lived the life of other living beings. Man's superiority is thus the result of his spirituality. He is not merely a more efficient animal. He even seeks to identify himself with the divine power. His future depends to a large extent upon this spiritual development. Thus, spiritual development is also accepted as one of the aims of human education. Religious education is introduced solely for this purpose.

10. *Total development.* Man is a complex being, made up of such physiological parts as the motor organs, sense organs, nervous system, etc., such processes as intelligence, emotions, feelings, etc., the social, cultural and other aspects of personality. In view of this complexity, it is believed that education must seek to develop every aspect of the human individual. He is trained to make the best use of his body. Efforts are made to develop his intellectual, moral, aesthetic, social and cultural aspects. Some people believe that this is the ideal of human perfection.

11. *Training for civic life.* It has already been explained that, in civilized societies, human life is identical with social life. Hence, education seeks to train the individual to live as a citizen and to fulfil all his obligations to society.

12. *Training in international living.* The individual of today is not restricted in his movement by the boundaries of his country. In the West, in particular, people commonly move from one country to another. It is now commonly felt that if man is to rise above his present level, he must be prepared to discard his narrow nationalistic leanings and adopt more universal or international attitude. Since this is a new situation, another objective has been imported into the mandate of education, and that is, it must prepare the educand for international living.

IMPACT OF SOCIAL IDEALS AND SOCIAL LIFE

(a) **Social Life and the Aims of Education.** In the history of human civilization, one can see considerable changes in the pattern and form of social life, as new attitudes and scientific and technological developments made their impact. Social life today is so different from the primitive social life because of technology. The recent remarkable developments in science and technology have led to important changes in human values. As a consequence, one of the aims recently given to education, in most civilized countries, is to provide technical and professional training. In addition to the technological developments, economic changes have also influenced social life considerably. Industrialization and urbanization have influenced economic change. Increases in population have only added to the complexity of economic problems. For this reason education is faced with the problem of providing such training as will improve the practical and vocational skill of the individual so that he may be able to earn his livelihood and also make his contribution to national development.

The democratic values of equality, fraternity and liberty are now part of social life In almost every country of the world. The social instinct of most people today refuses to discriminate between one person and another on the bases of caste, class, creed, community, sex, etc. Everyone wants freedom and demands an equal share of the opportunities in every sphere of life. It has been experienced everywhere that true liberty and equality are Impossible without spreading the feeling of fraternity. Consequently, one of the chief responsibilities of modern education is to generate a character which will help the educand to become a useful member of a democratic society.

(b) **Relation between Social Ideals and the Aims of Education.** In any country the social ideals are determined by the form of government and the ideas of its great individuals. In modern India, social ideals have been formed by the ideas of such great individuals as Aurobindo, Vivekananda, Rabindranath, Mahatma Gandhi, Dayananda, on the one hand, and by the suggestions of various government committees on the other. Much the same can be seen in the case of the civilized countries as England, America, Germany, France, etc. The objectives of education are formulated by the ideas of leading thinkers and the plans of the government.

The influence of social ideals can also be seen in the form of the prevailing social philosophy. This social philosophy is seen in the form of materialism, utilitarianism, idealism, fascism, communism, democracy, and other philosophical attitudes. These attitudes are seen not only in the thinking only of a few people, but also as a powerful force in the form of an ism, when it influences and sways entire societies. These social philosophies influence and change the ideals of education. This is as follows:

(1) *Idealism.* In idealistic societies, of which one example is ancient Indian Vedic society, the greatest emphasis is laid upon the propagation of religious, moral and spiritual ideals. In this case, the more permanent objectives are considered more important than the more immediate ones. Efforts are made to achieve a complete development of the human personality and also to create the best possible synthesis between the basic elements of the individual and the society. Most of the objectives of this kind of education tend to be universal.

(2) *Realism.* The philosophy of realism suggests that in determining the objectives of education, the immediate needs of society should be kept in view. This attitude encourages technological, economic and scientific education which can help in the material development of the nation.

(3) *Materialism.* A society which accepts the materialistic philosophy sets no store by moral, religious or spiritual values. Consequently, education is fashioned to achieve the physical and mental development of the individual.

(4) *Pragmatism.* Pragmatic thinking encourages a pattern of education in which every individual gets the opportunity to develop all his abilities and capabilities to their fullest extent.

(5) *Fascism.* Fascism accepts the complete authority of the state, and argues that the state is the end, and the individual only the means to that end. Consequently, education is designed to train the individual merely to serve as the instrument of the state. In this case, he is taught to work in the interests of the state and to be prepared for the greatest sacrifices he is called upon to perform.

(6) *Communism.* Communist societies normally stress the value of the realistic aims of education. Communist thinking is primarily materialistic in its value orientation, with the result that idealistic objectives are considered unimportant. Labour is accorded the greatest importance. The aim of education is concerned with labour from every aspect, the economic, political, social and even aesthetic. Educational institutions are mere instruments of state policy. The ideas of the state are propagated among the educands everywhere, and no one has the liberty to oppose or to criticise them. Consequently, the objective of education is to propound communist ideals to the educands.

(7) *Democracy.* One example of a democratic society is the modern American society. The two fundamental principles of democracy are that the individual is an end in himself and that he should conduct himself in such a way that his conduct promotes the welfare of all. Liberty, equality and fraternity are the ideals of democracy. Such a society allows the greatest possible freedom to its members and tries to provide equal opportunities to all. The aim of democratic society is the maximum good of the maximum number. Consequently, education has the following objectives in a democratic society:

(i) Creating respect for human personality in the new generation.

(ii) Assisting the students to obtain control over the means of education and, according to the time and ability available, to gain control over the greatest possible extent of social heritage.

(iii) Helping the student to pay attention to general welfare and to learn the difficult art of self-development.

(iv) Developing in each individual the ability to think in terms of the established categories of truth.

(v) Assisting the students in understanding the nature of democracy and in aiming at the progress of society as the goal of life.

It is thus seen, that educational objectives in a democratic society are framed to assist in the spread of democratic ideals. India is a democratic republic. Here, also-education aims at instilling the ideal of democratic life in the educands at every stage of education.

From the foregoing account of the various forms of social life and social ideals, and the objectives of education conforming to each one of them, it is evident that the aims of education are not permanent but changeable. Hence, it follows that if we want to create a particular pattern of social life and social ideals in a society, it is necessary that the educational pattern should conform to that kind of social life. Most educationists level criticism at the existing pattern of education for this reason. As long as the ideals and objectives of education continue to stray away from the social ideals, it is necessary to offer criticism to guide them back. This is necessary because, in the final analysis, the one single aim of education is to try and make every individual the ideal member of an ideal society.

VOCATIONAL AIM OF EDUCATION

Dewey, an American educationist, has commented that education is meaningful only when it aims at some vocation or employment. In the present age, some kind of educational qualification is essential for almost every job. As a result, very extensive educational qualifications become necessary for good jobs which carry big salaries. Economic independence is essential in the present day world, and for this reason parents are determined to educate their children so that they can become economically independent.

And, in fact, there can be no reason for denying this. Every individual should depend upon himself for his means of support. In the case of developing countries like India, technical and professional training is of the greatest importance. If the investments made on education do not help in the economic advancement of the country, such expenditure cannot be justified. Every young man is faced with the question of earning his bread. If his education does not prepare him for this, there is little reason to commend such an education. No educationist can deny the vocational aspect of education. In India, the earning of one's livelihood is not merely an economic necessity, but a spiritual duty.

Advantages

It is clear from the above description that the vocational objective of education is an important aspect of it, and it has the following advantages:

1. *Solution of economic problems.* India is today facing such grave problems as unemployment, poverty, famine, etc. Our economic problems are our greatest difficulties. On the other hand, most Western and Asian nations accept the vocational aspect of education, and it is seen that these nations are self-dependent and prosperous. They enjoy great respect and power in the world. Hence, technical and vocational training is of the greatest importance, since only such training can help to solve the economic problems of any country.

2. *Dynamism.* The principle of activity applies to the vocational aim of education. Dewey has commented that education imparted in this way makes use of the child's tendencies and habits, pays attention to their interests and awakens their minds. It tests the mind, excites the intelligence and puts an end to lethargy and inactivity.

3. *Moral, intellectual and cultural development.* As far as the vocational aspect of education is concerned, it is connected with earning money. For this reason, one can expect a high moral, intellectual and cultural level from an educated individual. If the educated individual fails to win economic independence, he tends to be immoral in his behaviour, degenerate in his intellectuality and indifferent to the arts and sciences.

Limitations

In view of these advantages of vocational objectives, most educationists in India are in favour of it. Efforts are being made to expand the facilities for technical and professional training in the country. Even the kind of basic education suggested by Mahatma Gandhi aimed at making the individual financially independent. But if the earning of one's bread is considered the sole aim of education, it leads to many difficulties. The major ones are the following:

1. *Absence of liberal education.* Liberal education plays an important part in the individual's development, since it alone is responsible for his intellectual and cultural development.

2. *One-sided attitude.* Although vocational guidance and professional training aimed at economic independence are important forms of education, it cannot be denied that education must also be responsible for the individual's character development, spiritual development, development of his personality, etc. If education aims only at vocational proficiency, it represents a one-sided approach.

3. *Materialism.* If education has vocational proficiency as its only objective, it becomes materialistic, at the cost of religious, moral and intellectual values. Materialism also leads to an increase in self-interest, violence and cut-throat competition which are detrimental to society and individual both.

It is evident from the foregoing discussion of the vocational objective of education that although it is an important objective, it cannot be considered the sole aim of education, even if it is considered the most important.

CHARACTER DEVELOPMENT

Philosophers of education have always considered character formation as one of the most important objectives of education. Among these philosophers are Plato, Aristotle, Herbart and Pestalozzi. Herbart has gone to the length of saying that the very fundamental nature of education is implicit in morality. He argues that education is essential for moral development since the moral individual must be free. Independence is bestowed by reason, and reason is obtained by education. The educational system in ancient India laid great stress upon forming the character of the student. Yajnavalkya suggested that only that is education which enhances the individual's usefulness for society and provides him with a good character. At that time, the educand was compelled to obey the rules of cleanliness of behaviour, self-control and regularity. Education in ancient Greece had the same objectives. Even today, educationists agree that education must aim at forming the character of the individual.

But it must be remembered that no two thinkers have defined character in the same way. McDougall, the psychologist, defines it as an organisation of sentiments, in which one particular sentiment governs all the other sentiments of the individual. From the psychological point of view, an individual whose sentiments are not governed by a governing or driving passion, has a disorganised personality. The higher the governing passion, the higher is the individual's character. It must also be kept in mind that, basically, character does not imply moral character. It has been interpreted in this sense only after Immanuel Kant, the German philosopher, who explained it in this way. In ancient Greece, the word character was taken to mean the moulds used for making coins. In order to prevent the minting of false coins, each one of these moulds was designed to avoid possible forgery. The word retains this meaning even in modern English usage. For this reason, some people use the term ethical character to distinguish between good and bad characters. Skinner has commented that the character of an individual, as the word character has been defined by history, Implies all that which renders a man or a woman unique, unlike all other human beings. Accordingly, then, character includes all those qualities and peculiarities of a person which help to distinguish him from all others.

Nevertheless, in actual fact, character can be seen only as an organisation of sentiments. The Hindi equivalent of this word refers, to a great extent, to the qualities of the personality. Values which a person considers important are concerned with his sentiments. For example, the sentiments of patriotism, love for mother or philanthropy are concerned with the values of sacrifice, service or kindness.

The sentiment of self-respect plays an important role in character formation. Most of the qualities concerned with the development of character are acquired by the individual, as he lives his life in society. This process of character formation starts in childhood. The child's environment, made up of his family life, the society and culture to which he is exposed, plays an important part in his character formation.

There can be no two opinions about accepting character formation as the objective of education. Now that the world has been made much smaller by rapid transport and communications, the obedience of ethical rules is important not only in an individual's conduct but also in the behaviour of nations. With the development of nuclear weapons, man possesses fantastic destructive power, which has endangered the existence of the very race. In the absence of morality he may be inspired to use these weapons. Wars can be avoided not by the rules of an international agency but by the morality of the leaders of the more powerful nations. In these conditions, it is imperative that education in every part of the world aims at the development of moral character.

Even if character is interpreted in more liberal terms, without limiting it to the concept of a moral character, it remains one of the major aims of education. Man cannot develop if his character is allowed to remain dormant. Character is the basis of his individual qualities, since he expresses his individuality through his character. Character is thus an essential characteristic of a developed individual.

It is evident from the foregoing discussion that the major objective of education should be the formation of character. But in India's present condition, education should also aim at enabling the individual to earn his livelihood. Education cannot aim exclusively at character formation. A fool cannot be ethical. Knowledge is essential to morality. For this reason, education must also aim at imparting knowledge. In the same way, one cannot survive on good deeds and good words alone. The educated individual must also aim at developing the individual's personality. If character formation is accepted as the major aim of education, it would benefit society, but education must also seek to enhance the individual's individuality.

It is evident from this that character formation is an important objective of education, but by no means the only one.

THE UNIVERSAL AIMS OF EDUCATION

Roughly speaking, education has two kinds of aims — the universal aims, and the specific aims. Universal aims tend to remain the same, irrespective of the time and place. One of the universally accepted objectives of education is the comprehensive development of the human personality. From the earliest times to the present day and in every country of the world education has aimed at developing the abilities and tendencies of human beings in such a way that they may be able to achieve maximum adjustment, both personal and social. Human nature does not change with time and latitude, and for that reason education has some universal aims. To take one example, the principle that a healthy mind needs a healthy body is a universal maxim, and a universal aim of education. For this reason, education everywhere includes mental and physical training. Similarly, everywhere individuals make families after entering adult life, and in order to ensure their survival, they have to adopt some means of earning their livelihood. Consequently, another commonly accepted aim of education is to train the individual so that he can occupy himself usefully and profitably. And, since man lives in society, it is essential that there should be adjustment between one man and another, because without it society cannot survive. Education therefore, must ensure that men and society develop in such a manner that the occasions of clash and conflict are reduced to a minimum. Clearly, then, there are certain objectives of education which remain the same in all places and at all times. These are as follows:

1. *Specific aims of education.* But, the aims of education are also conditioned by the social ideas, circumstances and changes that occur at a particular place and time. Hence, the aims of education also change with the circumstances. This change and adjustment is essential because education is the tool with which the society, and the individuals in it, can be made more efficient, satisfied and adjusted. And this can be possible only if the aims of education are changed to suit the circumstances. The example of India will clearly establish this.

2. *Aims of education in ancient India.* The attitude prevailing in ancient times was that education should indicate the ways and means of defeating the pains created by the man's passions. Self-knowledge was believed to be the only way of becoming independent of one's passions. Yajnavalkya, one of the greatest philosophers in the period of the Upanishads, believed that education must aim at developing a moral character. This attitude is best explained by Shankaracharya who believed that only that which brings liberation or salvation is education.

3. *Aims of education in modern India.* The old attitude outlined above cannot be applied to the present period in India. One reason for this is that the contemporary political, social and economic conditions differ completely from those existing in the past. In the past, India was considered the golden bird because there was no shortage of food. The schools then were the monasteries of the saints, situated outside the towns. Such schools were helped by the state and the society, with the result that the scholarly educator could devote his entire life to mental and spiritual development. Today, India is one of the backward countries in which there is a shortage of the means of survival. Before worrying about achieving complete literacy, the nation is more concerned with arriving at a stage of economic independence. Almost everybody has to wage a terrible battle against others to satisfy his own physical needs. If education does not prepare the man to earn his own bread and that of his family, and to fulfil the common needs of his dependents, his education will be useless, however spiritual it may be.

The modern individual is less concerned with salvation and liberation than his ancient counterpart because he is more engrossed in solving the more material problems of life which surround him. Survival is his first concern. If he does not survive, the problem of development will not trouble him at all. The modern individual has to exert his mind and his body to ensure own survival. Thus, it is evident that, as far as India is concerned, it is essential that education today must aim at training for livelihood. Mahatma Gandhi's comments on this subject are very illuminating. He pointed out that India's most immediate concern was to win liberation from his slavery by making the greatest possible efforts, be they educational, economic, social or political. Three-fourths of the battle lay in making this effort. He did not object to higher education: in fact, he supported it. But he objected to the kind of higher education which was being imparted in the country. He said that he had provided for the best libraries, the best laboratories and research facilities in his plan. He felt that an entire army of chemists, engineers and other specialists would be needed, an army which would be dedicated to the task of fulfilling the various needs of a people who were growing daily more conscious of their rights and their requirements.

EDUCATION FOR A DEMOCRATIC NATION

The objective of education in India is to try to achieve the aims laid down in the Constitution. A democratic nation aims at instilling a love of liberty, equality and fraternity in its people. And, if India is to be made a truly democratic nation, education should aim at developing these qualities. Hence, education aims at the total and independent development of the individual. But in this development it is essential that personal liberty should be in consonance with social justice. Social justice is based on equality. It provides every citizen with the opportunity to pursue his own development without prejudicing the interests of others. One implication is that the government must provide the poor people with the opportunity and the help to get an education which will raise them to same level as the others, because without this help they cannot secure such education for themselves. And without it, equality will have no meaning.

The most important democratic objective and ideal of education is the evolution of the sense of fraternity because democratic life is impossible without it. This feeling of brotherhood makes little of the differences generated by caste, race, class, profession, sex, nation, etc. and gives rise to a genuine love of humanity and human beings. The future of any democracy depends entirely upon its fiiture citizens and the quality of leadership. Hence, one of the important functions of education is that it should train the educands in democratic leadership. It is a truism that students are the future leaders of the nation. Education, therefore, must evolve ways and means of training these prospective leaders in the norms of democratic life. For this, it is essential that the student community itself must evolve a democratic pattern, and it must be burdened with much of the responsibilities of running the educational institutions in order to get practical training in social living.

Education for Creating a Prosperous Nation

If India is to develop into a prosperous nation, education must pay attention to the following objectives:

1. *Professional training.* Education must see to it that the educand is provided various kinds of scientific and technical education so that he can make a positive contribution to the nation's economic and technological progress. For this technical and scientific education is required.

2. *Character building.* The prosperity of a nation depends upon the character of its citizens, not upon their individual and respective knowledge. One of the reasons of the widespread and endemic corruption that is seen in the Indian economic sphere today is the lack of character. Hence, education must also seek to develop social and moral qualities in the educand so that he should be inspired to employ his talents for the benefit of society. Patriotism is an important element in character-building. At present there are many Indians who have got the opportunity to receive scientific and technical education in foreign countries, at the cost of their own nation. But these people do not return home to put their talents at the disposal of the country, because they sell themselves for the remuneration they receive abroad. This attitude reflects the absence of love for one's country. What is required is that the training received at the cost of the nation's wealth should be employed for the benefit of the nation. Besides, this training should be put to the best possible use. For example, if the doctors of the country refuse to go and live in the villages where they are most required, there is little hope of the nation becoming prosperous.

3. *Proper utilization of leisure time.* It has been found that the average Indian villager makes no sensible and profitable use of the spare time at his disposal. If this time is put to constructive use, it will help in the development of the individual's personality and also contribute to the nation's prosperity.

4. *Military training.* One important condition of developing India into a prosperous democratic nation is that it must have the capacity to face and rebuff any military challenge. For this it is desirable that education must help every young man and woman to receive military training. Such a training will help in time of national emergency because trained men and women will be able to form an effective second line of defence. Besides, this training has its uses in peace time also since it helps in evolving such social qualities as discipline, self-control, obedience, interest in community projects, etc.

It is evident from the foregoing account that education in India should aim at evolving democratic qualities, providing professional, industrial, scientific and military education.

EDUCATION FOR SOCIAL CHANGE

Any system of education is profoundly influenced by the processes of social change. In the present period one can clearly see the impact of such tendencies of social change, as industrialization and Westernization, on the society as a whole and consequently on the pattern of education. A tendency towards Westernization, an imitation of the Western mode of life, is one of the most notable trends in Indian society. As a consequence, one can see this change in the ways of living, of thinking and even in the ideals and values of life of the students at the secondary and higher levels of education. Many people are of the opinion that the aim of education is to facilitate the educand's adjustment to a changing society.

But this attitude to education is inappropriate. The aims of education are not determined by social changes. They are based upon a conception of human nature, and they aim at attaining certain permanent aims. On the one hand, education socializes the individual and thus provides him with the ability to adjust to society, but on the other it also develops his personality so that he can challenge society and seek to improve it. It is education which provides the leaders, reformers and revolutionary thinkers. If education falls in line with social change and prefers to be guided by it, then it cannot be a means of achieving social progress. Neither will it be able to institute changes in society. Hence, it is desirable that education should seek to change society, and not be guided by social changes. Education is the means of evolving new values in the new generation, of equipping the young people with the faculty of critical evaluation so that he can assess the society around them, and improve it where necessary. It is this training which compels the educated individual not to take anything for granted but to subject it to a searching analysis, think of all the conceivable alternatives and institute some social change, should it be desirable. Hence, education is a means to continuity as well as to change and progress. On the one hand it is influenced by social changes, but on the other it must keep a level head amid chaos, and guide future social emancipation.

EDUCATION FOR LEISURE

Some people are of the opinion that the best education is the one which teaches the educand many ways of spending his leisure usefully and constructively. Although many people never tire of delivering lengthy speeches on the importance and nobility of work, it is seen that all that is best, permanent and really valuable in human life is the creation of leisure, not of normal occupation. Although at first sight this appears to be contradictory, in fact this is true. One sees that many of the implements of human civilization, such as scientific instruments, things of day-to-day use, huge buildings and bridges, factories etc., are the result of dedicated and persistent effort. But on the other hand, the various objects of culture, such as literature, music, art, religion and philosophy, are the creation of leisure. If all the people of the world devote themselves to brutish effort, it might lead to physical development, but it would negate cultural development. Hence, now it is believed that apart from the material pursuits of life, the individual must have sufficient leisure so that he may do something in the direction of self-development. The importance of leisure for human life is thus evident.

But cultural development does not automatically follow if leisure is provided. The role of education will be seen here. One can perceive the difference if one observes the different ways in which the educated and the uneducated people around one spend their leisure hours. The uneducated can be seen consuming their leisure in useless gossiping, smoking, quarrelling, sleeping, indulging in alcohol or at the most spending their time in visits to the cinema or rarely the theatre. On the other, the educated individual puts his leisure to better use because, in addition to the physical needs of earning money, eating, satisfaction of the sex drive, the educated person also feels the need for increasing his knowledge, self-development, discretion, religious contemplation, etc. Evidently, then, it is only the educated person who can utilize his leisure properly. And, in fact, only those nations have led the others in cultural activities whose individuals have enjoyed the proper proportion of occupation and leisure. It is for this reason that modern India has not been able to emulate the cultural development of its past eras, because in the past the individual had education, leisure and time for philosophical, moral and spiritual contemplation. The knowledge attained by the Greek philosophers Socrates, Plato and Aristotle could be disseminated only among those who had the leisure to listen to these great thinkers and who had enjoyed an education which trained them to use their leisure in this kind of work.

Education trains one in the proper use of leisure. One of the best examples of this is old age. After people have retired from their professions, the educated people spend their leisure in a much better way than their uneducated counterparts. The same is true of old women. Uneducated people often find it difficult to pass time while the educated people have so much work that they are always conscious of a shortage of time. But here it must be remembered that the term 'educated' does not mean holding a formal education consisting of degrees obtained from colleges and universities. As a matter of fact, a survey conducted twenty years ago about the leisure habits of teachers of a famous University revealed that a large proportion of leisure time was spent in sleeping, gossiping or seeing films. But this does not disprove the foregoing statement in any way. The truth of the matter is that the term 'educated' should be used only for those people who spend their leisure time properly. Proper utilization of leisure includes such activities as self-development, religious activities, activities leading to intellectual development, literature, interest in and devotion to the arts, social service, etc.

But the above description is not intended to create the impression that the sole aim of education is to teach the proper utilization of leisure. It is one of the many objectives of education. If it is accepted as the only aim, it would lead to numerous difficulties. If this is assumed one would be naturally faced with the questions: Is education intended only for those who can afford to enjoy? Should no education be provided to those who find little leisure to enjoy after fighting for their bread? It is obvious that education is essential for such people also. If the proper use of leisure is accepted as the chief aim of education, then the following three difficulties crop up:

(1) This circumscribes the field of education, for it is limited only to those who have leisure, while in fact it should be provided to every one in a democratic society.

(2) Education must also have certain other objectives, such as training an individual to earn his livelihood, achieving a balanced development of personality, self-consciousness, cultural development, etc.

(3) As has already been pointed out, even many formally educated individuals can be seen misusing or wasting their leisure.

Despite the above criticism, the proper use of leisure and training for it is an important aspect of education. In this connection the following things should be kept in mind:

(1) The educated person has a larger choice of activities to pursue in his leisure time, such as literature, music, arts, etc., which are closed to the uneducated individual.

(2) Evidently, this objective of education encourages cultural development.

(3) Education helps to improve the constructive ability of individuals so that they can contribute to the progress of society.

(4) If this is accepted as an objective of education, it will be seen that education improves the interests of individuals and develops the mind.

Hence, training in the proper use of leisure is one of the important aims of education, though not the only one.

AIMS ACCORDING TO SECONDARY EDUCATION COMMISSION

In cogitating upon the aims of education, the Secondary Education Commission, in 1952, attached the maximum importance to the development of democratic citizenship. In its report, the Commission commented that "The educational system must make its contribution to the development of habits, aptitudes and qualities of character which will enable its citizens to bear the responsibilities of democratic citizenship and to counteract all those fissiparous tendencies which hinder the emergence of abroad national and secular outlook." Thus the Education Commission pointed out that education must on the one hand, aim at the development of such habits, attitudes and qualities of character which may help individuals to become ideal citizens of a democracy. On the other, it must train the individual to face and to overcome all those obstacles which bar the path of democracy, such being the disruptive and disorganising influences of regionalism, linguism, communalism, casteism, and the like. Another one of the aims recognized by the Education Commission was the training for leadership. This, too, is an important objective of education because the future of democracy depends upon the quality of leadership provided to the masses. These leaders are elected by the citizens. But if the citizens do not have adequate training in citizenship, they fail to elect the right leaders, with all the obvious evil consequences which fail to the lot of the country. It is for this reason that universal and compulsory education has been accepted as the fundamental condition of a democracy. On the other hand, it has been granted that education must also train men and women in leadership so that they can guide the country in various spheres. These ideas were reiterated by the Kothari Commission in 1964, for it is said that education must aim at strengthening democracy. And this is possible only when education imparts training in responsible democratic citizenship.

EDUCATION FOR CITIZENSHIP

It is evident from the foregoing discussion that accepting citizenship as one of the major aims of education is of particular importance for democratic nations. If a dictatorial system of government prevails in a country, then training in citizenship is not very significant because in such a country, the citizens play a very small role in the administration of the country. On the other hand, democratic countries depend upon their masses for development in every sphere, and it is no exaggeration to say that success or failure of the country depends upon the citizens. Bertrand Russell astutely observed that democracy should not even be thought of in a country in which the masses are uneducated. If democracy is to be a success, it is essential that the people of the country be educated in responsible citizenship. It must be remembered that the training in citizenship is provided not so much by schools and other educational institutions as much as by lectures, radio, television, newspapers and institutions of self-government. Even the different political parties can make a lot of positive contribution in this direction.

Again, the foregoing description should not lead to the belief that training for citizenship is required only in a democracy and it is superfluous in other forms of government such as dictatorship, fascism or communism. It is true that in societies of this kind, the citizens are not called upon to share in the responsibilities of government as much as in a democratic set up, but even here some training in citizenship is essential. There is a difference between democratic citizenship and citizenship in these forms of government. For example, communist governments do not encourage their citizens to think much because the average citizen there does not have the right to raise his voice against his government.

Essential Elements in Education for Citizenship

In order to fully comprehend training in citizenship as an important objective of education, it is essential to understand the qualities and abilities that such an education must seek to generate in the educand. Some important aspects are the following:

1. *General knowledge of the various problems of individual and social life.* Man's life, whether personal or social, is beset with various kinds of problems in all its aspects and forms such as the economic, political, moral, spiritual, physiological, mental, etc. Education should aim at equipping the individual with some general knowledge regarding all these problems so that he may not have any extraordinary difficulty in facing them. General knowledge in itself is important in democratic countries, because the individual citizens are expected to help in the progress of the country in every sphere.

2. *Socialization.* Socialization is the prerequisite for evolving the qualities of responsible citizenship. In the absence of socialization the individual cannot fulfil his responsibilities as a citizen. In fact, he has little obligation to discharge his duties in the first place. After the home, the college or the university is the next important medium of socialization. Here various programmes can be organised to develop such qualities as mutual co-operation, friendship, social service, sacrifice, sympathy, etc. These help in individual's socialization and thus prepare him for the role of the citizen.

3. *Total development.* Every democratic nation must provide for the comprehensive development of its masses if it wants ideal citizens. Hence, education should aim at the all round development of the child, his physical, mental, moral, spiritual development. Only then can they be expected to devote themselves to the task of

serving their nation, of making an honest contribution to the nation's economic and spiritual progress.

4. *Fulfilment of political responsibility.* Only he is a good citizen who honestly and zealously fulfils his political responsibility along with the other obligations he has to society. For example, in an election, it is the duty of every adult man and woman to elect the best possible candidate to represent the electorate, so that the country may get the best leaders. Citizens should be aware of their responsibilities, be prepared to defend their rights and be willing to fulfil their obligations. Every individual must learn to think independently. As Walker has commented, education in a democracy does not imply that the individual should become a tool of the government. He has himself to be an administrator or prepare others for this role. Hence, individuals must be trained to become leaders themselves and also to elect leaders.

EDUCATION FOR CULTURE

One of the accepted objectives of education is cultural development. Before trying to understand this objective, it is essential to understand the meaning of the term culture. Indian philosophical tradition interprets culture as the series of impressions impinging on the individual which help to prepare him for various functions in life. Marriage for example, is a ceremony which impresses upon the individual the responsibilities of procreating and then looking after his progeny. In this manner, culture is a means of socialization, but it can also be interpreted as the end result of socialization, in which case it is a purifying process. It comprehends all that for which impressions and experiences are necessary. Western tradition interprets culture as social attraction and intellectual superiority. According to Sorokin and MacIver culture implies man's moral, spiritual and intellectual superiority and attainment. In the words of Bogardus, "Culture is composed of integrated customs, traditions and current behaviour-patterns of a human group. Culture is the stock-in-trade of a group. It is an antecedent complex of values into which every individual is born. It is a medium within which individuals develop and mature." Hence culture comprehends all that is implied in social heritage. As Alexander A. Goldenweiser has expressed it, "Our attitudes, beliefs and our judgements and values; our institutions—political and legal, religious and economic; our ethical codes and codes of etiquette; our books and machines, our sciences, philosophies and philosophers—all of these and many other things and beings within themselves and in their multi-form inter-relations." This definition of culture contains a detailed account of all factors. Culture is generated and acquired. It is a unique quality of the human race, and it is transmitted from one generation to the next, as a mental phenomenon. It is social rather than individual, and it helps to satisfy certain needs.

Cultural Objective of Education

It is clear from the foregoing explanation of the term culture, that if culture is accepted as the objective of education, then certain specific things may be expected of education. The first factor in the cultural objective of education is the transmission of the social heritage from one generation to the next. Education aims at imparting the values, traditions, customs, patterns of life, etc., of the particular social group to the child, so that he can conform to these patterns and make his own contribution to the cultural development of his group. In the second place, the objective of education is to lend sophistication, grace and polish to the child's behaviour. But in this respect there are differences of opinion. Hinting at this difference, Vivekananda commented to an American lady, "Madam! In your country it is the tailor who makes a man cultured and gentleman but in my country it is the character which makes a man cultured and gentleman." Recognised patterns of behaviour, such as greeting a stranger, showing respect to one's elders, showing love and affection etc., vary from culture to culture. Hence education aims at acquainting the child with the patterns recognised in his own society. Obviously, then, culture can be interpreted liberally as well as narrow-mindedly. In its more superficial and limited sense, culture implies the mode of dress, external manifestations of behaviour, etc. But in its broader and more liberal sense culture implies values, thinking, self-development, etc. Consequently, the possession of a certificate of formal education is no guarantee of culture, because culture can be found only in that individual who has achieved some degree of self-development, both mental and spiritual, and has some notion of the values of life, From this standpoint, it is possible to distinguish between various levels of cultural attainment.

Criticism

As has been indicated earlier, culture is the unique quality which separates the human beings from the animals. Consequently, cultural development is a very significant objective of education. In fact it would not be wrong to consider it the single most important objective. If culture is lacking, it would in fact be improper to consider a person even educated. Cultural development is the standard of self development, which is the primary objective of education. But it is difficult to accept cultural development as the sole objective of education because of certain inherent difficulties, the more important ones being:

1. This leads to the neglect of the professional and the other aspects of education, and consequently such an education would not prepare a man to earn his livelihood.

2. If only the educated person is believed to be cultured, it leads to an unnecessary complex of pride and superiority over those who are uneducated, and by definition, therefore, uncultured. Hence, it is not proper to identify the educated with the cultured, as long as education is not interpreted in the most liberal sense.

3. This would lead to a greater distance between various social groups because the majority of educated people prefer to spend their time in cultural activity, at the expense of all physical effort. Naturally the distance between them and the class of manual workers increases and leads to disorganisation.

4. Acceptance of cultural development as the objective of education may also lead to a blinding to reality and concrete problems of life. It is true that literature,

music and art play an important part in human life but developments in this field cannot be achieved without corresponding and in fact antecedent progress in the economic and physical fields.

Briefly, then, cultural development is an important objective of education but in addition to this education also has certain other objectives, such as training the individual to earn his livelihood, developing awareness of citizenship, development of character, etc. It is necessary to attach appropriate importance to each one of these, if the comprehensive aim of education is to be understood.

SYNTHESIS OF VARIOUS AIMS OF EDUCATION

Even the educationists of the fairly remote past were interested in the various objectives of education, and consequently many different aims were ascribed to education. On the other hand, there has always been a distinct tendency to synthesize all these various aims into a single comprehensive aim. One example of this inclination is the aim Herbert Spencer ascribed to education, the aim of providing completeness to life. In general, other educationists have accepted that the general aim of education is a balanced development. Certain other educationists believe that education should aim at the complete development of human personality, but by including social qualities in this they also hint at the development of the social aspect which promotes adjustment between the individual and society. Hence, it is evident, that the various aims of education are not mutually exclusive or contradictory and it is therefore possible to synthesize the different aims and arrive at a single objective. But for this it is necessary to glance at the various possibilities and alternatives.

Complete Living

Herbert Spencer believed that the general aim of education was training for complete living. He pointed out that education must be so designed as to develop every aspect of human life and to enable the individual to adjust to every possible circumstance. He must have knowledge of the various responsibilities that he must fulfil towards himself, his friends, his society and his nation. He must also be taught to fend for himself in the economic jungle, and also to spend his leisure time constructively.

If one has to understand the concept of complete living properly, one must understand the concept of life. Spencer uses the term 'life' to imply five kinds of activities—the action of self-defence, the action of apparently protecting life, the action of protecting one's progeny, the action of safeguarding society, and the action of spending one's leisure. Education must aim at generating proficiency in each one of these activities. For this he devised a specific syllabus. For the first two kinds of activities he considered knowledge of physiology, physics, language, mathematics and geography essential. Knowledge of child psychology and home science can be relied upon to provide proficiency in protecting the progeny. Protection of society can be achieved through knowledge of history, economics and sociology. Leisure can best be spent after getting knowledge of the various arts. Spencer has thus provided a syllabus which helps the individual to perform the more important functions with the least effort, and which also achieves the objective of complete living. But a detailed analysis of this theory proves that it is in fact not as comprehensive as it appears to be. In fact, it is one-sided and inclines away from complete living. The following arguments are designed to bring out these weaknesses:

1. *A biological prejudice.* Spencer's theory evinces a definite bias in favour of the sciences and a bias against the arts because his philosophy was based on biological interpretations.

2. *A biological definition of completeness.* The completeness of life has been variously defined by different thinkers. Spencer's concept of the complete life does not satisfy the intellectually inclined thinker because of its biological prejudice. To give but one example, Spencer does not make any provision for religious training while many thinkers cannot conceive of a complete life which is devoid of religion. Besides, in the absence of religious training, it is difficult to provide any strong foundation for moral education.

3. *Neglect of literature and art.* Although Spencer has thought of some disciplines as fit for leisurely perusal, he has attached little importance to literature, music and the arts by considering them fit only for leisure. It must be remembered that these disciplines have value not only as means of utilizing leisure, for they have a definite contribution to make to the development of an individual's character and personality. It is improper to consider them as fit for leisure only.

4. *Unpsychological arrangement of the subjects.* Some thinkers have objected to Spencer's arrangement and ordering of the various subjects on the ground that it is unpsychological because it pays little attention to the individual aptitude of the educand by providing a common educational programme for all. Modern educationists are in favour of selecting particular subjects according to the aptitude of the individual child. Separate individuals make their own unique contribution to the progress of society because each person differs from every one else, and this difference becomes apparent soon after birth. The educationist and the teacher must provide each child with the opportunity to develop his own specific interests and abilities so that he can make some appropriate contribution to society.

It is evident, thus, that while complete living is acceptable as the aim of education, Spencer's conception of it is biased, narrow and too limited to be accepted. This aim could be more acceptable to many other thinkers if it attached sufficient importance to the spiritual aspect, along with the biological aspect.

Harmonious Development Aim

The harmonious development of the various aspects of human beings is the aim of education suggested by some philosophers. The human personality is made up of many aspects, such as the physiological, the mental, etc. In addition to this, each individual is born possessed of certain instincts. Education, according to this approach, must aim at a harmonious development of these aspects and instincts. Such a development amounts to a balanced development, which precludes the possibility of the greater development of any one aspect at the expense of another. Hence it leads to the creation of a balanced personality.

Apparently, this aim of education appears to be very attractive because it cannot be doubted that there are many facets of the human personality. It is therefore desirable that education should seek to develop each one adequately. But this approach is beset with certain difficulties.

1. *Lack of clarity.* The implications of harmonious development do not seem to be very clear. If it implies external development, it will provide with superficial knowledge of many subjects and profound knowledge of none. On the other, if harmony is intended to mean internal development, it would be difficult to decide the various extents to which each of the internal powers is to be developed. It is impossible to achieve the maximum development of every ability. It is frequently seen that excessive development in one direction is accompanied by lack of development in most other aspects. Different individuals possess different abilities to varying extents, and their respective development also therefore differs.
2. *Absence of any standard.* There is no way of measuring or evaluating this harmonious development. It is difficult if not impossible to determine if the individual's abilities are being adequately developed or not.
3. *Contradiction of individuality.* Man is a complex animal who is possessed of many processes and abilities. It is neither possible nor desirable that each of these qualities should be developed to the same extent. This will eliminate individuality from human beings.
4. *Difficulty of synthesising the syllabus.* If harmonious development is accepted as the aim of education, a further difficulty lies in deciding upon the subjects to be taught, and the extent to which each should be taught, in order to achieve the desired objective. Philosophers who accept this ideal have not elucidated this aspect of the matter.
5. *Difficulties pertaining to adjustment with the social environment.* As the social environment changes, different abilities of the individual come into play to achieve adjustment. Consequently, the abilities which are rarely called up tend to deteriorate and even vanish. Modern societies make little call upon the physical capabilities of the individual. Consequently, these abilities are not developed to the extent to which they were developed in more primitive societies. In such a situation, it is difficult to understand how this concept of education can show the way.
6. *Absence of practical guidance.* Any ideal objective of education fails to provide practical guidance. It is an abstract concept which must be clarified before it can be applied in practice.

Despite these shortcomings, this aim of education hints at the need for paying attention to the development of every aspect of the child's personality and for preparing him to face every possible situation. He must be allowed to develop the abilities which he will be required to use in his life. Harmonious education aims at this. The only real difficulty lies in determining the extent and proportion in which the different capabilities are to be developed.

ADJUSTMENT OF THE SOCIETY AND INDIVIDUAL

All the various objectives and aims of education can be divided into two broad categories — individual aims and social aims. Consequently, if education is oriented to the development of both society and the individual, it will have an aim which comprehends all these aims. Some educationists have emphasized the personal or individual aims of education while others have inclined towards the social aims. Critical analysis of both will help in understanding how the two can be synthesized.

Social Aims of Education

Since man cannot hope to exist outside society, it is desirable that education must have some social aim also. Certain scholars have insisted upon this aspect of education to such an extent that they have denied any importance to the individual aspect. Hegel believes in the complete sovereignty of the state and permits it complete authority over the individual. The state has complete control over the various parts of education, the syllabus, the methods of teaching, administration, organisation of institutions, etc., and it seeks to use each one of these in such a manner that it can train the individual to become a useful instrument in the hands of the state. Examples of this kind of education can be found in ancient Sparta. The individual was believed to have no independent status, since he was born for the benefit of the nation. He was expected to live only for his country. Spartan leaders were primarily concerned with strengthening their country through education of this kind, so that they could defend their territorial integrity. Literature and the arts did not concern them to any great extent. Much of the nation's energy was consumed in imparting military training to every young man. Hence, their educational system aimed at producing soldiers. This practice was carried to extremes, inasmuch as all infants thought to be incapable of becoming soldiers were killed off. Young men were encouraged to engage in physical exercise of every kind. Independent thinking of any kind was looked down upon. Administration was given great attention. Briefly, they desired to generate and develop all those qualities which are required in physical conflict. There was a very rigorous system of punishment. Literary education was considered to be of secondary importance, while training in music extended only to patriotic songs. The education of women was also given some attention, but their importance lay only as sources of good soldiers.

Education of this kind came to the front again in modern Germany. After the defeat of Germany in 1806, German thinkers meditated upon ways of saving their country. They concluded that this could only be done through education. This thinking spread to the field of education, and expressed it self through the insistence upon the teaching of national history and imparting of military training. Thinkers like Hegel and Fichte stressed the sovereign and supreme authority of the state, in direct opposition to any individual rights. Education became a medium of disseminating the ideas of the government among the educands. This trend culminated in the establishment of the Nazi cult and government, and later on in occurrence of the world war. Education on this pattern is seen emerging at various points of history in many different countries.

Individual Aims in Education

It is evident from the foregoing description that the social aims of education should not be stressed to the utter exclusion of the individual aims, since it leads to many distressing consequences. Contrary to this many thinkers have been influenced by numerous factors to stress the importance of the individual aims of education. Development of the individual's personality was an accepted aim of education both in Ancient Greece and India. The emphasis waned a little during the Middle Ages. But the modern period has seen a resurgence of this interest in the individual. It is manifested in an education which is completely child-oriented. Factors influencing this are the following:

1. *Effect of biological sciences.* The biological sciences suggest that every living being is distinct from every other living being, that each one has certain peculiar and unique characteristics, that its natural development means only the development of these unique characteristics. Hence, education aims at development of the individual abilities of each child.

2. *Effect of psychology.* Modern psychology places a lot of emphasis upon individual differences. Every child differs from every other child in respect of its colour, form, nature, interest and mental abilities such as intelligence, thinking, etc., and its personality. The aim of education is to develop each child in conformity with its special abilities. Success in life depends to a great extent upon development of this kind. As the result of this psychological concept, it is believed that education must seek to develop the individual abilities of each individual. Consequently, education has become child-oriented.

3. *Influence of the progressives.* According to T.P. Nunn, the progress of the world's rooted in the development and progress of the individual personality. The world has progressed only because some individuals have contributed to it according to their special abilities, If such gifted individuals had not existed, progress in any sphere of activity would have been impossible. Hence, education should aim at individual development if it seeks to contribute to social progress. In the words of T.P. Nunn, "Nothing good enters into the human world except in and through the activities of individual men and women and educational practice must be shaped to accord with this truth." Hence, the aim of education is to develop the abilities of men and women as individuate. Only this can help the world in progressing. And this alone will produce the leaders in various spheres and make progress possible.

4. *Effect of democratic ideas.* Democracy stresses the freedom of the individual. American educationists attach the greatest importance to the independent development of the individual, and hence they concede very few rights to the state to interfere in this matter. Democracy aims at providing the greatest freedom and equality to all individuals. Hence, it is believed that the democratic state should provide facilities for all individuals to develop in any direction they

conceive to be useful to themselves. The state has to pay particular attention to that class of individuals who cannot get education of their own accord. For this reason democratic societies make special arrangements for the education of the backward, orphaned and physically handicapped children. Teachers and students in educational institutions are free to think and express their own ideas, because, as Bertrand Russell has suggested, "Education of the individual is a finer thing than the education of the citizen." Education must not only seek to produce fine citizens but also fine individuals. The educational system should be so designed that it helps to develop the individuality of the child.

The emphasis that is nowadays placed on the individual aims of education does not imply total neglect of the social aims. It is in fact a synthesis of the individual and social aims. It is impossible to conceive of one in the total absence of the other. There is no human being outside society and society is made up of human beings. Hence, even if education is designed to aim at social service or training for citizenship, it implicitly promotes the interests and the individuality of the human being. It will be in keeping with the context to recount the ideas of some eminent educationists.

THE CONCEPT OF SOCIAL SKILL

In America, Professor Bagley believes that social skill is the aim of educational behaviour. Explaining the concept of social skill he has pointed out the following qualities which can be said to characterize the socially skilful individual:

(1) Economic efficiency or the ability to bear one's own financial burden.

(2) Prohibitive or negative morality, or the willingness, on the part of the individual, to sacrifice those wishes, the satisfaction of which would endanger or hinder the fulfilment of economic skill of other people.

(3) Willingness to desist from the satisfaction of those drives and desires which make no direct or indirect contribution to social progress.

In this approach to education, the individual's activities are evaluated from the standpoint of social duties. After the First World War, American thinking on the subject has inclined towards the individual's contribution to society. Social service has been the recognised aim of education ever since. Educational institutions felt it necessary to acquaint the individual with the duties and responsibilities of the citizen, while even the teaching of history was oriental to the fostering of social consciousness. Considerable stress was placed on cooperation and sacrifice. Much the same thing can be said about India, too. There is little doubt that this approach to education placed great stress on the social aspects. On the other hand, the supporters of individualism argue that progress is retarded if social service or training for citizenship are accepted as the aims of education. As in the case of all other social institutions, the educational institutions, too, are allowed to exist because they assist in the individual's personality, it is not fulfilling the aims of education. It is the duty of the state to provide any educational system which will promote the individual's development in every way. The state can claim any right of control over education only to the extent to which it does not interfere in the freedom of the educationists and the educands. This is the concept which prevails in modern democratic societies.

SELF-REALIZATION

Self-realization as the aim of education presents a synthesized ideal which comprehends the individual and social ideals, since both aspects of self-realization are important. Self-realization is not merely the manifestation of one's self but the complete development of the individual. Individualism should not be considered a contradiction of the social environment because the social aspect cannot be separated from human nature. In fact, the concept of a spiritual personality comprehends both the social and the individual aims of education. As J.S. Ross has argued, "The only meaning of the individual aim in education that is worthy of our acceptation is the development of valuable personality and spiritual individuality." Euken suggests that the aim of education is to make the personality superior. The adjustment or synthesis between the individual and the society is possible only in a democratic structure. The individual develops properly only through the medium of society. As J.M. Baldwin has commented, "The real self is the bipolar self. Personality develops only in society, since outside society it is not possible to evolve those characteristics which are unique in human beings. Personality has no meaning when it is separated from the social environment. And social service is the finest medium of achieving self-realization. Only free and independent individuals can achieve social ideals. The Christian religion accepts this concept of personality. Indian religions also stress the unbreakable bonds between society and the individual.

The concept of self-realization as an educational goal has been described after the one-sided description of the social and individual aims of education in order to make it clear that both social and individual aims can be synthesized in this goal of self-realization. This aim of education is supported by modern sociology, psychology, ethics and democratic principles.

4

AGENCIES OF EDUCATION

Sir Godfrey Thomson has written, "The whole of environment is the instrument of man's education in the widest sense. But in that environment certain factors are distinguishable as more particularly concerned: the home, the school, the church, the press, the vocation, public life, amusement and hobbies," Generally, of course, the process of education continues from birth to death, but some specific institutions play a more important part in it. All of these institutions are the agencies of education, and they include all those factors, bases, places or institutions, which have an educative influence upon the child. Hence, the institutions, agencies and bases of education mean the same thing, and should be interpreted as such. These institutions of education have been variously classified by different educationists. Some of the major classifications are the following:

1. *Active and Passive agencies.* Among the active agencies of education are home, schools, religious institutions, society, state, club, social welfare centres, etc. Here the educator and the educand, the audience and the speaker, the citizen and the leader, deliberately come into contact with each other and also react to each other. Consequently, the process of education forges ahead. Among the passive agencies of education can be enumerated radio, television, films, newspapers, magazines, etc. These are called passive because the process of education set into motion by them is not mutual but one-sided, because only the audience or educand is actively participating. The other element, the agency itself, remains inactive, and hence only the educand is himself influenced without influencing the source of his education.

2. *Brown's classification.* In addition to the formal and informal classification, to be mentioned later, Brown has divided the agencies of education into the commercial and uncommercial. The commercial agencies have a commercial objective while the uncommercial have social welfare as their objective. Hence, the press, films, radio, television, magazines, etc., are the commercial agencies of education. On the other hand, sports clubs, scouts and guides institutions, adult education centres and social welfare centres, etc., are the uncommercial agencies of education.

3. *Formal and Informal agencies.* The most recognised and well known classification is the division into the formal and informal agencies of education:

(a) *Formal agencies.* In the words of Henderson, "As the child watches, imitates, participates, in the activities of living he is being informally educated. When he is being consciously and intentionally taught, that is formal education." In this manner informal education is unconscious whereas formal education is conscious and deliberately imbibed. Informal education is unsystematic while formal education is systematized. Among the agencies of formal education are those institutions which have a predetermined location, time, plan and curriculum as well as trained educators. The best example of such institutions is the school. Such agencies are brought into existence by the state or society. In such institutions discipline and administration is created by the application of set rules. It is possible to use such agencies to provide education to a large number of educands simultaneously, according to a predetermined plan. At least specific education cannot be provided in the absence of these institutions, but it must be realized that education provided through these agencies is rather lifeless and theoretical, or bookish. It sometimes takes the educand far away from the realities of life. In addition to schools, libraries, lecture theatres, recreation centres, museums, etc., are also enumerated among the formal agencies of education. Pointing out the significance of the formal agencies, Dewey has remarked, "Without formal education it is not possible to transmit all the resources and achievements of a complex society. It also opens a way to a kind of experience which would not be accessible to the young, if they were left to pick up their training in informal association with others, since books and the symbols of knowledge are mastered." But he is also aware of the shortcomings of formal education. Dewey comments, "Formal education easily becomes remote and dead—abstract and bookish." The importance of formal agencies of education is thus evident.

(b) *Informal agencies.* The informal agencies of education are those in which education is provided informally and unconsciously. These lack all formality, rules, systematization, preplanning, premeditation or training. All of them perform the function of educating the educand indirectly. Most of them are independent of the control of any individual or institution. Education provided by them does not follow any set pattern. Besides providing education, they also perform certain other functions and fulfil many other needs. Education provided by them is devoid of any pretension and formality. It is natural and subtle. Among the agencies of informal education are family, society, state, radio, press, cinema, magazines, television, etc. Dewey believes that the informal agencies of education are more important than the formal ones, for he believes that they are natural. One example of this is education through communal living. Living in a group, the child thinks of many things. The sphere of his experience is being rapidly enlarged, for he is being subjected to many new stimuli. Under these circumstances his imagination develops and he becomes conscious of new responsibilities which provoke him to think. Even though the influence of these informal agehcies is subtle, it is definitely very comprehensive. In the development of the child's personality and character, the informal agencies play a very significant role. The major benefit derived from them is that they do not restrict the child in any way. The child develops naturally.

Despite these advantages, the informal agencies cannot completely replace the formal ones, because in the absence of a definite plan of education, much time and energy is wasted over things which ultimately prove useless. Besides, these informal agencies cannot be employed to give specific education or knowledge of a very complex kind. Again, definite and certified education cannot be provided through informal means.

It is evident from the foregoing account of the advantages and disadvantages of formal and informal agencies of education that both are essential for the development of the individual and of society. As social structures become progressively more complex and population increases, the importance of the formal and informal educational agencies also increases. Consequently, it has come to be believed that there is intimate relationship between the formal and informal means and agencies of education. When formal education increases to a great extent, it tends toward abstraction and lifelessness and then it needs the assistance of the informal agencies to infuse new life into it. For this reason, modern educationists believe that college and family are complementary factors in the child's education. Dewey has correctly commented that in the modern age, "One of the weightiest problems with which the philosophy of education has to cope today is the method of keeping a proper balance between the informal and the formal, the incidental and intentional modes of education." Neither of the two should be stressed at the cost of the other. On the one hand various kinds of schools and colleges should be established to provide formal education, while on the other the informal agencies must also be exploited to make up any deficiencies left in the formal mode. Even in colleges and schools, excessive emphasis should not be upon book learning. It is for this reason that modern schools design their curriculum so that sufficient time is given to extra-curricular and social activities. For the same reason, it has been found desirable that educators and parents should meet from time to time.

FORMAL AGENCIES OF EDUCATION

The different kinds of schools and colleges are enumerated among the formal means of education. The English word 'school' is derived from the Greek 'skhole,' which means leisure. Hence school implies a place of leisure where people gather during their leisure time for the purpose of developing themselves. In Ancient Greece, young men and women used to collect in schools during their leisure time to receive education from famed scholars and philosophers. These same schools later on took the form they have at present. In a school education is imparted to the educand by trained educators, at affixed time and place, according to a predetermined syllabus. Different schools are intended for different kinds and levels of education, for example, primary, secondary and higher education, university education, etc. Among professional institutions are medical colleges, engineering colleges, etc. The function of the school is to achieve the physical, mental and character development of the educand, to develop in him a social consciousness, the qualities of citizenship. It must also aim at cultural development and the imparting of professional or industrial training. From this standpoint, it is seen that schools in India suffer from many defects, which have to be removed. If a school is to be successful in achieving its aims in the present age, it must have intimate relationship with the family on the one hand and the state or government on the other. Both must give it their wholehearted support and co-operation.

INFORMAL AGENCIES OF EDUCATION

The major agencies of informal education are the following:

1. *Home or family.* Pointing out the significance of the informal means of education, as part of the educational system Raymont has commented, "Teachers are not the only educators, and schools and colleges are not the only educational institutions. The other institutions though for good or ill, are unquestionably educational in their effects." This is most true of the family, for the family makes a sizeable contribution to the child's education, irrespective of the quality of this education. In families which provide a defective environment, the child develops many bad traits of character. On the other hand, the importance of good families as contributing factors to the development of great personalities need hardly be explained. The difference that is seen among all the educands studying in schools and colleges is due to their varying family background. Mazzinni was quite correct in saying that the child's first training in citizenship is in the mother's lap and the father's affection. Accepting the importance of the family as a factor in the child's education, Montessori called his schools the home of children. Locke attached greater importance to education at home than to school education. Comenious opined that the home is the centre of all kinds of education for the child. Froebel is correct when he says that the education imparted at home is both effective and natural Pestalozzi also felt that the home is the child's first school. Raymont says, "Two children may attend the same school, may come under the influence of the same teachers and the same organisation, may pursue the same studies and perform the same exercise; and yet may differ *totocaelo* as regards their general knowledge, their interests, their speech, their bearing, and their moral tone, according to the homes they come from." The family looks after the child's physical development, lays the foundations of his character, gives him religious education, acquaints him with the realities of life and provides the right kind of environment for the development of his interests, tendencies, motivations, intelligence and other processes. It is the most important agency of the child's socialization. Besides, in many families some kind of professional and practical education is also imparted to the child. It is for this reason that co-operation between the family and the school is considered an important aspect of the child's education.

2. *Community.* The community is also an important informal agency for the child's education. Moving out of the family, the child automatically takes up the membership of various groups in community and through them develops various aspects of his character and personality. Playing in the group, he develops his mind and body. He also experiences moral, social and cultural development. Many institutions in the society provide him with professional and vocational training while different political groups look after his political training.

3. *State.* The modern welfare state is responsible for the overall development of all its citizens. That is why modern states pay so much attention to education and formulate national policies for education. The state shoulders the responsibility of establishing different kinds of schools. In many states free and compulsory education is provided, and even where this is not so, almost all educational institutions are aided by the state in one way or the other. The state provides able and trained teachers by establishing training colleges for them. The state also provides military training. Besides, research cannot be carried on without the help of the state. In a democracy, the state trains every individual in responsible citizenship. Although most sociologists oppose complete governmental control of education, everyone agrees that without state help education would fail. State also plays an important role by retaining control over literature and encouraging it to evolve along acceptable lines. The state also looks after the education of physically and mentally handicapped children by establishing special institutions for such children.

4. *Religion.* From very ancient times, various educational institutions in almost every country have been shouldering the responsibility of educating the populace. In India, most schools were organised either within or very near the places of worship, for example, temples, mosques, etc. All the education was imparted by the chaplain of these places of worship. Although almost all modern, welfare states are also secular, it is an acceptable practice to assist religious institutions where they contribute to the educational effort.

5. *Library.* There is little need to elaborate the role played by libraries in disseminating education. Libraries are the collection of the knowledge of centuries summarised in books. Many people maintain personal libraries but these do not fulfil all needs. Hence, the state and local self-governing bodies undertake the responsibility of establishing libraries. In almost all countries modern governments spend vast sums of money to establish big libraries.

6. *Reading Room.* In most modern towns, one finds reading rooms in addition to the libraries. These are established by the state and other institutions. These reading rooms provide many daily, weekly and monthly newspapers, all kinds of magazines, which are available to the public which can come there and read them. It is not possible for every individual to subscribe individually to such a large number of magazines. For this reason, the reading room plays a significant role in education.

7. *Museums.* Museums are very useful in imparting education in such subjects as history, geography, biology, anthropology, etc. It is for this reason that one finds well stocked museums and zoos in many big cities of the world. The knowledge that an individual can gain by roaming around in these institutions is not available to him anywhere else. It is a psychological principle that the thing seen is remembered longer than the thing heard. For this reason museums can contribute a lot to an individual's education. There are many museums and zoos in many Indian cities.

8. *Cinema.* Cinema is one of the important informal agencies of education in the modern world, for it is an important form of audiovisual education. By means of this it is possible to see incidents, individuals and objects as if with the eye itself. It is therefore very useful when one wants to acquaint the educand with things, places

and incidents occurring in foreign countries. It can be done by taking the educand to any cinema hall and exhibiting the appropriate film. It is evident, therefore, that this agency can easily be employed for the teaching of history, geography, civics, political science and comparable subjects. The government in India has inspired and financed the production of many entertaining and informative film documentaries concerning the revolution in agriculture and industry that is taking place in the country today. Newsreels also help in the dissemination of news and ideas. For example, the cinema has played an important role in educating the illiterate public about family planning. Apart from newsreels, even the commercial films have a tremendous impact upon the personality, character, behaviour and many smaller things of the young men and women of the country. It has been seen in America that the incidence of crime has gone up after films about crime became popular there. In India also a comparable trend is noticeable. Most films being produced today are concerned with the exhibition of the latest fashions, and this has had a detrimental effect upon the thinking of the younger generation. Hence, the government is faced with the task of encouraging the production of good, illuminating and elevating films, and also with the responsibility of preventing the production of films which cater to the baser instincts of men and women, films concerning sex, crime, etc. In many states, students have been legally barred from seeing films during the matinee show. This is not a very psychological way of shielding the younger generation from the ill-effects and bad influences of film going. They can see the same films later in the evening, and still imbibe the same ideas. Preventing students from seeing films during college hours will achieve nothing more than to increase attendance in colleges. There is no doubt at all that cinema has a comprehensive influence upon the moral, religious and intellectual development of adolescents. The main cause of this is that in viewing the film, the members of the audience unconsciously identify themselves with the hero or the heroine and hence suffer the same experience through which the hero passes. They can be observed exhibiting the same emotions which are controlling the figure on the screen. It would be no exaggeration to say that if the cinema is exploited to the greatest extent as a medium of education, then there is no other informal agency which can be more influential than the cinema.

9. *Drama.* Although the popularity of the cinema has done much to reduce public interest in drama, in fact cinema can never completely replace dramatic performance. In a dramatic performance the actor, through his concrete presence and acting, arouses certain emotions in his audience. Drama has certain drawbacks in that, unlike the cinema, it cannot exhibit scenes, places and incidents far removed from the location of the theatre. In spite of this limitation, there is little doubt that the drama can be a very effective medium for the powerful presentation of many ideas and behaviour patterns. But from the educational standpoint, drama is more significant from the point of view of those children who can take active part in it. It does not compare in this respect with films because children cannot participate in films. For this reason, almost all colleges and schools have some or the other dramatic society in which the educands produce plays. Acting is itself an art, and it can only be learnt through drama. Besides, drama also promotes interest in singing and dancing. Participating in drama is useful because it helps

a person to outgrow stage fright, or the fear of appearing before an audience. This promotes the ability to work in group. Acting also helps to reflect clearly the differences in the personalities of the actors and actresses. In certain cases, it has been seen that proximity of boys and girls during stage performances has led to certain undesirable consequences, but such incidents can, by and large, be prevented if the educators are conscious of their responsibility and handle the situations psychologically. Drama has also proved to be a useful medium for letting out or expressing many repressed drives and feelings. In the form of Psycho-drama, dramatic performances can actually be used to get rid of many of the child's abnormalities. Finally, the teacher himself, in order to be a successful educator, must indulge in some acting, because only then can he present his subject forcefully to the class and influence his audience.

10. *Newspapers and Magazines.* The contribution of newspapers and magazines to the education of people in general is far greater than that of any other informal agency because they can be circulated over a far larger area than can be covered by films, dramatic societies, television, etc. Today, the progress of education in a country is computed by the number and quality of magazines and newspapers published there. It is a matter of no little pride that after Independence, the number of newspapers and magazines, in English and in local languages has been going up steadily. This has been made possible by the rapid increase of literacy among the people. In the last few years many children's magazines have been published. These play a considerable part in the child's education. Magazines concerning sports and games provide considerable information in that sphere, while certain magazines provide information about health and how it can be maintained. There has been literally a flood of magazines concerning films, although it is difficult to class these among the better magazines. Besides these, a considerable number of weekly, monthly and magazines of other frequency add to the knowledge of the people. Apart from English and Hindi newspapers, newspapers in almost all regional languages are being published in the country, the latter having the advantage of being able to reach the masses living in the villages. And in fact, newspapers play the greatest role in making democracy a success. No other form of informal education can be compared with these as far as political, economic and social education is concerned.

11. *Radio.* In the west, the radio has been almost completely supplanted by the television, but in India it is still very much in vogue. It is pleasant to note that transistor radios can now be seen in even the remotest villages, and have become so common that they are carried everywhere, to work, to play, to social gatherings, to travel. The radio amuses as well as instructs. The All India Radio, the national radio network, has conceived and executed a number of programmes to achieve these ends, amusement, pleasure and education. Among their programmes many are aimed at the agriculturists, children, uneducated women, students, those Inclined towards light or classical music, towards humour and laughter, towards serious discussions on current topics and scientific subjects, etc. Most of the programmes broadcast over the radio are so full of information and also effective

that if one only has the patience to listen to them, one would find unprecedented progress in one's education. Aware of this significance of the part that the radio can play, the Indian government has provided public radio sets for each panchayat so that the villagers can collect in the building housing of the panchayat and listen to various programmes of interest to them. Radio is a very good medium of political education, in particular. Before the last general elections the All India Radio arranged for the leaders of various political parties to speak on the radio and explain the aims, objectives and plans of their respective organisations so that the uneducated people could assess the merits of each party and select the representative of the party most aligned to their own way of thinking. This was an important step forward in the political education of the electorate. As a consequence, one finds the opposition parties creating an uproar whenever it seems that the broadcasting system is becoming unduly sympathetic towards the ruling party. Efforts are being made to neutralize the broadcasting organisation, politically, so that it should not become an organ of the ruling party alone, but should develop into an agency for disseminating information, knowledge and amusement. By means of the radio, people who are separated by long distances from the centre of things can listen to all kinds of cultural programmes while relaxing at home. In this it is not even necessary to open one's eyes or to sit up, as is necessary in the case of television or cinema. But if the radio is to be made an effective agency of informal education; there is considerable need for overhauling its programmes. AIR pays considerable attention to the suggestions put forward by its listeners in this connection, and it also consults experts from time to time.

12. *Television.* As has already been mentioned, television has become an important means of informal education in most advanced countries. Colour television has also been introduced so that it has now come nearer to reality. Most men and women spend their leisure time in front of the television, and thus absorb a lot of knowledge and information without having to make any great effort. Most of the programmes exhibited over the television are so life-like that one hears of people dying of heart failure while watching boxing matches and other exciting events. Television was extensively used to inform people about man's recent journey to the moon. The launching and various other stages were televised for the benefit of the people. In India, the effective range of television is far too small at present, and most of the programmes put on the screen have a long way to go. Faster development in this direction would be very much desirable, but progress has been hampered by many difficulties. Once these are removed, it will be observed that television is the most effective means of imparting social, economic, political and even professional training. Closed circuit television, a more modern form of television exhibition, is being extensively used in the training of medical students. In this the operation taking place in the operation theatre is televised so that students sitting in the classroom can view it. In this way more students can be accommodated than would be possible in any operation theatre.

13. *Scouting and Girl Guides.* The scouting and girl guide movement has made an important contribution to the education of young boys and girls, for it teaches

them social service through giving first aid, swimming, cooking, guiding the physically handicapped, pitching camps, returning lost children to their parents in big fairs, etc. This helps the child to understand the human body, to develop his personality and character and also contributes to his moral progress. Such institutions can be seen in schools the world over. They are even more useful in that they do not indulge in political discrimination.

14. *Social Welfare Centre.* In addition to the scouting and girl guide movements, Brown considers social welfare centres as media of informal education. Social welfare centres and social education centres have been set up in India as part of the community development projects. These have been established in rural as well as urban areas. By taking part in it, men and women receive education of different kinds, learn various skills and thus generate the ability to achieve financial independence.

15. *Educational Tours.* Nowadays, much importance is being attached to educational tours as means of providing education in history and geography. In such tours the educands accompany the educator to far away places of historical or geographical significance. This has its entertainment value, apart from the information it provides. In many universities, educational tours have been made a compulsory part of education in history so that this education may become more life-like. Educational tours awake in the educand a greater awareness of the various movements occurring within the country, and also help to bring him nearer to nature. Tours are also considered an important part of industrial training, for the educand learns much by visiting industrial establishments.

Other Informal Agencies

In addition to the above agencies of informal education, different societies also have other institutions which are doing valuable work in this direction. Labour welfare committees, women welfare committees, cooperative societies, village panchayats, development block committees, and the like are concrete examples of this. Apart from this exhibitions of various kinds—art, science, industry, railways, postal, etc., do much to increase awareness of these spheres among the public. Nowadays international exhibitions have also become very popular. In such exhibitions, nations put up their respective pavilions to show their achievements and progress in various directions so that people viewing them can learn how far a particular country has progressed in a particular direction. One such exhibition was organised in Japan in 1970. The cause of higher education is also served by the committees and associations for various subjects—mathematics, history, biology, philosophy, etc., which hold international meetings from time to time in order to exchange views. And, the coffee houses in many large towns are no less important than educational institutions because among their clientelle are leading doctors, lawyers, literary figures, artists, impoverished politicians, who gather together to discuss all kinds of things. This helps to disseminate information and improve understanding of all affairs. Many towns also have literary associations which do much valuable work by encouraging and felicitating important literary figures. Professional associations, one example of which is the Indian Chamber of

Commerce and Industry, also play a significant role in educating public opinion by holding seminars and discussions. So, in this manner, different institutions contribute to the cause of education in their own way by providing information to the people.

Relationship between the Formal and Informal Agencies

Finally, it is necessary to keep in mind that the formal and informal agencies of education are complementary. Those aspects of education which are not attended to in schools are taken care of by the informal agencies. Even educational institutions employ many of the informal agencies for education—reading rooms, libraries, dramatic societies, cinema, films, institutions for military training, scouting and girl guides, etc. Besides, a school education is definitely incomplete if it is not complemented by education at home. For this reason, it is now an axiom of education that parents and educators should be given opportunities to meet each other so that they can consider the problems of their wards and think up ways of solving them. Many schools now celebrate parents day in which the parents of educands come to the school, meet teachers and discuss the various problems that face both the parents and the educators. In addition to this, school must also take the assistance of the community in spreading education, because the school is a special association created by the community through which it passes its acquired and accumulated knowledge to the younger generation. Without the co-operation of the state, it is difficult to establish or maintain an educational institution. Not only does the state make arrangements for the training of teachers and establishment of various institutions of special education, it also provides financial help to institutions otherwise not concerned with it. Inspectors appointed by the government inspect even the non-governmental institutions in order to ensure a uniform standard of education. In the absence of such control, most educational institutions would probably go to the dogs. In the field of higher education, most universities and research scholars would probably stop work if the government did not establish national libraries and provide grants for the creation of local libraries. It is therefore evident, that the formal and informal means of education supplement each other's efforts, and both should be exploited to the fullest extent to help the cause of education.

SCHOOL AS THE MOST IMPORTANT AGENCY

The school is considered the most important agency of education on the basis of the following arguments:

1. School is the sole agency of education as this term is generally interpreted. It is difficult to call a person educated if it is known that he has never been through school or college. Even if the individual does not take the trouble of obtaining the highest degrees, he should have been to school to gain elementary knowledge of mathematics and language.
2. Schools and educational institutions are believed to be the only media through which the national educational policy can be put into actual practice. When a national educational policy was laid down after independence in India, main attention was paid towards increasing the number of schools.

3. Without the assistance of the school, the family cannot by itself perform the task of educating child, and for this reason alone do parents send their children to schools. Earning one's livelihood is one important objective of education, and for this the child has no alternative but to go to school. It is not at all surprising that family businesses and occupations should have come to an end and that women should also be going out of the home in search of jobs. In consequence, it is no longer possible for the parents to educate their children without external help. It is better therefore to leave this task to the school.

4. Most of other means of education are capable of being turned to ulterior use, of use as the means of spreading political thought of a particular school, while school is the only one which provides real education. Schools and colleges have no aim but education. Magazines, radio, films, newspapers, etc., can be perverted as media of political propaganda of a definite school of thought. This reduces their importance as agencies of education.

5. School is the only educational agency which seeks to develop the individual's body, mind, morals, religious thinking and spiritual contemplation. It aims at complete development. Most of the other agencies can hope to develop any one or the other aspects of a person's personality. Libraries and reading rooms provide only mental education. The radio does not help in improving the body but schools and colleges also provide opportunities for physical, mental, moral and spiritual development.

6. Schools are also the chief media of conscious or intentional education. Their sole aim is to provide education, just as it is the sole aim of the educators, men and women, who work there. These educators are professional people trained to educate. These individuals devote much thought to the objectives and means of education, analyse the novel experiences which fall to their lot during the course of actual teaching, and make use of such experiences to improve their efficiency. No other individual can find or even hope to find so much time to devote to education. Neither is such a person an expert in teaching. Obviously, the school should be accepted as the best medium of imparting education.

7. In the case of certain specialized forms of education, it is impossible to achieve anything in the absence of schools and colleges, for example, medical, engineering and technical education. Colleges are the only media of providing training in these specialised spheres and in academic learning at the highest level.

8. One criterion of the importance of an agency of education is the extent to which it makes a contribution to education, but another criterion is the possibility of its being substituted by another. If this criterion is applied to the various agencies of education, it will be seen that school is the only one for which there is no substitute, and hence it is indispensable. The state, family, library, cinema, social welfare centres, in fact none of these agencies can hope to replace the school. Even if the child is educated within the family, such education is limited to primary education or training in the hereditary occupation. The family cannot provide more education than this. On the other hand, even some agency of education is not available after formal education has been completed, the absence does not constitute such a great handicap. Hence, school is the most important agency of education.

5

EVALUATION OF THE CURRENT EDUCATIONAL PATTERN

The Radhakrishnan Report of 1948-1949 hinted at the social aims of colleges when it said that the educational institution should introduce the educand to community life, provide useful information, and help to develop the necessary habits of intellectual work. It was also indicated that the current pattern of education did not fulfil our social requirements. The following shortcomings were noticed:

1. *Lack of objectives.* The prosperity of any nation depends upon the success of its system of education. The education in a country should conform to the national interest. From this standpoint, Indian education, particularly higher education, is entirely inadequate. Most educands receiving higher education were not aware of the reasons for receiving it. As a consequence, this aimlessness led to indiscipline, lack of sociability, etc., and also made it difficult for the educand to play a useful role in society once he had left college.

2. *Defective syllabi.* The current system of education was rendered obsolete because the syllabi had not been brought up-to-date. Consequently, the question provided through them could not possibly satisfy the contemporary needs of our society.

3. *Miseconomy.* Concerning the uneconomic performance of higher education, the Universities Commission had commented that a very large quantity of public funds was being wasted every year. What was even worse that this miseconomy involved a further waste of the time, effort and money of the parents of each student, and yet achieved nothing better than a total indifference to the frustration of the student's ambitions and hopes. This misuse of public funds is proved by the fact that there are larger number of educated unemployed in the country than uneducated unemployed. Evidently, if this education cannot train a man to earn his own livelihood, it can hardly be expected to turn him into a social asset.

4. *Specialization.* Modern education pays little attention to comprehensive and all round development of the educand. Higher education provides him with considerable information on one subject, but also deprives him of the opportunity of finding out anything about any other subject. As Mr. KG. Saiyeden has remarked, a narrow-minded unimaginative specialization leads to students of science being completely ignorant of art and poetry and students of the arts being incapable of understanding how science and scientific methods have transformed the world in which they live. But it cannot be forgotten that it is difficult for such one-sided personalities to adjust in society. Such individuals find it difficult to fulfil their

responsibilities devolving upon them from a variety of social relationships. For this reason, specialization in education hinders the fulfilment of social needs.

5. *English being the medium of education.* Considered from the social standpoint, education in India can claim to be a success only if it produces individuals who are capable of having a sense of oneness with their countrymen, rich or poor, educated or uneducated, villagers or city dwellers. This can be done only if education is imparted through the mother tongue or the national language. But since English is the medium of instruction in many states it leads to an alienation between the educated and the average Indian not similarly educated. Gandhiji also commented on the role of English as the medium of instruction in India. He said, "To inflict English on children is to stunt their natural growth and perhaps to kill originality in them." He also remarked that it had sapped the nation's power, weakened people, separated them from the common mass and made education unnecessarily expensive. The harm done to country by this education is only too evident.

6. *Defective system of examination.* The system of examination at every level of education — primary, secondary, intermediate, university — is very defective. In fact, it does not provide any real clue to the ability of the educand. It indicates nothing more than his ability to memorize bookish knowledge, of which it is an adequate test. It does not suggest the level of development he has achieved. Consequently, the educated individual possesses a fund of knowledge, but his personality does not develop.

7. *Encouragement to individualism.* Modern education encourages the spirit of individualism and leads to the expression of such anti-social traits as indiscipline, obstinacy, irregularity, misuse of authority, sexual misbehaviour, etc. It is seen that the uneducated individual is possessed of more social sense than the educated. Such an education is not only inadequate but positively harmful for society.

In view of the above shortcomings, the defectiveness of the present system of education and its failure to satisfy current social requirements need hardly be debated further. Very few, if any, educated people evince any desire for social service. On the contrary, the more educated the individual, the greater is his selfishness, pretension, egoism. If education is to serve the ends of society, it must get rid of the shortcomings outlined above. After India achieved her independence, a number of commissions appointed for the purpose of reviewing the system of education have pointed out the above defects time and again. The government has done something to eliminate these defects, but an educational system which will satisfy our society's requirements is a far cry. For this it is essential that the system of education must conform to the requirement of the nation and also that arrangements be made for free and compulsory primary education, adult education and basic education.

SCIENTIFIC AND TECHNICAL EDUCATION

The present age is an age of science. The progress of any nation depends to a large extent upon its scientific progress. And, for scientific progress, it is essential that the country must possess scientists of all branches in a large number. For this scientific education is essential. Science has been responsible for important technological developments in the fields of production and commerce. Absence of technical know-how within a country is reflected in the lower level of production in every field and also in the failure of the products to compare favourably with products prepared outside. Consequently, a nation cannot make its mark in international trade which, in turn, leads to a worsening of its economic condition. Hence, technical education is a necessity in every country in the modern age.

Imitation of Western countries in this respect

Almost all scientific discoveries and technological development have taken place in the Western countries. It cannot be denied that in the long past, India was more technologically developed than any of the Western countries, but this old knowledge can be of no particular use in the modern era. Hence, it has become essential that one should imitate the West in respect of technical and scientific knowledge and learning.

Education in the Present Indian Context

The single most pressing problem facing the country today is the economic situation. So far it has been found difficult to grow enough food to feed the growing population. This is not because the land here is less fertile than elsewhere, but the simple reason that the Indian farmer is ignorant of modern developments and continues to rely on the traditional methods of agriculture and farming. It has, therefore, been necessary to depend on Western countries for vital food supplies. It is, therefore, essential that all technical innovations in the field of agriculture should be made known to the farmer. At present India is one of the poorer countries in the world and the average income of an Indian is far less than that of an average citizen of one of the progressive nations of world. As a result, the average individual finds it difficult even to fulfil his physical requirements. This leads to failing health, increasing diseases and consequent waste of the nation's labour wealth. Science has done much to save wealth, time and effort by technological improvements in the fields of production, exchange, transport and communications. Without adopting these innovations, it is impossible for the country to progress.

It is obvious that in view of the present condition of the country, education should aim primarily at disseminating the science and technology of the West. Gandhiji had this in mind when he started that Indian education should be based on industrial education. Scientific and technical education is essential not only for curing the country of its economic ills but also for protecting it against invaders.

It is evident from the brief history of vocational and technical education given above that it faces certain special problems in the country. Some of these problems are the following:

1. *Unemployment among trained individuals.* In the recent past there were loud complaints from many sections of society that there are not enough institutions for technical and vocational training in the country. Even today there are some

demands to open more such institutions in certain parts of the country, but at the same time people are aware that there is widespread unemployment among technically trained graduates and technicians. Besides, many of the people apparently employed are only inadequately or improperly employed. This has created a very redoubtable situation which suggests that there was no correlation between the increase in technical training and actual industrial progress. It has already been pointed out that all modern progressive nations carry out surveys to determine the number of trained people required in each sphere of industry before entering on a programme of providing institutions for their training. These institutions are used to fulfil this demand for technical training. Although this idea was accepted in principle in India also, in actual practice no relation was maintained between the demand and supply of technically trained personnel. In the Fourth Five Year Plan the government had decided to provide employment to such people and also to control admission to all such colleges as well as colleges providing general education.

2. *Shortage of technicians at the lower level.* On the one hand, one finds a large number of qualified engineers without employment while on the other there is an acute shortage of trained technicians at comparatively lower levels of work. Most of the craftsmen and mechanics are not trained individuals. Even today one finds acute shortage of properly trained mechanics for maintenance work in motor vehicles, small machines, electrical appliances, etc.

3. *Absence of cooperation between the state, industry and education.* At the root of both the above problems is the lack of co-ordination and planning between the government, industry and education, because this imbalance of demand and supply is clear evidence of lack of planning. If technical education is to be really useful to the nation, it is essential that there should be co ordination between these three sectors so that their education should train the right number and right kind of individuals for which there is a demand in industry. The government can then really accept responsibility for finding employment for these trained personnel.

4. *Defects of administration.* To a considerable extent, the difficulties and problems of technical and vocational education in this country are enhanced by the administration, where sometimes one finds one man doing the job of three while at other times one finds two or more people engaged on a task which can easily be performed by one person. In both these conditions, the quality and quantity of work suffer, apart from the unpleasant experiences which the trained individual has to suffer. Many times politicians interfere in the work of highly skilled technicians and specialists, and as a result one finds many industrial and technical programmes suffering unimaginable losses. This also leads to dissatisfaction among the workers. Unless these problems of administration are solved, it will not be possible to create a climate conducive to the trained individuals.

5. *Narrow curriculum.* As far as possible, the curriculum for technical education should also include teaching of several subjects keeping in mind that the technician is also a human being. In recent years, attention has been paid to this aspect, and

one finds that the syllabi of most engineering colleges and technological institutes includes studies of social sciences and the humanities.

6. *Problem of the medium of education.* It is essential that the mother tongue should be the medium of education at the lower and middle level of technical education because educands coming in at this level do not have sufficient linguistic skill to study through the medium of English. But unfortunately even today, there is little or no technical literature available in Hindi or any regional language, with the result that it has been impossible to use them as media of technical education. The government is engaged in the task of creating a vocabulary of technical terms in Hindi and other regional languages, which encourages one in the hope that it will be possible to grant technical training through this medium in the near future.

7. *Shortage of trained teachers.* In the sphere of vocational and technical education there is an acute shortage of trained educators. In order to overcome this difficulty it is necessary to make the profession more attractive by offering high salaries to the staff of institutions engaged in this kind of education. Then, possibly people may find it more attractive and profitable to stay in the country than to settle abroad. Under the existing circumstances, a very high percentage of the trained talent migrates to foreign countries where the prospects are much better.

8. *Education after leaving school.* Another difficulty is that fairly soon after leaving school and taking up some job the trained individual finds that he is lagging far behind in knowledge because he cannot keep up with more recent advances in knowledge and technology. It is, therefore, desirable that some arrangement for refresher courses for these people should be made so that they can keep up with the growing knowledge.

9. *Lack of practice in laboratories.* Generally speaking, there is definitely a shortage of well equipped laboratories and workshops in the country, but even where they are available they are not put to sufficient use. Most of the education imparted to the educand is of a theoretical nature, with much less emphasis upon practical work and practice. But research laboratories can only be increased when the industrialists cooperate with the government. Another aspect of this problem is that such laboratories should make use of the equipment manufactured within the country instead of depending exclusively upon exports.

10. *Insufficient research.* Compared to the more progressive nations, India spends far less on research in technology. In Russia and America the amount spent on research is 2.8% of the national income while in India the amount invested in research is only 0.2% of the national income. In the absence of continuous research and new inventions, both technical education and industrial progress suffer. Hence, there is every need for encouraging research on the materials available in the country.

There is no doubt that some attention is being paid to the solution of these difficulties of technical and vocational education in the country, but undue interference by politicians and the government's inherent lethargy have only aggravated the situation. If anything positive is to be achieved, co-operation between the government, industrialists and directors of education is unavoidable. Unless some co-ordination is reached in the thinking of these three parties, there is no hope of progress in vocational and technical education. Neither will there be any chance of the trained people finding sufficient and proper employment. The one ray of hope is that the government has professed a keen interest in the problem of the trained unemployed and has promised some relief. The future of the country inevitably depends upon producing a larger number of technically proficient individuals and upon the proper utilization of their talents in the industrial sphere.

SECONDARY EDUCATION

The Secondary Education Commission appointed by the Central Government in 1952 made a survey of the objectives of secondary education and also an analysis of the defects of the prevailing system of education. According to this Commission, the following defects can be seen in the existing pattern of secondary education:

1. Existing secondary education is far removed from real life.
2. School education is narrow and one-sided, and is unable to train the total personality of the educand.
3. English being the medium of education, little attention has been paid to the teaching of other subjects.
4. Pressure of the examination kills the educator's enthusiasm and also his desire to experiment. He is concerned only with completing the course set down in the syllabus, so that many insignificant parts of the syllabus are stressed, to the exclusion of the more important aspects.
5. Large size of the classes renders impossible any direct contact between the educand and the teacher, and as a result indiscipline is becoming very common.
6. No attention is paid to developing the educand's character.
7. Defective techniques of teaching are adopted with the result that the child's development is being hindered.

The defects that were pointed out by the Education Commission more than a decade ago, exist today without any significant improvement. These defects can be found in an even more aggravated form in private educational institutions. Apart from this, the most noticeable thing about education in the country today is lack of direction and purpose. There is little relationship between life and the curriculum decided for education so that even after completing his secondary education, the education is ill-fitted for anything in life. Indiscipline and low standard of teaching are also common features. There is little, if any, social and community life in the school. Much of the effort is being wasted, as is evident from the high percentage of failures. In such a situation, secondary education can benefit from a complete overhaul.

Characteristics of a Good Secondary School

The success and efficiency of any school can be judged by the extent to which it is successful in achieving the aims of education laid down for that specific level of education. Hence, the good secondary schools are the ones that have succeeded in achieving the aims of secondary education. The Secondary Education Commission appointed by the Central Government has thrown considerable light on the objectives of secondary education, its curriculum, its techniques of teaching, organisation, etc. These will help us to determine the characteristics of a good secondary school. The more important features are the following:

1. *Development of democratic qualities.* Secondary schools must try to evolve democratic qualities in young boys and girls so that in later life they can become ideal citizens of the country and thus contribute to its progress and development.

2. *Development of professional skills.* The aim of secondary education is not to prepare the educand for higher education but to impart to him certain professional skills which he can employ in order to earn his livelihood and thus raise the standard of economic prosperity in the country.

3. *Development of personality.* While passing through the secondary education stage, the educand is at the crucial point of his personality development because of his tender age. Hence, only those secondary schools can be called good which provide for the physical, mental, social, intellectual, spiritual and moral development of the educand through a variety of extra-curricular programmes.

4. *Development of leadership.* The success of democracy and prosperity of the country depends upon the availability of the right kind of leadership in every sphere of life. Hence, the good secondary school must train the educand in right kind of leadership through discipline and an adequate social environment.

5. *Dynamic techniques of teaching.* Good secondary schools always adopt dynamic techniques of teaching in which the educand gets the greatest opportunity to be active. Teaching techniques should be modified according to the intelligence level and psychological needs of the educand. Extra-curricular programmes and games should be considered an essential part of the school's activities.

6. *Guidance and advice.* In good secondary schools, arrangements are made to provide individual, personal, educational and vocational guidance to the educands. Teachers and psychologists cooperate with the educand to solve most of his problems. Besides, it is better to decide upon some particular professions at the secondary stage, and for this, guidance should be provided to the educand.

7. *Adequate and hygienically ventilated buildings.* A good secondary school possesses adequate and properly ventilated buildings, because these are no less important than the text books or the educators. If attention is paid to these things, the physical environment favours education.

8. *Proper methods of examination and evaluation.* In a good secondary school objective tests are employed for evaluating the educand's performance. This evaluation is achieved not only by means of the annual examination but also by the monthly report of the educand's progress. A good secondary school adopts a scientific attitude to the problem of examination and evaluation.

9. *Good conditions for the educators.* Finally, the success of the secondary school depends upon its teachers, and for this reason they must be given every

opportunity and facility for developing their personalities and adding to their knowledge. Besides, they must be allowed to play an important part in the administration and organisation of the school. Arrangements must be made for their training and payment of adequate salaries. They must also be consulted in drawing up the curriculum. In this manner, only good teachers can form a proper foundation for a good secondary school. If the educators are good, there will be constant improvement in the techniques of teaching and evaluation, and this will contribute to the development of the educand's personalities and characters.

Role of Government

In modern democratic States, both the Central Government and local governing bodies must play their respective roles in the development of secondary education. In this connection, the Indian Secondary Education Commission has spelled out the respective responsibilities of both the governments. The Central Government must undertake the responsibility of laying down the objectives, curriculum, organisation, etc., of education. The education commission has pointed out that the Central Government must establish training centres for guides and career teachers to which the State governments can send their candidates for training. The Central Government must also undertake the task of preparing the best possible text-books, and by publishing them establish the standard to be imitated by other publishers. It should also organise committees of specialists to determine the objectives of secondary education, apart from determining the organisation, curriculum, mode of selection of educators, etc., for the secondary schools.

But the real responsibility for secondary education actually rests with the state governments, because it is the State government which organises secondary education in the State. In Uttar Pradesh, the State government has established a Secondary Education Commission, under the control of an Education Director. This director of education effectively controls education in each area through a deputy director whose function is to keep an eye on the functioning of schools in his area through the medium of inspectors. The Board of High School and Intermediate Education in the State lays down the curriculum for all the schools and also makes arrangement for examinations of the educands studying in the government schools and also in the numerous private run schools and inter colleges. These latter institutions are also subject to check and control by the inspectors, and they are financially aided by the government.

Diversified Curriculum

The multipurpose school, as is suggested by its name, is established for a variety of purposes which far exceeds the objectives of the average school. Its aim is not merely to prepare its educands for certain examinations but also to provide them with some kind of professional training in order to render them economically independent. For this reason, the educands studying in such schools have to undergo training in some kind of manual skill. While in the average school, efforts are made for the development of the educand's character and personality, the multipurpose school is also concerned with the development of social qualities and qualities of citizenship in its educands. For this purpose, the activities laid down in the curriculum are supplemented by other cooperative activities such as literary groups, music and dramatic societies, games and physical exercises, students groups, scouting, labour donation, social service, Red Cross and first aid, etc. By means of such activities, efforts are made to develop various interests in the educand. Many multipurpose schools also make arrangements for adult education and rural welfare programees. In an agricultural country like India such schools have their own importance, but unfortunately their number is still very small. Most of the schools in the country are intended for general education in which the main objective is to help the student pass a particular examination. It would be better if all the secondary schools situated in villages are converted into multipurpose schools.

SYSTEM OF EXAMINATION

Under the present system of examinations in this country, all the students are put in a single hall, at the end of each session, and answer books are distributed to each of them. At the appointed time, the question papers are distributed to them, following which during the space of two or three hours the student is expected to answer a required number of questions. Finally, the answer books are gathered and sent to an examiner whose appointment in that capacity is previously confirmed. Sometimes, the examiner is other than the person who sets the examination paper. If the student's attempt in the answer books is considered worthy of being awarded 33 per cent marks by the examiner, he is deemed to have passed the said examination. If he fails to secure these marks, in the eyes of examiner, he is deemed to have failed to pass the examination. The individual who does not succeed is compelled to spend another session in the same class.

Defects of the Examination System

There is hardly any need to point out that the existing examination system is not conducive to the proper development of children. The following are some of its shortcomings, that have been time and again pointed out by various educationists and commissions appointed for the purpose.

1. *Students do not study throughout the whole year.* For the present examination system, the student is not compelled to exert himself through the entire session, but achieves competency for it by labouring only through the last few weeks before the examination. In this manner, the student does not attain any real ability or capability even though he passes the examination. He forgets a lesson just as soon or as rapidly as he learns it. During the first two or three months of the session, it is a rare student who is seen at his desk. In this manner from the educational viewpoint, a major portion of a student's time is totally wasted.

2. *Studying from question-answer books and key books.* In the present context, a student's ability is gauged from the scores he obtains in the examinations. And for obtaining good marks in the examinations, there is no need to wander into a maze of extensive reading and comprehensive knowledge. In every examination paper, the student is required to do four to six questions out of nine or ten that are set. The consequence is that even without having gone through more than one-third

of the course prescribed for study, the average student finds three or four questions that he is in a position to answer. And four to ten pages of writing are considered adequate in answer to each question. Thus, why should the student bother himself with reading bulky books that are likely to cause him untold misery and confusion? And the best books do not even include any clue as to the precise answer that would suit a particular question which is likely to be asked in the examination. Often, most of the students write out the answers to questions asked in previous years in the examinations for which they are preparing. This is considered one of the best methods of preparation for examination. And if now the student discovers a book in the market that provides answers to all examination questions, then where is the need to write out these answers himself? Hence, the student instead of bothering to burden his brain with the actual text-books, studies help books and succeeds in the examination. The books in question-answer form are not sufficiently brief so that the student desirous of further economising upon the effort to be expended in the examination can turn to a perusal of guess papers which include answers to possible examination questions in a total of approximately fifty to sixty pages. If the guess work turns out to be exact or if the student is lucky, he is sure to pass the examination. It is only too painfully evident that the student who passes his examinations in this manner possesses no knowledge whatsoever of his subject and the object of examination is as far as possible from being fulfilled.

3. *Fear of examination.* In the modern examination system the examination is taken at the end of the session with the result that the student is fearfully conscious of the examination right through the session. Teachers and students alike are normally engaged in the study of text-books, there being little or no time for the student to engage in the study and perusal of any general books, not directly pertaining to his curriculum. He is also in no position to develop any real interest in other things. The natural result is that the student is not aware of anything outside the course that is prescribed. And, no curriculum or book, can ever provide complete knowledge of any subject. For such comprehensive knowledge, it is essential that many books be studied and that this study be supplemented with the necessary experience of actual practical life. Under the present examination system, the fear of examination does not conduce to any extensive study.

4. *Success in examinations a matter of luck.* In the way examinations are conducted at present, success is more a matter of luck than of anything else. His entire future is to be decided in two or three hours. No matter what skill a student has gained in his subject through constant labour during the entire session, his effort is completely wasted if for some reason or the other he fails to exhibit his skill in these three hours. Some students fail to attend the examination through some contingency such as illness during the examination period, or an accident or any other human involvement. On the other hand, even though they are in a position to attend the examination, they fail to give their best performance. The only consequence in such a case is that their whole year's effort is wasted.

5. *Mechanical method.* In this way, the existing system of education is a machine in which conclusions are reached, while no importance being attached to the human

elements involved. Hence, people have devised new methods of succeeding in this mechanical set-up. Some students do not bother to put in more than a few weeks' efforts for the examinations, during which they do nothing more than make a cursory study of guess papers and question-answer forms. As a result, they are in a position to come to grips with the paper, even though there is no element of mastery involved. And in subjects in which the question paper outdoes expectation, and unexpected questions crop up, the contingency is overcome by fraternizing with the examiners and having their marks surreptitiously increased. And in the case of such a success in any examination, it is only natural for the individual to be devoid of any skill whatsoever in the subject in which he has passed the examination.

6. *Defects concerning evaluation of answer books.* Under the present system of examination, a student's achievement in any subject is measured by the marks that he obtains during the examination. Hence, his fortune depends upon the Mr evaluation of his effort in the answer book. Such a method is susceptible to numerous faults, some of them being enumerated below:

(i) If the teacher's mental condition is disturbed he does not evaluate the answer books correctly. What most often occurs is that the first copies in the bundle sent to him are examined with due care, but as he gradually tires and reaches a stage of growing exhaustion, the subsequent copies are gone through as a matter of necessity and duty.

(ii) It is only too apparent that all copies are not examined from the same standpoint or standard. Of course, different examiners would award differing marks to the same copy, but even if the same examiner is asked to examine the same copy, it is quite likely that he will award it different marks on different occasions.

(iii) The maximum number of marks that any student may be awarded depends upon the examiner's mental tendency. It is a common case that the subject in which the examiner himself has never managed to score more than 60% marks in any examination that he has taken, is one in which no student will ever be awarded high marks by such an individual since he is convinced that none is equal to him, let alone anyone being superior to him. On the other hand, other examiners are very liberal and are even capable of awarding marks upto 90%. If all the answer books of a particular subject were to go to one and the same examiner, there would be some saving grace, but it usually happens that the number of students studying a subject runs into thousands so that the examiners of it are also numerous. If an individual's copy falls into the hands of strict examiner, he is not likely to score well at all, while a less deserving candidate may score better than him if the latter's copy happens to have gone to a very liberal person. And this seems to be playing with the children's or student's career and capacities.

(iv) It often happens, that due to a very great variety of causes, the examiner has very little time at his disposal to examine the copies. One of the causes in such a case is the delayed arrival of the answer books themselves, but more often it is a case of the examiner's being busy or just careless. One natural outcome of such practice is that the teachers pay half their fee to have the answer books examined by other less qualified and in some cases completely unqualified individuals. Some teachers are so lacking in ethical sense that they have their wives and students do the work of examining the copies, even though they cannot be imagined to be qualified for the work. It is easy to understand the extent to which some innocent students suffer as the result of such behaviour on the part of teachers.

(v) Many of the examiners are completely prejudiced or biased in their thinking, having only the most incomplete knowledge of their respective subjects. Secondly, some teachers even fail to understand the actual implications of the question asked in the question paper. It is only to be expected in such circumstances that there is no justice done to the student.

7. *Long examination period.* The present examination system allows the period of examination to spread over the very considerable period of at least a month. It is often seen that students get some two weeks between two individual examination dates. Such a long period of inactivity has the worst effect upon the student's attitude towards the examination as it tends to lull him towards the seriousness of the matter. Secondly, the provision of time periods between various papers is not at all proportionate. He gets no more than a few hours between two papers while between another two he has a few days at his disposal. Evidently, the opportunity available for the preparation of each subject is unequal.

8. *Wrong objective.* The present aim of examination is to obtain marks in order to get a degree, not the desire, to gain skill in any subject. Hence, the main attention in any examination is concentrated upon getting good marks so that one can have proof of one's ability or skill. There are many methods of obtaining an adequate number of marks in the examination, though all of them are not formal. One of the simplest is obtaining a certificate of success in an examination without actually appearing in it, irrespective of the fact that discovery of such an incriminating fact leaves them open to criminal action in a court of law. And the objective behind obtaining a certificate or degree is no more than securing a remunerative position that offers financial security in life. Thus, students who are not particularly desirous of securing a good status in life are often careless of studying hard to obtain a degree since they require no such passport to the good things of life. As a result of the contaminated and one-sided objectives of education existing at present, the system is riddled with defects and an inherent and chronic corruption.

9. *Defects of the essay system.* Under the existing scheme of examination, the student is required to answer each question in the form of an essay, with the result that the educational system has acquired all the defects inherent in the essay system. In this method, the students pay much greater attention to learning answers to question than to understanding the subject and delving deep into it. In the examination hall, they do no more than reproduce these well learned and remembered answers on the answer books. Once the examination is over, the

facts learned for it are as expeditiously forgotten, since once they have been put in the answer book, they no longer possess any importance for the student. One natural outcome of this method is that even though the student may have done exceptionally well in the examination, he is more or less blank in all the subjects that he has made a pretense of studying.

Suggestions for Improving the Examination System

Many thinkers, educationists and education commissions have pointed out the above defects in the existing scheme of examinations in this country, but there are many difficulties that hinder the complete replacement of it. The main difficulty is financial besides which the extremely large number of candidates makes it difficult to evolve a different examination system for them. Hence, the practicable solution is to maintain the existing scheme of things and make efforts to effect definite improvements. Main suggestions in this respect are the following:

1. *Certificates should not be required for services.* If the tradition of requiring certificates for various jobs and services is given up, and the individuals are separately tested for qualities that the job requires, then people will give up the race for obtaining certificates and degrees, and turn their attention to developing qualities required in the professions of their choice. It must, of course, be kept in mind that this method is not practicable in all professions, nevertheless, it should be used in as many as admit of its use.

2. *Improvement in the evaluation of answer books.* The method and system of examining and evaluating answer books should be improved. The remuneration of evaluating copies should be enough to induce the examiner to attend to them himself, and to do this work efficiently and well. The time allowed to the examiner for evaluating the answer books should be sufficient to allow him to work in peace so that no haphazard work results from hurry or strain. There should be a definite standard of references concerning the answer of different questions. Every examiner should be required to send copies that he has examined as samples so that his standard of judgement can be measured, and he should be requested to evaluate the remaining copies similarly.

3. *Terminal or monthly examinations.* Nevertheless, the student's knowledge of his subject cannot be properly gauged once in a year in a sitting of only three hours. For this it is essential that the teacher should examine the students in the class every fifteen days or a month in the subject matter that he has taught till then. The results should be announced on the basis of these monthly tests as well as the annual examination. This method will compel the students to spread their labour over the whole year.

4. *Examination in other aspects of development.* The aim of education is not only to impart information but to achieve the complete development of the individual. It is only information that is examined in the present examinations. Hence, it is essential that the child's physical, emotional and social development also be examined, even though the marks obtained therein may not be made the reason

for detaining him if he fails. Yet, these marks will help in advising and improving him. If the children understand that it is essential for them to pass in these respects also they themselves will try harder to improve themselves.

5. *Re-examination of those who fail to attend regular examinations.* Examinees, who, for one or the other legitimate reason such as disease, accident, etc., fail to attend their examination at the regular time, should be given a chance to be examined once the reason for their abstaining from the regular examination has been confirmed. Their efforts during the entire year should not be allowed to go waste.

6. *Discouragement to rote learning.* Questions in the examination papers should be such as discourage the practice of rote learning but encourage the expression of the student's skill in the subject. Questions should vary radically from year to year so that the practice of basing preparation and guess papers on questions asked in previous years and then rote learning answers to them is discouraged and ultimately discarded.

7. *Wide range of question papers.* Questions in the examination paper should cover every aspect of the curriculum even if more than one questions are given, and the solution of one is required. Such methods will induce the students to study all that is prescribed rather than making a selection from it.

8. *Equitable distribution of examination period.* During the period of examinations, the distribution of papers should be equitable and proportionate, the normal period of inactivity not stretching over more than one or two days. Only one paper should be set for one day.

9. *Increase in the number of examiners.* The number of examiners should be considerably increased so that all of them can conveniently judge a smaller number of copies in the period of one or two weeks provided them for the purpose.

10. *Punishment for corrupt practices.* Strict measures should be adopted for punishing all examiners who resort to corrupt measures in passing examinations or obtaining certificates.

Finally, the fundamental fact that must be pointed out is that the improvement in the existing scheme of examination depends upon the teachers themselves. It is for them to encourage the students in their classes to attain high degree of skill and efficiency in the subject rather than to prepare them for the examinations. In educational institutions, the principal teacher can specially attend to this aspect of the matter. Co-operation between teachers and the various examining bodies can help to improve the system of examinations.

6

CURRICULUM

Meaning of Curriculum

The term 'curriculum' is of Latin origin and it implies an athletic ground, thus indicating that curriculum is the ground through which the educand has to pass in order to reach a definite goal. In the past the term was taken to mean a collection of knowledge and skill. It did not then imply the educand's needs, but instead the knowledge and skills of the specialists working in different spheres. But the modern interpretation of the term is clarified by Bent and Kronenburg, who suggest that the curriculum is the organized form of subject matter, specially prepared to meet the requirements of children. Hence, now curriculum includes those experiences and activities which provide the student with the knowledge and the skills he will require in facing the various situations of real life. Obviously, the term 'curriculum' cannot be restricted to a list of books, because it must include other activities, the environment of the school and numerous other elements not taught by books. In the words of Bent and Kronenburg, "Curriculum, in its broadest sense, includes the complete school environment involving all the courses, activities, reading and association furnished to the pupils in the school."

Definition of Curriculum

It will be easier to understand the concept of curriculum by glancing at a few definitions given as follows:

1. *Curriculum is experience.* In the words of Munroe, "Curriculum embodies all the experiences which are utilized by the school to attain the aims of education." Thus the various subjects included for study in a curriculum are not intended merely for study or rote learning but to convey experiences of various kinds. The concept has been defined in more or less the same terms in the report of the Secondary Education Commission in these words, "Curriculum does not mean only the academic subjects traditionally taught in the school, but it includes the totality of experiences that a pupil receives through the manifold activities that go on in the school, in the classroom, library, laboratory, workshop, playgrounds and in the numerous informal contacts between teachers and pupils." Another definition of curriculum as experience is provided by Crow and Crow, "The curriculum includes all the learner's experiences in or outside school that are included in a

programme which has been devised to help him develop mentally, physically, emotionally, socially, spiritually and morally." It is obvious, then, that the aim of curriculum is to provide experience to the educand so that he may achieve complete development. By calling the curriculum an experience, the fact is made explicit that it includes not merely books but all those activities and relationships which are indulged in by the educand both inside and outside the school. Hence, the syllabi specified by the authority should not be taken to mean curriculum.

2. *Curriculum is a means or tool.* It is apparent from the foregoing definitions that curriculum is not an end in itself, but a means to an end, because it is created in order to achieve the aims of education. That is why one finds that different educationists have suggested different kinds of curricula to conform to the aims and objectives ascribed to education. Explaining the concept of curriculum as a tool of education, Cunningham writes, "The curriculum is the tool in the hands of the artist (the teacher) to mould his material (the pupil) according to his ideal (objective) in his studio (the school)." Here the educator is compared to an artist and the curriculum as one of the instruments or tools used by him to develop the educand according to and in conformity with the aims of education. It is evident that the curriculum will change with every change in the aims of education.

3. *Curriculum is environment.* The most comprehensive definition of curriculums given by those who conceive it to include the total environment of the school. In the words of H.L. Laswell, "The curriculum is made up of everything that surrounds the learner in all his working hours." In fact, the curriculum has been described as "the environment in motion." In modern times, this term is interpreted in this more liberal sense because there is no questioning the fact that the child's education is influenced by not only books but the playgrounds, library, laboratory, reading room, extra curricular programmes, the educational environment, and a host of other factors. In the school both the educator and the educand are part of the curriculum because they are part of the environment, while in the family the child and his parents are part of the educational environment. Hence, the formation of the curriculum is not restricted to making a list of subjects or text-books but must include a complete definition of the total environment in which the child is expected to progress and achieve the goals of education.

4. *Curriculum includes all activities.* It is stated in the *Twentyninth Year Book of the National Society for the Study of Education,* U.S.A. that, "The curriculum may be defined as the totality of subject matter, activities and experiences which constitute a pupil's school life." Elaborating the same concept further, H.H. Horne says, "The curriculum is that which the pupil is taught. It involves more than the acts of learning and quiet study; it involves occupations, productions, achievement, exercise, activity." Pragmatists, too, have included the entire range of the educand's activities in the curriculum because according to them the child learns by doing.

In the light of the various definitions of curriculum given above, it is possible to arrive at a definition of the terms which includes all the points mentioned in these definitions. Briefly, the curriculum is the means of achieving the goals of education. It includes all these experiences, activities and environments which the educand receives during his educational career. Such a definition of curriculum comprehends the educand's entire life, a contention borne out by all modern educationists who believe that the child learns not only inside the school but also outside it, on the playground, at home, in society, in fact, everywhere. That is why there is nowadays so much insistence on the participation of the parents in the child's education and on not restricting the environment of the curriculum to the school environment but taking it to mean every possible kind of environment encountered by the child. Besides, it includes all those activities which the child does, irrespective of the time and place of these activities. It also includes the entire range of experiences that the child has in the school, at home, in the world at large. Considered from this liberal standpoint, one finds that in preparing the curriculum one has a much wider background than would otherwise be possible.

The Aims and Objectives of Curriculum

Clarifying the aims and objectives of curriculum it has been pointed out in the report of the Secondary Education Commission that, "The starting point for curricular reconstruction must therefore be the device to bridge the gulf between the school subjects and to enrich the varied activities that make up the warp and woof of life." Hence, the curriculum should be so designed that it trains the educand to face the situations of real life, a curriculum can be said to have the following major objectives:

1. *Synthesis of subject and life.* The aim of the curriculum is to arrange and provide those subjects for an educand's study which will enable the educand to destroy any gulf between school life and life outside the school. The opinion of the Secondary Education Commission has already been quoted.

2. *Complete development.* The aim of the curriculum is to achieve the physical, mental, social, moral, religious, spiritual, in fact, complete development of the educand. Hence, while determining a curriculum it is essential to see whether it will make such a complete development possible.

3. *Development of democratic values.* In all democratic countries, the curriculum of education must aim to develop the democratic values of equality, liberty and fraternity, so that the educands may develop into fine democratic citizens. But this development should not only aim at national benefit. The curriculum must also aim at introducing a spirit of internationalism in the educand.

4. *Satisfaction of the educand's needs.* In defining curriculum, many educationists have insisted that it must be designed to satisfy the needs and requirements of the educand. It is seen that one finds a great variety of interests, skills, abilities, attitudes, aptitudes, etc., among educands. A curriculum should be so designed as to satisfy the general and specific requirements of the educands.

5. *Realization of values.* One aim of education is development of character, and what is required for this is to create in the educand a faith in the various desirable values. Hence, one of the objectives of education is to create in the educand a definite realization of the prevailing system of values.

6. *Development of knowledge.* In its most common connotation, the term curriculum is taken to mean development of knowledge or acquisition off acts. And, very frequently, this is the aspect kept in mind while designing a curriculum. But it must be remembered that it is not the only objective, although it is the most fundamental objective of a curriculum.

7. *Creation of a useful environment.* Another objective of curriculum is to create an environment suitable to the educand. Primarily, the environment must assist the educand in achieving the maximum possible development of his faculties, abilities and capabilities.

8. *Addition to knowledge.* In the contemporary educational patterns that curriculum is believed to be suitable which can create harmony, between the various branches of knowledge so that the educand's attitude should be comprehensive and complete, not one-sided.

9. *Harmony between individual and society.* In a democracy such social qualities as social skill, co-operation, the desire to be of service, sympathy, etc., are very significant because, without them, no society can continue to exist. On the other hand, development of the individual's own character and personality are also very important. Hence, the curriculum must create an environment and provide those books which enable the individual to achieve his own development at the same time as he learns these social qualities.

Curriculum and Syllabus

The relationship between curriculum and syllabus is made very clear by the foregoing description of the aims of curriculum. Curriculum is not merely syllabus, because the latter is only verbal, book-oriented and theoretical, while the former is not. Syllabus places more stress on learning and memory. On the other hand, the scope of the curriculum is much greater for it comprehends every aspect of the edueand's life, seeks to satisfy all his requirements and to develop every aspect of his personality. Hence, the syllabus is part and parcel of the curriculum, but the two terms should not be treated as synonymous. In addition to the syllabus, the curriculum also includes various kinds of extracurricular activities and all the various parts of the educational environment. Despite this the syllabus is treated as the basis of curriculum in the school, although it is improper to restrict the curriculum in this manner.

Bases of Curriculum

It is everywhere seen that the form of the curriculum undergoes a change whenever the aims of education are altered to suit changed conditions in society. For this reason, it is necessary to define the various bases of curriculum, of which the more important ones are the following:

1. *Aims of education.* One finds differences of curriculum according to the differing aims of education determined by the different philosophies of education such as idealism, realism, pragmatism, etc. If the aim of education is to bring about an industrial revolution then the curriculum will place more stress on industrial

activity but if education seeks to build the character of the educand, the curriculum will naturally lay a heavy emphasis upon the study of those subjects which help in character formation. If the curriculum aims at preparing the educand for future life and enabling him to earn his livelihood, it must include those subjects which give the educand some professional skill.

2. *Philosophy of education.* Another basis of the formation of curriculum is the philosophy of education. Difference in philosophic concepts leads to changes in the curriculum. Philosophy considers such fundamental and profound questions as man's place in the universe, the aims of nature, the aims of society, the relationship between man and society, etc. In every philosophy the answer derived for these questions is different, and this difference lends colour to the curriculum.

3. *Sociological basis.* In recent times, the curriculum has always been profoundly influenced by the discoveries of the various social sciences. This constitutes the sociological basis of education.

4. *Psychological basis.* But the most important basis of curriculum formation is the psychological one. In modern times so much research has been conducted in the sphere of educational psychology that it has become an independent branch of psychology. These researches have had great impact on the shaping of curricula and this is only natural since the curriculum is only a means to the educand's development. Hence, it should be shaped by the psychology of the educand.

Basic Principles of Curriculum Construction

Different educationists have expressed their own views about the fundamental principles of curriculum, the difference being created by their different philosophies of education. Briefly, the main principles of curriculum construction are the following:

1. *Principle of Utility.* T.P. Nunn, the educationist, believes that principle of utility is the most important principle underlying the formation of a curriculum. He writes, While the plain man generally likes his children to pick up some scraps of useless learning for purely decorative purposes, he requires, on the whole, that they shall be taught what will be useful to them in later life, and he is inclined to give 'useful' a rather strict interpretation. As a general rule, parents are in favour of including all those subjects in the curriculum which are likely to prove useful for their child in his life and by means of which he can be made a responsible member of society.

2. *Training in the proper pattern of conduct.* According to Crow and Crow, the main principle underlying the construction of a curriculum is that through education the educand should be able to adopt the patterns of behaviour proper to different circumstances. Man is a social animal who has to constantly adapt himself to social environment. Therefore, education must aim at developing all those qualities. In the educand which will facilitate this adaptation to the social milieu. The child is by nature self-centered, but education must teach him to attend to the needs and requirements of others besides himself. One criterion of an educated individual is that be should be able to adapt himself to different situations with which he is

confronted. In this context, the term conduct must be understood in its widest sense. Only then can this principle of curriculum construction be properly understood. All our activities in social, economic, family, cultural environment constitute behaviour or conduct, and it is the function of education to teach us how to behave in different situations.

3. *Synthesis of play and work.* Of the various modern techniques of education, some try to educate through work and others through play. But a great majority of educationists agree that the curriculum should aim at achieving a balance between play and work. In other words, the work given to the educand should be performed in such a manner that the child may believe it to be play. There is difference between work and play. That is why parents want to engage the child in work instead of allowing him to play all the time, but the child is naturally inclined to spend his time in playing. Keeping this in view, T.P. Nunn has written, "The school should be thought of not as a knowledge monger's shop but a place where the young are disciplined in certain forms of activity. All subjects should be taught in the "play way", care being taken that the "way" leads continuously from the irresponsible frolic of childhood to the disciplined labours of manhood."

4. *Synthesis of all activities of Life.* In framing a curriculum, attention should be paid to the inclusion, in it, of all the various activities of life, such as contemplation, learning, acquisition of various kinds of skill, etc. In the individual and social sphere of life, every individual has to perform a great variety of activities, and his success in life is determined by the success of all these activities. Hence, the curriculum should not neglect any form of activity related to any aspect oflife. A curriculum constructed on this basis will be both comprehensive and closely related to life. In other words, it should include all the activities that the educand is likely to require in later life.

5. *Principle of individual differences.* Modern educational psychology has brought to light, and stress the significance of individual differences that exist between one individual and another. It has been discovered that people differ in respect of their mental processes, interests, aptitudes, attitudes, abilities, skills, etc., and these differences are innate. All modern education is paidocentric, that is, it is centred around the child. Psychologists insist that the curriculum should be so designed as to provide an opportunity for complete and comprehensive development to widely differing individuals. One of the basic qualities of such a curriculum is flexibility, for it must be flexible in order to accommodate educands of low, average or high intelligence and ability, and to provide each one a chance to develop all these abilities to the greatest possible extent.

6. *Constant development.* Another basis for curriculum construction is the principle of a dynamic curriculum based on the realization that no curriculum can prove adequate for all times and in all places. For this reason the curriculum should be flexible and changeable. This is all the more true in the modern context when new discoveries in the various branches of science are taking place everyday. Hence, it becomes necessary to reshape the curriculum fairly frequently in order to incorporate the latest developments.

7. *Creative training.* Another important principle of curriculum construction is that of creative training. Raymont has correctly stated that a curriculum appropriate for the needs of today and the future must definitely have a positive bias towards creative subjects. And, one of the aims of education is to develop the creative faculty of the educand. All that is finest in human culture is the creation of man's creative abilities. Children differ from each other in respect of this ability. Hence, in framing a curriculum attention must be paid to the fact that it should encourage each educand to develop his creative ability as far as is possible.

8. *Variety.* Variety is another important principle of curriculum construction. The innate complexity of man and the many facets of his personality make it necessary that the curriculum should be varied, because no one kind of curriculum can develop all the faculties of an individual. Hence, at every level the curriculum must have variety. It will, on the one hand, provide an opportunity for developing the different faculties of the educand, while on the other, it will retain his interest in education.

9. *Education for leisure.* One of the objectives ascribed to education is training for leisure, because it is believed that education is not merely for employment or work. Hence, it is desirable that the curriculum should also include a training in those activities which will make the individual's leisure more pleasurable. A great variety of social, artistic and sporting activities can be included in this kind of training. Besides, educands should be encouraged to foster some or the other hobby so that they can put their leisure to constructive and pleasant use.

10. *Related to community life.* Curriculum can also be based on the principle that school and community life must be intimately related to each other. One cannot forget that the school is only a miniature form of community. Hence, the school curriculum should include all those activities which are performed by members of the larger community outside the boundaries of the school. This will help in evolving social qualities of the individual, in developing the social aspect of his personality and finally helping his final adaptation to the social environment into which he must ultimately go.

11. *Evolution of democratic values.* The construction of a curriculum in a democratic society is conditioned by the need to develop democratic qualities in the individual. The curriculum should be so designed that it develops democratic thinking and creates a positive faith in democratic values. The programme devised in the college should lead to the development of the individual and social qualities in the educand so that he may be able to participate usefully and successfully in democratic life. In all the democratic societies of the world, this is the chief consideration in shaping the curricula for primary, secondary and higher education.

It is evident from the foregoing account of the various bases of curriculum construction that this should be duly conditioned by careful thinking on all aspects — individual and social, variety, play and work, earning of livelihood, leisure, etc.

Importance of Curriculum Construction

The following advantages are derived when the curriculum is constructed for various levels of education:

1. *Achievement of educational aims.* The curriculum is constructed carefully in order to achieve the aims set for education, and therefore its advantage is that it helps in achieving these aims. In the absence of a curriculum it would be impossible to do anything systematically.

2. *Limits of teaching and learning.* In order to implement the educational programmes properly in different schools, it is necessary to determine in advance the body of knowledge to be acquired by the educands at different levels of education, and also the amount of teaching to be done by the educators. This can only be fixed on the basis of the curriculum. It helps in determining the work of the educator as well as that of the educand.

3. *Dissemination of knowledge.* The aim of education is the dissemination of knowledge, and this is also the aim of the curriculum. By studying the various subjects laid down in the curriculum, the educand acquires a quantity of knowledge in conformity with his abilities and level of intelligence. Different kinds of curricula are constructed for imparting education at different stages in the child's mental development.

4. *Development of character.* The curriculum of contemporary education aims not only at the dissemination of knowledge, but also at the development and formation of character because the child is kept in a social environment which encourages the development of all humane qualities in him. This improves the child's conduct and leads to development of character.

5. *Development of personality.* The various aspects of the educand's personality undergo change and development when he studies the various subjects prescribed in the curriculum, acquires different kinds of experience and adjusts or adapts to different sets of circumstances.

6. *Development of citizenship.* In almost all modern States, development of citizenship is considered to be one of the major responsibilities of education, and the curriculum is designed with this end in view.

7. *Discoveries and research.* At the highest level of education, the curriculum is designed to encourage research and make inventions.

7

TEACHING DEVICES

A great variety of teaching techniques are being used in modern Indian schools. There is no rigidity concerning this, because the educator chooses his technique to suit the occasion, the subject, the class, and a number of other factors. A. H. Garlick has clearly explained that the educator begins by deciding the subject he wants to teach. He then follows it up by selection and proper arrangement of the subject matter and finally arrives at the question of the method he should adopt to teach the subject to his pupils. It is here that he is faced with deciding between the advantages and disadvantage of the great variety of methods. Sometimes he turns to explanation, at others to exposition, at yet other times he is compelled to resort to lectures or to story telling. In his teaching he must also makes use of many illustrations and vivid examples. Briefly, the main methods of teaching are the following:

1. Asking questions and answering.
2. Illustration.
3. Narration.
4. Exposition.
5. Description.
6. Story-telling.
7. Lecture.
8. Text book reading.
9. Explanation.

ASKING QUESTIONS AND ANSWERING

Meaning

The oldest and the most famous of the various techniques of teaching is Socratic method of asking questions and answering them. In this method the intelligent educator allows his pupils to express their own ideas, stimulating them to think by interposing questions in their recital. If the students fail to provide an answer, the educator himself answers the difficult questions. The lesson is concluded when the educator sums up the subject matter which has been taught through the long series of questions and answers. Pestalozzi expressed the opinion that this Socratic method is very important. He based his own method of education on this technique, even though his method is very recent.

Required Abilities of Education

The difficulty of this method lies in the asking of appropriate questions. Though even the biggest fool can ask an unanswerable question, the question asked in the classroom must have some educative value. Asking such questions is no less than an art. This art, which is one aspect of the technique, is acquired through continuous practice. What is really required is complete awareness of the purpose of asking a particular question. The educator himself must possess the following abilities in order to phrase his questions skilfully:

1. *Accurate and comprehensive knowledge of the subject.* In order to ask appropriate questions, the educator must have comprehensive knowledge of the subject, as otherwise the questions are likely to be useless. It is only this knowledge which tells the educator the questions he must ask in order to teach something.
2. *Ability to analyse the subject.* The teacher's ability in asking questions depends upon his ability to analyse the subject matter and to locate the areas of difficulty inherent in it.
3. *Knowledge of the educand.* Before embarking on questions, the educator must have knowledge of the educand's psychology so that the questions should conform to the latter's mental level, abilities and motivation.
4. *Experience.* Much of the facility, variety and accuracy of the questions depends upon the educator's experience.
5. *Mental ability and decisiveness.* In order to ask the right questions, the educator himself must have mental ability and the power to arrive at a decision quickly.
6. *Power of expression.* Linguistic ability is essential in asking questions. The educator must also have experience in modulating his voice properly.

Reasons for Asking Questions

The various reasons for asking questions are the following:

1. *Motivation.* Through questions motivation is created in the educand by arousing his curiosity, focusing his attention and awakening his interest.
2. *Knowledge relating to the educand.* The object of many questions is to find out the educand's problems, attitudes, aptitudes, knowledge, etc. Hence, one of the objectives of asking such questions is to provide the teacher with adequate knowledge concerning the educand.
3. *Relating to old knowledge.* Another reason for asking questions is to relate the new knowledge given to the educand to the old knowledge he has received. This helps the educand to assimilate the new information.
4. *Locating difficulties.* The only way of finding out the student's difficulties in learning a subject is to ask him questions. This is essential, because without removing difficulties, teaching cannot be effective.
5. *Test of knowledge.* One set of questions can be specially devised to test the knowledge that the individual educand has grasped so far, It is believed that greater accuracy in the answers of one educand, than of another, indicates a better grasp of what is being taught. In our own examination system, questions are asked for this purpose.
6. *Co-operation and active participation of educands.* If the lecture on any subject is interrupted frequently to ask questions to the educands, they are compelled to

attend to what is being said and perforce to remember it also. Hence, educands are asked to answer questions in order to ensure their active participation in teaching.

7. *Means of development.* Asking questions can also be means of the intellectual and social development of the child. Social development depends on asking questions and receiving answers, because this increases mutual contact. If educands are permitted to ask questions freely, it helps in their free development.

8. *Localising around the basic lesson.* Another objective of asking questions is to localise or concentrate the subject matter around the basic subject. It sometimes happens that the educator wanders from the subject he is teaching. In such a situation the question asked by the educator or the educands once again focus his attention on the subject matter.

9. *Practice and repetition.* Another reason for asking questions is to allow the educand to apply his knowledge. In answering questions, the educand has to make use of the information he has acquired and this helps him in retaining it.

10. *Practice and repetition.* Yet another aim of asking questions is to repeat the subject matter and give the educands practice. The text books prescribed for various levels of education are equipped with a set of questions at the end of each chapter. These questions are intended to provide practice and repetition. That is why these questions are frequently entitled 'questions for practice'.

11. *Encouragement to thinking and observation.* Sometimes the questions are deliberately framed in such a way that the answers to them cannot be found either in the educator's lecture or in any text book. In order to answer them the educand has to depend upon his observation of things, objects, individuals and surroundings which form part of his environment. He is also compelled to think about such tilings. Such questions have particular importance when they are used to encourage independent thinking and originality of ideas. Educands with a greater degree of creativity rarely need such stimulus for they are in the habit of observing things of life and thinking about them.

12. *Increase in self-confidence.* This method has the advantage of adding to the educand's self-confidence because when he answers questions successfully, he realizes that he has understood and learnt the lesson.

It is clear from the foregoing account that this method of asking and answering questions is valuable both for the educator and the educand. It is not essential that a particular question must have only one specific reason behind it. It may be motivated by a number of reasons, even a few of which have not been included in the preceding account.

Important Factors in Questioning

Apart from the aims and the language of the question, the manner in which it is asked is also significant. If the manner of questioning is faulty, the question will not fulfil the purpose for which it was asked. Hence, in asking questions, the teacher must remember the following points:

1. *Seriousness.* Questions should always be asked seriously. It is improper to laugh, show anger or smile when asking questions.

2. *Attracting attention.* Questions should be asked to arrest the educand's attention when it shows signs of wandering away from the subject being taught.

3. *Proper frequency.* The frequency of questions should be so managed that they should not be too far apart in order to avoid lassitude or disinterest and not so close together as to give the educand no time to think at all.
4. *Proper interval.* The interval between questions can be determined by the complexity of the subject matter and the intelligence of the educands.
5. *Proper distribution.* Questions should be distributed over the entire lecture so that students are compelled to attend to each part of it.
6. *Entire class.* Questions should be asked to the entire class so that every individual is forced to exercise his mind.
7. *No side issues.* Questions should not be prefaced with side issues, they should be clearly stated so as to avoid wastage of time.
8. *No repetition.* Questions should not be repeated as a matter of habit. If this is done, educands do not pay attention to it the first time, confident that it will be repeated. It should only be repeated as an exception, not as a general rule.
9. *Neither too simple nor too difficult.* The subject matter of the question should conform to the knowledge and intelligence level of the educand, neither too simple, nor too difficult. If the questions are too simple, they will not require any mental effort, while excessively difficult questions will cause excessive strain on the educand's mental faculty, without achieving the desired result.
10. *Varied form and language.* The form and language of the questions should be varied in order to bring in variety and avoid monotony and disinterest.
11. *Collective thinking.* Even if the question has been satisfactorily answered by the first educand, the educator must continue to ask the same question to the other educands so that all the aspects are clarified by the thinking of all the educands.
12. *Encouragement.* The question should be accompanied by repeated comments which encourage the students to answer the question. This builds up the confidence of the educands and makes them feel that they can answer the question if they try.
13. *Proper language and subject matter.* The language and subject matter of the question should be determined beforehand. If the educator repeats the same questions in different words, it creates the impressions that either the educator has no self-confidence or that he has made no preparation. In both the cases the impact on the educand is undesirable.

It is clear, therefore, from the above description, that the questions should be carefully asked, keeping in mind the language, the style, purpose, etc.

Traits of Proper Answers

In this technique of asking and answering questions, the answers are just as important as the questions. On the one hand, it is essential that the questions should be presented in the best possible way, and on the other, it is equally important that educands should be trained to answer questions properly. In the modern examination system, the educand's character, ability, mode of thinking, knowledge, in fact, everything is judged by the answers that he provides to the questions asked in the examination. Hence, the educator must train the educand to give the right kind of answer, and in order to do this, he himself must be aware of the qualities a good answer must possess. The following are these qualities:

1. *Appropriateness.* The first quality of a good answer is that it must answer the question without going into long and purposeless digressions. But the answer can be appropriate only when the educand's ideas are clear. Lack of clarity in ideas communicates itself to the answer and makes the answer inappropriate.

2. *Completeness*, When the answer is complete, it helps the audience or the reader understand the subject. Hence the words used in the answer must convey the same sense to the listener that they convey to the user, the sense in which the latter has used them. Incomplete answers should not be accepted. The teacher must insist upon the educand's completing his sentences and providing a complete answer.

3. *Linguistic qualities.* Language is the medium in which answers are given and in order to make language intelligible it is necessary to follow certain rules of grammar. Hence, the language of the answer should be grammatically correct. Besides, it must also be simple and clear, because there is no virtue in using difficult language. The only purpose in answering a question is that the answer should provide the information which is being called for. And since language is a medium of expressing ideas, the educand must be trained in the correct use of language so that he can express his ideas with clarity and precision. As far as possible, the language of the answer should be pure, not mixed with a large number of obsolete or uncommon words or foreign expressions. Again, the educand should be taught to avoid hyperbolic language because his aim is not to impress the listener with his command over the language. But the use of long and crude words should also be avoided, and in answering questions economy of expression should be exercised. Verbosity, again, is no virtue.

4. *Order.* The answer must also have properly ordered parts, the arrangement being determined by the order of the various parts of the question. If the answer is not properly ordered, it cannot be said to be good or accurate.

5. *Quickness.* When questions are being asked verbally, there is some value in the answer which is made rapidly and quickly. If the educand takes unnaturally long time in answering the question, this detracts from the merit of the answer.

6. *Proper tone.* The proper tone also plays a vital role in the answering of questions, because an unusually high tone has a bad effect on the listeners. Hence, there is no need for the educand to shout his answer, just as much as there is no need to speak in an inaudible whisper. The educator should train the pupils to answer questions in an even and balanced tone of voice.

ILLUSTRATION METHOD

In the illustration method of teaching, a subject is explained by providing examples of facts or experiences of which the educands are already aware. In this technique is implicit the principle of proceeding from the known to the unknown. Very often concrete illustrations and examples are used to explain some abstract idea or theory. In this is implied a progress from the concrete to the abstract. In the same way many known facts are cited as example to help the educand to understand facts of which he is as yet unaware. The principle underlying this situation is the progress from the known to the unknown. In each case, the real aim in providing an illustration is to create an association, the right background for presenting new knowledge. This method of teaching has many advantages, among which are the following:

Advantages

1. *Overcoming difficulties.* Illustrations and examples help to overcome the difficulties faced by the educand in understanding the subject. Thus, his ideas are clarified and he is enabled to understand something which had eluded his comprehension.
2. *Assists in elaboration.* Illustrations help in the explanation and elaboration of abstract concepts and many scientific principles, because verbal explanation becomes more concrete so that the complex subject is somewhat simplified. For this reason, teaching by illustration is considered essential for the teaching of many sciences.
3. *Encourages interest and curiosity.* Illustration tends to increase the educand's interest in the subject and to enhance his curiosity to know more about it. In the absence of interesting illustration, the teaching of science becomes drab and monotonous. Illustrations also provide the correct distraction for the student so that the process of learning becomes interesting and compelling.
4. *Helps memorizing.* Illustrations not only help in teaching and understanding but also in memorizing or retaining the subject. It helps recall because concrete facts are easier to memorize and recognise than abstract ideas.
5. *Assists observation and experimentation.* The presence of numerous illustrations during a lesson sharpens the educand's observation. Besides, the teaching of many sciences is done through experiments which serve as illustrations. The educator performs experiments in the presence of the educands in order to help them to understand the subject.
6. *Mental Practice.* If many illustrations are provided, they provide fine mental exercise and practice to the educand in the subject concerned because increased interest and attention lead to greater observation and better retention and recall.

NARRATION

Meaning

One important method of teaching is the verbal narration of something by the teacher. It is the narration of some incident, story, or even in a lively and interesting style. The success of the narration depends upon the educator's own power of expressions, his verbal felicity, his gestures and facial expressions, etc. It is an art that is normally acquired after long practice. The narrative technique involves the use of the imagination to make a subject both comprehensible and interesting, and although people confuse the technique with the story telling method, the two are not identical. All narratives do not take the form of story-telling. The teaching of history, geography or civics can be done through the narrative method, but this is not story-telling, because here it is a narrative of facts and places, not of individuals and events. It differs from plain and simple description inasmuch as it aims to create a vivid picture in the educand's mind.

Traits of Effective Narration

In order to make an effective use of the method of narration the educator should keep in mind the following traits of effective narration.

1. *Presentation of a lively picture.* Narration must succeed in creating a vivid mental picture of the subject in the recipient's mind, because the success of the

technique depends upon the vividness of this picture. The educator must make use of his imagination. But this must be supported by a sizeable vocabulary.

2. *Engaging style.* The effectiveness of the method depends upon the interesting style of the educator. It is here that one finds a difference between one educator and another because while one can make a subject interesting, another may turn it into something unbearably drab. If the style is interesting, it catches the educand's interest and maintains his curiosity.

3. *Simple language.* Success in narration depends to a great degree upon the language used. It should be simple and clear.

4. *Demonstration.* In order to make the narration lively, it is better to use some teaching aids and apparatus, such as maps and charts in the case of history and geography. The teaching of mathematics is greatly facilitated by the use of diagrams and graphs. In the case of social sciences the educator has to draw upon his fund of stories, jokes, etc., to illustrate his subject matter. Demonstration or illustration not only makes the subject more comprehensible but also makes it more interesting, thus improving the concentration of the audience. Even the blackboard can be extensively used for this purpose.

5. *Appropriate speed* The speed of narration must be appropriate. Every educand should be able to understand all that is being said. Going too fast or too slow is not desirable.

6. *Systematic presentation.* When the subject of narration is divided into many parts and presented systematically and in an orderly manner, the educand is greatly helped in his understanding of the subject. For this, the main idea should be split into many pieces and arranged systematically. The process of learning can be improved by asking questions at the end of each step in the narration. This should be followed by making the educand arrive at a conclusion, which should be used as the basis for the next step. This informs the educator of the extent to which his audience is following him while it helps the educand to summarize and thus memorize the subject matter. The asking and answering of questions leads to the educand's active participation.

7. *Loud, clear and sweet tone.* Since the narration is done verbally, the educator's voice and tone play an important role in it. He should speak in a loud, clear and pleasant tone. If this is not done the subject becomes drab and uninteresting. He should also vary his tone as the tone of the narrative itself changes.

8. *Dramatic style.* As far as possible, the educator should try to make the narrative more lively by resorting to gestures, facial expressions, bodily postures, etc. in keeping with the subject matter. But this dramatic presentation should not be so overdone as to make it theatrical and ridiculous.

9. *Narration for teaching.* Narration is not merely for narration or for the student's pleasure. Its aim is teaching, and if the educator finds that the method does not succeed in teaching anything he should abandon the method and choose another.

10. *Narrator's Background.* Success of the narration depends not only on the words but also on the speaker's own background, character, enthusiasm, self-confidence, knowledge, personality, etc. Hence, the educator must try to develop his personality and character, keeping this in view.

11. *Question-answers.* In order to make the narration more lively, it should be interrupted with questions and answers. This keeps the educands on their toes, and does not allow them to become lethargic.

12. *Absence of sermonising.* It is not proper to fill the narrative with long sermons, because children are averse to listening to them, and thus they soon ignore what is being said. As far as possible, the narration must make each point quite clear. There is no advantage in circumlocution.

The narrative can be successful in the class depending upon the educator's ability. It is definitely more powerful than written matter because the educands take more interest in it. It creates a very vivid and clear picture in the child's mind, and a powerful narration creates feelings of respect and affection for the educator. Besides, the narrative can be used to guide the educands, because the intelligent educator can illustrate the narrative by mentioning incidents from real life and also including in the narration guidelines of how the educand should behave in such situations.

Traits of Defective Narration

Despite the above advantages of the narration method, it also suffers from certain defects. The following are the more important traits of defective narration:

1. *Passive education.* In this method the educator alone is active, because the educands make up only an inactive audience.
2. *Not concerned with comprehension.* Very frequently the educator is more concerned with concluding his narration than with the comprehension of the educand. He rarely bothers to find out if they have understood anything. The method should be supplemented by the question-answer technique in which the educand must be encouraged to ask the questions. He may otherwise be afraid of interrupting the educator.
3. *Improper language and speed.* If the language is difficult and the narration is carried out at high speed, the educand understands almost nothing. This has the inevitable effect of the educand losing interest in the narration.
4. *Not lively.* If the narration is not lively, loss of interest is the only result.

Suggestions for Improvement

It has already been pointed out that the use of various suggestions given above — interesting style, large vocabulary, use of teaching aids, etc. — can safely take care of these defects and the method can become a powerful medium of instruction. As far as possible, the educator should resort to the language of everyday, spoken in a natural and unaffected style. It is not necessary for the educator to memorize every part of the subject. Even if he remembers the main points, he can successfully narrate the subject. During narration the educator should keep in mind the objective of the narrative, and to this end, he should repeat the main points.

DESCRIPTION

A.H. Garlick expressed the opinion that description implies the use of words or symbols to represent some object. It is the process of creating a picture in words and for that reason, it is also called verbal artistry. In a description the external qualities — colour, form, shape, nature, qualities — of an object are described in order to acquaint the listener with the object. The qualities most desirable in the educator, if he indulges in description, are accurate observation and a good memory. Some people have the innate ability to describe things, but other people can achieve effective descriptions only after long practice. The success of a description depends upon the vividness of the mental image it can create in the listener's mind, and for this it is essential that no part of the described object should be neglected. Besides, the language employed in the described object must also be in keeping with the mental level of the audience so that it has no difficulty in comprehending the description. In order to make a description effective the educator must keep in mind the following factors:

How to make description effective?

1. *Proper order.* Before embarking on a description it should be divided into a number of steps and the steps arranged in a proper order. This makes the description easier and also helps the audience in understanding it.
2. *According to mental ability.* The description must be in keeping with the mental ability of the audience, because if it is too simple it will not interest the audience, and if it is too difficult it will not be comprehensible.
3. *Appropriate language.* The language employed in the description should be simple, clear and in keeping with the mental level of the audience. There is no need to make it too technical or too literary.
4. *Proper speed.* The description should be made at proper speed. Excessive slowness leads to boredom and too much speed makes for confusion and lack of understanding.
5. *Proper size.* The size of the description must also suit the level of the audience. Young children cannot concentrate on a long description. Hence, it should be condensed or elaborated according to the needs of the audience.
6. *Interesting style.* The style of description should be interesting so as to maintain the interest and curiosity of the audience.
7. *Contextual.* A description should include only relevant facts. Excessive and inappropriate examples and illustrations only detract from the merit of the description, because they engage the attention of the audience without allowing it to concentrate on the subject.
8. *Illustration.* In order to make a description more vivid, illustrations and apparatus should be used. Apart from the black-board, the educator should also make use of models, maps, pictures, etc.
9. *From the known to the unknown.* Sometimes the educator has to describe an event with which the educands are unfamiliar. In order to make such a description concrete, the educator must try to relate the unfamiliar elements with elements and facts known to the educands.
10. *Dramatic style.* In order to make the description more lively, the educator should employ the dramatic method of gestures, changing facial expressions, postures of the body, etc. But the acting should not proceed to the extreme of becoming ridiculous and laughable.

11. *Questions and answers.* In order to keep the audience on its toes, it is better to intersperse the descriptions with questions. In order to answer the questions, the educand is compelled to listen the description and to try and remember it. At the same time, the educator must permit educands also to ask questions so that they can express their difficulties. This will inform the educator of the success or failure of the description.

12. *Relation between part and whole.* The description must be so designed that the educands can easily establish a relationship between the whole and its various parts. This helps in memorizing the subject. In order to achieve this end, it is often, found advantageous to conclude the description by giving a brief resume of the entire description.

13. *Self-confidence.* The greater the self-confidence of the educator, the more powerful will the description be, because this self-confidence will generate confidence in the audience.

In general, of course, teachers tend to be good at describing things, but by keeping the above points in mind, every teacher can attain greater skill at using the method of description.

STORY-TELLING

The most psychological method of teaching young children is to tell stories to them. Stories are definitely useful in the teaching of such subjects as history, civics, etc. and are known to be so, but they prove even more useful in the teaching of morals and religion. Compared to the other techniques, that of story telling has the following advantages.

Advantages

1. *Satisfies curiosity.* Children have an inborn curiosity to learn about various objects and people. The educator can take advantage of this curiosity to tell the children many things through the medium of the story.

2. *Interesting.* There are very few people who object to listening to stories. Children in particular enjoy being told stories and hence a story can be used as an interesting medium of education.

3. *Assists memory.* It is always easier to remember a subject one finds interesting. Hence, things taught by a story are remembered more easily.

4. *Entertaining.* For children, education must also be entertaining, and this is possible only through story telling. This makes the child enjoy his education.

5. *Inspiring.* By the use of selected, good and psychological stories much can be done for developing the child's personality and character because stories are stimulating and inspiring.

6. *Development of character.* Moral education cannot be given in sermons. It is better and more effective to tell inspiring stories to the child so that he is presented with a good example which he may strive to follow.

Factors in Successful Story-Telling

In order to take advantage of the technique of story-telling, it is essential to present it psychologically, and, in any case, story-telling is an art, albeit an art which can be acquired through practice. The more important factors in successful story-telling are the following:

1. *Identification with the story.* The more the teacher can forget himself in telling the story, the better it will be. But this is possible only when he himself finds the story interesting. For this reason, it is advisable that the educator should tell only those stories which first interest him.

2. *Sufficient knowledge.* Only that story can be powerful and impressive which the educator remembers in all its details. But, the story must be told in the educator's own words. It should never be read out, because this is the surest way of boring the audience.

3. *Dramatic presentation.* In presenting the story, the educator should enact the various expressions and emotions described in the story and carry out the actions and gestures which are a part of it. This creates a concrete picture in the child's mind and helps him to remember the story.

4. *A. Adequate language.* The language used in telling the story should be simple and within the comprehension of the audience.

5. *Interesting style.* The style of story-telling should be natural, life-like, interesting and varied.

6. *Systematic presentation.* A systematic presentation and proper ordering of sequences is absolutely essential. If the educator forgets some part and returns to it later on, after having described some future event, the educands are likely to lose the thread and become irritated. Hence, the educator must remember the sequences of events very clearly.

7. *Confirming to the mental level.* Different kinds of stories interest children of different ages. Very young children are usually interested in stories of magic and adventure, stories which are awe-inspiring. Adolescents find such stories disgusting. But in all such stories, action should be the main element, although the stories are to be selected according to the age group of the audience.

8. *Purposeful.* In telling the story, the educator must always keep in mind its purpose. If this is not done, then the purpose will remain unfulfilled.

9. *Necessary atmosphere.* In order to tell the story, it is necessary to have a calm and peaceful environment. From the psychological standpoint, the right environment for story telling is one of curiosity and expectation.

Apart from these suggestions which should be kept in mind, one should consult books on psychology in order to learn the art of story-telling. The educator must critically analyze his own style, language, acting, etc., in order to eliminate the errors he finds.

LECTURE METHOD

Meaning

The lecture method is perhaps the most commonly applied technique of teaching in colleges and universities. In this method the educator makes careful preparation of his subject, and then communicates this knowledge to his class in the form of a continuous monologue known as the lecture. More often than not he is not concerned with whether his educands are comprehending his speech at all. One finds that a majority of the educand's business lies in taking down notes of the lecture being delivered. Most educators who receive university education and turn to school teaching tend to use this technique even with young children. This is very unjustifiable, because the lecture method may be appropriate for higher education, but it is unsuitable for the teaching of children at the primary and secondary levels. Even at the higher levels of education, this technique should be employed only as one of the many techniques, not as the only method which can be used to advantage.

Shortcoming at Primary and Secondary level

At every stage of education, the most immediate aim of teaching is that the subject should be understood by the educand. And, if this can be achieved by the lecture method it should be employed. But if it is found that even at the university level the lecture method is not the most beneficial, there can be no reason for continuing with it. In actual fact, one finds that very few educators care whether even one member of the class is listening to their lecture. Hence, they are not bothered about making their lecture powerful or effective. The most obvious advantage of the lecture method seems to be that it can teach a large number of educands simultaneously without necessitating the use of other aids. But the normal criterion behind its application is that the educator finds it the simplest method, apart from the pleasure he may derive from expressing himself and thus deriving some satisfaction. At the primary and secondary levels of education, the technique manifests the following shortcomings:

1. *Inactive method.* This is the most inactive or negative of the various techniques of teaching since all that the educand is required to do is to listen patiently. Obviously, it cannot bring forth the same advantages that the more active methods can.

2. *Indifference of the educator.* In most cases, the educator using the lecture method evinces a total indifference to the interests, attention, progress, etc., of the student. He thinks that his sole concern is to deliver the lecture without concerning himself about the advantage the educand derives from it.

3. *Absence of concentration.* In such a situation, most of the students pay little attention to the speech of the lecture, and while they are bodily present in the class, they are mentally absent.

4. *Unpsychological.* Psychologically speaking, the true function of education is not to stuff the child's mind with information, but to encourage the child to acquire this information actively, and for himself. The lecture method is unpsychological in that it chooses the first alternative, and the wrong one. Being inactive, the educand listens to the lecture but assimilates very little of it.

5. *Absence of active knowledge.* Any piece of information or knowledge can be permanent and effective only when it is acquired through one's own effort. In the lecture method, the knowledge is gratuitously offered to the educand by the lecturer.

6. *Rapid speech.* Very frequently, the educator's speed in talking is far greater than can be desirable, with the result that the educand cannot hear some things, cannot understand other things while of the remainder most are not concerned with his own experience, and so completely beyond his comprehension.

7. *Absence of teacher-taught relationship.* The lecture method affords little if any scope for any relationship between the educator and his pupils, while almost all educationists agree that an intimate relationship should exist between the two.

8. *Use of auditory powers only.* It is generally believed in psychology that the process of learning becomes more rapid if it involves the use of all the sense organs. The lecture method exercises only the auditory powers of the educand, and hence fails to make any impact.

In spite of these defects, this is the most commonly employed method of teaching in the country today. At the university level and other institutions of higher learning this is the only method that is being used, a situation which calls for serious thought.

BOOK READING METHOD

Meaning

At every level of education, certain text books are prescribed in the syllabus. These books form the basis of examination, and it is considered to be the duty of the educand to memorize the subject contained in them. Consequently, educators resort to the reading of these books in the classroom doing nothing more than just reading through them and explaining the parts which appear, to them, to be difficult for the student to comprehend. Sometimes one of the educands is asked to do the reading while the educator again explains the more difficult portions. Another variation on this pattern is to ask different educands to read different portions of the lesson. Some educators interrupt the reading by asking questions, but only to assure themselves that the educands are listening to the reading. This is perhaps the most defective method of teaching which could be devised, because it is a complete contradiction of all psychological principles of teaching as well as of learning. The rationale behind the adoption of this technique is that it economizes on the teacher's efforts, and also that it convinces the educands that the work has been done according to the syllabus.

Defects of Book Reading Method

Of the many defects that are inherent in this method, the following are only the more glaring ones:

1. *Violation of a principle of teaching.* The more important among the principles of teaching are the principles of active participation, of linking with life, of interest, of selection, the book reading method violates every single one of these principles.

2. *Inactive method.* In this method also most of the educands sit inactively. Hence, this does not compare favourably with the active methods of teaching.

3. *Boring method.* This method is entirely monotonous and repulsively boring. Educands soon ignore the educator and his speech.

4. *Lack of practice.* In this method there is no opportunity to either repeat a lesson or to practise it.

5. *Narrow attitude.* This method can provide very little knowledge to the educand because it is limited to the knowledge contained in the book.

It is evident from the list of its defects that this method should not be adopted at any stage of education. The only thing of importance one can derive from it is the negative suggestion that no books should be prescribed for teaching. Only a subject should be prescribed, and it should be left to the educator to gather information on the subject and to teach it.

EXPLANATION

What is Explanation?

The word explanation is used in a variety of ways, for explanation of something may be in words or in full sentences. In its scientific connotation the term implies the search for general principle, deduction and integration while in the field of education explanation is taken to mean translation of difficult and unfamiliar terms into words better known to the educand, relating unknown facts to known ones for the educand's ease, education of implied meanings through the use of apt illustrations, etc. In general explanation is taken to mean the simplified presentation of a complex or difficult subject. This is done to facilitate the educand's understanding and retention of the subject. But this explanation is the task only of that individual who has knowledge of the subject and the educand's psychology. Besides, the educator must also be blessed with the power of expression and an extensive vocabulary. Explanation in one subject differs from explanations in another. In philosophy, for example, explanation is primarily concerned with abstract concepts which have to be related to the more concrete experiences of the educands in order to make them comprehensible. In an explanation the illustrations offered must be relevant, in keeping with the context, and in conformity with the intelligence level of the educands.

Possible Defects of Explanation

In order to be an expert at explanation, it is necessary to be aware of the possible defects of this method which are the following:

1. *Excessive explanation.* This is the temptation which the good educator must guard against. Very frequently the educator is tempted not merely to explain something but to give the educand a comprehensive idea of the educator's own knowledge, with the result that the educator, instead of explaining anything, takes a test of the educand's patience. Explanations if necessary, must be brief, relevant and precise.

2. *Unnecessary explanations.* Some educators tend to explain words, sentences and incidents which require no explanation. This is not merely ridiculous, it is also wasteful. The educator must be judicious in this choice of what must be explained.

3. *Explanations at the wrong place.* Explanations should be forthcoming from the educator as and when they are necessary. It is unjust on the part of the educator

to preface his teaching with a series of explanations, leaving the educand in utter confusion because he is not aware of what is being explained. In the same manner, to avoid explanation when it is actually required is equally unfair, because this fails to resolve the educand's doubts and difficulties.

4. *Useless explanation.* That explanation can be called useless which does not help the educand in understanding the subject.

Explanations themselves take many forms. Difficult words and involved ideas are explained through simplification. Words are also defined. Sometimes the meaning of a word is explained by suggesting a synonym while at other times the meaning is indicated by first presenting the object to which it relates and then utter the word, Complex actions are demonstrated and thus explained. Sometimes words are explained by mentioning their sources, the roots. It is for the educator to choose the method most appropriate for his needs. An explanation is correct when it is pure, clear and systematic. Hence, it should possess these qualities.

In order to take advantage of the explanation technique of teaching, the educator should keep in mind the following facts:

1. *Proper size.* An unnecessarily long explanation becomes uninteresting and boring while the very short explanation does not explain enough. Hence, the explanation should be relevant and proportionate.
2. *Simple language.* The purpose of explanation is achieved only when its language is pure and simple.
3. *Demonstration.* In order to make the explanation lively the educator should make use of apparatus and teaching aids.
4. *Questions and answers. During the explanation and at the end of it, the* educator should encourage questions from students in order to remove their difficulties and also to test their comprehensions.
5. *Experience.* Things mentioned as part of the explanation should be available to the educand so that he can experience them.
6. *Removal of doubts. An* explanation is really complete only when the educand's doubts on the subjects have been finally resolved.
7. *Interesting style. As far as possible the style of education should be* interesting and adapted to the educands mental level.
8. *Natural.* The explanation should be naturally presented.
9. *Absence of sermonizing.* An explanation should not be intended to be a sermon. It should aim at assisting the educand to understand.
10. *Appropriate.* The explanation should suit the subject and the occasion.

8

INNOVATION IN TEACHING

MICRO TEACHING

Meaning

1. *Mush (1968).* Micro teaching is a "teaching and education technique which allows to apply well defined teaching skill to a carefully prepared lesson in a planned series of five minutes, encounters with a small group of real classroom student, often with an opportunity to observe the performance on video tape."

2. *Dwight Allen and Kenn Ryan (1989).* "Micro-teaching is a system of controlled practice that makes it possible to concentrate on specific teaching behaviour and to practise teaching under controlled conditions."

3. *Me Aleese and Unwin (1970).* The term "Micro-teaching is most often applied to the use of closed-circuit television (CCT) to give immediate feedback of trainee teacher's performance in a simplified environment." Micro-teaching is best viewed as a form of simulated teaching usually incorporating reduced complexity and some feedback placed "along a simulation spectrum ranging from the purely abstract text-book teaching practice through the actual classroom teaching."

4. *Clift and Others (1976).* "Micro-teaching is the procedure which reduces the teaching situation to simpler and more controlled encounter achieved by limiting the practice teaching to specific skill and reducing teaching time and class size."

Characteristics

In the light of the above-mentioned definitions may be concluded the following characteristics of micro-teaching:

1. *Real teaching.* Micro-teaching is real teaching. However, it focuses on developing teaching skills.

2. *Scaled down teaching.* The following outline is characteristic of scaled down teaching:

   (i) Scaling down the class size to five to ten pupils.

   (ii) Scaling down the duration of period of five to ten minutes.

   (iii) Scaling down the *size* of the topic.

   (iv) Scaling down the teaching skill.

3. *Individualized device.* It is a highly individualized training device.

4. *Providing feedback.* It provides the feedback for trainee's performance.
5. *Device for preparing teachers.* It is a device to prepare effective teachers.

Assumptions

According to Allen and Ryan, micro-teaching is an idea at the core of which lie the following five essential propositions or assumptions:

1. *Real teaching.* Micro-teaching is real teaching. Although the teaching situation is a constructed one in the sense that teachers and students work together in a practice situation, nevertheless, bonafide teaching does take place.
2. *Reduced complexities.* Micro-teaching reduces the complexities of normal class-room teaching. Class size, scope of content and time are all reduced.
3. *Focus on training.* Micro-teaching focuses on training for the accomplishment of specific tasks. Included among these tasks are the practice of technique of teaching, the mastery of certain curricular materials, the demonstration of teaching methods.
4. *Increased control of practice.* Micro-teaching allows for the increased control of practice. The rituals of time and students are manipulated. In the practice setting of micro-teaching a high degree of control may be built into the training programme.
5. *Expanding knowledge of results.* Micro-teaching very much expands the normal knowledge of results for feedback dimension in teaching. The trainee engages in a critique of his maximum insight into his performance, several sources of feedback are put at his disposal. He analyzes aspect of his own performance in the light of his goals with the guidance of a supervisor or colleague. The trainee and the supervisor go over student response forms that are designed to elicit students' reactions to specific aspects of his teaching. If the supervision has video-tape available, he may use video-tape playback to show the teacher how he performs and how he may improve. All his feedback can be immediately translated into practice when the trainee reteaches shortly after the critique conference.

Comparison with Traditional Teaching

1. *Simple* versus *complex teaching.* While micro-teaching is simple, traditional teaching is relatively complex and threatening.
2. *Specification of objectives.* In micro-teaching the objectives are specified in behaviour terms.
3. *Providing feedback.* While in micro-teaching important feedback is provided, in traditional teaching feedback is not provided.
4. *Size of class.* While in micro-teaching the class is divided into small groups of five to ten pupil-teachers, in traditional teaching the class consists of fifty to hundred pupil-teachers.
5. *Duration.* While in micro-teaching the duration is five to ten minutes in traditional teaching the duration is fort is to sixty minutes.
6. *Patterns of class-room interaction.* While in micro-teaching patterns of class-room interaction may be objectively studied, in traditional teaching the pattern of class-room interaction cannot be objectively studied.

7. *Practising skill.* While in micro-teaching the pupil-teacher practises only one skill selected for practice, in traditional teaching the pupil-teacher practises whole complex teaching behaviour.

8. *Role of supervisor.* While in micro-teaching the role of the supervisor is specific and well defined to improve teaching, in traditional teaching the role of supervisor is vague and not useful to improve teaching.

9. *Awareness.* In comparison to traditional teaching micro-teaching develops more awareness among student-teacher with regard to professional training.

10. *Score.* In university examination micro-teaching results in better score than their counterparts in conventional teaching.

Objectives

The following objectives of introducing Micro-teaching in Colleges of Education have been enlisted by Duggal and Sharma:

1. Initiating the teacher trainees to analyse and develop teacher behaviour under laboratory conditions.
2. Landing the novice teachers gradually in the real class-room after gaining enough confidence.
3. Imparting intensive training in the component skills of teaching to teacher trainees at pre-service level.
4. Involving the academic potential of teacher trainees for providing feedback to the peers.
5. Reducing the work-load of teacher educators with the involvement of peer-supervisors.
6. Reducing the burden upon practising schools while having practice of teaching skills under simulation conditions in colleges of Education.
7. Exploring the human resources to the maximum and making them economic with regard to time, money and material.

Steps in Micro-teaching Procedure

Micro-teaching procedure involves the following steps:

1. *Defining the skill.* To provide the knowledge and awareness of teaching a particular skill is defined to trainees in terms of teaching behaviour.
2. *Demonstrating the skills.* The specific skill is demonstrated by the experts or shown through video-tape or film to the teachers trainee.
3. *Planning the lesson.* With the help of his supervisors the student-teacher plans a short (micro) lesson in which he can practise a particular skill.
4. *Teaching the lesson.* The pupil-teacher teaches the lesson to a small group of pupils (*i.e.* 5 to 10 pupils). The teaching is observed by the supervisors or peers. Video-tape or audio-tape are televised at close circuit television (CCIV).
5. *Discussion.* Teaching the lesson is followed by discussion to provide the feedback (suggested improvements) to the trainee. The videotape or audio-tape may be displayed to the trainee to observe his own teaching activities. The awareness of his own teaching performance provides the reinforcement to the pupil-teaching.

6. *Replanning.* The pupil-teachers replan the lesson in order to practise the small skill effectively in the light of the discussion and suggestion.
7. *Reteaching.* This replanned lesson is retaught to another small group of students of same class for the same duration to practise the same skill.
8. *Rediscussion.* The reteaching is now followed by discussion of suggestions, and encouragement to the teaching performance. The feedback is again provided to the trainee.
9. *Repeating the cycle.* The cycle is repeated till the desired level of skill is achieved.

To conclude, in micro-teaching the pupil-teacher tries to complete the 5 R's *viz..* Recording, Reviewing, Responding, Refining and Redoing.

Principles

The following principles underlie the technique of Micro-teaching:

1. *Principle of practice.* 'Practice makes a man perfect' is an oft quoted proverb. If activity is repeated again and again, it is learnt effectively. Microteaching provides practice in each small task of skill for the pupil-teacher gains mastery.
2. *Principle of reinforcement.* Since long the value of reinforcement in the learning process has been acknowledged, it involves teacher encouraging pupils' responses, using verbal praise, accepting their responses or non-verbal ones like a smile. In micro-teaching lessons reinforcement encouragement is given to the pupil-teacher from time to time for his better performance with the feedback, as well as he attains satisfaction and his performance is improved. Reinforcement and feedback stimulate him for better learning and better teaching.
3. *Principle of experimentation.* Micro-teaching was born in an experiment. Experiment consists of objective observation of actions performed under controlled conditions. Therefore, controlled conditions are necessary in micro-teaching The pupil-teacher and the supervisor conduct experiment on teaching skill under controlled conditions. Variables such as time, content, students and teaching techniques may be manipulated or controlled. Since the very beginning, microteaching has been used as means of research. Those aspects of micro-teaching that render it valuable as a training technique also render it valuable as a research tool.
4. *Principle of evaluation.* A proper evaluation of pupil-teacher's work may become an effective motivation for better learning and better teaching. The supervisor evaluates each micro-lesson. In micro-teaching, self-evaluation is also allowed. With the help of video-tape recorder the teacher-trainee may evaluate his own performance. Improvement can be made on the basis of self-evaluation.
5. *Principle of precise supervision.* The supervision accompanying microteaching is highly specific and precise. The supervisor pays full attention to one point at a time. Both the supervisor and the teacher are clear about the aim of the micro-lesson ahead of time. The supervisor possesses an observation schedule which he fills up while supervising. He makes an assessment on a rating scale. Rating is a method in which the expression or opinion concerning a particular trait is systematised.

6. *Principle of continuity.* Micro-teaching requires continuity. The teacher learns and re-learns the skill of teaching. Its unique features are: Discussing Planning-Teaching-Feedback-Replanning-Reteaching till mastery is attained.

Role of the Supervisor

Micro-teaching supervisor is essentially a teacher. His role is to increase and refine performance of the skills that serve as the objectives. The responsibility of the supervisor in micro-teaching is two-fold:

1. *Developing ability to perform a skill.* The supervisor should help the trainee develop ability to perform a skill. The supervisor discharges the following functions in this role:

(i) The supervisor helps the trainee in discrimination of the skill and reinforces his performance of it.

(ii) The supervisor tries to understand the behaviours that constitute the skill and to become sensitive to the cues that signal when the skill should be performed.

(iii) The supervisor reinforces his behaviour when the trainee performs the skill or begins to approximate the performance of it.

2. *To understand the application of skill.* The supervisor could help the trainee to understand as to when the skill should be applied. Having a repertory of reinforcement skill does not ensure good class-room application. Good performance depends on when and where the skills application are used. The supervisors, therefore, must help the trainee in making these professional decisions. This role of the supervisor relates to the application of skill.

3. *Working with trainees.* Each supervisor is assigned between 6 to 10 teacher trainees at the start of the session in micro-teaching and he works with this group.

4. *Visiting schools.* The supervisor visits his trainees in the school and prepares a special schedule of micro-teaching lessons in the practising schools. This requires special arrangements. The period allowed is only between five to ten minutes. The pupils discuss with the supervisor after the lesson.

5. *Supervising the lesson.* The supervisor supervises the lesson. He notes the improvements which are to be made by the pupil-teacher in the presentation of the lesson.

6. *Evaluating the lesson.* The supervisor evaluates the lesson and gives feedback.

Evaluative Instruments

The teaching skills developed through micro-teaching lessons should be evaluated by the peers or supervisors. The rating schedule is used as criterion measure. Stanford Teacher Competence Appraisal Guide (STCAG) is the most popular evaluative instrument for assessing the effectiveness of micro-teaching.

Allen and Ryan (1969) have given the following evaluation sheet for assessing the skill of reinforcement. This consists of four dimensions of the reinforcement skill:

1. *Rewarding correct responses.* The correct responses of the students could be praised or rewarded by saying 'fine' 'good,' 'excellent', etc.

2. *Using non-verbal cues.* To encourage his students the teacher should use non-verbal cues such as smile, etc.

3. *Giving credit.* The teacher should give credit to students answering a question partly correct.

4. *Referring to positive aspects.* The teacher should refer to positive aspects of a student's previous responses.

The observer records these four dimensions in terms of frequency if the teacher has used the category a number of times. The categories are assessed on scales ranging from three to seven points. The STCAG consists of a number of scales rating the broad aspects of a teacher's performance.

Aids and Apparatuses

The folio wing, aids and apparatuses are used in micro-teaching:

1. *Obserrvation schedule (check-list).* The observation schedule may be used in the form of check list or questionnaire. It should include all items to be observed.

2. *Cassette tape-recorder.* A cassette taper- recorder may be used for recording the entire conversation in the class-room. It can be used for appraising one's own self or by supervisor.

3. *Video-tape recorder.* Use of Video-tape recorder has both the advantages of sight and sound.

4. *Close-circuit television.* The entire class-room programme can be seen in. another room and show n to the other group through close circuit television while it is taking place. Thus all the staff-members and pupil-teachers can see the lesson without disturbing the class with the help of Close Circuit Television.

5. *A movie film.* The entire programme can be recorded with the help of a movie film which may be seen again and again.

6. *One-way screen.* One way screen may be used for some purposes.

7. *Two monitors.* Two monitors should be available for assistance.

Advantages

Micro-teaching is distinguished by the following advantages:

1. *Modification of teacher behaviour.* Micro-teaching is an effective device for the modification of teacher behaviour.

2. *Knowledge of teaching skills.* By the use of micro-teaching the knowledge and practice of teaching skills can be given.

3. *Developing teaching skills.* Micro-teaching experiences develop the specific teaching skills such as reinforcement skill, explaining skill, skill of using blackboard, skill for using audio-visual aids, skill for class management, etc.

4. *Developing teaching efficiency.* Micro-teaching is found useful for developing teaching efficiency in pre-service and in-service teacher education programme.

5. *Improving teaching practices.* This technique is a training device for improving teaching practices and to prepare better and effective teachers.

6. *Individual training.* By Micro-teaching the training of teacher becomes individualized. Each trainee makes progress in developing teaching skills at his rate depending on his ability.

7. *Regulating teaching practice.* The technique permits increased control and regulates teaching practice.
8. *Real teaching.* Micro-teaching is real teaching. It may be one either in real class-room conditions or simulated conditions.
9. *Reducing complexities.* Micro-teaching reduces the complexities of normal class-room teaching by scaled down teaching, class size, scope of content and time are all reduced.
10. *Focus on teaching.* Micro-teaching focuses attention on teaching behaviour to modify and improve in the desired direction.
11. *Analysing one's own teaching performance.* This teaching is an economical device and the use of video-tape enables the trainee to analyse his *own* teaching performance.
12. *Continuous reinforcement.* In Micro-teaching the mechanism of feedback device can be combined with other devices such as simulated social skill training and interaction analysis device which provide continuous reinforcement to the trainee's performance.
13. *Research tool.* In the end, Micro-teaching is a useful research tool which may be used by teacher candidates to study teaching even during their training.

Limitations of Micro-Teaching

In spite of the above-mentioned advantages, Micro-teaching suffers from the following limitations:

1. *Costly.* An effective micro-teaching system requires tape-records, Videotapes and Close Circuit Television. Therefore, it is costly for Indian school.
2. *Narrow scope.* Micro-teaching provides opportunities for developing only a few skills (say 20 to 25). However, in reality, teaching requires more than these skills.
3. *Disturbs existing time-table.* Micro-teaching disturbs the existing timetable of practising schools by calling small groups for a few minutes (say five or ten).
4. *Presentation in parts.* A very small content is presented. This in five or ten minutes separates or breaks the lesson.
5. *Difficulty in actual practice.* Micro-teaching is difficult in actual practice in a class of 5 to 10 pupils. The pupil-teacher may not feel any difficulty. He may gain a lot of confidence. But in the class of fifty or more he may fail to teach.

SIMULATED TEACHING

In 1968 Cruickshank developed a system denoted by several terms such as Role-playing, Artificial teaching, Pilot training, laboratory method, clinical method and inductive scientific method. This was simulated teaching. It is one of the techniques being used currently in India as well as in other countries for the modification of teacher behaviour. Thus class-room roles are simulated under this approach. Behavioural problems and class-room managements are better handled through simulated teaching.

Definition of Simulation

(i) *Thomas and Deemer.* "To simulate is to obtain the essence of teaching without the reality."

(ii) *Harman.* "Simulations contain the important parts of, but not all of, reality. Simulations do not have to look like the real-life counterpart, but they do have to "act Mike the real thing."

From the above mentioned definitions it is clear that when a *simulation* includes important aspects of reality, it omits other elements of the real life situation. Unimportant elements from real life are subtracted when simulations are designed. There is a reduction of information from the real life in the case of simulated displays. This information is in some sense unnecessary for the learning of the task. Simulation may be explained in the following equation:

Simulation = Real life — irrelevant task elements.

(iii) *Webster's Dictionary.* "Giving the appearance or effect of; to have characteristics of."

(iv) *Tansey.* "Simulation is an all-inclusive term. It contains those activities which produce artificial environments or which provides artificial experience for the participants in the activity."

To sum up, simulation may best be defined as a role playing in which the process of teaching is enacted artificially and an effort is made to practise some important skill of communication through it. Under this technique the pupil-teacher and the students simulate a particular role and try to develop an identity with the actual class-room environment. Thus, the whole simulated teaching programme becomes a training in role perception and role playing. Simulation is the basis of sensitivity training, socio-drama, role-playing and psycho-drama.

Assumptions

The following are the assumptions upon which Simulated Social Skill Training (SSST) is based:

1. *Teacher behaviour is modifiable.* The first assumption is that the teacher behaviour is modifiable by the use of feedback devices.

2. *Patterns of teacher behaviour are essential.* Yet another basic assumption is that there are certain patterns of teacher behaviours which are essential in effective teaching. These behaviours may be described and practised like any other skill while the observer identifies those behaviours the teachers practise those patterns of teaching behaviour.

3. *Teacher behaviour has taxonomy.* The teacher behaviour has its taxonomy. According to Karl Openshaw and others the taxonomy of teacher behaviour is developed by the use of simulated technique as:

(i) Source dimension, (ii) Direction dimension,
(iii) Function dimension, (iv) Sign dimension.

4. *Social skills are developed.* The fourth and the final basic assumption is that social skills are developed by practice and imitations in a group. The members of the group have an opportunity to practise in controlling and improving their own behaviour for teaching purposes.

Activities

1. *Role playing.* The simplest of the activities included in the all-embracing term simulation is role playing. Essentially it is one or either of two following types of activities:

(i) Act of being someone else.

(ii) Act of acquiring experience in a set of activities in which the actor seeks to acquire or to increase his competence.

In role playing the role assumed is one in which the actor portrays either a fictitious role or an actual role, but performs that role in an artificial environment, By definition the role portrayed may be one with which the actor has little or no familiarity at the start of simulated situation or of relationship among real life participants of a social process. Alternatively, the role playing may be used to assist the participants to gain some perception of the actions, attitudes or situations of another person. The role played by the participant may be one in which the actor desires to acquire competence. Alternatively it may be one in which the actor has previously acquired some familiarity, but desires to improve his level of competence.

2. *Socio-drama.* Socio-drama uses role playing as a means to enable the role players to seek a solution to a social problem which is posed for them. The problem may be one extracted from the real world. Alternatively, it may be one designed to present a selected situation for solution. Irrespective of this type of situation, the role players are required to devise an acceptable solution to the situation presented.

Socio-drama may be distinguished from role playing only in the objective which is sought. Role playing seeks to provide competence and understanding in a particular role for a person who plays that role. On the other hand, Socio-drama seeks to utilize role playing as a means of devising a solution to a problem situation which is prescribed for the role players. This problem may be fictional or it may be an abstraction from real life.

3. *Gaming.* An added element in the technique of Socio-drama is Gaming; an element which demands the development and choice of strategies (or decision making) and some type of pay-off-rewards of deprivations dictated either by chance or by the choice of strategies. These decisions and the rewards are subject to the strictures of rule known to all players. The situations employed in Gaming involve outcomes which are affected by decisions made by one or more decision. Gaming may be designed in a manner which allows chance to affect the outcome, or the chance may be prohibited.

Steps in Simulation

Flanders has recommended the following steps in simulation:

1. *Selecting pupil-teachers.* First of all a small group of pupil-teachers is selected. Letters A, B, C, D, etc. are assigned to each person in the group. Role assignments are rotated by letters so that each individual has a chance to be an actor or observer.

2. *Selecting and discussing skills.* Now, the skills to be practised are selected and discussed. Topics of conversation are suggested that fit the skills.

3. *Deciding considerations.* In the third step, such as to who will start the conversation, who will intervene, who will step the interaction and when it will be stopped are decided.

4. *Deciding procedure of evaluation.* Next, the procedure of evaluation, kind of data to be recorded and the method of recording, etc., are decided.

5. *Conducting practice session.* First practice session is conducted and the actor is provided with feedback on his performance. The procedure of the second session is changed, if necessary, in order to improve the training procedure.

6. *Prepared to change the procedure.* One should be prepared to change other procedure and the topic and move on the next skill, if need arises, so as to present a meaningful challenge to each actor to keep his interest as high as possible.

Simulation in Teacher Training

1. Craikshank developed a teacher training system which is capable of presenting the student with different simulated problems relating to teaching. The various steps in teacher training are the following:

2. *Introducing the participant.* If he were a new teacher in a school, the participant is introduced into the situation.

3. *Providing information.* The participant is provided with information and opportunities to solve the problems of a new teacher.

4. *Exposing solution of problems.* Now, the participant is exposed to a variety of potential solutions to particular problems.

5. *Observing other results* The participant is given the opportunity of observing the results of his chosen line of action.

6. *Introducing to the situation.* The participant is introduced to the situation by film-strips.

7. *Giving the materials.* Now, the participant is given the materials that teaching going in the school's world actually receive, these materials include the school rules and regulations, curriculum hand-book and record cards of all students in the class.

8. *Presenting problems. Then the participant is presented with problems in* role playing situations, written incidents of combinations.

9. *Responding.* After the presentation of each problem the participant responds on an Incident Response Sheet.

10. *Identifying, locating and implementing.* Now, the participant identifies the factors influencing the problems, locates the relevant information, suggests appropriate course of action, communicates and implements a decision.

11. *Small group discussions.* Now follow small group discussions which consider the analysis and decide the action.

12. *Large group discussion.* The objective of these discussions is to push the analysis of the teaching problem, and not to come up with the 'right' answer.

Types of Simulation

Norman has identified the following types of simulation:

1. *Identity simulation.* In this simulation, the actual system is used as model.

2. *Replication simulation.* In this simulation, an operational model of the system is used in its usual environment.

3. *Laboratory simulation.* In this type of simulation, replication is employed in the laboratory, with features of the real system represented.

4. *Computer simulation.* This type of simulation is an abstract representation of the real system with the use of a computer.

5. *Analytical simulation.* This type of simulation uses mathematical modes and attempts to get solution by analytical means.

Precautions in Devising a Simulated Situation

While devising a simulated situation the following precautions should be observed:

1. *Clear objectives.* The objectives should be clear and precise.
2. *Motivation in advance.* The students should be motivated in advance.
3. *Role involvement.* The students should be involved to perform certain roles.
4. *Flexibility in approach.* There should be flexibility in approach.

Advantages of Simulated Teaching

The following are the advantages of simulated teaching:

1. *Device for motivating student.* Simulated teaching is a device for motivating students. To quote Cruickshank, "The technique provides reinforcement to students to develop teaching skills and avoid any risk of actual class-room encounter."

2. *Analysis of teaching problems.* Simulated teaching provides opportunities to student teachers to study and analyse critical teaching problems.

3. *Insight into behavioural problems.* Simulated teaching helps students in understanding behavioural problems of class-room, it helps in developing an insight to encounter them.

4. *Forging link between theory and practice.* A major advantage of using simulated teaching is that it forges close links between theory and practice.

5. *Factual and conceptual knowledge.* Simulated teaching enables students to acquire factual and conceptual knowledge and to retain the knowledge acquired.

6. *Means to conceptual knowledge.* Simulated teaching serves as a social laboratory. It provides opportunities to the students to exercise the social skills acquired. It helps in utilizing an artificial environment knowledge previously acquired. It leads to gaining some comprehension of the complexities of selected social processes.

7. *Interesting and enjoyable.* Last but not the least, the simulated teaching is interesting and enjoyable to students.

Uses in Problems of Teaching

According to Flanders simulated teaching maybe used to solve the following problems of teaching:

1. To ask open or close questions at the appropriate time.
2. To ask a question which *lifts* the current level of abstraction or a question which lowers it.

3. To ask questions from the areas in which concepts and logical connections have been expressed by the students previously.

4. To summarize what students have said previously.

5. To ask a question which may move the discussion to the next step in a logical sequence of problem solving.

6. To make the appropriate use of ideas expressed previously by the students.

7. To make constructive use of positive and negative feelings of the students.

8. To provide reasons for using 'praise' or blame.

9. To predict the consequences which follow from alternative actions.

10. To assist pupils to compare consequences of alternative actions through speculation before discussions are arrived at.

11. To guide constructive discussions.

12. To clarify the first steps needed to start work in ways that are in accordance with the interests and abilities of one's pupils.

13. To organize pupil's ideas in terms of teaching objectives for reinforcing selectively those ideas which are in target.

14. To demonstrate and explain rules of logic in class-room discourse.

15. To assist pupils to maintain consistency in the meaning of words and to assist to distinguish matters of facts, opinions and values.

Limitations of Simulation

In spite of the above uses, simulated teaching suffers from the following limitations:

1. *Difficulty for beginners.* New participants may face some difficulty in asking different kinds of questions. A simple task such as ''open'[5] and[4] 'closed'' questions may provide an *introductory* challenge.

2. *Incorrect recording.* It is possible that during an exercise, the observer may record incorrectly.

3. *Misconception.* The most common error in serious skill training is the misconception that adults may play the role of pupils.

To sum up, it may be said that simulation may be used to make a powerful tool in solving some of the problems that hinder effective teaching. It may also impart teaching of certain skills which are necessary for teaching and its effectiveness. It goes without saying that simulation exercise can be improved in a systematic experimentation around it. However, simulated social training (SSST) may be given a fair trial.

PROGRAMMED LEARNING

Programmed learning has been announced as an innovation in educational techniques. It has a long past but only a short history.

What is Programmed Learning?

1. *Susan Markle.* "Programmed learning is a method of designing a reproducible sequence of instructional events to produce a measurable and consistent effect on behaviour of each and every acceptable student,"

2. *Harold W. Bernard,* "Programmed learning refers to the arrangement of instructional material in progressive sequences."

3. *Michael J. Apter.* "Programmed instruction is a method of instruction in which the information to be taught is broken into small units which are to be presented to the student (usually in written form) in a carefully planned sequence. Each unit or 'frame', contains not only information but is also terminated with a question."

To include on the basis of the above definitions programmed learning is a method of individualized instructions in which the educand receives information relating to his own needs in progressive sequences but in small units. The educand remains active and proceeds at his own rate. He knows immediately whether he is right or wrong. Thus, programmed learning is a method which makes effective use of programmed books, language, laboratory, teaching machines, films, radio, television, tape-recorder and the teacher.

Characteristics

Negative Characteristics

1. *Not a test.* It is a teaching method and not a test. It helps the students in learning the material.

2. *Not an audio-visual aid.* It is not a part of the new technology of education.

3. *Not a Panacea.* It is not *a* technique of imparting knowledge. The educands learn at their own rate. The gifted educands learn quickly and backward educands learn at a slower rate.

Positive Characteristics

1. *Individualized instructions.* It is a method of individualized instructions. It is information presented according to individual needs. It maximizes the rate ana depth of learning. It motivates the students and fosters understanding.

2. *Logical sequence of material.* The subject-matter of programmed learning is presented into logical sequence of small steps. By proceeding in small steps, the possibility of committing error is eliminated.

3. *Interaction between the learner and the programme.* In programmed learning emphasis is laid upon interaction between the learner and the programme. It requires that the learner should be active.

4. *Immediate knowledge of results.* Programmed learning provides immediate knowledge of results. At each step the educand is informed of how he is doing. He immediately knows whether his answer to a question is right or wrong.

5. *Organized nature of knowledge,* Programmed learning lays emphasis upon the organized nature of knowledge. It requires continuity between the easier concepts and the difficult ones.

6. *Learner's own speed.* The learner moves at his own speed in programmed learning situation. Thus, learning takes place at individual rather than general rates.

7. *Constant evaluation.* Constant evaluation is possible by the record of student's responses in a programmed material. It is possible to improve the quality of programmed materials through checking the number of errors at each steps. Thus

student's progress may be evaluated by looking into the various types of responses produced by the learner.

Fundamental Principles

1. *Small steps.* A programme is made up of a large number of small and easy steps. One learns better in small steps, since the likelihood of errors is reduced in small steps.
2. *Active response.* Programmed learning is based on the principle of active response. A student learns better if he actively participates in the lesson and he learns best if he is actively responding while learning.
3. *Immediate confirmation.* As the student learns best if his answer is confirmed immediately, therefore, immediate confirmation serves as a kind of motivation or reinforcement.
4. *Self-pacing.* In programmed learning each student proceeds at his own rate or pace. It is common knowledge that some students naturally learn more rapidly or more slowly than others. One learns most effectively if one learns at one's own pace. This principle is based on individual differences in the process of teaching and learning.
5. *Evaluation.* Constant evaluation is yet another fundamental principle of programmed learning It helps students to learn and grasp the material given in each frame. The aim of this arrangement is not to test the student but to improve the quality of programmed materials through checking the number of errors at each step.

Types of Programming

The following are the main types of programming:

1. *Linear Programming.* This was developed and used by Skinner and his associates. In the linear style the subject matter is divided into very small steps, each of which is called a frame. Each frame, in its turn, requires the student to do something. When the student has given his response, he confirms it with the correct response provided in the programme. There is provision for self-pacing. Therefore, the linear programmed learning has all the principles mentioned below:
   (i) Information given in small steps.
   (ii) Active responding by the student at each step.
   (iii) Immediate knowledge of results.
   (iv) Self-pacing.
2. *Branching Programming.* The branching or instrinsic style (method) of programming was invented by Norman A. Crowder. He defined it as a programme which adapts to the needs of the students without the medium of an extrinsic device such as computer. The frame size and the amount of information given is larger than that of linear programme. The student starts by multiple choice questions designed to test the student's learning of the material. If the student chooses the correct answer, he is told that his answer is right and he is led to the next learning item. If his answer is wrong he has to go through a discussion where he is told what was wrong with the answer. He is then taken to the original item and allowed to select the right response again.

Branching programmes may be produced for use on a teaching machine or in a book form. The book form is known as a scrambled text because the pages do not follow in a normal sequence. The student is directed to different pages of the book according to the choice of the answer. He is instructed to press a particular button on a teaching machine according to the choice of the answer. The programme is presented on the film which is seen by learner on screen. An error counter records each incorrect answer chosen.

3. *Mathetics Programming.* The term 'mathetics' has been derived from the Greek *math* meaning To learn'. Thomos F. Gilbert originally formulated the basic concepts of mathetics. As K. P. Pandey puts it, "Mathetics is defined as the systematic application of reinforcement theory to the analysis and construction of complex repertories which represent mastery of subject matter." The unit for mathetical sequence is called exercise. The size of exercise is determined by the rise of the step a student can reasonably take at the moment. In order to determine the effectiveness of the courses of instruction, a detailed analysis is made of the behaviour of the student and the responses indicated. In writing mathetical programmes the basic steps are the following:

(i) Data collection and task analysis. (ii) Prescription for mastery.
(iii) Characterization and lesson plan. (iv) Exercise writing.
(v) Editing.

Steps in Preparation of Programme

Following are the steps in the preparation of a programme for learning:

1. *Selection of Units.* Selection of a unit to be programmed is the first step in preparation of programme. The programme should begin with a small unit as far as possible. The student should not have a tendency to select a very wide and general topic. In a very wide and general topic he will commit mistakes and meet frustration.

Lysaugth and Williams have suggested the following six criteria for the selection of unit to be programmed:

(i) *Programmer's own field of study.* The topic selected for a programme should belong directly to programmer's own field of study.

(ii) *Ease.* Ease in the handling of material is another criterion for the selection of a unit to be programmed.

(iii) *Length.* Another criterion for the selection of a unit is its length. Length of the unit should be determined according to the desired objectives for the subject-matter. Instead of programming a full course in mathetics or grammar it is better to take a unit of the course.

(iv) *Depressed level of learning.* Notorious stumbling blocks of learners must be programmed.

(v) *Logical order of material.* Logical order of material is an important criterion to be followed in the selection of a topic to be programmed.

(vi) *Special student needs.* Special student needs are also an important criterion in selecting a topic for programme.

2. *Writing assumptions about learners.* Characteristics of the learners or the audience for whom the programme is being prepared should be written fully

and accurately. The programmer should mention assumptions about their age, interests, abilities or skills, ambitions and background. The assumptions about learners should be written in objective, concrete and specific terms. Cumulative records, achievement tests, intelligence tests, aptitude tests, case history and above ail personal experiences of the programme as a teacher or learner prov e useful in Slaving a complete picture of the learners.

3. *Defining instructional objectives.* Instructional objectives should be defined in behavioural terms. The following points should be kept in mind in this connection:

(i) *Guide for selection of subject matter and teaching method.* Statement of instructional objectives should provide a guide for selecting the subject-matter, the teaching methods and the material to be used during instruction.

(ii) *Guide for evaluating instruments:*

(a) *In terms of student performance.* Each objective should be stated in terms of student performance rather than teacher performance.

(b) *In terms of terminal behaviour.* Each objective should be stated in terms of learning process rather than learning product.

(c) *In terms of one general outcome.* Teaching should be so stated that it includes only one general learning outcome rather than a combination of several outcomes.

4. *Defining pre-requisite knowledge and skills.* Pre-requisite knowledge and skills should be defined in behavioural terms. It helps to draw line of demarcation in respect of elements of the mastery or terminal behaviour which the programmer wants to develop. A careful study of prerequisite knowledge and skills should be prepared in terms of an empirical study conducted on representative sample of learner for whom the programme is being prepared.

5. *Preparing a criterion test.* A criterion test shows the entire range of terminal behaviour which has to be developed through the programme. It determines the success or the failure of the programme. While developing a criterion test the programmer should think very carefully about the situations which will evoke desired behaviour. The whole structure of criterion test should be reviewed by a person expert in the subject-matter as well as in techniques of testing. After this the entire test should be administered on a representative group of subjects. The choice of words, the use of language and relevance of each test item should be properly analysed. To quote Dr. K. P. Pandey, "A Good criterion test is one which reflects representative elements of the universe of behaviour which have been considered as the terminal behaviour."

6. *Developing contents.* In the end, specific outline of content to be programmed should be developed. At this stage the programmer should write the complete information. He should list all the relevant examples, concepts, illustrations *i.e.*, diagrams, maps, charts, etc., which are to be included in the content of a programme. The authenticity of the subject-matter should be ensured. The order in which instructional matter is to be presented should also be decided. Subject-matter should also be presented according to the level and needs of the students.

Use of Programmed Learning

In India, programmed learning is now being used in the following different areas:

1. *Industries.* Indian industries like TISCO, TELCO, Gujrat State Fertilizers Company Ltd. of Baroda, Gujarat Refiner and Jyoti Ltd. of Baroda are using programmed learning for their trainees. Some of the training officers of these industries have also joined courses on programmed learning.

2. *Defence.* Indian Army, Navy and Air Force are taking interest in the programmed learning movement. Recently, a three day seminar was conducted for the officers of Indian Military' Academy. Four officers of Indian Military Academy attended programmed learning course which was held at Poona in 1969, Two officers of Indian Air Force attended programmed learning course at Mysore in 1970. In 1969, the Army Cadet College. Poona conducted a full course on programmed learning at Poona. A course on programmed learning w as conducted for the Officers of Army Education Centre, Pachmarhi.

3. *Agriculture and Family Planning.* Agriculture and Family Planning Departments are showing keen interest in developing programmed learning materials. A number of programmes have been developed for family planning purposes. Different types of programmes have been developed such as pictoprogrammes and group programmes.

4. *Languages Learning.* Language learning is posing a serious problem for schools and colleges in India. Programmed learning projects have been taken up at different centres to produce self-instructional materials for teaching different languages for schools.

5. *School education.* Programmed learning may be used in the following aspects of schools education:

(i) Single Teacher Schools. (ii) Correspondence courses.
(iii) Gifted students. (iv) Backward students.
(v) Supplementary reading. (vi) Second language specialists.

TEAM TEACHING

The term team teaching is a recent idea in the field of education yet concepts underlying this method are not new. The Leoncasttrain Plan, The Dalton Plan, Writs Platoon System, Hosic's Co-operation Group Plan — all these contain varying traces of team teaching. Educators from various areas agree that, if organized properly, team teaching approach to education, is highly beneficial in India where there is shortage of subject teachers particularly in science and mathematics. The problem of scarcity of able teachers in rural areas may be solved, by introducing team teaching.

Definition of Team Teaching

1. *J. T. Shaplin.* 'Team teaching is a type of instructional organization, involving teaching personnel and the students assigned to them in which two or more teachers are given responsibility, working together, for all or a significant part of the instruction of some group of students.

2. *M. B. Naik.* "In a team teaching method, two or more teachers make a plan of the subjects co-operatively, carry it out, and also evaluate its effects on the students periodically."

3. *Michael J. Apter.* "Team teaching involves bringing together a number of classes whose teaching is then the joint responsibility of the teachers of these classes who now constitute a team."

From the above listed definitions it may be concluded that the team teaching involves a group of teachers who are jointly responsible for the planning and instruction of a course whether at the elementary, secondary or at college levels. The group of teachers may be few as two or as many as five or six teachers depending upon the nature and objectives of the course, the size of the class, and the facilities to be used. All the teachers of the team cooperatively develop a programme of instruction and share in teaching, evaluation and course improvement.

Essentials of Team Teaching

1. *To combine sections.* A number of sections of a particular class are combined to meet at the same hour in a big class for a particular subject, say physics.
2. *To make a team of subject teachers.* Subject teachers of those sections make a team and they choose one of them as leader of the team to teach physics.
3. *Common assembly of teachers.* On every working day, all the members of the team have a common assembly. Hence they discuss the methods used by the fellow-teachers while teachers make a plan for the next day and share the classroom experience of teaching physics.
4. *Imparting idea of team teaching to students.* Before the sections are combined an idea of effective use of team teaching methods should be given to all the students concerned.
5. *Imparting large group instructions.* At the beginning of the school year it is essential to give large group instructions for about four or five weeks in order to find out the levels and abilities of the students. Such a large group may be exposed to two or more subject teachers initially.
6. *Division into ability groups.* The large group is now splitted into three or four ability groups. Various methods like use of audio-visual aids, programmed learning, extra coaching, extra special home work may be employed according to the ability level of each group. Intelligent students may be given extra practice and learning material of higher level.
7. *Duties of team teachers.* Team teachers take it in turns to give lectures to a big class. While one teacher is teaching in a big class, other teachers should take care of other things such as home work correction, helping the slow learners, preparation of teaching aids like maps, charts and models, maintenance of discipline, complaints of the students, out-going and incoming of the students, fees and supervision of work of the students in the class. Thus, the teacher who is teaching focuses his attention on teaching only and he is not at all disturbed. It should be noted here that there must be a close relationship between the subject-matter covered in the big and small groups.

Guiding Principles in the Team Teaching

Kenneth has mentioned the following guiding principles in team teaching:

1. *The size and composition of the group must be appropriate to its purpose.* For some purposes it may be most convenient and most effective to assemble two or

more classes and pupils. For other purposes much smaller groups are desirable. For others again, individual tutoring and private stud) are essential. For some purposes steaming and setting may offer the best solution. For others fixed ability groupings may be preferred. It is wrong to suppose that reduction in the size of classes will act as a panacea. There is no magic number whether it be 40, 35 or 20 for calculating the right size of the class. The number may be according to the needs of the learning situation. The concept of the fixed size class is obsolete.

2. *The time allotted to any group should be appropriate to its purpose.* A fairly fluid time-table is essential. Since the pupils interests cannot be switched on and off, it follows that all lessons should not be of the same length.

3. *The learning environment should be appropriate to the activities of the group.* For 'straight' lesson the conventional classroom may still be the best place. But it is not the only learning place that is needed. Laboratories, libraries, workshops, listening and viewing rooms and individual study materials are also needed. The physical lay out of the typical school rarely provides all these things.

4. *The nature and extent of the supervision of the group activities depends upon the purpose of the group.* The arrangement whereby one teacher takes charge of the class works tolerably well so long as chalk and talk remains the rule. However, there are many situations where the teacher cannot be expected to carry on single-handed. As the occasion demands, he needs the assistance of his colleagues, either as consultants or as actual fellow workers.

5. *The duties assigned to teachers should be appropriate to their special qualifications and interests.* A teacher who gives a first-rate lecture may not necessarily make a good use of discussion group or take up remedial work with backward pupils. Some teachers have a flair for expounding their subject to a large audience, other for sympathetic attention to the individual pupil's difficulties. Ideally, every teacher should assume the role for which he is best fitted.

Factors Influencing Success

1. *Co-operation between team teachers.* One of the important factors for the success of team teaching is full co-operation between the team teachers and their willingness to accept criticism from each other.

2. *Co-operation of the head of the institution.* Full co-operation of the head of the institution is invariably necessary.

3. *Availability of suitable rooms.* Small and big classrooms should be easily available.

4. *Availability of Audio-visual aids.* An important factor contributing to the success of team teaching methods is the availability of effective audio-visual aids required for large group instructions.

5. *Teacher's willingness.* Teacher's willingness to change from traditional system to team teaching is a factor for the success of this method.

6. *Proper planning.* Lastly, the pre-requisite success of team leaching depends upon proper planning. While assigning duties to team teachers their interests and abilities should be kept in mind. Some teachers present material better than others; some are more effective in the laboratory while others may prepare visual-aids

and construct tests etc. In his book *The Teaching and the Curriculum* Grannies Joseph C. has given following outline of planning process:

(i) Reading of the general topic of the proposed unit by teachers.
(ii) Survey of the written Material and other resources.
(iii) Teacher's individuality.
(iv) Teacher's key lesson for collective planning.
(v) Construction of team learning and evaluation of exercise.
(vi) Periodic meeting for collective planning.
(vii) Daily planning on a contingency basis
(viii) Co-ordination of team's daily plans.
(ix) Leader's help to teachers to set up favourable conditions in classroom.

Advantages of Team Teaching

The following are the advantages of team teaching as compared to the traditional methods:

1. *Better Planning.* In the traditional methods two separate teachers were required to spend time in planning the same units for two different classes in two different rooms. In team teaching, on the other hand, each teacher can devote more lime to planning for preparing his unit since he has more time for that purpose.

2. *Improvement in technique of teaching.* In team teaching teachers are given opportunity to observe each other's teaching and improve their technique of teaching. In traditional teaching, on the other hand, they are devoid of the opportunity of observing the lessons of other teachers.

3. *Better teaching presentation.* In team teaching specific teaching presentations to the combined section are made by the team teacher who is best qualified in that particular field of subject. This is not so in the traditional method.

4. *Better atmosphere for teaching.* In team teaching the teacher presenting a lesson has better atmosphere for teaching since he is not disturbed by so many interruptions. In traditional class-room teaching, on the other hand, he is disturbed by so many interruption.

5. *Useful for brilliant students.* In team teaching, sometimes the brilliant students are segregated. They are given extra work and thus they do not lose interest as they do in traditional classroom teaching.

6. *Useful for slow learners.* In team teaching slow learners are properly and separately attended. In traditional teaching, they are generally disregarded.

7. *Solution for shortage of subject teachers.* Team teaching may help in solving the problem of shortage of trained teachers. This method of teaching would prove to be very helpful and effective in rural areas for primary and other levels. Since it is becoming very difficult to get good trained teachers in subjects like science and mathematics, two or three teachers specialised in three or four subjects can teach in teams.

9

SOCIOLOGY OF EDUCATION

DEFINITION OF EDUCATIONAL SOCIOLOGY

The following definitions of educational sociology will make it easier to comprehend the nature, scope and importance of the subject:

1. *Brown*. "Educational sociology is the study of the interaction of the individual and his cultural environment." It is evident from this definition that it studies the effect of the cultural environment on the individual, and also the ways and means by which this cultural environment can be changed.

2. *Carter*. "Educational sociology is the study of those phases of sociology that are of significance for educative processes, especially the study of those that point to valuable programme of learning and control of learning processes." Putting it simply, this discipline is sociology in the field of education. It carries out experiments to make the application of sociological principles more active and effective.

3. *Ottoway*. "Educational sociology starts with the assumption that education is an activity which goes on in the society and the society in its turn determines the nature of education". Modern educationists agree that the process of education is made possible by the family, school, community and other parts of society. The educational system of a society will bear resemblance to the nature of society itself although this does not imply that society cannot be changed through education. In fact, both society and education influence each other and educational sociology makes a study of this interaction.

RELATION TO EDUCATIONAL PSYCHOLOGY

As is apparent from the term, educational psychology is the psychology that relates to education; or to put it differently, it is the science concerned with behaviour pertaining to education. It is also the scientific study of human behaviour in conditions that take their particular form from education. Putting the same differently, educational psychology is the science that applies the principles of psychology concerned with human behaviour and experience to circumstances predominantly educational. In the words of Skinner, "Educational psychology utilizes those findings that deal specifically with the experiences and behaviour of human beings in educational situations".[1] Apparently, educational psychology is intimately concerned with human personality.

Education is the process of mental development. Hence educational psychology is concerned with the development of mental processes along with the various social processes. Judd, a famous educational psychologist, wrote, "Educational psychology may be defined as the science which describes and explains the changes that take place in individuals as they pass through various stages of development from birth to maturity." Educational psychology, being more than an academic pursuit, besides studying the process of development, also puts forward suggestions for its acceleration.

The process of development is dependent upon and grounded in two factors: maturity and learning. Hence, educational psychology is concerned with the study of both these factors. As Crow and Crow express it, "Educational psychology describes and explains the learning experiences of an individual from birth through old age".[2] In this way, educational psychology is the psychology of learning, towards which the educational psychologists have contributed by making intensive studies of the factors and conditions determinant of learning.

Briefly, educational psychology makes a psychological study of human development, maturity and learning, and applies the scientific conclusions of this study to actual teaching conditions in order to attain the ends of education. The modern educational psychologist is a specialist in his own right and is deeply engrossed in researches into behaviour sign A cant to education.

It is believed that there is intimate relationship between the sociological and the psychological tendencies in modern education. Such educationists as Pestalozzi, I lerbart and Froebel, who encourage the use of psychology in education, also admit the influence of sociological factors in the child's development. Pestalozzi wanted the education of the child to be such that it could lead to the welfare of the family and the nation and society, along with the child's own welfare. According to Herbart, the aim of education is the moral development of the individual so that he can develop the ability to bring about social welfare. Thus, both Herbart and Pestalozzi wanted to educate the child for social welfare. Even the thinking of Froebel reflects some sociological inclination, for he conceives of the school as a miniature society. In kindergarten education, he has placed special emphasis upon the social aspect of education. Thus, the proponents of the psychological tendency in education believe the social aim to be important, while, at the same time, those in favour of the social objectives of education do not in any way detract from the importance of psychological elements in education. Obviously, then, both the tendencies complement each other. In educating the child, therefore, it is important to pay attention to both his psychological and his social conditions, for neither is less important than the other. The child enters the world possessed of the psychological elements, but these psychological elements develop in the social environment. Hence both must be studied in the child's education.

The scientific tendency in education places a lot of emphases upon the importance of science. Spencer was one of the proponents of science, and he has

1. Skinner, C.E., *Educational Psychology*, Prentice Hall Inc., New York (1951), p. 14.
2. Crow, L.D. and Crow, A., *Educational Psychology*, Eurasia Publishing House Pvt. Ltd. (1964), p.7.

said that science should be made the basis of education. Education, according to him, aimed at preparing the individual for the complete life. He believed that knowledge of the various physical and social sciences must supplement knowledge of literature, art and music. Sociology and psychology are important social sciences. Hence, the scientific, sociological and psychological tendencies are intimately related to each other. All three of them aim at the complete development of the individual in order to make him a useful member of society. These tendencies differ only in respect of the emphasis they place on their respective spheres. All three of them want to fashion education in such a manner that it should culminate in the happiness of the individual and the welfare of society. Both the sociological and the scientific tendencies have stressed the social objectives of education, both have opposed the traditional methods of discipline and both have demanded radical changes in the curriculum. Both are opposed to social distinctions and both want the child to study the natural and the physical sciences. But, despite these similarities, the two differ from each other in the following respect:

(1) While physical scientists believe science to be supreme, the sociologists believe society to be the most important.

(2) The scientist may also be an individualist but the sociologist is invariably in favour of social approach.

Despite these two minor differences, both aim at social welfare. Because individual and society are two aspects of a single fact, and are therefore supplements to each other, the scientific and the sociological tendencies of education are also complementary.

VALUE OF THE SOCIOLOGY OF EDUCATION

1. Stress on professional or vocational education. The sociological tendency lays stress on enabling the child to earn his livelihood through professional education.

2. Opposition to individualism. The sociological tendency was born out of reaction to individualism. It stresses the importance of society, as against the individual.

3. Social progress as the aim of education. Social welfare is the aim ascribed to education by the sociological tendency. Children should be trained only for this through a system of free and compulsory education. This should make them responsible members of society.

4. Faith in democracy. The sociological tendency also evinces faith in democracy. In a democracy, education is based on the co-operation between the stale and society, and besides, the success of democracy depends upon the education of its' members.

5. Clarification of social problems. The sociological tendency clarifies social problems and suggests ways and means of solving them through education. Many social reforms can be brought about by education, and it can create an entirely new generation which may be free of the defects inherent in the older generation.

6. Raising the standard of social life. The sociological aim of education is to raise the standard of social life by achieving the child's comprehensive development. Education must train the individual to fulfil his social responsibilities. If it fails to do this, education cannot be said to have any utility.

7. Importance to social sciences. The presence of the sociological tendency in education has led to greater importance being attached to the social sciences, so that the child can understand social phenomena and problems, and thus be enabled to make some positive contribution to social welfare.

8. Importance to social life in the school. Social life within the school has been recognised as important because of the sociological tendency. It is now suggested that authorities should encourage the formation of committees which train the child for later social life.

9. Education as an agency of social progress. According to sociologists, education is the best means of social control, social change and thus, finally, of social progress. All social changes that may become necessary for social progress can be easily brought about through education. Social control becomes a measure of self control through education because education socializes the individual.

INFLUENCE OF SOCIOLOGY IN EDUCATION

It is evident from the foregoing account of the sociological tendency in education that sociology has had widespread influence upon the meaning, objectives, functions of education, the curriculum, the methods of teaching, the school organisation, etc. These influences can be briefly enumerated as follows:

1. Meaning of education. According to educational sociologists, education is a social process which socializes the child and causes certain changes in his behaviour. In this way, even in defining education, the sociologists have stressed its social aspects,

2. Objective of education. According to them, the objective or aim of education is to evolve those social qualities and a social feeling in the child which will enable him to understand his responsibility to society and nation, and to become the ideal citizen of his country, and train him to fulfil his duties. Such aims of education as education for citizenship and education for social life are influenced by the sociological tendency.

3. Functions of education. Elucidating the functions of education, the educational sociologists have stressed the social functions of education. In his *Brief Course in the History of Education* Munro lays down the following four functions of education:

(*i*) *Spread of knowledge.* The first function of education is to provide various kinds of knowledge to the child. This develops the child's mind, and without this no other development is possible.

(*ii*) *Social control.* The child undergoes a process of socialization in educational institutions and is thus subjected to social control. But social control through education eventually becomes self control for the child so that he has no difficulty in accepting it. Hence, in every society, schools instil the elements of social control into the younger generation through the process of education.

(*iii*) *Protection of the social heritage.* Education is one important medium of transferring social heritage and culture from one generation to the next, because it is through education that the new generation is acquainted with the culture and civilization of society. And it is through education that the new generation is taught to adopt this culture. The new generation makes its own contribution to this social heritage, intensifies it and, in its turn, passes it on to its successor.

(*iv*) *Social development.* Social development is also one of the important aims of education because, without this individual development is not possible. The school is itself a miniature form of society, for in the school the educators try to create an ideal social environment in order to inculcate the best possible picture of society in the minds of the educands. After leaving the school, the educand retains this picture of the ideal society in his mind and tries to recreate it in reality. Through education the individual develops the qualities required for the ideal member of society, and when most of the members of society have these qualities, it is only natural that society will develop.

4. Organisation of curriculum. Educational sociologists have provided a number of valuable suggestions about reorganising the curriculum of education. They suggest that the curriculum should be based mainly on social ideals and values, and should provide for the introduction of social subjects and collective activities. The curriculum should be revised from time to time, according to the needs of the society, because it should always educate the individual to be the member of society and to fulfil his responsibilities towards the family. Hence, sufficient importance must be attached to professional and scientific subjects in the curriculum, which should be flexible and variable so that it can be made to accommodate all social changes and social necessities.

5. Methods of teaching. The sociological tendency also laid stress on the inclusion of social elements in the methods of teaching so that education can evolve essential social qualities in children, Some examples of this are the Dalton method, the Project method, etc. Educational sociology gives suggestions for changes in teaching methods from the viewpoint of social dynamics.

6. Administrative techniques. Before the impact of the sociological tendency, efforts at administration and discipline were individualistic but the sociological influence laid stress on the social or collective methods. Collective methods stress the fact that administration and discipline should be collective, not individual. It is desirable to create such an atmosphere in the college that social discipline should naturally emerge in the educand so that he may not indulge in activities harmful to the individual or the society at large. In this way, community feeling was made the basis of discipline. It is seen in many circumstances that much better discipline can be established through the influence of social control and public opinion than is possible through individual methods.

7. Child education movement. As a result of the sociological tendency, there began a movement for the education of infants. Many infant schools were established in America and in many European countries. Most of them aimed at providing education to the children of labourers. In England, Robert Owen drew attention to the ill-effects of not educating the children of the labour class.

8. Monitor method. The influence of the sociological tendency can be clearly seen in the monitor method introduced by Dr. Andrew Bell. In this method the onus of teaching fell on the children, for children of higher classes were required to teach children of junior classes. As a result one single educator could teach a much larger number of educands. On the basis of this monitor system, many monitorial schools were established in a number of countries.

9. Adult education movement. The sociological influence insisted upon the fact that no individual in society should be left uneducated, and hence many movements for adult education began; schools and colleges for such people were run during evening and nights. Much important work has been done in this direction in India.

10. Social education. The sociological tendency has also made a very strong impact in the field of social education. Social education of the individual implies an education which acquaints the individual with every aspect of his environment and trains him to fulfil his responsibilities as a citizen. Social education aims not only at the complete development of the individual but also at evolving social unity and other social ideals in him. Agencies of social education are literacy, lectures, exhibitions, meetings, tours, etc. In India much useful work has been done in the villages towards providing social education.

11. Responsibility of the state. According to the sociological tendency, it is the responsibility of the state to provide education. Hence, it is for the state to make every individual, through education, capable of earning his livelihood, of developing his personality, of fulfilling his social duties. Without proper education of the masses, democracy can never be a success. Hence, the state should provide primary, secondary, university and professional education.

THE SCOPE OF SOCIOLOGY OF EDUCATION

Educational sociology, as the name indicates, is the sociological study of educational institutions and processes. It may be defined as the study of education from the sociological standpoint. It is the study of the inter-relationship of education and the social system. It centres upon the study of social institutions and their role in education. It includes the inter-relationships of education with kinship, social stratification, attitude to knowledge, interactional relationship besides the organisational pattern of educational institutions, the teacher-pupil relationships, the teacher-teacher relationships and finally student-student relationships. The meaning of sociology of education will be further clarified in the following chapter.

The scope of sociology of education, as is clear by its definition given above, includes almost all the elements of general sociology with particular reference to education. Thus it includes the study of relationship of education to the other aspects of social system particularly kinship, social stratification, political organisation, knowledge and attitudes to knowledge.

1. Education and kinship. Both education and kinship are important institutions of socialisation in a society. Every society introduces gradual socialisation of a child through complex processes which give the child individual identity and the ability to acquire social status and fulfil roles according to it. In the kinship system the most important role towards socialisation is performed by parental family. The school transfers knowledge from one generation to another and develops intellectual ability. Both kinship and educational institutions develop the value system in a society.

Family is an enduring association of parents and children. Its primary functions are the satisfaction of the members and the socialization of the child.

It is a social agency for the education and protection of the race. It is in the family that the child acquires such important qualities as sincerity, sympathy, self submission and consciousness of responsibility, etc. It is the character developed in the family which helps the child in becoming an important and responsible member of society. In every family, the child gets an opportunity for free expression of thoughts and development of his entire personality; Psychologists have incontestably proved that the proper development of the child is impossible without a good environment in the family. The tendencies and habits which he acquires in the family, he finds impossible to shed later on. According to Freud, the viewpoint of a child towards the elders in the family determines his attitude and viewpoint towards the elders in society. The child's first school is his home and family. The child's education should be in the hands of the parents in family. The parents should participate in all the child's activities. A child learns much by imitating his superiors. Mahatma Gandhi and such thinkers paid personal attention to the development of their children. It is the family which imparts practical education to the child concerning the customs in society, conduct, other important elements of culture, preservation of health, love, sympathy, co-operation, etc. According to M.S. Gore and I.P. Desai, "The points of contact between the educational and the kinship systems are thus many and varied. The extent to which the two systems support each other and, the extent to which they work at cross purposes in any given society is a point of examination and study for the sociologist of education. He is further interested in determining the conditions under which the two systems are likely to support or conflict with each other".[3]

2. The school as a social system. After the home, the child is exposed to the school which also influences him, for the school is nothing less than a miniature society in him. It socializes him, gives him an opportunity to manifest his qualities, instructs, drives and motives and helps to develop his personality. For the child, the educator's personality and character provide a model which he strives to copy, thereby consciously or unconsciously moulding his personality'. This is true only of those teachers who succeed in arousing in the child's mind an attachment and love for themselves. Every little action, every movement, speech, etc., impresses itself on the child's mind. On the other hand, he is often repelled by some teachers, and he wants to contradict them through every act. This repulsion may be conscious or unconscious, but it drives the child away from such a teacher. The child is attracted by the other teacher who wins his sympathy, and it is from this teacher that the child wants to win praise and appreciation. He fears the frown of this teacher, he imitates him persistently. Apart from the teacher the child is also influenced by his colleagues, and his status and role in his school group plays a large part in determining the status and role he is to occupy in society in later life. During the process of education, the child's personality develops under the impact of the other personalities with whom he comes into contact, in the school the child is disciplined. He is aware that disobedience brings immediate punishment, but too strict a system of discipline restricts the child's

3. M.S. Gore, I.P. Desai and Suma Chitnis, *The Sociology of Education in India*, NCERT, 1967, p.7.

mental growth and may even drive him to criminal activity. On the other hand, complete absence of control may either make him liberal, free and independent or impulsive and impish. Besides, the cultural programmes of the school also help to refine his attitudes.

In this manner, the human personality is profoundly influenced both by the home and the school. Of the two, the family influence lasts for a longer time and is more comprehensive.

3. Education and social stratification. Social stratification, whether open or close, is very much concerned with education. Social mobility is very much influenced by castes, religious groups and classes. All these influence the mental progress of the child through education. Thus social stratification governs the type of education which a particular individual will be able to secure. This is clear from the influence of castes, religious groups and classes upon education in India:

(*i*) *Influence of castes.* Under the Hindu social organisation, it is caste which determines the individual's status and position in the social hierarchy. One finds elements of the caste system even among the Muslims. In the caste, the professions and occupations of the lower castes are predetermined and fixed, and the child aims at adopting the occupation of his own caste. Since the child is almost compelled to adopt the same profession as his forefathers, he is inevitably exposed to the rules of unteachability which operate between his caste and a superior caste. This creates very undesirable prejudices and gives rise to narrow mindedness in the child. Although there are some advantages in adopting the hereditary occupation, it is undeniably unscientific in that it fails to consider the individual differences of the children and does not consider the actual suitability of the child to that particular occupation. The caste system has had the effect of splitting the society into many small segments, and this fragmentation obviously hinders the development of national unity. Besides, it is also responsible for the child's awareness of discrimination and distinction between individuals and the consequent feelings of superiority and inferiority. In this way, the presence of many different castes hinders the child's mental progress.

(*ii*) *Impact of religious groups.* In India one can see many religious groups such as Hindus, Muslims, Christians, Buddhists, Sikhs and Jains, etc. Most of these religious groups have established and are maintaining many religious schools in which general religion is taught, along with their own respective religious teachings. Most of these schools try to inculcate a particular set of religious principles in the educand. In many ways the teaching of religious principles can be of benefit to the child and the community, but when teaching in the school contradicts or ridicules teaching in another school, it naturally gives rise to a consciousness of differences between one religion and another. The immediate consequence of this is communalism which is instilled into the child's tender mind, and this prevents him from identifying himself with other members of the nation, and thus national unity suffers. The best course is to inculcate the general principles of religion, stressing the fact that all religions are one and the same, for without this, religion can only lead to narrowminded thinking.

(*iiii*) *Impact of classes.* Social class has the most potent influence on the child. On the one hand, we find a steady breakdown of discrimination based on religion and caste, but on the other we find a growing consciousness of the class one comes from, thus intensifying the feeling of difference. This awareness, that one belongs to the lower, middle or upper class is communicated to the child also. Consequently, children coming from the lower classes start with the feeling of inferiority, of being poor, of deprivation of the good things of life. In reaction to this inferiority, many of them turn to criminal activity, because children from the upper classes find pleasure in displaying their superiority which has already created in them pride and vanity and a number of other ignominious emotions and sentiments. Comparatively, the child from the middle classes is less susceptible to either extremes. The emotion for superiority on the one hand is reduced by consciousness of inferiority on the other, and this explains the reason why most middle class children show better performances in academic work than children from either of the two other classes. Some political ideologies also reinforce this awareness of the difference of class. It may have some dubious advantages, but it cannot be denied that on the whole it has a detrimental effect on the child's development, and that it practically obviates the possibility of ever generating any humane sentiments in them.

4. Education and the political system. In modern societies, one finds that education is provided in government controlled institutions as well as privately managed institutions. Many educational institutions are also controlled and managed by religious institutions. And even among the government or state controlled institutions, one finds that some are administered by the central authority and others by state or local self-governing bodies. Another aspect of the state control of education is to determine the spheres which the state should take under its own wings and the areas which can be safely left to the control of the people. In the present day, every government, be it totalitarian or democratic, must contribute to education. There is no doubt that in a democracy the government is elected by the people, but it cannot be denied that the people themselves cannot evolve an educational pattern which may look after the educational needs of every individual. And, at the same time, it is also realised that democracy cannot be successful in the absence of universal education. Hence, modern democratic states play a large part in educational planning and organisation.

Having accepted that the state must exercise control over the educational system, it becomes necessary to determine the extent to which this control should be exercised. Historically viewed, education has been carried on in every state through a variety of means and agencies. On the one hand, one finds colleges and schools run by individuals for profit while on the other one comes across institutions created by religious groups or philanthropists who have collected funds from private individuals for this purpose. In addition, one finds state aided institutions in every country. Even J.S. Mill, who objects to state control of education, has admitted that the state should establish some ideal educational institutions which may serve as models and which may inspire the people to create similar institutions. Mill objects to the state control of education on the ground that the state tries to educate the people along lines which supports own ideology and thus it controls the ideas of the people. This belief is not completely without logic and supporting evidence, because communist states do try to control the thinking of the younger generations by intellectually feeding them on communist literature. It amounts to slow brainwashing. Much the same tendency has been seen in the past in totalitarian states which also try to control the thinking of the people by making educational institutions the centres of states propaganda. This is unfair and improper. In fact, state control in education should be exercised with the sole purpose of preventing encroachment upon the political and social independence and freedom of the people, because this is essential for a proper development of personality. In the second place, the state has at its disposal unlimited means and resources which enable it to arrange for education on a large-scale, something which is beyond the reach of private individuals and groups of individuals. Briefly speaking, it is desirable that state control of education should be guided by the principle of the least possible infringement of the liberties of the people. The welfare state provides for education on precisely this principle. With the establishment of democratic government, the sphere of education is widening rapidly with the result that the responsibilities of the state are increasing. The state imposes taxes on the people in order to finance education and then compels people to send their children to schools and colleges. It also supervises educational arrangements in institutions not controlled by it to ensure uniform standards, and also to provide financial aid to them.

Aldous Huxley has remarked, "If your aim is liberty and democracy, then you must teach people the arts of being free and of governing them selves' Democracy can never be successful without education. Wherever democracy has been unsuccessful, it has been because of the lack of education. In a democracy the government is composed of the elected representatives of the people and if the people are uneducated they can never elect the right leaders and consequently can never create the right kind of government. In fact, it is impossible even to hope for democracy in the absence of education. It is difficult to expect a citizen to behave responsibly if he is not even aware of his rights and duties. Bertrand Russell has commented, "Democracy in its modern form would be quite impossible in a nation where many men cannot read". The truth of the matter is that education is a prerequisite of democracy. Only after proper education should the citizen be invested with his democratic rights. As Fichte, the German philosopher, has commented, "Only the nation which has first solved in actual practice the problem of educating perfect men will then solve the problem of the perfect state". Although Fichte made this comment in the context of autocratic states, it cannot be doubted that the perfection of even a democratic state can be judged only by the extent to which it contains educated people. As Hetherington puts it, "Democratic government, at least, demands an educated people". Throwing light on the objectives of education in the 1949 meeting of the universities commission, Dr. S. Radhakrishnan stressed the fact that the democratic state recognises the importance of the individual, and it is the process of development of this individual which is called education. Hence, education is absolutely necessary for establishing a democratic society. Dewey has pointed out that democracy is inconceivable without education, because education alone can generate and instil the qualities which democracy demands as a prerequisite. Philosophers of the ancient Greek city state were aware of the significance of education. Both Plato and Aristotle laid stress on the importance of education for the success of democracy. Ernest Barker comments, "To Plato education was the most important function of the state and the department of education the most important state department which was particularly advocated for producing the philosopher king to improve the men's minds for becoming virtuous beings". Plato, in his famous text, *The Republic,* stressed not only the importance of education for democracy tut even formulated a plan for the education of men and women which made all kinds of development: physical, mental, moral and aesthetic-possible. Aristotle was of the opinion that the aim of the state is to make possible the achievement of the highest moral level and this can be reached through education alone. Thus, education is the most important function of the state. From one point of view, the state itself is a school in which the individual learns citizenship. Aristotle suggested that the aim of education is to produce good citizens. These truths were known not only Greeks but also to Indian thinkers of ancient times. India has been the home of democratic ideals and principles from ancient times. Hermitages and places of worship were used as schools in which the sages tried to create ideal citizens who could become useful members of society. But the modern age needs democratic education far more than was needed in ancient Greece or ancient India because modern democracies are so vast and their problems so complex that the education of citizens is even more imperative today.

5. Education and the attitude to knowledge. The sociologist is interested in the social attitudes towards the sources, the limits and the validity of knowledge. With the change in these social attitudes one finds a considerable interest in the interaction among educators and the educand in educational institutions. In the ancient times knowledge was limited and attained through some limited means. It was acquired by few and individually circulated on the basis of Guru-Shishya relationship. Therefore the attitude towards knowledge was of awe and reverence. The teacher was feared and respected, his word was the law. Teachers refused admission to a student purely on personal grounds. The student, on the other hand, considered knowledge to be a treasure deposited with few persons who must be obeyed in order to learn. He had high respect for knowledge since most of the knowledgeable persons belonged to high caste or high social status. Thus the teacher-taught relationship in ancient India or Greece was very much governed by attitude to knowledge.

This attitude to knowledge has considerably changed in the modern times. The growth of knowledge in all directions, the substitution of new and sometimes absolutely opposite theories for the older ones, have led to the growing realisation that no knowledge is final. Knowledge is unlimited and can be achieved by innumerable means. The one single factor that has come out to be the most certain concerning knowledge in our own time is the realisation that no knowledge is final and no means the only means of knowledge. In every field of knowledge today multisided, holistic, integral and total approach is considered to be wiser. All statements are taken as tentative. All theories are merely probable. Again, the fast growth of knowledge is making the old attitudes irrelevant. For example, in the early wake of science, scientific knowledge was considered to be most certain and the scientific attitude used to challenge religious and spiritual experiences. With the growth of so many theories in different branches of knowledge, scholars used to adhere to this or that ism. But today scholars work in areas rather than of ism. Most of the scholars today are realising that the knowledge attained by non-scientific, intuitive, psychic or spiritual methods is no less or more valid than scientific knowledge. The world of knowledge is drifting towards a pluralistic, catholic, agnostic, mystic, holistic and integral approach. Therefore the student's approach towards knowledge is altered. He is an agnostic if not a cynic. This agnosticism or cynicism has flown to him from the teacher himself. The data of knowledge is much more complex to be finally explained by a single formula or even by a conglomeration of formulae. The sociologist is interested in knowing how this change in the attitude to knowledge influences teacher-taught relationship, inter-teacher relation, teacher's role in society, teacher-administrator relationship, in brief all interaction with in the educational system.

6. Interaction within educational system. The most important area in the scope of sociology of education is, however, social interaction within the educational system. The educational system involves three social constituents: teachers, students, and in a small measure the society or the community at large. All these constituents constantly change within themselves and in their interaction. The educational sociologist analyses the factors of this change, obseives the direction of change and finds out cause-affect relationship. A deeper analysis of the interactions within the educational system will give a better insight in the scope of sociology of education.

(*a*) *Teacher-administrator relationship.* At the fringe of the social organisation in the educational institution is the teacher-administrator relationship. The administrator is the employer or agent of the employer. He is the leader, the supervisor and the guide of the teachers. With the authority vested in him, he gives rewards and punishments for successes and failures. Therefore, the personality and the way of teaching is very much influenced by teacher-administrator relationship. The nature of the administrator changes according to the types of management. In government institutions the government officer is the administrator. In aided institutions the management is constituted by a president, a secretary, a nominee of the government and influential members elected by the donors constituting the general body of management. The executive body works for a limited term and is elected by the general body. It is answerable to the government, the general management body and the public at large. In practice the secretary wields most of the power. If his behaviour is autocratic it has an adverse effect upon the morale of the teachers. If he acts democratically it has a healthier influence upon the teachers.

(*b*) *Teacher-teacher relationship.* In every educational institution today there are more than one teacher. Therefore, the educational sociologist is interested in knowing teacher-teacher relationship. This relationship may be fraternal or marred by rivalry. While the fraternity results in co-operation, team spirit and goodwill, rivalry leads to mudslinging, favouritism and factionism. Even in small institutions or university or college departments two or more camps may be found among teachers giving vent to jealousy and rivalry against each other. The groups are based upon castes, religion, region, language, nationality, seniority, qualification or cadre. These groups may be seen from primary to university level involving dissensions among students seeking favour from this or that camp.

(*c*) *Student-student interaction.* The interaction among students is governed by age, classes, sex, study habits, extra-curricular activities and so many other factors. The most intimate interaction is provided by the classroom situation. Interaction everywhere may be cohesive or divisive. It may increase co-operation or conflict. The most important dimension for improving interaction is provided by extra-curricular activities, the debating societies, the dramatic clubs, literary associations, teams for sports and games and batches of excursions. All these provide scope for more intimate relationships resulting in deeper interactions. Sometimes teachers by favour or disfavour, create groups among students and increase jealousies and rivalries. The educational sociologists analyses the conditions of student-to-student interactions, the cohesive and divisive forces, the consequences, the factors of social change and social control, etc.

(*d*) *Teacher-taught relationship.* The most important field of interaction within an educational system is the teacher-taught relationship. Formerly, this relationship was familistic, today it is contractual. Formerly, the teacher himself laid downs the rules of admission, syllabi, teaching schedules, teaching methods and practically every detail of education. Today, the rules and syllabi are framed by experts or the government bodies while schedule is prescribed by the principal or the time-table incharge. Therefore, the teacher is confined only to teaching of his subject according to time-table. He is appointed on his job on a particular salary scale and under certain conditions. Teaching today is a profession with all its advantages and limitations.

The following are the factors governing teacher-taught relationship:

(*i*) *Age.* The distinction of age creates respect on the part of the younger and leadership on the part of the elder. In teacher-taught relationship the distinction of age is inverse with the level of education. Thus it is maximum at the primary level and minimum at the university level. The bigger age gap allows for the development of teacher-taught relationship based upon respect, fear and reverence. The smaller age gap makes for more intimacy, love, affection and more interaction between teacher and taught.

(*ii*) *Teacher's status.* In some societies the hereditary status of the teacher is high. He is an all knowing and infallible person. He may punish or reward according to his own judgement. In modern democratic societies, however, the authority of the teacher is eroded along with the authority of the administrator. Therefore, there are more interactions in the present-day institutions in comparison to the institutions of ancient past.

(*iii*) *Status and attitude of knowledge.* If these are marked by a certain finality the teacher wields more authority over the students. If these are tentative and probable, as it is today, the authority of the teacher is proportionately eroded.

(*iv*) *Mode of acquiring knowledge.* Formerly, teacher's words were unquestionable. He commanded total loyalty. Today, however the mode of acquiring knowledge is multiple, tentative and creative. Therefore, teacher-taught relationship has become more informal, less based upon fear and more intimate.

(*v*) *Image of the teacher in society.* Formerly, the image of the teacher was almost the highest in the society. Therefore even the princes used to touch feet of their teachers. If a scholar came to a court even the king left his seat. Today with the contractual system of education, the teacher is a professional person if not a poor member of society. With the erosion of the image of the teacher in society, the interaction between the teacher and taught has considerably changed.

(*vi*) *Self image of the teacher and the student.* The self image of today's teacher is a professional person delivering goods, making out his living and at the most pursuing knowledge. He is one among equals, never superior and occasionally even inferior. The self image of the student, on the other hand, is no more of a submissive disciple obeying his teacher but an individual making the best of education to further his own aim in life.

(*vii*) *Role of the teacher.* The teacher-taught relationships change according to change in the teacher's role in education. Formerly, he was independent and sovereign. Today he is subordinate and dependent upon the management, the government, the wider community and even the student. This role again changes on various levels of education such as primary, secondary and university. It also changes according to the type of management of the educational institutions, the private, the religious or the government management. This role again is governed by personal traits, seniority, qualifications, cadre, economic condition and innumerable other factors. The educational sociologist analyses the change of role and the consequent changes in the teacher-taught relationships.

(*viii*) *Mode of standardisation.* As most of the educational institutions today receive financial aid, the government lays down uniform modes of standardisation about the syllabi, the teaching methods and the evaluation techniques at various levels of education. Sometimes there is an examining body governing all the students in a state such as U.P. Board of Secondary Education. Each university arranges for examination and evaluation of all the students of all the colleges affiliated to it. This mode of standardisation has eliminated the value of personal qualities and scholarship of the teachers. The teachers and the students now concentrate upon text-books and even help books with the sole aim of preparing for the examination and achieving better success.

In the end it may be noted that the scope and type of interaction between the educators and the educand is today becoming more and more complex and changing fast. This requires an occasional review by the sociologists of education.

10

SOCIALIZATION AND FAMILY

Socialization is the process whereby an individual learns to behave in accordance with social traditions and mores. The human child possesses a tendency towards imitation. The child develops according to the environment in which he lives. The individual tries to win the praise of the group in which he lives. Man is a social being. He, of his own nature, tries to adopt the culture of society. Man becomes what he is by socialization and it is by virtue of this that he is believed to be superior to animals. Socialization brings balance to his personality because the social aspect of personality also is very important. Through socialization the individual learns to control himself in the interest of society and realizes his responsibility towards others. Socialization develops in him the community feelings and he learns to cooperate with others.

Individuals influence each other by means of imitation, suggestion and sympathy. In addition to these, social institutions and associations also carry out the individual's socialization. The individual is influenced by many processes in society, praise and blame, cooperation and conflict, submission and ascendency. These help to form his personality and individuality. Education is the most prominent means to socialization.

Socialization in the Family

The family plays perhaps the most dominant role in the individual's socialization. The child finds much to learn in the behaviour of his family members, parents, relatives and friends. He imitates them in their mannerisms, behaviour, cliches, etc. He tries to avoid such activities which result in punishment or which are considered bad in the family. It is the family environment which forms his good habits and it is in the family that he acquires criminal tendencies. In the book *New Light on Delinquency and its Treatment* Healy and Bronner have written that juvenile delinquents mostly hail from families which at one time or another, have suffered some hindrance in the fulfilment of social relations. Psychoanalysts, prominent among them are Freud and Adler, have proved that a man behaves in society according to whatever he has become in the family. Termann, the author of *Psychological Factors in Marital Happiness* has said that only those individuals can make marriage a success whose parents were contented. The preface writer of *Women of the street*, a searching book on London prostitutes, has stated that the problem of prostitution is the problem of the parent-child relationships. Boys and girls are spoiled when family contentment and peace are lacking. Many similar circumstances give birth to many thieves, murderers and prostitutes.

Other Influences in Socialization

But it is incorrect to believe socialization to be dependent exclusively on the family. Other institutions and associations outside the family also wield influence on the development of man. When the child has grown a bit, he leaves the sanctity and protection of his home to go out and plan, at such a time he is very susceptible to the influence of his playmates. The child in the school, is in addition to the effect of education, vulnerable to the influences exerted by the personalities of his teachers and friends. In much the same way, young men and women learn to conduct themselves and to give expression to their views, such a process being an outcome of education and constant association with teachers, the unique environment, fellow collegiates, etc. Following college education, the individual's occupations and marriage are important factors of socialization. Both men and women are strongly influenced by the personality of their life partner, and their future depends upon this to a large extent. In this way, the child in the family becomes successively the protector, husband and father. These new responsibilities and rights teach him very much. In brief, socialization is a process which begins at birth and continues unceasingly until the death of the individual. Like education it too is an incessant process.

Thus family exerts maximum influence, then come the play groups, school, religious group, children club, community and larger cultural patterns. Interaction is maximum with pals, then with friends and casual acquaintances.

NEED FOR SOCIALIZATION

The question why is socialization necessary for the development of the individual is best answered by the examples of human beings who were for some reason, nurtured outside society. Human beings of this kind are described by Gesell in his work *Wolf children and Human child* and by Davis in his essays. In 1920, in India, two children were found in a wolfs den, of which one was eight years old and the other couple of years younger. The second died after the lapse of only a few months while the first continued to live for six years. She was named Kamla. The girl was completely innocent of the modes and ways of human behaviour. She walked on all fours, growled like a wolf and could not speak. She became nervous at the sight of human beings as undomesticated animals tend to do. In this way, due to the absence of socialization she possessed none of the characteristics of human being save for her bodily structure. She was taught to speak, wear clothes and eat. In this way, she could learn some human behaviour due to the influence of socialization after a period of some years.

Socialization is not the exclusive but a prominent source of individual's development, because heredity also has its importance. The development of the individual, with the spread of culture through socialization, is impossible. The 'self' of the individual develops only due to socialization. Every social relationship of the individual contributes to this process of socialization. The problem of man's socialization is very complex and it has not yet been completely solved in any human society. In the words of Davis, "The improvement of socialization offers one of the greatest possibilities for the future alteration of human nature and human society"

WHAT IS SOCIAL DEVELOPMENT?

In defining social development, Sorenson has written, "By social growth and development we mean the increasing ability to get along well with oneself and others."[4] Thus social development is the ability or skill by means of which an individual maintains order and system in his relation with other beings in his neighbourhood, besides adapting his behaviour to them. Man is a social being influencing the conduct of others and being influenced by their behaviour, in his turn. Social relationships depend upon the mutual adjustment between such behaviour. Interests, attitudes, habits, etc., bear much importance for this mutual behaviour. Development of all these elements is part and parcel of social development in general. During the different stages that an individual passes, social circumstances in his immediate neighbourhood, his relations with others and their expectations of him undergo constant change. Social development increases the ability to adjust to one's present social circumstances and to behave in accordance with the wishes and desires of other people. If adult men or women were to be seen playing with dolls, it would be considered socially undesirable and improper whereas it is perfectly reasonable for a child to indulge in this sort of entertainment. Due to social development, the individual's conduct conforms to the requirements of his age, his social status and social functions. In the words of Powers, "Social development can be defined as the progressive improvement, through directed activity, of the individual in the comprehension of the heritage and the formation of flexible conduct patterns of reasonable conformity with this heritage."[5] In this manner, stress is laid upon unceasing progress and development. The individual's social circumstances are constantly undergoing change. Hence, the individual must perforce change with these circumstances. This is the process of his actual social development.

Characteristics of Socially Matured Individual

Having understood the behavioural patterns of a person mature from the social standpoint, it will, become easier to comprehend the implications of social development. An individual, mature from the social standpoint, is one who cooperates with all those with whom he comes into contact, and contradicts them only when such a course of action becomes inevitable. He is never ill-mannered, choosing instead to appear very well mannered, considerate, and friendly to all and sundry. Consequently he has a large circle of friends. An adult, who has attained that stage, as required by the social standpoint, evinces great interest in art, study, games, etc. He studies the works of the greatest authors, and takes interest in games and forms of recreation suitable to his station in life. His activities and conduct are

4. Sorenson, H., *Psychology in Education*, Mc-Graw Hill Book Co., New York 1954, p. 209.
5. Powers, F. F., *Educational Psychology*, Prentice Hall Inc., (1945), pp. 102-3.

scrupulously in conformity with his age and sex. He mixes with people easily, yet occasionally prefers some solitude. He has the power of independent decision and judgement. He gives every evidence of being well balanced and adjusted within himself and in his behaviour towards other individuals.

Socially Undeveloped Individual

On the contrary, an individual who is undeveloped or immature as looked at from the social standpoint, is one who hesitates in society and shows signs of being embarrassed. He experiences nervousness when in the presence of others. He depends to a large extent upon the decisions of his mother and is attached to her, having a very small circle of friends and acquaintances. He finds it difficult to carry on with others.

It is evident from the above description that social development comprehends physiological and mental status, qualities of personality and emotional development.

Having understood the meaning of the phrase social development, one is now in a position to study and understand the child's social development in infancy.

FAMILY AND SOCIAL DEVELOPMENT

Human personality develops in a social environment. In the childhood the personality of an individual is very susceptible to change and variation. He can be turned in practically any desired direction. The famous psychoanalyst Freud has contended that the personality of man is formed in his childhood and the period after that marks only its development. In view of the fact that the experiences, habits, etc., acquired in childhood are so extremely important, the family situation also becomes important because the childhood of the individual is spent within the precincts of the home. The family situation can be regarded as comprehending three factors: (1) Relation of parents to child, (2) Order of the child's birth, and (3) Presence of brothers and sisters and other members in the family. The important role played by the family in the formation of the child's personality can be clearly realized after these three aspects have been studied.

Relation between Child and his Parents

Having affected a psychological analysis of the importance of the parent-child relationship the psychoanalysts have tried to show why the child is influenced to such a great extent by his parents and the relation in which he stands with them. According to Freud the parents are particularly present before the child as ideals. They are more powerful and strong and can perform all activities efficiently. The child effects an identification with his father unconsciously. He wants to become as his father. It is often seen that the young child dons the clothes of his father and imitates his manner of walking and talking. The child behaves precisely as do his mother and father. Besides identification, the second element in this is that of imitation. The child learns much by imitation. There are many activities that the child learns to perform merely by observing and imitating the older members of the family. For the child, the parents are as examples and it will be very difficult to prevent children from indulging in activity in which the parents themselves indulge particularly when they do so in front of the child. This difficulty arises because he feels that what the parents are doing should be done. In this both identification and imitation are included. The child also receives suggestions from his mother and father. The activities in which the mother and father indulge automatically suggest themselves to the child. In this way, the process of identification is not the only process that is activated in the relationship between the child and the parents but is supplemented by the process of imitation, suggestion and sympathy. According to Freud, the viewpoints of the male and female child towards their parents are not identical. Freud believes that the sex instinct is innately given in the individual and is present at birth. In his opinion, the child does not suck his mother's breast merely because he is hungry but also because it gives him pleasure. His mother is not exclusively the source of his nourishment but also the basis of his feelings of pleasure. Freud has further postulated the instinct for heterosexuality in children. Accordingly, the male child loves his mother more while the female child shows greater attachment to the male parent. The mother is the boy's beloved. Hence, naturally the father becomes his opponent and sometimes he sees that he is deprived of his mother's love only because of his father's presence. Often his mother loves him and goes to his father when the latter comes. Consequently, the boy regards his father as a rival. On the one hand, he respects the father because he is the ideal, on the other, the child also hates him in his capacity of opponent.

Criminal Tendency and the Parent-Child Relationship

The misbehaviour of the parents or their neglect of the children are important factors due to which children often become juvenile delinquents. According to the report *Women of the Street,* an important research on the prostitutes of London, the problem of prostitution has its origin in the relationship between the child and the parents. Often when the child is deprived of parental love and is sternly punished frequently he is filled with the desire to revolt and disgust so much so that he runs away from the home when he gets the opportunity to do so. Once away from the home he falls into criminal ways. If neglected by his parents the child feels helpless and alone as a result of which he develops many kinds of complexes. The child becomes a delinquent also when the parents try to conceal too much from him. For example, the children are very apt to ask their parents as to where they came from or where the younger children came from and they are often misled. When they come to know of their true source from servants or from their friends they develop a sense of insecurity because they are deeply hurt when they come to know that their parents do many things that they would not have the children know. This sense of insecurity often lures children into sex crimes.

Need for Balance

In this way, both excessive neglect and excessive love and affection are not to be desired in the relationship between the child and parents. Both are the origin of difficulties concerning the personality and all kinds of problems take root in the mind of the child. Similarly, it is harmful both to place absolute control on the child as well as to leave him to his own mechanisms almost entirely. If the child is given too much freedom he does not develop any respect for authority and cannot be governed. If he is placed under excessive control, his personality is not allowed to develop and he is obsessed with a sense of inferiority and sometimes even turns to crime. The truth of the matter is that if the child is to be disciplined and educated a bitter pill must be swallowed. It is very difficult to bring up a child. In this connection it is necessary that there be much balance and understanding. Then, there can be no one universal rule that can apply to all children. Some children are amenable to greater control while others respond to a lighter degree of authority. On the other hand, all children are not similarly influenced by authority just as all children do not react in the same manner to parental love or neglect. All that has been said before is true in a general way but it is also open to exceptions.

Influence of Discrimination

Sometimes parents discriminate between their children in behaving towards them. They have unlimited love and affection for one while another receives only scolding and punishment. Sometimes it is the beautiful child that is loved while the ugly one is neglected and disregarded. Whatever the reasons at the root of this discriminatory behaviour it is bad because it arouses feelings of hatred for each other among the children. When the child observes that his brother or sister is being loved more than he is, he becomes anxious to revenge this injustice. Sometimes he is even seen possessed of aggressive tendencies. He also tries to harm the other children in one way or the other. He is seen to be disappointed, insecure, fearful, etc. But it is also possible that the child may try to win the admiration and love of others in society and at school by appearing to be better than others in order to make reparation for the deficiency in family love that has been accorded to it. Whatever the outcome, it is completely undesirable and psychologically unjustified to indulge in this kind of discrimination between the children.

Effect of the Character of Parents

The personality of the child is also appreciably influenced by the moral thoughts and conduct of the parents because usually the child looks upon his parents as ideals on which to mould his life. In order to inculcate morality in the children the parents should place an example before them in the form of their own exemplary behaviour. There are very few children who can mould their behaviour according to social values and conceptions even when they have seen their parents indulge in theft, sexual immorality, falsehood, deception and other forms of misconduct. In Miss Eliott's study the parents in 67 per cent broken homes and 44 per cent unbroken homes were indulging in immoral behaviour. If the mother indulges in prostitution her daughters have no inhibition against it and they would have no difficulty in imitating her and proceeding towards immorality and corruption.

Effect of the Mutual Relation of Parents

The personality of the child is further open to another important influence, *viz.*, the mutual relation between husband and wife. If the husband misbehaves towards the wife then the child, particularly the male child, takes exception to it and this increases his hatred for the father. This can, under certain circumstances, lead to terrible consequences. Similarly, if the wife misbehaves with husband, the female child in particular is likely to dislike it and hence she hates her mother. Constant conflict and quarrelling between husband and wife leads to the creation of an atmosphere of insecurity in the home which is not at all conductive to the development of the child's personality. If the relations between husband and wife are good the children have a good and encouraging ideal before themselves which they can imitate to good effect. They then try to be good themselves. It is only natural for the child to develop some personality defects if the relation between his parents is not good.

Effect of the Broken Family

When the relations between the husband and wife deteriorate, the family is reduced to a broken family. This is because the relations between no two members retain their original charm and goodness. A broken family is one in which the family relations have been severed. Family does not mean the living together of some individuals but rather the intimate and profound relations that exist between them. In the absence of this intimacy the family is disbanded and in the broken family juvenile delinquents are reared and brought up. In the broken family the children are not looked after or cared for. According to some specialists, the broken family tends to create the criminal tendency in the female children more than it does in the male child. In Bombay there were 386 boys and 169 girls under the child care society. Of these two boys and two girls had their parents in jail serving sentence for some or the other crime while 2 boys and 5 girls were victims of harsh behaviour and 5 boys and 6 girls were victimized by immoral insecurity. In the broken family the relations between the husband-wife, parents-child and brother-sister do not remain healthy. Hence it is natural for boys and girls to tread the path of mistakes, crime and degradation.

The personality of the child is susceptible to the influence not only of the relationship between itself and its parents but also by the personality of his brothers and sisters. This influence seems to be more pronounced in the case of girls because they are not quite as exposed to external influences as the boys are. If the older children in the family indulge in criminal activity the younger are very likely to follow suit or at least to be profoundly influenced. If the sister is a criminal or indulges in immoral acts, the younger sister will also imitate her or at least she is, likely to do so. The individual is socialised in the family. If the child finds other children in the family who are not much older or younger than it then the child finds a good atmosphere in the family. If there is only one child in the family then it does not find this social atmosphere which is so conductive to its development and its development is to some extent adversely affected. But this deficiency can be compensated if the parents play with the children.

Effect of the Financial Status

The financial condition of the family also influences the development of the child's personality. If the financial condition is good and the parents can adequately satisfy the needs of the children then the children are generally not possessed with the sense of inferiority and want and they do not turn to crime. But it the financial condition of the family is extremely bad the personality of the child suffers. Merrill has written that if the income of the family is low the children also have to work and their education is thus left incomplete. The child's personality does not react very appreciably to the conditions of work. Many of the desires of the poor children are left unfulfilled in order to satisfy which they turn to criminal activity. Poverty induces feelings of dissatisfaction and inferiority. But this does not warrant the conclusion that the poverty of the family will inevitably have a harmful effect upon the child's personality. Sometimes the children, both male and female, become delinquent even though, and sometimes because, the financial condition of the family is very good. On the other hand, the children of the poor learn the lesson of self-reliance from the very start.

From the foregoing description of the parent-child relationship and the effect of various family conditions on the personality of the child it is evident that they are very important. In fact, it is these elements that are responsible for the development of the main characteristics of the individual's personality.

Family has a Nuclear Situation

Family is the first institution in the history of man. In the ancient age men lived in small families, which lacked any kind of organisation or permanence. But they served to fulfil simple biological and psychological needs. Generally, the family consisted of husband and wife and their offspring. The powerful men possessed many wives and thus they lived in big families with their wives and children. When man became oriented in agriculture, many families formed a group and stayed permanently at some place for farming. When these people started partaking of each other's pain and happiness as neighbourly gestures, social relations increased and in this way many families formed a community and the next step was the creation of nation. In this way family is that primary group which slowly evolved into nation.

Family is a fundamental unit of human society. Its foundations rest upon man's biological and psychological needs. In the modern age, many functions of the family have shifted to other institutions but nevertheless, there are many biological and psychological needs which man cannot satiate without a family. Havelock Ellis in his penetrative essays, has shown that the importance of mother's milk for the child cannot be obtained in any other manner. Psychologists have proved that the absence of family affection has a serious impact upon the child's development. Sexual passions can be satisfied even outside the family but it can never be the source of emotional fulfilment. That 'man is a social animal' implies that man cannot live without a family. Thus family is a fundamental unit of society.

The family has a nuclear situation in human society. In primitive societies the entire organisation is based on family units while the division of labour in society is also based on the family. In the complex structure which is society today, the family has lost some of its importance, but even today the activities of most members are for the family or contiguous to it. It is seen that people work and labour more for the comfort of their wives, children and other members of family than even for personal comforts. Thus even now the family is the nucleus of a major part of man's activities.

Society Depends upon Family

Proper social organisation depends upon proper organisation of families. If the families disintegrate in some society, then the society will never be safe. One major cause of social disorganisation is family disorganisation. Families develop the characters of the members of society. Freud and other psychologists have proved that a child, when a man, exhibits the same character and mental tendencies which he acquires in the family. In the opinion of Adler, a man's role in the family determines his role in society.

Family Socializes Individual

In this way, a person is socialised in the family. Defining family, Merrill writes, "Family is an enduring association of parent and offspring whose primary functions are the socialization of the child and the satisfaction of the members". According to Dewey and Tufts the family is a social agency for the education and protection of the race. It is in the family that the child acquires such important qualities as sincerity, sympathy, self-submission and realising responsibility, etc. It is the character developed in the family which helps the child in becoming an important and responsible member of society. Wright was quite correct in stating that in every family, the child gets an opportunity for free expression of thoughts and developing his entire personality. Psychologists have incontestably proved that the proper development of the child is impossible without a good environment in the family. The tendencies and habits which he acquires in the family, he finds impossible to shed later on. According to Freud, the viewpoint of a child towards the senior in the family determines his attitude and viewpoint towards the elders in society. The child's first school is his home and family. According to R.G. Collingwood, the child's education should be in the hands of the parents in family. The parents should participate in all the child's activities. A child learns much by imitating his superiors. Mahatma Gandhi and such thinkers paid personal attention to the development of their children. It is the family which imparts practical education to the child concerning the customs in society, conduct, other important elements of culture, preservation of health, love, sympathy, co-operation, etc.

It is evident from the above account that family is the primary and fundamental unit. Confucious remarked quite correctly that if you want to improve society improve its families. Society will improve automatically when the families improve.

Family is the Conveyor of Traditions

The family moulds the character and personality of the individual. It is through the family that society imparts its culture to the individual. Thus, the family is very important in the form of socializing agency. In the essay, *The Family Conveyance of Tradition,* Paul Schreker wrote that a particular Junction of the family is to sanction children. Like marriage, the institution of family is constituted by different elements of culture. It is due to this reason that it has religious, judicial, political, artistic and linguistic aspects. Whenever a new thought impresses itself on an age the family takes a new form in order that the upbringing and mental tendencies may be harmonious to that thought. Politics and law were dominant in Rome, so the family organisation there was such as to ensure the upbringing of children in harmony with the culture. Today, thc economic order is predominating. So the family has changed its form, it makes the mental tendencies concur with the new culture. In this way, the family makes individual harmonious with the culture of society. In the family, the child acquires knowledge about the current customs, mores, traditions, etc.

Social Control Through the Family

A social life is a web of relationships. In order to maintain these relations properly a system of rights and duties is organised which will avoid any conflict between the members of society and allow them to develop as complements to each other. In order to avoid any breach of this harmony between the individuals in society, the society applies numerous kinds of control on the individual. They are taught to obey the elders, have sympathy for the young and for others. A strict control over sex relationships is necessary for maintaining the social order, otherwise disintegration will spread over the complex social life of today. Relationships between men and women will lose their solidarity. Illegitimate children will be born with no one to look after them.

Although the anthropologists Mead and Malinowski have discovered societies where control over sex relations is inordinately lax without disturbing the social order but such an order is completely contradictory to the thinking of today's cultured person. It is the family which does this work of controlling sex passions for society . In all cultures, the families exercise some degree of control over the unmarried members till they attain the matrimonial state. In the same way, the family acts as a preventive to individual in keeping him from the habits and crimes like drinking, theft, etc. Not many parents could like their children to embark on careers of crime. Even the worst person tries to prevent his children from adopting similar habits and consequently any objectionable behaviour on the part of children is punished and laudable effort suitably rewarded. They thus drop bad habits and learn good tilings. In this way the making of a good citizen in society depends upon the parents.

In every society some values and ideals are regarded as high and signs of culture. Whichever person exhibits these in greater measure is respected in society. For example, Indian society treats religious and spiritual qualities as supreme and a person who is possessed of them is appropriately respected everywhere. Besides, in India, premarital and extramarital sexual relations are controlled as a necessary measure. The responsibility of creating these values in the individual, which are treated highly in society, lies with the family. It is true that the character of every person is different from any other by nature but the family environment also has a big hand in forming them. Most of the famous religious persons of the world like Gandhi were deeply influenced by some one religious person in their respective families. In the making of great men the mothers have always had a major part to play. The differences in the ideals of people related to different cultures are born in their families.

11

PEER GROUP AND EDUCATION

According to *Oxford Concise Dictionary* peer means equal. Thus peer group is the group of equals. Such is a social group. A social group is that aggregate of persons which is like a unit and whose members have some common aims, interests, stimulations and emotions together with mutual social relations and social interactions. Through the medium of all these, members of a social group influence each other and are tied to each other. According to Bogardus, "A social group may be thought of as a number of persons two or more, who have some common objects of attention, who are stimulating to each other, who have common loyalty and participate in similar activities

CHIEF CHARACTERISTICS OF GROUP-LIFE

Just as to classify the groups is a difficult task, similarly to point out the characteristics of group-life is also a difficult problem. Even then some characteristics of group-life can be described. These are as follows:

1. The members of a group are related to each other. Simply a gathering of persons cannot be called a group. The members of the group should be inter-related. In fact, this web of social relation is called a group. Cuber has written, "A group is any number of human beings in reciprocal communication". MacIver and some other sociologists have also admitted the social relations to be the fundamentals of the group-life.

2. Group implies a feeling of unity. A feeling of unity is essential for every group. By virtue of such feeling, members of a group treat each other as their own and a sense of sympathy between them develops.

3. Members of a group have a sense of we-feeling. By a sense of we-feeling, the members of group help each other in performing their duties; and they defend collectively against the harmful powers. They treat others as the outsiders and try to make their group prosperous and self-sufficient.

4. The interests of the group members are common. A group includes those persons who are related to each other in such a way that they should be treated as one. For it, the interests of the persons of a group should tend to be common because, this similarity promotes unity.

5. There is similarity of behaviour in a group. As the interests, ideals and; values of the persons of a group are common, similarly, the behaviour of the persons also tends to be similar. A social group is not merely a group of persons, but it is a continuation of their behaviour.

6. Control of group over the actions of the members. The main reason behind the similarity of behaviour in group-life is that actions of the members are controlled by the group. In each group there are some customs, norms and procedures which are acceptable to every one and the dissenting members of the group given punishment. Even if the group fails to punish a person disobeying these, he shall be severely criticised by public. In this way, every one has to obey the social norms. In fact, without some norms, the existence of group-life is practically impossible.

7. The members of a group are affected by its characteristics. Each group possesses some social characteristics which separate it from the similar and dissimilar groups. These characteristics affect the members constituting the group. The effect may be of different nature for different persons, but still all the members are affected by the group.

8. Common values. Each caste has its own specific common values as help to distinguish it from other castes and also tie its members in the thread of unity. In this way, the social values of the Brahmins and the Shudras, the Kshatriyas and the Vaishyas, can be seen differing considerably. The caste panchayats are very vigilant in enforcing the obedience to these social values and people who deviate from them or transgress their bounds are exterminated from the caste. They are subjected to social isolation and ostracism. They cannot marry again into the group. In a similar vein the example of the family can also be considered. The social values of the members of a family are common and are traditionally respected and communicated to the succeeding generation? They are clearly expressed in the mutual behaviour of the members. Thus, members of the social group are bound together in the tie of common values.

9. Mutual obligation. The relationship between the members of a social group is further strengthened through their mutual obligation, besides their common social values. The family is a fine example of this. In the family, all the members have complementary obligations to each other. Children obey the orders of parents and try to conform to their desires. Husband and wife love each other. The husband fulfils the needs of the wife, while the wife obeys the orders of the husband besides cooperating with him in all activities. In this way, the members of the family are bound to each other by the ties of mutual obligation.

10. Mutual expectations. In a social group, the members are entitled to expect love, sympathy and co-operation from others. In the family the husband expects his wife to love him while his wife expects reciprocation of this affection. When this desire is turned into despair, the family relationship is destroyed and divorce is imminent. In the same way, the parents expect their offspring to accede to then wishes while the children expect from their parents love and sympathy coupled with help to rise in future. The disintegration of the family sets in when these desires are not fulfilled. While the family is a much close knit social unit, even the neighbourhood is related to each member through mutual expectation. In ail social groups that human beings form, members have expectations of each other. If the people of one's own clan were not to share in one another's joys and sorrows, then what is the use of any clan. All individuals hope that in times of joy and sorrow the people belonging to their clan will participate and render the occasion befitting of a social being. And so long as this mutual expectation is being fulfilled, the organisation of the group is maintained intact. If in any school, the student were to refuse to show obedience to his teacher and the latter were to abstain from helping the student in his pursuit of knowledge, how long can such a school last? Thus, a social group retains its existence only as long as its constituent members fulfil their responsibility by satisfying the mutual desires among them.

The example of the family as a social group can serve to illustrate the forementioned characteristics of group-life. Among the members of the family there are relationships such as husband-wife, father-son, brother-sister, etc., and all of them work for the interests of the family in a mood of mutual co-operation. Each member treats every other member as his own, and despite all the differences that there may be between their attitudes and tendencies, they share some common ideals and values. It is because of the common interests that the family works as a well knit unit. Family control is exercised on each member. Disobedience of the laws of the family leads *to* serious altercations between the head of the family and the children while even the senior members do not escape censure. Each member bears the indelible stamp of his family characteristics. The characteristic is so prominent that the study of an individual's behaviour affords some clue as to the type of family in which he must have been bred. These characteristics of the group life are to be found in other groups, in greater or lesser degree.

Social organisation is the organisation of social groups. And social groups are the units of social organisation. Hence the organisation and the disintegration of social organisation is dependent upon the integration or disintegration of the social groups. The social group, as is evident from the term applied to it, is a group the basis of which is social relationships. The family, for example, is a social group.

The above discussion of group-life may be useful in understanding how to create group-life in school. Social consciousness can be created by arranging social programmes. Guardians may also be invited to participate in several such functions. Group songs and group parade are also useful. Celebration of national festivals in school affects the tone of social life. This tone is improved by means of discipline, co-operation, moral level and mutual relationships. The teachers should present good examples and improve their relations with the students.

LEADERSHIP AND EDUCATION

Qualities of Leadership

In the analysis of leadership, the greatest importance, from the practical viewpoint, is that of the qualities of leadership. While this knowledge of the qualities of a leader on the one hand reveals the kind of person the leader is, it also on the other hand, shows the qualities that an individual should possess if he wants to become a leader. Once again, different scholars have attributed different qualities to leaders. Some of the important views will be described here.

Constituents of Leadership

In connection with leadership, Pigors regards the following as indispensable:

1. Common cause 2. Leader 3. Follower 4. Present situation.

Qualities of leadership according to Allport. Allport has included the following in the qualities of leadership:

Trait of ascendence, 2. Physical power, 3. High mobility, 4. Erect, aggressive carriage, 5. Tonus, 6. Tenacity, 7. Face to face mode of address, 8. Reinforcement of energy, 9. Restraint, 10. Inscrutability, 11. Expansiveness in the field of action, 12. High intelligence 13. Understanding, 14. Keenly susceptible to social stimulation, 15. Tact, 16. Zeal, 17. Social participation, 18. Character, and 19. Drive.

Coffin's classification. Charles Bird has recounted no less than 79 qualities in a leader, but in this long list of qualities, many of the qualities have been repeated. Coffin has tried to place these qualities in some limited classes. According to Coffin, the qualities of a leader can be included in the following classes:

1. Intelligence. Sharp intellect, insight, intellectual far-sightedness, skill and acuity.

2. Moral Sensitivity. Honest, just, proper decision, benevolent viewpoint, moral outlook, selfless and idealistic, love of truth.

3. Imagination. Secularism originality, imagination, foresight, curiosity, comprehensive interests and flexibility.

4. Restraint. Restraint, self-control and profundity.

5. Drive and determination. Inspiration, enthusiasm, mobile or dynamic personality, candidness, aggression, desiring name and fame, bravery, determination, patience, concentration, the tendency to pursue to an end.

6. Responsibility. Respected, candid, charactered, believable, organised, aware of duties, lover of work, concentrated.

7. Self-reliance. Awareness of purpose and direction, self-reliance, confidence, the ability to take decision, enthusiasm and unvarying decision.

8. Dynamic physical characteristics. Physical power, shape, ability, tonus, straight body, etc.

9. Imperturbability. Balance, optimism, benevolence, patience, decisive, energetic and positive nature.

10. Social responsiveness. Adaptability of social motivation, taking part in social activities, friendliness, affection, sociability, extrovert tendency and influence on others.

11. Easy maintenance of good relation with others. Acuity, sympathy, co-operation, humanity and a knowledge of human nature.

Coffin has further done the job of making these 11 classes even more brief by dividing all the qualities into three classes:

1. Planning. 1. The ability to know problems. 2. The ability to evolve plans for solving these problems.

2. Organisation. 3. The ability to organise the necessary objects and individuals to ensure the success of the plans. 4. The ability to organise the entire system and have it function as one unit. 5. The ability to introduce sudden changes.

3. Persuasion. 6. The ability of distributing responsibility among different individuals for the implementation of the plan. 7. The ability of successfully examining the entire plan. 8. The ability of keeping his own control on the entire system or organisation.

All Qualities, Physical and Mental, are Needed for Leadership

From the various opinions on the different qualities which a leader should necessarily possess that have been described above, it is evident that it is not sufficient for the leader to be the master of only physical qualities. Here it must be remembered that in the animal world the most powerful animal is the leader but in human society physical power alone is not sufficient. Yet the importance of the qualities of physical power and an attractive personality is not inconsiderable. One can often see intellectual ability and attractive physical personality going together in the human leader. By his experiments, Partridge has proved that all the individuals who scored the highest in the Army Alpha tests were tall, attractive and of an independent nature. This view, held by Partridge is one-sided, because one often finds a complete lack of physical charm in intellectual giants and leaders. One only need be reminded of Socrates and Chanakya. On the other hand, it would be equally incorrect and baseless to state that in the modern world, only intellectual achievements are enough to bring leadership to an individual. Actually, in order to become leader, an individual should be possessed of many qualities of the personality and in particular skill in behaving, in addition to physical and intellectual qualities.

Education for Leadership

But the mere fact of the existence of these qualities in an individual is not sufficient as insurance of successful leadership. It is true that the leader possesses in innate form the qualities of leadership, but as Plato observed correctly they also require to be educated. In a democracy, leaders can be discovered and created through the medium of education and public programmes. For this, responsible tasks should he entrusted to the men and women of the younger generation. They should, be given the opportunity of coming forward and expressing themselves. Youth festivals should be organised in order that the youngsters may be able to display their qualities. In this way, when there will always be new leaders to replace the older and retiring leaders, the society and the nation will be able to progress constantly and at a fast pace.

12

SCHOOL AND EDUCATION

A child's personality is influenced by his school, where he comes into contact with his teachers and his colleagues. At home the child's ideals are his parents and in school he forms his ideals around his teachers. A child hates a teacher who is cruel and uses the stick. He tries to revenge himself on such a teacher, but if the teacher is kind and considerate the child loves and worships him. Both the personality of the teacher and his behaviour toward the child influence the child's personality. A teacher is bigger than the child in size as well as in mental stature and he can make many demands upon the child. For this reason the child likes the idea of developing to the same size as the teacher. At home the child identifies himself with his parents while in school he identifies himself with his teacher but only when the teacher has a magnetic personality. If the teacher's own personality is not very strong he does not have much influence upon the child. On the other hand, the teacher's way of thinking and moral conduct influence the child's thinking and behaviour. The teacher's standard of living, modes of behaviour, conduct, etc., all affect the student. Putting it briefly, every quality, good or bad, of the teacher that is manifest in his behaviour towards the child, leaves some influence upon the child's mind.

Influence of Playmates and Classmates

Normally, the child's class-fellows in school are his playmates and friends, though, sometimes, the child makes friends with children belonging to other classes. A child studying in a higher class normally behaves in a highhanded manner towards the child of a lower class. The same thing happens when two children of different age levels come into contact. An older child's behaviour towards his junior may be either loving or cruel, for in any case the younger child treats the older with fear and respect. Another factor is the competition in matters of study that occurs between children, for it can, on the one hand, induce the child to develop emotions of jealousy, hatred and disgust, while on the other it may inspire him to greater effort and independence.

Influence of Group on the Child

Individual influences do count but the most important influence upon the child in school is the influence of the group of his colleagues in the playground. Children tend to form groups with those boys and girls either with whom they play or the ones with whom they indulge in mischief. These groups compete with each other, while within the group there are always wrangles for leadership. Within each group, each particular child occupies a definite place and plays a distinct role. Each group has a complement of recognised members and an encourage of those who attach themselves to the group. There is a leader within the group whose intimate friends form the inner circle of the group. It is the function of the leader to look after the functioning of the gang, to do the thinking for the gang and to be its mainstay and its moral support. In certain groups the brain is provided by one child and the action by another. It is for the brain to draw up the plans and for the dare devil to carry them out. Another common feature of such groups is the comedian or jester whose sole function is to play the fool and to keep his group amused. It is possible for such groups to have one child playing the role of the scape-goat. Functions within the group are allocated according to the ability or the capacity of each individual child. In fighting gangs the strongest boy automatically assumes the mantle of leadership while in mischievous groups the most intelligent boy becomes the leader. A child's role in any such group coincides with his personality, while the performing of this role influences his personality.

SOCIAL ISOLATES

Because of some physiological or psychological shortcomings some children find it impossible to mix with other children of their own age or to make friends with them. Hence, in their social life, such children tend to be isolated, and this isolation has the worst effect upon their mental, social and moral development. They tend to exaggerate their feelings of inferiority and to address their sense of self-respect and self-confidence. The development of their character suffers in the process.

There can be many causes of social isolation. Physical handicap can be one cause. Defects of hand, foot, eye or of speaking can hinder the child. Feeble children also tend to avoid other children. Abnormality, physiological or mental, obstructs the socialization of the child and prevents him from mixing in the group.

A social isolate is the child who cannot make his own friends in society. For this he has to depend upon his parents or teachers. And such help should be forthcoming. He should be introduced to other children who can accept him into their group, but even then care should be taken that these children should not indulge in any activity which should make the isolate wish to run away. Such children are extremely emotional and even the slightest misbehaviour disturbs them considerably. If the child suffers from no physiological or mental abnormality but is still an isolate then his isolation arises from emotional causes, the majority of which have their origin in the family environment. The family environment may be made unbearable if the parents are extremely excitable, destructive, vicious or corrupt. A healthy family environment is the first requirement for the healthy social development of the child.

SOCIAL STRATIFICATION AND DEVELOPMENT

Social stratification is a common feature in every social group, for different individuals occupy different social groups. In some societies these groups are based on social prestige, as is the case in India, where there are caste groups. In other societies they may be based on the economic status in which case there will be the low income, middle income and high income brackets. Generally speaking, the child is not conscious of the group to which he belongs, and it is seen that if children from different groups are allowed to mix informally they do not give any indications about their groups. However, in almost every case one finds the influence of the parent's group on the child. Parents themselves constantly tell their children about the groups and the relation in which they stand to each one of them. People belonging to the poor group tell their children to stay away from the children not belonging to their income brackets. In India individuals belonging to the higher castes do not allow their children to mix with the children of the lower castes, or the so-called untouchables. It is, putting it briefly, the parents who are responsible for developing class consciousness in their children, and later on this has a very profound influence upon the socialization of the children. In America it has been found that while many white children do not feel the least inhibition in playing with Negro children, their parents instill into them various kinds of fear associated with the Negroes. Thus a deep-rooted prejudice against the Negroes is created in the children's minds. Similar tendency can be seen among the Hindu and Muslim communities in the country. It is now apparent that children are influenced by social stratification only because of their parent's teaching.

ROLE OF COMPETITION

Competition is an important factor among the various stimuli that encourage the child to work. This stimuli does not function for children less than two years of age. By the age of six the workings of this stimulus can be seen clearly. In this manner, the child's earliest behaviour pattern shows objectivity but later on he develops the tendencies of competition and co-operation. In the early stages this competition is limited to winning the love and attention of the parents. It can occur when the child wants toys and other things to play with. Before the age of three this tendency does not play an important role in fashioning the child's pattern of behaviour. During this period the child is kept occupied with his toys and has little patience with what other children are doing. Gradually, he develops a feeling of competition. This occurs in most cultures, but in certain cultures where this tendency in children is looked down upon, the child does not develop it to any great extent. Obviously, the tendency to competition is the result of social and cultural environments. Besides, even in one culture the same child may show a spirit of competition on one occasion but not on another. Or, one child may have a deep desire to compete while another may be indifferent. There can be many factors responsible for this variation, among them the child's order of birth in family, the behaviour towards him of his parents and other relatives, result in any competitive activity.

The spirit of competition plays an important role in the child's development. In individual competition the child exerts all his energies in getting ahead of the other child and this improves the rate of his development. When the child is a member of a group competing with another, his energies are directed at securing victory for his own group. This improves his community spirit. It has been observed in a series of experiments that wherever there is scope for comparison with another's performance the child improves his own performance owing to competition. If the spirit of competition can be intelligently employed, it will yield positive results. But this can be done if the difference between the competitions is not very large, because if one is far more powerful and accomplished than the other, then the inferior competitor is likely to lose his self-confidence in the process of competing. It is this factor which controls the independent child's choice of competitors. Left to himself the child will move among children of his age and capacity so that he can compete with them. It is essential for the parents and teachers to remember that healthy competition can take place only within a group with a small range of individual differences.

Competition must necessarily be healthy. In healthy competition the child is inspired to work more than he is accustomed to and to do better than the others in his group. For this he has no need to employ dishonest means, so long as the competitor is not much better than he is. Healthy competition does not contradict co-operation, in fact, it encourages cooperative enterprise. It is, then, best to encourage healthy competition rather than to stop or to increase it. Parents and teachers can create circumstances in which the child can compete. Care must be taken to ensure that competition does not rise to a level where the child is forced to adopt improper means.

ROLE OF DISCIPLINE

There can be no two opinions about the importance of discipline in an organisation but the definition of the term discipline itself has raised some problems. Educationists differ in their opinion of it. It becomes important, therefore, to be sure of what discipline means. An unscientific definition of discipline would normally include such activities as obeying the rules of the college, respecting the teachers, arriving in the class on time, abstaining from conversation during lectures, not damaging college property, doing all work required by the teacher, not quarrelling with one's juniors, avoiding the use of unfair means during an examination, non stealing, etc. And, in fact, each of the above activities is directly concerned with maintaining the organisation of the college in its normal condition.

Difference between Discipline and Order

There is subtle but distinct difference between discipline and order because no discipline can exist without an order. Discipline, on the other hand, comprehends much more than order. In the words of T. P. Nunn, "Discipline is not an external thing like order but something that touches the inmost springs of conduct. It consists in the submission of one's impulses and powers to a regulation which imposes form upon the chaos, and brings efficiency and economy where there would otherwise be ineffectiveness and waste". Real or actual discipline is, therefore, seen to rest on character. Training in order is the training of character. Outlining the difference between discipline and order Rusk, the educationist, has pointed out that while order denotes the child's behaviour at home or in school, discipline is taken to mean the training of character, which is far more comprehensive than order.

Object of Discipline

In the words of Welton, "The aim of all true discipline is the training of conscience which consists in cultivation of the goodwill and development of moral insight". Training in discipline is given to develop a man's moral insight. And training of insight implies the development of a goodwill in the child. Disciplined children accept good work and avoid bad. If the insight develops, the child's moral insight also develops and he learns to judge what he should do and what he should not. A disciplined child does not have to be told to do this and not to do that, whether he is at home, in the school, in society or anywhere. He can judge for himself and he does what is right and avoids that which is bad. Discipline aims at underlining the importance of morality in education. Herbart, another educationist, has remarked that the objective of education is morality, meaning that education aims at making the child moral. And this aim can be achieved only when the child develops a sense of morality.

Discipline in the Classroom

Some people think that the teacher who has the quietest class maintains discipline most effectively. There is no doubt that a disciplined class in not noisy but the mere fact of absence of noise does not make a class disciplined. Discipline is not merely staying quiet, for it comprehends many other things. Some teachers have recourse to suppression to maintain quiet in the class. There may be quiet in the class but it cannot be said to be discipline. The following methods may be adopted to maintain discipline in the class:

1. Interesting method of teaching. It is desirable for the teachers to teach even the most arid subject in such a manner as to make it interesting for the students. If this does not happen, the students soon get tied up, they yawn in the class and if possible make a lot of noise. If the mode of teaching is effective, the students take a natural interest in the subject and discipline is automatically maintained.

2. Alertness. Discipline also depends upon the degree to which the teacher is alert. If the teacher is himself inclined to sleep or yawn in the class, there is little possibility of his maintaining interest and discipline among the students. When he is himself wide awake the students tend to behave because they are conscious of his eyes upon them and they realise that he will object to any undesirable activity on their part. If there is real discipline the students behave not because they are afraid of being punished but because they want to cooperate with the teacher.

3. Definite rules of behaviour in the class. If discipline is to be maintained, there must be definite rules of behaviour in the class of which the students should be made cognizant on the first possible opportunity. It sometimes happens that the student does things he should not do only because he is not conscious of these rules. If, for example, the teacher has pointed out that students should raise their hands and attract his attention if there is any difficulty the students will do so and there will be no disturbance during his teaching. Neither will the students feel that their difficulty has not been explained to them. After he has framed the rules the teacher should see whether the rules are being obeyed. If he finds any students disregarding the rules he should advise the students to change their mode of behaviour. This forces the students to realise that there are some rules of behaviour in the classroom and that decorum must be maintained.

4. Creating a sense of responsibility in the students. Self discipline is based on the sense of responsibility. Hence in order to maintain discipline in the class the students should be encouraged to be responsible. It should be made clear to them that keeping peace in the class, following the rule, keeping the furniture in order, etc., are all their responsibility. The task of keeping order and peace in the classroom should be left to the students so that they can create discipline themselves.

5. Impartial behaviour. Some teachers are partial to some students in the obedience to rules, and where they would punish some students they let others go scot free. This partiality is very dangerous because there can be no discipline if the teacher behaves inconsistently. Both the student who is discriminated against and the one who is discriminated in favour tend to get out of hand because in either of them the attitude towards the teacher takes an undesirable turn.

6. Training in discipline. Finally, students should be told about the advantages of discipline and order in the class. It helps to maintain discipline. The students should also be told how orders or laws should be obeyed. It is at times desirable to ask make their suggestions about improving discipline in the class. This will make them feel that establishing discipline is their own task and they will be encouraged to co-operate with their teacher.

Methods of Discipline

Norman MacMunn has analysed the different ways of maintaining discipline in the class in his work *The Child's Path of Freedom.* The main methods are the following:

1. Repression. In the past, repression was used to create discipline in the schools the world over. Gradually, psychologists raised their voices against this treatment with the result that this method is looked down upon everywhere.

2. Impression. In this method of establishing discipline the teacher makes use of his personal impression instead of punishment. He treats the children with love, in return for which he gets their affection and respect. Children behave themselves with such a teacher.

3. Emancipation. Another method which differs from the methods of repression, is that of emancipation. In this method the child is left to himself and is allowed to see for himself which actions are desirable and which are not. If this is done he will naturally learn to distinguish between right and wrong, and will avoid Undesirable activity. Proponents of this method have hinted at the mode of teaching discipline through nature. If the child puts his hand in the fire it is immediately burnt by the fire. Nature punishes without warning.

ROLE OF REWARDS

Meaning of Reward

Reward literally means that which is given to an individual in return for what he has done. Under this definition even punishment would become a negative reward. But more usually reward is not interpreted in such a liberal manner and is taken to mean only positive award. Reward, therefore, is the good and proper consequence of good and desirable actions. It can take the form of some concrete physical prize or even merely psychological satisfaction at having done a thing well.

Kinds of Rewards

Reward can take almost any form, but the more common ones are the following:

1. Oral reward. Oral rewards are given in the form of praise. The praise may even take the form of a certificate, a medal or a shield. It can also be praise, done individually or in public.

2. Physical reward. Schools and colleges have a tradition of giving things as reward. Such useful objects as books, sports, equipment, clothes, hair oil, soap, comb, are normally given.

Each of the two above forms of reward have their own significance. Oral reward or recognition has the effect of satisfying the self-respect of the child and of encouraging him to repeat such activity in future. Its drawback is that words of kindness are forgotten, sooner or later. On the other hand, if the words of praise are concrete in the form of a cup or shield or some other form of reward, they will continue to encourage the child in his future life. In this connection books have their own significance because they not only impart knowledge to the child but can be retained by him for long periods. Sports equipment is the next best choice because it is liked by almost all children and also helps to enhance his prestige in the eyes of his friends. He can also derive pleasure by using this equipment and can also thereby improve his health. Equipment meant for outdoor games is better than that for indoor games. In fact, anything that has utility can serve as a reward, but that which has durability also is better than another which can be used up quickly.

Aim of Reward

The aim of giving a reward can be judged from the significance that such an act has. These aims are:

1. Encouraging correct and proper activity. Education aims at directing the child's activity towards a desirable end and preventing it from turning towards the undesirable. Prevention is affected through the medium of punishment and encouragement for good activity through the medium of reward. Rewards delight the child for the moment, but they also serve as an incentive for repeating the activity which brought about the reward. Rewards help to instill the right habits in a child and to improve his character,

2. Recognition of desirable activity. It is only natural for a child to be recognised as the author of some desirable action after he has done it. He desires such recognition from the teacher or parent. Rewards are the token of this recognition, and once recognition is granted the child can hardly wait to do it again. Recognition is directly linked with self-expression. A child desires to express himself and also to have this self-expression recognised by his teachers,

3. Setting good examples to other students. As a normal rule, rewards and awards in colleges are presented in a big gathering in which all students are present. Sometimes the parents of the students are also invited to join in the celebration. When the child goes forward to receive his cup, shield or certificate while his friends, parents and well-wishers look on, he feels delighted and very pleased with himself. At the same time the other students are also spurred on to do something which will put them in a similar position.

4. Encouraging healthy competition. Healthy competition is an important factor in communal life. Students try to do better than their neighbours, and they do better than they would otherwise if the concrete result of this competition is present before them. It is often seen that the bright students in a class compete hard for the first position because of the prize that goes with this position. They also exert themselves in the sports field because they are aware that the winner will receive a prize and a lot of cheers. Awards have played an important role in encouraging healthy competition in studies and in game. Besides, awards can be given not only for mental and physical excellence but also for moral excellence, for if a tradition for giving an award for the best behaved student is established in the college it will encourage the students to make a good job of it. Awards can help the child's development of character by encouraging him to excel in all walks of life.

5. Encouraging hard work. If a child wants to win some award it is necessary for him to put in a lot of hard work. Hence, when there is some reward, the child tends to work hard in every sphere, the mental, physical and the ethical or moral.

Principles for Giving Awards

If benefit is to be derived from the giving away of prizes it is desirable that some system should be followed. It is essential to take care of the following aspects:

1. Reward based on ability. In the first place, the reward should be directly proportionate to the student's ability and the student should realise that he unquestionably deserves the reward being given.

2. Limited number of awards. If almost every student in the school or college can win one prize or the other the entire system of prizes loses its value, for it then fails to stimulate competition. Prizes therefore should not exceed five in number.

3. Prize subsequent upon effort. It is never proper to give a prize for some quality acquired by birth. Prizes should be given for things which involve effort and hard work, and the prize should be given for the maximum effort shown. It should also be realised that winning a prize entails effort as well as talent.

4. Three or four prize distributions in a year. If primary and secondary schools have three or four prize distributions in a year it will help to maintain the enthusiasm of the students at a high pitch during the entire year. They will continue to compete with each other and their effort will not suffer due to lack of encouragement. This will help the teaching and the maintenance of standard.

5. Prizes for least interesting work. If prizes are allocated to activities in which every one naturally takes interest nothing useful is achieved for the incentive is already there. It is desirable to keep prizes for subjects which are important in their own right but which normally do not arouse interest in the student.

6. Prize should not have high exchange value. It is not desirable to have a prize which is itself worth a lot of money. A student should not desire to obtain the prize merely because it is valuable in terms of money. But at the same time the prize should not be so cheap as to arouse no enthusiasm in the student.

7. Encouraging healthy competition. In making arrangements for prize the teachers should take care that this should not lead to jealousy, hatred, formation of rival groups and other undesirable associations. The aim of having awards is to create a spirit of healthy not unhealthy competition.

8. Prizes should be announced well in advance. Before the competition begins students should have sufficient notice of the fact that there is a prize. This will provide them with sufficient time to work and will also keep them organised and hard at work for a longer period.

9. Impartiality in awarding a prize. It is absolutely essential that the person or persons entrusted with awarding the prize are completely impartial. If some partiality or discrimination takes place it not only robs the prize of its importance but creates ill feeling among the students.

10. Prizes should coincide with individual and communal feeling. Prizes should be such as to arouse the individual and communal interest of the student. It is for this reason that some awards are set aside not for individual performance but for the performance of a team as a whole, whether it is a sports team or a class. Inter school and inter-college competitions help to develop a healthy community spirit.

ROLE OF PUNISHMENT

Punishment means the pain and suffering caused to students with a view to improving administration and curing ills. Punishment can also take two forms—physical and mental. Physical punishment is given through the medium of causing pain to the body. This pain may be mild or severe. Milder forms of physical punishment are asking the student to stand on his seat or in a corner, forcing him to run around a field twice and similar punishments which do not cause too much suffering. Severe physical punishments can take almost any form, but among the better known are pulling the ears, beating with a stick, slapping, pinching, punching, or even giving a severe thrashing in the presence of the entire school. Mental punishment can be given by admonishing, criticising, demeaning, or a variety of other methods. At times, this mental or physical punishment is further supplemented by economic punishment in the form of fines.

Objectives of Punishment

As a general rule punishment can have three main objectives—taking revenge, curing a fault or improving, or setting an example for other people so that they may not do such a thing. Punishment meted out in the college may have anyone or even more of these three motives behind it. At times the students who disturb the discipline of the college are punished in front of an assembly of all students so that other students may be discouraged from following their footsteps. Punishments of this kind are often severe for they have far-reaching consequences, and without severity they lose their meaning. At the school level it is quite common for the headmaster to call a meeting of the entire school and then to proceed to thrash the recalcitrant students severely. The very sight of this is often enough to deter most of the other students from such activity. In the present-day, however, almost all punishment aims at improving the student and curing him of his bad habits. Mental punishment in any case has no other objectives, because it can neither serve as an example to others nor can it be used for revenge. Many teachers inflict mental or physical punishment upon their students when they feel that they have been insulted. Such activity is absolutely improper and an individual capable of it has no right to be a teacher. There can be no doubt that students have been known to injure the dignity of the teacher, and it is only natural for the teacher to feel infuriated. But although he may desire to get a little of his own back by pushing the student, such a desire can hardly be said to be proper. Punishment should be meted out only when the student can be improved by it, or when such punishment will set an example before the other students and guide them along the right path.

Excessive Use of Punishment

During the middle ages punishment was a common thing while in India even today excessive punishment is not unknown. In rural areas in particular it is common. If a student fails to turn up at school three or four boys are sent to bring him there, and they do so by dragging or beating him. When he finally does arrive he is then set upon by the teacher who literally makes a puly out of him. He is then forced to stand in the corner in a bent position with a brick balanced on his back. Many schools follow a standard procedure for convincing the students that punctuality is the king of virtues. The headmaster closes all approaches to the schools and takes up his position at the gate with a thick rod in his hand. All students arriving late are welcomed at the gate by the headmaster, given a sound thrashing and then allowed to proceed to the class, with a hefty kick to speed them on their way. After this few students would dare to be late again, and if one is there is every chance of his playing truant from school rather than risking the punishment. This tradition of inconsiderate punishment is not restricted only to primary and secondary schools but even to high schools and intermediate colleges. Besides, the tradition is not peculiar to India, because worse examples of excess in this direction can be found in the history of education in many western nations. Prof. Cubberley has written of a school master named Haubberley who appears to have had a Teutonic taste for a variety of things. This master has recorded that in his 51 years and seven months of teaching life he administered 9,11,527 strokes with the cane, 1,24,010 strokes with a stick, 20,989 strokes with a ruler or a piece of rope, 1,36,715 strokes with the hand, 10,23 5 strokes on the face, 7,905 ear boxings, and 11,15,800 slaps on the head. In addition to this he had a vocabulary of 2000 abusive terms some two-thirds of which were taken from the German language while the rest had been invented by the teacher himself. This example proves the extent to which mental and physical punishment was inflicted upon the students. Excessive punishment is normally inflicted when there is a desire to suppress the individual punished. It is taken for granted that individual is, by nature, a cheat and bounder and that if he can be prevented from doing his dark deeds it is only through the fear of punishment.

Consequences of Excessive Punishment

There can be many consequences of excessive punishment, almost the only desirable one being that it may frighten the individual into submission. It may result in permanent injury or even, in some extreme cases, in death. There can be no doubt that when other children see punishment of this order being given, they are inspired to stick to the straight and narrow path of virtue. Mental punishment is no less harmful than physical punishment. It has been seen that students commit suicide after they have been criticised and ridiculed beyond endurance by their teachers. And, on the other hand, it has also been observed that if the teacher limits himself to criticism and ridicule, the students imagine that he is either a fool or incapable of administering physical punishment. In such cases they become even more unmanageable.

Propriety of Excessive Punishment

Generally speaking, it may be said that excessive punishment can never be justified, particularly if it is physical punishment. It should, therefore, never be used to excess. Among its consequences are impaired hearing, loss of limbs and even death. Further, it can only succeed in creating feelings of hatred and revenge against the teacher in the student's mind. There have been cases where a student has been compelled to revenge himself upon the teacher and to bring about the latter's death. Such reactions can have no value and they reflect upon the system of education as a whole. Even the students who are deterred from anti-social activity when they see another student being punished, do not have any feelings of love or respect for the teacher. They are inspired only by fear and disgust.

Similar consideration applies to the subject of excessive mental punishment. If the student commits a mistake he should not be ridiculed or criticised so severely that he may be compelled to seek revenge or that he may develop a permanent inferiority complex. This can only have a bad effect upon his character. And all such influences only serve to encourage indiscipline, not to discourage it.

These considerations should not create the feeling that punishment should be given up. Adequate punishment is desirable and at times even necessary. There are some students who, if they are not thrashed, grow impudent and feel that nothing can happen to them, whatever they may do. This confidence leads them to do things which are completely undesirable. Such students must necessarily be taught that there is a divinity that shapes our end, even if the divinity takes the form of a ruler or cane. If students who disturb the discipline of the college go unpunished the rules and regulations of the college lose their meaning for such students. If the importance of the rules is to be brought home to the erring students it is necessary that there should be provision for punishment. What is important is that this punishment should then be administered without discrimination.

Principles Underlying Punishment

Punishment should be administered only on principle, so that it may not lose its meaning. The following things should be kept in mind—

1. Punishment should be such as to improve the erring students.
2. Punishment should be example to other students so that they may be deterred from following the same path.
3. Punishment should never be excessive.
4. Punishment should be in direct proportion to the magnitude of the misdemeanour.
5. Physical punishment should be administered by the headmaster, but this individual should not display any anger. Punishment should be an act of justice.
6. Punishment should not take the form of ridiculing or insulting a student.
7. Punishment meted out to the student should be recorded in his report book and sent to the parent.
8. There should be no discrimination while punishing a student.
9. For all violations of discipline there should be fixed punishment. In all such violations the punishment must be inflicted upon the culprit. When the punishment is fixed the student either accepts the inevitable or decides to behave himself.

Finally, it can be said that if the above points are kept in mind in framing punishment in the college the students will definitely improve. Good examples will be set to the other students. The success of all punishment depends to a great degree upon the psychological insight and intelligence of the teacher.

THE SCHOOL AS A SOCIAL SYSTEM

Sociology of education particularly studies the school as a social system. The social organisation in the school consists of different roles and statuses for the educator and the educand. Among the teachers also there are different statuses and roles according to their seniority, qualifications, special skills and the position of the heirarchy of the school. The headmaster in every school occupies a pivotal position, more responsibility, more administrative power and therefore the most important role. Similarly, among the educands also different students occupy different statuses and roles in the schools according to their seniority, special skills and allotted responsibilities, etc. For example, the chief prefect is overall incharge of the discipline among the students. Similarly, there are so many prefects who maintain discipline in the school. Every class has a monitor who maintains law and order in the classroom in the absence of the teacher and complains to the teacher about the defaulter student.

As a social system the school aims to prepare the students to occupy social roles according to their capacities after leaving the school. In India most of the rural youths finish their studies after high school. Some of them do not go beyond the middle schools. Therefore the functions of the middle schools and the high schools in transmitting knowledge, skills and socialisation are very important. As a social system the first function of the school is to transmit knowledge and skills to the younger generation. The technical schools transmit knowledge concerning so many traits. The agricultural institutions tell the sons of cultivators about better means of cultivation. All the schools impart knowledge of 3r's, reading, waiting and arithmetic. This is necessary in order to help every male and female to skillfully manage the household affairs and also matters concerning every day life.

Besides transmitting knowledge, the school as a social system transmits culture to the younger generation. The customs and traditions, rules of etiquettes and manners are taught both by instruction and by example. The rules of the school discipline the educands and give them training in good manners. The mechanism of rewards and punishment makes this training a success. Most of the schools transmit the culture of their area in the younger generation. However, the urban public schools mostly transmit culture of the West which is not a healthy sign. This alienates the student from the culture all around him. Each school must train the educands in regional and national culture. However, efforts must be made to maintain human culture everywhere.

The younger generation learns future roles by means of perception and identity formation both in the family and in the school. Extra-curricular activities in the school are important to develop individual differences and particular skills of the educands. Thus some of them may develop social leadership qualities, other political leadership traits and so on.

An important function of education is the development of the individuality of the student. This individuality is developed by the development of individual skill and the allotment of roles and statuses according to it. This should not be based upon favours and prejudices. As a social system the school is the best place to teach equality, liberty and fraternity to the younger generation. It is the best preparation around for practice of democratic traits in the wider social situation.

THE CULTURE OF THE SCHOOL

Each school has a particular culture. This can be noticed in the comparison in the private and public schools, the rural and urban schools, the schools in the tribal areas, the boys and the girls schools, etc. Culture is constituted of the norms, customs, traditions, rules of behaviour, attitudes, etc. All these are reflected in the social life of the school. While in the outer society culture is transmitted without much change and refinement, in the school particular attention is given to transmit refined elements of culture. This is done through various means of socialisation and the allotment of different statuses and roles to different students.

The school is an important place for achievement. Students are accorded prizes, awards, statuses and roles according to their scholarly attainment and achievements in the sports and extra-curricular activities. It teaches hierarchy and functions according to it. The behaviour of the teachers among themselves and their behaviour towards the headmaster serve as examples to the student about behaviour among equals and the behaviour towards the seniors.

THE SCHOOL AS A SOCIAL ORGANISATION

Social organisation is a network of statuses and roles In a school, the headmaster is at the top of the hierarchy. His word is the law. He delivers the goods. He is responsible for the smooth functioning of the school. In other words, he is the head of the government of the school. Should he decide to act as an autocrat, the school will not develop democratic traits among the students. Usually the de facto power of the headmaster is exercised through teachers and responsible students. Every class-teacher wields authority in matters concerning his class. He is helped in this process by the monitor, the prefect and other teachers. Thus the social organisation of the school should be dynamic and well adjusted. The extra-curricular activities are very important for all-round development of the school as a social organisation. The school management consists of representatives of the public who help the headmaster and the teachers to carry out various functions in the school as a part of general community. If the parents are invited to the school function, the co-operation between the school and the community as limbs of social organisation increases. This is particularly necessary at the nursery and the elementary level.

The most important task of the social organisation is socialisation. This socialisation requires acting according to allotted roles and statuses. The schools provide scope for the development of leadership qualities among the students particularly through the extra-curricular activities. Under the supervision of the teachers, they gradually learn to cany out responsible activities. The headmaster and the teachers should allow more and more freedom to the students and it makes them more responsible. They should follow, the principle of least interference in the social relationships among the students. They are responsible for the socialisation of the students towards the community. They should impart the knowledge of social customs and traditions and develop values of society among the students. Thus the school serves as an agency of cultural transmission. It weans the child from the family and makes him more independent. As the student progresses from nursery to high school he becomes more self-reliant, more individuated and a better adjusted person. The teachers should be competent, take interest in the activities of the students and provide maximum facilities. So much depends on their presenting proper examples because social learning very much depends upon role perception. The students should learn social commitment. This requires favourable examples from the teachers and the headmaster. Competence, responsibility, straightforwardness, skill and dynamism are created among the students by the social organisation of the school. As the educand learns commitment to his roles so he becomes a better member of society after leaving the institution.

The school is an important centre for promoting social mobility. It presents an example of the fulfilment of social justice. It is a place where every social custom and tradition is analysed, evaluated and even questioned before acceptance is granted to it. Therefore the school presents the forum for bringing about desirable social changes. If the new generation learns the defects of the pernicious customs and traditions, it fights for their change and replacement in the wider society. This is particularly true about the high schools.

THE SCHOOL AND SOCIETY

Society is a system or organisation of mutual relations between human beings, implicit in certain communities and institutions. The school is a group and education an institution. Evidently, the school is an important part of society. Here we mean a specific society, not the general concept of society, which is an abstract notion. And a specific society implies a group of human beings living within the limits of a definite country and which is characterised by a specific culture. The school is related to this specific society. It is for this reason that different educationists have defined the objectives of education differently for different nations. In the past, in India the objective of education was salvation, while at about the same time in China education was intended for scholarship. As time passes, the aims of education in a society change when its cultural patterns undergo change. For example, in modern China, the objective of education is to acquaint the educand with the ideology of Mao Tse Tung and to use him as a tool for implementing this ideology in practice.

Explaining the intimate relationship between society and school, T.P. Nunn, the famous educationist, writes, "A nation's schools, we might say, are an organ of its life, whose special function is to consolidate its spiritual strength, to maintain its historic continuity, to secure its past achievements, to guarantee its future. Through its schools a nation should become conscious of the abiding sources from which the best movements in its life have always drawn their inspiration, should come to share the dream of its nobler sons, should constantly submit itself to self criticism, should purge its ideals, should re-inform and redirect its impulses". This comment clearly indicates that the relationship between society and school is characterised by the following elements:

1. Schools keep the moral power of the society secure, and also maintain the social heritage of society. This social heritage is handed on by the schools to the following generation.
2. Schools also protect the historical continuity of society. Schools perform the function of acquainting the new generation with the ancient myths and legends, and maintaining the patterns of behaviour in the form of traditions and customs.
3. Schools also help to keep alive the society's achievements in the past, and transfer it to the younger generation through the teaching of history and the social sciences.
4. Schools are the guardians of the society's future, because educands are the future leaders of the nations. Schools shape the future of the country by achieving the complete development of these leaders. It is for this reason that the educator is often referred to as the architect of the nation.
5. Through the medium of the school, the members of society are acquainted with those motives and inspirations which formed the basis of all the literary achievements of the past. This is achieved through the teaching of literature.

6. Schools also encourage considerable discussion and exchanges of opinion on the functioning, methods of working, customs and traditions existing in various parts of society. These elements are analysed and subjected to criticism in order to decide whether they should be retained or thrown out. In this way, schools are the source of social change.
7. Through the medium of the school, leaders in various spheres such as engineering, medicine, legal profession, teaching, literature, etc., are trained. In this sense the progress of society depends upon the progress of the schools.

It is evident from the foregoing account of the intimate relationship between society and school that development and progress of schools is essential for the progress of society. Before introducing any change in society on a large scale, it can be experimented within the school and its nature and consequences observed. It can then be introduced into society.

Impact of Society on School

It is evident from the intimate relationship that exists between society and school that both influence each other. The various points to be noted in the impact of society on school are the following:
1. All the individuals, educators and educands, found in schools come from society, and hence it is only natural that their thinking should influence life in the school. It is generally accepted that the kind of family an educand comes from can be judged from his conduct in the school.
2. Society is a dynamic and changeable structure. One can see the effect of various social changes on schools.
3. Social conduct, or conduct in society, also has an influence upon the conduct of educand in schools. If social conduct deteriorates, there is no way of shielding the student from this deterioration and consequently conduct in school will also reflect a fall in standard.
4. The curriculum of the school is determined according to the needs of society, because parents always send their children to school in order to prepare them for society. They are given education so that they may become useful members of the society.
5. The life of the school is profoundly influenced by all the major institutions of society, such as family, religion and economic institutions. From this standpoint one can compare the schools in Communist Russia with the schools of democratic America.
6. All the education that the educand imbibes in school through books and lectures, actually emanates from society, because books are little more than the accumulated experiences and thoughts of the greatest figures in society.

Impact of School on Society

Society is influenced by the school in as great a measure as it itself influences schools. In this respect, the following points are to be considered:
1. Schools produce the future leaders for ail the society. It follows that the type of school will determine the calibre of leaders, and their calibre in turn will determine the nature of society that they will create.

2. The school, like the family, is a social institution which socializes the individual and provides him some experience in social control. Therefore, the individual will learn to accept the kind of social control that is imposed on him in school, and will also demand similar social control from society. For this reason, there is a great insistence in democratic countries that the atmosphere in school should also be democratic so that the educand can get used to democratic norms of social control.

3. It has already been stated that the school plays an important part in social change because it subjects all the customs, traditions, mores, practices, etc., of society to continuous criticism. As a result of this criticism some of these are maintained and others rejected. This determines the direction of future social change.

4. It is the function of society to provide useful citizens to society, and if society wants to be independent, it is necessary that the school should provide it with citizens who are capable of being independent and self-reliant.

5. By exercising their right of criticism, the educands eliminate the weaknesses of society and thus prepare a blueprint for its future reformation and improvement.

Contribution of Society to the Moral Development of Children

Education amounts to a complete development of the child and an important aspect of his development is moral development. Society can play a positive role in the child's moral development in the school. In this connection, the following things should be noted:

1. If society itself is well organised, the child's personality will also be balanced and his moral development becomes possible.

2. The patterns of moral behaviour exhibited in the family and other social institutions can help to encourage the child to behave in the same manner.

3. The child's moral development can take place more rapidly and positively if the educator is assisted by other members of society.

Responsibility of Society in Making the School Effective

The extent to which society can play an active part in making the school a powerful and effective medium of purveying education is evident from the impact it has on the school. It is clear that society has great responsibility in this direction. The following points should be noted in this connection:

1. Society should undertake to construct appropriate buildings for schools and also provide for their decoration and maintenance.

2. It is the responsibility of society to see that educators get respect in society and that their needs are well looked after.

3. When invited by the school, various members of society should attend the school functions and take an enthusiastic part in it.

4. The society should not hesitate in providing any and everything which the teacher demands as essential to the complete development of the educand.

5. Society should also look into the examination system, the curriculum, etc., of schools, should subject it to criticism, should examine it from the standpoint of contemporary needs of society and should suggest changes if necessary.

Responsibility of the School towards Society

Just as the society has certain responsibility towards the school, in the same way the school also has certain obligations to society which it must fulfil In this connection Prof. M.V.C. Jeffreys writes, "The school can do nothing better for the education of citizens than to make its boys and girls members of a true community in which are combined liberty and order, freedom and responsibility, in which human personality is respected for its own sake, regardless of age or other irrelevant circumstances; which recognizes the authority of reason and experience, not of fear and status; and where liberty of thought has its complement in the responsibility for making one's own choice of opinions and love rather than neutrality is the guarantee of intellectual freedom". Broadly speaking, the school can do the following tasks for society:

1. Assisting the progress of society in every possible way.
2. Training the children to live in a community.
3. Providing enough technical or scientific training as will enable them to earn their own livelihood and be independent.
4. Generating all qualities of good citizenship in the student.
5. Setting into motion and further'assisting all programmes of social reform.
6. Encouraging the students to purge the society of its bad customs and habits.
7. Contribution to the development of folk culture by participating in and celebrating social occasions and festivals.
8. Developing such high moral characters and balanced personalities in the children that they should become useful members of society.
9. Taking the advice of parents and guardians in order to help in the complete development of their children, and also to warn and guide the parents about possible future problems.

Means of Bringing Society and School Close to Each Other

The importance of close cooperation between school and society is evident from the foregoing discussion. The following are the means by which this can be done:

1. Schools should frequently organise cultural functions of a kind which can make it possible for various members of society to attend and participate in them.
2. The relationship between society and the school can be given a more firm foundation by running social welfare schemes or adult literacy schemes in the schools to educate the old and illiterate members of society.
3. Co-operation can be farther increased by forming committees consisting of teachers and parents.
4. Schools should win financial assistance and co-operation in other forms from various senior members of society for the organisation, provision and development of the school.

13

THE COLLEGE IN THE SOCIAL STRUCTURE

In the social structure of a society the college occupies a very important place. It provides trained personnel and developed males and females to the society. The technical colleges prepare the students for occupational roles. Thus the colleges are connected with the general social structure. Immediately after finishing the college studies the boys and girls enter matrimony and profession. The success in these is initially guaranteed by the training at the college. Therefore the college student must be prepared for adult roles. Various types of colleges such as arts colleges, science colleges and technical colleges occupy slightly different positions in the structure of the society. The technical colleges particularly prepare for vocations while the colleges of humanities prepare the students for general roles. The college is a forum not only for the discussion of intellectual matters but also for analysis of social political affairs. Discussions and debates on all these develop critical attitudes among the coming generation. It encourages independent thinking and the demand of social and political reforms.

The college promotes development of autonomy and the formation of identity The college provides opportunities of the development of these traits. After leaving the college as a person gets married and establishes his own family he is helped by his training in the college. Sometimes the colleges open opportunity for knowing and selecting life partners. This depends on the disciplined and free atmosphere in the mixing of males and females in the college.

The social structure of the college is organised by the principal at the apex, the professors, the tutors, the administrative staff and finally the students. The everyday affairs are run by the principal with the help of a council of management. As the government gives financial grants therefore it exercises control over the expenditures and general functioning of the college through inspectors and officers of the education department of the state.

There is a hierarchy of statuses and roles among the professors according to seniority and administrative positions. The authority of the principal is exercised through the heads of the departments in administrative matters. While in smaller colleges the principal may directly interfere in the functioning of a teacher, in bigger colleges, this is done through the heads of the departments. While most of the colleges are governed by rales framed by the university to which they are affiliated, the autonomous colleges are free in their selection of syllabi and mode of examination. However, most of the colleges are affiliated with some university. The nominees of the university occupy an important place in the management of the college. During examinations the nominee of the university watches the conduct of the examination and reports to the university. The curriculum is framed by Boards of Studies of the University in order to ensure uniformity among the colleges affiliated to the university. However, each university organises its own boards of studies and enjoys autonomy in this connection. As the colleges are governed by the rules framed by the university they are part and parcel of university education.

The students are the most important part of the social structure of the college. They are divided into two categories. Those who live in the hostels are called hostellers or hostelers, while those staying outside the college are known as day scholars. Hostels are governed according to the college rules. The warden maintains discipline and supervises all sorts of activities in the hostel. Therefore the hostelers are more strictly governed than the day scholars. The college provides facilities for the development of skills and abilities through different types of teaching. It develops general abilities and leadership qualities through extra-curricular activities such as study circles, debating unions, discussion groups, sports councils, N.C.C. and other provisions. It provides facilities for activities started on the initiative of the teachers and the students. It organises sports, athletics and excursions to various parts of the country. The social structure of the colleges of arts, sciences, law, medicine, engineering, agriculture, technology, education and commerce, may be a bit different in their routine activities but the general traits described so far are applicable to all these.

Functionally, the college is a social system. It selects and differentiates the students on the basis of achievements in different directions. It puts a premium on academic excellence. It promotes development and exposes the students to various activities. It encourages creativity and critical faculty. It develops responsibility and provides occasions for taking up independent decisions. It promotes qualities of team work as well as initiative and leadership. It provides opportunities for development of friendship among same sexes and also among different sexes. The friendship among different sexes provides opportunity to select life partners and lays the foundation for a successful marriage and happy family. Thus in the modern societies each male and female passes through the college life to become an adult prepared to accept various roles and statuses in the wider society outside.

FACTORS RELATED TO COLLEGE ATTENDANCE

A good college must be well attended. The attendance in a class is the index of the success of classroom teaching. If the attendance in a class is poor it is a reflection upon the teacher and his teaching method. Besides the interesting teaching method, attendance is also influenced by relevance of the matter taught to the students. If the lecture delivered is not relevant to the curriculum most of the students decide to play truant. Therefore, the management and the principal must look to college attendance and analyse the factors related to it. The most important factors are as follows:

1. Quality of teaching. As has been already pointed out, attendance is an index of the quality of teaching. Therefore, one finds a higher percentage of attendance in a better college and in a better class in the same college.

2. Facilities offered. Attendance also depends upon facilities offered to the students. If the classrooms are congested and small so many students will not attend lectures. If the college does not provide minimum facilities such as canteens, drinking water, suitable places to sit, reading rooms and libraries, common rooms for girls and boys, mixed and separate and neat and sufficient buildings and open lawns and attractive natural environment, most of the students will like to pass their time outside it. On the other hand, if these facilities are ample the students will be within campus even in their spare times and sometimes even in holidays.

3. Teacher-taught relationships. The college is a social system. Therefore, the most important single factor governing college attendance is the teacher-taught relationship. If this relationship is informal and warm there is better attendance. If it is formal and rude the attendance is thin. It is a common observation that some teachers are more loved and respected by their students who do not want to miss any class and therefore attend almost cent-per cent. On the other hand, teachers whose method is uninteresting, formal and lacking warmth have a thin attendance in their class. Besides the differences among colleges in the attendance rates, there is difference in the attendance rates in different departments in the same college. As a rule as the number of students grows the rate of attendance falls. The teacher-taught ratio should not be allowed to rise beyond a certain level as it adversely affects attendance. The size of a class should not be bigger than the prescribed limit necessary for good teacher-taught relationships. The subjects which are more interesting are better attended. The teachers who are better psychologists and bigger scholars attract more attendance to their lectures.

4. Time-table. An important factor related to college attendance is the timetable. It should be suitable for the day scholar both boys and girls. It may be modified if a good number of students are working in offices during day time. It should not be late in the night particularly as this may cause difficulties to the girl students to attend classes. It should also change according to changing weather and climate of the region. It should have sufficient provision for leisure, particularly during the lunch hour. It should have sufficient spacing so that the students may easily attend the next class after finishing the present work.

5. The curriculum. An important factor related to college attendance is the curriculum. It should be moulded according to the needs and tastes of the educands. It should be made interesting and involve practical work. It should be made more attractive by provision for extra-curricular activities.

WHO WILL GO TO COLLEGE?

Now, who will go to college? Obviously, those who pass the high school. These are generally teenage boys and girls who successfully pass out high school and intermediate colleges. But passing alone is not the criterion. So many brilliant boys and girls have to stop their studies after high school due to lack of facilities.

Therefore, who will go to college also depends on the facilities offered by the government and the colleges. Besides, the poor parents cannot meet the expenses of college education. Therefore, who will go to college depends upon the financial condition of the family. Again, the employment situation is also important in this connection In India most of the girls are married after passing through the schools. Therefore few go to college. Again, in rural areas most of the young men take up their family occupation after high school or intermediate and therefore do not go to college. Thus the colleges are mostly attended by urban youths and the unemployed young men for the suburban villages. This situation may be changed by governmental measures such as provision of scholarship to all the meritorious students particularly those coming from poor families.

VARIOUS TYPES OF COLLEGES

The most important types of colleges may be categorised as follows:

A. Categorisation According to Academic Levels

1. Degree Colleges. As is clear by the term, these colleges provide education up to degree level in arts, sciences and technical subjects.

2. Post-Graduate Colleges. As is clear by the nomenclature, these colleges provide education in humanities, sciences, commerce, engineering and medicine up to post-graduate level. These colleges have independent departments for every subject, organised under a head of the department and two or more lecturers. The time-table of each department is framed separately, particularly at the post-graduate level. Most of the post-graduate colleges include degree education in the subjects offered by them.

B. Categorisation According to Types of Education Provided

1. Arts Colleges. These colleges provide education in arts subjects such as literature, economics, political science, geography, history, psychology, sociology, economics and languages, etc.

2. Science Colleges. While the arts colleges prepare for B.A. and M.A. degrees, the science colleges prepare for B.Sc. and M.Sc. degrees. The science colleges provide teaching in physical sciences, such as Physics, Chemistry, Botany, Geology, Zoology, etc.

3. Medical Colleges. These colleges provide education in different branches of medicine, organised in separate and independent departments under a head, one or two professors, one or more readers and several lecturers, well-equipped laboratories and libraries and the attached outpatient departments with all the facilities for practical medical training. These require huge grants from the government. The admission is made through competitive examinations on a highly selective basis. Sufficient provision is made for scholarships to deserving and poor students. Most of the students are hostellers. Therefore, facilities for hostel accommodation are available on a good scale. The colleges prepare for M.B.B.S., M. S. and M.D. degrees.

4. Colleges of education. These colleges prepare for B.Ed., and other degrees required for trained teacher. These are also known as teachers training colleges. Admission to these colleges is made on a highly selective basis depending upon academic merits of the candidates. The government provides special aids to these colleges.

5. Law colleges. These colleges prepare for L.L.B. and L.L.M. Degrees. Most of them work in the evening because a good number of students are employed during day time. Most of the law teachers are allowed to practise as advocates in the courts. The law colleges in India are generally part and parcel of arts or science colleges and governed by their management. Therefore establishment of independent law colleges will be a progressive step.

6. Technical colleges. Colleges of engineering are the most developed, richest and the most important colleges in a country. Their staff is highly paid and well qualified. Each department is located in big buildings with suitable workshops and all facilities. The government not only gives huge grants for buildings and equipments, books and libraries but also for scholarships to deserving and needy students. Admission is made on a highly competitive basis. The campuses are usually extending to several kilometres since almost all the students are hostelers. The hostels of engineering departments, like the hostels of medical students offer better facilities of boarding and lodging. These colleges prepare the students for B.E. and M.E. or B. Tech and M. Tech, degrees in various branches of engineering or technology.

7. Specialised colleges. Besides the above categories of the subjects of teaching, there are some specialised colleges, teaching special subjects such as home science, performing arts, music, dance, acting, photography, painting, etc. These colleges may be private, governed by some trust or established by the government. They prepare the students for diploma in the field of their specialisation. They provide practical training and sometimes even arrange for the employment of their students.

HOW MANY SHOULD GO TO COLLEGE?

Different committees surveying the quality and quantity of the students of the colleges in India, complain about the low quality of the student with the consequent result of growing educated unemployment. As most of the urban youths have no courage to take up self-employment ventures, most of them go on adding one degree after another to their qualifications. This makes them unable to take up any vocation other than white collor jobs, which are not sufficient to cope with their growing number. Besides the boys the highly educated girls also do not find employment easily nor are they easily adjusted in matrimony. In no progressive country education is so much lopsided with such a large number of students in the colleges. In most of the countries the youths take up vocations and employment after finishing their high school education and getting in specialised institutions. In India, on the other hand, most of the students passing through high schools thoughtlessly and almost spontaneously seek admission to the colleges. Failing to get admissions to specialised medical and engineering colleges they flock to the colleges of arts and sciences and stay there sometimes for half a dozen years seeking this or that degree. These degrees do not brighten their employment chances. Therefore, one finds a lot of frustration among educated youth in India. This is due to lack of proper planning.

Only those should be admitted to colleges who have necessary physical, mental and financial equipment for the purpose. Failing this they only create problems for those who have these with them. Therefore, the government should restrict admissions to colleges through different measures. This will improve the quality of education and reduce so many problems. On the other hand, initiative from the teachers and the college managing bodies is equally necessary. Delinking of jobs and degrees will help this process.

GROWTH OF COMMUNITY SENTIMENT IN COLLEGE

Modern psychology does not credit the existence of any group mind distinct from the mind of the individual, but in group situations the laws of group behaviour are freely employed. A college is a psychological group. Qualities such as discipline and cooperation can be evolved in the students only after some community feeling has been injected into them. William McDougall has pointed out several conditions that are necessary for the development of a group mind. They can be put to good use in developing community sentiment in colleges. They are:

1. Permanence of the group. A college, in its role as a group, should possess certain degree of permanence or physical stability. Naturally, some students join the college every year while others leave it, and some change is always going on in the shape of additional buildings, staff members changing their colleges, etc. But despite this change there is some permanence for the average student who spends two to four years in one college while in exceptional cases this period even extends from ten to twelve years. If the teachers in a school are not unnecessarily changed at a rapid rate and some of the college rules are maintained, the students derive a sense of permanence and the realisation that the college has a distinct nature. This can help them to develop a community feeling, which is part of their greater community feeling comprehending their society as a whole.

2. Study of the form of the group by members and the member's understanding of its duties and functions. Each student is a member of the college group. He can have community feeling for it only if he learns to regard it as a group, realises the duties that he has to perform as a student, and has knowledge of the college's rules and methods of working. For this reason it is desirable for the teachers to introduce their new students every year to the institution as it is, what it stands for, how things are run in it and what is expected of the newcomers. It is only in these circumstances that each student will be able to play his role in achieving the ideals of the college.

3. Contact with other groups. Community feeling does not develop only by taking part in the functions of one's own group. It is necessary that members of different groups should intermingle. Occasions for such contact can be developed by organising debates, discussions, dramatic performances, games and sports. But on all such occasions it is necessary that the feelings of the contestants for each other should be those of friendliness and respect. Should these feelings be lacking, the healthy development of any community feeling is not easy. In all such programmes students come to regard themselves as representatives of a particular college, with which they identify themselves. It is for the honour of this institution that they have to fight. Community feelings will inevitably result.

4. Development of community tradition. In a college, as in every other group, the members keep on changing every year but the community life of the group can be maintained for years at a time if a community tradition is developed. Old students who keep up their contact with their old college play an important role. Old Boys Associations can perform a useful function by renewing contact with the newer generation of students and by holding meetings and thus keeping alive the traditions of the colleges. Many colleges and universities are famous for some particular tradition. Some colleges can boast of a fine tradition of discipline while another college may be producing the best students. If the old students and teachers are successful in keeping up these traditions every year the newcomers are encouraged to do their best.

5. Division of labour among members. In every group different individuals are entrusted with the performance of different duties. Without this division of labour the life of the group cannot run smoothly. In a school or college, in particular, it is desirable that individual students should be entrusted with the task of looking after the discipline, the gardens and lawns, the classrooms, the library and the reading room, etc., and of organising cultural programmes. If the student is compelled to perform such functions he learns to shoulder responsibility and to take decisions on his own. Besides, he feels some personal interest in the functioning of the college and this gives vitality to his understanding of the community spirit.

14

SOCIAL FUNCTIONS OF EDUCATION

By laying stress on the individual aims of education one does not imply total neglect of the social aims of education. Man lives in society. He is socialized by his contact with his family, the neighbourhood, friends and relatives. He imitates the behaviour of others and thereby arrives at his own distinctive organisation of gestures and actions. His physical and psychological needs are satisfied through his contact with other people. Therefore, obviously, the social aims of education are also very important, and without them, education can even be said to be incomplete. These social aims are the creation, generation or development of those qualities in the individual which facilitate his adjustment with other members of society. Some of these qualities are sympathy, pity, kindness, love, brotherhood, service, etc. Possession of these qualities makes the individual a useful member of society. The school is a miniature pattern of society, it exercises social control over the individual. It aims at protecting the social heritage of society and transmitting it to the younger generation. Through its discipline it exercises social control over individuals and thereby makes them capable of introducing reforms in society. For this reason M.K. Gandhi pointed out that though he attached much importance to the individual, it should not be forgotten that man is a social animal. He has risen above his immediate circumstances only by learning to adjust his own individuality to the needs of social progress. Unqualified individualism is no better than barbarity. Man has learnt to steer between unqualified individualism and social control. Both the individual as well as the society progress when man deliberately submits to social control for the welfare of society as a whole. Thus, the individual and social aims of education are supplements. This is further clarified by the words of Gandhiji, "A nation cannot advance without the units of which it is composed advancing, and conversely, no individual can advance without the nation of which it is a part also advancing". All modern educationists agree on this synthesis of the individual and social objectives of education. The goal of self-realization is achievable only through the medium of education, self-sacrifice and service. Roosevelt also said that the criterion for judging an individual's ability and education is the extent to which he has shared in the progress of his nation or society. The Mudaliar Committee, appointed by the government to examine the state of secondary education in India, also suggested that the aim of our education is to form the character of the citizens of democratic India, to improve their practical or professional skill in order to achieve the nation's economic progress, and to develop their artistic, literary or cultural tendencies for the complete development of their personalities. Rabindranath's concept of the universal man presents a fine synthesis of the individual and society. Education in Shanti Niketan was based on the principle of self-education, and in this principle universality is considered as important as liberty and completeness. According to this concept, the individual should break the shackles of his individual personality and try to identify himself with the universal soul.

Social Environment in Education

The importance of the social environment as a factor in the development of human personality has been established by many sociological and psychological studies. Children brought up in an animal environment clearly established that man cannot develop without a social environment. A child studied by Averon spent 11 or 12 years of life roaming in the jungle. Later on, Itard, the famous educationist, tried to make him a normal human being, but, without success despite unlimited patience and skill. The social environment, part of man's total environment, is more important than the natural environment because a child's values and ideas evolve out of the ethos in which he lives. This development of values is made possible by the individuals surrounding the child, their ideas, values, experiences, needs, instincts, etc. Knowledge of these helps the child to understand the basic features of human nature and to realize that, despite his individual differences, he, too, is a human being. From this standpoint, literature acquires tremendous significance because it provides the individual man with different kinds of experience and knowledge. The real impact of the social environment is felt through those intimate relationships which spring up between the educand and his colleagues, and also between him and the educators. The educator and the educand should be bound to each other by strong ties of love and sympathy. The educand should be trained to discharge his responsibilities, fulfil his duties and do some service to society. This he can be taught through a variety of cultural programmes, social gatherings, in fact, any positive activity involving a group. In addition, the student should also be encouraged to participate in social service campaigns which embrace society as a whole, not merely his own limited circle within the school. This entire social environment generates social qualities in the individual, creates good sentiments in him, gives him higher ideals and increases his personal stock of happiness through love and achievement.

Education and Man's Future

All contemporary social thinkers who think in terms of internationalism as something superior to nationalism, which they consider too narrow, believe that education is the finest agency for developing this sentiment. Bertrand Russell and Rabindranath were correct when they argued that if mankind aspires to rise above narrow parochial and national interests, to put an end to everyday conflict between nations, and to avoid the horrifying consequences of a nuclear Third World War, then it will be essential to establish, in every country, an educational system which will create a new generation of beings, entirely above differences between individuals, convinced of the truth of internationalism and world brotherhood. This educational system must be such that it can persuade individuals to forget differences of caste, creed, race, country, etc., and think of the world as one huge family. Dr. Radhakrishnan also stressed that we must work for international unity. We should try to raise a new generation which has faith in the sublimity of intellectual or spiritual life, in purity, in love for all mankind, in peace. The aim of education is to make individuals useful for the world. Only when this ideal is faithfully accepted by every country will it be possible to erase conflict and war from this planet. For this, it be necessary to base education, on the one hand, on liberty and freedom, and, on the other, on a reverence for humanity. This done, all educated human beings will regard other human beings as ends in themselves and will make possible such changes in social institutions that no individual will be exploited as a means. Different educationists have suggested different schemes for education, according to the importance they attached to different social and individual aims of education. One can find convincing differences between the education in democratic America and the education in Nazi Germany and Communist Russia. This difference is reflected in the society and individuals created by the two systems. Hence, it is clear that we will have to introduce those changes in education which will enable us to create individuals and a society according to our ideals. With the recent strides in science and the growth in human consciousness, it has now come to be believed that it is essential for mankind to create a society in which all human beings will rise above the differences of sex, caste, religion, community, nation, and will respect humanity, consider every individual an end in himself, and permit every person to strive for his own development. The success, the pleasure, the glory of both man and his society lie in the realization of this dream. Hence, the importance of education for the complete development of man and society is evident.

STABILITY AND CHANGE

The functions of education in the sphere of social change are outlined as follows:

1. Assistance in adopting social change. Whenever some social change occurs, it results in changes in the pattern of doing some work. This change is easily adopted by some people while others find it very difficult to adjust themselves to this change. It is the aim of education to make all good changes easily accessible to every person. In India, a large majority of people found it difficult to reconcile themselves to the changes that occurred in the institutions of family and marriage, but the educated minority soon realized the advantages of these variations. Hence, it was this section of the people which adopted these changes very soon. Later on, as education spread to other sections of society, the importance and value of these changes came to be recognised more universally. For this reason, it is now generally accepted that before bringing about any social change in society, it is necessary to create a receptive temper of mind among the people. Otherwise, there is invariably some resistance to change.

2. Overcoming resistance to change. Certain factors make it easy for some social innovation to be adopted and accepted, but on the other hand, certain factors create resistance to acceptance. The best way of overcoming such resistance is education. Through the medium of education, the importance of social change is convincingly explained to the people so that they are purged of their prejudices and blind faith, and thus enabled and also strengthened to accept something new.

3. Analysis in change. But society does not progress with any and every change, and neither does the individual. Progress occurs only when the change leads the society to more desirable social values. And for this, analysis and criticism of social change is essential. Only the educated individual can make valid criticisms and offer constructive suggestions, because it is education which invests the individual with the capacity to use his intelligence, to distinguish between right and wrong and to establish certain ideals. Education determines the values which act as a criterion for the analysis of social change. Through this analysis and criticism, undesirable social changes are prevented and desirable social changes encouraged. In every society, this is achieved only through the efforts of rational and educated people.

4. Emergence of new changes. Since the educated class is constantly engaged in an analysis of contemporary Society, it also makes frequent suggestions for improvement. It is on the basis of such suggestions that social reform movements are set into motion. The flood of social reform movements that was witnessed at the turn of the century was due to modern education. Educated people made a study of western societies and their institutions compared both with our own, and agitated public opinion towards the abolition of many social evils such as child marriage, objections to widow remarriage, unequal rights to women, the custom of women committing sati, etc. Only through education could the importance of such changes be made apparent to the people. It was through education alone that public opinion could be turned in favour of these changes. Hence, it is the educated class in every society which initiates, guides and controls movements for social reform.

5. Leadership in social change. If social change is to be directed properly, it is necessary to have able leadership, well acquainted with the complexity of the problem. Such leaders can be created only through education. For this reason social welfare workers must first be educated before they are unleashed on society. On the one hand education creates in them a consciousness of social change, while on the other it teaches them to distinguish between the good and the bad. Education in India must be able to create appropriate leadership at every level if social changes conducive to democracy are to be introduced.

6. Educating the people for social change. Only a properly organised system of education can generate in the people of a society the ability to adopt some social change. As a result of education, individuals learn to analyse their customs and traditions to criticize them, and to cooperate in movements for social reform. The educational system has played a major role in bringing about revolutionary social changes in England, France, America and Russia.

7. Advances in the sphere of knowledge. New researches and inventions all depend upon education, because only the educated individual can search for new things in every sphere. Only such people can help in the progress of non-material culture. Fresh discoveries in the sphere of knowledge provide the right basis for criticism of society. Then the need for change becomes apparent. Thus education contributes to social change by bringing changes in knowledge.

It is evident from the above account that educationists, educators and schools have a tremendous responsibility in social change. Defective education leads to defective social changes. Hence, if society is to change in the right direction, it is essential that attention be paid to the educational system because this alone can create future generations of critics of change and leaders of reform.

15

EDUCATION, STATE AND COMMUNITY

Aristotle defined the state as a commune of families and villages whose aim is a complete and self-reliant life. But this definition was appropriate only to the city state, because the modern state is not limited only to villages. Modern thinkers point out four essential characteristics of the state-population, a definite geographical area, a government and complete sovereignty. Briefly, then, the state can be defined as an organised human group living in a definite geographical area and having its own sovereign government.

EDUCATION AND THE POLITICAL SYSTEM

Before going on to a detailed analysis of the relationship between the state and education, one must see the extent to which the state can play a part in social life. In other words, one must see how far education is a subject of state control, guidance and assistance. In modern societies, one finds that education is provided in government controlled institutions as well as privately managed institutions. Many educational institutions are also controlled and managed by religious institutions. And even among the government or state controlled institutions, one finds that some are administered by the central authority and others by state or local self governing bodies. Another aspect of the state control of education is to determine the spheres which the state should take under its own wings and the areas which can be safely left to the control of the people. In the present-day, every government, be it totalitarian or democratic, must contribute to education. There is no doubt that in a democracy the government is elected by the people, but it cannot be denied that the people themselves cannot evolve an educational pattern which can look after the educational needs of every individual. And, at the same time, it is also realised that democracy cannot be successful in the absence of universal education. Hence, modern democratic states also play a large part in educational planning and organisation.

Rights of the State

Before elucidating the rights of the state with respect to education, it is necessary to understand that there is considerable difference of opinion on this subject. Most of the theories and opinions on this subject can be divided into the following classes:

1. Individualism. Hobbes, Locke, Bentham, J.S. Mill and Herbert Spencer attached greater importance to the individual than to the state in the organisation of society. Hence, these philosophers are not in favour of state interference in education. Hobbes favours the policy of *laissez-faire* and suggests that the administration of education should be left to independent citizens. He agrees that state control of primary education is desirable and proper but he objects to state interference in higher education. Bentham is of the opinion that the state exists only to increase the happiness and contentment of the citizens, and therefore the state should interfere in education only to the extent to which such interference will lead to an increase in the sum total of happiness. He suggests that primary education should be compulsory in every country, that the state should provide the schools and colleges, but the state should not have any monopoly in education. The state must also not try to discourage private educational movements. Spencer believes that social progress is based on the principle of struggle for survival, and from this he argues that it is the duty and responsibility of the state that it should assist the people in their struggle for survival. Yet, even in this assistance, the state must take care not to restrict the freedom of the individual. Raymont has summarised the opinions of the individualist philosophers in these words: "In fine, there has been a strong tendency amongst English political thinkers from Locke to Spencer towards distrusting the intervention of the state beyond the absolutely necessary limits, though opinions have differed considerably as to how far those limits should extend". Putting it succinctly, individualist thinkers favour the adoption of the *laissez-faire* policy by the state. There is also no doubt that even after putting education in the hands of the people, the state will still have to take special steps for the education of some sections of the people, who cannot make arrangements for their own education. Besides, the state will also have to step in to put an end to the conflict in the sphere of education between various classes of society.

2. Collectivism. Collectivist thinkers oppose the views of the individualists. This school of thought has been subscribed to by such eminent thinkers as Matthew Arnold, Carlyle, Ruskin, Edmund Burke and others. Carlyle and Ruskin vigorously opposed the concept of *laissez-faire,* and suggested in contrast a complete state monopoly of education. Thinkers of this school suggest that the state's responsibility does not end with protecting the people. It must also contribute to their growth and development in other spheres also, and for this it has the fight to take complete control into its own hands. The state should be given comprehensive rights to protect the nation and its people from external aggression, to apply in practice the national policies, to punish the criminals, to increase and equitably distribute national wealth, to tax the people, to provide means for protecting the health of the people, to emancipate culture by proper control, etc. In the field of education, the state has the responsibility of providing free and compulsory primary education. In this sphere the state has complete rights, and it must exercise these rights. Hence it is the state which should control the educational system in the country.

3. Totalitarianism. Collectivist thinking in its extreme form becomes totalitarianism, which theorizes that the participation of the state is the most comprehensive form of human communities. In fact, the boundaries of the state and the society are identical, and therefore state should have complete control over education. According to Hegel, complete development of the child is impossible in the absence of an education for citizenship, provided by the state. Totalitarian thinkers are of the opinion that the child should not only be educated by the state, but also for the state.

4. Pluralism. Propounders of this philosophy want to delimit the powers of the state by a written constitution, for they are in favour of the independence of citizens. It is suggested that the extent of the state's powers should be clearly defined, so that other institutions like the family, church, etc., can make important contributions to education. Thinkers of this school, therefore, favour the establishment of privately controlled as well as state controlled educational institutions. The educand is not merely a citizen but also an individual, and hence his education must represent the combined effort of the family, religious institution and others, in addition to the effort of the state. State monopoly over the education of children is not considered desirable.

5. Anarchism. Thinkers belonging to this school are opposed to the existence of any kind of governmental or state authority in society, and for that reason the very question of state control of education does not arise. Anarchism argues, from the absence of any central authority, that the individual's development is best achieved in a condition of complete freedom. Such a condition naturally leads to mutual co-operation between individuals, and this is the precondition of proper development. The parents naturally and instinctively educate their children, without being forced to do so. Similarly, the child also does not have to be compelled To receive education. Everything in the field of education can be done by voluntary co-operation, without any external pressure.

6. Welfare state. Most of the views expressed above are extremist in nature. The concept of the welfare state is an attempt at achieving some balance between the widely divergent views about the authority of the state expressed in these philosophies. In the present age, the state is believed to aim at welfare of the citizens. In view of this, it becomes the duty of the state to make provisions for the best possible kind of education. Wherever the people have failed to create educational institutions, the state should step in and fill the vacuum. In addition to this, it is desirable that the state should retain some control over education in order to achieve the welfare of the people. For example, it can compel parents to send their children to school, if the parents are not inclined to view this with favour. But state control should be accompanied by state assistance also. The state should arrange for universal and compulsory education, at least at the primary level. It must also provide suitable textbooks to the students, or encourage other people to produce such books. The state has the authority to impose taxes upon the people to collect funds for educational purposes. It is the duty of the state to determine the proper syllabi for state institutions as well as other institutions controlled by private groups of individuals. Some anarchist and individualist thinkers may oppose state control of education to this extent, but there is no denying the fact that the people cannot successfully put into effect a complete educational programme.

Raymont presents a balanced view when he comments, "We observe that education, like the other beneficial influences at work in a civilised community, may be conducted by all or any of three means: first, by voluntary effort with a view to profit; secondly, by voluntary effort arising from philanthropic or religious motives; thirdly, by the agency of the state".

Limits to the Control of Education

Having accepted that the state must exercise control over the educational system, it becomes necessary to determine the extent to which this control should be exercised. Historically viewed, education has been carried on in every state through a variety of means and agencies. On the one hand, one finds colleges and schools run by individuals for profit while on the other one runs across institutions created by religious groups or philanthropists who have collected funds from private individuals for this purpose. In addition, one finds state aided institutions in every country. Even J.S. Mill, who objects to state control of education, has admitted that the state should establish some ideal educational institutions which should serve as models and which should inspire the people to create similar institutions. Mill objects to the state control of education on the ground that the state fries to educate the people along lines which support its own ideology and thus it controls the ideas of the people. This belief is not completely without logic and supporting evidence, because communist states do try to control the thinking of the younger generations by intellectually feeding them on communist literature. It amounts to slow brainwashing. Much the same tendency has been seen in the past in totalitarian states which also fries to control the thinking of the people by making educational institutions the centres of state propaganda. This is unfair and improper. In fact, state control in education is exercised with the sole purpose of preventing encroachment upon the political and social independence and freedom of the people, because this is essential for a proper development of personality. In the second place, the state has at its disposal unlimited means and resources which enable it to arrange for education on a large scale, something which is beyond the reach of private individuals and groups of individuals. Briefly speaking, it is desirable that state control of education should be guided by the principle of the least possible infringement of the liberties of the people. The welfare state provides for education on precisely this principle. With the establishment of democratic governments, the sphere of education is widening rapidly with the result that the responsibilities of the state are increasing. The state imposes taxes on the people in order to finance education and then compels people to send their children to schools and colleges. It also supervises educational arrangements in institutions not controlled by it to ensure uniform standards, and also provides financial aid to them.

Functions of the State in the Field of Education

Explaining the functions of the state, MacIver and Page have pointed out that there are certain functions which the state alone can perform, others which can be performed by others but not so efficiently as by the state, and yet others which are best left to other agencies, apart from those which the state does not have the ability to perform. The provision of education falls into the first and second of the above four categories, because not only is the state the best equipped for this task, it is in fact the only agency capable of coping with the educational problems of populations of remarkable size. The state alone can provide universal education to such a large number of people. The functions of the state in the sphere of education can be summed up as follows:

1. Provision of proper schools. The state should establish different kinds of schools—primary, secondary, higher learning and professional colleges—so that the local requirements of the people can be fulfilled. In addition to this, the state must also correlate these various institutions in such a way that the effort at education is not wasted.

2. Making primary education compulsory. At least at the primary stage, the state should make all education compulsory, free and universal. This kind of education, at least the elementary education, is absolutely necessary for the mental development of the people. Hence, the state should compel parents to send their children to schools.

3. Providing finances for education. The state must plan for and provide the finances required for education. Some people have advanced the argument that the provision of free and compulsory primary education will reduce its value in the eyes of the people. While this may be true, the state is faced with the necessity of doing so, because the private sector has failed to provide primary education for the masses. It is now accepted that every modern state must provide free and compulsory education to all children in the country. Apart from primary education, it has been experienced that private resources are never sufficient to provide proper secondary and higher education to adequate numbers of students. Even here institutions have to seek the assistance of the state. In addition to the creation of primary and secondary schools and universities and professional colleges for higher learning the state helps the cause of education by providing scholarships and financial help in different forms to poor but brilliant students. In many western countries the number of students receiving state aid in one form or the other frequently rises to fifty per cent of the total number enrolled in the university. In India, this stage has not been achieved and consequently many brilliant students are deprived of the opportunity to study.

4. General control and guidance. One important aspect of state functioning in the sphere of education is control, inspection and guidance of individual institutions. The state government officials construct syllabi for various levels of education, with the help of educationists and other learned people. In the same manner, the state does not take independent decisions about educational matters, but seeks the advice and guidance of experts. The state should normally not interfere in teaching methods, but leave it to experienced teachers, researchers and scholars. Besides, the state can also not profitably guide the techniques of evaluating educational ability. This, too, is the task of the teacher and the educationists. All that the state can lay down, in the way of guidance, is that some method of evaluating educational ability must be introduced at each level of education. The state may also require this method to be so accurate, dependable and valid that it may serve as a basis for evaluating the individual's fitness for various tasks.

5. Providing skilled educators. It is clear from the preceding paragraph that there is little the state can do in the absence of skilled educators. Hence, it is a major responsibility of the state to provide such educators. Even if the national educational policy has been created by brilliant thinkers and incalculable effort has gone into its creation, it will fail to achieve anything if there are no skilled educators to implement it. The responsibility of the state does not end with putting up buildings for schools, filling such schools with educands and making arrangements for the administration of the institution. As Raymont has pointed out, "Educational salvation lies, not in bricks and mortal;, nor in sumptuous equipment, nor in paper curricula, nor in elaborate machinery of whatever kind, but in the subtle influence of informed men and women upon the pupils committed to their care. A good teacher, in sympathy with his work, and doing it under reasonably liberal condition of service will achieve better things in a barn than a bad or dissatisfied one will achieve under the best of external circumstances". Hence, it is desirable that the state should take upon itself the responsibility of providing trained and qualified teachers, and of seeing that their conditions of service create the satisfaction so necessary for the job. The educand's mental health depends very greatly upon the mental health of his educator. More often than not, in most non-governmental educational institutions one finds conditions of work which are not at all conductive to mental balance, for example, varying scales of pay, physical conditions of work, absence of opportunity to progress, etc. The state should investigate all such conditions and improve them, and also enact legislation which secures the rights of people working in private institutions.

6. Training in citizenship. In the sphere of education, one important function of the state is to train young men and women in citizenship. For this, the state must create institutions for training in science, industry, agriculture, etc. The cultural training and advancement of the people can be provided for by creating art galleries, cultural committees, means of recreation, etc. Now-a-days, states send cultural delegations to other countries. Another way in which the state can help in improving cultural standards is by facilitating the international exchange of teachers and students. In a democratic society it is necessary for the state to maintain a healthy level of social living, by creating conditions conducive to the physical and mental development of its people, and by assisting all private agencies engaged in similar work. Political training is also essential in a democratic country, because political awareness must be created if proper leadership is to emerge. It is for the state to exploit all means of communications — newspapers, radio, television, cinema, etc.,— in order to acquaint every individual with the latest in political, economic and social thinking, and also to inform him of all economic and industrial progress taking place within the country. In this way, it can be seen that the political education of people living in a democratic country depends entirely upon the co-operation of the state.

COMMUNITY AND EDUCATION

Responsibility of Community Towards Education

It is clear from the foregoing discussion that community has great responsibility towards education, for it itself is a medium of education. As Crow and Crow has commented, "A community cannot expect something for nothing. If it wishes its young people to serve their community well, it must provide whatever educational advantages are needed by the young people, individually and collectively, to prepare themselves for that service". Briefly, the community has the following responsibilities towards education:

1. Educational control. In a democratic state, education should be controlled by the state because only then can they ensure that democratic ideals will be instilled into the young men and women receiving education. Hence, it is the leaders of society who give decisions regarding the curriculum, general organisation and administration, finances, methods of examination, etc., of the schools.

2. Control of schools. The duty of the community does not end with providing finances and other means with which to establish schools. The community must also undertake the responsibility of selecting those individuals who can be relied upon to run the schools in a way in keeping with the ideals of the community. Besides, educators influence the life of the community very greatly, and hence the community must also ensure the correct selection and appointment of educators.

3. Co-operation between educators and citizens. Modern educationists are of the opinion that the educator should establish contact not only with the parents of his wards but also with the leaders of society, so that educators, parents and leaders can get together and decide the curriculum, the ideals of education, the manner of day-to-day administration of schools, etc.

4. Providing the informal means of education. Outside the school, there are many agencies such as reading rooms, dramatic societies, museums, libraries, etc., which contribute in an important measure to the education of the child. Besides, the child's education cannot be really complete unless society also produces a mass of good literature and allows scope for the expression of artistic creativity. All such provisions can only be made by the community. It is for the leaders of society to collect funds to provide such informal means of education. Funds for this can be obtained from the state as well as from philanthropically inclined persons.

Educational Impact of the Community

It is evident from the foregoing account of the educational responsibilities of the community that it has a comprehensive educational impact. In this connection the following points are noteworthy:

1. Impact on physical development. In every country there are certain agencies of local self government, for example municipalities, which are responsible for public hygiene and sanitation. Even at the international and national level some such committees are formed to safeguard the health of the citizens, because physical health is directly dependent upon public hygiene. In most big towns, citizens contribute liberally to the establishment of public hospitals which serve the poorer sections of society which are themselves incapable of paying for medical services. In addition, many societies also provide gymnasia and other facilities for physical exercise. In India gymnasia have been traditionally attached to various places of worship so that young people can bring to physical health the devotion often given to worship. Here young people were encouraged to attend such gymnasia and to take care of physical health under the guidance of physical culture experts and religious leaders. There apparently seems to be a decline of interest in this direction over the last few years, but nevertheless even now one finds such gymnasia attached to temples, etc. Every educated community takes care of the physical well-being of its young by making provisions for nutritious food, occasions for rest, plenty of physical exercise, etc.

2. Impact on mental development. The community can play an important role in the mental development of its citizens by providing musical competitions, cultural functions, dramatic performances, seminars, etc. Besides, every enlightened community also builds libraries and reading rooms and encourages people to use them because mental development is hastened in the process of acquiring knowledge. All such means of mental development are now considered necessary adjuncts of any civilized community.

3. Impact on cultural development. Every community has its own distinctive customs, modes, mores, modes of behaviour, traditions, ideals, etc., which are transferred to the younger generation through the process of socialization. This socializing process has so profound an influence upon the individual citizens that one can find distinctive patterns of behaviour evolving in them which serve to distinguish them from members of any other community having a different set of ideals, customs and traditions, etc. In order to maintain the vital force of society, it becomes necessary to make some changes in these adjuncts of culture from time to time. Here, too, the leaders of the community have to assert themselves. It is for them to reflect on the existing state of affairs, to analyse and see the defects, to suggest ways and means of changing the cultural complex in order to affect improvements. Besides, the culture of a community also undergoes natural change and transformation by coming into contact with other cultures. Hence, community is the best medium of cultural development.

4. Political impact. In the words of Crow and Crow, "The political ideology of a community is reflected in the extent to which educational opportunities are offered to all its members and in the responsibility assumed by its political leaders for the educational progress of the citizens of the community". One can conceive the political impact of the community on citizens by comparing the political thinking of the citizens of democratic America and communist Russia. In a communist country the community aims at spreading communist ideology among the people while in a democratic state the community is inclined to develop democratic ideals among the people, and all its efforts are directed towards such development.

5. Economic impact. Different kinds of industries, jobs and professions develop only in a community, not in the solitude of an individual. The child examines his own ideas and the conduct of various individuals involved in different occupations. In the process he learns many forms of behaviour through imitation and this arouses his curiosity regarding many different professions and occupations. Frequently one finds that adolescents develop some interest in one or the other profession. On the other hand, some professions are practically inherited in that they are learnt within the family. Other professions can be learnt with the help of neighbours, family members, the community, etc. In certain cases the profession of an individual is determined by the community, for it is the community which decides the profession to be adopted by the child when he reaches adulthood. In India, for example, in the past, the profession of an individual was determined by his caste. Although now nobody pays attention to the claims of the caste system in this connection there is no denying that the choice of profession is often limited by the type of people one comes into contact with the local institutions and committees, which conditions one's thinking. It is from them that one learns how to earn one's livelihood. It is therefore evident that the community influences the economic life of the individual to a very great extent.

6. Moral and character development. Community has an impact not only on the physical and mental development of the individual, but also on his moral and character development. Every society has its own code of ethics which differs in some degree from that of other societies, and this difference is reflected in the behaviour of its citizens. In order to see this effect of the community on the moral development of the individual, one can compare members of a civilized community with those of a tribal society and see the difference between their moral ideas and characters. Whatever the difference between the moral levels of two communities, there is no community which is completely devoid of any moral values and standards. Even the most backward society has some primitive moral code and it tries to instil these moral ideas into the younger generation in it. It is the community which provides the environment for the character development of the child. If this environment is favourable it will create good character while on the contrary one will find defective character formation if the environment itself is defective. Hence, in this respect the duties of the community are self-evident.

7. Impact on social development Community is responsible for developing the community sentiment among its members, and this community sentiment creates in them a we-feeling and a sense of responsibility towards the community which brings with it awareness of certain duties. Most of the intelligent people in a community try to create responsible citizens out of their young children. It is the society which socializes the individual. In Indian society the individual's socialization is achieved through a variety of religious functions deliberately intended to create social consciousness in the child participating in the function. This awareness of the society around one is manifested in each individual's desire to win the praise of the members of the community and an equally strong desire to avoid winning their criticism and disrespect. He is afraid of being ostracized. But it must be remembered that development of social consciousness does not imply a blind following of the traditional rules and customs of society. Many people do reflect upon the nature and value of all these customs, and if they find them defective they raise their voices against such customs and vigorously arouse people to getrid of them. This is the beginning of social reform movements, and if members of the community cooperate with the revolutionaries, social reform takes place. But all this takes place within the society, because, the process of development and improvement of society occurs within the society, not outside it. Hence, the community plays an important part in the individual's social development.

8. Educational impact All the various influences that can be seen emanating from the community have an educational impact, inasmuch as they help the process of education. Apart from this, the community also has some impact upon formal education. The different classes of the community contribute to establish educational institutions. In India, one finds various institutions financed and run by Hindus and Muslims, and among Hindus by Brahmins, Jats, Sikhs and other religious groups. Generally, such institutions aim at educating children belonging to their own communities. In addition such communities also try to provide the informal means of education such as reading rooms, libraries, dramatic societies, etc.

Educational Importance of the Community

It is evident from the foregoing account that the community makes important contribution to both formal and informal forms of education. The child develops first within the limited sphere of his own family and then steps out into the larger surroundings of the community which unconsciously influences his language, thinking, modes of living, habits, ideas, etc. In fact, every aspect of his development is consciously or unconsciously influenced by the community. In the words of Francis J. Brown, "Changing the behaviour of individuals is not enough, education must seek to modify community patterns of behaviour through close and constant interaction with the total culture of the community". From the very beginning, the child's behaviour, habits, his dress, etc., are all determined by the community. It is the community which determines his attitudes towards various religions, tribes, classes, individuals and objects, and in this way community aids the family in socializing the child but it differs from the family in that it continues to influence the child even after the family has stopped doing so. The community's approved patterns of behaviour are enforced on the individual through school discipline, while the moral and ethical code of the community is reflected in the personalities of the teachers which also influence the individual.

In India, from very ancient times, the community has played a very significant role in the education of men and women. And even in present-day education, one can see the impact of the community in every sphere. A democratic government was established in the country after it won independence, and this government presented democratic ideals to the country. The government also put forward the suggestion of universal and free education. It also undertook the task of establishing educational institutions to provide education at every level. Some of this burden was taken over by some communities. Libraries, reading rooms, museums, art galleries, dramatic clubs, etc., have been established in all the large towns. The community is playing a steadily increasing role in education in the country.

INTER-CULTURAL UNDERSTATING

India is a big country in which one finds groups distinguished from each other on the basis of language, religion, race, mode of dress, etc. There are numerous racial groups living in different parts of the country who not only possess different cultures, but possess cultures which do not resemble civilized groups. One finds differences of living standards, language, style of dress, etc., among the people living in different parts of the country, but even more remarkable is the difference in values of life and ideas. In fact, that which is called Indian culture is not a single culture, but a composite culture made up of the synthesis of numerous cultures. This was born even before Aryan civilization, and other cultures have added to it from time to time. In view of the numerous instances of conflict which have been seen recently due to linguism, regionalism, communalism, casteism, etc., it can be said that schools have failed to create unity and mutual sympathy among the different groups. These influences are also seen constantly working in the country in the garb of partiality for a person of one's own region. This has led many educationists to reflect upon this issue and to give valuable suggestions.

Inter-cultural understanding implies particular attitude, the attitude of understanding members of another culture, of recognising their merits, of sympathising and being liberal towards them. And since India contains many different cultures, inter-cultural understanding is essential, for, in its absence, conflict can never be curtailed. This inter-cultural understanding can be created through education. An emotional unity is the first essential thing for this. Besides, in the absence of inter- cultural understanding, it is impossible to generate a genuine internationalism which is necessary in view of the substantial differences between the numerous cultures found in different parts of the world. And, as long as human beings do not rise above their petty differences and understand all human beings to be members of the same group and learn to appreciate other cultures, international understanding cannot be created. The following suggestions are put forward for creating inter-cultural understanding:

1. Study of cultural anthropology. Cultural anthropology, one branch of anthropology, provides knowledge of the origin of various cultures, their development and their inner content. By studying the fundamental elements of this discipline, educands can comprehend the different cultural patterns and characteristics which are found. By studying the origins of various cultures, they will be able to understand that differences in culture arise out of the different circumstances in which the cultures are born. This will lead to a more charitable and liberal attitude to cultural differences.

2. Encouragement to tourism. Travelling to different parts of the country is a valuable experience in that it helps one to realize that despite the obvious differences in various groups, all of them are Indians. This promotes inter-cultural understanding.

3. Encouraging mutual meetings. Indian universities regularly organise cultural programmes in which students from different universities present cultural shows. Such meetings give the young people to meet young people of other cultural groups, with the result that they get a chance to understand the other culture. This helps to free their minds of narrow thinking.

4. Propagating the theory of unity in diversity. People who believe either in the destruction of diversity in order to create uniformity or in the destruction of unity to maintain diversity forget that unity in diversity is a natural characteristic of human society as well as of the entire creation. Happiness lies in following this principle. If this principle is accepted, internationalism will be encouraged, but not at the cost of nationalism. Today, all the different cultures that are growing in the country must be allowed to flourish. None of them should be destroyed, because each represents a specific pattern of adjustment with the environment existing at a particular place, and hence it has its own value. Each culture is the product of the local conditions, climate and natural environment, and represents an adjustment to that environment. Therefore, each culture must be given the opportunity to grow further. But this does not necessarily imply that the country will inevitably be divided into numerous different cultural groups or that this should be allowed to happen. Cultural unity can be promoted even after maintaining cultural variety and identity. This cultural unity can be created by using education to promote intercultural understanding. If people can be made to realize that both unity or conformity and diversity or individuality are part of the theory of unity in diversity, it will be possible to take care of and eradicate much of the prejudice, partiality, differences, etc., that arise out of cultural differences.

In addition to the above measures, it is possible to utilize many other things for the purpose of creating inter-cultural understanding, Young men and women can, for example, be encouraged to establish contact with members of other cultures through the medium of pen-friendship. Even inter-cultural marriages can be of immense value in this respect. It is possible to create situations in which members of different cultures come into contact with each other. Tourism, in particular, should be encouraged. Young students can tour the country in groups and thus acquaint themselves with the different cultures existing in remote parts of the country. It is possible to generate a liberal, sympathetic and kind hearted attitude towards other cultures among the younger generations through the medium of magazines, literary publications intended for the young, and other similar channels. Exhibitions of literature and art can achieve the same thing. Films can also make valuable contributions in this respect. Besides, once the teachers themselves have understood the importance of this aim of education, they will provide many illustrations to their students to create intercultural understanding.

LANGUAGE PROBLEM IN INDIA

Different languages are spoken in different parts of the country in India, while in some parts several languages are in use at the same time. Among the many languages spoken here are Hindi, Urdu, Punjabi, Gujarati, Marathi, Assamese, Kashmiri, Tamil, Telugu, Malayalam, Kannada, etc. Hindi is the language of the majority of the people, and other people are also learning it, but this has not hampered the development of literature in the other languages. To take but one or two examples, the literature in Punjabi, Gujarati or Marathi is in no way inferior to or less developed than the literature in Hindi. In itself, the presence of so many languages is no particular disadvantage because the development in each one of them contributes to the totality of national literature. There is no harm in each linguistic group trying to improve its own language, but when the difference of language is made the basis of conflict and tension, many difficulties arise. Linguism is the tendency which encourages a linguistically united group to extol the virtues of its own language to the denigration of all other languages and linguistic groups. This tendency is as harmful for the nation as any other ism. This linguism is at the root of the language problem in India and it is steadily becoming more virulent and intense. One finds a terrible conflict in Punjab on the question of Hindi and Punjabi. In Assam this has even led to bloodshed. The Bengali speaking people protest against what they consider to be the imposition of Hindi upon them. Apart from these regional languages, other languages such as Hindi, English and Urdu are made the cause of demonstrations, conflicts and violence, and consequent tension. More often than not, the disturbances for language are only masks for definite political objectives. In fact, most of the people instigating disturbances and action on the basis of language are politicians and not literary figures. For example, in Punjab, the demand for the recognition of Punjabi was only an off-shoot of the main demand for a Punjabi state.

Linguism obscures all clear thinking on the language problem, and makes it impossible to adopt an objective attitude to it. Certain fundamental problems are at the root of linguism—which language should be the link language in the country, which language should be considered the national language, what status should English have in the pattern of education? etc. Other related questions concern the status that should be given in the educational pattern to the regional language and the efforts that should be made to develop Hindi as the national language. Because of regional affinities, people advocate the case of their own language as the national language.

In 1956 the Central Education Recommendation Commission suggested the trilingual formula to solve the language problem, a formula which was approved by the Chief Ministers of all the states in 1968. It was provided in this formula that at the secondary level, the educand shall be required to learn three languages, his mother tongue or regional language, Hindi and English. This suggestion was objected to on the ground that it attached too much importance to English when most educationists are in favour of using a foreign language as an alternative. The Kothari Commission, which was constituted in 1964, suggested in June 1966 a variant of the tri-lingual formula, but it still attached very great importance to English. In this connection it must be pointed out that in 1953 the Mudaliar Commission had recommended the teaching of two languages at the secondary stage, the mother tongue and a national language. Actually, the language problem has its root in the fact that although Hindi is accepted as the national language in the Constitution, it is not so in fact. The problem is being perpetuated because most politicians responsible for solving it have too many different opinions. Any solution to it can be expected only when people get rid of their prejudices on the subject and consider it objectively and scientifically.

16

SOCIAL STRATIFICATION AND EDUCATION IN INDIA

On the one hand, one finds numerous groups in contemporary Indian society, distinguished from each other on the basis of language, religion, race, caste, tribe, geographical location, etc., while on the other, one also finds distinct economic classes. The processes of secularization, westernization, acculturation, industrialization and urbanization have led to remarkable changes everywhere. The impact of the West is evident enough, but it is accompanied by frantic attempts to rejuvenate ancient Indian values. The increasing complexity of economic problems has had the effect of economic classes leaving indelible marks on the personality of children. Increasing political awareness is another factor which is clearly evident. The most clear outcome of the interaction of all these tendencies is that the young generation has been presented with a fantastic variety of alternatives and differences of opinion, the extent of variety by its very nature rendering extremely difficult any determination of right and wrong. This disorganization of values is manifested through such undesirable activities as indiscipline, juvenile delinquency, pessimism, destructive and murderous tendencies, etc. In such a situation, the first duty of the educational organisation is to supplement the clear presentation of all possible alternatives before the younger generation with active encouragement in the choice of one alternative, so that there is some positive guidance.

Hence, education must not merely inculcate secularism, realism and liberality in the educand, but must also provide him with the ability to distinguish the right from the wrong. The young people are subject to a multiplicity of influences emanating from various sources, and for this reason it is essential that there should be some unity in all this diversity. The absence of such a unity will have disastrous consequences in the form of personality and social disorganisation. The first step in this direction is the creation of character, which will grant an adolescent the determination to be guided by his own opinion. It is essential that old and traditional values be explained to the younger generation in the interest of continuity with the older generation, but this should not preclude consideration of new values which can lead to progress and development. Education can thus fulfil the needs of society only if it adopts a comprehensive and dynamic curriculum, a dynamic methodology of teaching and a dynamic philosophy of education.

CHARACTERISTICS OF INDIAN SOCIETY AND THE MODERN CONTEXT

In order to understand the social foundations of education, it would be interesting to glance at the characteristics of Indian society. The main features are the following:

1. Caste system. Caste can be defined as a hereditary intermarrying group which determines the individual's status in the social stratification by his occupation, etc. In defining caste it is necessary to highlight its characteristic features. Intermarriage is an essential feature, for its members cannot marry outside their group. There are similar though less rigid limitations and restrictions on the dietary habits of the members of a caste. The occupations of most of the castes are determined, and it is not possible to transfer from one caste to another. The Brahmin has the highest place in the social stratification of castes.

It is evident from the foregoing account that caste is not identical with class, because in a class, stratification is free, not rigid. Membership of the caste is determined by birth while the membership of the class is based on status, standard of living and other objective factors. Members of the caste do not necessarily have any caste consciousness but members of a class have a class consciousness. Class is much more flexible than caste, which is completely rigid. Compared to the class, caste groups have greater social distance between them, and it is not possible to transfer from one group to the next. Similarly, caste division is also much more rigid in that members of one caste cannot mix or eat and drink with the members of another. In this manner the caste system presents a bigger obstacle to the progress of democracy. In the medieval period the caste played an important role in the organisation of Hindu society—it organised the Hindu society, it maintained social and political stability, helped in begetting good offspring, looked after social security, looked after the mental security of the members, functioned as a trade union, determined laws about education, provided technical training, maintained and transmitted hereditary knowledge of mechanical and technical processes, maintained the religious life, etc. The caste system continued to exist due to certain characteristics of Hindu society, such as religious influence, static society, rural social structure, geographic division, differences between tribes, absence of education, etc. But in the present-day the caste structure is being weakened by many factors. Modern education, social reform movements, political movements, industrialization, means of communication and transport, increase in the value attached to money, emergence of new social classes, a modern system of laws, etc., are all helping in the decline of the traditional caste structure, but despite this one finds a steady increase in casteism also. Casteism is actually being encouraged by elections fought on the basis of caste, and it is being kept alive by petty politicians. In the modern context, the caste system is proving immeasurably harmful to society. The separation and division in society caused by untouchability is in fact due to casteism, which is causing social disorganisation in many other ways also. It is dividing the Indian society into a number of fragmented groups. Discrimination on caste grounds causes serious difficulties in the development of the individual, and this helps to maintain the inequalities of distribution of wealth and the means of production. Because the sculptors were believed to belong to the low castes, the art of sculpture has suffered a serious below. Very often the protection of women is hindered in the name of protection of caste. Besides, the caste system is responsible for a number of other problems such as child marriage, denial of widow remarriage, dowry, etc. Hence, the caste system is proving a very serious obstacle to social progress and the establishment of a democratic society. It is opposed to nationalism because it encourages casteism. In view of the situation, many sociologists have suggested many ways of eliminating caste system. But what is required even more than the elimination of the caste system is its refashioning or modification so that it may help in fostering the sentiment of nationality and also encourage the growth of democracy. The first step in this direction is to remove caste discrimination in the new generation through education. Co-education will also encourage intercaste marriages. Another way is to get rid of surnames which indicate the caste of a person. It is also necessary to keep strict control over caste meetings and caste associations. Ways must be found of stopping caste considerations from taking a part in political elections. In this way, the existing caste system is proving a hinderance to the development of democratic ideals through education, and in order to prevent its ill-effects from poisoning society, it is necessary that educational institutions should take the first step.

2. Social classes. Classes in society are as common in India as they are in any part of the world. Class is a status group, and in any society the social status of one group always differs from that of another. In the words of MacIver, "A social class is any portion of community marked off from the rest by social status". The foundation of the class is the class consciousness. In every case, the member of one class is perfectly conscious of his own status in respect to and as differentiated from the status of some other group. For this reason, the child's developing mind and personality always bear the stamp of the social class in which he originated. Many schools cater to the children of one particular social class because members of other classes cannot bear the expenses of educating children in such schools. Class consciousness also tends to hinder the growth of democratic values, and for this reason the school should provide an atmosphere which may encourage the sense of equality and underplay differences between children of different social classes. It is difficult to increase the sense of brotherhood as long as class distinctions exist. But class consciousness cannot be eliminated without putting an end to economic disparity and other inequalities. For this social and economic reforms are essential.

3. Religious groups. Another characteristic feature of the Indian society is the number of religious groups and communities found here—Hindus, Muslims, Christians, Parsis, to name only a small number. Even among Hindus there are a number of smaller communities such as the Sanatan Dharma, the Arya Samaj, etc. The Jains and the Buddhists also believe themselves to be separate communities, while the Shias and the Sunnis among the Muslims also claim to be distinct communities. Every one of such religious communities tries to strengthen the communal or we-feeling among its members and tries to help them progress in many ways.

That they do something positive cannot be denied, but this also cannot be compared with the harm done by promoting communal feelings, since these stand in the way of developing any national sentiment. Certain religious groups are so fanatically opposed to certain other groups that communal rioting between them is a regular feature, and it starts on the smallest excuse. Many political parties take advantage of this, and in order to secure their own advantage they keep on encouraging communalism. Apart from the damage to life and property during communal disturbances, considerable damage is done to the attitudes of the younger generation because the entire social atmosphere is vitiated. Without putting an end to this communalism it is impossible to achieve the moral, spiritual and intellectual development of children. As long as it exists, it is also impossible to create any national unity or to create an atmosphere suitable to the development of democratic values and concepts.

4. Variety of languages. Another feature of Indian society is the presence of more than a dozen languages and an almost impossible number of dialects. Although this variety is conducive to cultural prosperity, it also affords a useful opportunity to those who want to arouse linguistic sentimental attachments and create differences. As a result there have been very destructive riots and conflicts in many parts of the country, leading to loss of life and property, both public and private. If linguism spreads rapidly, it only injures the mental development of the young people because they begin to hate other languages and refuse to learn them. Linguism also leads to hatred of the literature in the other tongue. Hence, this emotion also blunts moral and intellectual development.

5. Many cultures. Although from the earliest times, it has been granted that India had a single culture, in fact, this unity covered a remarkable diversity. India is such a big country that it should properly be called a sub-continent, and in different parts of this country, different cultures have been independently evolving. While all of them share certain common characteristics, they also differ from each other in many respects which influence the children brought up in them. There can be no denying that cultural variety adds to cultural prosperity but it can also encourage social disorganisation when the distinctions are used to create differences. In more recent years, political interests have inspired many people to demand separate states on the basis of these cultural differences. In some cases these demands have gone so far as to express a desire for secession from the Centre.

6. Excessive population. The population in India is growing at such a rapid pace that the excess of population has become a very complex and frightening problem. In such a situation it is becoming increasingly difficult to provide the necessities of life, proper education and a proper environment for everybody.

7. Poverty. As a result of the large population, the country is suffering from endemic poverty which serves to offset all the advantages of education.

8. Disorganisation of the joint family. The joint family system is rapidly breaking down in modern Indian society, and it is being replaced by centralized families, with the result that the individual is now subject to the influences of a different kind of family. Before making any national plan for social reformation, it is essential to keep this change in mind.

9. Disorganisation of values. The present-day society in India has lost all its faith in the traditional Indian values under the impact of westernization, secularization, urbanization and a host of similar influence. But the lost set of values has not been replaced by any more recent pattern and consequently one finds complete disorganization of values. This is acting as a serious impediment to moral and spiritual development.

10. Marital disorganisation. One finds a steady increase in the cases of disorganised marriages due to the system of dowry, increase in divorce rate, change in the functions of the family, marriage between incompatible people, etc. Marital disorganisation invariably has a bad effect on the development of children.

11. Materialism. Compared to the ancient Indian society, the contemporary social organisation is decidedly more materialistic. This is leading to individual and social disorganisation on the one hand, and to evil effects upon the social, moral, spiritual and intellectual development of the younger generation on the other.

12. Politicization. After Independence, political influences have penetrated every sphere of life with the result that the sole motive governing every action is that of self-interest and self-aggrandizement. Even in education, political interest can be found at practically every level. This again is functioning as a very serious obstacle to all progress.

13. Social disorganisation. Indian society is being rapidly fragmented into small units because of the influence of regionalism, linguism, casteism, untouchabil- ity, communalism, etc. As a consequence, one finds social disorganisation everywhere. This has a detrimental effect on the development of children.

14. Individual disorganisation. For the last few years, the tendency to indulge in various kinds of intoxicants is growing among the younger generation, more particularly among the students. The character level of students is falling rapidly under the influence of alcohol, opium and other intoxicants and viewing of immoral films. Combined with this is the uncertainty about the future, which only tends to aggravate abnormalities, mental tensions and personal disorganisation. All these are serious problems for the educational planners.

15. Economic difficulties. Compared to the conditions existing in ancient and medieval India, there is far greater unemployment today. This has a direct impact upon the minds of education. Besides, economic difficulties make it impossible to achieve the ideal of universal education.

EFFECT OF INDIAN SOCIETY ON CHILD DEVELOPMENT

Having seen the chief characteristics of Indian society, it is now possible to study the effect Indian society is likely to have on the child's development, and for this we will study its effect on each individual aspect of development.

1. Effect on physical development. Considerable attention has always been paid to bodily development in India from the very ancient times. Some kind of physical training has always been an inevitable part of school education, the tradition of yogic and other exercises starts from ancient times. In modern school, efforts are made toward the physical development of the edueand through such institutions as Scouting, Girl Guides, A.C.C., N.C.C., N.C.C.R., etc, in addition to which many schools also provide special training and guidance in some sports. Most of the contemporary Indian thinkers, among them Aurobindo and Vivekanand, have stressed the importance of physical education, but despite such physical education it is found that the health of the educands is generally below average. The poverty of the Indian nation is clearly reflected in their dull and weak faces and it is only poverty which prevents the state from providing free nourishment to educand. Education itself is so expensive that most families find it an almost intolerable burden. In addition to this, dietary habits also influence the health. As it is, the food taken by Indians is lacking in many of the nourishing elements, besides which milk is very expensive and few people can afford to take it in the requisite quantity although it is essential. Again, one finds very few means of entertainment and recreation in Indian society. The result of this is that although the student can be compelled to abstain from the matinee shows at cinema halls, he cannot be prevented from spending his leisure time in reading pornographic literature or in taking intoxicants. Cigarettes and other intoxicants are in common use in the lower and middle classes of Indian society. Children and adolescents imitate their seniors and also take to smoking, thus injuring their health. Another factor is the greater importance attached to smart, shiny and highly colourful clothes than to rich and nutritive food in many middle class families. Most of the young men and women living in cities are completely averse to physical effort of any kind. Their condition is made worse by a polluted atmosphere, absence of sanitation and unhygienic living conditions, shortage of nutritious food, poverty, irregular living habits, etc. Urban children are particularly subject to all these shortcomings, and thus their health is falling rapidly. The pity of it is that little if any effort is being made to check this landslide. There is little hope that one can foster for the coming generation when the fixture parents themselves suffer from so many shortcomings. In actual truth, although much importance is attached to physical education and training in theory, in actual practice, there is little physical education. Then, it is found that young men and women who complete the entire course of education, spending sixteen or seventeen years in schools and colleges, are far worse off in respect of health than those who study for a short time and then immediately adopt some career. As long as the educated class of the country suffers from such debility, there is little chance of any development or progress in the country.

2. Effect on mental development. Mental development is intimately related to physical development. Even when the child exists in embryo in the mother's womb, his health is influenced by the health of his mother, and if some nutritive elements are lacking in the nourishment conveyed to him, his mental development is retarded along with his physical development. After emerging from the womb, the child is influenced by the family. In India, little can be said in favour of the family if one considers the influence it exercises on the child's mental development. The child's mind is negatively influenced by the constant poverty, family disturbances and quarrels, quarrels between his parents, the large number of family members and other problems arising from this, frequent visitation of disease, etc. This is further complicated by the constant presence of such mental attitudes as casteism, communalism, etc. The prejudice of communalism is fostered in his mind from his earliest days and it is very soon supplemented by thoughts of untouchability. Not much later he is exposed to the realities of his family status as determined by its income, and the evil-effects which emanate from this. Today the country provides the highest training and education in the spheres of agriculture, medicine, engineering, the arts, technology and almost any conceivable branch of learning, devised to develop the young and growing mind. But how many people can really derive any benefit from such institutes of higher learning? Poverty effectively deprives even the most intelligent children of poor families of the highest education, for there is almost no arrangement of any financial assistance for them. Apart from this, the education provided in modern schools is also not free of defects, for it does nothing more than prepare the child for a profession or a job, and even that is often not available to the individual. In villages, many children do not attend even primary school. Most poor people are compelled to send even the youngest children out to some occupation so that they can augment the family income. In such conditions, it is futile to hope for the mental development of children. In recent years, radios, newspapers and other media of mass communication have just begun to penetrate to the villages, but as compared to the villages of Western countries, such means of mental development are still in short supply. In addition to this, such disorganising and disruptive tendencies as regionalism, linguism, etc., are only making minds more narrow and limited. What, then is the occasion for surprise if one finds little originality in most spheres? Even after so many years of independent national life, we have not been able to give a national status to Hindi. In addition, the conditions existing in the country are not conducive to the development of the literature of any language. English is still very influential and it carries with it a definite mental slavery. As a result of all these factors, mental development cannot be independent and unrestricted.

3. Effect on emotional development. Although many of the elements of Indian culture have succeeded in checking the growth of abnormalities of personality and mental disease, the present condition of society cannot be considered to be favourable to the emotional development of the coming generation. Increasing poverty, increasing population, family and marital disorganisation, uncertain future, rapidly increasing commodity prices and other such factors influence the growing mind at a very early age and fill it with various kinds of fears and repressions. As a result of such sentiments as casteism, linguism, regionalism, communalism, etc., children begin early to hate many sections of society and also to fear them. How can brotherhood develop under such conditions? The committee for national integration has given certain suggestions for evolving emotional unity and integration among the people, but all this amounts to letting off steam because all this activity is being countered by the encouragement to disruptive forces for political ends. Hatred and fear are being progressively encouraged, with the result that conditions are deteriorating further. All these factors add up to create a very unhealthy atmosphere for the emotional development of the younger generation and consequently one can see all the elements of individual disorganisation in the students of today—such elements as indiscipline, violence, disrespect, excessive sexual indulgence, crudity, use of intoxicants, gambling, etc.

4. Effect on moral development. Want of something and poverty are both mortal enemies of moral development and both of these elements can be seen in most Indian families. The situation in towns is much worse than in rural areas because children see so many scenes of violence and crime, immorality and cruelty, that they cannot avoid them. Apart from any other influence, the cinema alone is responsible for a great degree of moral depravity and degradation, and it is next to impossible to shield young boys and girls from its influence. The film industry is more concerned with making huge profits than with the influence their films are likely to have on the moral fibre of the people. And hence, art is used as an excuse to cover up exhibitions of immorality, sexual indulgence and violence, all of which tend to undermine the moral character of adolescents. In villages, poverty effectively takes care of any moralistic leanings, and they, too, are called upon to face many odd circumstances. Because of their ignorance and lack of education, they are not even aware of their rights, besides which justice in Indian courts is neither inexpensive nor expeditious so that they may be encouraged to fight for their rights. Those who do struggle for their rights are soon destroyed and worn out, and those who do not, succeed only in existing. The moral level of the villagers is lowered by lack of education, lack of sanitation and hygiene, insecurity, communalism, casteism and untouchability. One sometimes feels that the impersonal atmosphere of the towns is perhaps better and easier to contend with. In cities one finds certain areas designated as criminal areas, and children living here are taught the fundamentals of crime in their very early years. In cities like Bombay a very large number of juveniles are becoming involved in the illicit liquor, prostitution, gambling and other such evils which encourage juvenile delinquency on a large scale. The state can do little in such cases, and it is doing even less. The morals of the younger generation are further endangered by the disorganised set of moral and social values, caused by widespread differences of opinion about man-woman relations, sexual aberrations, earning of wealth, exploitation, social values, the aim of life, the duties of the individual, relationships between members of the family, etc. It is difficult for the youth to decide what is wrong and what is right in any of these matters, and it is only natural that in the absence of any guiding principle they should feel obligated to follow on the smooth flow of instinctive needs and their satisfaction. This kind of disorganisation of personality and character throws a lot of responsibility upon the leaders in the social, educational, economic and political spheres. It can also be alleged that many leaders connive at this growth in moral degeneration because their interests are linked with this deterioration. The problem is so complex that moral and religious preaching in schools will do little to stem the rot. What is required even more is to somehow do away with the set of circumstances which are responsible for lowering moral standards. Morality is not something to be taught, but a model to be presented by the conduct of elders, teachers and parents in the society. Moral education alone can never raise moral standards by itself. If a family is disorganised, the children cannot be saved by moralistic preaching. Characterless teachers cannot possibly achieve any moral improvement in the educand, and there can be no denying that the teaching posts are sometimes manned by individuals who have no moral values themselves and who do not hesitate even one minute to spread immorality among the educands. At the university level there is such great prevalence of nepotism, corruption, sexual indulgence and aberration, that if the truth be told, many parents would refuse to send their children for higher education to such institutions. Academic freedom is now merely a cloak for narrow mindedness. Even educational institutions are not free from the poison of casteism, communalism, linguism, regionalism, so much so that educational institutions are in fact playing a major role in spreading such disruptive sentiments among the younger generation. Briefly, there is a totality of circumstances which can only prevent any moral development in the child, and a detailed analysis of all of them would require a book of phenomenal size.

5. Social development The ideal of seeing oneself in all others has been part and parcel of Indian culture for ages, and as a consequence one finds that in India, particularly in the rural areas, there is a considerably high level of social exchange, organisation and adjustment. This is more true of the past than of the present, because in more recent years the detrimental effects of communalism, linguism, regionalism, etc., have been evident. They have cut into this social exchange and destroyed social feeling. Poverty and corruption have helped this disruptive process, and as a consequence one finds a very high incidence of disagreement, civil litigation, violence, theft, dacoity, prostitution, etc., in the villages, and sometimes even in the towns and cities. Social control practically ceased to exist, and has been replaced by selfishness and individualism. Materialism has practically replaced interest in religion. One finds that educated or literate villagers have even less of the social consciousness than their uneducated counterparts because they are less amenable to social control. In the urbanized areas this lack of social consciousness is evident in the impersonalism, materialism, selfishness, business like approach and corruption of the highest order, supplemented by a refusal to recognise even one's next door neighbour. As the city grows in size, this social consciousness seems to decrease in direct proportion, while in certain areas, such as the industrial and criminal infested areas, it has practically vanished. The disorganisation of the joint family has also been responsible for this deterioration in social feeling, a process which is being only encouraged by marital disagreements, maladjustment, etc. In schools and colleges one can see much the same kind of thing in the relationship between teacher and taught, and teacher and the school organisers. In the face of such disruptive factors, little can be done by organising a few isolated social programmes. Similarly, the efforts made by the committee for national integration are rapidly negated by the activities of political parties which are intent on spreading mutual hatred and jealousy among the various communities, social groups, classes, etc. On the one hand, people advocate the adoption of short programmes for encouraging social consciousness but on the other they themselves are responsible for growing gangsterism, groupism and other such anti-social activities within the school. All these are doing considerable harm to social development.

6. Effect on aesthetic development. The child's aesthetic development depends very much upon the beauty of the surroundings in which he is brought up, the beauty of the home, the school, the neighbourhood. In school his aesthetic development is helped along by some elementary training in the various arts, drawing and painting, singing, music, dramatics, etc. Many schools in the country provide specialized training in the arts. Efforts are also sometimes made to make the school buildings attractive and aesthetically appealing. But in actual fact the paucity of means makes such steps difficult and often colleges are not able to maintain beautiful buildings or lawns. In many cases one finds that the school or college presents an appearance little better than some factory. Yet, it must be remembered that it is the home which plays a larger part in the aesthetic development of the child, and in this respect the homes of a majority of children compare unfavourably with the school these children attend. Leaving aside the deliberate attempts at beautification, which require a definite economic standard, one finds that frequently children come from homes which do not even provide sufficient space for the large family to live cleanly and in normal privacy. In villages, one often finds the family and the domestic animals practically sharing a common shed, thus living in almost inconceivably unhygienic surroundings. How much aesthetic development can one expect from the child who spends much of his day playing naked in the dirty and dusty street outside his house. Towns are not much better than the villages in this respect, for many houses are not well lit, clean, located in densely populated areas, serviced by narrow, dark and appalling lanes. Little aesthetic progress ban be expected from children living in such homes.

7. Spiritual development. It has been the fond belief of many generations that Indian culture is basically spiritual, and that this inherent spirituality is steadily vanishing widen the impact of such modern tendencies as westernization, urbanization, industrialization, that spiritual values are being rapidly replaced by more material and secular values. This process is also being hastened by other co-operating factors such as endemic poverty, illiteracy, corruption, a numbing dirtyness, widespread communalism. Some educationists have advised the adoption of some kind of religious instruction in schools, and have been trying to convince the government that this would not constitute a violation of its professed secularism. Some political parties, the communist party among them, are violently averse to the adoption of any such moral or religious instruction, and one finds that religious instruction has not been so far introduced in the curriculum of most schools. In cities and towns, much of the religious teaching is hiding only certain vested interests of a social or political nature. Another thing which must be considered is the influence of science and technology and the great frequency with which religious riots between different religionists take place upon the basic faith in religion itself. Both have sought to weaken man's faith in religion, but despite this the introduction of religious instruction in schools will have some beneficial effect on the child's spiritual development. Otherwise, there is little if anything to hope for, because the atmosphere and environment existing in the country would discourage any kind of interest in spiritual matters. Certain other educationists have advocated the propagation of ancient Indian cultural and moral values through courses in ancient history. In fact, the entire system of education can be successfully Indianized by teaching all subjects in the Indian context, and thus the ancient values can once again be made popular. Although many private institutions are engaged in useful work in the direction of spiritual development of the younger generation, the state, too, must be convinced that the adoption of religious teaching in schools is not a reversal of its policy of secularism so that it can also play its part in introducing such education in institutions controlled or aided by it. Almost all educational philosophers of the country have supported this suggestion for moral instruction.

8. Effect on cultural development. In the good old days of ancient India, education sought first of all to make the child cultured and civilized, but in the present-day, educational institutions are concerned merely with acquainting the child with the various subjects put on the syllabus. The institutions care little whether the child acquires any culture in the process of education or not. Besides, the shortcomings that could be made up at home are not compensated because of the consistently widening generation gap and absence of social and family control. Society in general also provides a model only for such disruptive tendencies as classism, individualism, all of which promote selfishness, absolute liberty and disregard of laws. One finds little consideration and respect in the relations between teachers and students, parents and children, adults and young. Freedom and the rights of the individual are the call of the day, and they are only excuses for unbridled violence and indiscipline. Again, selfish politicians are encouraging instead of trying to arrest the process. Cultural development suffers another setback when the young see their elders raising their voice and hands against constituted authority in the form of the government. Even the social, educational, political and other circumstances obtaining in the country are not conductive to cultural development of any kind. Hence, one finds almost no cultural development in the present generation of children.

Having considered the impact of the Indian environment on the various aspects of the child's development, it is evident that considerable social reform will have to be undertaken, if the child's comprehensive development is to be ensured. This entire treatise was not to say that such conditions obtain in India alone, because such defective environment exists in many countries. Yet; instead of deriving consolation from this fact, it is better to try to improve things in our own country as best as we can, and according to our own lights. In trying to achieve the development of the child's character, care must be taken to see that it carries the imprint of Indianization, for such characteristic development is natural. If proper social conditions and a healthy environment is to be created, in order to faciliate the child's development, it will be necessary for parents, teachers and administrators to cooperate. In fact, the process of education as a process of complete development is not different from the process of universal progress. If there is any drawback or shortcoming in any part of the country, it inevitably has an adverse effect on the development of the younger generation. Educational institutions are only a normal part of the social organisation, and hence they can achieve nothing by isolating themselves from the social pattern. Hence, if the educational policy is to be successful, it will have to be treated as part of the programme of general development.

EDUCATION AND SOCIAL MOBILITY

One finds many castes, religious groups and social classes in India. These form important elements in the child's social environment and they influence his development. This influence can be briefly described as under:

1. Influence of castes. Under the Hindu social organisation, it is caste which determines the individual's status and position in the social hierarchy. One finds elements of the caste system even among the Muslims. In the caste, the professions and occupations of the lower castes are predetermined and fixed, and the child aims at adopting the occupation of his own caste. Since the child is almost compelled to adopt the same profession as his forefathers he is inevitably exposed to the rules of untouchability which operate between his caste and a superior caste. This creates very undesirable prejudices and gives rise to extreme narrow mindedness in the child. Although there are some advantages in adopting the hereditary occupation, it is undeniably unscientific in that it fails to consider the individual differences of the children and does not consider the actual suitability of the child to that particular occupation. The caste system has had the effect of splitting the society into many small segments, and this fragmentation obviously hinders the development of national unity. Besides, it is also responsible for the child's awareness of discrimination and distinction between individuals and the consequent feelings of superiority and inferiority. In this way, the presence of many different castes hinders the child's mental progress.

2. Impact of religious groups. In India one can see many religious groups such as Hindus, Muslims, Christians, Buddhists, etc., and some people have gone so far as to consider the Sikhs and Jains as distinct groups although, in fact, they are part of the Hindu community. Most of these religious groups have established and are maintaining many individual schools in which general religion is taught, along with their own respective religious teachings. Most of these schools try to inculcate a particular set of religious principles in the educand. In many ways the teaching of religious principles can be of benefit to the child and the community, but when teaching in one school contradicts or ridicules teaching in another school, it naturally gives rise to a consciousness of differences between one religion and another. The immediate consequence of this is communalism, which is instilled into the child's tender mind, and this prevents him from identifying himself with other members of the nation, and thus national unity suffers. The best course is to inculcate the general principles of religion, stressing the fact that all religions are one and the same, for without this, religion can only lead to narrow-minded thinking.

3. Impact of classes. Social class is the most potent influence on the child. On the one hand, we find a steady breakdown of discrimination based on religion and caste, but on the other we find a growing consciousness of the class one comes from thus intensifying the feeling of difference. This awareness, that one belongs to the lower, middle or upper class, is communicated to the child also. Consequently, children coming from the lower classes start with the sense of inferiority, of being poor, of deprivation of the good things of life. In reaction to this inferiority, many of them turn to criminal activity, because children from the upper classes find pleasure in displaying their superiority which has already created in them pride, vanity and a number of other ignominious emotions and sentiments. Comparatively, the child from the middle classes is less susceptible to either extremes of emotion for superiority on the one hand is reduced by consciousness of inferiority on the other, and this explains the reason why most middle class children show better performances in academic work than children from either of the two other classes. Some political ideologies also reinforce this awareness of the difference of class. It may have some dubious advantages, but it cannot be denied that on the whole it has a detrimental effect on the child's development, and that it practically obviates the possibility of ever generating any humane sentiments in them.

It is neither possible nor desirable to eliminate religious groups, classes or castes from society in order to protect the child from the evil influences of these social institutions. It is more practical to try to create an environment, at home and in school, which would counter such influences, or at least not reinforce them. The educator can take upon himself the duty of explaining to the child that discrimination on the basis of any one of these is artificial, and that it is not a sound criterion for distinguishing between one human being and another. This will help to make the children more humane and liberal in their approach.

17

EDUCATION AND MODERNIZATION IN INDIA

In the words of S.N. Eisenstadt, "Historically, modernization is the process of change towards those types of social, economic and political systems that have developed in Western Europe and North America from the seventeenth century to the nineteenth and have been spread to other European countries and in the nineteenth and twentieth centuries to the South American, Asian, and African continents".[1] Modernization is the characteristic feature of modern society.

CHARACTERISTICS OF MODERNIZATION

The process of modernization becomes evident from its characteristics. Following are its chief characteristics:

1. Social mobilization. Social mobilization is that process by which the old social, economic and psychological elements are transformed and new social values of human conduct are set up. The social mobilization is a peculiarity of modernization.

2. Social differentiation. Another feature of modernization is social differentiation. In this process there is increase in the complexity in social, political and economic activities and there is progress in the activities of individuals in various fields. Industrialization is a result of modernization. In politics the administrative complexity in the central and local bodies is a characteristic of modernization. The political power gets dispersed among adults. Thus modernization is a way to democratization. As a result of modernization new trends in philosophy, religion, science and literature become visible. Briefly, an increase in modernization leads to a progress in social, economic, political and cultural fields, there is more differentiation in these.

3. Structural differentiation and change. Another characteristic of modernization is structural differentiation and continuous change. In the social and economic fields old organizations break up yielding place to new. In political field new parties emerge. The cottage industries are replaced by big industries. The new means of production develop. Many new professions develop. The 'production becomes more complex.

1. Eisenstadt, S.N., *Modernization: Protest and Change*, Prentice-Hall of India Pvt. Ltd., New Delhi, 1969, p. 1.

4. **Change in organizational and status system.** A feature of modern society is the emergence of a number of specialized organizations. Secondly, there is greater division of labour. Thirdly, the organizations based on close kinship lose in importance. With the acceleration in the speed of change the status of individuals and families undergoes change. New classes emerge in society. From the cultural and economic viewpoint there come into being three classes, namely, upper, middle and lower.

5. **Urbanization.** The phenomena of urbanization and modernization are interlinked, one leads to the other.

6. **Social and political movements.** An important feature of modernization is the emergence of new social and political movements which aim at the transformation of society. This transformation becomes imperative in order to make man adjust to fast changing conditions. These movements also aim at casting off orthodoxy and paving the ground for change to modernity. In order to attain the new aims, a change of outlook becomes imperative.

7. **Comprehensive and multi-sided education.** An important aim of modernization is the spread of education. In modern society it is tried that all should be educated. Besides academic education under modernization, the need for technical and professional education becomes acute, therefore, many technical and professional institutes spring up to meet this demand.

8. **Development of international co-operation.** Lastly, the development of international co-operation is the aim of modernisation. The national movements gave birth to many nations. For the development of mutual relations among nations, a League of Nations and later U. N.O. came into existence.

MEANS OF MODERNIZATION

After discussing the characteristics of modernization, the means of modernization will now be discussed:

1. **Industrialization.** In modern countries industrialization is going on at fast pace. The Western countries, in particular U.S.A., have helped underdeveloped countries in industrialization. In order to meet the demands of fast growing population, every country must perforce become industrialized. Therefore, India is fully resolved to bring about fast industrialization.

2. **Urbanization.** The fast growth of population of this country in the last 50 years has led to fast urbanization in India. The fast industrialization and consequent urbanization has led to many ticklish problems like slums, crimes, etc. In order to solve these problems town planning is imperative.

3. **Secularization.** Secularization is a consequence of urbanization. The people of India have adopted the ideal of secularism according to which everybody is free to follow the religion of his choice. Modern society is pluralist. Compassion and tolerance are the chief characteristics of modernization.

4. **Rise of new social classes.** The traditional social classification in India is based upon caste system. The caste is incompatible with the egalitarian social values. Under it the status of a person is determined by his birth. Whatever may have been

the merit and use of caste system in the past, there is little doubt that in the modern society it is an obstructive force; it is retrograde; it is against the democratic values. Due to current politicization the importance of caste system is growing; but from all other viewpoints its value and importance is declining. Today, both in the towns and villages, the people are divided into classes which are based upon economic and political rather than caste considerations. The distinction between lower, middle and high classes is exclusively economic. The classes based on economic considerations are non-hereditary. A low class person, by dint of his labour and application, may belong to upper class to-morrow. The importance of money and possessions in modern society is paramount. With increasing politicization there is now clear-cut demarcation between those in power and those out of it. Mostly, economically better off, persons are politically also better off, but this is not essential. The political leaders class in India is other than the economically rich but the economically rich support politicians with money and use them.

The industrialization is giving rise to an organised labour classes and the communist thinking is creeping in Indian society. With the organization of labour class the capitalist class is also getting organized and they have formed many associations to protect their interest. While there are all India labour organizations there are also all India associations of the capitalists.

5. Social change. Modernization accelerates the pace of change; it is quickened. The change is both the characteristic and goal of social change. Change is a cultural goal towards which every society advances. The change must be towards the achievement of greater human dignity and greater social equality. It is progress towards democratic values. The social change can be seen in diverse fields. On the one hand, social movements have greatly changed our ideas and concepts about various social matters and on the other youth movement has brought about revolutionary change in the thinking and aspirations of youth. The youth movement can be seen all over the world, this is an important characteristic of modernisation and the pace of modernization gets accelerated by these movements. The youth movement is a rebellious against the traditional values and is a harbinger of new shape of things to come. Today, a particular attention is being paid to encourage youth movements at the university level. From time to time youth functions and festivals are held in the universities in which young persons from all over the country participate. This encourages national integration and also shows the basis for building up the future. In India the youth movements can be seen in the form of student movements. The youth are demanding the right to participate in the administrative affairs of the universities. The modern youth is busy evaluating the educational curriculum and also the efficacy and utility of examinations. These matters become a bone of contention among the students and university authorities.

6. Westernization. The trend towards modernization in India can be seen in the form of a movement towards westernization of the society. The trend towards westernization can be seen in all fields. In social, economic, political, cultural, religious and educational spheres, India is following the example of the West. Even those who are in favour of retaining the traditional values also want to utilize the good traits of the Western system. They want a synthesis of Western and Indian values. The westernization leads to modernization. In the social sphere we are following West in matters like dress, lifestyle and town-planning, etc. The latest fashions of the West are quickly followed by the Indian elite. There is more of westernization in the technical and scientific spheres than in the social spheres. This has given rise to cultural lag. In the social fields we are still sticking to the obscurantist values of casteism, communalism and parochialism.

7. Democratization. In the field of politics the most characteristic feature of modernization is the process of democratization. India is becoming progressively democratized. There is in India universal adult franchise. Everybody above a certain age is entitled to elect his representative. Everybody is equal before law and enjoys equal rights and privileges. In the economic sphere an attempt is being made to reduce economic disparities. The compulsory primary education is aiming at universal literacy. All political parties are wedded to the value of equality, liberty and freedom. There may be differing viewpoints regarding the means to attain these values but there is no dispute about their validity and acceptance as the ultimate goals of political endeavour. Though it is undeniable that there was a tradition of democracy in the ancient India, but the modern democratic tradition in India is following the West. In the promotion of democracy in the West, U.S.A. in particular, has helped a great deal.

EDUCATION AND MODERNIZATION

S.N. Eisenstadt has rightly pointed out, "Perhaps the best starting point for the analysis of the characteristics in the educational institutions in modern societies is the pattern of demands for and the supply of educational services that tended to develop with modernization."[2] In the words of Yogendra Singh, "...education has been one of the most influential instruments of modernization in India. It has led to the mobilization of people's aspiration for nationalism, liberalism and freedom. It alone has been responsible for the growth of an enlightened intelligentsia which carried forward not only a movement for independence but also a relentless struggle for social and cultural reforms."[3]

The most important function of education is modernization. Modernization is a comprehensive concept aimed at capturing, describing and evaluating profound qualitative and quantitative changes in society. It describes the transition of a society from medieval to modern culture. It stands for progress beyond tradition. Modernization according to some sociologists is based upon European and American models. As compared to urbanization, industrialisation, westernization and Europeanization, modernization presents a more complex process and a more complex result. In the intellectual sphere it is an awareness that it is possible to see a rational explanation of physical and social phenomena. Thus, it is represented by positivism and empiricism and rationalism. In the field of religion it is expressed in secularism. Its approach is this-worldly. In philosophy it is expressed in humanist thought. It includes social mobilization and differentiation

2. *Ibid.*, p. 16.
3. Yogendra Singh, *Modernization of Indian Tradition*, 1973, p. 106

and specialization in individual and institutional activities. In political field it stands for democratization. In ecology it is characterised by advancing degree of urbanization. But the most important feature of modernization as related to education is cultural. In cultural sphere its symptoms have been pointed out by A.R. Desai as follows:[4]

1. Growing differentiation of the major elements of cultural systems, "The spread of literacy and secular education, a more complex, intellectual and institutional system for the cultivation and advancement of specialized roles based on intellectual disciplines".
2. Emergence of a new cultural outlook characterised by emphasis on progress and improvement, on happiness and spontaneous expression of abilities and feelings, on the development of individuality as a value and efficiency.
3. Emergence of a new personality orientation, traits and characteristics revealed in greater ability to adjust to the broadening societal horizons: some ego-flexibility; widening spheres of interests; growing potential empathy with other people and situations; a growing evaluation of self-advancement and mobility; a growing emphasis on the present as the meaningful temporal dimension of human existence; a growing awareness of dignity of others and an increased disposition to respect them; a growing awareness in the individual that "his world is calculable, that other people and institutions around him can be relied on to fulfil their delegation and responsibilities," growing faith in sciences and technology and a growing awareness that, "rewards should be according to contribution and not according to either whim or special properties of person not relating to his contribution".
4. Finally, modernization implies, "the ability of society to develop an institutional structure capable of adjusting to continually changing problems and demands". The emergence of such a flexibility constitutes, according to Prof. Eisenstadt, the central issue and challenge of modernization.

Education is the most important instrument of modernization since modernization includes[5]:

1. Directed change in the system of attitudes, beliefs and values, and also in the institutional complex, to enhance the acceptability of modern technology and its organizational and operational framework.
2. Growth of the infrastructure essential to the adaptation to technology of foreign origin to specific national needs; and
3. Laying the foundations of institutions and organizations which could, in time, assume responsibility for independent innovation and technological growth to the country's needs and problems.

In view of the abovementioned changes required by modernization the functions of education in this direction may be achieved by the following:[6]

---

4. Desai, A.R., Need for Revaluation of the Concept, in Desai, A.R. (Ed.): *Essays on Modernization of Undeveloped Societies*. Vol. I. Thacker and Co., Bombay, 1971, pp. 462.-63.
5. *Ibid*, Vol. II, p. 506.
6. *Ibid.*, pp. 507-08.

1. By enlarging the cognitive map of those exposed to it, education suggests alternatives to tradition, brings into focus the rewards implicit in them, and indicates—roughly at least—the paths through which the new goals with their attendant regards can be achieved. It broadens mental horizons, raises expectations and predisposes people to make experiments.
2. As an instrument of socialization it can project new images and values. Purposively used, it can be a help in obliterating attitudes and behaviour patterns that are dysfunctional to programmes of modernization.
3. By providing ideological articulation it can promote the development of national consciousness and can help people see their needs and their problems in a national perspective. This can stimulate the creation of a national consensus at least on major issues.
4. Education provides a highway to elite status of the educand. The educands provide a reference model to the masses, who, in imitation of the former, take the first steps away from tradition. Modernizing elites are almost always the products of modern or semi-modern school/university systems.
5. Problems—solving leadership—scientists and technicians, management experts and administration—with the requisite knowledge and skills, can only be expected to emerge out of the educational system. Large-scale programmes of modernization demand specialists of several types at different levels and look to the educational system for a steady flow of technocrats, planners and managers to operate them.
6. Education is a mobility multiplier. Although its impact is on the immobility of thought ways, in the long run it does alter rigid forms of social stratification. Modernization requires both types of mobility.

In sum, with proper planning and under efficient direction, education can make a meaningful contribution to the attainment of modernization. It can be harnessed to diffuse attitudes and ideologies required for the adoption of modern technology and its associated values and organizational premises, to provide personnel to operate and sustain the programmes of modernization and to create capabilities for adaptation and origination of new technology.

MODERNIZATION AND INSTITUTIONAL EDUCATION

Researches have been conducted in West and India about the role of educational institutions in bringing about modernization. Most of them have shown a positive correlation between the two. However, Saunders, in his study *Education and Modernization in Brazil* has found that it undermines modernity. He remarks: "Brazilian schools, especially at the primary level where their impact on personality development is greatest, tend to stifle rather than develop the personality traits on which modernization depends, and from which the society must draw its innovators".[7] Lerner in his research work *The Passing of Traditional Society Modernising the Middle East* (1963), on the basis of his study with adult samples of

7. Saunders, John V.D. (1969), "Education and Modernization in Brazil". In: Eric N. Barklanoff (ed.). *The Shaping of Modern Brazil.* Baton Rogue: Louisiana State University Press .

six developing countries, asserted that literacy is the basic personal skill underlying the modernization process. Joseph A. Kahl in his research, *The Measurement of Modernism: A Study of Values in Brazil and Mexico* (University of Texas Press, 1968), pointed out significant correlation between education and modernization. Reporting results of the Harward's project on the social and cultural aspects of economic development, covering Argentina, Chili, India, Pakistan, Israel, and Nigeria, Inkeles concluded that, "Education is the most powerful factor in making men modern".[8] In their study based on 5 national probability samples of adult age, 20 and older, drawn from the U.S.A., Finland, Japan, Mexico and Costarica, Waisanen and Kumata, concluded positive correlationship between education and various indicators of modernity.[9]

Examining the immediate effects of schooling on people's modernity Armer and Youtz concluded, "Western education leads to the modernization of perspectives in traditional, non-industrial societies".[10] After a study of 591 seventeen years old males in Kano City in Nigeria they maintain," 'Western education does indeed have a definite effect on value orientations of youth that is largely independent on test factor".[11] This has been collaborated by S.L. Sharma in his work *Modernizing Effects of University Education* published by Indian Council of Social Science Research in 1979. This conclusion has been again supported by articles in a special number of *International Journal of Comparative Sociology* (1974, XIV, 3-4). In this special number, researches conducted independently in various parts of the world, showed remarkable uniformity in concluding that schooling promotes attitudinal modernity in developing societies.

Besides the relation of schooling and modernization researches have been conducted about the effect of higher education on modernity. Williamson, studying university students in the United States, Germany, Japan and Columbia, concluded that while Americans and Columbians are at the conservative end the Japanese are on the other end of the scale of rationalism-traditionalism developed by Kahl.[12] Similar researches were conducted by some other notable sociologists in the West including Silberman (1970), Greer, (1972), Smith and Inkeles (1966), Sack (1973), etc. In India studies concerning schooling and social change were conducted by A.R. Desai, (1952), G. S. Bhatnagar (1972), and Margaret L. Cormack (1961). Cormack made a full length study of Indian students concerning social change. She concluded, "They are not considering values, attitudes and attitudinal change. They are concerned with certificates, degrees and employment".[13] Thus Cormack

8 Inkeles, Alex (1969), "Making Men Modern". *American Journal of Sociology* 75 (2): 208- 225.

9 Waisanen, F.B. and Hideya Kumata (1972), "Education, Functional Literacy, and Participation in Development." *International Journal of Comparative Sociology*, XIII (1): 21-35.

10 Armer, Michael and Robert Youtz (1971), "Formal Education and Individual Modernity in an African Society." *American Journal of Sociology*, 76 (4): 604-626.

11 Ibid.

12 Williamson, Robert C. (1970), "Modernism and Related Attitudes: An International Comparison Among University Students". *International Journal of Comparative Sociology.* XI (2): 130-145.

13 Cormack, Margaret L. (1961), She who Rides a Peacock, p. 2278.

maintained negative correlation between higher education and social change in India. She found little evidence of change orientation among her respondents. Similar conclusion was reached by B. V. Shah (1964) in his study *Social Change among College Students of Gujarat* (Baroda: Maharaja Shivaji Rao University). Y.B. Damley in his study *College Youth in Poona,* however, found some positive correlation between higher education and individuation, a trait of modernization. But he himself admits, "It is not a study of the general body of students. Therefore, no generalizations can be drawn about the nature of the student's behaviour or thinking".[14] M.S. Gore, I.P. Desai and Suma Chitnis found encouraging evidence of the relation between education and modernization. According to them, "The state, sex and educational level of the respondents were all important variables in determining the modernity of student sample".[15] Similar conclusion was reached by Malik and Marquette in their study *Changing Social Values of College Students in the Punjab.* They concluded that, "...an overwhelming majority of Punjab youth favours the abolition of such traditional institutions and caste and untouchability and strongly approves of a general social revolution in India'.[16] In his book *Education in Social Change* Sullivan found that, "Factors other than experience at a particular training college appear to be operative in changing that student's outlook towards traditional social practices".[17]

The latest study in this connection was however made by Dr. S.L. Sharma published by ICSSR (1979) under the title *Modernizing Effects of University Education.* On the basis of a study of 3437 students in the 34 teaching departments of Panjab University during the academic year 1934-74, Dr. Sharma reached the following important conclusions concerning the relationships of modernization and education:

1. The level of higher education is of no consequence as an explanatory variable of student modernity.
2. There is the lowest percentage of moderns in the humanities, followed by social sciences and professionals with the highest percentage in the science faculty.
3. Males are more modern than females.
4. High status students are more modern than low status students.
5. There is a significant and positive correspondence between level of student modernity and that of their reference teachers, provided the latter preferred character-building role, over other roles, favoured no social distance in their relations with students and reported greater interpersonal interaction with students
6. There is a weak though positive relationship between years of hostel exposure and modernity's course.

---

14. Damle, Y.B. (1966), *College Youth in Poona: A Study of Elite in the Making,* Mimeographed Poona: Deccan College, p. 13.
15. Gore, M.S., I.P. Desai, and Suma Chitnis (1970), *Field Studies in the Sociology of Education,* New Delhi, NCERT, p. 584.
16. Malik, Yogendra K. and Jesse F. Marquette, 1974. "Changing Social Values of College Students in the Punjab," *Asian Survey* 14 (9): 795-806.
17. Sullivan, Edward Eugene, *Education in Social Change,* Bombay, Asia Publishing House, 1968.

7. Age is found to be inversely related to student modernity. Boys out scored girls in modernity.
8. Caste has no bearing on modernity.
9. A significantly larger percentage of high modernity cases hails from medium size families with 4 to 6 numbers.
10. Family type has no association with modernity.
11. Socio-economic status of the family has a significant though weak positive relationship with modernity.
12. Father's education and occupation are only weakly related to student modernity.
13. Father's income has a moderately strong positive association with modernity.
14. There is no relationship between parental modernity and student modernity.
15. Students with early urban background are not more modern than those with rural background.
16. Those who have lived longer in urban setting are more modern than those with fewer years of urban dwelling.
17. The initial exposure to cosmopolitan city like Chandigarh makes not much difference in modernity.
18. Duration of urban exposure is positively associated with modernity.
19. Early residential background and modernism of the city have no influence on student modernity.
20. There is a significant and positive relationship between media exposure and modernity.
21. There is a strong positive relationship between extent of exposure to other cultures and level of modernity.
22. Constant exposure to other cultures significantly increases the negative effect of education on modernity.
23. The convent and or public school educated students are more modern than the government and/or aided school educated.
24. The type of schooling is the best predictor of modernity with the convent or public school educated being most modern.
25. Early socialization variables account for greater variance in student modernity than the later socialisation variables.
26. Developmental variables are more powerful than structural variables in explaining student modernity.
27. Educational variables, particularly schooling background, tops the list of explanatory variables.[18]

On the basis of the above conclusions Dr. S.L. Sharma points out inverse relationship between the level of higher education and the student modernity. He gives the following reasons for this surprising fact:

18. *Op. cit* pp. 184-193.

1. The present higher education stresses mere transmission of information to the neglect of inculcating ability to think for one self. It stresses mere skill acquisition to the neglect of generating this position, for skill formation. It neglects character training and stresses mere certification for white collar jobs.
2. The system of higher education in India lacks an articulate social ideal.
3. The present educational system has not changed in the life of goals set by the Constitution of free India.
4. The present system of education is not a source of characterological transformation.
5. The course content of the present higher education does not lead to modernisation.
6. The cognitive and value content in conjunction with the social context of the present higher education is not relevant to the cultivation of modernity.
7. Our teachers are not so modern as to influence the student. They are not interested in character building and social training. They are unsure of what the community expects from them. The persistent authoritarian orientation limits the power of teachers to act as agents of student modernity.
8. The objective conditions in our educational institutions such as overcrowded classes, low teacher-pupil ratio, impersonal character of teacher-taught relationship, render the task of change orientation on the part of the teacher the more difficult. Small classes are better for such influence than large and unwieldy classes
9. The lack of freedom for the teacher to design his own courses restricts considerably his potential for induction for social change. In the words of Dr. S.L. Sharma, "Our teachers thus presented a case of double failure as socializers of student modernity; first, they lacked strong modernity orientation, and second, they failed to modify their role orientations so as to bring them in line with modern norms"[19]
10. The extra academic component of campus climate restricts its relevance to modernity.
11. Routinization of educational experience is a possible reason for the failure of higher education as a modernizer.
12. The overgrown structural fonnat of higher education is a significant reason for its failure to modernize.
13. The built-in traits of present higher education such as under emphasis on the value element in its course content, are responsible for its poor performance.

Dr. Sharma suggests the following three objectives as the aims of higher education to make it a better instrument of modernization[20]:

1. To prepare skilled manpower for a developing economy;

19. *Ibid.*, p. 198.
20. *Ibid.*, pp. 209-210.

2. To re-socialize people in the values conducive to socio-economic development; and

3. To inculcate in man a creative self-awareness, an ability to think for himself and a sense of critical judgement.

He suggests that three areas should be particularly modernised: the reorientation of the content, the recasting of the teaching-learning nexus and improving the quality of education. The quality of early education should be improved. Group extracurricular activities should be encouraged. A secular-rational and egalitarian man should be created. To conclude, "Besides providing the highly skilled manpower to a technico-industrial economy, higher education in our view can lay down the foundation of socio-economic development in the following ways: 1. by imparting to the younger generation the requisite psychological dispositions which are regarded as helpful for development; and 2. by instilling in students a reflective ability and a capacity to make rational decisions.[21]

TWO PATTERNS OF MODERNISATION

In his paper Social Change and Educational Policy published in *The Sociology of Education in India* (NCERT, 1967), Professor A.R. Desai accepts two patterns of modernisation of a traditional society pointed out by Don Martingale-exogenous and endogenous. He defines these two patterns by pointing out that, "An exogenous factor is one arising outside the social system, and endogenous is one arising internal to the social system".[22] Both these factors initiate and shape social change. They determine the nature of leadership and its basic aim. These in their turn determine the objectives of education, the structure of the machinery of education, technical and other means of spread, the allocation of finances of education and the nature of personnel executing it.

Historically, the modernization process worked differently in the capitalist and the non-capitalist countries. In U.S.A. it grew in three phases merchantilist, *laissez faire* and monopoly. It developed a massive formal education system. This system though basically the same, changed according to changing circumstances in each country. Not only in Europe but also in Africa, Asia and Latin America the modernization process transformed the politico-economic and socio-cultural structures. However, the colonial hold on these nations was maintained. Thus modernization in colonial countries was brought about by the foreign rulers and exogenous factor. In communist countries on the other hand, modernization developed on non-capitalist lines aiming at the establishment of a social structure based upon collective ownership and meeting the assessed needs of the citizen. After the Second World War these countries developed a modern educational system different from that evolved in capitalist countries. The countries liberated from colonial subjugation engaged in modernization according to their specific

21. *Ibid.*, p. 213.
22. Op. Cit., p. 91.

conditions aiming at over coming backwardness by rapid industrialisation and social institutional reconstruction. According to Professor A.R. Desai, "The two patterns of modernization, *viz.*, modernization on the capitalist and the non-capitalist basis have the following implications for their educational systems:

(i) They provide different aims and approaches to the content of education and to the communication process.

(ii) They result in different attitudes towards education.

(iii) They determine different methods of providing finances for education.

(iv) They also generate different patterns of organisation of education.[23]

In capitalist countries education was considered as a commodity purchased by the consumer at different prices in the market. Thus it depends on the purchasing capacity of the family and group that the individual gets a particular type of education. In non-capitalist countries, however, education was considered a vital need and a fundamental right and therefore provided as free communal service by the society. Besides the aims and approaches and attitude, the methods of providing finance for education also differed in capitalist and non-capitalist countries. In capitalist countries finances for education were provided by individuals, private societies, endowments and the government. Thus the government is one of the competing financiers though being the supreme it frames laws to regulate education market. It reserves certain aspects of education which are essential for the community. It also takes such measures as are required to safeguard the educational interests of the handicapped and backward groups. In non-capitalist countries, however, the entire responsibility for educational finance is the burden of the state. Finally, there are two patterns of organisations of education in capitalist and non-capitalist societies. In the former it is made of an amalgam of the heterogeneous bodies and groups providing finances. In non-capitalist countries there are no diversities and conflicts in several agencies controlling education as the total control is in the hands of the state in the name of the society.

23. *Ibid.*, pp. 93-94.

18

SOCIAL CHANGE AND EDUCATION

WHAT IS SOCIAL CHANGE?

Social change is the change in society. Society is a web of social relationships. Hence, social change is a change in social relationships. It is the change in these which alone we shall regard as social change. What are social relationships? Social relationships include social processes, social patterns and social interactions. These include the mutual activities and relations of the various parts of society. In the words of Jones, "Social change is a term used to describe variations or modifications of any aspect of social processes, social patterns, social interactions, or social organization. Thus, social change is a change in the social organization. It is in this sense that Davis has written, "By social change is meant only such alternations as secure in social organization—that is, the structure and functions of society." Social change can be observed in every society. Describing social change in detail, Merril and Eldredge have said, "Social change means that large numbers of persons are engaging in activities that differ from those which they or their immediate (forefathers) engaged in some time before".

Society is composed of a vast and complex network of patterned human relationships in which all men participate. When human behaviour is in the process of modification, this is only another way of indicating that social change is occurring. Human society is constituted of human beings. Thus, whatever apparent alteration in the mutual behaviour between individuals takes place is a sign of social change. This fact of social change can be verified by glancing at the history of any society. Man is a dynamic being. Hence, society can never remain static. It undergoes constant variation.

FACTORS OF SOCIAL CHANGE

What are the factors due to which social relationships undergo constant alterations? Some writers consider diffusion to be the main factor of social change while some other writers consider invention in a similar capacity. Actually, both diffusion and invention have a hand in the change which besets social relationships Roughly, the main causes of social change are the cultural, technological, biological, population, environment, psychological and other factors.

1. Cultural factors. The main cause of social change is the cultural factor. Changes in the culture are accompanied by social changes. Max Weber has proved this hypothesis by a comparative study of religious and economic institutions.

Actually, no one can deny that changes and variations in culture inevitably influence social relationships. Culture gives speed and direction to social change and determines the limits beyond which social changes cannot occur. This, however, does not warrant the conclusion that there is no distinction between social and cultural change. Actually, the filed of social change is limited in comparison with the field of cultural change.

2. Technological factors. The technological factor has immense influence in social change. To quote Ogburn, "Technology changes society by changing our environments to which we in turn adapt. This change is usually in the material environment and the adjustment we make to the changes often modifies customs and social institutions. In this way, the incessant increase in new machines and methods due to new discoveries has had a very great influence upon social relationships. The form of society is undergoing change as a result of the development and invention of electric, steam and petrol driven machines for production, the means of transport and communication and various mechanical appliances in everyday life. Even institutions like family and marriage have not remained immune to the effect of these developments. The explicit effects of technological advance are labour organization, division of labour, specialization, high speed of life, increase in production, etc. In the modern age technological factors are among the predominant causes of social changes.

3. Biological factors. Biological factors too have some indirect influence upon social change. Among the biological factors is the qualitative aspect of the population related to heredity. The qualitative aspect of population is based upon powerful and great men and mutation. Hence, biological factors play a part in social change to that extent. In addition to this, the biological principles of natural selection and struggle for survival are constantly producing alterations in society.

4. Population factors. Even changes in the quality and size of the population have an effect upon the social organization as well as customs and traditions, institutions, associations, etc. Increase and decrease of population, a change in the ratio of men and women, young and old, have an effect upon social relationships. Decrease or increase in the population has an immediate effect upon economic institutions and associations. The ratio of men to women in a society affects marriage, family and the condition of women in society. In the same way the birth and death rates, etc., also influence social change.

5. Environmental factors. The geographists have emphasized the impact of geographical environment upon human society. Huntington has gone so far as to assert that an alteration in the climate is the sole cause of the evolution and devolution of civilizations and cultures. Even if these claims of the geographists are to be discarded, it cannot be denied that floods, earthquakes, excessive rain, drought, change of season, etc., have significant effect upon social relationships and these are modified by such natural occurrences.

6. Psychological factors. Most sociologists regard psychological factors as important elements in social change. The cause of social changes is the psychology of man himself. Man is by nature a lover of change. He is always trying to discover new things in every sphere of his life and is always anxious for novel experiences. As a result of this tendency, the mores, traditions, customs, etc., of every human society are perpetually undergoing change. This does not mean that man always considers the new to be superior to the old. While he is always attending to what is new and unique he also wants to preserve what is old. The form of social relationships is constantly changing in the process of interaction between these two tendencies. New customs and methods which replace the old traditional customs are being formed. Old traditions are respected but time demands change and adaptation to changing conditions. Change is the law of life. When changes do not occur at the appropriate time, revolutions take place, wars are fought, epidemics spread and changes are violently introduced.

7. Other factors. In addition to the abovementioned factors, another factor of social change is the appearance of new opinions and thoughts. For example, changes in the attitudes towards dowry, caste system, female education, etc., have resulted in widespread social variations and modifications. In fact, a majority of the social revolutions take place as a result of the evolution of new ways of thinking. Similarly, war is also a cause of social change because it influences the population, the economic situation and ratio of males to females, etc. In the same way, social changes are introduced by the advent of great thinkers as Gandhi and Karl Marx, etc.

RESULT OF SOCIAL CHANGE

The form of each aspect of social life is being continually transformed due to the effect of the abovementioned factors which cause social change. New institutions and associations are being formed and destroyed in the social, economic, political, cultural and verily, in all spheres. The form of family, marriage, state, religion, culture, educational system and economic and social structures, is continually changing and transforming, as a result of which, a change occurs in the life of the individual and subsequently in his relations with others. To take an example, the result of social change can be well understood and realized by studying the history of the objectives, structures, forms, importance and functions, etc., of the family from the early past to the present-day. Similarly, all the changes and differences that can be seen between the tribal society and the present-day society can be attributed to social change.

EDUCATION AND SOCIAL CHANGE

The functions of education in the sphere of social change are outlined as follows:

1. Assistance in adopting social change. Whenever some social change occurs, it results in changes in the pattern of doing some work. This change is easily adopted by some people while others find it very difficult to adjust themselves to this change. It is the aim of education to make all good changes easily accessible to every person. In India, a large majority of people found it difficult to reconcile themselves to the changes that occurred in the institutions of family and marriage, but the educated minority soon realized the advantages of these changes. Later on, as education spread to other sections of society, the importance and value of these changes came to be recognized more universally. For this reason, it is now generally accepted that before bringing about any social change in society, it is necessary to create a receptive temper of mind among the people. Otherwise, there is invariably some resistance to change.

2. Overcoming resistance to change. Certain factors make it easy for some social innovation to be adopted and accepted, but on the other hand, certain factors create resistance to acceptance. The best way of overcoming such resistance is education. Through the medium of education, the importance of social change is convincingly explained to the people so that they are purged of their prejudices and blind faith, and thus, enabled and also strengthened to accept something new.

3. Analysis of change. But society does not progress with any and every change, and neither does the individual. Progress occurs only when the change leads the society to more desirable social values. And for this, analysis and criticism of social change is essential. Only the educated individual can make valid criticisms and offer constructive suggestions, because it is education which invests the individual with the capacity to use his intelligence, to distinguish between right and wrong and to establish certain ideals. Education determines the values which act as a criterion for the analysis of social change. Through this analysis and criticism, undesirable social changes are prevented and desirable social changes encouraged. In every society, this is achieved only through the efforts of rational and educated people.

4. Emergence of new changes. Since the educated class is constantly engaged in an analysis of contemporary society, it also makes frequent suggestions for improvement. It is on the basis of such suggestions that social reform movements are set into motion. The flood of social reform movements that was witnessed at the turn of the century was due to modern education. Educated people made a study of western societies and their institutions compared both with our own, and agitated public opinion towards the abolition of many social evils such as child marriage, objections to widow re-marriage, unequal rights of women, the custom of women committing sati, etc. Only through education could the importance of such changes be made apparent to the people. It was through education alone that public opinion could be turned in favour of these changes. Hence, it is the educated class in every society which initiates, guides and controls movements for social reform.

5. Leadership in social change. If social change is to be directed properly, it is necessary to have able leadership, well acquainted with the complexity of the problem. Such leaders can be created only through education. For this reason social welfare workers must first be educated before they are unleashed on society. On the one hand, education creates in them a consciousness of social change, while on the other, it teaches them to distinguish between the good and the bad. Education in India must be able to create appropriate leadership at every level if social changes conducive to democracy are to be introduced.

6. Educating the people of social change. Only a properly organized system of education can generate in the people of a society the ability to adopt some social change. As a result of education, individuals learn to analyse their customs and traditions, to criticise them and to cooperate in movements for social reform. The educational system has played a major role in bringing about revolutionary social changes in England, France, America and Russia.

7. Advances in the sphere of knowledge. New researches and inventions all depend upon education, because only the educated individual can search for new things in every sphere. Only such people can help in the progress of non-material culture. Fresh discoveries in the sphere of knowledge provide the right basis for criticism of society. Then the need for change becomes apparent. Thus, education contributes to social change by bringing changes in knowledge.

It is evident from the above account that educationists, educators and schools have a tremendous respectability in social change. Defective education leads to defective social changes. Hence, if society is to change in the right direction, it is essential that attention be paid to the educational system because this alone can create future generations of critics of change and leaders of reform.

19

SOCIAL CONTROL AND EDUCATION

Social control is the control of society over the individual. Some of man's tendencies are beneficial to society while others are detrimental to its interest. There can be no question of controlling the beneficial tendencies. Thus, social control is exercised by society over the undesirable or harmful tendencies of man. But is social control merely negative? Is controlling some tendencies its sole function? No, social control creates those conditions in which man can be socialised and be prevented from performing anti-social activities. Some control comprehends all those processes, methods, mores, patterns, etc., which render assistance in this work. In this way, the term social control is fairly comprehensive. This is not governmental control. Governmental control is based upon law and is enforced upon the individual externally. Social control is self-control. It keeps on changing in accordance with the changes in society.

DEFINITIONS OF SOCIAL CONTROL

The various definitions of social control, as provided by the sociologists, are not identical. Some main definitions are the following:

1. Brearly. "Social control is a collective term for those processes and agencies, planned and unplanned, by which individuals are taught, persuaded or compelled to conform to the usages and values of the group to which they belong." It is clear from this definition that social control includes those laws by which an individual behaves in concurrence with the mores of group.

2. Gillin and Gillin. "Social control is that system of measures, suggestion, persuasion, restraint and coercion by whatever means, including physical force, by which a society brings into conformity to the approved pattern of behaviour a subgroup or by which a group moulds into conformity its members."

3. MacIver and Page. "By social control is meant the way in which the entire social order coheres and maintains itself, how it operates, as a changing equilibrium."

4. Gurvitch and Moore. "Social control can be defined as the sum total or rather the whole of cultural patterns, social symbols, collective spiritual meanings, values, ideas and ideals, as well as acts or processes, directly connected with them, whereby, inclusive of society, every particular group and every participating individual member overcome tensions and conflicts within themselves through temporary equilibria and take steps for new creative efforts."

This definition of social control is adequately comprehensive. It has taken into account both the negative and creative aspects of social control and has indicated the means and processes of social control.

TYPES OF SOCIAL CONTROL

1. Karl Mannheim's View. Different sociologists held differing views upon the types of social control. Karl Mannheim has accepted the following two types of social control:

(i) *Direct social control.* This is the control exercised upon the individual by the reactions of the people living in proximity. Such control is found existing in the family, neighbourhood, play group, and other primary groups. An individual is deeply influenced by the opinion and views of his parents, colleagues, neighbours and those who work with him. His behaviour is determined or controlled by their criticism, derogation, praise, suggestion or persuasion, etc. This is direct control.

(ii) *Indirect social control.* This is the control exercised upon the individual by factors which are separated from him. Control of the individual by secondary groups is of this type. Its prominent means are traditions, institutions, customs, rationalised behaviour, changes in situations and social mechanism, etc. The means of social control are invisible and subtle. In the existing complex society, the influence of the opinion, law, custom, etc., is controlled in this way. It is not that there are no individuals behind this control but these individuals are not seen by the persons affected.

2. Kimball Young's View. Kimball Young has divided social control into two classes from the viewpoint of methodology. In this way, social control has been divided into the following two types:

(i) *Positive.* Reward has an immense value upon the activities of an individual. A large part of the population of society desires to be rewarded by the society. And, consequently, they constantly endeavour to conform to the traditions, mores, values and ideals accepted by the society. For this, they are rewarded in the form of social recognition, fame, respect, etc.

(ii) *Negative.* Under this are comprehended those types of social controls in which a person is prevented from doing something by threat of punishment, while it encourages the people to indulge in certain types of activity by promising reward, it also discourages and prevents people from many activities by fear of punishment, which can be moderate, severe, physical or verbal or in any other form. Examples of verbal punishment are defamation, criticism, ridicule, etc. An example of physical punishment is extradition from caste. Fear of these punishments helps to prevent people from violating the socially approved customs, traditions, values and ideals, etc.

3. Other Views. In addition to the abovementioned forms of social controls, two other forms, formal and informal, have also been recognized. The formal types are those which are specifically designed for control, and include government, law, police, army, jail, penal code, etc. Informal social control includes those methods which develop by themselves according to the needs of society such as, mores, traditions, customs, social ideals, etc. Hayes has accepted two forms of social control: (a) Control by sanction—In this social control is effected by awarding the obedient and punishing the miscreant, (b) Control by socialization and education.

AGENCIES OF SOCIAL CONTROL

It would have become evident from the foregoing description of the various types of social control, that there are many direct and indirect, formal and informal means of social control. Among the important means of social control Ross has enumerated family, educational system, belief and religion, social suggestion, social ideal, ritual and festival, art, leadership, law and administration besides physical force. Giddings has accepted the importance of belief, social direction or guidance, religion, social ideals, social festivals, art, leadership, intellectual factors, education and propaganda, law and administration and force, as means of social control.

SOCIAL CONTROL AND EDUCATION

According to Ruskin, "Education consists in making people polite what they ought to be". The ideals and patterns in these are promoted through education. Here the word "education" is used in a comprehensive sense. It is only in this meaning of the word that the sociologist studies or contemplates it. Education teaches man to live according to Nature. Education gives him ability to succeed in his struggle for existence. Education is an art of adaptation. For man, adaptation is more social than natural. Hence, education adapts man to society. In this way, education is an important means of social control.

Education is in the family, school, playground, club, office, in fact, everywhere. At every place the individual is taught something and socialized. In the family, in school, on playground, he learns to follow the opinion and advice of others and learns to comply with the traditions and mores. Theoretical education, *viz.*, reading and writing, serves to form the intellectual base for all this and with practical education he learns to put this into practice. The organization or system of society is disrupted and thrown into confusion when the educational system contradicts or when the activity of education does not function correctly and social control fails to function. Hence, education is a necessary condition for the proper exercise of social control. In the absence of an appropriate and organized education social control remains merely an arbitrary pressure which cannot continue for long. Without proper education the harmony of the individual and society is not merely difficult but well nigh impossible. Education makes social control normal . It makes social control self-control and the individual does not experience its burden.

20

DESCHOOLING SOCIETY

Some of the recent books in which the credibility of the educational system of the world has been threatened on account, *i.e.*, its general irrelevance and meaninglessness are *School is Dead* by Everett Reimer, *Pedagogy of the Oppressed* by Paul, Freire, *Compulsory Mis-Education* by Paul Goodman, *Teaching as Subversive Activity* by Charles Weingartner and Neil Postman, *How Children Fail* by John Holt and *The Under Achieving School* by John Holt and *DeSchooling Society* by Ivan D-Illich. Thus Ivan Illich, Paul Goodman, and John Holt, etc., are firmly convinced that educational institutions have polluted our consciousness. They have, therefore, questioned the very existence of the educational institutions. There is fair consensus among educational planners, educational thinkers and policymakers that knowledge imparted in educational institutions is neither effectively nor efficiently organized to fulfil the needs of the present and those of the forseeable future. Instead of opening the possibilities of individual evolutionary growth, educational inputs seem poised to create greater fragmentation of human society. The task which education has to address itself is how to liberate the individual from various kinds of bonds and tyranny to enable him to develop an integrated personality and live in harmony with the Nature, the self and the society. The new educational system will have to be open-ended, multifaceted, experimental and innovative.

SCHOOL AS FALSE UTILITY

A school is the most insidious of all the false utilities. Attitudes are already changing. The proud dependence on school is gone. Many teachers and pupils, taxpayers and employers, economists and policemen would prefer not to depend any longer on schools.

WHY DESCHOOLING?

1. Poor students lag behind. Even with schools of equal quality a poor child can seldom catch up with a rich one. Even if they attend equal schools and begin at the same age, poor students lack most of the educational opportunities which are casually available to the middle-class child. These advantages range from conversation and books in the home to vacation travel and a different sense of oneself, and apply, for the child who enjoys them, both in and out of school. So the poorer student will generally fall behind so long as he depends on school for advancement of learning.

2. Over dependence on school. School appropriates the money, men and goodwill available for education. It discourages other institutions from assuming educational tasks. Work, leisure, policies, city living and even family life depend on schools for the habits and knowledge.

3. Neither learning nor justice. Neither learning nor justice is promoted by schooling because educators insist on packaging instruction with certification. Learning and the assignment of social roles are melted into schooling.

4. Most learning outside the school. A major illusion on which the school system rests is that most learning is the result of teaching. It is true that teaching may contribute to certain kinds of learning under certain circumstances. But most people acquire most of their knowledge outside school, and in school only insofar as in a few rich countries, school has become their place of confinement during an increasing part of their lives.

5. Teachers less skilled than craftsmen. Skilled teachers are made scared by the belief in the value of licences. Certification constitutes a form of market manipulation and is plausible only to a schooled mind. Most teachers of arts and trades are less skilful, less inventive and less communicative than the best craftsmen and tradesmen.

6. Recognition of two faced nature of learning. The deschooling of society implies a recognition of the two faced nature of learning. As an insistence on skill drill alone could be a disaster, therefore, equal emphasis must be placed on other kinds of learning. But if schools are the wrong places for learning a skill, they are even worse places for getting an education. This is so since school does both because it does not distinguish between them. School is inefficient in skill instruction because it is curricular. In most schools a programme meant to improve one skill is always chained to another irrelevant task. History is tied to advancement in maths and class attendance to the right to use of the playground.

7. Two realms. The very existence of obligatory schools divides any society into two realms, some time spans and processes and treatments and professions are academic or pedagogic, while others are not. This power of school to divide social reality has no bounds, education becomes unworldly and the world becomes non-educational.

8. Learning in practice. Everyone learns outside school, to speak, to think, to love, to feel, to play, to curse, to politick and to worry without interference from a teacher. Even children who are under a teacher's care day and night are no exception of the rule. Orphans, idiots and school teacher's sons learn mostly outside the educational process planned for them. Teachers make a poor showing in their attempt at increasing learning among the poor parents who want their children to go to school are less concerned about what they will learn than about the certificate and money they will earn. Middle class parents commit their children to a teacher's care for learning what the poor learn on the streets.

Educational research demonstrates that children learn most of what teachers pretend to teach them from comics, from chance observations, and above all from mere participation in the ritual of school.

9. Wrong motivations. Pupils have never credited teachers for most of their learning. Bright and dull alike have always relied on rote reading. Both are motivated by the stick or by the carrot of a desired career.

10. Job for school teachers. Schools create jobs for school teachers, no matter what their pupils learn from them.

GENERAL CHARACTERISTICS OF DESCHOOLED SOCIETY

1. Purposes. A good educational system has three purposes. It provides all what they want to learn with access to available resources. It empowers all who want to have what they know to find those who want to learn it from them. It furnishes all who want to present in issue to the public with the opportunity to make their challenge known.

2. Application of constitutional guarantee. Such a system would require the application of constitutional guarantee to education. Learners should not be forced to submit to an obligatory curriculum, or to discrimination based on whether they possess a certificate or a diploma. The public should not be forced to support a huge professional apparatus of educators and buildings through a regressive taxation which in fact restrict the public's chances for learning by the services the professional is willing to put on the market.

3. Modern technology. It should use modern technology to make free speech, free assembly and a free press truly universal and, therefore, fully educational.

4. Less restrictive educational artifacts. The market for learners would be much more various and the definition of educational artifacts would be less restrictive. There could be tool shops, libraries, laboratories and gaming rooms. Photo labs and offset presses would allow neighbourhood newspapers to flourish. Some storefront learning centres could contain viewing both for closed-circuit television, others could feature office equipment for use and for repair. The jukebox or the record player would be commonplace, with some specializing in classical music, others in international folk tunes, others in jazz. Film clubs would compete with each other and with commercial television. Museum outlets could be networks for circulating exhibits of works of art, both old and new, originals and reproductions, perhaps administered by the various metropolitan museums.

5. Hidden curriculum and Open Learning. To understand deschooled society, we must focus on the hidden curriculum of schooling. We are not concerned here with the hidden curriculum of the ghetto streets which brands the poor or with the hidden curriculum of the drawing room which benefits the rich. We are rather concerned to call attention to the fact that the ceremonial or ritual of schooling itself constitutes such a hidden curriculum. Even the best of teachers cannot entirely protect his pupils from it. Inevitably, this hidden curriculum of schooling adds prejudice and guilt to the discrimination which a society practises against some of its members and compounds the privilege of others with a new title to condescend to the majority. This hidden curriculum serves as a ritual of initiation into a growth oriented consumer society for rich and poor like. School is not, by any means, the only modern institution which has as its primary purpose the shaping of man's vision of reality. The hidden curriculum of family life, craft, health care, so-called professionalism, or of the media play an important part in the institutional manipulation of man's world vision, language and demands. School enslaves more profoundly and more systematically, since only school is credited with the principal function of forming critical judgment, and, paradoxically, tries to do so by making learning about oneself, about others, and about nature depend on a prepackaged process.

Everywhere the hidden curriculum of schooling initiates the citizen to the myth that bureaucracies guided by scientific knowledge are efficient and benevolent. Everywhere this same curriculum instils in the pupil the myth that increased production will provide a better life. And everywhere it develops the habit of self- defeating consumption of services and alienating production, the tolerance for institutional dependence, and the recognition of institutional rankings, in spite of contrary efforts undertaken by teachers and no matter what ideology prevails the hidden curriculum of school does all this.

6. Open Learning System. The system accepts the learner and his surroundings as the environment for learning. It concentrates on enriching that environment. The system seeks, obtains and maintains the active co-operation of the community and regional resources which can be important factors in enriching the learning environment. It diminishes the dependence of the learner on a single resource. It treats learning as a continuing activity. It includes living, working, recreating and learning.

7. No need of degree. The system is capable of enabling learners to participate in the programme of learning and instruction without imposing traditional academic entry requirements, without the pursuit of an academic degree or other certification as the exclusive reward.

8. Practical objectives. The planning of new educational institutions ought not to begin with the administrative goals of a principal or president, or with the teaching goals of a professional educator, or with the learning goals of any hypothetical class of people. It must not start with the question, 'What kinds of things and people, learners want to be in contact with in order to learn'. The system requires, formulation of learning objectives in such a way that they can serve the basis of decisions in instructional designs including evaluation and in such a way that it will not only be known to the students but they also participated in decision-making.

9. Role of extra-curricular activities. It is a process of learning that is not enclosed or encumbered by barriers, that is accessible and available, not confined or concealed and that implies a continuum of access to opportunity. Most learning happens casually, and even most intentional learning is not the result of programmed instruction. Normal children learn their first language casually, although faster, if their parents pay attention to them. Most people who learn a second language will do so as a result of odd circumstances and not of sequential teaching. They go to live with their grand parents, they travel, or they fall in love with a foreigner. Fluency in reading is also more often than not a result of such extra-curricular activities. Most people who read widely, and with pleasure, merely believed that they learned to do so in school, when challenged, they easily discard this illusion.

10. Advent of 'Brave New World'. Deschooling could mean the advent of a 'brave new world' dominated by well-intentional administrators of programmed instruction. Deschooling could take place in either of two diametrically opposed ways:

(i) The first would be the expansion of the mandate of the pedagogue and his increasing control over society even outside school. With the best of intentions and simply by expanding the rhetoric now used in school, the present crisis in the schools could provide educators with an excuse to use all the networks of contemporary society to funnel their messages to us, for our own good.

(ii) On the other hand, the growing awareness on the part of governments, as well as of employers, taxpayers, enlightened pedagogues and school administrators, that graded curricular teaching for certification and has become harmful could offer large masses of people an extraordinary opportunity: that of preserving the right of equal access to the tools both of learning and of sharing with others what they know or believe.

GOALS OF EDUCATIONAL REVOLUTION

But this would require that the educational revolution be guided by following goals:

1. To liberate access to things by abolishing the control which persons and institutions now exercise over their educational values.
2. To liberate the sharing of skills by guaranteeing freedom to teach or exercise them on request.
3. To liberate the critical and creative resources of people by returning to individual persons the ability to call and hold meetings—an ability now increasingly monopolized by institutions which claim to speak for the people.
4. To liberate the individual from the obligations to shape his expectations to the services offered by an established profession by providing him with the opportunity to draw on the experience of his peers and to entrust himself to the teacher, guide, adviser or healer of his choice. Inevitably, the deschooling of society will blur the distinctions between economics, education and politics on which the stability of the present world order and the stability of nations now rest.

WORK EXPERIENCE AND SOCIALLY USEFUL PRODUCTIVE WORK

Vocationalisation, Work Experience, Socially Useful Productive Work, Basic System—The underlying philosophy behind all these concepts is the same, i.e., relating education to productivity and providing work experiences. These terms provide a redefinition of educational thinking in terms of a society launched on the road to industrialization.

WORK EXPERIENCE

Work experience is a participation in productive work in school, in the home, in a workshop, on a farm, in a factory or in any other productive situation.

The Education Commission (1964-65) observes, "The concept of work experience is closely related to the philosophy underlying basic education. The programme of basic education did involve work experience for all children in the primary schools, though the activities proposed were concerned with indigenous education and the village employment pattens. If in practice basic education has become largely frozen around certain crafts, there is no denying the fact that it always stressed the vital principle of relating education to productivity. What is now needed is a reorientation of the basic education programme to the needs of a society that has to be transformed with the help of science and technology. Thus, work experience must be forward looking with the character of the new social order".

SOCIALLY USEFUL PRODUCTIVE WORK

According to the Ishwar Bhai Patel Committee (1978), "It may be described as purposive, meaningful manual work resulting in either goods or services which are useful to the community. Purposive, productive work and services related to the needs of the child and the community will prove meaningful to the learner". The Committee has further observed, "The purpose of demarcating a distinct curricular area as Socially Useful Productive Work is to emphasize the principle that education should be work-centred, as the concept of Socially Useful Productive Work is to be developed in the light of the Gandhian philosophy of Basic Education, in and through work."

1. Aim of Socially Useful Productive Work. The Committee observes, "The Aim of this curricular area is to provide children with opportunities of participating in social and economic activities inside and outside the classroom enabling them to understand scientific principles and processes involved in different types of work and in the setting in which they are found in the physical and social environment".

2. Planning and criteria of selection. The Committee stresses that this work must not be performed mechanically but must include planning, analysis and detailed preparation at every stage, so that it is educational in essence. The criterion for selection of activities should thus, be that the work involved is:

(i) Productive

(ii) Educative and

(iii) Socially useful

3. Lack of usefulness in work experience. In the view of the Committee, the programmes of work experience which were introduced as a result of the recommendations of the Kothari Commission with the objective of relating education to productivity lacked the component of social usefulness and in practice were not even casually correlated to other subject areas.

4. Three phases. The Review Committee has stated the three phases of the Socially Useful Productive Work:

(i) Study of the world of work through observation and enquiry,
(ii) Experimentation with materials, tools and techniques, and
(iii) Work practice.

5. Six areas of work situation

(i) Health and Hygience
(ii) Food
(iii) Shelter
(iv) Clothing
(v) Culture and recreation and
(vi) Community work and social service.

6. Merits of the programme

(i) *Reduction of gap in work and education.* The Committee feels that if 'Socially Useful Productive Work' is given a central and dominant place in the curriculum, the gap between work and education will be reduced, the school will not remain isolated from the community and the gulf that divides the affluent from the weaker and poorer section of the community will be bridged. Such a scheme, will provide equality of opportunity for working and learning to all children, irrespective of caste, creed, sex and economic status.

(ii) *Control on migration.* The Committee further hopes that those who receive education under the new scheme will not migrate from the village to the towns, deserting the community which had nurtured them and spent money on their education.

(iii) *Bridging gulf between rural and urban.* The Committee envisages that the new pattern will assist in checking the cleavage that has been created between the so-called educated and the rural masses and which has resulted in lack of harmony.

(iv) *Check on educated unemployed.* The Committee thinks that the introduction of 'Socially Useful Productive Work' will avert the paradoxial situations in which national resources are spent on the education of the villagers only to help them join the ranks of unemployed.

(v) *Right direction.* The Committee strongly feels that the reaffirmation of the Gandhian concept of work education is the very step in giving the right direction to the present system of education. Therefore, it asserts that the work education must find a central place in the school curriculum.

(vi) *Education through work.* The Committee makes it clear, "We are not advocating education plus work but education in and through work as this is the basis of the Gandhian philosophy of Basic Education."

(vii) *Following natural instinct.* The Review Committee points out that the merit of education through work is that it follows the natural instinct of man to translate 'thought into activity and activity into thought'.

(viii) *Coordination.* The Review Committee has further observed, "At the risk of sounding pedantic we would like to stress the close co-ordination of the senses and thought and also the reciprocal influence between brain activity and material creative activity".

(ix) *Socially Useful Productive Work—Subjected to Related Activities.* The socially useful productive work should, as far as possible, be allied to the elective chosen by the students, allowing also for any other kind of work depending upon the facilities available in the neighbourhood. The students who are studying Home Science, for instance, work with the community for improvement of the nutritional status of the population, utilizing the local products for developing cheap and wholesome diets. The students of Chemistry may undertake useful work of soil fertilisers and water, removal of pollution, utilization of wastes, etc. Those of physics may similarly work on rural electrification, improvement of small and cottage industries, etc. Biology students may serve in primary health centres and promote other health measures or help farmers, horticulturists, etc., for improving productivity. Political Science students may work with Panchayat Administration, local bodies, etc., for purpose of improving various services to the community.

21

TEACHER'S ROLE IN SOCIETY

The process of education is a triangular process in which there are three points—the educator, the educand and the subject of education. In order to be able to teach, the educator must establish some relationship with the educand, based on his knowledge of the latter. For this relationship to be meaningful it is essential that the educator himself should be conversant both with the subject he is teaching and the psychology of the educand. Education aims at teaching the educand and providing him with some information. Teaching assists the educand in his adaptation to his environment and helps to make him active. Through education, training of the emotions is accompanied by an inspiration to learn. Briefly, then, teaching is intended to prepare the educand for future life.

PRINCIPLES OF TEACHING

All educationists agree that at the root of the teaching there are some fundamental principles which govern the process, and that the teacher must be aware of these principles. For example, such factors as the educand's chief interest, the directions of his distraction, his mental ability, the basic laws of learning, etc., all influence the process of learning and teaching to a very great extent. Naturalists tried to base all techniques of teaching on some natural laws, while the idealists presented some principles—such as, from simple to complex, from the known to the unknown, from the concrete to the abstract, from the whole to the part, etc. Despite these differences, all educationists agree that the educator must keep in mind the following principles while he is teaching:

1. Principle of activity. Pragmatic thinkers lay particular emphasis upon the principle of activity, for they believe it to be the most important factor in learning. In the words of W. Ryburn, "One of the most important facts about children, which we have to remember throughout our teaching work, is that children are naturally active." Thus our first general principle of teaching methods, such as the Project method, method of Basic Education, Dalton Plan, Montessory and Kindergarten method is that these are based on the principle of learning by doing. The process of learning is an active process, and nothing can be really learnt by inactively listening or looking on as a mere spectator. Hence, in the school, the child should be given every chance to be active. This also has another advantage.

When the child is active physically, his mind is also more active than otherwise, and hence he acquires things more easily. For example, the child will not learn to play if the game is described to him, but he learns it rapidly if he is made to participate in it. The same is true for other subjects such as history, geography, civics, agriculture, etc., which are taught in schools. When given a chance to do something himself, the child takes a greater interest in the activity, and is therefore better prepared to learn it. For this reason, it is always suggested that the teaching of various subjects should be accompanied by various kinds of programmes which compel the educand to participate actively. Experiments in psychology have clearly indicated that the principle of learning by doing applies not only in childhood but also in adult life. Among adults, too, the individual is more eager to learn when he is actively participating in some activity. Knowledge increases only when it is used. In the words of Comenius, "What has to be done must be learned by practice". All kinds of artistic skill, such as dancing, sculpture, music, painting, etc., are all learned through actual practice.

2. Principle of motivation. Educational psychology has made educators aware of the fact that motivation is the most significant factor in the process of learning. In the absence of motivation, the educator cannot elicit any useful response from the educand. There is a lot of wisdom in the proverb that you can take the horse to water but you can't make it drink. In much the same way, the educand learns something only when motivated to learn it, because it is motivation alone that can awaken interest in him. Once interest has been aroused in a particular direction, the educand is motivated to learn it. Creation of a strong motive for learning is more than half the educator's task. If this motivation is absent, the educator can try his best but it will be remarkable if he drives anything into his pupil's head. Motivation depends upon the child's innate tendencies. One example of this is curiosity, which is manifested in the child's constant desire to learn about things which make up has environment. This curiosity of the child can be exploited to facilitate the processes of learning and teaching. The teacher's real task lies in his pupil's curiosity in the subject to be learnt, for, once this has been achieved, the educand can be safely left to himself to learn all there is to be learnt about the subject. Apart from curiosity, the child is possessed of many other tendencies of which play is another important one. This, too, can be exploited for education, as it has been in the playway of education in which the child is taught through games of various kinds. Play takes away much of the tension of work and renders it easy. Motivation for learning can also be induced by making use of such tendencies in the child as dedicating himself, assertiveness, conflict, competition, etc.

3. Principle of linking with life. Dewey, the famous educationist, expressed the opinion that education and life are two aspects of the same fact. In tribal societies the processes of living and education are not separated but as social structures become more complex, the process of education tends to be separated from life. At times, it can move so far away from life that whatever happens inside the school seems to bear no relation to the life outside the school. That is why educationists keep on reminding people that life inside the school must keep in contact with life outside it, for education to retain any meaning. Hence, one of the important principles of education is that it must have tenacious links with life. All that is taught to the child can remain in his mind only if it establishes some association with all that he has learnt before. The teaching of arithmetic, for example, can be made more meaningful if it is linked to the child's everyday activities outside the school. The teaching of geography, for example, should have its beginning in the teaching of local photography. If civics is to be taught, then it is best to begin by telling the pupils about the local municipal board or any other self-governing body. This principle must be applied to all the other subjects that are taught in the school. If the subjects taught are linked with objects of real life, the educand is helped in his later adjustment with life when he leaves the school.

4. Principle of interest. Another important principle underlying teaching is the principle of interest. Educational psychology tells the educator that he cannot make his teaching effective unless he arouses the pupil's interest in the subject being taught. Hence, the educator must begin his task by arousing this interest, because this will create the necessary inspiration in the child. He will be willing to learn and thus facilitate the teacher's work. There are certain disciplines which naturally interest the educand, but where there is a question of choice among alternatives, as far as possible, attention must be paid to the educand's own inclinations and interests. To put it differently, one must teach the child only that which the child prefers to learn, and conversely, one must create interest in a subject before forcing it on the child. Either of these two approaches can be adopted, depending upon the circumstances.

5. Principle of selection. The principle of selection also plays a significant part in the teaching process. The successful teacher always determines beforehand the subject that he wishes to teach a particular class, the extent to which he would prefer to teach and the method he would like to adopt. Hence, the technique of teaching and the limits up to which a general subject like geography, history, civics, agriculture, painting, language, or mathematics, etc., is to be taught are determined well in advance. The rules governing this selection are determined by the educator's own judgment and understanding of his pupil's psychology. And, the greater his knowledge of psychology, the better will be his selection.

6. Principle of definite aim. Just as education in general must have an aim, each different lesson taught to the educand should also have its distinct objective. This helps to achieve clarity and precision in teaching, and also focuses the educand's attention. It is the objective of the lesson which determines the technique of teaching. The educands should also be aware of this aim of education so that they may know what the teacher is trying to tell them and also the direction in which they are progressing. Not knowing this objective, they tend to ignore many of the important aspects of the lesson, because they fail to attach due importance to each part. Hence, in order to give a definite and clear form of teaching, it must also be given an aim.

7. Principle of planning. Having determined the aim and the subject of teaching, it is next necessary to plan the technique which is to be employed in this. Proper planning leads to economy of time and efforts, because then the aim can be achieved easily and rapidly. Its utility lies in the fact that, even before beginning the task of teaching, the educator is aware of the difficulties he is likely to face, so that he is also fully prepared to face them. He also arranges his subject matter so as to achieve maximum clarity. But here one must make a qualification. Before embarking on the task of teaching, the subject matter should never be fitted into a rigid framework. The framework must be flexible enough to accommodate any change that may become necessary during the course of teaching. Hence, the planning and the plan adopted should be flexible and changeable.

8. Principle of division. According to this principle, the subject-matter should be divided into different steps so that it can easily be presented to the class in an ordered and systematic manner. But the division must allow of easy transition from one stage to the next. It is advantageous to the educand also because when the matter is presented in steps, the educand finds it easier to grasp and understand clearly. This principle of division forms part of the principle of planning.

9. Principle of individual differences. Modern educational psychology has now firmly established that children differ from each other due to innate differences of intelligence, aptitude, attitude, interest, mental faculties, etc. Hence, obviously it would be impossible to teach all educands by the same techniques and standards. It is true that educator normally adopts a technique and standard in conformity with the average intelligence of his class so that much of what he teaches is grasped. But this is only a make-shift method because it does no justice to either the more intelligent or the less intelligent section of the class. The paidocentric education insisted upon today makes it necessary to pay special attention to those educands who are either far above or far below the average level. It is, therefore, necessary that the educational technique must be varied to conform to their respective responsibilities.

10. Principle of democratic behaviour. In democratic countries in particular, the principle of democratic behaviour conditions the process of teaching, because the very justification for the teacher's existence lies in his ability to produce citizens capable of living in a democratic society. In such conditions it is desirable that most of the work should be done by the educands themselves, the educator acting merely as his guide. What is more important is that the social environment of the school should itself encourage the development of democratic qualities. The educand must have complete liberty to ask questions, allay his fears, resolve his doubts, so that he can achieve a high level of mental development, which would otherwise be impossible. The curricular and extra-curricular programme of the school should never be rigid. It should be flexible enough to allow the educand to progress along the lines indicated by his natural inclinations.

11. Principle of creativity and entertainment. All modern educationists suggest that the process of teaching must be creative and entertaining. Its creative nature allows the child to express his own individuality and the possibilities of entertainment offered by it make it more interesting for the student to learn.

TEACHER'S TRAINING

Need of Training

Teaching is not something that anybody can do without any kind of training. For efficient teaching it is necessary that the educator must have education of the highest level accompanied by training in techniques of teaching, principles of teaching, solution of educational problems, curriculum, organization of the school, etc. Different kinds of training is required for teaching at the different levels of education, and with this end in view, the kind and nature of training required for teaching at the primary, secondary and higher levels of education, have been determined. In ancient India the educand learnt the art of teaching from his own teacher without going to any independent teacher training establishment. The problems of training teachers arose when the British government in India set up a department of education to look after the educational needs of the country.

Kinds of Teacher Training

Different levels of training are required for teaching educands at different levels of education, and for this purpose different institutions are required. In India teachers concerned with teaching at the primary level and middle schools, are trained at normal training schools. Teachers for the high school level are trained in training colleges. In the universities, the B.Ed. and M.Ed. classes are intended to train individuals for teaching and functioning as principals in high schools and intermediate Colleges. In addition to this, the country also has various institutions for providing special training in the teaching of home science, art, physical education, etc. But in view of the growing demand for trained teachers in all these spheres, one is obliged to say that the provisions for teacher's training in the country are wholly inadequate.

Problems of Teacher Training

The following is a brief account of the difficulties facing the training of teachers in the country:

1. Absence of any co-ordination between schools and training schools. In India, the training that is imparted to the trainee in the teacher's training schools bears little relation to the kind of teaching actually required in the schools, and hence this training does little to prepare him practically for teaching. K.G. Saiyeden has pointed out that instead of the theories learnt by the trainee and his actual conduct in the classroom, becoming synthesized and complementing to each other, they have in fact become two separate and disconnected facts.

2. Absence of a balance between theory and practice. It is desirable that there should be a balance between principles and practices taught in the training colleges. In actual fact, training in most centres is concentrated on theoretical teaching without providing adequate opportunity for putting these theories into practice and thus testing them.

3. Defective curriculum. What is really desirable is that training colleges should teach only those subjects which are required for teaching in the schools, but in actual fact it is found that this basic principle is never in mind in determining the curriculum of the training college. As a consequence, the trainee studies many subjects which he is never required to teach.

4. Absence of freedom. In most training colleges, the trainees have little freedom to develop their independent personality. Their only immediate concern is to pass the examination somehow and to obtain their certificate of merit.

5. Neglect of human values. Little or nothing is done in the course of day-to-day training during the session to make the trainee aware of the ideals guiding human behaviour. K.G. Saiyeden has pointed out that when the attention is centred on minor details and technical necessities due to narrow mindedness, all view of the relation between the school and society and the awareness of the actual problems of living is lost sight of.

6. Defective selection. As a general rule one finds that the number of applicants for admission to such colleges is far in excess of the sets or accommodation available. As a result the individuals selected are chosen for reasons other than their merits. Very often, no less than half the trainees in the B.Ed. classes are selected on recommendation and personal contact. As a result, many very able individuals are deprived of training.

7. Problems of in-course training. The problems besetting the in-course training through refresher courses, short-term courses, committees, summer institutes, are different in nature, inasmuch as they centre around the curriculum, selection, difference in theory and practice, etc.

SUGGESTIONS FOR IMPROVING TEACHING

Educationists and education commissions have frequently pointed out the need to improve the attractiveness of education as a profession. Dr. S. Radhakrishnan said that the teacher has an important place in society, for it is his lot to transmit intellectual tradition from one generation to the next, to maintain technical efficiency and to prevent the torch of culture from burning out. He guides not only the individuals but the entire nation. Drawing attention to the pitiable lot of teachers in the country, Dr. Sampurnanand, the former chief minister and also education minister of U.P., commented, "The nation must realize the difficulties and the feelings of the teachers who are expected to provide men of ability and character and leaders in every sphere of life while they themselves have to work under conditions not calculated to foster either efficiency or self-respect". The Kothari Commission for education suggested that better salaries must be paid to teachers at all levels of education. In addition to this, the commission also advanced the following suggestions for improving the lot of teachers:

(1) A Model Act should be prepared to control appointment of teachers to the universities.

(2) The post of principal in the school should be held only by an educated individual.

(3) When the teacher's ability improves, he should be given higher salaries.

(4) In the universities, special additional posts should be created for scholars.

(5) After every five years, the pay scales and dearness allowance rates should be reconsidered according to the change in prices.

(6) A teachers welfare fund should be established, and the teachers themselves should be asked to contribute one and-a-half per cent of their income.

(7) Retirement benefit should be extended to every class of teacher.

(8) The age of superannuation should be 60 to 65 respectively in schools and colleges.

(9) Teachers should also be given travel concessions so that they can tour the country every five years or so.

(10) Teachers should be given freedom to fight elections and to fight for civil rights.

(11) In order to give national recognition to brilliant teachers, the number of awards should be increased.

Despite the very concrete suggestions laid down by the Kothari Commission almost no active measures have been undertaken to improve the profession of teaching and render it more attractive. In many schools, even today the teacher is not paid a fixed salary, and appointments to most institutions are controlled by recommendations rather than merit. In many schools, the trained teachers are not given salaries according to grades determined by the government. In many cases, the management committees have remarkable extensive powers to terminate the service of teachers, thus rendering the teacher completely insecure. There is little reason for a brilliant and qualified individual to come to education when he is faced with poverty and insecurity. Hence, it is necessary that the state and the people must cooperate to remove these difficulties.

22

EDUCATION AND ECONOMIC ORDER

Economics may be defined as a scientific study of man in relation to his wealth getting and wealth spending activities. It studies the unlimited wants of man and the limited resources with which he wants to fulfil these wants. Economics deals with the resources of environment and studies how economic goods satisfy the wants of man, are produced, consumed, exchanged and distributed. Thus, production, consumption, exchange and distribution form the basic aspects of economics. Economics is concerned with land, labour, capital and organization. It explains theories, laws and principles connected with agriculture, trade, industry, banking, commerce, capital investment, manpower planning and everything that concerns the economic life of the nation.

ECONOMIC ASPECTS OF EDUCATION

The following points explain the economic aspects of education:

1. Education as Economic Good. A 'good' can be included under the scope of economic good only when its availability is limited and it is capable of allocation. Following are two types of economic good:

(i) *Material good.* A material good is physical and tangible.

(ii) *Non-material good.* A non-material good is a service rendered that satisfies a human want.

Education is a non-material economic good. It is service rendered to satisfy a human want. It is limited and capable of being allocated to individuals.

Education is a Producer's and Consumer's Good as given below:

(i) *Producer's good.* Producer's good is a good used in the process of producing other goods.

(ii) *Consumer's good.* Consumer's good is a good used by a consumer to satisfy his wants.

Education is both producer's good and a consumer's good. It gives satisfaction to the person who consumed it. It helps in the production of more goods. Education in the form of a producer's good is acquired for the purpose of becoming a teacher, lawyer, engineer or mechanic, or for any other profession or vocation, the main purpose of which is to produce a material or non-material good. At the same time it is consumed by those who receive it in the satisfaction of some of their wants. Again, education becomes a consumer's goods when the purpose of acquiring knowledge is to enrich a person's life by increasing his capacity to use, enjoy or appreciate any material or non-material good that satisfies human want.

2. Education as Industry. A country's government spends its gross national income of different sectors of the economy such as agriculture, industry and education every year expecting more returns than the previous year. The share for education is increasing every year in both developed and developing economics. Thus education is indeed a 'growth industry' which provides employment and services needed by the total economy as any other industry contributes to the gross national product of the country. It contributes substantially to the total economy of the country, and without it the economy would be all too poor. Again, education produces non-material goods which satisfy human wants. Education, as it produces goods necessary for human welfare, is amenable to demand supply and cost benefit analysis.

3. Education as Human Capital. Capital is anything that involves costs but yields a stream of income over time. It is the key to the production of income and consequently to economic growth. It consists largely in its power to produce or accumulate income immediately or in the long run. H.G. Johnson classified capital in the following four categories:

(i) *Capital goods.* These render specific services to production or consumption by the owner.

(ii) *Human capital.* This is labour, the important characteristics of which is that both inherently and by legal tradition, control over the use of the capital is vested in the individual embodying the capital regardless of the source of finance or the investment in it.

(iii) *Social capital.* This is collective capital, the important characteristic of which is that for reasons of inherent necessity or administrative convenience its services to production or consumption are not charged to individual users but are paid for by taxation of the community at large.

(iv) *Intellectual capital.* This is knowledge, the important characteristic of which is that, once created it is a free good, in the sense that use of it by one individual does not diminish its availability to others.

Essentially, education is human capital as it directly promotes the quality and capability of human beings. It contributes to intellectual and partly at least makes social capital. Economics considers human beings as a form of capital due to following reasons:

1. There are costs associated with development and formation of human capital.
2. The costs of skilled human resources add incrementally to the national product.
3. Expenditure on human resources which increase the national product also increase the national wealth.

Factors affecting human capital formation are investment in formal education, improved health, on the job training, manpower rehabilitation, migration, etc.

Formal education raises the economic value of the human capital by raising the future earning power and current asset value of human beings.

IMPACT OF ECONOMICS UPON EDUCATION

Areas of impact of economics upon education are the following:

1. Aims of education. Economics determines aims of education. Besides knowledge aim, cultural aim, character aim, spiritual aim, social aim, harmonious development of personality as an aim, vocational aim is one of the important aims of education.

2. Importance of education. Economics explains the importance of education in so far as the economic growth of the country is largely based on educational development.

3. Education as a means. Economics teaches man to be a better producer both for his personal good, and for the good of the country. It further points out that education is a means for that end.

4. Education as an investment. Education is itself an investment in economic terms. It removes poverty, as it produces skilled labour and creates right attitude to work and development. It creates awareness for better living.

5. Education as a guarantee of economic security. Education determines professional values, the wage structure and guarantees economic security of the people.

6. Education and economic status. Economic status of a person is determined by education. Education helps him in possessing a good earning capacity and leading a good economic life.

7. Education and economic prosperity. Economic development of the country depends on education. Economic prosperity of the country is directly proportional to the educational development of the people.

EDUCATION AND ECONOMIC GROWTH

What is Economic Growth?

Economic growth is identical with prosperity and better life. Faster economic growth helps the people of a country to enjoy higher standards of living. It leads to better social services. It gives more aid to the people of other countries. Economic growth means increase in the net national income during a given period of time. Some economists take increase in per capita income as an indicator and a measure of economic growth. Following are some definitions of economic growth:

1. Marshall. "The result of the labour acting on the natural resources of a country which produce within a given period of time a certain, non aggregate of commodities after avoiding double counting."

2. Mayer and Baldwin. "Gross National Product and per capita income."

3. Schumpeter and Hicks. Economic growth implies a growth in Gross National Product.

Role of Education

The system of education and the economic growth in a given social set-up are inter-related. One cannot exist without the other. Deterioration in education results in slow economic development. On the other hand, slow economic development will affect educational system and standards. According to B.G. Tilak, the relationship between education and economic growth is a two-way process—one of a reciprocal nature, of mutual contribution. In his book *The Economics of Education* John Vaizey has humorously and rightly described this relationship like a "chicken and egg". Harbison and Myers opine that education is both the seed and the flower of economic development. To sum up, the role of education in economic growth is as follows:

1. Production of material wealth. According to Alfred Marshall, "Education makes a man more intelligent, more ready, more trustworthy in his ordinary work; it raises the tone of his life in working hours and out of working hours; it is thus an important means towards the production of material wealth". Education is now universally accepted as a very useful productive activity which promotes national prosperity and national welfare in various fields. Thus, it produces material wealth.

2. Development of talents and virtues. An accelerated and higher level of economic welfare depends on bringing about fundamental changes in both the mental outlook and technical knowledge and skills. An awakened mind, right knowledge, appropriate skills and desirable attitudes are the great levers of economic development. Conceived and imparted correctly, education produces these talents and virtues. It yields an automatic bonus in the 'growth process' and the 'change process'. It releases the dynamism and forward flowing energy, which are the assets for a developing country. The constructive urges of man are aroused through education. Better organizational skill and sharp inventiveness are the direct results of education, it aims at the harmonious development of 3 H's (head, hand and heart), This will produce integrated personalities, who are assets to the economic progress.

3. Development of human resources. The development of human beings is the key resource of economic development. Human resource has both quantitative as well as qualitative aspects—quantitative in terms of effective man-hours and qualitative in terms of skills, knowledge and attitudes of human beings, on whom depends the tempo of development of a country. In a developing country every man's outlook and his level of education must change. With more investment in human capital (education) there will be more improvement in skills, knowledge and attitudes.

Karl Marx pleaded for education on the ground that, "It is counter balance to the inhuman results of the division of labour". According to Harbison and Myers, "The educational process of human resources development is necessary for the transformation of social and political institutions, for which the people of modernizing countries strive. Economic contribution of education could be interpreted in terms of human capital through education. Education improves man-power engaged in production. This improvement achieves higher and higher targets of growth and production in all areas and aspects of industrial development and economic prosperity.

4. Quantitative and qualitative improvement. The role of education in economic growth has both quantity and quality dimensions. Educational innovations and research are necessary and must be encouraged in planning to provide quality labour, efficient administrators, well trained teachers and various other professionals, with dedication and an experimental outlook. The role of education in discoveries and inventions should be supported further with necessary finance.

Education has the power to improve quality. It adapts human resources and makes them more productive. In USSR in 1920's, it was estimated that the work of the people who had received primary education was almost one-and-a-half-time more productive than that of illiterate workers of the same age doing the same work; and that the work of those who had received secondary education was twice as productive, while that of graduates was four times a productive.

Japan has been able to make very rapid economic progress in the twentieth century, in spite of the late arrival in the field, large density of population and paucity of natural resourses. The explanation may be found—at least partly—in the fact that she has been stepping up her public expenditure on education since World War II. Compared to Mexico and Brazil (rich in natural resources), Denmark and Switzerland (low in natural resources) have higher per capita income because of the effective system of education in the latter. By spending more than half of the national wealth on education, USA has attained great heights of economic prosperity in return. The economic progress of Netherlands is also due to her educational pattern. Thus, economic prosperity of modern advanced countries has proved that the most effective means for prosperity is education. By their efficiency and dynamism educated persons contribute to national prosperity and growth of national income.

23

Values and Education

WHAT ARE VALUES?

Values relate to the aims of human life. For the achievement of the aims men frame certain notions and these notions are called values. In the words of W.H. Kilpatrick, "That out of man's capacity for goal seeking behaviour arise his wants and efforts and out of these come in consciously chosen ends (goal) and means. Because ends conflict man is led to put his goals against each other. When this is done critically enough values emerge". According to Mr. Henderson, "It has been pointed out that man acts to satisfy his wants, anything which satisfies a human want becomes thereby a value. To say, then that our conducts is motivated by our value is another way of saying that we act to satisfy our wants".

DETERMINATION OF VALUES

Educationists had propounded the following principles about the determination of values:

1. Hedonistic view of life. The value of a thing is due to the fact that the thing has power to satisfy our wants.

2. Perfection theory. Any thing has value if it relates to the perfection of life for which a man endeavours in his life.

3. Utility of theory. Anything which has utility is valuable.

4. Order theory. Anything which is helpful in organizing society is called value.

5. Existence theory. Value is helpful in existence.

6. Experimental theory. Values are experiments in present and past as well.

7. Part and whole theory. Values are felt sometimes partly and sometimes wholly.

8. Objective and subjective theory. Values are determined by the notions of individuals and also by the circumstances in which he lives.

9. Emotive theory. Man's emotions are expressed by his nature. These emotions change according to the circumstances. Thus by virtue of his emotion man determines his values.

These values have certain characteristic like subjectivity, objectivity, material or abstract, elasticity, etc. These values aim at perfection, self-realization, satisfaction, perfection and development of integrity and cohesion, etc.

Education and Values

According to Reid, "Education is part of life, and nearly our question about values and education are inseparable from larger question of values in life. Values are embodied in educational practice". Thus education develops a sense of discrimination between good and bad. This discrimination is based on values. And these values are tested in schools.

To quote W.H. Kilpatrick, "The teacher must have an essential part of his professional equipment, which is here called "map of value". Such a map consists of his hopes, aims, ideals, all the criticised values which he will use as aims in hiding these things. Teaching should aim continually on keeping this aggregate of values, alive and growing but especially it should include all that the teacher hopes for student to learn so as life for them becomes as rich and fine as possible". In other words, "Aims are an end in themselves and values are the product". Values of education are the same as of life. These educational values are individual as well as social.

Contribution of Educational Values

Educational values contribute the following advantages for individual and social life:

(1) Development of healthy and balanced personality.
(2) Capacity to earn livelihood and acquired material prosperity.
(3) Development of vocational efficiency.
(4) Creation of good citizenship.
(5) Reorganization and reconstruction of experience.
(6) Adjustment with the environment and its modification.
(7) Fulfilment of the needs of man.
(8) Development of character.
(9) National integration and national development.
(10) Values for leaders and skilled workers.
(11) Promotion of social efficiency.
(12) Cultural values.
(13) Utilization of leisure.

Therefore educational values play a significant role in the life of man. Through them one is able to lead his personal and social life successfully. To sum up in the words of J.S. Brubacher, "Hence the ultimate aim of education is self-realization, the fulfilment of man's instinctive potentialities for many in addition to the realization of eternal life. All proximate aims of education take their direction from the aim which itself stands imperishable and eternal".

RELIGIOUS EDUCATION

The aim of contemporary education is not only the mental, physical, and social development of the individual, but also his religious and moral development, which is why modern educationists have stressed the importance of moral education for the country. Vivekanand said that religion is the basis of education, although here he does not imply his own or some one else's religion. This comment also implies that the aim of religious education is not to propound the theories of any one particular religion but to create faith towards universally accepted religious values. The presence of religious faith helps the individual to face all kinds of adverse conditions with the belief that he can progress at least a little, irrespective of the darkness of the outlook. Hence, religious faith helps man in his progress, raises him to a high level, and also assists him in developing democratic qualities. Religion is the foundation of all moral character, because without religion man cannot have faith in truth, beauty and goodness. The freedom that we want to grant the child through education is not possible without religion. Besides, even culture has no meaning in the absence of religion which also acquaints us with the final goal of life. Without knowing this goal, education cannot progress. Religion is the basis of true humanitarianism.

It is evident from the foregoing comments that religion should be given its appropriate place in the curriculum for education. Vivekanand has recommended that modern science should be used to awaken the educand's knowledge. History, geography and literature should be taught to the educand along with the teaching of religion which must be used to teach them the greatest truths. Dr. S. Radhakrishnan also supported the teaching of religion at the various levels of education. He said that we will have to plan for a rational religion for our conflict ridden emerging humanity, a religion that does not ridicule man's soul filled with unrestrained individualism and hesitation born out of conflict. We have to present a new philosophy of God with which we can fight against those doubting communities of men who are fighting against each other to establish their supremacy on men's souls. Rabindra Nath Tagore also expressed sympathy with this viewpoint in granting the greatest importance to a humanitarian religion in education. Pointing to the basic humanitarian religion that is at the base of all religions Tagore said that these religions differ from each other in moral value, but each one is inspired by the same tendency. In these religions, man looks for his highest ideal, which he calls God. They try to discover it in some personality of human character. Mahatma Gandhi has also attached the greatest significance to religious education, and he has advocated that educands should be acquainted with the basic elements of all religions. Sri Aurobindo has considered religious education to be the most important aspect of education.

Aims of Religious Education

The introduction of religious education leads to many advantages. It also has some objectives, the main ones being the following:

1. Moral development. James Ross has opined that without a religious education, the highest moral development of the educand is impossible because religion is the foundation of moral development and character. All the religions of world have stressed the need for developing moral qualities, and for this reason religious education is essential for developing the educand's moral character.

2. Refinement of human values. One aim of religious education is to distinguish between the divine and the material, and to give a divine touch to human values. In this way, religious education refines human values and thus puts humanity on the path to higher ideals.

3. Socialization. Social service is recommended by every religion of the world. In the Gita people are advised to act with a view, not to personal gain, but to add to the prosperity of the humanity. By inspiring man to forget his own narrow interests and to think of humanity at large, religious education continues the process of socializing the individual.

4. Development of democratic values. Religious feeling relates man on one side with God and on the other with human beings, and by showing that the same God exists in every human being, it encourages the development of the democratic qualities of liberty, fraternity and equality. In the absence of this sense of fraternity, equality has no meaning. It only remains a legal concept, not reality.

5. Cultural development. Religion is an important part of culture, and for that reason religious education contributes to man's cultural development. In fact, cultural progress of a group is measured by its religious development. Dr. S. Radhakrishnan has laid special stress on the contribution of religious education to the cultural development of the individual.

6. Sense of respect for man. Another objective of religious education is to induce a sense of respect for humanity in the educand. The basis of religion is the synthesizing element, and this is the basis also of education and culture.

7. Proper attitude. The aim of religious education is to achieve the complete development of the child's personality and to induce in him the correct attitude to life and the universe. In the words of V.T. Thayer, "The school must therefore concern itself with the whole child and no child can become whole without instruction in religion".

Mode, Form and Subject Matter

The method and form of religious education is clarified by its objectives mentioned above. The question is how religious education can be imparted and what should be its subject matter. In this connection it is essential to remember the principle that religion is acquired, not taught, for it is not a subject to be learnt, but to be realized and translated into life. That is why Vivekanand has suggested that religious education should be preceded by an account of the ideals of great men such as Rama, Krishna, Mahavir, etc. Religion means continued progress on the path to service and worship despite the greatest handicaps and obstacles. According to Vivekanand, one example of this is the ideal of Hanuman. He has advised the young men of the country never to let weakness fall upon the mind. In such a situation they should think of Mahavir and Mother Goddess and they will find that this weakness vanishes immediately. Vivekanand felt that the country needs a kind of religious education which achieves synthesis with science on the one side and teaches the lesson of patriotism, sacrifice and service, on the other.

According to Sri Aurobindo, there is little to be gained by paying more lip service to religious education unless religious education is actually transferred to real life and a tendency to worship, contemplation, self-control and abstinence does not grow. Spiritual development can be helped to a certain extent by worship, prayer, and the celebration of various religious festivals. The educand must be educated in his religious duties, prayer and contemplation and in every school the educands must be initiated into the ideals of service to and living for God, humanity, the country and other countries. Religious education does not necessarily imply that the child should be forced to read all religious texts, as suggested by Mahatma Gandhi, Vinoba Bhave and other thinkers. This is also not necessary for religious tolerance. Study of different religions is not as important as actual application of the various principles of religion, and it is equally undesirable to foist any particular religious practice on every individual. Hence, the curriculum of religious education should centre around the basic elements of religion.

Religious Education in a Secular State

Some people opine that religious education should not be encouraged by the state in a secular country like India, and they argue that religious education should be given by religious institutions and society, not by the school. This attitude has no justification because education must aim at the complete development of the individual, an aim that cannot be fulfilled in the absence of religious education. A secular state does not imply a state which is hostile to or indifferent towards religion, because all that the term secular implies is that the state shall not insist upon the adoption of any particular religion, because there is no state religion. It is correct to assume that the government should not try to spread any particular religion, but it must also be remembered that religious education cannot be equated with the deliberate campaigning for some particular religion. All that is required in religious education is that the educand should be taught the basic elements which are at the root of every religion, thus developing the educand's faith in moral character, religious values and humanitarianism. And, since India is also a democratic country, it has a great stake in the development of democratic values, which also depend upon religious education. Hence, religious education has its significance even in a secular state because it is the most powerful medium for developing democratic values. But religious education in a secular state must be carefully planned so as not to injure the sentiments of any particular sect of religionists, and also to avoid giving undue importance to any one religion. Every educand must be given the freedom and opportunity to profess his own religion, but he should be accompanied by acquaintances with other religions, since this alone is the way to religious tolerance. True religious feeling can be evolved in the educand by telling him about the lives of all the great religious leaders and founders. The subject matter of religious education should be designed to conform to the level of training and intelligence of the educands. A religious life is a life with a purpose, the same purpose which religious education has.

MORAL EDUCATION

The aim of education is the complete development of the child, a development in which moral development occupies an important place. Man's greatest characteristic is his character. Vivekanand has defined character as the sum total of an individual's instincts, the inclinations of his mind. Man is made by his thoughts. One finds that children develop characters according to the ideas presented to them during their growth. For this reason they should be initiated into the ideals of sacrifice, hard work and contemplation. Good thoughts lead to a sound determination and this in turn puts the man on the path to good life, and he is filled with strength of soul which inspire him to adhere to this path. In order to form character, it is necessary to pay attention to subtle and small things, for character is manifested through habits. Character can, therefore, only be improved by improving the habits of the individual. For this both determination and courage are required. Vivekanand had said in a resonant voice that one must form one's character and express one's true nature, the enlightened pure element in oneself. One must also look for the same element in every other individual.

According to Sri Aurobindo moral education is the education of the heart, without which no individual can be completely human. But this moral education cannot be imparted through lectures and text-books because the basis of this education is proper feelings, proper conduct and the development of proper habits of thought, feeling and action. The task of education is to guide, direct and suggest to the child, without interfering with his activities in any way. Teachers should present the highest ideals but must also remember that moral education is imparted through imitation and setting examples rather than through discipline. In ancient India the child acquired moral education only by imitating his teacher. The modern teacher, therefore, must also have the highest ideals. In addition, moral education takes place through moral conversation and behaviour. Senior educands should be required to read literature which encourages the purest emotions in them and inspires them to attempt at the highest ideals. In order to give moral training to the child, the latter should be acquainted with the means of distinguishing between the right and the wrong. The various emotions of the child are not to be suppressed but sublimated. Mahatma Gandhi, like Sri Aurobindo, believed that development of character is the aim of education, for which, in his opinion also, moral education is essential. Dayanand believed that education of any kind is impossible without the practice of abstinence. Dr. S. Radhakrishnan also said that moral education is absolutely necessary for any education. In Indian culture very great importance has always been attached to moral character. No education is complete without moral education, and this morality is the foundation of man's fixture, and therefore the seed of this must be sown in the school. Dr. S. Radhakrishnan said that we must create the proper social order but we must also keep in mind that the individual does not become complete only by achieving economic prosperity. In order to become a complete individual the pleasure and beauty of the soul is essential. This soul must be brimming with love, faith, and the willingness and ability to serve humanity reborn.

From the foregoing account of the opinions of various philosophers, it is evident that moral education is as much a part of education as religious education is. In this connection, it is stated in the report of the Secondary Education Reorganization Committee for U.P., "That moral and humanistic education should form an integral part of our education; students should be taught the fundamental truth common to all religions. Illustrations of these fundamental truths should be taken from all religious and ethical movements with a view to emphasizing their essential unity."

WHAT IS CULTURE?

In anthropological literature the term culture is used in many senses, but in general writings it is used to indicate social charm and intellectual superiority. Even some sociologists believe cultured individuals to be the leaders of society. According to Sorokin and MacIver, culture implies man's moral, spiritual and intellectual achievements. In the words of Bogardus, "Culture is composed of integrated customs, traditions and current behaviour patterns of human group. Culture is the stock in trade of group. It is an antecedent complex of value into which every individual is born. It is a medium within which individuals develop and mature." In Indian society the individual is prepared for performing various functions in society at a very early age by a series of impressions deliberately made upon his mind. For example, the ceremony of marriage places upon the individual's shoulders the responsibility of procreating and thus ensuring the continuity of the race. Culture includes all those elements for which ceremonies and their consequent impressions are required. It is the process of purification. In ancient India Sanskrit was believed to be the language of the educated people, and this too is intimately concerned with culture, because the Hindi synonym is 'samskriti'.

Man and Culture

In the words of Kroeber, "In short, a cultural fact is always a historical fact; and its most immediate understanding, and usually the fullest understanding of it to which we can attain, is a historical one. To a large degree calling culture superorganic or super-individual means that it yields more readily to historical interpretation than to organic or psychosomatic explanations." Thus, Kroeber calls culture super-organic and super-individual in the sense that it is amenable to a historical interpretation or a more apt interpretation than the biological or psychological interpretation of culture. This viewpoint makes it amply clear that although human beings create culture, it is not the creation of single individual. The same thing has been stated by Majumdar and Madan in these words: "Human beings, it must be realized, are perhaps equally the creator of cultures as they are its creatures and careers." Hence, culture guides mankind, and while it renders him free from many causes, it also, to certain extent, enslaves him. It is evident that Majumdar and Madan have also accepted culture as super psychic and super social. Kroeber's viewpoint on culture is considered to belong to the category of cultural determinism according to which culture is the determinant of man's activity, not itself dependent upon man. But this concept of cultural determinism is no less imbalanced and one-sided than biological or geographical determinism. Kroeber's belief that culture is super-organic arid super-individual is acceptable only to the extent that culture is not the creation of anyone individual but of a community of human beings. But it is difficult to agree with him in the belief that culture is the final determinant of all human activity.

CULTURE AND EDUCATION

The intimate relationship between culture and education is evident from the fact that one of the major aims of education is to impart to the child his cultural heritage, the social heritage. In any human group, the various elements and parts of culture evolve after thousands of years of the experience, and these are handed down as a whole to the succeeding generations. Hence, every individual is born into a particular culture which provides him with definite patterns of behaviour and values which guide his conduct in different walks of life. He has thereby saved the necessity of making fresh experiments every time. Obviously, then, culture plays an important part in man's life. By understanding the nature of its importance, it will be easy to understand how the education of various elements of culture can help man. The main features of the contribution of culture to man's life are the following:

1. Adaptation to the natural environment. Everywhere, man lives in a definite natural environment to which he must necessarily adapt himself. Without doing this, he cannot exist. All the experiments and inventions that he makes in the process of this adaptation form an important part of the culture. Due to differences in the natural environment of different communities, there arise differences in their cultures also, and it is on this basis that a distinction is made between primitive and developed cultures. In all the tribes of India, the members behave in certain distinct and specific ways in order to adapt to their respective environments. These modes of behaviour are taught to the younger generations. It is these modes of behaviour which go to make up culture.

2. Adaptation to the social environment. Culture also includes customs, traditions and the pattern of current behaviour, etc. Inherent in it are our beliefs and ideas, decisions, values and social institutions. All of these help the individual to adapt to his social environment, but it must be remembered that all these elements undergo gradual changes as the social environment itself changes. Culture determines the patterns of social control, through which the individual is subjected to the coercion of the group. Hence, the advantage in communicating the culture of the group to the child through education is that he is thereby acquainted with the traditions, customs, values and patterns of conduct prevailing in his group. This knowledge enables him to adapt to the social environment and thus achieve his socialization.

3. Development of personality. The personality of an individual is manifested through his pattern of behaviour. The behaviour is always profoundly influenced by the culture of his group. Anthropologists have established as a fact that one finds differences in the basic behaviour patterns of individuals belonging to different cultures and differences in behaviour corresponds to difference in culture. Some people are more aggressive while others are submissive. One finds imprints of Western culture in European and American culture. Culture influences the physical, mental, social, emotional, moral and aesthetic aspects of the individual. Individual effort leads to important changes in culture, but the behaviour of the average individual is determined by culture.

4. Socialization. Culture plays an important role in socializing the individual, and for this reason the quantity and direction of socialization differs from one society to another. Every society has its own ethos, and this is communicated to the individual in many different ways. Ralph Linton has pointed out three ways in which the individual can participate in culture. In the first place, he participates universally in culture, that is, he adopts the habits, ideas and emotional patterns that prevail among the adults of that group. In the second place, the individual specifically participates in culture by adopting those elements of culture which are found among some specific organization or specific group of people. And finally, in the third place, the individual's participation in culture turns to the alternative elements in which he adapts those elements which are found only in a small number of individuals. It is this participation in the third, the alternative aspect, that lends individuality to the personality of each person. George H. Mead expresses the opinion that in adopting his culture the individual's ego passes through three stages analogous to the three stages of education. In the first stage, the individual imitates other people around himself, normally unconsciously. He is found smiling at others. In childhood, the infant acquires his culture through imitation. In the second stage, the children imitate different individuals in society in their play. After this the third stage of acquiring culture is the stage of games where the individual learns to control his behaviour. In the environment of the playground, the individual cannot behave wilfully, since he has to conform to the norms of the game. Hence, he gradually begins to adopt the ideals, principles and beliefs of his group, and it is only this kind of individual who is called cultured.

Education of Culture in the Family

The child's cultural education begins at home, and it is in the family that he participates in the elements of culture and passes through the various stages of cultural development explained by Mead. The parents and other members of the family educate the child in the various means of culture such as traditions, customs, values, belief, etc. It is in the family that the child first learns to distinguish between right and wrong. The various impressions impinging upon his mind in the family environment help to make the child cultured. In Indian society a variety of religious ceremonies are performed to initiate the child into cultured life. Comparable religious practices are found in other cultures also. Patterns of moral and religious behaviour are also learnt in the family. Good behaviour is imbibed from the behaviour of adult members of the family, because the child invariably imitates the behaviour of the adults and brothers and sisters. One can find the clear imprint of family influence upon the lives of the greatest men who have contributed to their respective cultures. A part of the cultural training in the family is unconscious, but a large part of it is consciously imparted to the child by the adults.

Cultural Education in the School

Now-a-days, it is the school which has taken over the function of culturally educating the child, just as it educates him in every other way. Schools in different countries educate the child according to their own cultures because through their text-books they seek to acquaint the child with their own values, mores, ideas, customs, etc. Various extra-curricular programmes are also intended to impart culture to the child. These programmes take the form of games of various kinds, dramas, community songs, dances, discussions, debates, tours of various parts of the country, etc.

Generally speaking, of course, both the family and the school undertake the task of communicating the society's specific culture to the younger generation, but nevertheless one does find minimal differences between the cultures of individuals belonging to different ranks of the same society. Hence, this education in culture is limited not only to training in the culture of the society as a whole, but also of a more limited culture belonging to the specific class and level in society. This social and economic class culture distinguishes between children belonging to different strata of society. Hence, cultural education comprehends both the general or extensive culture as well as the numerous sub-cultures existing within the extensive culture. Cultural education is important inasmuch as it helps the individual to adapt to his natural and social environment, to develop his social personality, to enable him to conduct himself fruitfully in this intercourse with other members of the society. Apart from this, the individual is also assisted by culture he adopts from social institutions and learns to conform his behaviour to the accepted norms. He finds in this culture distinctive patterns of behaviour designed to meet the various contingencies of social life. It is through this training that he becomes a useful member of society.

Education in Liberality to Other Cultures

Cultural education must supplement knowledge of one's own culture with the liberality of approach for other cultures which is so essential for understanding and sympathising with them. In the absence of this liberality, members of one culture believe themselves to be either superior or inferior to members of other cultures, with the result that tension is enhanced. This tension can even find violent expression. This is a major cause of many communal riots that frequently disrupt the peace in India. It is, therefore, desirable that the children should not only be taught their own culture but also be taught to appreciate other cultures. This is essential if the organization of society and world peace is to be maintained.

For this, some attention should be paid to other cultures also while imparting training in the various aspects of one's own culture. While teaching the child about the religion of his own group, for example, it is necessary to tell him that despite the obvious differences the same elements are also to be found at the root of other religions. The child should be made to understand that cultural differences are the manifestation of the different natural environments, but that this is no reason to believe one culture to be superior or inferior to another. There is no magnificance or denigration attached to differences in the natural environment. It is more creditable for every human group to lead its life according to this own culture. Therefore, it is never proper to foist the culture of one group upon another. When the child comprehends the true causes at the root of cultural differences, he can adopt a more liberal and sympathetic attitude to other cultures, and also avoid the mistake of considering his own culture to be the best one.

Education in the Proper Use of Leisure

One important aspect of cultural education is training in the proper use of one's leisure. That man is a cultured animal can be judged from the manner in which he spends his leisure, and it is only this which really distinguishes between the cultured and the uncultured individual. Hence, children should be educated to use their leisure from cultural attainments, such as literature, music, art, self-development, etc. It is for this reason that educationists have insisted upon supplementing education in science with some education in humanities also.

The relationship between education and culture is clear from the foregoing account.

24

EDUCATION FOR INTERNATIONAL UNDERSTANDING

NEED FOR AN INTERNATIONAL ATTITUDE IN EDUCATION

Internationalism implies the awareness of all human beings as members of a single human society, irrespective of national boundaries and other differences. The modern period has seen a remarkable transformation of the means of transport and communications, the tremendous spreading to education, the notable increase in the mutual contact between citizens of the world. As a consequence the world has shrunk in size, which in itself has led to local problems influencing areas and people far removed. For example, it is now being recognized that the excessive increase in poverty in any one part of the world is almost certain to affect the economic conditions of other countries as well. If peace and prosperity are to be created in one country, it becomes necessary to create good living conditions all over the world. Now that man has set foot on the moon, there is an increasing demand for international understanding. Besides, the two world wars of the century have enforced the useful lesson that, in this age of nuclear weapons, the people of the world have to live and die together. Communist and non-Communist countries both feel that they cannot hope to maintain their status in the world, unless they make efforts to spread their ideology in other countries. The failure of the League of Nations depressed the desire for internationalism. For this reason its successor, the United Nations, is aiming at co-operation not merely in the field of politics but also in the economic, educational and cultural spheres. UNESCO, one specialized body of the UNO, is dedicated to the spread of international understanding through the medium of education in every part of the world.

INTERNATIONALISM IN MODERN INDIAN EDUCATION

Modern educational philosophers in India have supported the notion of internationalism for a specific and unique reason. This attitude is based on the philosophy of the ancient Upanishads which taught that God lives as soul in the bodies of all human beings, irrespective of differences of race, nation, area, sex, etc. Vedanta philosophy provides the strong foundation for it. Sri Aurobindo was a staunch internationalist, in spite of his very emphatic expression of nationalism. He expressed the opinion that, just as the ideal nation is one in which the individual's freedom and perfection is harmonized with the development and organization of society, the freedom and development of an international society should be harmonized with the development and perfection of humanity in its entirety.

Of the many modern thinkers, Rabindra Nath Tagore expressed such vehement support for internationalism that people misunderstood him and took him to be opposed to nationalism. His creation, Shanti Niketan, is the concrete manifestation of the international attitude in education. Dr. Radhakrishnan, the chairman of the Indian Universities Commission, drew attention to the need for an international attitude in education. He expressed regret at the failure of the current educational system to propagate feelings of internationalism and universal brotherhood. An educational system should be such that it may create a new generation of individuals who believe that all human beings are brothers and that differences of caste, region, community or nation have no significance. True education leads to internationalism. Dr. Radhakrishnan commented that we must make efforts for the unity of the world. We should try to create a new generation which has faith in the nobility of intellectual life, in purity, in a feeling of brotherhood towards humanity, in love and peace. There should be no national educational plan which proves an obstacle in the growth and spread of this feeling. In fact, there is no opposition between nationalism and internationalism, but if it becomes necessary to make comparisons, both Rabindra Nath Tagore and Dr. Radhakrishnan incline towards internationalism. Education must aim at making every man and woman a citizen of the world, by developing within each one such thinking, concentration, insight and intellectuality or spirituality that they can perform useful roles in life. Peace in the world can be expected only when this ideal is pursued by education in every country. These ideas of Dr. Radhakrishnan have found echoes in every part of the world, and there is consensus of opinion among educationists everywhere that training men and women in internationalist! through education is the only way of avoiding a Third World War.

PROPAGATION OF INTERNATIONALISM BY UNESCO

The role of UNESCO in spreading internationalism is notable. This body is a special organ of the UNO dedicated to the spread of international understanding. It has been said in its constitution that "since wars begin in the minds of men it is in the minds of men that the defense of peace must be constructed". The breadth of its scope can be judged from its name, the United. Nations Education, Scientific and Cultural Organization. In order to achieve its goal of spreading international understanding, it performs the following functions:

1. This organization transmits knowledge of the literature, art, science, etc., of one nation to all other nations.

2. It also provides many opportunities to thinkers, scientists, teachers and artists to meet each other and exchange ideas and put forward creative plans for promoting world peace and justice. Efforts are made to prevent the people from being influenced too much by narrow parochial thinking.

3. UNESCO also seeks to improve the mutual relations between various nations and remove fear, suspicion and lack of confidence between them.

4. Considerable financial aid is given by UNESCO to improve the teaching facilities in backward and exploited countries.

5. UNESCO also provides guidance in modifying texts prescribed in various syllabi in order to make the books more internationally oriented. The organization does its best to root out illiteracy and lack of education from the poor countries.

6. In order to promote international understanding, UNESCO provides facilities to students and teachers to visit abroad and to exchange views and also gain experience in international living.

7. It also organizes art and literature exhibitions at the international level to promote feelings of love and friendship.

8. Research is also encouraged by UNESCO, for it provides financial help and other facilities to researchers.

It is evident from the varied functions of UNESCO that the organization is particularly aiming at creating an international feeling in education but this objective cannot be achieved by UNESCO alone. For this it will be necessary to make proper arrangements for education in many countries.

SYNTHESIS OF THE NATIONAL AND INTERNATIONAL POINTS OF VIEW

Here it is essential to understand how the national and international standpoints can be synthesized and reconciled with each other. Nationalistic feeling attaches importance to the nation's interests. Inspired by such feelings individuals are even willing to lay down their lives in order to protect the honour of their nations. It is only by awakening such feelings that many nations have gathered so much military power and have attempted to extend their own frontiers. But, if carefully examined, it will be seen that this is a distorted form of nationalism. In its best form nationalism does not oppose internationalism. It has helped various nations to collect power in their hands in order to throw of the yoke of a foreign nation. Nationalism has played a vital role in throwing out colonialism. But despite these great advantages and positive qualities, nationalism underwent a change and became colonialism itself. As a result of the nationalistic feelings, people focused their eyes on their own country and lost interest in anything other than their own sectarian interests. Just as any interest turns into an ism by becoming narrow and thus harms the more liberal interests, in the same way, this narrow minded nationalism has become an obstacle in the development of internationalism. It is this nationalism which inspired many nations of Europe to establish big colonies in Africa and Asia. Later, Germany and Italy became jealous of the English and French colonies, a feeling which manifested itself in the First and Second World Wars. After the First World War, an international organization known as the League of Nations was established, but it came to a premature end due to the narrow nationalism of its members. It was the precursor of the United Nations Organization which came into being after the second experience of a global conflict.

Despite the lessons learnt earlier, many nations continue to constitute a very grave threat to international peace because of their own interests. One concrete example of this is South Africa which continues to exercise its policy of apartheid, despite the many warnings given by the UNO. It is now universally felt that it is only the distorted form of nationalism which hindered the growth of internationalism.

On the other hand, healthy nationalism is a boon to internationalism. As has already been pointed out, it is only nationalism which has inspired many nations to throw off foreign rule. It is nationalism which has helped even the smallest nations of the world to raise their heads and stand proudly by the side of their mightier brothers. In fact, nationalism can be used or misused by human beings. The two international wars of the present century should be sufficient to teach human beings that there is need for balance and synthesis between nationalism and internationalism. There is a parallel to be drawn here. Individuals sacrifice the interests of family, race, town, etc., for the benefit of the nation, because they realize that these also gain when the nation gains. In the same way, national interests can be allied with international goals. National interests can be restricted for this, and it cannot be questioned that progress of isolated groups also depends very much upon the progress of the world as a whole. This fact must be realized first of all by the rich, powerful and the prosperous nations, because on them lies the onus of the world's development. In fact, it is the realization of their responsibility which is persuading the rich nations to extend a helping hand to their poor neighbours, but when some political strings are attached to the aid given, it defeats the purpose of encouraging internationalism. It must be remembered that there would be no international feeling in the absence of a national one, for it is the latter which inspires the former. No nation should become an obstacle to the progress of another nation in trying to achieve greater prosperity for itself. Secondly, progressive nations must help the underdeveloped ones. The principle of Panchsheel is a fine example of a synthesis between the nationalism and internationalism, but for this peaceful co-existence itself is not enough. Active co-operation is more important.

MEANS OF INTERNATIONAL EDUCATION

In order to encourage the growth of internationalism, it is necessary to make suitable amendments and modifications in the objectives of education, in the syllabus, and the methods of teaching. The following suggestions have been put forward:

(A) Aims of education. With the intention of spreading international feeling, the following aims of education should be paid special attention:

1. *Development of independent thinking.* Education must help every student to think for himself so that he should not blindly accept every statement favourable to his own country, and blindly reject everything in favour of another. He must be able to arrive at an independent judgment of the worth of some fact relating to his own country or another.

2. *Developing a feeling of world citizenship.* Education must also seek to teach children that they are citizens of a world state. When this feeling is developed in them, they will have no difficulty in rising above national interests and understanding international interests, which they will try to achieve.

3. *Creating faith in humanity.* Rabindra Nath Tagore, the strongest supporter of internationalism among the contemporary Indian educational philosophers, based his concept of internationalism upon the philosophical background of humanitarianism. Humanity is the true religion of human beings, while all the great religions are only different forms of it. All great religions have placed great stress upon the equality of human beings. Human perfection has been accepted as the goal of human life. Once this concept is understood, it becomes easy to have faith in humanity and to love all human beings irrespective of their country.

(B) Syllabi. The following changes in syllabi are suggested, if an international feeling is to be created:

1. All syllabi should include paintings, literature, music, etc., which are typical of different countries.

2. The children should be acquainted with all attempts at humanitarian work carried out in every part of the world.

3. Efforts should be made to overcome narrow-mindedness and blind faith in children through a scientific education.

4. The teaching of geography should be supplemented with knowledge of the singleness of the world.

5. The teaching of history should concentrate primarily on the efforts of great figures who have contributed to the history of the world.

6. In teaching civics, the educator should explain to the student not only the rights of citizen but also the rights and duties of a person to the international community as a whole.

7. Teaching should not be restricted to bookish teaching alone, but must also extend to visits to different parts of the country and also to other countries.

8. Pen-friendship should also be encouraged.

(C) Methods of Teaching. Certain suggestions about the changes and improvements in syllabi also imply some changes in teaching methods, if education is to have an international impact. The points to be noted in this connection are:

1. *Stress on world citizenship.* During the process of teaching, it is desirable to stress points which may help in evolving an all encompassing love and world citizenship.

2. *Stress on similarities.* The teaching of history, geography and civics, should concentrate not upon the differences between and tensions among nations but on the similarities so that sympathy for other nations and nationals is awakened in the mind of the educand.

3. *International viewpoint of educator.* But an international viewpoint cannot be generated in the educand if the educator himself lacks it. When the educator is

possessed of it, he will inspire the educand through his conversations, his ideas, training, and by setting an example. Hence, the first step in the process is to educate the educator.

4. *International contact.* The various committees for the various sciences and arts that are constituted at the university level should be encouraged to develop contact with national and international institutions of the same kind. What is really required is international contact at all levels of life and among people of every walk of life, scientists, scholars, literary figures, teachers, doctors, in fact, every profession. Such contacts can be evolved by international meetings of local committees concerned with different professions, and also through mutual exchange of scholars and learned people.

Finally, it has also been suggested that every national plan of education in every country, must make a specific provision for developing international feeling through education. Educators and educational institutions should be given specific instructions concerning this. Only this will awaken sufficient enthusiasm in local institutions, and only thus can the aim of international education be fulfilled.

SPREADING INTERNATIONAL EDUCATION

Apart from the formal education of colleges and schools, certain other media can also be useful in spreading international feeling, the major ones being:

1. Pen-friendship. Quite a few of the contemporary magazines, in all parts of the world, more particularly, the magazines meant for children and adolescents, carry this kind of information. Such magazines publish the reader's interests, age, hobbies other relevant information and sometimes even a photograph of the person interested in pen-friendship. Thus, many children and adolescents form pen-friends in all parts of the world, and later on exchange pictures, postal stamps, books and other things. Pen-friendship is thus the most important means of increasing feeling for people of different parts of the world.

2. Exchange of gifts. Another modern practice is the sending of gifts by the children of one country to the children of other countries, India, for example, has gifted elephants to the children of other nations. Such actions strengthen international feeling by attracting children of one country to another. Sometimes, some gifts packets are also distributed in schools. These packets contain things that the children can use. It is only natural that when the children get these gifts packets, they harbour kind and friendly feelings for the donor. The American Redcross distributes such gifts parcels among Indian children from time to time.

3. International competitions. Now-a-days cultural competitions over the display of dance, drama, art, music, etc., take on an international colour because people from many countries participate in them. This brings people into contract with the result that the world seems like a vast home.

4. International exhibitions. Such exhibitions also play an important part in promoting international understanding, because they help to acquaint people with the art and culture of different countries.

5. Cine films. People derive a lot of information by seeing foreign films, because they see their mode of living. Besides, it also encourages the feeling that human beings are the same everywhere, in their happiness, pain, pleasure, problems, joys and sorrows. This helps international understanding.

6. Radio and television. Radio and television play practically the same role as films because foreign programmes help the audience to understand life in other parts of the world.

7. Literature. Now-a-days, the literature of almost every country is available in every other country of the world. This can help in increasing acquaintance with life as it is lived in different parts. In addition to such literature certain books specialize in compiling the stories of lives, characters, interesting incidents and surprising objects in various parts of the world. This is a kind of international literature.

8. Contribution of universities. Finally, it can be said that universities are the most important medium of propagating international education because they provide opportunities for the meeting of artists, scientists, literary figures and scholars. This creates international understanding at a very high level.

9. Various institutions of UNO. Many institutions of UNO, more particularly., UNESCO, are engaged in directly and consciously promoting international understanding and the growth of international feeling. It is desirable that their sphere should be further expanded, and that more nations should participate in their programmes so that their objectives can be achieved more easily.

SUGGESTIONS FOR INTER-CULTURAL UNDERSTANDING

Inter-cultural understanding implies particular attitude, the attitude of understanding members of another culture, of recognizing their merits, of sympathizing and being liberal towards them. And since India contains many different cultures, inter-cultural understanding is essential, for, in its absence, conflict can never be curtailed. This inter-cultural understanding can be created through education. An emotional unity is the first essential thing for this. Besides, in the absence of inter-cultural understanding, it is impossible to generate a genuine internationalism which is necessary in view of the substantial differences between the numerous cultures found in different parts of the world. And, as long as human beings do not rise above their petty differences and understand all human beings to be members of the same group and learn to appreciate other cultures, international understanding cannot be created. The following suggestions are put forward for creating inter-cultural understanding:

1. Study of cultural anthropology. Cultural anthropology, a branch of anthropology, provides knowledge of the origin of various cultures, their development and their inner content. By studying the fundamental elements of this discipline, educands can comprehend the different cultural patterns and characteristics which are found. By studying the origins of various cultures, they will be able to understand that differences in culture arise out of the different circumstances in which the cultures are born. This will lead to a more charitable and liberal attitude to cultural differences.

2. Encouragement to tourism. Travelling to different parts of the countiy is a valuable experience in that it helps one to realize that despite the obvious differences in various groups, all of them are Indians. This promotes inter-cultural understanding.

3. Encouraging mutual meetings. Indian universities regularly organize cultural programmes in which students from different universities present cultural shows. Such meetings give the young people to meet young people of other cultural groups, with the result that they get a chance to understand the other culture. This helps to free their minds of narrow thinking.

4. Propagating the theory of unity in diversity. People who believe either in the destruction of diversity in order to create uniformity or in the destruction of unity to maintain diversity forget that unity in diversity is a natural characteristics of human society as well as of the entire creation. Happiness lies in following this principle. If this principle is accepted, internationalism will be encouraged, but not at the cost of nationalism. Today, all the different cultures that are growing in the country must be allowed to flourish. None of them should be destroyed, because each represents a specific pattern of adjustment with the environment existing at a particular place, and hence it has its own value. Each culture is the product of the local conditions, climate and natural environment, and represents an adjustment to that environment. Therefore, each culture must be given the opportunity to grow further. But this does not necessarily imply that the country will inevitably be divided into numerous different cultural groups or that this should be allowed to happen. Cultural unity can be promoted even after maintaining cultural variety and identity. This cultural unity can be created by using education to promote inter-cultural understanding. If people can be made to realize that both unity or conformity and diversity or individuality are pan of the theory of unity in diversity, it will be possible to take care of and eradicate much of the prejudices, partiality, differences, etc., that arise out of cultural differences .

In addition to the above measures, it is possible to utilize many other things for the purpose of creating inter-cultural understanding. Young men and women can, for example, be encouraged to establish contact with members of other cultures through the medium of pen-friendship. Even inter-cultural marriages can be of immense value in this respect. It is possible to create situations in which members of different cultures come into contact with each other. Tourism, in particular, should be encouraged. Young students can tour the country in groups and thus acquaint themselves with the different cultures existing in remote parts of the country. It is possible to generate a liberal, sympathetic and kind-hearted attitude towards other cultures among the younger generations through the medium of magazines, literary publications intended for the young, and other similar channels. Exhibitions of literature and art can achieve the same thing. Films can also make valuable contributions in this respect. Besides, once the teachers themselves have understood the importance of this aim of education, they will provide many illustrations to their students to create inter-cultural understanding.

25

Education in Democracy

Aldous Huxley has remarked, "If your aim is liberty and democracy, then you must teach people the art of being free and of governing themselves". Democracy can never be successful without education. Wherever democracy has been unsuccessful, it has been because of the lack of education. In a democracy the government is composed of the elected representatives of the people and if the people are uneducated they can never elect the right leaders and consequently can never create the right kind of government. In fact, it is impossible even to hope for democracy in the absence of education. It is difficult to expect a citizen to have responsibility if he is not even aware of his rights and duties. Bertrand Russell has commented, "Democracy in its modern form would be quite impossible in a nation where many men cannot read". The truth of the matter is that education is a prerequisite for democracy. Only after proper education should the citizen be invested with his democratic rights. As Fichte, the German philosopher has commented, "Only the nation which has first solved in actual practice the problem of educating perfect men will then solve the problem of the perfect state". Although Fichte made this comment in the context of autocratic state it can be judged only by the extent to which it contains educated people. As Hetherington puts it, "Democratic government, at least, demands an educated people". Throwing light on the objectives of education in the 1949 meeting of the Universities Commission, Dr. S. Radhakrishnan stressed the fact that the democratic state recognizes the importance of the individual, and it is the process of development of this individual, which is called education. Hence, education is absolutely necessary for establishing a democratic society. Dewey has pointed out that democracy is inconceivable without education, because education alone can generate and instil the qualities which democracy demands as a prerequisite. Philosophers of the ancient Greek city state were aware of the significance of education. Both Plato and Aristotle laid stress on the importance of education for the success of democracy. Ernest Barker comments, "To Plato education was the most important function of the state and the department of education the most important state department which was particularly advocated for producing the philosopher kings to improve the men's minds for becoming virtuous beings". Plato, in his famous text, *The Republic* stressed not only the importance of education for democracy but even formulated a plan for the education of men and women which made all kinds of development physical, mental, moral and aesthetic possible. Aristotle was of the opinion that the aim of the state is to make possible the achievement of the highest moral level and this can be reached through education alone. Thus, education is the most important function of the state. From one point of view, the state itself is a school in which the individual learns citizenship, for Aristotle suggested that the aim of education was to produce good citizens. These truths were known not only to the ancient Greeks but also to Indian thinkers of ancient times. India has been the home of democratic ideals and principles from ancient times. Hermitages and places of worship were used as schools in which the sages tried to produce ideal citizens who could become useful members of society. But the modern age needs democratic education far more than was needed in ancient Greece or ancient India because modern democracies are so vast and their problems so complex that the education of citizens is even more imperative today.

Importance of Education in Democracy

The importance of education for a democratic state is fairly evident from the foregoing account. The following things call be stressed in this connection:

1. Knowledge of rights and duties. If democracy is to be a success, it is essential that every citizen should be aware of his rights and duties because only then can he take active and productive part in the affairs of the state. This knowledge of rights and duties can be obtained only through education. Education socializes the individual so that he develops consciousness of duty.

2. Development of humane qualities. If the ideal of brotherhood is to be achieved by a democratic state, it is necessary for it to develop humane qualities in its members. Kant's moral concepts throw important light on this. Only through education can such qualities as a high moral character, sociability, benevolence, patience, pity, sympathy and brotherhood, etc., he developed in the individual.

3. Faith in democratic ideals. In order to make democracy a success, it is essential that its citizens must have faith in the democratic ideals. And this can be brought about only when they are adequately educated because it is only the educated person who realizes that the sole purpose of life is not the satisfaction of gross physical desires. The ideals of freedom, liberty, brotherhood are more valuable and necessary. No one but the educated individual can understand the circumstances and needs of another person before passing judgment on him. Only such a person can accept the idea of equality after recognizing human values as being the end to be achieved.

4. Fulfilment of political duties. In a democracy the government is elected by the people, and hence the responsibility for electing a good government develops upon them. And, if the people are unable to understand their political rights or to fulfil their political responsibilities, it is foolish to hope for a democratic government. This ability to recognize where one's duty lies can come only through education. Educated people can properly assess the qualities and shortcomings of the various individuals who are fighting the elections, and of the various political parties and their plans and policies which they profess. In India, the absence of education is a big handicap in creating a truly democratic state because during elections the ignorant people are persuaded to vote for the wrong persons, with the result that the governance of the country has failed time and again. Corruption is rampant. The Mudaliar Report points out that if democracy is anything more than voting blindly then every individual must accept the task of independently thinking about all social, political and economic problems before deciding upon the party he wishes to support. But this is possible only when the entire electorate is educated to think independently.

5. Protection and transmission of culture. In any state, ideals can be achieved only when change is accompanied by a parallel continuity, and this continuity with the past is maintained only through culture, the social heritage, which is passed on to the new generation through the medium of education. Hence, education is also required for transmitting culture to future generations and for protecting it.

6. Preventing exploitation. The ideals of democracy are opposed to exploitation of every kind, but if political, social and economic exploitation is to be eliminated from society, it is essential to have universal and compulsory education. In its absence, the rich and powerful people will never give up their advantage and habit, while the poor will never become sufficiently conscious of their rights or their ability to organize together and counter this exploitation. Educated people in a country are aware of their rights and they have the intelligence and training to fight exploitation or violation of their rights. Hence, education is the only real foundation on which democracy can be based.

Education for Democracy in India

All these important aspects of democratic education hold true in India also. India is not merely a modern democratic state but a country which is traditionally inclined towards democracy. A democratic constitution was adopted after Independence. In 1938, Jawaharlal Nehru had said, "The Indian National Congress stands for independence and a democratic state". This objective was achieved after Independence with the establishment of a democratic society. The Indian Constitution seeks to establish a popular government in the country on the basis of democratic principles outlined earlier. For this every citizen must participate in the administration, through his right to vote and to be elected. Every individual is guaranteed and given equal status and opportunity, because no one is discriminated against on the basis of religion, race, caste, community, sex, or on any other grounds. The government is responsible to the people and its elected representatives.

In order to achieve this objective of democracy, education is as necessary in India as anywhere else, a truth which the Indian people have been quick to realize. In the words of Dr. F.W. Thames, "Education is no exotic in India. There has been no country where the love of learning had so early an origin or has exercised so lasting and powerful an influence. From the simple poet of the Vedic age to the Bengali philosopher of the present-day there has been an uninterrupted succession of teachers and scholars". Not only did the Indian Constitution accept the ideals of democracy, it considered education the prime responsibility of the state. In Article 45 of the Constitution it has been stated that every state must arrange for the provision of free and compulsory education to all children up to the age of 14, within ten years of the date of inception of the Constitution. After the achievement of independence, a new phase began in the history of education.

Articles 29 and 30 of the Constitution give fundamental rights to every individual in connection with education and cultural development. According to Article 29, every Indian national living in any part of India will have the right to maintain his own specific language, script and his culture. No person can be refused right of admission to any educational institution, established by the state, by reason of religion, race, caste, language or any other similar consideration. According to Article 30, every minority community will have the right to establish and maintain educational institutions of its own choice, irrespective of whether the minority is a linguistic or religious one. The state will also not refuse aid to any such institution created by a religious or linguistic minority. Articles 45 and 46 determine the policy for education as part and parcel of the directive principles. According to Article 45, the state will make efforts to provide free and compulsory education, within ten years, to every child below the age of 14. According to Article 46, the state will pay special attention to the educational and economic interests of all backward classes, especially the scheduled castes and scheduled tribes. It also entrusts the state with the duty of protecting backward classes from social injustice and exploitation of every kind. The Indian Constitution laid the foundation for a federal government in which the functions of the state and central government are distinctly defined. Both the central and state governments have some duties with respect to the education. It has been realized that there must be co-ordination between the central and state authority on education for a balanced development of the country. The modern Indian state is a welfare state whose objective is the complete development of its people. This welfare can be achieved only through education. Little surprise therefore if all the leaders of the nation stress the importance of education as a first step to improve the future of the nation.

OBJECTIVES OF EDUCATION, ACCORDING TO THE SECONDARY EDUCATION COMMISSION

The democratic ideals which the existing educational policy is hying to achieve are outlined most precisely in the Secondary Education Commission's explanation of the objectives of education.

1. Development of democratic citizenship. The success of democracy depends largely upon the people's awareness of their rights and duties and the extent to which people fulfil their responsibilities. Education aims at developing this ability in the people, because education teaches the man to think and distinguish between right and wrong. He can understand social, economic and political issues and reflect on the possibility of solving such problems. He can decide upon the political party or the leadership which should be entrusted with the task of forming a government and undertaking administration. He does this thinking of the problems facing the country and considering the ability of each group or leader to face such problems. He can express his ideas and suggestions through lectures, essays, articles, etc. He can organize new movements or constitute various kinds of committees to solve the problems facing the country. It is the duty of the state to insist upon a syllabus which can be expected to generate such democratic awareness among the children being educated.

2. Training in skilful living. Democracy can be said to have succeeded only if it can translate the democratic ideals to its society. And, for this, socialization of individual through education is essential. It is desirable to develop such social qualities as collective feeling, co-operation, discipline, tolerance, sympathy, brotherhood, etc., in the individual. Education must also aim to create faith in social justice and willingness to rebel against injustice. Education helps people in adjusting to each other, and the educated individual is generally tolerant and liberal. Although he may differ from other people in their opinions, he has the ability to adjust to such people because he can understand their attitudes. Hence, education is the only means of removing the obstacles in the path of democracy, and also of achieving some adjustment between people who differ from each other in respect of language, race, caste, religion, sex, etc.

3. Development of personality. The success of a democratic society also depends upon whether mature men and women from the majority of minority in its population. Democracy can succeed only if most of its members have developed mature personalities, because a mature person has gone through physical, mental, social, ethical and spiritual development. And education is nothing more than this comprehensive development. Hence, education should aim at the development of all aspects of the educand's personality through various kinds of training. Keeping this in view, most schools and colleges now provide many kinds of extra-curricular training, which supplement all that is taught as part of the curriculum.

4. Developing vocational skill. The Secondary Education Commission has pointed out that another aim of education is to develop some vocational skill in the educand. No nation can progress in the absence of economic progress. The first duty of the state is to provide a system and means of educational skill to the educands so that they can earn their livelihood at the same time as they contribute to the nation's economic growth. The country urgently needs skilled craftsmen, engineers, doctors, teachers and administrators. For this, specialized colleges are required. Every child should be given the right to choose a profession of his own liking, and opportunity to acquire the highest training and education in this profession.

5. Developing leadership. The success of a democracy depends upon the capabilities of the leadership. The democratic government is a decentralized government, for that reason it requires skilled leadership of administration. The democratic government is run by the elected representatives of the people who should be possessed of special qualities. Expert leadership is required for development and progress in every sphere—political, social, economic, artistic, scientific and cultural. Education should aim at evolving such leadership because without doing this education cannot make any real contribution to democracy, for, then it is leaving unfulfilled one of its important responsibilities.

The element of leadership can be encouraged through many kinds of curricular and extra-curricular activities in schools.

Apart from these objectives of education laid down specifically by the Secondary Education Commission, it is desirable to reflect upon some other objectives, which have significance in view of the fact that India is a democracy. In fact, the aims of education vary a little bit with the level of education—the primary , secondary and university education—a fact which has been recognized by the different education commissions established from time to time. The aim of education, at the primary level, is to develop the child's mind by presenting the fundamental elements in the various areas of knowledge, and also to give him an opportunity to develop all his abilities— physical, mental, moral, motor, creative imagination, etc. At this stage attention should be paid to physical development no less than mental development, but attention must also be paid to the burden such an education place on the child. The education imparted should not become a burden.

At the secondary level, attention should be focused on discovering the interests and abilities of every adolescent, and then developing such abilities. Education should be concerned not merely with the general welfare of society but also with the self-realisation and personal development of each individual.

Recommendations of Indian Universities Commission

The Indian Universities Commission has laid down the following objectives of university education in the country:

(1) Providing leadership in politics, administration, professions, industry and commerce.

(2) Training the intellectual leaders of culture and creating inventors.

(3) Causing spiritual development in the educands.

(4) Protecting the culture and civilization of the country and instilling the youth with the ideals of this culture.

(5) Discovering the inherent qualities of individuals and developing them through training.

Development of Emotional Integration

For the success of democracy, education must have an additional objective of promoting emotional integration among the citizens of this country which has an unlimited variety of races, tribes, languages, religions, communities, etc. Without this the ideal of brotherhood cannot be realized, besides, such a situation also encourages the growth of disorganizing and disruptive forces which hinder the country's growth.

Prerequisites for Democratic Education

In India it has been recognized everywhere that education must have the foregoing objectives for the success of democracy, although one is aware of the absence of any concrete step in this direction, upon the present. In order to achieve a higher level of democratization in the educational pattern it is essential to pay attention to the following things:

(1) Efforts must be made to put an end to the discrimination practised in educational institutions established by religious groups. This discrimination is based on caste and religion. The selection of educands, the appointment of teachers, the fashioning of the syllabi are all apparently influenced by caste and

communal considerations. All such things must be prevented. The state should penalize all such institutions by refusing them grants and other financial aid to compel them to give up such undemocratic practices.

(2) Regional considerations and affiliations are also seen influencing the selection of candidates and appointment of teachers in many parts of the country. Such practices cannot be prevented without the intervention of the central authority.

(3) Arrangements should be made for the teaching of Hindi, the all India language, and English, the international language, in addition to the language being taught in each region and State. Some people oppose the teaching of English while others are averse to learning Hindi. But it must be realized that Hindi is essential for developing nationalism while without English we cannot participate in any movement for internationalism. Both of them are important for achieving the democratic ideal, and it is to be regretted that the centre gives little evidence of clear thinking on the issue.

(4) The syllabi at all levels of education—primary, secondary and university levels—need to be reformed in order to lay greater emphasis upon democratic tendencies through the proper teaching of history and geography. Democratic tendencies should be actively encouraged.

(5) In most Indian schools and colleges, the working conditions and pay scales of teachers are far from satisfactory. Few universities provide sufficient facilities for research and higher studies. Appointments of teachers are made more on the basis of personal considerations than on the actual merits of each individual. So long as such conditions are allotted, to exist, there is little hope for democracy. Hence, it is desirable that the government should study the situation, punish the culprits and provide more facilities for teachers and research enthusiasts.

(6) In order to achieve the objectives of nationalism and internationalism, students and teachers should be given facilities for domestic and foreign travel, because such facilities are practically non-existent at present.

(7) At each level of education, the educand should be acquainted with ancient Indian culture and knowledge. Little has been done in this direction so far.

Improvements in Syllabi

If democratic ideals are to be achieved, the syllabi at every level need to be drastically changed. The following things should be considered in this connection:

1. Wide based syllabi. In order to achieve the democratic ideals discussed earlier, and also to achieve the comprehensive development of the child's personality, it is desirable that the syllabi at the primary, secondary and university levels should be wide based. The educational pattern in India has been evolved after keeping this point in view, but it is regretted that the shortage of means has made implementation difficult.

2. Variety and flexibility. At the various levels of education, the curriculum should be flexible and varied, not rule-bound and rigid. This is desirable, because only then can the curriculum accommodate the brilliant as well as the average educand. At the secondary and university levels this is all the more essential because the syllabus must provide each educand with a reasonable choice for selecting subjects that he would like to study. It must also be flexible in order to permit some minor adjustments according to the level of educands studying it.

3. Based on local requirements. India is a large country with a remarkable variety of races and tribes, languages and dress, etc. The syllabi should take into account local requirements. It would be better to give primary education to the children residing in different parts of the country in their respective mother tongues. At the secondary level and later at the university level the educand should be given an opportunity to learn both Hindi and English. Ignorance of English will handicap them and leave them ignorant of a very big chunk of knowledge.

4. Creating a social consciousness. The curriculum should invariably provide certain programme which can be expected to create social consciousness and a desire for responsible community life. But this sentiment for community life should be in keeping with the sentiments of nationalism and internationalism.

5. Earning one's livelihood. The syllabus must include the teaching of subjects which the student can study and later on turn to account for earning his livelihood. In deciding the syllabi for the teaching of professional subjects, it is essential to keep in mind the situations the educand will be required to face in practical life and also the extent to which the present syllabus is helping to prepare him for those situations.

Improvements in School Administration

Another aspect of educational reform is introducing the following changes in pattern of school administration in the country. The pity of it is that little if any work has been done in this direction:

1. More rights to teachers. Educators should have greater say in determining the policy of the school, in preparing the syllabus and in other matters pertaining to the school. The educator must experience a sense of being free from shackles so that he may be able to work enthusiastically.

2. Greater freedom to educators. Educators should be given greater freedom in framing the syllabus, in selecting the methods of teaching, studying, research, etc. Without freedom little creative and original work can be expected. Only when the educators are given freedom to act and to think for themselves can they be expected to make new discoveries in science, literature and art, etc.

3. Democratic environment in schools. Co-operation and brotherhood should form the basis of relations between the educator and the administrators or organizers of the school, between the vice-chancellor and the teachers of the university, etc. The principle of equality should not be sacrificed in the name of discipline, for the latter is perfectly possible even when every one is treated as equal. Defects should be removed and faults rectified democratically and liberally, not in an authoritarian manner.

4. Improvements in the conditions of the educator. The educator is also an important element in the teaching pattern, like the educand. The working conditions of teachers can hardly be said to be satisfactory in this country. Arrangements should be made for training them adequately, and their selection should be made on merit, not on personal considerations and whims of the powers that be. They should be encouraged to study further and go in for research work. Their scales of pay should be made equal to the scales of pay of people who are as well qualified as they are. Payment should be made on the basis of equal pay for equal work. Their work should be free from interruptions from the administrative staff. Seminars and institutes should be organized from time to time in order to improve their efficiency by informing them of the latest discoveries in their respective spheres.

Improvement in Methods of Teaching

In a democracy, even the teaching methods adopted inside the school should be essentially democratic. In this connection, the following suggestions can be given:

1. Encouraging co-operation. All work should be done with the co-operation of the principal and the head of the department, between the head and the educator, between the educator and the educand, and between one educand and another. This helps to evolve the sense of co-operation and sense of community so essential for democracy.

2. Stress on activity. According to John Dewey, one of the most famous exponents of democratic education, the child should be taught by actually doing some action. By taking an active part in the process of teaching, the educand learns self-control, self-discipline and self-inspiration, all of which are essential for the success of democracy.

3. Independence. Liberty is the fundamental principle of democracy, and hence the democratic method of teaching also has no place for any external pressure. It permits the educand to ask any questions coming to his mind, to express his own opinion and to make any criticism which suggests itself to him. Democratic education aims at training the individual to think for himself. Great stress is placed on the child's independence in all modern teaching techniques, such as Montessory method, Project method, Dalton method, Heuristic method, etc. In all such democratic techniques the teacher serves only as the guide whose task is to encourage, guide and direct the child who learns for himself and moves on the path of knowledge.

4. Based on all-round development. Teaching methods in a democratic society should be so designed as to promote and encourage development of every aspect of the child's personality. Care should be taken to see that no aspect is repressed, so that all-round comprehensive development becomes possible. The democratic citizen would be handicapped by a lopsided development of personality because it would render him unfit for performance of duties in one sphere or the other. In proportion to the greater rights given to a citizen in democracy, his duties and responsibilities also tend to be greater than those of an individual in some other society. Hence, education must be so designed as to create such abilities in the child as self-dependence, self-reliance, dedication to duty, ability to fulfil responsibilities, etc.

Establishing Discipline

Discipline has special value in the democratic pattern of education because the educands passing through the phase of education have themselves to grow up and take part in administration. They have to consider the success of democracy. In other patterns of government so much discipline and training in discipline are not quite so necessary. The greatest discipline is self-discipline, it is self-control, it involves changes in one's own tendencies and desires, according to the demands of the community and the society. It is absolutely essential for the members of a democratic society to be disciplined. And this is possible only when school and university students are taught the lesson of discipline. In schools the educator should be impartial in his behaviour towards all the educands. Most of the work of the school should be performed by the educands, under the guidance and supervision of the educators. Self governing units such as students' unions, students' committees, and students' parliaments should be created so that the educands may be trained in democratic activities and life. He should be able to take active and intelligent part in such activities. The educand's activities should be hindered or obstructed by his own organizations and institutions, not by the official administration. Social control will thus teach them to be disciplined. The teacher must prove himself to be a model of discipline. Even the state should avoid unnecessary interference in the working of educational institutions. Finally, it can be said that only the voluntary co-operation of the educators, guardians and administrators can help to create a truly democratic environment in schools in which the educand can learn to be disciplined.

26

EDUCATION FOR SOCIALISTIC PATTERN OF SOCIETY

Definition of Adult Education

In the words of Mukherjee, "Adult education may be defined very broadly so as to include all instruction, formal or informal, to adults". According to K.G. Saiyeden, "Adult education includes political and civil as well as moral education". What was called adult education before winning Independence is today called social education. But the aims of social education are more comprehensive than those of adult education. Its main aim is to bring a socialistic pattern of society through education.

WHAT IS SOCIAL EDUCATION?

The erstwhile education minister Maulana Abul Kalam Azad explained the meaning of adult education while inaugurating the UNESCO seminar on village adult education in 1949. He said that social education implied education for making a man complete, it will make him literate so that he has access to the knowledge of the world. It will tell him how he should adapt to his environment and how he should take maximum advantage of his physical circumstances. It will teach him handicrafts and more efficient method of production so that he may achieve economic prosperity. It will teach him the fundamentals of personal and social hygiene so that this domestic life may be happy and prosperous. And finally, this education will train him in citizenship so that he may be able to cooperate with his government in making the country strong and in establishing peace in the world for all of which some knowledge is essential. In the beginning, social education or adult education was interpreted only in the sense of granting literacy to the unread adult, but now it has come to comprehend every kind of education for the adult. In the words of Biharee, "Social education is the stimulation in each citizen of a greater awareness of the advantages of the pattern of society as conceived in the constitution and a persistent desire for progress towards a pattern socially, economically and culturally".

PURPOSE OF SOCIAL EDUCATION

In the past, adult education limited itself to creating some limited literacy in the adult so that he could read and write letters, read religious texts and comprehend accounts. But social education today is far more comprehensive. In this connection, the following aims of social education have been stated in a booklet *Social Education in India* published by the government of India. The following are the aims set down there:

(a) Individual aims. Social education, from the individual standpoint, aims at the achievement of the following objectives:

(1) Mental development of adults.

(2) Development of their professional ability.

(3) Their physical development.

(4) Development of their social skills.

(5) Their cultural development.

(6) Their self-development.

(b) Social objectives. Social education has the following social objectives:

(1) Development of social unity.

(2) Protection and development of national resources.

(3) Organization of co-operative communities and institutions.

(4) Inclusion of the social ideal.

AIMS OF SOCIAL EDUCATION

It is evident from the foregoing list of the purposes of social education that its aim is very comprehensive. After Independence, a committee was appointed under the chairmanship of Mr. Mohan Lal Saxena to advise the government on the expansion of adult education in the country. This committee re-christened adult education and called it social education, and determined the following aims for it:

(1) To awaken the citizens towards their rights and duties, and to encourage the feeling of social service among them.

(2) Creating love for democracy among the citizens and training them in democratic government.

(3) Acquainting the citizens with the problems confronting the country and the world.

(4) Creating a feeling of respect and admiration for Indian culture through the teaching of history, geography and culture.

(5) Providing the citizens with an opportunity for cultural mixing and getting pleasure through organization of songs and dramatic activities.

(6) Acquainting the citizens with specific moral values through community discussions and teaching.

(7) Providing necessary knowledge of language and arithmetic and encouraging the spread of knowledge.

(8) Educating the citizens to use their leisure for economic production and prosperity through teaching handicraft and other skills.

(9) Continuing the educational programme among the citizens through the use of libraries, discussions, educational committees and public universities,

(10) Creating a sense of co-operation among the citizens.

FIVE-POINT PROGRAMME

The government evolved; a five-point programme to achieve these targets of social education:

(1) Spread of literary.

(2) Education in health and hygiene rules.

(3) Training in industry and professions for economic progress.

(4) Awareness of rights and duties along with feeling of citizenship.

27

THE DISTURBED CAMPUS

The phenomenon of student unrest started in India with the agitation of 1905 led by Calcutta and Dacca students to oppose the partition of Bengal. This marks student involvement in agitations. As a part of national struggle it was encouraged by all political parties and welcomed by the public. Therefore, since then the students' participation in national political movement in India increased at every stage particularly in Quit India Movement in 1942. Most of the national leaders were students during the period of national struggle. They left the colleges and the universities to participate in National Movement at the call of their beloved leaders M.K. Gandhi, J.L. Nehru and B.G. Tilak, etc.

Student Unrest in the World

Students' involvement in politics is nothing new. In Germany, Russia and France a large number of students participated in political activities in the 19th century. In 20th century the student activities in South Korea were effective in changing the Iron regime of Syghman Rhee. In Japan the students demonstrated against Prime Minister Kishi. In Indonesia and Vietnam the students protested against US interference. In England and America one occasionally witnessed student demonstration against expansion of nuclear weapons. Peace marches are a usual scene. A large number of students in Afghanistan are fighting as gorilla against Russians. In Dacca students have several times strongly demonstrated on national issues. In USSR, however, the phenomenon of disturbed campus is not traceable. On the other hand, in almost all the other countries of the world one finds students' participation in demonstrations, strikes, processions and mass meetings.

Role of Political Parties in India

In India by the participation in national struggle the students learned agitational methods of protest and realized the power of student unity. After the country achieved independence this experience was utilized to highlight students sentiments on local, regional, national and even international issues. Since the political parties were in the habit of using students as the youth power in political agitations, most of the political parties encouraged students organizations on political basis. Thus, while BHU has been dominated by rightist students, JNU is the centre of leftist activities. Congress-I, BJP, Janata and DMKP all the political parties have been maintaining their student wings since Independence in India. Therefore, it is quite understandable that the disturbed campus is not a temporary phenomenon. Disturbance is only a symptom, a fruit whose roots are being nourished by all the political parties.

Growth of Youth Power

This, however, does not mean that the students have themselves no political consciousness and that whatever they do is at the instigation of the political parties. Leadership is a phenomenon which is nourished and grown in institutions of higher learning everywhere. This is necessary for the growth of youth leadership in the country. This is most welcome though when it takes wrong turns it becomes a headache to the government and the people alike. In recent years several universities have witnessed growth of student power. In most of the universities the student unions have their own buildings, budget extending to thousands of rupees and all the paraphernalia of a political party. During the period of elections the whole campus and even the city is on siege. All types of methods of propaganda are utilized. Vote catching devises are practised even more shrewdly as compared to the techniques of general elections. Propaganda material worth lakhs of rupees is utilized. Posters come up on all the walls of the city. Hundreds of vehicles of all types are utilized. Money flows from the capitalists and the political parties. And when the winners celebrate they are blessed by the benign presence of the national leaders belonging lo the political parties to which they owe allegiance.

The Modus Operandi

After the leaders are elected, they take stock of the situation local, regional and national. If the issues are not pointed enough, even the flimsiest issue is taken up for starting agitation. It is not because there is something to do that the political activities go on but because the leaders have to justify their election and to show their presence that issues are created. This, however, does not mean that all the activities are baseless. Some student activities have undoubtedly cleaned the campus, made the teachers more responsible and kept the administration awake. From time to time the student leaders do the cathartic function of unwailing the mask from the face of the administrators and powerful teacher politicians to show them m their tine colours. This service is of signal importance.

INDISCIPLINE

Indiscipline is the initial symptom as well as the result of a disturbed campus. While discipline is the adherence to rules and regulations, indiscipline is their contravention. According to the report on the problem of student indiscipline in India m 1960 presented by the committee appointed by the UGC to investigate student indiscipline, "Indiscipline is mass moral turpitude and collective defiance of authority and the use of techniques in seeking redress of real or imagined grievances which are not appropriate for students to use". This definition was formulated alter a close study of the disturbed campus. The acts of indiscipline noted by the committee involved discourtesy to teachers, misbehaviour towards women students, student riots, damaging college building, disruption of the normal life of society, squatting on tram lines and rail tracks, stopping and burning the buses, physical violence against this or that individual and group and a host of other activities resulting into disruption of the educational process, growth of violence and general elimination of peace and order. These acts of indiscipline started on any issue and led by the student leaders followed by thousands of enthusiastic students. The committee called these techniques inappropriate. This is far from convincing since it suffers from the dual standard, allowing the use of these techniques to political leaders and disallowing them to students. This double standard is far from convincing to the student leaders.

Multisided Phenomenon

Thus the phenomenon of the disturbed campus is multisided. Physically, it may be seen in acts of violence, damages to property, impediments in the normal working of the educational institutions, mass meetings, hunger strikes, agitations, processions, etc. The psychological aspect, however, is more important. This is made of power mongering on the part of the leaders and frustration among the students. So many lapses on the part of the government administrators result in a sense of frustration on the part of the students. One of the most glaring factor creating frustration is the phenomenon of educated unemployment. The student leaders, on the other hand, are constantly on the look out to take an issue to show their power to the student community on the one hand and to the administrators, the government and the public on the other. It is notable that it is from the ranks of these student leaders that some of the most famous national leaders in India have grown. Their example serves to encourage the ambitions of every student leader. By taking up an issue he makes promises to the student community and exercises pressure by threats and coercion upon the administrative authorities.

Psychological Factors

In brief, the following psychological factors work at the root of the phenomenon of disturbed campus:

1. Loss of faith in aim of education. As more and more students become disillusioned about the goals of education in the colleges and universities, they withdraw from studies and involve themselves in union activities.

2. Loss of faith in the means. Even if the goals sought by educational institutions may be sound, loss of faith in the means of education may result into frustration. This may be concerning any part of the educational machinery such as admissions, appointment of teachers, discipline among teachers, time-table, curriculum, methods of teaching, rules of discipline, rules concerning hostels, efficiency of the general administration and finally the mode and validity of examination and evaluation methods. It is a truism that in India at present all these aspects of education are full of problems which do not appear to be solved in near future.

3. Lack of internalisation of values and attitudes. It is well known that without teacher's involvement in the process of education, no betterment in educational institutions is possible. This involvement, however, requires several conditions. If so many teachers are known to be having side jobs, running tuition shops, doing insurance business or things like that, they can hardly have any involvement with teaching in the educational institutions. This involvement requires more conscientiousness among teachers. The teachers themselves should be free from politics before asking the students to do so. If the teacher unions are functioning like labour unions how can they suggest anything different to the student unions. The repressive techniques of the research guides can only help to increase frustration rather than any real creative work among the research students. But while the teachers know that there is no necessary correlation between teaching methods and evaluation techniques their enthusiasm in teaching cannot be maintained, unless the teacher-management relationship, the teacher-principal and the teacher-student relationship is improved. The involvement of the teachers is not possible if the teacher-taught ratio is beyond a certain proportion. No educational institutions can remain undisturbed without solving this problem. Therefore, the values and attitudes demanded from the students should be first created among the teachers. And before asking for involvement on the part of teachers, suitable conditions for its natural growth must be created.

ANALYSIS OF THE PHENOMENON

In *The Sociology of Education in India,* NCERT (1967) Mr. S.H. Asthana and Suma Chitnis have analysed the phenomenon of the Disturbed Campus under two heads as follows:

(A) The Educational System, its Goals, Failure and Indiscipline

1. Goals of education. The minimum goals of education is training for earning a livelihood. The maximum goal of education is socialization, diffusion of knowledge, values, attitudes and norms of relationships, required for playing adult roles in society. In a healthy system of education both these goals must be realized.

2. Failures of educational system. The abovementioned goals have not been realized. The growing number of educated unemployment clearly shows failure of our educational system to provide livelihood. During British regime even a matric fail could find a job. Now persons with post-graduate degree are unemployed in a great number. And this number is constantly growing. This failure may be attributed to the following causes:

(i) *No accurate assessment of manpower needs.* As there is no accurate assessment of manpower needs there is no correlation between the number of educated persons and the number of employment opportunities growing every year. Expansion in education has been more rapid than generation of job opportunities.

(ii) *Prejudices.* Caste, region, language, religion and nationality have been the basis of appointment in non-government and even government agencies. Therefore, the organization has failed to provide livelihood on the basis of merit.

(iii) *Irrelevance of Education to Occupation.* A general criticism of the present educational system is about irrelevance to occupations other than white-collar

CAUSES OF YOUTH TENSION IN INDIA

ıre the causes of widespread indiscipline among the youth in tl

xity. The youth of today is in a dilemma because he does not kno
ıd what is wrong. Most of the teachers express such completel
pinions on moral problems that the educand is confused. O
e finds very strong arguments being advanced for a materialisti
some teachers, while other educators are found supporting th
n with equally valid arguments. The confusion is made worse b
nions on the subject of religion also. Some educators are devou
e other are complete atheists. On the one side are the educator
he ancient ideal of abstinence as the sole means of developin
e other, one finds more liberal educators who believe that th
sexes and social intercourse, etc., are the most important formativ
racter development. They argue that sex is natural and there i
restraint. It is only something natural that the educand shoul
left completely adrift when he is faced with such contradictor
sequently, he finds it difficult if not impossible, to act accordin
inciple. He has no choice but to do as he likes, and one finds tha
endencies are being manifested in the form of indiscipline.

educators. Most of the youth forming part of the existing
ture are completely lacking in ideals. Some of the causes of this
he bad economic conditions of the educators, uneven and often
king conditions, nepotism and favouritism in appointments,
social prestige, etc. But, whatever the causes, it cannot be
majority of teachers at the primary and secondary level of
lividuals without ideals and principles. In fact, many of them
erate and there is little cause for surprise if indiscipline among
s when they are guided by such individuals. But, it must also
hat the government is also very much to be blamed for this
cently, the staff at the primary level in U.P. went on strike to
ds for increase in pay. It was argued by the educators that the
not expect good teaching at the salary it offered to the educator.
ountered this with the suggestion that it wanted the educands
leals. If the government itself exhibits such lack of concern
mental principles which guide civilized life, it can blame only
tuation created in the country by increasing indiscipline.

m of education. After India had won her independence, a
es and commissions have criticised the existing system of
nted out its defects. In spite of this the system continues till
duced by the East India Company with a view to producing
aff. There has been no change for the better, in fact, there has
erosion of standards. Corruption at all levels is not rampant

jobs. The values created by academic education do not create initiative and necessary qualities of character such as national integration, equality, patriotism, democratic attitude to life, etc.

(iv) *Lack of national integration.* Casteism, communalism, linguism and parochial tendencies are fast disintegrating Indian society. Far from eliminating these tendencies, the education sometimes encourages them. For example, in most of the colleges and universities linguism, regionalism and casteism are rather the rule than exception. Communalism, though not much rampant, may also be seen particularly in the educational institutions organized and run by a particular community. Unless national integration is maintained the conflict among various groups of students and teachers is inevitable.

(v) *Absence of democratic values.* It is an irony that the student unions which were primarily established to fulfil the demands of democratization of education have themselves become source of the disturbed campus. Equality may be declared in policy but it is not properly practised. Liberty takes the form of indiscipline and rowdy behaviour. Fraternity is conspicuous by its absence. In the words of S.H. Asthana and Suma Chitnis, "Democracy, to many, is voicing an opinion insisting on one's rights, student unions give an excellent exercise in these qualities. But the more important concept of democracy as a partnership of free men, united in the common purpose of national development, does not emerge".

Unfortunately the example of academic fraternity set by the teaching community is far from encouraging this value among the students. Most of the university departments in every residential university exhibit cut throat factionism among teachers. This factionism sometimes goes to the extent of teacher's activities against the research students and disciples of rival colleagues. Every university department has become a den of favoritism, in-fighting, casteism, communalism, regionalism, hatred and jealousies. In this atmosphere no youth can learn democratic values. Team work is a phenomenon unknown to Indian scholars. While in the West most of the valuable academic advancement has been achieved through team work, in India hardly a group of scholars can see eye to eye on any problem. Seminars exhibit leg pulling and personal aggrandisement, vain show and mannerism rather than any solid contribution to knowledge. Lectures are organized to oblige friends. Examinerships are exchanged. Ph.Ds. are distributed on clique basis. Appointments are made on the basis of personal favour. In the face of such a low level of character and behaviour among gurus, it is small wonder that the new generation learns that opportunism, nepotism, politicking, wire pulling, back-biting, cut-throat competitions and ruthlessness are the values and traits required for progress in life. It has been rightly lamented by Asthana and Chitnis, "The academic community in India is not a partnership in quest of knowledge. Mutual response between teachers and administrators swings between the two extremes of callous flouting of authority and a subservience that smothers self-respect. A mood of lethargy and pessimism prevails".

(B) Norms, Sanction, Values and Attitudes

Change in Norms

Formerly, it was the norm in education that the teachers were respected. According to Indian philosophy of education academic achievements are correlative to respect toward teachers. This norm has been now reversed since education is linked with payment of fees. The modern students have hardly any respect towards their teachers, the idea of serving the teacher is beyond their comprehension. This discourages the teachers to give their best to the student. The modern teacher is stimulated by the challenge he faces in the class. The old teacher was encouraged to give his best because of his love and sentiment of service, dedication and sacrifice for the academic cause. Thus, the norms both on the part of teacher and the taught have been reversed.

Change in Sanctions

Formerly, the teacher's attempt to maintain discipline was sanctioned by the administration, the community and even by the students themselves. Even corporal punishment was appreciated. Today attempts to discipline the students do not receive sanction from the community and the students. The administration is helpless against the strength of the student unions. It is a common feature in the universities that rustication of rowdy student leaders is opposed by student unions tooth and nail. It sparks off protests, strikes and even violence. The students turn a deaf ear to the teachers, the principal and the vice-chancellor. The parents do not approve punishment any more. Corporal punishment is opposed by the parents.

The most important sanction to discipline in education comes from social ethos. Formerly, the social ethos emphasized reverence for elders. The children were asked to obey their parents and teachers. Today the emphasis is on freedom—freedom to think, freedom to act, freedom to react and even freedom to all kinds of indiscipline. In almost every sphere of life today the only value is self regard or selfishness. In the absence of the sanction of the social ethos discipline cannot be created in educational institutions.

Change in Values and Attitudes

Indian society was formerly authoritarian. In the wake of democratic values authoritarianism has been substituted by liberty. Not only in the field of education but in marriage and family modern boys and girls do as they like. The age of marriage is growing, making norm for twenty to twenty-five for girls and twenty-five to thirty for boys. Till then boys and girls stay in universities and colleges. Therefore, they learn all types of individual ways of behaviour and conduct. They are not governed either by parents or by teachers. The media, the film, literature, radio, television and everything else are laying emphasis upon personal choice irrespective of what it means to others. Therefore, the values of equality and fraternity have been often set back by liberty. In fact, of the three democratic values, fraternity is the proper basis for equality and liberty. Liberty, on the other hand, cannot be the basis of equality and fraternity. Unfortunately, the modern

youth lays emphasis upon liberty as the
wonder that he is only concerned with him

In Indian axiology Dharma was the hig
subordinate to it. Moksha was the ideal of
It has now been substituted by a one-sidec
only values to be cherished. According to
are provided by destiny, Dharma and M
the present world everywhere Dharma an
and Kama are actively pursued. The histo
human societies has shown that mammoi
and final decay. This is the inevitable
such circumstances the youths learn to
emphasis is rather on smartness than cul
knowledge than scholarship. Therefore,
exception. Scholarship, simplicity and l
Not excellence but success is the goal. N
aims to be achieved. The modern stud
on fashion, excitement, novelty, speed a
are gradually breaking all norms of dec
no level. All means are adopted for self-a
M.K. Gandhi are being used in educatic
of goals which are far from decency, di

Conclusions

The analysis of disturbed campus in In
is revolt against oppression most of it
it may be attributed to exuberance of
and even crime. While some of it aim
most of it is for the calculated benefit
of it may genuinely represent uprisin
inroad of political parties into camp
not even by the union leaders but by
While some of the budget of the stud
the student, most of it is met by secre
interests. Therefore, it goes without
corrective measures.

Basically the disturbed campus
unrest in India is a phenomenon
educators, defective system of educa
educators, repressive policies of t
teacher-parent relationships and fi
An analysis of these causes of youth
of curing them.

The following a
country:

1. Moral perple
what is right ar
contradictory c
the one hand, h
philosophy by s
cause of idealisn
the differing op
religionists whil
who believe in t
character. On th
casual mixing of
influences in cha
no need for any
be stupefied and
alternatives. Con
to any rational pr
his more animal

2. Lack of ideal
educational struc
materialism are t
insufferable worl
absence of any
doubted that the
education are inc
are morally degen
educands increase
be remembered t
situation. Fairly r
support its deman
government could
The government c
taught 3R's not i
towards the funda
itself for difficult s

3. Defective syste
series of committe
education and poi
today. It was intro
qualified clerical st
only been a steady

but accepted as another fact of life. Accepting bribes to give better marks, co-operating with another educator to give better marks to his candidate, favouritism in the evaluation of doctoral research theses, are some of the common practices. In fact, one can sum up the entire situation by saying that now, there appears to be no correlation between hard work and study, writing the collect answers in the examination answer books and getting good marks. There is, therefore, no occasion for surprise if one finds that the educand's only aim is to secure degree by fair means or foul. Apart from the system of examination, the education system is further eroded by such defects as an impractical teacher-taught ratio in the classroom, absence of extra-curricular programmes, the prescription of sub-standard text-books, etc. It is only manifesting one's ignorance if one imagines that indiscipline can be removed when the education system is so beset with defects.

4. Political gangsterism. Most of the colleges and universities in the country have become nothing more than hotbeds of political gangsterism and polemic. Most of the students unions are dominated by stooges of some political parties, and they are concerned only with achieving their own ends by using the students unions. Such influences not only lead to gangsterism in the institution, they also create the possibility of misusing the students for political ends. One finds that during elections, political parties become even more active in their efforts to woo the educands to their side. There is no denying that political parties have played a sufficiently destructive role in bringing about indiscipline and the consequent problems although it would be unfair to imply that political interference is the sole cause.

5. Grouping among educators. If an individual takes it upon himself to attend the functions and gatherings of teacher's unions of some institution on three or four occasions, he will soon arrive at the conclusion that the groupism found among teachers perhaps exceeds that which is found among the members of any other professional group. Students are not only aware of this groupism, but they are deliberately made aware of this, because in many cases they are directed by one group to observe the activities of the other group of educators and to report it to the first. Thus, the educand becomes conscious of existing rivalry between the various groups among his educators. All this has a very detrimental effect on the educand's mind, because he feels that such activity must be justified.

6. Repressive policies of the state. Clashes between the students and police have become a regular feature in almost every state. One hears of many incidents in which the police thrashed the students, carried out a baton charge, entered the college campuses, destroyed property, attacked students inside the colleges, even resorted to firing and killing students. Lack of discipline among the students cannot be compared to revolution and rioting, and it should not be treated as such. At the root of it there are some causes which have to be understood and then eradicated.

Adoption of a repressive policy only adds fuel to the fire, and ultimately this fire spreads from one part of the country to another, until it engulfs most of the country.

7. Social disorganization. Social disorganization is a condition in which the organization, control and mutual co-operation that normally exists between various social institutions and committees deteriorates and practically ceases to exist. This kind of disorganization leads to the disorganization of such fundamental institutions as marriage and finally, ultimately leading to personal disorganization. Indiscipline is just one instance of this kind of disorganization. Hence, one cause of the indiscipline found among students today is the general disorganization of society.

8. Absence of teacher-parent relationship. In a more normal situation, the absence of relationship and contact between teachers and parents is another cause of indiscipline. Both the teacher and the parent are unaware of the difficulties of each other, and thus they blame each other for the defects of the students without making any effort to improve the student. In fact, the responsibility for the student's indiscipline must be equally divided between the student, the parent and the teacher, but mutual co-operation and contact between the latter two can solve this problem to a great extent.

9. Psychological causes. At its root, indiscipline is a psychological defect of character. Among its more prominent causes are abnormalities concerning sex, inferiority and superiority complexes, feelings of insecurity, absence of any aim, etc. All these factors contribute to the frustration of the educand, which is converted into violence. This violence is manifested in the facts of indiscipline which are universally condemned. The responsibility for giving rise to such psychological symptoms rests upon bad and morally degenerate films and literature, lack of character among the educators, social class distinctions, absence of any normal relations between girls and boys in the college, neglect of moral education, etc.

The most important factor among those outlined above is the defective nature of the system of education, because all other causes have their origin in the basic shortcoming. The existing system of education cannot do with some small changes. It needs to be completely overhauled, in fact, scrapped and replaced by a different system altogether. It should be made to conform to the cultural characteristics of the nation, education should be imparted through the medium of the national language, and it must incorporate better working conditions for the educator, and a more efficacious and reliable system of examination.

MEANS OF CURING YOUTH TENSION

The means of curing youth tension can be inferred from the foregoing account of its causes. The following suggestions have been made in this regard:

1. Improvement in the teacher's condition. This comprehends increase in salary, better conditions of work, more just and impartial selections and appointments, reasonable prospects of advancement, etc. If these conditions are met, the educators will be able to live satisfactory lives and thus they will be encouraged to impart some idealism to their educands.

2. Presentation of right ideals by the educator. Since almost all educands initiate their educator both consciously and unconsciously, it is necessary that the educator must present the correct ideal in every sphere of conduct.

3. Improvements in the system of education. As far as possible the defects in the system of education pointed out by various committees and commissions should be removed immediately.

4. Improvements in the examination system. Education achieves development of the total personality. The examination, therefore, must test this development, not merely the memory, as it does at present.

5. Preventing political influence in schools. No political party should be given the chance to penetrate school and college life.

6. Control of unwarranted state interference. More often, than not, the vice-chancellors appointed to the universities are appointed on any consideration except that of merit. These appointments are made by the government, and hence are illustrations of undue state interference in education. It is undesirable for the state to interfere in the working of education in this manner.

7. Protection of the independence of educational institutions. Of the many incidents of violence and destruction by the students in the recent past, many were inspired by the entry of the police into college compounds, either without the permission or in violation of the express command of the college authorities. All educationists agree that no government employee has the right to enter the premises of the educational institution without the permission of the principal. If this rule is not violated it would be easier to prevent manifestations of youth unrest from becoming violent and destructive.

8. Contact between educators and parents. Another method of curbing youth unrest is to encourage contact between educators and parents so that they can meet and discuss the problems of educands and thus remove the causes leading to indiscipline.

9. Moral education. Most thinkers agree that absence of moral education is responsible for youth unrest and character defects of the educands. In any case moral education will definitely curb indiscipline.

10. Creation of proper atmosphere in colleges. The psychological factors at the root of youth unrest can be eliminated by creating the proper atmosphere in schools. As far as possible, the atmosphere should resemble that of a large family in which the relations between boys, girls, educators, students, etc., would be morally and psychologically healthy.

Youth unrest is a complex problem having its social, political and psychological aspects. In order to remove it, these aspects must be understood and the co-operation of educators, parents and state must be used to solve this problem.

IMPROVEMENT OF STUDENT UNIONS

The role of student leaders in campus is not negative. Student unions cannot run on the pattern of labour unions. Instead of aiming at students' unity and demand of students' rights, they should rather aim at furthering the cause of education and strengthening teacher-taught relationship. This, however, requires a periodical survey of the needs and demands of the students by the government and the administration and prompt remedy to them. Restriction on admission of blacklisted students is a necessary condition for checking indiscipline on the campus. The following suggestions may be advanced for the better organization of student unions:

1. Students' participation in management. In the college governed by managing committees the student leaders may be given representation in the managing committees so that they may get their demands directly fulfilled without any confrontation with the principal.

2. Limitation on expenses. There should be restriction and proper auditing of budget of student unions. If evidence for spending much beyond income is clear, enquiry should be made into the extra source of income.

3. Restriction on activities in public. The activities of student unions should be confined within the campus. They should be restrained to do anything in city.

4. No permission for litigation. All the controversies concerning students should be decided by principal, the Vice-Chancellor and the district administration. At no time the students union may be permitted to go to court for pressing its demand.

5. Proper permission for activities. The students union is governed by campus rules. They should give prior information and seek sanction for every activity from the principal in the college and the Vice-Chancellor in the university. Activities should be organized not only by prior information but prior sanction.

6. Correlation of manpower needs an educational planning. This point has been repeatedly emphasized by every education commission. Educational planning includes educational guidance. Manpower planning depends on vocational guidance. Vocationalisation of higher education is necessary for practical use of educational facilities. Job efficiency should be the criteria for organization of courses, method of evaluation and modes of instruction.

7. Better teacher-taught relationship. Peace on the campus depends on proper teacher-taught relationships. This requires satisfaction and involvement of the teachers as well as the taught. This depends upon proper policies concerning admission, curriculum, methods of teaching, administration, evaluation, appointments and general facilities.

8. Better socialization. This requires elimination of parochialism, casteism communalism, linguism, regionalism and factionalism from the campus. On the other hand, national integration should be propagated by all means.

In the end it should be remembered that some sort of disturbance is a part of the normal life in the campus. It is only when indiscipline crosses limits that action should be taken. Prevention is always better than cure. This is particularly true in the case of educational campus.

jobs. The values created by academic education do not create initiative and necessary qualities of character such as national integration, equality, patriotism, democratic attitude to life, etc.

(iv) *Lack of national integration.* Casteism, communalism, linguism and parochial tendencies are fast disintegrating Indian society. Far from eliminating these tendencies, the education sometimes encourages them. For example, in most of the colleges and universities linguism, regionalism and casteism are rather the rule than exception. Communalism, though not much rampant, may also be seen particularly in the educational institutions organized and run by a particular community. Unless national integration is maintained the conflict among various groups of students and teachers is inevitable.

(v) *Absence of democratic values.* It is an irony that the student unions which were primarily established to fulfil the demands of democratization of education have themselves become source of the disturbed campus. Equality may be declared in policy but it is not properly practised. Liberty takes the form of indiscipline and rowdy behaviour. Fraternity is conspicuous by its absence. In the words of S.H. Asthana and Suma Chitnis, "Democracy, to many, is voicing an opinion insisting on one's rights, student unions give an excellent exercise in these qualities. But the more important concept of democracy as a partnership of free men, united in the common purpose of national development, does not emerge".

Unfortunately the example of academic fraternity set by the teaching community is far from encouraging this value among the students. Most of the university departments in every residential university exhibit cut throat factionism among teachers. This factionism sometimes goes to the extent of teacher's activities against the research students and disciples of rival colleagues. Every university department has become a den of favoritism, in-fighting, casteism, communalism, regionalism, hatred and jealousies. In this atmosphere no youth can learn democratic values. Team work is a phenomenon unknown to Indian scholars. While in the West most of the valuable academic advancement has been achieved through team work, in India hardly a group of scholars can see eye to eye on any problem. Seminars exhibit leg pulling and personal aggrandisement, vain show and mannerism rather than any solid contribution to knowledge. Lectures are organized to oblige friends. Examinerships are exchanged. Ph.Ds. are distributed on clique basis. Appointments are made on the basis of personal favour. In the face of such a low level of character and behaviour among gurus, it is small wonder that the new generation learns that opportunism, nepotism, politicking, wire pulling, back-biting, cut-throat competitions and ruthlessness are the values and traits required for progress in life. It has been rightly lamented by Asthana and Chitnis, "The academic community in India is not a partnership in quest of knowledge. Mutual response between teachers and administrators swings between the two extremes of callous flouting of authority and a subservience that smothers self-respect. A mood of lethargy and pessimism prevails".

(B) Norms, Sanction, Values and Attitudes

Change in Norms

Formerly, it was the norm in education that the teachers were respected. According to Indian philosophy of education academic achievements are correlative to respect toward teachers. This norm has been now reversed since education is linked with payment of fees. The modern students have hardly any respect towards their teachers, the idea of serving the teacher is beyond their comprehension. This discourages the teachers to give their best to the student. The modern teacher is stimulated by the challenge he faces in the class. The old teacher was encouraged to give his best because of his love and sentiment of service, dedication and sacrifice for the academic cause. Thus, the norms both on the part of teacher and the taught have been reversed.

Change in Sanctions

Formerly, the teacher's attempt to maintain discipline was sanctioned by the administration, the community and even by the students themselves. Even corporal punishment was appreciated. Today attempts to discipline the students do not receive sanction from the community and the students. The administration is helpless against the strength of the student unions. It is a common feature in the universities that rustication of rowdy student leaders is opposed by student unions tooth and nail. It sparks off protests, strikes and even violence. The students turn a deaf ear to the teachers, the principal and the vice-chancellor. The parents do not approve punishment any more. Corporal punishment is opposed by the parents.

The most important sanction to discipline in education comes from social ethos. Formerly, the social ethos emphasized reverence for elders. The children were asked to obey their parents and teachers. Today the emphasis is on freedom—freedom to think, freedom to act, freedom to react and even freedom to all kinds of indiscipline. In almost every sphere of life today the only value is self regard or selfishness. In the absence of the sanction of the social ethos discipline cannot be created in educational institutions.

Change in Values and Attitudes

Indian society was formerly authoritarian. In the wake of democratic values authoritarianism has been substituted by liberty. Not only in the field of education but in marriage and family modern boys and girls do as they like. The age of marriage is growing, making norm for twenty to twenty-five for girls and twenty-five to thirty for boys. Till then boys and girls stay in universities and colleges. Therefore, they learn all types of individual ways of behaviour and conduct. They are not governed either by parents or by teachers. The media, the film, literature, radio, television and everything else are laying emphasis upon personal choice irrespective of what it means to others. Therefore, the values of equality and fraternity have been often set back by liberty. In fact, of the three democratic values, fraternity is the proper basis for equality and liberty. Liberty, on the other hand, cannot be the basis of equality and fraternity. Unfortunately, the modern youth lays emphasis upon liberty as the highest value. Therefore, there is no wonder that he is only concerned with himself.

In Indian axiology Dharma was the highest value while Artha and Kama were subordinate to it. Moksha was the ideal of life. This was an integral value system. It has now been substituted by a one-sided value system of Artha or Kama as the only values to be cherished. According to Indian wisdom while Artha and Kama are provided by destiny, Dharma and Moksha are the values to be pursued. In the present world everywhere Dharma and Moksha are left to destiny and Artha and Kama are actively pursued. The history of cultural development in different human societies has shown that mammon worship leads to cultural degeneration and final decay. This is the inevitable result of the present-day culture. In such circumstances the youths learn to fulfil their aim by hook or crook. The emphasis is rather on smartness than culture, mannerism than character, general knowledge than scholarship. Therefore, mediocrity is the rule and excellence is exception. Scholarship, simplicity and hardwork are no more necessary values. Not excellence but success is the goal. Not Dharma but Artha and Kama are the aims to be achieved. The modern student aims at enjoyment. The emphasis is on fashion, excitement, novelty, speed and enjoyment. Heterosexual relationships are gradually breaking all norms of decency and restraint. Student politics knows no level. All means are adopted for self-aggrandisement. The techniques taught by M.K. Gandhi are being used in educational campus all over India for achievement of goals which are far from decency, discipline and even student welfare.

Conclusions

The analysis of disturbed campus in India shows several features. While some of it is revolt against oppression most of it may be termed indiscipline. While some of it may be attributed to exuberance of youth, most of it is delinquency, vandalism and even crime. While some of it aims at general welfare of student community, most of it is for the calculated benefit of a clique of student leaders. While some of it may genuinely represent uprising of Indian youth, most of it is due to the inroad of political parties into campus. Most of the union activities are guided not even by the union leaders but by their political mentors outside the campus. While some of the budget of the student unions is covered by contributions from the student, most of it is met by secret donations from political parties and vested interests. Therefore, it goes without saying that the disturbed campus requires corrective measures.

Basically the disturbed campus in India is the result of youth unrest. Youth unrest in India is a phenomenon exhibiting moral perplexity, lack of ideal educators, defective system of education, political gangsterism, groupism among educators, repressive policies of the state, social disorganization, absence of teacher-parent relationships and finally, the psychological defects of character. An analysis of these causes of youth unrest in India will pave the path to the means of curing them.

CAUSES OF YOUTH TENSION IN INDIA

The following are the causes of widespread indiscipline among the youth in the country:

1. Moral perplexity. The youth of today is in a dilemma because he does not know what is right and what is wrong. Most of the teachers express such completely contradictory opinions on moral problems that the educand is confused. On the one hand, he finds very strong arguments being advanced for a materialistic philosophy by some teachers, while other educators are found supporting the cause of idealism with equally valid arguments. The confusion is made worse by the differing opinions on the subject of religion also. Some educators are devout religionists while other are complete atheists. On the one side are the educators who believe in the ancient ideal of abstinence as the sole means of developing character. On the other, one finds more liberal educators who believe that the casual mixing of sexes and social intercourse, etc., are the most important formative influences in character development. They argue that sex is natural and there is no need for any restraint. It is only something natural that the educand should be stupefied and left completely adrift when he is faced with such contradictory alternatives. Consequently, he finds it difficult if not impossible, to act according to any rational principle. He has no choice but to do as he likes, and one finds that his more animal tendencies are being manifested in the form of indiscipline.

2. Lack of ideal educators. Most of the youth forming part of the existing educational structure are completely lacking in ideals. Some of the causes of this materialism are the bad economic conditions of the educators, uneven and often insufferable working conditions, nepotism and favouritism in appointments, absence of any social prestige, etc. But, whatever the causes, it cannot be doubted that the majority of teachers at the primary and secondary level of education are individuals without ideals and principles. In fact, many of them are morally degenerate and there is little cause for surprise if indiscipline among educands increases when they are guided by such individuals. But, it must also be remembered that the government is also very much to be blamed for this situation. Fairly recently, the staff at the primary level in U.P. went on strike to support its demands for increase in pay. It was argued by the educators that the government could not expect good teaching at the salary it offered to the educator. The government countered this with the suggestion that it wanted the educands taught 3R's not ideals. If the government itself exhibits such lack of concern towards the fundamental principles which guide civilized life, it can blame only itself for difficult situation created in the country by increasing indiscipline.

3. Defective system of education. After India had won her independence, a series of committees and commissions have criticised the existing system of education and pointed out its defects. In spite of this the system continues till today. It was introduced by the East India Company with a view to producing qualified clerical staff. There has been no change for the better, in fact, there has only been a steady erosion of standards. Corruption at all levels is not rampant but accepted as another fact of life. Accepting bribes to give better marks, co-operating with another educator to give better marks to his candidate, favouritism in the evaluation of doctoral research theses, are some of the common practices. In fact, one can sum up the entire situation by saying that now, there appears to be no correlation between hard work and study, writing the collect answers in the examination answer books and getting good marks. There is, therefore, no occasion for surprise if one finds that the educand's only aim is to secure degree by fair means or foul. Apart from the system of examination, the education system is further eroded by such defects as an impractical teacher-taught ratio in the classroom, absence of extra-curricular programmes, the prescription of sub-standard text-books, etc. It is only manifesting one's ignorance if one imagines that indiscipline can be removed when the education system is so beset with defects.

4. Political gangsterism. Most of the colleges and universities in the country have become nothing more than hotbeds of political gangsterism and polemic. Most of the students unions are dominated by stooges of some political parties, and they are concerned only with achieving their own ends by using the students unions. Such influences not only lead to gangsterism in the institution, they also create the possibility of misusing the students for political ends. One finds that during elections, political parties become even more active in their efforts to woo the educands to their side. There is no denying that political parties have played a sufficiently destructive role in bringing about indiscipline and the consequent problems although it would be unfair to imply that political interference is the sole cause.

5. Grouping among educators. If an individual takes it upon himself to attend the functions and gatherings of teacher's unions of some institution on three or four occasions, he will soon arrive at the conclusion that the groupism found among teachers perhaps exceeds that which is found among the members of any other professional group. Students are not only aware of this groupism, but they are deliberately made aware of this, because in many cases they are directed by one group to observe the activities of the other group of educators and to report it to the first. Thus, the educand becomes conscious of existing rivalry between the various groups among his educators. All this has a very detrimental effect on the educand's mind, because he feels that such activity must be justified.

6. Repressive policies of the state. Clashes between the students and police have become a regular feature in almost every state. One hears of many incidents in which the police thrashed the students, carried out a baton charge, entered the college campuses, destroyed property, attacked students inside the colleges, even resorted to firing and killing students. Lack of discipline among the students cannot be compared to revolution and rioting, and it should not be treated as such. At the root of it there are some causes which have to be understood and then eradicated.

Adoption of a repressive policy only adds fuel to the fire, and ultimately this fire spreads from one part of the country to another, until it engulfs most of the country.

7. Social disorganization. Social disorganization is a condition in which the organization, control and mutual co-operation that normally exists between various social institutions and committees deteriorates and practically ceases to exist. This kind of disorganization leads to the disorganization of such fundamental institutions as marriage and finally, ultimately leading to personal disorganization. Indiscipline is just one instance of this kind of disorganization. Hence, one cause of the indiscipline found among students today is the general disorganization of society.

8. Absence of teacher-parent relationship. In a more normal situation, the absence of relationship and contact between teachers and parents is another cause of indiscipline. Both the teacher and the parent are unaware of the difficulties of each other, and thus they blame each other for the defects of the students without making any effort to improve the student. In fact, the responsibility for the student's indiscipline must be equally divided between the student, the parent and the teacher, but mutual co-operation and contact between the latter two can solve this problem to a great extent.

9. Psychological causes. At its root, indiscipline is a psychological defect of character. Among its more prominent causes are abnormalities concerning sex, inferiority and superiority complexes, feelings of insecurity, absence of any aim, etc. All these factors contribute to the frustration of the educand, which is converted into violence. This violence is manifested in the facts of indiscipline which are universally condemned. The responsibility for giving rise to such psychological symptoms rests upon bad and morally degenerate films and literature, lack of character among the educators, social class distinctions, absence of any normal relations between girls and boys in the college, neglect of moral education, etc.

The most important factor among those outlined above is the defective nature of the system of education, because all other causes have their origin in the basic shortcoming. The existing system of education cannot do with some small changes. It needs to be completely overhauled, in fact, scrapped and replaced by a different system altogether. It should be made to conform to the cultural characteristics of the nation, education should be imparted through the medium of the national language, and it must incorporate better working conditions for the educator, and a more efficacious and reliable system of examination.

MEANS OF CURING YOUTH TENSION

The means of curing youth tension can be inferred from the foregoing account of its causes. The following suggestions have been made in this regard:

1. Improvement in the teacher's condition. This comprehends increase in salary, better conditions of work, more just and impartial selections and appointments, reasonable prospects of advancement, etc. If these conditions are met, the educators will be able to live satisfactory lives and thus they will be encouraged to impart some idealism to their educands.

2. Presentation of right ideals by the educator. Since almost all educands initiate their educator both consciously and unconsciously, it is necessary that the educator must present the correct ideal in every sphere of conduct.

3. Improvements in the system of education. As far as possible the defects in the system of education pointed out by various committees and commissions should be removed immediately.

4. Improvements in the examination system. Education achieves development of the total personality. The examination, therefore, must test this development, not merely the memory, as it does at present.

5. Preventing political influence in schools. No political party should be given the chance to penetrate school and college life.

6. Control of unwarranted state interference. More often, than not, the vice-chancellors appointed to the universities are appointed on any consideration except that of merit. These appointments are made by the government, and hence are illustrations of undue state interference in education. It is undesirable for the state to interfere in the working of education in this manner.

7. Protection of the independence of educational institutions. Of the many incidents of violence and destruction by the students in the recent past, many were inspired by the entry of the police into college compounds, either without the permission or in violation of the express command of the college authorities. All educationists agree that no government employee has the right to enter the premises of the educational institution without the permission of the principal. If this rule is not violated it would be easier to prevent manifestations of youth unrest from becoming violent and destructive.

8. Contact between educators and parents. Another method of curbing youth unrest is to encourage contact between educators and parents so that they can meet and discuss the problems of educands and thus remove the causes leading to indiscipline.

9. Moral education. Most thinkers agree that absence of moral education is responsible for youth unrest and character defects of the educands. In any case moral education will definitely curb indiscipline.

10. Creation of proper atmosphere in colleges. The psychological factors at the root of youth unrest can be eliminated by creating the proper atmosphere in schools. As far as possible, the atmosphere should resemble that of a large family in which the relations between boys, girls, educators, students, etc., would be morally and psychologically healthy.

Youth unrest is a complex problem having its social, political and psychological aspects. In order to remove it, these aspects must be understood and the co-operation of educators, parents and state must be used to solve this problem.

IMPROVEMENT OF STUDENT UNIONS

The role of student leaders in campus is not negative. Student unions cannot run on the pattern of labour unions. Instead of aiming at students' unity and demand of students' rights, they should rather aim at furthering the cause of education and strengthening teacher-taught relationship. This, however, requires a periodical survey of the needs and demands of the students by the government and the administration and prompt remedy to them. Restriction on admission of blacklisted students is a necessary condition for checking indiscipline on the campus. The following suggestions may be advanced for the better organization of student unions:

1. Students' participation in management. In the college governed by managing committees the student leaders may be given representation in the managing committees so that they may get their demands directly fulfilled without any confrontation with the principal.

2. Limitation on expenses. There should be restriction and proper auditing of budget of student unions. If evidence for spending much beyond income is clear, enquiry should be made into the extra source of income.

3. Restriction on activities in public. The activities of student unions should be confined within the campus. They should be restrained to do anything in city.

4. No permission for litigation. All the controversies concerning students should be decided by principal, the Vice-Chancellor and the district administration. At no time the students union may be permitted to go to court for pressing its demand.

5. Proper permission for activities. The students union is governed by campus rules. They should give prior information and seek sanction for every activity from the principal in the college and the Vice-Chancellor in the university. Activities should be organized not only by prior information but prior sanction.

6. Correlation of manpower needs an educational planning. This point has been repeatedly emphasized by every education commission. Educational planning includes educational guidance. Manpower planning depends on vocational guidance. Vocationalisation of higher education is necessary for practical use of educational facilities. Job efficiency should be the criteria for organization of courses, method of evaluation and modes of instruction.

7. Better teacher-taught relationship. Peace on the campus depends on proper teacher-taught relationships. This requires satisfaction and involvement of the teachers as well as the taught. This depends upon proper policies concerning admission, curriculum, methods of teaching, administration, evaluation, appointments and general facilities.

8. Better socialization. This requires elimination of parochialism, casteism communalism, linguism, regionalism and factionalism from the campus. On the other hand, national integration should be propagated by all means.

In the end it should be remembered that some sort of disturbance is a part of the normal life in the campus. It is only when indiscipline crosses limits that action should be taken. Prevention is always better than cure. This is particularly true in the case of educational campus.

28

NATIONAL EMOTIONAL INTEGRATION

The consciousness of nationality is generated in the younger' generation through education, and hence there is a profound relationship between nationality and education. In India, when the revolt against the British government was awakened, all national leaders demanded the formation of a national educational programme. They argued that the educational programme of the country should be modified to suit the requirements of the nation. In 1921, Mahatma Gandhi expressed his views on this subject in Young India, criticising the existing educational pattern introduced by the British people. He too demanded that the educational pattern must be modified to suit the demands of the nation. His reasons for adding manual work to cducation wcrc sound sincc hc knew that cducation must pay its own way in a poor country like India. Rabindra Nath Tagore conducted an experiment in Shanti Niketan to produce a novel kind of human society in which the problems of the individual and the community, the nation and the world, could be solved simultaneously. Swami Dayanand insisted upon reforming education to suit the educational pattern that existed in ancient times. On the other hand, Annie Besant's educational plan, which included the establishment of primary schools, lower middle schools, higher middle schools, high schools for general education, high schools for general science, commercial schools, technical high schools, agricultural high schools, etc., was more directly in touch with the problems of contemporary India.

Madan Mohan Malviya established the Hindu University at Kashi in order to realize the ideals of education which prevailed in ancient India. In addition to these individual and specific efforts, all other educational philosophers of the time, including Sri Aurobindo, Vivekanand, etc., favoured the modification of the educational pattern in order to make it conform to ancient Indian values, ideas and thinking. In more recept times, in his report of the Universities Commission, Dr. Radhakrishnan pointed out the defects of the existing pattern of education, and suggested that it should be refashioned to fulfil national needs. It is only because of the feeling of nationality that most educationists have objected to the use of English as a medium of instruction in the country. Everyone has stressed the need for education to be a character building process, because without this the fixture of the nation will always remain dark. Dr. Radhakrishnan has said that the fixture of the nation is made by character. No country can be great if its inhabitants have low character. If we want to create a great nation, we must educate our young men and women in such a manner that they should possess the force of character. We must have men and women who see themselves reflected in other human beings. This has been said in our sacred texts.

Stressing the need for an education for nationality, the Kothari Education Commission has said that the objective of our system of education should be to develop national consciousness. For this we must develop the knowledge of our cultural heritage, but we must also submit this cultural heritage to revaluation. At the same time we must have faith in the future towards which we are moving.

Development of Nationalism in the New Generation

The following suggestions can be given for generating nationalism in the younger generation:

1. Development of a national language. The first prerequisite for developing nationalism is the development of a national language in the country. In India, this position can be occupied only by Hindi. When the succeeding generations learn Hindi and use it, the feeling will gradually take root that India is one nation.

2. Development of a national literature. Development of a national language will lead to the development of a national literature. With the propagation of Hindi in every part of the country, a new literature will be created, which will be read everywhere. Apart from encouraging national unity, it will also enable the people to create a literature which encourages national power and protects the cultural heritage of the country.

3. National educational programme. In India the spread of education is the responsibility of both the central and the state governments but as yet, it has not been possible to formulate a national programme of education, with the result that one can see considerable disparity in the various parts of the country. In order to evolve a feeling of nationalism the country should have a unified educational programme which should be flexible enough, to take within its purview the differences that exist between one region and another. This will lead to a certain similarity in the education in all parts, and make possible the application of a single curriculum through which national literature on the all India scale can be created.

4. Observance of national festivals. The feeling of nationalism can also be strengthened by enthusiastic observance of national festivals, Independence Day, Republic Day, Children's Day, Teacher's Day and the birthdays of all great men.

5. Respect for national symbols. Another way of fostering the feeling of nationalism is to generate and show respect for national symbols such as the national anthem, the national flag, the national bird, etc.

6. Improvements of curriculum. In order to help the development of the national sentiment, it is desirable that the teaching of history, civics, etc., should be conducted in such a way that it helps national sentiment. This can be done by preventing the publication of any material in text-books and other media of publication which hurts national sentiments and pride. The government seizes all copies of such material and punishes the publishers and authors.

7. Co-operation of political parties. It is impossible to generate nationalism if the political parties fail to cooperate. Many political parties not only hinder the growth of this sentiment, but actively engage in activities calculated to harm the national interest. Such political parties owe their allegiance to other nations, show no respect for national symbols and spread anti-national feelings among the people. As far as possible, political parties should be prevented from indulging in such activities.

8. Co-operation of teachers. Education for nationalism can never be really successful without the active co-operation of teachers. For this reason, the educators must themselves possess this feeling, because then they can set an example for the educands. It will then be even easier to grow the national sentiment among the younger generation.

Synthesis of Nationalism and Internationalism

Now-a-days many thinkers object to the use of education for fostering the national sentiment because they have come across many bad effects of narrow nationalism in many countries and seen that education for nationalism has stood in the way of the growth of internationalism. The education for nationalism that was given in Italy and Germany, for example, was completely opposed to internationalism. It is in connection with this one-sided education that Bertrand Russell pointed out that children are taught to exhibit complete devotion and worship to the state of which they are citizens. The lesson taught to them is that worship of the state consists in doing as directed by the state. For this they are taught distorted versions of history, politics and economics so that they should not be critical of the blind national faith expected of them. They are acquainted with the evil actions of other nations but not of their own although the truth is that each nation has been unjust to other nations. It is unquestionably true that if the facts of history are distorted in order to propagate the sentiment of nationalism it is undesirable. But this danger is not peculiar to nationalism alone. It is true of almost all human relations that as they become deeper and stronger they also become narrower, and that they impede the growth of any liberal attitude. If, for example, an individual has intense love for his family, this may come in the way of his loving his nation, but this does not imply that love for nation can exist only at the cost of love for family. Proper and healthy love for the family does not impede love for the nation, it helps it to grow. In the same way healthy nationalism also does not preclude the possibility of internationalism. As Dr. Louise has said that it is essential to strengthen one's love for one's motherland, but this does not make it proper to violate the canons of humanity, for the external benefit of one's own nation. It is obvious, therefore, that education must not only propagate nationalism but must also encourage internationalism. The plan for national education presented by such eminent educationists as Mahatma Gandhi, Sri Aurobindo, Vivekanand, Rabindra Nath Tagore, etc., has kept this in view, that nationalism and internationalism should grow harmoniously. That is the reason why Rabindra Nath Tagore's Shanti Niketan turned into an ideal institution for education in internationalism. According to Tagore the educand's aim is to reach the level at which there is no distinction between nationalism and internationalism.

Obstacles in the Development of Nationalism

The progress and growth of nationalism in India is being impeded by certain elements and obstacles, the more important ones among which are the following:

1. Casteism. Casteism is the most restricted form of narrow interests. As a result of this, not only the country but even Hindu society has been fragmented into small pieces, each one of which is concerned only with preserving its own interests, without caring for those of other groups. In the presence of this casteism, nationalism is a far cry. Even the unity of the Hindu social organisation is difficult to maintain. Hence, it is necessary to get rid of casteism, although it is not necessary for this to destroy the caste system .

2. Regionalism. In contemporary India, regionalism and regional loyalties have spread so much that even the political unity of the country is being threatened. Some states have expressed the desire to secede from the Union, because they believe themselves to be separate nations. Such tendencies should be suppressed with a strong hand because otherwise national unity may be damaged beyond repair.

3. Communalism. In India today, there are still many Muslims who do not accept India as their country. At the root of this is communalism, and because of their blind faith in their own community they believe the country to belong to Hindus, although it belongs to everybody. It is impossible to evolve nationalism without first putting an end to the mutual distrust of the different communities. For this active steps must be taken in educational institutions .

4. Linguism. Another expression of the disorganising influences at work in the country is linguism. With independence came the problem of deciding a national language, because a national language is essential for maintaining the unity of the nation. Compared to other languages Hindi is best equipped to fulfil this role, but many people object to this because of narrow political interests. In addition, the people of some states are not willing to accept any language but their own. This controversy turned violent and led to considerable bloodshed. An early solution of this problem is desirable if nationalism is to foster in the country.

5. Classism. Most people in India create distinctions among themselves on the basis of economic and social classes. Communist influence has encouraged class hatred to such an extent that various classes fight for their own interests, even at the cost of the national interest. Class interest is also manifested in the form of untouchability. This class struggle is a serious impediment to the growth of national sentiment, and it must be eliminated from the minds of the younger generation.

The purpose behind recounting these obstacles to national sentiment is to point out that both negative and positive steps must be taken. Nationalism can be spread among the younger generation by following the suggestions given earlier and also by removing these hindrances. Mutual co-operation between the people, government and educators is of the essence. It is impossible to improve the country's future without increasing the sentiment of nationalism, irrespective of industrial and scientific progress. The future of the nation is dark unless a high national character of the people is formed.

The unity of a nation depends upon the extent to which its various members look upon themselves as members of the same group. National unity or integration does not automatically follow upon living within the same geographical boundaries. Emotional integration is necessary for this unity. As is evident from the term itself emotional integration is the unity, identity or similarity of emotions. If it exists, then individuals feel related to and concerned with each other, despite any external differences. It is emotional integration which keeps members of a family organised. In colleges, this emotional integration is generated through various communal programmes. It promotes a sense of community and impedes the progress of disorganizing tendencies.

In India one finds marked differences in the living standards, dress, customs, religion, culture, etc., of the various people existing in different parts. India's large size is emphasized by these differences, but one result of this is that when a person goes from one part of the country to another, he is almost a foreigner there. This has led to regionalism, expressed in the desire of people of one region to promote their own regional interests at the expense of the interests of other regions. Regionalism has gained tremendous momentum because it has been linked with linguism. Linguism is the prejudice of the speakers of a particular language to develop their language, to the detriment of any and all other languages spoken in different parts of the country. Casteism or radical distinction between the Hindus and Muslims has led to deterioration of social organisation in the country. Untouchability is an offshoot of casteism. Religious communities have been known to come into violent conflict with each other, thus leading to considerable damage to public and private property, and bloodshed on a large scale. Communalism is responsible for the hatred which one religious group fosters for another. Putting it briefly, regionalism, linguism, casteism, communalism, etc., are the disruptive and disorganisation influences which have divided Indian society into various groups. It is impossible to hope for a solution of the problems in the absence of emotional integration. And if these problems remain unsolved, democracy will also remain a dream.

Unity in Diversity

Generally speaking, the extent of diversity found in India tends to create the impression that it is not a country but a subcontinent. But this does not imply that unity of integration is impossible in such a situation. One finds distinct and different racial characteristics among the inhabitants of different parts of the country, because differences of complexion, size, shape, etc., are clearly evident. It can be clearly seen that there is gradual decline in the physical stature of the inhabitants as one moves from Punjab to Assam. If other examples are necessary, it can be seen that there are all kinds of complexions in this country. In the north complexion varies from darkly wheatish, dark, yellow, pink and even runs into mixtures of these colours. Inhabitants of the Andamans are jet black while colour of those of the South Dravidians is a shining black, in direct contrast is the rosy white complexion of the Kashmiris. Turning to languages, one finds that the Indian Constitution has granted recognition to Urdu, Bengali, Assamese, Oriya, Punjabi, Gujarati, Marathi, Sindhi and numerous other languages, in addition to Hindi. Besides, Telugu, Kannada, Tamil and Malayalam have been accepted as the four Dravid languages. Sanskrit has also been given special consideration as the original Aryan language. Differences exist not only at the level of language but also in respect of dress, religion, culture, etc. Tribes of the north-east, central districts and the south differ from each other in their modes of life, their social and psychological characteristics, etc., to such a great extent that one can find among them different cultural and social regions. If one travels from east to west, and then back again, one will find clearly perceptible differences in complexion, dress, customs, modes of life, dietary habits and other aspects of culture, even at very short distances. But despite these differences of region, race, language, tribe, etc., the existence of a national unity cannot be questioned. One finds this inner unity or integration in all the people spread over the landmass limited by the Himalayas on the one side and the Indian Ocean on the other, the Burma Hill on the east and Pakistan on the west. This inner unity is the basis of emotional integration. Despite the more obvious and superficial differences, prosperity increases. It is this inner unity which Sir Herbert Rizley described when he commented that, at the root of the apparent diversity of physical and social type, language, custom and religion that immediately strikes the observer coming to India, is a definite similarity of identity of inner unity of life from the Himalayas to Cape Comorin. This inner integration or unity is the basis of Indian culture. All the saints of the past were aware of this unity, although they were no less aware of the obvious differences. It is for this reason that India has always been treated as a single unit, even in the remote past. It has been customary to refer to all the people residing in different parts of the country as Indians, even though one could see the differences of religion, culture, languages, etc. In fact, the very name Bharatvarsha denotes not merely geographical boundaries but actually the ideal of a cultural unity. During the Middle Ages, India was always treated as one unit. That India is accepted as the mother by all Indians is only due to a feeling of oneness and identity.

Efforts for Emotional Integration

It was this question of emotional integration which inspired the Central Education Ministry in 1961 to organise a committee for emotional integration under the chairmanship of Dr. Sampurnanand. This campaign to increase emotional integration had the solid foundation of belief in the principle of unity in diversity. All that is needed is that the younger generation should be educated in this direction through various kinds of programmes. Speaking at the inauguration of the Indian Integration Committee, Shri K.L. Shrimali, explained the significance of education and commented that if we want to generate national consciousness in our people, we will have to plan our education accordingly. Education must be so designed as to encourage each participant to think of himself as a responsible part of the Indian nation. Education must take upon itself the responsibility of awakening the younger generation to the truth that, despite obvious external differences, all Indians are the same, emotionally.

Keeping in mind the objective outlined above, the Emotional Integration Committee gave the following suggestions:

1. Reorganization of syllabi. In order to reorganise and reshape the syllabi of colleges and universities to accord with the needs of the nation, the committee made the following suggestions:

(i) At the primary stage, stress should be laid upon nationalistic stories, poems, songs, etc.

(ii) At the secondary stage, in addition to the other subjects being taught, special attention should be given to the study of national literature, social studies, moral and religious guidance and extra-curricular activities.

(iii) At the university level, the syllabi should include the various social sciences, languages, literatures, cultures and arts. Teachers and students should be given facilities to travel to various parts of the country.

2. Encouragement to extra-curricular activities. Besides imparting formal knowledge to the students, the teachers must provide them with the opportunity to take part in such extra-curricular activities which are important from the standpoint of emotional integration. Besides, such programmes must also represent the entire nation. Such programmes help in the development of we-feeling, a feeling of unity and sympathy. One example of such programmes is the Inter University cultural festivals, in which teachers and students participate from all parts of the country.

3. Improvement of text-books. It is desirable that text-books on various subjects, and especially on history, should be amended and improved. They should be designed to encourage a sense of emotional unity with people living in other parts of the country. This will also help to check the growth of communal feelings. But it should also be remembered that such amendments should not be made at the cost of truth because such violence to truth is not necessary. That the country is one is an undeniable truth. What is required is an expression of this truth.

4. Improvement concerning language and script. In this connection the committee on Emotional Integration made the following recommendations:

(i) The use of the Roman script should be permitted to increase knowledge of Hindi in certain areas.

(ii) International numerals should be used in every field of knowledge.

(iii) Arrangements should be made to teach the Devanagri script where it is not known.

(iv) Hindi text-books should also be provided in the regional scripts. Dictionaries using both Hindi and the regional languages should also be prepared.

(v) At the university level, study of Hindi and English literatures should be encouraged so that integration is encouraged and divisive forces checked.

(vi) The rights of the minorities should be protected in formulating a language policy.

In addition to the above list of suggestions, the Committee for Emotional Integration also made certain other suggestions. In schools the daily programme should be started after a community prayer and a ten-minute talk, either by the principal or by some respected person, on some subject which may encourage emotional integration. Another way of encouraging emotional integration is to organise a mass meeting of the school once a year and asking the students to take an oath to increase emotional integration. Besides, all subjects and activities likely to lower awareness of differences should be encouraged. In this manner it is possible to create a climate in which all people feel that they are members of one nation. On the negative side, all efforts must be made to destroy all elements which tend to obstruct the growth of emotional integration.

Suggestions for improving Emotional Integration

Apart from the suggestions outlined above, education can be used in the following suggested ways for improving emotional integration in the country:

1. Development of an all-India language. The first condition for increasing emotional integration in the country is that an all-India language should be evolved. Hindi is the only language capable of performing this role. Hence, it is desirable that knowledge of this language be made compulsory for every citizen. Government should extend every facility for developing Hindi literature. The development of a national language will not prejudice the interests of regional languages. They should be allowed to pursue their own course. But all communications between the Centre and the States should be conducted in the all-India language. Applicants for administrative jobs in the government should be required to know Hindi, although they may be allowed to take the examination in their regional language.

2. An all-India educational policy. Education is the most effective tool for spreading emotional and national integration. For this reason a national educational plan should be devised. This plan should aim at providing every child with knowledge of the ideas of great men, poets, leaders, religious thinkers, etc. Text-books should be prepared under the supervision of the Central government and provided by it, so that the younger generation may be brought up in an atmosphere of nationalistic fervour. Rules for the appointment of teachers, their pay scales and their conditions of forking should be common all over the country. The same syllabi should be applicable to all institutions in the country at the primary, secondary and university levels. All-India organisations like the NCC, Scouting, Girl Guides, etc., should be given appropriate encouragement. University education should be through the medium of the national language, even if the students are permitted to answer questions in their mother tongues. In this manner, the objective of national unity or integration can be achieved by evolving an all-India educational plan.

3. Programmes for increasing national unity. Many kinds of programmes can be devised for increasing national unity. For example, the cinema can be used to spread the feeling of national unity. Radio and television can also be used equally effectively. All-India competitions and meetings can be organised in various parts of the country to increase national unity. Such programmes help people living in different parts of the country to meet residents of other parts and learn their ideas and understand them. Travel facilities should be made more common and delegations and tours encouraged. During the last few years special trains made up of farmers of different areas, students and members of parliament toured the entire country. This helped the cause of national integration. Other programmes similar to these can be organised .

4. Development of intercultural understanding. In all the programmes outlined above, intercultural understanding will be promoted. This helps people to achieve liberality of attitudes to other cultures, an essential precondition of national unity in a country in which there are many cultures.

5. Efforts by teachers. Success of most of these programmes for increasing national unity depends upon teachers. As long as the teachers themselves do not rise above their petty narrow mindedness and create ideals, there is little hope of the students developing any emotional unity. Hence, it is desirable that national consciousness should first be stirred in the students. For this, teachers from various parts of the country should be encouraged to meet each other. This can be done through the all-India teachers organisation. Even otherwise, most of the problems of teachers are common all over the country, and when they meet each other they will get an opportunity to think over these problems and exchange ideas. At the same time, a national consciousness will awaken in them. Yet, attention must be paid to forestalling the development of a class consciousness among the teachers. The government can make a positive contribution in this direction by organizing lectures from time to time and distributing literature of this kind.

6. Governmental efforts. Governmental effort is essential for bringing success to all the projects outlined above, because without official blessing there is little that education can achieve. This cannot be doubted because there are many agencies which are working against the development of emotional integration. So long as the government fails to check agencies which encourage linguism, communalism, religious bigotry and other disruptive forces, education will not be able to achieve the goal. One of the first steps in this direction is control over disintegrative political parties. In every part of the country laws should be enacted to prevent any individual from giving expression to linguism, communalism, regionalism, casteism, untouchability, etc. This should be followed up by a strict application of these laws.

It is evident from the foregoing description of the measures for increasing emotional integration that these measures must be both positive and negative. Adoption of all these measures would be a positive step. The negative step of destroying all obstacles in the way of emotional integration is no less important. For this, teachers, administrators and guardians will have to work collectively.

QUESTION BANK

PRINCIPLES OF EDUCATION

Q. 1. Formulate a definition of education. Why is education regarded as a process of adjustment?

Q. 2. Distinguish between formal and informal education.

Q. 3. "Education has been defined and interpreted in many ways but these definitions are mostly complementary rather than contradictory." Explain?

Q. 4. What is Non-formal education? Discuss its nature, objectives and types.

Q. 5. Who are benefited from Non-formal education? What are its agencies? Distinguish between formal and non-formal education.

Q. 6. "Education is the process of Human Resource Development." Discuss this statement in the light of scope of education.

Q. 7. Is education a science or an art? Discuss the nature of education.

Q. 8. What are the aims of education? Distinguish between universal and specific aims of education.

Q. 9. Discuss the inter-relationship of aims of education and social life in the context of history of education in India.

Q. 10. Discuss the advantages and disadvantages of vocational aim of education.

Q. 11. Discuss the functions of education is human life.

Q. 12. Discuss the functions of education in national life.

Q. 13. Discuss the Formal and Informal Agencies of Education.

Q. 14. Evaluate the current pattern of evaluation and examination.

Q. 15. What is curriculum? What are its principles and bases?

Q. 16. What are the main devices of teaching? Explain any one device you like. Give reasons for your preference.

Q. 17. Explain the meaning and characteristics of Micro-teaching. Distinguish its assumptions and methods from traditional teaching.

Q. 18. "Simulation embraces three types of activities: role playing, socio-drama and gaming." Explain and point out assumptions and activities of simulation.

Q. 19. What is programmed learning? Explain its fundamental principles.

Q. 20. Define Team Teaching and point out its essentials and guiding principles.

SOCIOLOGY OF EDUCATION

Q. 1. Explain sociological tendency in education and point out its impact.

Q. 2. Define educational sociology and discuss its value.

Q. 3. Discuss the scope of sociology of education.

Q. 4. Explain the meaning of education in West and East and attempt a synthetic definition.

Q. 5. What are the aims of education? Distinguish between universal and specific aims of education.

Q. 6. Discuss how the aims of education are related to human life.

Q. 7. Discuss the inter-relationship of aims of education and social life in the context of history of education in India.

Q. 8. Discuss the advantages and disadvantages of vocational aim of education.

Q. 9. Discuss the aim of education as character development.

Q. 10. Discuss the functions of education in human life.

Q. 11. Discuss the functions of education in National life.

Q. 12. Distinguish and explain Formal and Informal education.

Q. 13. What is Non-formal education? Discuss its nature, objectives and types.

Q. 14. Who are benefited by Non-formal education? What are its agencies? Distinguish between Formal and Non-formal education.

Q. 15. Discuss the importance of school as an environment.

Q. 16. Explain the relationship of society and school. Discuss their mutual impact.

Q. 17. What is the responsibility of school towards society? Suggest means to bring society and school close to each other.

Q. 18. Explain the concept of de-schooled society. What is hidden curriculum and open-learning?

Q. 19. "The concept of Socially Useful Productive Work (SUPW) must find a central place in the new plan of education." Discuss this statement in the context of Indian Education.

Or

"Education should be work-centered." Elucidate this statement.

Or

Discuss ways and means of relating education to productivity.

Or

"The introduction of Socially Useful Productive Work will assist in checking the cleavage between the so-called educated classes and the masses." Explain.

Or

"Work Experience, Basic Education, Socially Useful Productive Work—all have the same meaning, though different names." Discuss.

Q. 20. Write short note on Education and Human Values.

Q. 21. "Religion and education are natural allies." Discuss the need, aims, modes and role of religious education in a secular state.

Q. 22. "Education without moral values is not education". Discuss.

Or

"Education without Ethics is blind." Discuss.

Or

"Ethics has much to do with education." Discuss.

Q. 23. Write short note on Culture and Education.

Q. 24. Explain the education of culture in Family, School and Society.

Q. 25. What are the chief characteristics of Group Life? How can these be utilized in education?

Q. 26. Write short note on leadership and education.

Q. 27. What is Community? What is its responsibility towards education?

Q. 28. Write short note on educational impact of the Community.

Q. 29. What is the educational importance of the Community? How will you develop community sentiment and leadership in the school?

Q. 30. Discuss the role of state in education. Do you agree with the demand that education should be nationalized? Give your reasons for and against.

Or

There being an intimate relationship between state and education, the state control of education is necessary. Discussfully and point out to what extent the State should control education.

Q. 31. Write an essay on the Disturbed Campus.

Q. 32. What is social change? What are its factors and results? Discuss the function of education in bringing about social change.

Q. 33. Point out the important features of social change in India during British period. Explain educational policy during British period.

Q. 34. What social changes occurred in post independent India? Discuss characteristics of Five-Year Plans and new educational policy.

Q. 35. Explain the meaning, types and agencies of social control and discuss the role of education in social control.

Q. 36. What is socialization? How is it realized in family and school?

Q. 37. Discuss the fundamental principles of teaching to be remembered by a teacher.

Q. 38. "Efficient teaching does not depend merely on the teacher." Explain and discuss the kinds and problems of teacher training. Give suggestions.

Q. 39. Explain the economic aspects of education.

Q. 40. What are the areas of impact of economics upon education?

Q. 41. Write a short note on Education and Economic Growth.

Q. 42. Write a short note on Technical Education.

Q. 43. "Democracy without education is blind." Explain and discuss the need and importance of education is democracy.

Q. 44. How can education be used to establish democracy in India? Discuss the views of secondary education commission and Indian universities commission in this connection.

Q. 45. What measures should be taken to establish democracy in India?

Q. 46. Explain the concept of emotional integration. How can education contribute to national integration in India?

Q. 47. Explainfully the meaning of "education for international understanding". Describe a few activities which can be undertaken in your school for its development.

Or

"Internationalism is a synonym for humanism, with the emphasis on what is universal in man—his strivings for self-expression within the larger community and for its ultimate benefit. National contributions must not be glossed over by internationalism in education. On the contrary they will be stressed, just as individual contributions are stressed in democratic society. But those contributions will be stressed as part of man's larger heritage and not as a nation's jealously guarded monopoly." Formulate, and comment on, some of the issues relating to nationalism and internationalism in education which the author has raised.

Q. 48. Suggest some measures for developing intercultural understanding through education among various groups in India.

Q. 49. Write short note on education and modernization.

Q. 50. Show the relationship of modernization and education in the context institutional education.

Bibliography

Alterkar A.S., 1957, Varanasi, *Education in India,* Nawal Kishore and Bros.

Agaham, Wiliard, *A Time for Teaching,* New York: Harper and Row, 1964.

Aiyar, S.P., "Education and the Traditional Society in India," *General Education Quarterly* (Vol. III, No. 1) October, 1965.

Anderson, C. Arnold. The Social Context of Educational planning Paris, International Institute of Educational Planning, UNESCO, 1968 (Fundamentals of Educational Planning No. 5).

...."The Modernization of Education," in *Modernization, The Dynamics of Growth,* Myron Weiner (ed.) Madras, Higgintothams, 1967.

Appadorai, A., "Integration Council and Its Task," *The Hindustan Times,* June 20, 1968.

Archer, R.L. *Rousseau on Education,* New York: Longmans, Green and Co., 1912

Arnstine, Donald., *Philosophy of Education: Learning and Schooling.* New York: Harper and Row, 1967.

Bardis, Panos D., "Education and Sociology in the United States of America," *Sociological Bulletin* (Vol. XIV No. 2), September 1965.

Barnett, George and Jack Otis. *Corporate Society and Education: The Philosophy of Elijah Jordan, Ann* Arbor, Michigan: University of Michigan: Press, 1962, 1961.

Battle, Jean Allen, *Culture and Education for the Contemporary World,* Columbus, Ohio: C.E. Merrill Publishing Co., 1969.

Biddle, Brue J., et. al. *Essay on the Social System of Education,* Columbia, Missouri: University of Missouri, 1966.

Brookover, W.B., *A Sociology of Education,* New York, American Book Co., 1955.

Burnett John., *Aristotle on Education,* 5th ed. Cambridge, Massachusetts: Harvard University Press, 1928.

Burns, H.W., (Ed.), *Education and the Development of Nation*, Syracuse, Syracuse University Press, 1963.

Butts, Robert F., *A Cultural History Education: Reassessing Our Educational Traditions,* 1st ed. New York and London: McGraw Hill Book Co., Inc., 1947.

Cale, Luella, *A History of Education: Socrates on Montessori,* New York: Holt, Rinethart and Winston, Inc. 1950.

Coleman, J.S., (Ed.) *Education and Political Development,* Princeton, Princeton University Press, 1965.

Damle, Y.B., "Socialisation for an Unknown Future" — paper presented to the *Seminar on "Higher Education, Technology and Social Change"* (December 1-3 1966). New Delhi Indian Institute of Technology, Department of Humanities and Social Sciences, 1966.

Damle, Y.B., "Education and Social Values" —paper presented to the *"Conference of Indian Sociologists'* (October 14-16, 1967) Bombay, Indian Sociological Society, 1967.

Deva Indra., "Contemporary Technology and the Image of Man" —paper presented to the seminar on "*Higher Education, Technology and Social Change*" (December 1-3,1966). New Delhi, Indian Institute of Technology, Department of Humanities and Social Sciences, 1966.

Deutsch, Martin, "Early Social Environment: Its influence on School Adaptation," in *The Social Dropout,* Washington, National Education Association, 1964.

Dewey, John, Democracy and Education: An Introuduction to Philosophy of Education *New York, MacMillan Co. 1916*—Freedom and Culture, *New York, G.P. Putnam's Sons, 1939.*

"Educational and Traditional Values — A Symposium," Education Quarterly, (Vol., 15 No. 58), June 1963, pp. 64-105 (See especially the contributions of Zakir Hussian, Mulk Raj Anand, Kamla Devi Chattopadhyaya, and A.R. Wadia).

Eisenstadt., S.N., *From Generation to Generation,* Chicago, Free Press, 1956.

Elkin, Frederick, *The Child and Society,* New York, Random House, 1960.

Erickson, Erick, H., (Ed.) *Youth: Change and Challenge,* New York, Basic Books, 1963.

Eron, Leonard D., et., al. "Social Class: Parental Punishment for Aggression and Child Aggression," *Child Development* (Vol. XXXIV, No. 4), December 1963.

Fletcher, S.S. and J. Welton., *Frebel's Chief Writings on Education,* New York: Longmans, Green and Co., 1912.

Forbes, Clarence A., *Greek Physical Education.* New York: Century Co., 1929.

Garforth, E.W., *Education and Social Purpose.* London, Old-burire, 1962.

Gittler, Joseph B., *Review of Sociology: Analysis of a Decade,* New York, John Wiley and Sons, 1957.

Goel, B.S., "Caste and Class Tensions in Indian Education" Conspectus, (New Delhi, Indian International Centre, Vol., No. 4), 1966.

Goodman, Paul., "The Universal Trap," in *Social Foundation of Education*: Current Issues and Research in Education. Dorothy Westby-Gibson (Ed.), New York, Free Press, 1967.

Gore M.S., Desai, I.P., and Chitnis, Suma, *Papers in Sociology of Education in India,* New Delhi, National Council of Educational Research and Training, 1967.

Gottlieb, David, "Social Class, Achievement, and College-going Experience," *The School Review,* (Vol. LXXX, No. 3), Autumn 1962.

Government of India, *Emotional Integration Committee: Preliminary Report,* New Delhi, Ministry of Education 1962.

Hansen, Donald A.,"The Responsibility of the Sociologist of Education" *Haward Educational Review,* (33), Summer 1963, p. 313.

Hansen, Donald A., "The Uncomfortable Relation of Sociology and Education," in *On Education: Sociological Perspectives,* Donald A. Hansen and Joel E. Gerstl, (eds), New York, John Wiley and Sons, 1967, p. 22.

Harley, Ruth, E., "Sex-Role Pressures and the socialisation of the Male Child," *Psychological Reports,* (Vol. V.) 1959.

Herriot, RobertE., "Some Social Determinants of Educational Aspirations," Harvard Educational Review, (Vol. XXXIII, No. 2) Spring 1963.

Husen, Trosten, "Home Background and Behaviour in the Classroom Situation," *Research Bulletin* No. 5, Stockholm Institute of Education, University of Stockholm, January 1956.

India, *Education and National Development: Report of the Commission* (1964-66), New Delhi, Ministry of Education, Government of India, 1966.

India, Ministry of Education, *Education in India* (Successive Years).

India, Ministry of Education, 1958, Indian University Administration: Report of a Conference of Vice-Chancellors *(Delhi).*

India, Ministry of Education, 1954, Report of the International Team on Secondary Education, *(Delhi).*

India, National Council of Educational Research and Training 1963-64, Physics, *The Physical Sciences Study Committee Text on High School Physics* (Delhi).

India, *Report of the National Committee on Women's Education* Ministry of Education, Government of India, 1959.

India, *Post War Educational Development in India*: Report by the Central Advisory Board of Education, New Delhi, January 1944.

India, Report of the: University Education Commission: *1948-49. Vol, I. Government of India Press, Simla, 1949.*

India, National Council of Educational Research and Training, *Review of Education in India*: 1947-61, Ministry of Education, New Delhi, 1961.

Inkeles, Alex and David H. Smith. 1974, *Becoming Modern,* Cambridge: Harvard University Press.

Inkeles, Alex, 1973, "The School as a Context for Modernization"

International Journal of Comparative Sociology XIV (3-4): 163-179.

Jindal, B.L., 1979, *School Type and Student Modernity,* Field work Monograph (Mimeographed). Chandigarh: Punjab University.

John, V.V., "The Freedom to Teachers," *The Hindustan Times,* November 10, December 1966.

Jesselyn, Irene M., *The Happy Child,* New York, Random House, 1965.

Kabir, Humayun, *The Indian Heritage,* London, Asia Publishing House, 1962.

Kahl, Joseph, A., "Educational and Occupational Aspiration of Common Man Boys *Harward Educational and Review* (Vol. XXIII, No. 3), Summer 1963.

Kerber, August and Smith, Wilfred (Eds.), *Educational Issues in Changing Society*, Detroit, Wayne State University Press.

Kimball, Solon T., "An Anthropological View of Learning," *In Social Foundations of Education: Current Readings* from the Behaviour Sciences (ed.) New York, Macmillan 1966, Vol. 166-271.

Kirk, Robert N., "Educating Slum Children in London," School and Society (Vol. 93, No. 2250), Mareh20,1965.

Kohn Melvin L., "Social Class and Parental Values," American Journal of Sociology (Vol. LXIV), 1959.

Kpnyon, Frederic G., *Books and Readers in Ancient Greece and Rome.* New York: Oxford University Press, 1932.

Lawrence, Evelyn, (ed.) *Friedrich Froebel and English Education,* New York: Philosophical Library, 1953.

Marrou, Henri I., *A History of Education in Antiquity,* Translated by George Lamb, New York; Sheed and Ward, 1956.

Malleiy, David., *High School Students Speak Out,* New York, Harper and Brother, 1902.

McClelland, David C., et. al., Talent and Society: New Perspectives in the Identification of Talent Princeton, *N.J., D. Van Nostrand Co., 1958.*

Mannheim, Karl and Stewart, W.A.C., *An Introduction to the Sociology of Education,* London, Routledge and Kegan, 1962.

McClelland, David C., *The Achieving Society,* Princeton, D. Van Nostrand Co., 1961.

Mead, Margaret, and Wolfenstein, Martha, (Eds.)., *Childhood in Contemporary Cultures,* Chicago, University of Chicago Press, 1955.

Mehta, Prayag, *Achievement Motivation in High School Students,* New Delhi, N.C.E.R.T. 1969.

Mekeel, Scudder, "Education, Child-Training and Culture," in *Education and the Social Order,* Blaine E. Marcer and Edvin V. Carr (eds.), New York, Rinehart and Co., 1968.

Mukherji, Shridhar N. *Higher Education and Rural India,* Baroda, India: Acharya Book Depot, 1956.

Mukherjee Kartick C. *Underdevelopment, Educational Policy and Planning* Bombay and New York: Asia Publishing House 1967.

Mukherjee, D.P. Problems of Indian Youth—A Collection of Papers, *Lucknow, 1945.*

Munshi, K.B., *Foundations of Indian Culture,* Bombay, Bhartiya Vidya Bhawan, 1962

Phillips, H.W., Sociology and the Planning of Education in Relation to Development, *Paris, U.N.E.S.C.O., 1964.*

Poignant, R., *The Relation of Educational Plans to Economic and Social Planning,* Paris, International Institute of Educational Planning, 1967.

....Social Change in Modern India, *Bombay, Allied Publishers, 1966.*

Radha Kumud Mukerji, 1951. *Delhi, Ancient Indian Education* (Motilal Banarsidas), Radhakrishnan, *An Idealist View of Life,* London, George Allen and Unwin, 1951.

Radhakrishnand, S., *Freedom and Culture,* Madras, G.A. Natesan and Co., 1952.

Rai, Lala Lajpat, *The Problems of National Education in India,* Delhi, Publications Division, 1968.

Raj Krishna, "Thought on Tradition and Modernity", *Quest,* (41), April-June 1964.

Ramanathan, G., *Education Planning and National Integration* Bombay, Asia Publishing House, 1965.

Rawat P.L. 1963, *History of Indian Education,* (3rd Ed), Ram Prasad and Sons.

Rodehover. Myles W., Axtell, William B., and Gross, Richard E., The Sociology of the School. New York, Thomas Y. Crowell Co., 1957.

Ruhela, S.P. *Sociology of Education: A Review of Researches* and Priorities, New Delhi, National Institute of Education, Department of Foundations of Education, 1967, (Mimeographed).

'A Preview of the Seminar on Sociology of the Teaching Profession in India' — presented to the Seminar held at the Tata Institute of Social Sciences, Bombay, February 5-10,1968 (Mimeographed).

'A Note one the Researchable Topics in Sociology of Education in India' — A paper presented to the Jamia Millia Teachers' College Seminar on 'Educational Sociology,' December 24-26,1968 (Mimeographed).

Field Studies in Sociology of Education, New Delhi, National Council of Educational Research and Training.

Ruhela, S.P. (Ed.), *Sociology of the Teaching Profession in India,* New Delhi National Council of Educational Research and Training, 1970.

[4] "Research Needs in the Sociology of Education," in *Research Needs in the Study of Education,* U. Shanker and S.P. Ahluwalia (Eds.), Kurukshetra, Kurukshetra University, 1968, pp. 17-25.

Rugg, Harold O. *Culture and Education in America,* New York: Harcourt, Brace and Co., 1931.

Ryan, Patrick J. *Historical Foundations of Public* Education Dubuque, Iowa: W.C. Brown Co., 1968.

Samuel, R.H. and R. Hinton Thomas, *Education and Society in Modern Germany,* London: Routledge and Kegan Paul Ltd., 1949.

Saiyidain, K.G., *The Humanist Tradition in Indian Educational Thought,* Bombay, Asia Publishing House, 196.

Sexton, Patricia, *The American School: Its Social Context.* Englewood Cliffs, New Jersey: Prentice-Hall, 1967.

Shah, A.B., Planning for Democracy and other Essays. *Bombay, Manaktalas 1967.*

Shah, B.V., "Sociology of Education — An Attempt at Definition and Scope," *Sociological Bulletin* (Vol. XIV. No. 2) September 1965, p. 65.

Sharma, R.N., *Philosophy of Education* (Hindi) Vinod, Agra, 1980.

Sharma, S.L., Modernizing Effects of University Education. *ICSSR. New Delhi, 1979.*

Silber, Kate., *Pestalozzi, The Man and His Work, London*: Routledge and Kegan Paul, 1965.

Sinha, M.R. (ed.), *The Struggles of Modern India*, Bombay, Asian Studies press, 1967.

Stanley, William O., *Education and Social Integration.* New York, Columbia University, Teacher's College 1953.

Vadekar, D.D., "The Indian Traditional Values and Their Indications for Education in India in the Age of Modern Science and Technology," *The Journal of the University of Poona: Humanities Section* (23), 1965.

Vakil, C.N., "National Integration: The Common Language" (Parti), *Times of India,* July 13,1961.

Vakil, C.N., "National Integration: The Roles of Hindi and English" (part II), *Times of India,* July 14,1961.

Waller, Willard., *The Sociology of Teaching.* New York: Wiley and Sons, 1932.

Ward, Herbert, The Educational System of England and Wales and its Recent History, *Cambridge University Press 1935.*

Westby-Gibson D., (Ed.) *Social Foundations of Education: Current Issues and Research,* New York, Free Press, 1967.

1

PHILOSOPHY: NATURE, PROBLEMS, SCOPE AND VALUE

Aristotle devised metaphysics to be studied after physics. Thus etymologically speaking, metaphysics means "after-physics". It is the last science, the science of sciences. It is also the first science, the mother of all sciences. He also calls it the science of being though such a science is impossible since science deals only with processes of phenomena. Philosophy deals with Being as much as with Becoming. Thus, it includes sciences within its ken. Man experiences eternity as well as change. Philosophy as an explanation of the total experience of man seeks the integral truth.

The rationalists, in the early dawn of modern philosophy, defined metaphysics as a knowledge deduced from self-evident principles. This attempt at rationalisation or mathematisation of philosophy sought to make it more exact. But metaphysics with thought as its instrument should never dream of being exact like mathematics since thought, though real, cannot be identified with Reality. To be inexact is both a weakness as well as the strength of metaphysics. The philosopher is a lover of knowledge and never a sole possessor of it. The complete comprehension of Infinite by finite, is a logical impossibility and yet the destiny of man lies in progressing for an ever near approximation to it. Human thought which always bifurcates Reality into form and essence, subject and object, "that" and "what", can never truly represent the Reality which is an all inclusive spiritual unity. Philosophy is not a matter of logico-mathematical deduction or induction.[1] The laws of geometry are not applicable to Metaphysics any more than they are applicable to chemistry or physiology. Every new field of experience has its own laws. Philosophy, the moment it loses touch with immediate experience of Reality, forgets its way in the wilderness of human ratiocinations which lead us nowhere.

The necessity of basing philosophy on experience was loudly proclaimed by the opposite school of empiricists represented by Locke, Berkeley and Hume. Locke pointed out that for its content the form and instrument of metaphysics is

1. "It is subtle even than chemical subtlety and therefore not to be deduced, induced, inferred or discovered by a reasoning which proceeds from a consideration of the elements of name and form and makes that its standard." — Sri Aurobindo, *The Advent*. Vol. X, No. 2, p. 95.

dependent on experience. This was a great corrective to rationalistic extreme and yet by confining metaphysics to mere sense experience, the empiricists shifted the balance in the opposite direction which led to the negation of all metaphysics. This is obvious, since if sense experience is the only experience, philosophy is a mere wild goose chase. To be itself, philosophy should widen its field to include all types of experience, religious, moral, scientific, spiritual, etc. Hume denied the supremacy of Reason. But if reason is a slave to passion, the refutation of reason, being itself a ratiocination, stands self-condemned. All refutations of reason are subject to hysteron—proteron. Hume's "criticism of rationalism and reductio adabsurdum of empiricism, however, gives a lesson which philosophy should not forget. Reason is its surest instrument but to get its data, it should rely on experience.

Kant combines the Baconian idea of the extension of knowledge with the Cartesian idea of certainty. But he also fights shy of all metaphysics in the ultimate sense. Only the metaphysics of Nature and metaphysics of knowledge is possible. Thus, it was left to Hegel to revive in full vigour the ultimate status of philosophy. The object of philosophy, according to him, is to search out the concept, the purpose, the significance of phenomena and to assign to these their corresponding positions in the world and in the system of knowledge. It systematises the values in a unified whole. Here, for the first time, we find a true view of Philosophy as a systematisation of values and facts. But, by the identification of Nature with Logic[2], Hegel arrives at an intellectualism which led Bradley to assert with a vengeance, "Metaphysics is the finding of bad reasons for what we believe on instinct."[3]

This curt remark is a timely warning to all who attempt at reduction of Reality to mere thought but its rejection of all metaphysical speculation as bad reasons appears to be too sweeping. The intellect is not rejected in Spirit but transformed into a better instrument to receive the truth.

Bergson's approach here seems to be more balanced than that of Bradley. Philosophy, according to him, must take into account not only sensory but also mental and intuitive experiences. It must be based on real experience[4] Bergson shows a true insight into the problem when he points out that the difference between various schools of philosophy is because of their fragmentary glimpse of Reality , supplemented by different kinds of intellectual interpretation and elaboration. He suggests that by mutual comparison and elimination of peculiarities, philosophers may grasp the universal character of basic Reality.[5]

---

2. "Hegel Preface to *The Philosophy of Right.*
3. Bradley, F. H., *Appearance and Reality* (Preface).
4. "Philosophy can only be an effort to dissolve again into the whole, the ocean of life in which we are immersed, whence we draw the very force to labour and to live and from which both matter and intellect originate. "
— Bergson, *Creative Evolution*, p. 202
5. "The object of Philosophy would be realised if this intuition could be sustained, generalised and above all, assured of external points of reference in order not to go astray"
— Bergson, *Ibid*, p. 252

Again, philosophy according to Bergson, ' 'does not only facilitate speculation, gives us also more power to act and live. For with it we feel ourselves no longer isolated in humanity, humanity no longer seems isolated in the Nature that it dominates."[6] Finally, Bergson is an anti-intellectualist only when by intellect he means the faculty in its usual capacity' in practical life, intellect working on data supplied by sense-perception. Otherwise, the intellect may co-operate with intuition by assembling the data of intuition and forming fluid concepts.[7] Intuition and Reason are equally necessary in philosophy.

Contemporary thought witnesses a chaos in the field of metaphysics. All sorts of arguments have been advanced to support widely divergent views of Reality. All kinds of reactions are raising head under high sounding names of 'isms'. All types of methods have been put to test. The purpose of Nature beneath all this burning cauldron of ideologies, however, seems to be the manifestation of an integral philosophy which may reconcile all and transcend all. and rouse itself from its dogmatic slumber. A true philosophy is an '*esprite de ensemble*' a synoptic vision of Reality. It is the intellectual search for the fundamental truth of things.

It is generally agreed by all that philosophy must be based on experience but as we have already seen, often the term experience has been limited to certain specific regions. The root fallacy underlying all the conflicting schools of philosophy is a shift from the centre to periphery, an exaltation of part as whole, a dogmatic denial of everything beyond the limited ken of intellect and finally, an unwarranted application of the logic of finite to the matters of the Infinite. "The work of philosophy" as Sri Aurobindo rightly points out, "is to arrange the data given by the various means of knowledge, excluding none, and put them into synthetic relation to the one truth, the one supreme and universal Reality."[8] Philosophy should be all comprehensive, affirmative, synthetic and spiritual. Philosophy, meaning love of wisdom (Philo=love, Sophia=wisdom) should be distinguished from mere opinion. Knowledge, as the Indians conceived it, is the knowledge of that by knowing which everything else can be known.[9] Thus, philosophy is the knowledge of Ultimate Reality . But Ultimate Reality, as Indian philosophy truly maintains, is not only Existence but also Consciousness and Bliss. Hence, philosophy, as the quest after ultimate truth, is science of value *par excellence*.[10] It should not only criticise facts but also satisfy human aspirations. It should synthesise value and existence, religion and science. To quote Sri Aurobindo, "It should be a discovery of the real reality of things by which human existence can learn its law and aim and the principle of its perfection"[11]

---

6. Bergson, *Creative Evolution*, p 285.
7. *Ibid*, p. 251.
8. Sri Aurobindo, *The Renaissance in India*, p. 72.
9. कस्मिन्नु खलु भगवो विज्ञाने सर्व मिदं भवति।

—Mundakopanisad, I. i. 3.

10. Maitra, S. K., *Sri Aurobindo Mandir Annual*, Vol. II, p. 61.
11. Sri Aurobindo, *The Human Cycle*, p.93.

DEFINITION OF PHILOSOPHY

A beginner in philosophy is perturbed to find that different philosophers have given different definitions of philosophy, While some philosophers have laid emphasis on psychological facts, others have given more importance to values. According to John Dewey, "Whenever philosophy has been taken seriously, it has always been assumed that it signified achieving a wisdom that would influence the conduct of life".[12] On the other hand, according to Windelband, philosophy is "... the critical science of universal values". While there is much difference in Indian and Western definitions of philosophy, one finds widely different definitions presented by Western philosophers also. Of these definitions some emphasize the critical aspect of philosophy while others lay emphasis upon its synthetic aspect. Some examples of these two types of definitions of philosophy are as follows:

(a) *Philosophy is a critical method of approaching experience.* Examples of this type of definitions are as follows:

1. "Philosophy is essentially a spirit or method of approaching experience rather than a body of conclusions about experience. "[13] — *Edgar S. Brightman.*
2. "It is not the specific content of these conclusions, but the spirit and method by which they are reached, which entitles them to be described as philosophical..."[14] —*Clifford Rarrat.*
3. "Were I limited to one line for my answer to it, I should say that philosophy is general theory of criticism."[15] — *C.J. Ducasse*

(b) *Philosophy is comprehensive synthetic science.* The following definitions of philosophy emphasize its synthetic aspect:

1. "Philosophy like science, consists of theories of insights arrived at as a result of systematic reflection."[16] —*Joseph A. Leighton*
2. "Philosophy is concerned with everything as a universal science." —*Herbert Spencer*
3. "Our subject is a collection of sciences, such as theory of knowledge, logic, cosmology, ethics and aesthetics, as well as a unified survey".[17] — *Roy Wood Sellars*

The above mentioned definitions of philosophy show that while some philosophers have mainly emphasized critical philosophy, others have defined it as a synthetic discipline. In fact, both these viewpoints are one-sided because philosophy is both critical as well as synthetic. Literally speaking, the word 'philosophy' involves two Greek words—*Philo* meaning love and *Sophia* meaning knowledge. Thus literally speaking, philosophy means love of wisdom. It should

12. John Dewey, *Democracy and Education*, p. 378.
13. Brightman E.S., *Introduction to Philosophy*, Henry Holt & Co., New York (1925), p. 9.
14. Barret, C., *Philosophy*, The Macmillan Co. (1935), p. 5.
15. Ducasse, C.J., *Philosophy of Art*, Dial Press, New York (1929), p. 3.
16. Leighton, J.A., *The Field of Philosophy*, Appleton Century Crofts, New York (1910), 9. 4.
17. Sellars, R.W., *The Principles and Problems of Philosophy*, The Macmillan Co., New York (1926) p. 3.

be noted here that this definition of philosophy is different from the sense in which the word 'Darshan' has been taken in India. The literal meaning of philosophy shows that the philosopher is constantly and everywhere engaged in the search for truth. He does not bother so much to arrive at final conclusions and continues with his search for truth throughout life. His aim is the pursuit of truth rather than its possession. Those who enjoy journey do not care so much about the destination, neither are they perturbed when the destination is lost in sight in spite of continued long journey.

In an effort to define philosophy, one arrives at the difficulty that there is no genus in this case and also no differentia. In defining a science one points out to the genus science and also to the particular area of the particular science which differentiates it from others. This is, however, not possible in the case of philosophy because philosophy is one and not many. Hence, in order to arrive at the meaning of philosophy you will have to discuss its problems, attitude, method, process, conclusions and results. In brief, *philosophy is a philosophical process of solving some characteristic problems through characteristic methods from a characteristic attitude and arriving at characteristic conclusions and results.*[18] Some might find this definition very vague and inadequate. But while defining science, do we not say that science is scienteing or that it is method? And can we understand this definition of science without understanding scientific method? When science cannot be understood without knowing scientific method, how can we hope to understand philosophy without knowing philosophical method? Again, in understanding the definition of science we are required to understand not only scientific method but also scientific attitude, scientific process, scientific problems and scientific conclusions because all these together form a science. Therefore, what is vague and inadequate if we say that in order to understand philosophy one must understand the attitude, problems, activity, conclusions and results peculiar to it? This will also clarify the distinction between philosophy and science which has been forgotten by many philosophers.

1. Philosophical problems. Each branch of knowledge gives rise to certain peculiar problems. In the early human life on this planet when man was struck with wonder at the natural phenomena or when he found complex and conflicting phenomena in life and was filled with discontentment at the existing order of things, it was the beginning of philosophy . While the philosophy of Vedas began in wonder, the philosophy of Gautam Buddha began in discontentment with the miserable world. In the West the early beginning of philosophy was in wonder while the modern Western philosophy had its origin in doubt. In the words of Patrick, "Although philosophy among the ancients began in wonder, in modern times it usually begins in doubt."[19]

This wonder and doubt gave rise to several types of problems. A general characteristic of these problems was that they were concerned with general and universal questions and not with the questions of particular nature. In this sense

18. Sharma, R.N., *Problems of Philosophy*, Kedarnath Ramnath (1982), p. 6.
19. Patrick, G.T.W., *Introduction to Philosophy*, Houghton Mifflin, p. 3.

the philosophical problems are different from scientific problems which have their origin in particular questions. Some examples of philosophical problems are: What is knowledge? What is world? Who has created the world? Is there a God? Who am I? What is the aim of my life? Why should I live? What is the purpose of the world? etc. In fact, a description of all the philosophical problems will almost form a book. Hence for our present purpose it is sufficient to say that philosophical problems are those which arise in the field of philosophy. Now, what is the field of philosophy? The philosophical field includes epistemology, logic, philosophy of science, semantics, metaphysics, axiology, philosophy of religion, social philosophy, political philosophy, philosophy of history, philosophy of education, etc. In brief the field of philosophy includes all knowledge but the philosopher raises questions of general nature only. For example, about the beautiful things his question will be what is beauty? Some philosophers have divided philosophical problems into the following three classes:[20]

(a) *Concerning knowledge and experience.* These include problems of epistemology, philosophy of science, semantics, etc.

(b) *Concerning reality or Existence.* This class includes problems of metaphysics, ontology, cosmology and theology, etc.

(c) *Concerning values.* These include problems of axiology, aesthetics, ethics, social philosophy, philosophy of religion, political philosophy, philosophy of education, economic philosophy, philosophy of history, etc.

In the above mentioned classification of philosophical problems it should be noted that problems of different fields of philosophy cannot be absolutely isolated from each other because in fact philosophical problems are not so much problems of a particular field as problems of a particular type. In other words, as opposed to the particular problems of science, these are general problems.

Philosophical problems may be viewed from two aspects — critical and synthetic. In the critical aspect the problem of philosophy is to critically examine the postulates and conclusions of different sciences. In the synthetic aspect, its problem is to present a complete world-view based on the conclusions of sciences. Thus, in brief, philosophy is a totality of some peculiar problems of which some are problems of philosophical sciences while-others are problems of criticism and synthesis of the postulates and conclusions of different sciences.

2. Philosophical attitude. Philosophical attitude begins in wonder or doubt. It is critical, reflective, tolerant, detached, continually progressive, directed by experience and reasoning and devoid of hurry in arriving at conclusions.

3. Philosophical method. The philosophical method is not exclusively employed by philosophers only. Every man, some time or the other, utilizes philosophical method in his thinking on philosophical problems. However, the philosophical method is mainly utilized by the philosopher. Secondly, the philosophical method is not absolutely different from scientific method. As has been already pointed out, philosophical problems have much in common with the scientific

20. Bahm, A.J., *Philosophy, An Introduction*, Asia, Bombay, (1964), p. 7.

problems. It goes without saying that in solving its problems concerning science, the philosopher utilizes the same methods of induction and deduction as used by a scientist. Thus, in the understanding of the philosophical method, these two methods must be discussed.

(i) *Induction.* The principles of different sciences are arrived at by means of inductive process. For example, in psychiatry, some general principles concerning mental diseases are discovered by observation of the behaviour of mental patients, its recording, its analysis, classification and finally generalisation to arrive at certain common principles. This is the method of induction. The philosopher does not act on the facts like the scientist. He has no laboratory work to do. He utilizes concepts and propounds new theories, e.g., materialism, idealism, etc. And then he tries to explain his experiences satisfactorily on the basis of these theories. As in science so in philosophy a theory is acknowledged to the extent it satisfactorily explains experience, otherwise it is substituted by another theory which is more successful for this purpose. The cure of bad philosophy is not the negation of all philosophy but the affirmation of a better philosophy. The failure of a particular philosophical theory does not mean the failure of philosophy itself because very soon a better philosophical theory substitutes the earlier and this process goes on *ad infinitum.* The process to arrive at a general proposition by means of several particular propositions is known as the inductive process and it is equally found in philosophical as well as scientific thinking.

(ii) *Deduction.* Deduction is the process to arrive at certain particular propositions from a general proposition. For example, All men are mortal. Socrates is a man. Therefore, Socrates is mortal. Deductions like this are occasionally made in philosophical thinking.

Besides the two abovementioned methods, philosophical thinking involves another method peculiar to it known as dialectical method.

(iii) *Dialectical method.* This is a natural method of philosophical thinking. It is a commonplace experience that when we think over a problem we arrive at certain positive facts. This is thesis. Now, after some time we come to know some facts which are contradictory to the thesis: this is anti-thesis. Thesis and anti-thesis cannot live together for long hence they are synthesised into a synthesis. This synthesis, arrived through antithesis is more comprehensive than the original thesis. Thus, knowledge grows in a dialectical process through thesis, anti-thesis and synthesis To illustrate, in the beginning a philosopher takes the world to be real as it is. As he progresses in the knowledge and experience he finds that the world is unreal When he proceeds further in the realm of knowledge and experience he finds that the world is neither real nor unreal but both. Tints, philosophical thinking proceeds from thesis, antithesis to synthesis, in fact, the dialectical process is the thinking of thought. In it the man re-thinks over his earlier thought and discovers hitherto unknown facts.

While searching for the solution of his problems the philosopher utilizes two methods with regards to his experience, analysis and synthesis. While some philosophers have exclusively emphasized the value of philosophical thinking, others have absolutely denied its value. It goes without saying that these two extremist views are equally one-sided.

(iv) *Analysis.* Analysis means the process of distinction between different elements involved in a particular state of experience so that they might be more clear. Realist philosophers have emphasised this procedure while absolutists have advanced arguments against it.

(v) *Synthesis.* This process involves connecting together the scattered elements in a particular experience which brings into light new patterns and facts. The Idealist philosophers have laid emphasis on synthesis. But, as has been already pointed out, philosophical thinking requires both analysis and synthesis. Analysis, therefore, cannot be banished from the field of philosophy, though it might be useless in certain conditions.[21] The contemporary school of Logical Positivism has taken analysis as the sole method in philosophy. Though the method of logical analysis solves many intricate problems in philosophy it does not negate the value of synthesis.

Thus philosophical method is multi-sided. Though the philosophers have sometimes emphasized this or that method exclusively, yet all the above mentioned methods have been found to be useful in philosophical thinking.

4. Philosophical activity. Once an eminent psychologist was asked what is psychology ? To this, he replied: psychology is what the psychologists do. Similarly, we can say, philosophy is what the philosophers do. The activity of philosophers is philosophising. Philosophising involves thinking, criticism and the process of solving the philosophical problems through different philosophical methods. Philosophical activity begins in a state of wonder, discontentment and doubt. In it the philosopher thinks over his own experience. This thinking is critical and the attitude is philosophical. In brief, philosophical thinking has the following characteristics.

(i) Philosophical thinking is gradually matured with the increase in knowledge and experience.

(ii) Philosophical thinking is concerned with philosophical problems.

(iii) Philosophical thinking utilizes philosophical methods and philosophical attitude.

(iv) Philosophical thinking is done in individual and group situation, alone and together with others.

(v) Philosophical thinking is comprehensive while non-philosophical thinking is one-sided.

In the end, the real nature of philosophical thinking can be known only after one himself takes recourse to it. The abovementioned discussion only points out its chief characteristics.

5. Philosophical effects. Different types of knowledge affect the individual and group differently. This effect of philosophy is as follows:

(i) *Effect on the philosopher.* The effect of philosophy can be seen in the life of the philosopher, in his expectations and aspirations, in his aim of life, in his bent of mind, and in his different activities.

---

21. See Spaulding, E.G., *The New Realism*, p. 155.

(ii) *Effect on group-life.* The effect of philosophy is seen not only in the life of the individual but also in group-life. The influence of democratic philosophy can be seen in the democratic societies of the world.

(iii) *Effect on civilization and culture.* In any time and place contemporary philosophical trends express the process of thinking in contemporary culture. Philosophical changes are the expressions of cultural changes. A comparison of the history of philosophy with the history of culture will prove this fact.

6. Philosophical conclusions. It has been said regarding philosophical conclusions that while a philosopher raises questions he does not answer them. Ordinarily, philosophical conclusions are the conclusions arrived at by the philosophers regarding philosophical problems where a question arises as to who is the philosopher. In answer to this question one may point out to the names of hundreds of thinkers who have presented widely different and mutually contradictory conclusions. A beginner in philosophy is very much perturbed to see this difference of opinion. He fails to understand as to which are the philosophical conclusions and which are non-philosophical. Another definition of philosophical conclusions may be given by calling them the conclusions of philosophical problems. Here it is difficult to prepare a final list of philosophical problems and even those which are quite well known have been solved in so many different ways that no definite conclusions can be derived.

A non-philosophical person may raise a question as to why philosophers so much disagree regarding the conclusions of philosophical problems. Will the philosophical thinking always be unconcluded? Can all the philosophical conclusions not arrive at any final truths? Now, while we find differences in the views of different philosophers we also notice that the same philosopher presents widely different views at different times. But this is not the case with the philosophers alone. As William E. Hocking has said, "Everybody has a philosophy and the differences between man and man are chiefly philosophical differences. I will say more than that; the difference between a man and himself is a philosophical difference by which 1 mean that people frequently fall into a philosophy which does not belong to them and leads them away from themselves because they borrow a philosophy from somebody else".[22] The truths of this statement can be ascertained by anyone who-looks to his own experience and thinking.

In fact the diversity of philosophical conclusions is not a weakness of philosophy. Different philosophers have thought over philosophical problems from different perspectives and however wide, integral and comprehensive a perspective might be, it always remains one-sided. The philosophical conclusions, therefore, are workable and limited. As the philosopher develops in his thinking, his philosophical conclusions are also modified and even changed. This does not mean that he is changing his position but only that he is visualizing new truths, which show the one-sidedness and limitations of the truths known earlier. In

22. Hocking, W. E., Philosophy "—The Business of Everyone, *Journal of American Association of University Women,* June 1937, p. 212.

fact, the philosophical aim is never completely achieved nor is the philosophical curiosity ever completely satisfied because if this is done then philosophical thinking will stop. Actually speaking, the aim of the philosopher is not so much to arrive at certain final conclusions regarding the philosophical problems as to sustain philosophical thinking. His efforts should not be evaluated on the basis of definite conclusions but by his philosophical insight, maturity and constant thinking. To Glaucon who asked, "Who are the true philosophers?" Socrates replied, "Those who are lovers of the vision of truth."[23]

The above discussion regarding philosophical conclusions shows that the main function of the philosopher is to raise philosophical questions and constantly think over them through philosophical methods and from philosophical standpoint. Hence it cannot be said that philosophy raises certain questions anu leaves them unanswered. If by leaving a question unanswered we mean the absence of any final answer to it then this is the case with the philosopher and this has been already discussed. But if leaving a question unanswered means absence of any efforts to solve it, it does not apply in the case of the philosopher. Thus, it goes without saying that the philosopher raises certain questions, meditates upon them through philosophical methods and tries to arrive at certain conclusions but does not take them as final and therefore continues with his philosophical reflections.

NATURE OF PHILOSOPHY

Whenever it is asked regarding a science as to w hat is its nature, it is said that it is scientific. Thus the nature of psychology, sociology, economics, political science and other social sciences is scientific. Similarly, if it is asked that what is the nature of philosophy a natural answer will be that it is philosophical. In order to understand the scientific nature of a science we have to understand scientific method, scientific attitude, scientific problems and scientific activities. Similarly, in order to explain that the nature of philosophy is philosophical, we will have to explain the philosophical problems, philosophical attitude and philosophical activities, etc. Philosophical problems are the general problems of different philosophical sciences. In its critical and synthetic aspects, the problems of philosophy are the examination and synthesis of the postulates and conclusions of different sciences. Philosophical attitude is reflective, curious, tolerant, guided by experience and reasoning and a persistent effort to reach the truth though never in a hurry to arrive at final conclusions. Philosophical methods include induction, deduction, analysis, synthesis and dialectical method. Philosophical activity begins in wonder, curiosity and discontentment at the existing order of things. This activity may be individual as well as social, alone as well as in group. The aim of this activity is to present a total world-view. Different philosophers arrive at different conclusions through philosophical methods. However different these conclusions might be, they are different from scientific conclusions as a class by the very virtue of the fact that they are philosophical. The philosophical nature of philosophy shows the effect on the individual, group and community. In brief, the philosophical

23. Plato, *The Republic*, Book VI, p. 485.

problems, philosophical attitude, philosophical method, philosophical activity, philosophical conclusions and their effect on the individual and society show that the nature of philosophy is philosophical. It follows that when we say that the nature of philosophy is philosophical we mean all these problems, methods, attitude, activity conclusions and effects characteristic of philosophy.

PROBLEMS OF PHILOSOPHY

Philosophical Problems are General Problems

Different types of questions give rise to the problems of different sciences. For example, if it is asked whether two and two make four, it is a problem for mathematics. If it is asked that in which year Akbar the Great ruled India, it is a problem for the historian. If it is asked as to what different types of climate are found in India, it is a question for geography. Similarly, the political, economic and social problems fall within the scope of political science, economics and sociology, respectively. The philosopher is not concerned with these particular problems. But does it mean that his problems are entirely unconnected with the problems of different sciences? No. In the different problems mentioned above, the questions of general nature will fall within the scope of philosophy. For example, questions like: What is space? What is time? What is beauty? What is right? What is good? What is knowledge? are philosophical problems. Thus, it is clear that philosophical problems are concerned with general questions rather than with questions of particular nature.

Types of Philosophical Problems

Philosophical problems are mainly of two types. On the one hand, there are problems of those studies which are known as philosophical sciences. These include Epistemology, Logic, Philosophy of Science, Metaphysics, Axiology, Aesthetics, Philosophy of Religion, etc. On the other hand are the problems which fall within the field of philosophy as a universal science. Both these types of philosophical problems will now be discussed in sequence.

Problems of Philosophical Sciences

As has been already pointed out, philosophical problems include problems of the sciences which are different from physical sciences in spite of tearing the name science. The main distinction between philosophical sciences and the physical sciences is that the former raise more fundamental and basic questions as compared to the latter. For example, Aesthetics is not so much concerned with the distinctions between beautiful and ugly objects as with the fundamental question about the nature of beauty and art. What is beauty? What is art? Does art lie in the artist or in his artistic expression? Similarly, other philosophical sciences raise fundamental problems in their own field. Broadly, the main problems of philosophical sciences are as follows:

(1) *Metaphysical problems.* Metaphysics is the science of existence or Reality. Its main problems are: What is Reality? Is the world one or many? What are the fundamental characteristics of creation? What is space? What is time? What

is matter? What is relation? What is cause and effect? What is the purpose of creation? Is the world progressing? Is there a God? Is change real or unreal? In brief, metaphysics discusses the three aspects of Reality, *viz.*, the world, the self, and the God. Some thinkers fail to distinguish between metaphysics and philosophy. Metaphysics is the main branch of philosophy. Thus, philosophy includes many other branches covering widely different fields than metaphysics. When a student of philosophy studies the philosophical thought of any philosopher, he has to study not only his thoughts about metaphysical problems but also about the problems falling within the field of logic, ethics, religion and epistemology, etc. However, it can be said that metaphysical problems constitute the central problems of philosophy.

(2) *Epistemological problems.* Epistemology is the science of knowledge and truth. Its problems are the fundamental problems of the process of knowledge. Is it not strange that though so many thinkers are busy in the acquisition of knowledge, not many think over the general questions concerning the nature of knowledge, its limits and the relation of knower with the known? These questions are raised in epistemology. Therefore, epistemology provides the basic foundation of knowledge. For example, an epistemological problem is concerning the question whether one knows the object outside him or only the content of his mind. Epistemology critically examines different methods to achieve different types of knowledge. Philosophers have discussed such problems since time immemorial and conclusions of philosophers like Immanuel Kant of Germany have proved to be epoch-making.

(3) *Logical problems.* Logic is the science of methods of thought and the implication of judgement. It studies the structure of thought, its laws and fallacies. What is thought? What is its relation with Nature? How does mind solve a problem? What are the natural methods of thinking? What is definition, hypothesis, division, explanation, etc.? How can we arrive at the meanings of a proposition? All these are the problems falling within the scope of logic. Thus, like epistemology, logic also provides fundamental basis to knowledge because every science requires thinking and logic is the science of correct or valid thinking.

(4) *Problems of semantics.* Semantics is the science of the meaning of words. It is concerned with the question about the relation of words and objects. In other words, it is a science of meaning of language. In it the different words, symbols, signs, etc., are analysed and their meanings fixed. It goes without saying that like epistemology and logic, semantics is also a basic science in the achievement of knowledge. Logical positivism, a contemporary school of philosophy, admits semantical problems as constituting the basic problems of philosophy.

(5) *Philosophy of science.* As has been already pointed out, philosophy is intimately connected with science and discusses their problems of general nature. For example, all the sciences believe in the postulate of causality. The philosophy of science critically discusses the concept of causality and finds out its truth and limitations. The philosophy of science also critically examines different scientific methods used in different sciences and finds out conditions in which they are

valid. The philosophy of science is mainly concerned with developing a world-view based on the conclusions of different sciences. Hence, in the modern times, the problems of the philosophy of science are considered to be very important. Even the philosophers who do not admit any value of philosophy in modern times, consider the function of philosophy of science to be very much valuable.

(6) *Axiological problems.* Philosophy is very much concerned with value. Axiology is the science of value. It discusses value from the philosophical point of view. Its main problems are: What is value? What are the fundamental values? What is good? What is beauty? What is art? etc. Without discussing these fundamental problems regarding values, we cannot solve many problems concerning values in our every day life. The philosopher synthesizes the facts with values in his *Weltanschauung.* While the philosophy of science discusses facts, the discussion of values falls within the scope, of axiology.

(7) *Problems of aesthetics.* Aesthetics is the philosophical study of beauty. Art creates beauty. Hence, the nature of art is an aesthetic problem. This, in its turn, raises many questions such as: Does art lie in the artist or in his creation of art? Is there beauty in music, drama, picture, statue, dance, woman or is it in our mind? The artist creates beauty, then is it in the content of his mind? What are basic characteristics of art? What are the criteria of judging beauty and art? All these are problems falling within the field of aesthetics.

(8) *Ethical problems.* Ethics is the science of good, the right and wrong. Its main problems are: What is right? What is wrong? What is good? What is conscience? What is responsibility? What are rights and duties and what is their interrelation? What is justice and how can it be attained? Thus, ethics discusses the ultimate good and explains rights and duties in its light.

(9) *Problems of philosophy of religion.* Philosophy of religion, as is clear by the title, raises philosophical problems in the field of religion. For example, Is there a common element in different religions? What are the fundamental elements of religion? What is the relation of religion with ethics? How far is religion based on Reality? What is God? Is God one or many?

(10) *Problems of social sciences.* While philosophy of science discusses problems of physical sciences, different branches of philosophy have been developed for discussing different problems of social sciences. The important among these social sciences are education, sociology, economics, political science, history, etc. Philosophy discusses the philosophical questions arising in these social sciences. This has given rise to different special branches of philosophy, *e.g.*, philosophy of education, social philosophy, economic philosophy, political philosophy, philosophy of history, etc. These philosophical disciplines based on social sciences raise general and fundamental problems in their field. For example, philosophy of education raises the fundamental question about the aim of education. Political philosophy discusses the nature of state and government, their rights and duties and their limitations. Social philosophy discusses the philosophical questions in the social relationships. Economic philosophy raises questions of fundamental importance in the fields of production, consumption and exchange. Philosophy

of history examines the nature of historical and cultural processes and finds out their place in the total cosmic process. Besides problems of these special branches of philosophy, there are some other philosophical problems concerning matters of social importance, for example, the philosophical basis of marriage, family, physical development and even of dress.

Problems of Philosophy as a Comprehensive Science

As has been already pointed out, philosophy also acts as a comprehensive science. In this aspect, its important problems are as follows:

(1) *Criticism of different sciences.* This philosophical problem is two-fold — (a) criticism of the basic postulates of different sciences, (b) criticism of the conclusions of different sciences. The critical analysis of the law of causality is an example of a problem of first type. A problem regarding the conclusions of different sciences arises in the form of the question whether man is determined by his circumstances or whether he is free. While psychology, biology and other social sciences conclude that man is determined by his circumstances and is bound to act according to them, jurisprudence, ethics and religion consider him free to act according to his will. Whether man is determined or free, this is an important question because it is closely connected with the concept of responsibility. A man can be held responsible for his acts before law only when he is free to choose among several alternatives. It is only then that his act can be considered to be wrong or unlawful and punishable. If a man is determined by his circumstances, the responsibility for his acts lies not on him but on his circumstances and he cannot be punished for what he has done. As different sciences have presented different conclusions regarding the question of man's freedom in his circumstances, this problem cannot be solved by sciences alone. On the other hand, different sciences present mutually conflicting conclusions on this issue. Such problems arising from the conflict in the conclusions of different sciences are philosophical problems. They are also considered philosophical because they are concerned not with any one particular science but fall within the field of several sciences and because each scientist is confined within his own limited field, no scientist can solve such problems. They are, therefore, left for the philosopher.

(2) *Synthesis of different sciences.* According to A. N. Whitehead, "Philosophy is not one among the sciences with its own little scheme of abstractions which it works away at perfecting and improving. It is the survey of sciences, with the special object of their harmony and of their completion".[24] Thus the problem of philosophy, as a comprehensive science, is to weld the conclusions of different sciences into a world-view. Without this the conclusions of different sciences will remain scattered and cannot present a complete picture. Thus man cannot arrive at a total world-view without the help of philosophy. A world-view based on science alone will be one sided, inadequate and deformed. The synthetic function of philosophy can be understood by the example of an elephant and several blind

24. Whitehead, A. N., *Science and the Modern World*, The Macmillan Co., New York (1926), pp. 126-127.

men. Each blind man touches some part of the elephant's body and takes it to be the whole animal because he does not know other parts of its body. The total picture of the elephant's body can be clear to a person who has eyes to see. The blind men will only form a distorted picture of the elephant. Similar is the case with scientists regarding the nature of the world. Each scientist presents a picture of the world according to the conclusions arrived at in his own field. Thus, different scientists interpret the world differently. While for the biologists the world is moved by biological laws, the psychologists lay more emphasis on psychological principles. Only a philosopher can give a total world-view by a synthesis of the conclusions of different sciences. Hence, the importance of the function of philosophy as a synthetic discipline.

(3) *Historical problems of the origin of sciences.* It is a widely known fact that every science originally had its beginning in philosophy. It is hence that philosophy is called the mother of all sciences. One finds the influence of the thought of ancient philosophers like Socrates, Plato and Aristotle in the fields of several sciences. Basically, both philosophy and science have their origin in man's curiosity and his wonder at the natural phenomena. The philosophers of the Vedas wondered as to how the hard, black cow gives soft white milk. They were amazed to see that though all the rivers flow to the sea yet the sea is never full. While these were philosophical problems, they were equally scientific. In the beginning of human knowledge, philosophy and science were intermixed. It was only after gradual specialization and subtle study that division of labour resulted in the form of different sciences, separated from the main stem of philosophy. These sciences were again divided into separate branches which were gradually considered to be independent sciences. As mother of sciences, philosophy also performs a much more important function. In the process of scientific progress, philosophy is always found at the apex. It always transcends science and goes further. It is hence that the philosophical problems of today become scientific problems of tomorrow. But does it mean that a time will come when the philosopher will be left with no problem of his own? No. The philosopher will always move further than the scientists, transcend scientific conclusions and discover new problems to think. These problems will be taken over by the scientists of tomorrow but then the future philosopher will again transcend sciences and discover further new problems for his philosophical reflection. Thus, new branches of philosophy will be born from the womb of philosophy and it will retain its title of the mother of sciences.

The above detailed analysis of the philosophical problems shows that philosophy is concerned with the general problems of physical and social sciences. Philosophy examines the conclusions and postulates of sciences, solves their conflict, synthesises them and presents new problems thus giving rise to new branches of science. It is clear that no description of philosophical problems can be considered to be complete and final because while on the one hand ever new problems arise in the field of new sciences, on the other hand the philosopher himself also raises new problems in new fields. A beginner in philosophy will be amazed to see the wide difference of opinion among the philosophers on the solution of different philosophical problems. On the basis of this difference of opinion, some conclude that the philosophical process is useless. But is the arrival at the destination the only reward of the journey? Those who enjoy journey are satisfied even while they do not reach the goal. In fact, the philosopher is a lover of wisdom, never a sole possessor of it. The culmination of philosophical process lies in an ever burning thirst for new knowledge and not in arriving at final conclusions.

SCOPE OF PHILOSOPHY

The above discussion of philosophical problems also clarifies its scope. Thus, the scope of philosophy can be divided into the following two parts:

(1) *Field of philosophical sciences.* The scope of philosophy includes different philosophical sciences such as metaphysics, epistemology, logic, semantics, philosophy of science, axiology, aesthetics, ethics, philosophy of religion, political philosophy, philosophy of education, philosophy of history, economic philosophy, etc. All these sciences are important parts of the field of philosophy.

(2) *Field of philosophy as a comprehensive science.* Philosophy is the science of sciences, the mother of all sciences. From this point of view, its scope includes the criticism and synthesis of the postulates and conclusions of the physical and social sciences.

(3) *Subject matter of philosophy.* The scope of philosophy clarifies its subject matter. Its subject matter includes the conclusions and postulates of all the physical and social sciences besides their general problems. In the words of C. D. Broad, "The object of philosophy is to take over the results of the various sciences, add to them the result of religious and ethical experiences of mankind and then reflect upon the whole, hoping to be able to reach some general conclusions as to the nature of the universe and as to our position and prospects in it".[25]

The above discussion makes it clear that the philosophical problems, scope and subject matter depend on philosophical sciences and the conclusions and postulates of different sciences.

BRANCHES OF PHILOSOPHY

While studying the philosophical thoughts of a philosopher, we study his thinking in different branches of philosophy. These branches of philosophy are as follows:

1. Epistemology. Philosophy is the search for knowledge. This search is critical. Hence, the first problem which arises before a philosopher is about the nature of knowledge and its limitation. Therefore, epistemology is the most fundamental branch of philosophy. It discusses philosophically truth and falsehood, validity of knowledge, limits of knowledge and nature of knowledge, knower and known, etc.

2. Metaphysics. This is the study of existence, reality or essence. Its main branches are as follows:

(i) *Cosmogony.* This is a study of creation. Is the world created, or is it eternal? How was world created? Why was it created? Who created the world? What is the purpose in creation? All these are the problems of cosmogony.

25. Broad, C. D., *Scientific Thought* Harcourt Brace Go., Mew York (963). p. 20.

(ii) *Cosmology.* The main problems of cosmology are: Is the world one or is it many, or is it both one and many?

(iii) *Ontology.* Ontology is the study of ultimate reality. Is the reality one — or is it many or is it both one and many? If reality is many, what is the relation between these many elements? All these are ontological questions.

(iv) *Philosophy of self.* This is mainly concerned with the philosophical analysis of self. What is self? What is its relation with the body? Is it free or does it depend on the body? Is it one or many? All these are problems of philosophy of self.

(v) *Eschatology.* The discussion of the condition of soul after death, the nature of the other world, etc. form the subject matter of this branch of philosophy.

3. Axiology. This branch of philosophy philosophically studies value. It has been divided into the following three branches:

(i) *Ethics. Ethics discusses the criteria of right and good.*

(ii) *Aesthetics.* Aesthetics discusses the nature and criteria of beauty.

(iii) *Logic studies truth.* The subject-matter of logic includes the methods of judgment, types of propositions, hypothesis, definition, comparison, division, classification and fundamental laws of thoughts, etc.

4. Philosophy of science. This branch of philosophy is concerned with the philosophical examination of the postulates and conclusions of different sciences.

5. Philosophies of social sciences. The philosophical problems in different social sciences give birth to different branches of philosophy of which the main are as follows:

(i) *Philosophy of education.* This is concerned with the aim of education and the basic philosophical problems arising in the field of education.

(ii) *Social philosophy.* This branch of philosophy discusses the philosophical basis of social processes and social institutions.

(iii) *Political philosophy.* This branch of philosophy is concerned with the forms of government, forms of state and other basic problems arising in the political field.

(iv) *Philosophy of history.* The subject-matter of this branch of philosophy is the nature of historical process, its purpose and its relation with the cosmic process.

(v) *Philosophy of economics.* This branch of philosophy studies the aim of man's economic activities and the fundamental problems arising in the economic field.

(vi) Besides the above-mentioned branches of philosophy based on sciences, there may be certain comparatively lesser branches of philosophy such as philosophy of physics, philosophy of commerce, philosophy of physical education, philosophy of marriage, philosophy of family, etc. These, however, are not sufficient to form independent branches of philosophy.

6. Semantics. The most important branch of philosophy, according to the contemporary school of Logical Positivism, is sementics which is concerned with the determination of the meanings of different words used in different languages.

PHILOSOPHICAL ATTITUDE

It is said that one day Gautama Buddha went out in the city and saw a dead body, a patient and an old man. He was much perturbed to see their miserable condition. His thinking was disturbed and he felt that the world is momentary and full of misery. His faith in the life was disturbed. He began to meditate upon the cause of misery in the world. He deliberated on various alternatives in this connection. For years together he remained wandering in the forests, meditating on the causes of misery and the ways to remove it. Though in the beginning he was much disturbed at the state of misery in the world but while meditating on its causes his attitude was detached and unemotional. His mind was open and his view comprehensive. He meditated on the experiences of his life and tried to find out root cause of misery and the ways to remove it.

The above mentioned situation shows the fundamental characteristics of philosophical attitude. Sometimes one finds a bit different philosophical attitude than that of Buddha. When the ancient sages of the age of Vedas wondered at the phenomena of Nature their philosophical attitude was that of wonder. On the other hand, the philosophy of the French philosopher Descartes began in doubt. He doubted in the efficiency of his sensations and perceptions. How can I know that my senses are not deceiving me? What is the proof that I exist? How can I be sure about the existence of the world around me? Thus, failing to find any solid proof of the existence of things around him and also of his own, Descartes' mind was full of doubt. This doubt was fundamental in his philosophical attitude.

Characteristics of Philosophical Attitude

The above mentioned example of the philosophical attitude of Gautama Buddha, the seers of the Vedas and Descartes, the father of modern Western philosophy, shows the following chief characteristics of philosophical attitude:

(1) *Sense of wonder.* Most of us are so much used to the world around us that we do not wonder even at things which are marvellous otherwise. The philosopher is a man who is given a childlike sense of wonder. He wonders at the system, sequence, variety and mutually contradictory phenomena in the world around him and tries to find out the cause behind all this. This was the beginning of philosophy in India and elsewhere.

(2) *Doubt.* Philosophical attitude is against dogmatism. It examines every belief, it doubts in everything not because doubting is a philosophical habit but because the philosopher is in search of some solid proof for the existence of things around him and also that of himself.

(3) *Criticism.* Thus, the philosophical attitude is critical. The philosopher does not accept a thing as it is but examines it and arrives at rational conclusions.

(4) *Reflection.* Critical thinking involves reflection. Hence the philosophical attitude is reflective.

(5) *Tolerance.* The philosopher is prepared to see every aspect of a problem. His mind is open and his standpoint liberal and tolerant.

(6) *Acceptance of the guidance of experience and reason.* The philosopher thinks in the light of his experience and with the help of his reasoning. He has no prejudice and preconception of his own. He is prepared to go wherever his reason might take him, however, this may hit at his hitherto held beliefs. It is hence that the great social reformer Sankara of India declared the world as Maya.

(7) *Absence of hurry in arriving at the conclusions.* The philosopher does not arrive at any conclusions unless he has some solid proofs for them. He does not worry about the amount of time involved in the process as he is in no hurry to reach the conclusions.

(8) *Detachment.* The philosopher is neither a sceptic nor a dogmatist. He reflects with a detached and unemotional attitude.

(9) *Persistence,* The philosopher ceaselessly persists in his thinking unless he arrives at some satisfactory conclusion. And because his conclusions are never final his search continues throughout his life.

To conclude, the philosophical attitude involves a sense of wonder, doubt, criticism, reflective thinking, tolerance, acceptance of the guidance of experience and reason, absence of hurry in arriving at the conclusions, detached attitude and a persistent effort for the search of truth.

As a comprehensive science, philosophy has two aspects — critical and synthetic. This synthetic aspect of philosophy is known as speculative aspect because the philosopher has to take recourse to speculation in his philosophical synthesis. The philosophical synthesis is not merely a putting together of bits of knowledge. It involves speculation. It is hence that the philosopher arrives at new truths and sees further than the scientist. The critical philosophy critically examines the postulates and conclusions of different sciences. On the other hand the synthetic philosophy presents a world-view by a synthesis of the conclusions of different sciences. The former type of philosophy is inadequate without the latter. The critical philosophy is discursive. The synthetic philosophy is constructive. The critical philosophy finds out the validity of the postulates of different sciences and examines their conclusions. It solves the problems which fall in the field of more than one sciences. On the other hand, the synthetic philosophy presents a total picture of the world arrived at by a synthesis of the conclusions of science. Thus, it synthesizes various sciences and also points out to those fields of knowledge where no research has been made so far. Thus it leads to the birth of new sciences. It is not that the critical philosophy examines the postulates and conclusions of sciences only, the philosopher also examines postulates and conclusions of other philosophers and presents a more comprehensive world-view by a synthesis of different philosophies.

PHILOSOPHY AND COMMON SENSE

Though the philosophical process is different from the process of common sense, it cannot be said that the two are entirely different. As Aldous Huxley has said, "Men live in accordance with their philosophy of life, their conception of the world." Common sense involves the intelligence required in understanding our day-today life. Life is impossible without it. On the other hand, in philosophy one solves the basic and general problems arising in his experience. While commonsense is concerned with particular questions it is inadequate with out the understanding of basic and general problems. Therefore, philosophy and common sense are mutually complementary. Common sense is certainly not the maximum of philosophy but it is definitely the minimum of it. The systematic form of common sense observations provide the basis for science and the systematization of scientific conclusions leads to philosophy. Thus while common sense is narrow, philosophy is comprehensive. It is hence that some Indian philosophers have equated common sense with ignorance. But ignorance is not the contradictory of knowledge. It points out to knowledge negatively. This shows the intimate relationship of philosophy and common sense. In his everyday life the man finds much conflict and contradiction in the matters of commonsense. When this conflict becomes excessive it gives rise to philosophical problems because the man is in need of going to the depth of the common sense problems and find out the harmony lying under the apparent contradictions. This is done by philosophy. Therefore, philosophy is not only required by the philosopher but also by the common man. The philosopher should never leave commonsense. By being a philosopher he should be rather more successful in his everyday life though while engaged in the philosophical process he might forget the world around him. However high may be the mind of the philosopher, his feet should always rest on the solid earth because ultimately man is the son of this terrestrial world and he has to grow here. Thus, it is clear that the philosopher cannot do without commonsense.

VALUE OF PHILOSOPHY

Philosophy influences both the personal and social aspects of human life. Most of the Western philosophers have considered the goal of philosophy to be the achievement of knowledge, but the aim of philosophy is not merely intellectual. It is true that philosophy gives us knowledge but, as Sri Aurobindo has pointed out, "Still the truth once discovered must be realisable in our inner being and our outer activities; if it is not, it may have an intellectual but not an integral importance; a truth for the intellect, for our life, it would be no more than the solution of a thought puzzle or an abstract reality or a dead letter". The existentialist school of our time has emphasised the life of the individual, his feelings, expectations and frustrations, in philosophical thinking. It is a revolt against logical and naturalistic system building, analytic intellect and dead thought which make philosophy a useless search for the ideas which are entirely unconnected with our practical life. Therefore, the contemporary school of pragmatism emphasizes the pragmatic value of truths. Humanism lays emphasis upon the Protegorian principle of *Homo Mertsura.* The instrumentalism of John Dewey explains knowledge and intelligence as instruments for success in life. Hence philosophy and life are closely connected. This can be seen particularly in the following points:

1. *Value of philosophy in personal life.* In our personal life we daily come across the problems when we have to decide between right and wrong. This decision

requires criterion of right and wrong or good and ultimate good. To present such a criterion is the job of moral philosophy. Thus, it is clear that we are in need of philosophy at every step of our life. Man cannot live a thoughtless life. He has to always think over many types of problems. Is it not strange that though many people think, few know the laws of thought and the ways of thinking? The laws of thought and the ways of thinking form the subject-matter of an important branch of philosophy known as Logic. A man may sometimes think properly even without any knowledge of logic but a knowledge of logic will definitely make his thinking better and more valid. In the modern times, everywhere in urban areas one hears talk about art. Many want to refine their lives. Many want to live amidst beautiful things and beautify their surroundings. But how many persons think about the basic questions as to what is beauty? What is art? These questions are raised by all important branch of philosophy known as Aesthetics. Many people are prepared to sacrifice their lives for the sake of their values. What is this value? What are the ultimate values? These questions are answered by Axiology. Everyman, some-time or the other, tries to know what will happen to him after death? Is there a world other than our own? What happens to the man when he dies? These questions are raised in Eschatology, an important branch of philosophy. Again, some thoughtful persons, when they reach at some crossing in life, think as to where they have to go? Why have they come to this world? What is the aim of life? Who am I? These questions are raised in philosophy of self. When the man looks at the towering tops of the mountains, murmuring sounds of the forests, pitch-dark nights, roaring oceans and ferocious earthquakes and other peculiar natural phenomena a question rises in his mind as to what is this world? What is its nature? How has it been made? Who made it? Why did he make it? All these questions are discussed in Cosmology and Cosmogony. Thus, numerous types of questions that are raised in our everyday life fall beyond the scope of common sense or science because they are basically philosophical questions. The value of philosophy in a man's life is, therefore, quite clear.

2. *Value in behaviour towards others.* Whereas philosophy influences personal life, it influences social life as well. Our behaviour towards others is determined by our philosophies. If a man considers others as ends in themselves, his behaviour will be different from that of those persons who consider others as mere instruments to achieve their own selfish ends. Every man has divine element in him, this is a philosophical attitude. Everybody is a thief, this is a different philosophical attitude. It can be easily understood that these different philosophical attitudes will lead to different types of behaviour towards others. In fact, it will not be an exaggeration to say that at the root of the behaviour of different persons, there are some philosophical difficulties. For example, the hatred of a communist towards a capitalist is the result of Marxist philosophy.

3. *Value in political life.* Philosophy also influences political life. Various types of political philosophies such as democratic socialism, communism, totalitarianism, anarchism, etc., lead to different types of government and state and to a lot of difference concerning human rights and the different aspects of political life.

4. *Value in economic life.* Every one has to earn money in order to earn his livelihood. The question is as to what is the aim of life. Is money an end or merely a means to it? This is a philosophical question and on the answer to it, depend not only the economic activities of the individuals but also those of nations. The form of production, consumption and exchange very much depends on the answer to this philosophical question. According to Gandhi, capitalists are the trustees of the capital of society. On the other hand, according to Karl Marx, the capitalists are the exploiters of the proletariate. These two different philosophical attitudes have widely influenced economic life.

5. *Value in social life.* Society is a web of social relationships. These relationships are found in different institutions such as family, marriage, business, etc., and in thousands of associations. All these are influenced by philosophy. For example, whether the wedlock between male and female is a social contract or whether marriage is a religious sacrament, this is a philosophical question on the answer to which depends the form, stability and result of marriage in a particular society. Similarly, the relationships between parents and their children in a family do not depend on the biological and psychological attachments alone but also on their philosophical attitude towards life. Whether the children should be brought up as ends in themselves or whether they are mere instruments for the progress of the family, this is a philosophical question the answer to which determines many important issues in a joint family. Similarly, what are the rights of society over the individual and do these rights have a limit? How far should the individual accept social control and how far can he evade it? All these are philosophical questions which have important social influence.

6. *Value in cultural life.* The philosophy of a nation is the index of its cultural progress. Thus, philosophy influences each aspect of culture. The forms of dance, music, art, literature, etc., are very much influenced by philosophy. A healthy philosophy will lead to a healthy attitude towards all these. To illustrate, Indian philosophy is mainly spiritual, therefore, one finds the stamp of spirituality on Indian dance, music, art, literature, etc. On the other hand, Western philosophy is materialistic and, therefore. Western culture bears the stamp of materialism. To quote John Dewey, "Thus philosophy makes a change of culture. In forming patterns to be conformed to in future thought and action it is additive and transforming in its role in the history of civilization".[26] This is expressed in even more clear terms by Archie J. Bahm when he says, "Without philosophy then there would be no civilization, and civilizations differ from one another as romantic, rationalistic, pacific, aggressive, mystical and mundane, partly because of their philosophical differences".[27]

The philosophy of a nation represents the infancy, adolescence and maturity of a nation's culture. Philosophical progress manifests cultural progress. In a nation where there is no philosophical progress, its culture is dead. Cultural revolutions have also coincided with philosophical crises. In Greece when Socrates was made to

26. John Dewey, *Philosophy and Civilization*, G.P. Putnam's Sons, New York, 1931, p. 6.
27. Bahm, A.J., *Philosophy — An Introduction*, p. 27.

drink hemlock it was not because of the enmity of people against him only but also because of his opposition to philosophy of the community of his time. Similarly, many other great men have sacrificed their lives by challenging the philosophies of their contemporary philosophers and thus changing it through their blood.

7. *Value in educational field* — Though now-a-days, the number of students of philosophy and departments of its teaching in Indian universities is gradually becoming less and less, no thoughtful person denies the value of philosophy in educational field. In the words of Blanshard and others, "The function of philosophy in universities is properly the same as its function in the cultural development of a society to be the intellectual conscience of the community".[28]

The most fundamental question in the field of education is concerning its aim? This question raises another question as to what is man, because what he is not, he cannot become. He can become only that which is already implicit in him. Man's nature is, therefore, a philosophical question on the answer to which have developed so many philosophies of education which are the foundations of different modern methods of teaching.

8. *Value in the field of knowledge.* In the modern times, many educated persons who swear by science, consider philosophy to be useless in the age of science because they are ignorant of the function of philosophy in the field of science. It can be said without exaggeration that without a philosophical basis, any knowledge is imperfect, because no total picture can be presented without the synthetic function of philosophy. Without this total picture there will always be tension in the field of knowledge which leads to philosophical activities. As Aristotle has said, "Whether we philosophise or not, we must philosophise". This has been expressed by Perry in somewhat different terms when he says, "Philosophy is neither accidental nor supernatural, but inevitable and normal".[29] Besides its synthetic function, another important function of philosophy is the criticism of the postulates and conclusions of different sciences. Whenever a scientist delves deeper in his own particular field, he reaches a depth where the process of his thinking is not scientific but philosophical. This can be seen in the thinking of many a great scientists of the world. The importance of philosophy in the field of knowledge is, therefore, quite clear.

From the point of view of different aspects of the individual and social life, and in different fields of knowledge, the discussion of the value of philosophy shows the utility of its study. In the words of J.W. Cunningham, "Philosophy thus grows directly out of life and its needs. Everyone who lives, if he lives at all reflectively, is in some degree a philosopher".[30] In the words of Chestertan, "The most practical and important thing about a man is his view of universe — his philosophy. The employee is at the mercy of the philosophy of his employer and the employer stakes his business on the philosophy of his employees".[31]

28. Blanshard and Others, *Philosophy in American Education*, Harper & Bros., New York (1945), p. 80.
29. Perry, *The Approach to Philosophy*, p. 22
30. Cunningham, J.W., *Problems of Philosophy*, p. 5.
31. Quoted by Hocking, *Types of Philosophy*, p. 4.

2

PHILOSOPHY AND EDUCATION

In order to comprehend the close relationship of philosophy and education the aspirant should first know the various branches of philosophy and then study their relationship with education. The most important branches of philosophy are: Metaphysics, Epistemology and Axiology. Again, the relationship of Philosophy and Education should be sought in different fields of education such as the aims and ideals, the methods of teaching, the curriculum, the school administration, discipline and finally evaluation. All these branches of education are based upon philosophical foundation. Needless to say that as the philosophical foundation differs so differ the aims and ideals, the teaching methods, the school administration and discipline in different educational systems. This will be explained in details in our study of the different systems of philosophy of education. At present, our discussion will be confined to provide a summary picture of the close relationship of philosophy and education.

METAPHYSICS AND EDUCATION

Aristotle developed the study of Metaphysics to be studied after physics. While physics studies the laws of the external form of existence, metaphysics thinks over the real essence of things. Its main problems are: What is the nature of existence? What is reality? What is truth? What are its different forms? Is the world one or many? What is time? What is substance? What is causality ? What is fact? What is the purpose or aim? What is change? What is novelty? What is similarity? Who am I? Is there a purpose in creation? Is the world determined or free? Is there a God? Has the world progressed? etc. Thus the subject-matter of metaphysics includes the self, the world, and the God. Its scope includes ontology, philosophy of self, cosmogony, cosmology and theology. Ontology is the science of reality.

The metaphysics, in brief deals with reality in man, world and hereafter. This has a close bearing upon the aims and ideals of education. The metaphysical attitude provides the educationists the proper perspective for devising aims and ideals of education. What we want to make out of man depends upon his nature and place in the universe. Again, the concept of self is the basis of the development of character, the central aim of education. Know thyself and be thyself is the universally acknowledged aim of education. The concept of world is directly concerned with the individual's relationships with society and nature. While Indian philosophy emphasises harmony between man and the world the Western philosophers have made too much of man's desire to overpower Nature. While the former philosophy has been the foundation of educational institutions like Vishwabharati or Sri Aurobindo's International University, the other approach is the philosophy behind the technological and scientific education of today. In fact the more integral is the world-view the more multi-sided will be the education based upon it. In the end, moral and religious education is based upon the metaphysical concept of God. This does not mean that moral education must necessarily be linked to religious education. It only shows that our explanation of the ultimate reality or the total reality, call it God or anything else, has important bearing upon education particularly its aims and ideals and therefore its means and plans.

The most important metaphysical theories which have influenced education are: Naturalism, Idealism, Pragmatism and Realism. Naturalism has been manifest in different types of theories such as Atomic naturalism, Scientific naturalism, Mechanistic naturalism and Historical naturalism. These will be discussed in detail in our chapter on Naturalism as a philosophy of education. The most important metaphysical theory in the field of education is idealism. Idealism has been subjective, objective, phenomenalistic and absolute. These will be discussed in details in our chapter on Idealism as a philosophy of education. The most influential metaphysical theory in today's field of education, however, is pragmatism. This is closely linked to Instrumentalism and Humanism. These will be discussed in our chapter on Pragmatism as a philosophy of education. In the end the metaphysical theory known as Realism has very much influenced education concerning science and technology. This will be discussed in sequence.

EPISTEMOLOGY AND EDUCATION

Epistemology is the branch of philosophy which is concerned with the discussion of the problems concerning knowledge. Its main problems are: What is the relation between the knower and known? Is the content of knowledge identical with the external object or is it different from it? How can we know that our knowledge is a real knowledge of the object? What are the limits of knowledge? What are the sources of knowledge? etc. Besides, the epistemologist raises certain other questions such as: What is knowledge? Is the knowledge of knower possible, if not, then what is known? If the known is an object then what is this object? Is the knowledge of the existence of an object possible without its being known? How can we distinguish between true and false knowledge? What is ignorance? Is it a form of knowledge or different from it? What is the process of knowledge? Do we know something which was already existent before our knowledge of it? What is the meaning of forgetting of knowledge? What is the basis of validity of knowledge? What are the errors possible in the process of knowledge? Is our knowledge definite or is the definiteness based purely on our feeling and faith? How is it that some beliefs are considered to be more valid than others? What are the distinctions between different types of knowledge? What are the relations of knowledge with science and philosophy?

The above mentioned description of epistemological problems clarifies the scope of epistemology. Its subject matter is the process, methods, object, characteristics, conditions, validity and fallacies of knowledge. Epistemology is the philosophical discussion of ail these problems. It should be remembered here that epistemology uses the philosophical methods of induction and deduction, synthesis and analysis. In it is adopted the philosophical attitude which is detached, tolerant, persistent and guided by experience and reasoning. One finds different conclusions presented by different epistemologists regarding epistemogical problems. While according to the realist philosophers knowledge is the knowledge of objects, the idealists define it as the knowledge of ideas. While some epistemologists think that the presence of object is necessary for knowledge, and therefore, every knowledge is a knowledge of both knower and known, others think that the knowledge of known is different from the knowledge of knower. Thus, we find realists, idealists and empiricists, rationalists and critical philosophers in the field of epistemological problems. About the possibility of knowledge one finds different approaches such as agnostic, sceptic and mystic. All these approaches have thrown light on different aspects of knowledge. Besides, different epistemologists have criticized the views of other fellow epistemologists and this discussion has given rise to an interesting literature. Kant's famous book *Critique of Pure Reason* is a permanent contribution to epistemological literature.

The explanation given above shows the importance of epistemology for education. Empiricist school of philosophy discussed the methods and value of empirical knowledge. Its opposite Rationalist school pointed out how some of the knowledge is innate. Scepticism shows the limits of knowledge. David Hume rightly pointed out that certainty can be possible only in mathematics and not in the field of sciences. Agnosticism shows the relativity of human knowledge. Criticism shows that our knowledge is neither *a-priori* nor *a-posteriori.* It shows that knowledge is synthetic, requiring sensibility, understanding and reasoning. Intuitionism shows that intellect and intuition are complementary. Mysticism shows the value of spiritual experiences in the field of religion. Pragmatism rightly maintains that the value of knowledge is in its use. Instrumentalism rightly points out that reason is an instrument for the satisfaction of human needs. Humanism rightly shows that the criterion of all knowledge is man himself and there is no ultimate knowledge. Experimentalism and relativism rightly point out that knowledge is experimental and relative. Thus all the schools of epistemology show the methods, limits and value of knowledge. They supply the necessary foundation for all knowledge, scientific and otherwise.

AXIOLOGY AND EDUCATION

Axiology includes three normative sciences: Logic, Ethics and Aesthetics. All these three are intimately related to education.

LOGIC AND EDUCATION

The term logic is derived from the Greek word 'Logos', which means reason or expression of reason in words, that is, discourse. Etymologically, therefore.

Logic is the science of reasoning or argument. According to Dewey and Stebbing reasoning is reflective thinking, and reflective thinking is a process of finding way out of some difficulty or problem by weighing the evidence on the basis of a tentative hypothesis and thereby reaching some conclusion. The reasoning can be either deductive or inductive. In the deductive reasoning we argue from a general principle to a particular conclusion. For example, we say that since all men are mortal, an X, who is a man, is mortal. But if we argue that since X, Y, Z, who are men are subject to death, every man must be subject to death, we are arguing inductively. In logic we study the general principles governing both types of reasoning. Accordingly, we may define Logic as the science of laws of thought and reasoning. According to Morris R. Cohen and Ernest Negel, "Logic may be said to be concerned with the question of the adequacy or probative value of different kinds of evidence Thus, according to this definition of logic, logic is concerned with both conclusive as well as partial evidence. Traditionally, logic was concerned only with conclusive evidence. These authors, however, represent the modern approach which includes not only conclusive but also partial evidence as the subject-matter of logic. In the words of Cohen and Negel, "Logic may, therefore, be also defined as the science of implication, or of valid inference (based on such implication)". Thus logic is not concerned with the factual questions such as about the psychological processes of reasoning actually happening in mind, etc. Factual questions are material issues. They crop-up in an enquiry along with the questions concerning the implication. While evidence includes facts it also includes premises and conclusions the relation between which is known as implication. The former is the subject-matter of physical sciences or human sciences, while the latter comes within the field of logic. In the words of Cohen and Negel, "Logic as a distinctive science is concerned only with the second — with the relation of implication between propositions. Thus the specific task of logic is the study of the conditions under which one proposition necessarily follows and may therefore be deduced from one or more others, regardless of whether the latter are in fact true".

The above discussion shows that logic is the basis of all knowledge. It is hence called the science of sciences. It studies various intellectual processes such as thinking, reasoning and judgement. All education is concerned with theory and practice. While the theory is arrived at by induction, the practice depends upon deduction. Both induction and deduction are the two important branches of logic. The knowledge of logic helps us in avoiding error and arriving at correct generalisation in every field of knowledge. It resolves doubts and points out fallacies. It is intellectual exercise necessary for all the serious students. The teacher must know logic in order to have successful communication.

ETHICS AND EDUCATION

According to philology, the word ethics is derived from the word Ethos, which means character. In this way, ethics is the science of character, habits of activity or behaviour of human beings. Ethics is also called Moral Philosophy. The word moral is a derivative from the Latin word mores' meaning conventions or practice.

In this way ethics literally means the science of convention or practice. Ethics is the science of human conduct. Habits and behaviour are related to the permanent peculiarities of human character. Conduct is the mirror of character. Thus ethics is the science of character or habit. It evaluates human habits, character and voluntary determinations and discusses their propriety or otherwise.

Ethics considers the duties of human beings. It is an ethical science and it pronounces ethical decisions upon conduct. There is a motive in conduct. In it there is voluntary determination. It manifests character. Character is manifested in determinations. Determination is the activated form of character. Therefore, it studies what is right and what is wrong in character. But the propriety of habits and determination can be determined by measuring them with the ideals of life. These goods too have classes. Supreme good determines the propriety of the immediate good. For example, every student must take the examination, it being his immediate good because he has laboured for it throughout the year. But in some conditions it may be improper to do so. To take an example, he may have to desist from taking the examination in order to nurse his mother. Here the propriety of the immediate good of sitting for the examination is determined by the supreme good of postulating the superiority of duty to oneself. Thus ethics is above all the science of the supreme good. It studies the ideals of human life. It shows what ought to be done and what ought not to be done. In the words of James Seth, As the science of the Good, it is the science *par excellence* of the ideal and the ought. "[1]

Ethics is the science of character. But it is different from the natural and factual sciences. It is a normative science. In Muirnead's words, "It is related not merely to temporal behaviour but to behaviour in the form of the basis of legal decision".[2] Its function is to give decisions on behaviour, whether the behaviour is right or wrong.

According to Mackenzie,[3] 'Ethics can be defined as the study of what is right or good in conduct. "In this definition ethics has been accepted as the study of both right and good. But there is difference between right and good. 'Rectus' the Latin word from which right has been derived, means straight or according to law. Thus, good behaviour will correspond to law. Good comes from the German 'gut', meaning that which is useful for the supreme good. In this instance, good is that which leads to supreme good. Mostly good is taken to mean an end, not a means to an end.

According to Prof J. S. Mackenzie, the study of ethics admits classification into at least four divisions: "(1) Psychology of ethical consciousness; (2) Sociology of an ethical life; (3) Theories of ethical criterion; and (4) The application of this criterion in ethical life".[4] These four divisions of ethics are the foundations of all education. The most widely accepted aim of education is man making or character building. As the science of character ethics analyses the psychology of ethical consciousness. It shows how different moral norms evolve in different

1. Seth, J., *A Study of Ethical Principles*, William Blackwood and Sons Ltd., London (1908), p. 37.
2. Muirnead, J.H., *The Elements of Ethics*, John Murray, London (1895), p. 33.
3. Mackenzie, J.S., *A Manual of Ethics*, University Tutorial Press Ltd., London (1929), p. 1.
4. *Ibid*., p. 25.

circumstances but then it examines the validity of these norms and provides solid basis for social ethos of the educand. It examines the theories moral of standard and shows the possibility of arriving at a correct ethical criterion. Ethics is not only theoretical, it also helps in the application of moral principles in actual life. Ethical activities are accompanied by a feeling of vice and virtue. Ethics details the criterion for this vice and virtue. Its scope includes the descriptions of good qualities and bad qualities. Due to the relation of good and bad to every human activity, the field of ethics includes the conclusions of other sciences and arts. Ethics gives moral judgments on these too. In this way, many psychological, political, economic, sociological, religious and philosophical problems come to be included in the field of ethics. Philosophical problems like the real form of human personality, voluntary nature of volition, immortality of the soul, the existence of God, and unity and the moral order in the universe, etc, are included in ethics. The sociological problem relating the relation between the individual and the society is also an ethical problem. In this way, in brief, it may be said that wherever there is human behaviour and human volitions, there is scope for ethics. In John Dewey's words, "The foremost conclusion is that morals have to do with all activity into which alternative possibilities enter. For wherever they enter, a difference between better and worse arises".[5]

AESTHETICS AND EDUCATION

Aesthetics is the science of beauty, as logic is the science of truth and ethics is the science of good. Education seeks to realise the true, the good and the beautiful. Therefore, It requires not only logic and ethics but also aesthetics. The aim of education is to realise all-round development of the educand. In this development moral and aesthetic developments occupy foremost place. While moral development requires knowledge of ethics, aesthetic development requires training in aesthetics. Aesthetics again, is the basis of all literary and artistic criticism. It supplies the philosophical basis to literature and art. As literature and art contribute significantly to education, the value of aesthetics in education is clear.

SOCIAL PHILOSOPHY AND EDUCATION

The term 'Social Philosophy' includes two words, social and philosophy. Literally, it is the philosophy of the society. What is society? Society is the network of social relations. Here society means general society, not any particular society, because philosophical view points towards universality even though, in actuality, it may become limited. Hence the subject of social philosophy is the human society as a whole. It does not concern itself with creatures other than the man for, in the first place, they do not have any society', and in the second place, if at all they have one, their society is fundamentally different from the human society. Social philosophy is not concerned with nature either, because the relations that exist between the objects of nature are different from social relations. The latter have mental or

5. John Dewey, *Human Nature and Conduct* in "The World's Great Thinkers Series, "The Social Philosophers," Edited By Commins and Linscott. p. 449.

psychic elements and are linked with consciousness. They are also coloured with feelings, emotions, instincts and passions. Bereft of these psychological elements, human relations are nothing more than the relations that exist between objects. Mere coexistence, either among the people of one nation or among the nations themselves, is not enough for social relations. In the field of social relations, social change and regulation cause integrative and disintegrative processes. Both similarity and dissimilarity are to be found in society though the former is more important. Unity in diversity is the basic trait of social relations. That explains why in the modern world, which is inhabited by various races, nations and states, etc., the consciousness of one world has become so powerful and the notion of world government so popular. Dissimilarity breeds inter-dependence among the social units, causes division of labour, differentiation and specialisation, and then leads to mutual co-operation and organisation. Society is to be measured not by men and their groups but by the interactions and inter-relations that exist among them. Precisely, these are the subjects studied by a social philosophy. It seeks to determine the facts and values involved in the network of social relations. It looks at the human society in all its perspectives, past, present and future; east, west and universal. Its approach is all-pervasive. It evaluates the human achievements in the light of eternal values and pronounces judgements upon them. It analyses various groups, committees, institutions, associations and their inter-relations from the philosophical viewpoint.

The social philosopher examines the basic principles of human behaviour and supreme values of human life, and thus prepares a solid ground for social sciences. Just as the philosophy of science provides philosophical basis for physical sciences, social philosophy provides philosophical basis for social sciences. It studies the philosophical questions involved in social phenomena and processes. It views the problems of the social scientist from the philosophical point of view, and evaluates the social facts in the light of supreme social values. Different social sciences study different aspects of social life. Social philosophy seeks to harmonise the different conclusions of different social sciences and to fulfil the chasm amongst them. Without social philosophy, the knowledge of social sciences would be incomplete and scattered. In regard to the analysis of supreme issues, every social scientist has to consult the social philosopher. For example, the impact of Plato's and Aristotle's social philosophy may be seen on the different social scientists. In modern times, American behaviourist thinker, William James, and the utilitarian philosopher, John Dewey, have exercised considerable influence on different social sciences.

The basic problem of education is now to secure man's development. For this it is necessary to know what is man. Social philosophy analyses human nature and finds out how far man is naturally social and how far not. While prescribing syllabi for educational institutions it is essential to keep in view what type of society we want to create. It is clear that social philosophy constructs the philosophical foundations of the educational system.

3

PHILOSOPHY OF EDUCATION

Our discussion of the concept of education and the concept of philosophy form the basis of arriving at the definition of philosophy of education. Thus philosophy of education is essentially a method of approaching educational experience rather than a body of conclusions. It is the specific method which makes it philosophical. Philosophical method is critical, comprehensive and synthetic. Therefore, philosophy of education is the criticism of the general theory of education. It consists of critical evaluation and systematic reflection upon general theories. It is a synthesis of educational facts with educational values. In brief it is a philosophical process of solving educational problems through philosophical method, from a philosophical attitude to arrive at philosophical conclusions and results. Thus it aims at achieving general and comprehensive results. This clarification of the definition of education will be further clarified by a discussion of the scope and nature of philosophy of education. It should be noted here that philosophy of education is a species of the genus philosophy, with the differentia that its proper scope is confined to the field of education. Thus it is philosophy in the field of education.

SCOPE AND NATURE OF PHILOSOPHY OF EDUCATION

The scope of a subject directly follows from its definition. Therefore, the scope of philosophy of education is concerned with the problems of education. These problems are general in nature, such as the interpretation of Nature, the world and the universe, explanation of aims and ideals, the relationship of the various constituents of the field of education. The main problems of philosophy of education include aims and ideals of education, analysis of human nature, relationship of education and state, educational values, theory of know ledge and its relationship to education, economic system and education, the place of school in educational system, the curriculum and the process of education and finally the relationship of education and social progress.

The above mentioned problems of philosophy of education constitute its scope and clarify its nature. Its scope includes a critical evaluation of the different aims of education held and propagated from time to time such as character building, man making, human development, preparation for adult life, development of citizenship, utilisation of leisure; training for civic life, training for international living, total development of personality, evolution of democratic society, realisation of social change, realisation of cultural man, adjustment of society and individual and finally self-realisation and spiritual emancipation. These and other aims of education presented by educational thinkers in different times and climes are scrutinised and evaluated. It should be remembered here that the chief function of philosophy everywhere is critical evaluation as well as construction. Thus philosophy of education critically evaluates different aims and ideals of education to arrive at the most sound and cogent aim of education. Here again, it is more concerned with the general and universal aim rather than any specific and particular aim of education. It is so since philosophy everywhere deals with most general. Again, philosophical process is comprehensive and total. Therefore, philosophy of education aims at presenting a synthesis of various aims and ideals of education.

The same philosophical attitude pervades the discussion of human nature in philosophy of education. A philosophical picture of human nature is a result of the synthesis of the facts borrowed from all the human sciences with the values discussed in different normative sciences. The philosophical picture, therefore, is more integral as compared to the pictcure of man drawn by biology, sociology, psychology, economics and anthropology and so many other human sciences.

The most important part of the scope of the philosophy of education is formed by the educational values. Value is typically a philosophical subject since it is more abstract than concrete, mental than physical, integral than one-sided, universal than particular. Philosophical treatment of values not only evaluates' them but also systematises them in a hierarchy. Educational values are determined by philosophical values. Educational values held by different philosophers have been derived from their world-view. Therefore, a scrutiny of the world-views, the specific function of philosophy, is necessary for any treatment of philosophical values.

Education deals with knowledge. It is determined by the source, limits, criteria and means of knowledge. The discussion of all these however falls within the jurisdiction of epistemology, an area of philosophy. Therefore, an important area of the functioning of philosophy of education is concerned with theory of knowledge. The most important service of philosophy of education to the cause of education everywhere, is the prescription of criteria for deciding the relationship of state and education, economic system and education, curriculum administration, discipline, progress, etc. These problems have led to the evolution of different philosophies of education. The criteria of judgment everywhere are determined by philosophy. Therefore, philosophy of education prescribes criteria of judgement in these fields.

The above discussion of the scope of philosophy of education also explains its nature. Thus, philosophy of education is an important branch of applied philosophy. Of the three divisions of philosophy, metaphysics, epistemology and axiology, philosophy of education falls in the third. It is, therefore, mainly concerned with educational values. As a branch of philosophy it utilises philosophical methods for the solution of philosophical problems with a philosophical attitude to arrive at philosophical conclusions. In this comprehensive process it includes facts concerning education and synthesises them with values.

PHILOSOPHY OF EDUCATION AND THE TEACHER

According to John Dewey, "Philosophy of Education is not an external application of readymade ideas to a system of practice having a radically different origin and purpose, it is only an explicit formulation of the problems of the formation of right mental and moral attitudes in respect to the difficulties of contemporary social life. The most penetrating definition of philosophy which can be given is, then, that it is the theory of education in its most general phases".[1] Thus the teacher gets his theory of teaching from the philosophy of education. Teaching methods are very much concerned with the philosophy of education the teacher holds. According to Spencer, only a true philosopher may give a practical shape to education. How he behaves with the students and how he communicates depends very much on how he defines the educands. Different philosophical systems of education have explained human nature in widely different ways. This very much governs the teacher's attitude to the method of teaching. Though philosophy is no substitute for the teacher's knowledge of the subject, it is certainly necessary for his enlightenment. In the words of Bertrand Russell, "Philosophy is to be studied not for the sake of any definite answers to the questions — but rather for the sake of questions themselves; because these questions enlarge our conception of what is possible, enrich our intellectual imagination and diminish the dogmatic assurance which closes the mind against speculation, but above all because through the greatness of the universe which philosophy contemplates, the mind also is rendered great and becomes capable of that union with the universe which constitutes its highest good".[2]

The most important contribution of the philosophy of education to the teacher is, however, concerned with the aims and ideals of education. Without philosophy of education the teacher will not have any sense of purpose in his teaching. This is not possible by science however we may eulogise the role of science in the present-day education. In fact, while science supplies the means, only philosophy supplies the ends. In the words of John Dewey, "Philosophy is concerned with determining ends of education, while the science of education determines the means to be used."[3]

Again, philosophy of education helps the teacher in the determination of the curriculum of education. Defining a philosopher Plato said, "He, who has a taste for every sort of knowledge and who is curious to learn and is never satisfied, may be justly termed a philosopher".[4] Philosophy provides a comprehensive and total view of the educational situation. It leads to integral approach. It is a total view-point. Therefore, it is a good prophylactic against all one-sidedness. Criticising the

1. Dewey, J., *Democracy and Education*, p. 386.
2. Bertrand Russell, *The Problems of Philosophy*, pp. 249-50.
3. John Dewey in *Sources of Science of Education*.
4. Plato, *Republic*. Book V.

anomaly of one-sidedness in our present educational system, A. M. Schlezinger has rightly pointed out, "We desperately need a rich emotional life, reflecting actual relations between the individual and the community".[5]

The world is faced today with two prominent approaches to life, the Eastern and the Western. These present two different cultural attitudes, two different philosophies of life. Mankind has made experiments for a proper human life in different climes and times. The modern man may do well by synthesising the wisdom of different cultures. An ideal teacher imbibes combination of East and West, philosophy and science. Explaining this viewpoint, Kewal Motwani has said, "Now two types of cultures, with vastly different ideologies and values have come face to face in India and are engaged in a deadly combat. India, with her rural, agricultural, handicraft culture, with an integrated view of life, with its emphasis on indefinable, qualitative values, on individual uniqueness, on dharma, on self-imposed poverty, on social synthesis, on a subjective, broad-based nationalism, on man and machinery of the government, on a life of religious experience and unfoldment, on power through repose is confronted by a culture that stands for machine and science, for an urbanised, industrialized order, for analytical view of life, with its emphasis on neuroses and complexes, for mass production, for quantitative values, for struggle for existence and survival of the fittest, for accumulation of wealth and economic imperialism, for assertive, arrogant nationalism, for democracy and dictatorship, for religion of scientific humanism and rationalism. India has sought the vision of the whole not of the parts, she has been interested in living not merely in the means of livelihood. She has combined philosophic contemplation with action; she has stood for beauty and dignity, not mere utility. But today the culture of machine and science has taken a firm grip of India and is slowly seeping into her soul".[6]

The complex modern civilization, overburdened with technology, is threatening a relapse into barbarism or an extinction of *Homo Sapiens.* Man is facing today the problems which are characteristic of the atomic age and bred by industrialism. Everywhere, we find chaos and frustration. Solutions have been offered from all sides. Science and international law have proved helpless. Thoughtful men are looking towards religion, morality and spirituality. As an author puts it, "The alternative with which we are faced is: either atrophy of our brain power; degeneration of man, decline of his intellectual and spiritual activities which become more and more mechanical and in the end slavery in new totalitarian regimes with over-centralised control; or a spiritual revolution; an awakening of man to the fact that he, after all, is a spiritual being, with inexhaustible spiritual powers; and a stem determination to defend his liberty and to subordinate the so-called progress of science and technology to the moral and spiritual end of humanity within a democratic order".[7] Therefore, the most essential thing for a teacher is his philosophy of education. The only remedy to

5. Schlezinger, A.M., *The Politics of Freedom*, 1950, p. 237.
6. Kewal Motwani, "*Sociology*" University of Madras Journal, July 1939, pp. 189-190.
7. F.H. Heinemann, *Hibbert Journal*, October 1957, p. 46.

cultural or any other type of one sidedness is the philosophical approach. This philosophical approach is expressed in integral viewpoint admirably summed up by Sri Aurobindo in these words, "The heart and the mind are universal Deity and neither a mind without heart nor a heart without mind is the human ideal".[8]

Warning against the neglect of philosophy of education on the part of the teacher Rusk maintained, "Teachers who assume that they can afford to ignore philosophy pay the penalty of their neglect, for their efforts, lacking a coordinating principle, are thereby rendered ineffective".[9] Philosophy is needed not only in the determination of aims and ideals and the curriculum but also in the actual day-to- day programme of educational practice. In the words of Adler, "Thus we begin to see, not only the distinct sphere of the philosophy of education, as answering questions, unanswerable by science, but also the need for a philosophy of education for without it there could be no certain determination of the basic practical principles, underlying the policies which direct actual day-to-day educational practices".[10]

In the end the teacher is not only supposed to have a sound philosophy of education but he is required to develop a philosophical viewpoint among his students as well. In the words of K.L. Shrimali, "Thus, not merely must the teacher have a philosophy of education, he must come prepared to develop among his students a philosophy of life".[11] The teacher provides information and knowledge to the educands but his personal stamp is always in the form of a philosophy of life. What the great teachers have given to the world is philosophy and not information.

METHODOLOGY OF PHILOSOPHY OF EDUCATION

The nature of a subject determines its methods. In the words of Sri Aurobindo, "The description of the status of knowledge to which we aspire determines the means of knowledge which we shall use".[12] Philosophy of education is concerned both with facts and values about all the aspects of human being, the world around him and his status in the cosmos. Such a comprehensive field cannot be dealt with mind alone. In the words of Sri Aurobindo, "What the mind conceives must be need not be the measure of will be".[13] This, however, does not mean the neglect of the importance of language and logic in philosophy of education. To quote Sri Aurobindo again, "A language has to be created which is at once intuitively metaphysical and revealingly poetical, admitting significant and living images as the vehicle of a close, suggestive and vivid indication".[14] While a rational method alone is not sufficient to realise the purpose of philosophy of education, the same is true about an empirical method as well. In the words of

8. Sri Aurobindo, *Views and Reviews*, p. 3.
9. Rusk, R.R., *Philosophical Bases of Education*, p. 9.
10. Adler, *In Defence of The Philosophy of Education*, 41st Year Book of the National Society for the Study of Education, p. 206.
11. Shrimali, K.L., *Better Teacher Education*, Ministry of Education, Government of India, 1954, p. 2.
12. Sri Aurobindo, *Synthesis of Yoga*, p. 351.
13. Sri Aurobindo, *Letters on The Mother*, p. 87.
14. Sri Aurobindo, *The Life Divine*, Vol. II, p. 43.

Sri Aurobindo, 'So long as we confine ourselves to sense evidence and physical consciousness, we can conceive nothing and know nothing except the material world and its phenomena".[15] Only a synthesis of reason and experience may give us an insight into the problems of philosophy of education. As Sri Aurobindo has rightly pointed out, "Every concept is incomplete for us and to a part of our nature almost unreal unless it becomes an experience".[16] Philosophy of education is both a criticism as well as realisation. Therefore, "In each case", as Aurobindo points out. "Understanding, discrimination, verification are necessary, but the subjective and the supraphysical must have another method of verification, than that which we apply successfully to the physical and external objective".[17]

Pointing out the function of philosophy Sri Aurobindo said, "It is an attempt to fix the fundamental realities and principles of being as distinct from its processes and the phenomena which result from those processes".[18] Therefore, neither synthesis nor analysis alone can be ideal methods of philosophy of education. Rational analysis is insufficient to solve the problems concerning educational values. To quote Sri Aurobindo, "All this labour of speculation has its utility in training the human mind and helping to keep before it the idea of something beyond and ultimate towards which it must turn. But the intellectual reason can only point vaguely or feel gropingly towards it or try to indicate partial and even conflicting aspects of its manifestation here, it cannot enter it and know it".[19] This, however, does not mean a total rejection of intellectual processes in the field of philosophy of education. Even in the field of psychical and spiritual development reason and logic may play some role. To quote Sri Aurobindo again, "Reason is not the supreme light and yet it is always a necessary light bringer and unless it has been given its rights and allowed to judge and purify our first infrarational instincts, impulses, rash favours, crude beliefs and blind prejudgments, we are not altogether ready for the full unveiling of a greater inner illumination".[20]

Therefore, philosophy of education cannot do without utilising intuitive method. The intuitive method is a knowledge by identity, a knowledge by intimate direct contact. In the words of Sri Aurobindo, it is inclusion, indwelling and identity. He has rightly said. "Intuition, therefore, is present at the beginning of things and in their middle as well as at their consummation".[21] This intuition is not only mental but psychical and spiritual. Explaining spiritual intuition, the sure foundation of any philosophy of education, Sri Aurobindo has said, "The spiritual intuition lays hold always upon the reality, it is the luminous harbinger of the spiritual realisation or else its illuminative light, it sees that which the other powers of our being are labouring to explore, it gets at the firm truth of

15. *Ibid,* Vol. I, p. 72.
16. *Ibid.*, p. 74.
17. *Ibid.*, Vol. II, p. 434.
18. *Ibid.*, p. 456.
19. *The Riddle of This World*, p. 24.
20. Sri Aurobindo, *Evolution*, p. 29.
21. Sri Aurobindo, *Letters*, Ist Series, p. 5.

the abstract representations of the heart and life, a truth which is itself neither remotely abstract nor outwardly concerte, but something else for which these are only two aides of its psychological manifestation to us".[22] Spiritual intuition does not negate the experiences gained through physical, vital or mental instruments. Whereas the latter seek to abstract one particular type of experience from the whole, it is a knowledge through whole being. "It is a direct vision, an authentic seeing, a comprehensive intuitive apprehension".[23]

Thus, educational philosophy utilises deductive and inductive reasoning, experiences of different types and the intuitions to arrive at inner as well as total truths. The utilisation of these methods however requires a constant development of the philosopher and the educator, his constant grappling with the actual problems arising in the everyday process of education.

NEED OF PHILOSOPHY OF EDUCATION IN MODERN TIMES

All modern educationists hold the view that not only should the educator be equipped with knowledge of a variety of subjects, but also that he should have his own philosophy of education, without which he cannot efficiently solve the problems that face in teaching from day-to-day. Fichte correctly pointed out that the art of education will never attain complete clearness in itself without philosophy. Hence, there is an interaction between the two, and either without the other is incomplete and unserviceable. Some people are so impressed by the achievements of science that they give a higher place to science than to philosophy in education. Psychologists are of the opinion that education should be based on psychological principles, while sociologists, impressed by the significance of social phenomena, suggest that education should be more influenced by their findings. But all these people forget that even sociologists and psychologists have failed to solve many difficulties that have arisen in connection with the aims of education, curriculum, teaching methods, discipline, etc. They have failed to provide a satisfactory criterion for determining techniques of assessment, standards of evaluation, selection of text-books or of teaching methods. In actual fact, there is no rivalry between educational philosophy and educational practice because philosophy gives adequate importance to the principles enunciated by psychology and sociology. The only real difference is that philosophy of education is concerned with more fundamental problems, that it delves far more deeply than any one science, that its attitude is far more comprehensive and liberal and that it is an attempt at synthesizing most of the viewpoints from which any phenomenon is examined. Hence, the educator can do nothing without philosophy.

The educator is often faced with problems in the sphere of education which can be solved only on the basis of his conception of the universe. Every behaviour or action has its own principles. Hence educational behaviour, too, must have its own principles. The principles underlying all educational behaviour are derived

22. Sri Aurobindo, *The Synthesis of Yoga*, p. 663.
23. Sharma, R.N., *The Philosophy of Sri Aurobindo*, IIIrd Ed. 1977, Kedar Nath Ram Nath, Meerut, pp. 57-58.

from philosophy of education. It is only through a philosophy of education that one determines the curriculum, the text-books, the methods of teaching, methods and standards of evaluation, the methods of maintaining discipline, etc. Hence the educator should study educational philosophy.

"The educational system which we attempt to set up," says G.D.H. Cole, "must depend on the kind of society we mean to live in, on the qualities in men and women on which we set the highest value, and on the estimates which we make of the educability of both of those who are endowed with the higher intellectual or aesthetic capacities and of ordinary people".[24] Philosophy of education is theoretical, the theory, however, aims at the guidance to practice. In the words of John Dewey, "Whenever philosophy has been taken seriously, it has always been assumed that it signified achieving a wisdom that would influence the conduct of life ".[25] Idealism has been the most ancient and the most prominent school in philosophy. In the words of Adams, "Idealism in one form or other permeates the whole of the history of philosophy",[26] This idealism has been the most fundamental theory underlying educational principles. In the words of Robert R. Rusk, "It bestows dignity and grandeur upon human life by emphasising the distinctiveness of man's nature, attributing to him powers, not possessed by animals, which issue in ideals—logical and aesthetic, it admits the existence of a Supreme Being, by its respect for human personality it provides the basis for democracy".[27]

The most fundamental question in the field of education is concerning its aim. This question raises queries about the nature of man and the possibility of its modification and transformation. Man's nature is very much concerned with his place in the cosmos. Therefore, the question of the aim of education is very much concerned with the question of the nature of the universe. Again, it is intimately concerned with the concept of culture prevalent in a society. This makes for the close relation between philosophy and education. In the words of Blanshard and others, "The function of philosophy in universities is properly the same as its function in the cultural development of a society, to be the intellectual conscience of the community".[28] Education is based upon the distinctions between animal and human nature. It has generally aimed to develop the characteristics peculiar to man. In the words of Robert R. Rusk, "Those powers and their products are peculiar to man, and differentiate him from other animals. They lie beyond the range of the positive sciences—biological and even psychological, they raise problems which only philosophy can hope to solve and make the only satisfactory basis of education a philosophical one ".[29]

Education aims at imparting knowledge. Knowledge, however, requires a global outlook and a synthesis of various types of informations and experiences.

24. Cole, G.D.H., *Essays in Social Theory*, p. 47.
25. John Dewey, *Democracy and Education*, p. 378.
26. Adams, *The Educational Theory*, Macmillan & Co.
27. Robert R. Rusk, *The Philosophical Bases of Education*, University of London Press, p. 154.
28. Blanshard and Others. *Philosophy in American Education*, Harper & Bros., New York (1945), p. 80.
29. Rusk, R.R., *The Philosophical Basis of Education*, p. 154.

This is a philosophical activity without which no education is possible. Therefore, the need of philosophical basis of education is rooted in the branch of philosophy known as epistemology. This has been expressed by Perry in somewhat different terms when he says, "Philosophy is neither accidental nor supernatural, but inevitable and normal".[30] Besides its synthetic function, another important function of philosophy is the criticism of the postulates and conclusions of different sciences. Whenever a scientist delves deeper in his own particular field, he reaches a depth where the process of his thinking is not scientific but philosophical. This can be seen in the thinking of many a great scientist of the world. The importance of philosophy in the field of knowledge is, therefore, quite clear. From the point of view of different aspects of the individual and social life, and in different fields of knowledge, the discussion of the value of philosophy shows the utility of philosophy of education. In the words of J.W. Cunningham, "Philosophy thus grows directly out of life and its needs. Everyone who lives, if he lives at all reflectively, is in some degree a philosopher".[31] In the words of Chesterton, "The most practical and important thing about a man is his view of universe — his philosophy".[32]

30. Perry, *The Approach to Philosophy*, p. 22.
31. Cunningham, J. K., *Problems of Philosophy*, p. 5.
32. Quoted by Hocking, *Types of Philosophy*, p. 4.

4

IDEALISM

Idealism is one of the oldest schools of thought in the world of philosophy, originating in human nature itself, continuing from the primitive man to his present counterpart in some modified form or the other, the metaphysical standpoint has overtones of spirituality since it believes that the ultimate existing element is spiritual in nature. The entire universe is an extension of the mind or soul. From the epistemological standpoint it is better called idealism, implying thereby that thought or ideal has greater validity than the physical object. From the normative standpoint it is accurately represented by the term idealism which means that it attaches greater importance to ideal than to facts in this world. Obviously, the term idealism connotes different concepts when placed in various contexts. Whatever the context, the word definitely represents a particular theory in philosophy.

Summing up the importance of idealism in the history of philosophy, Adams has remarked, "Idealism in one form or other permeates the whole of the history of philosophy".[1] The essence of idealism has been admirably explained in brief in the words of G.T.W. Patrick as follows: "Idealists refuse to believe that the world is a great machine. They deny the supreme importance of matter, mechanism and the conservation of energy, as explaining our world. They feel that somehow certain sciences, such as psychology, logic, ethics, aesthetics, have to do with things basal and intrinsic, that they are quite as much a key to nature's secrets as are physics and chemistry. They believe that the world has a meaning, a purpose, perhaps a goal, and that there is a kind of inner harmony between the heart of the universe and the soul of man, such that human intelligence can pierce through the outer crust of nature and penetrate to its inner being, at least in some measure". This explanation of idealism highlights its distinction from materialism.

Idealism has been also compared to realism. In the words of Brubachar, "Some realists take the view that mental functions can be reduced to bodily ones, while certain idealists make matter a function of the mind. The idealists arrive at their monism by pointing out that it is mind that is central in understanding the world".

CHIEF CHARACTERISTICS OF IDEALISM

The following are the chief characteristics of idealism:

1. Adams, *The Evolution of Educational Theory*, Macmillan & Co. (1912), p. 28.

1. The universe exists in spirit. According to idealism, the spirit is the fundamental constituent of the universe. It points out that only mental life can be known, because the mind is capable of knowing only its own states and its adjuncts. Every individual human mind is apart of the universal mind, outside which nothing exists. For this reason, rational or spiritual knowledge is the only true knowledge. By virtue of this distinction, philosophy and the other social sciences are far more important than the physical or natural sciences.

2. Mechanical explanation of the universe is inadequate. Idealists believe that the mechanical explanation of the universe is inadequate because it does not succeed in explaining human values. Idealists also refute the concept of mechanical determinism.

3. Teleological explanation of the universe. In the words of Stella V. Henderson, "Idealism emphasizes the spiritual side of man. Because, to the idealist, spiritual values are the most important growing out of metaphysical, idealism would emphasize spiritual growth". Idealism propounds that human life and natural phenomena have a common goal, and that both man and nature try to achieve this goal. This concept finds its best explanation in the contemporary Indian philosopher Sri Aurobindo's thought. Idealists do not challenge or deny the importance of science, but they do not completely accept its explanation of the universe since it finds no place for spiritual values.

4. Man is central in creation. Idealists point out that man is at the centre of the universe. In the words of Rusk, "It bestows dignity and grandeur upon human life by emphasising the distinctiveness of man's nature, attributing to him powers not possessed by animals, which issues in ideals — logical, ethical and aesthetic: it admits the existence of a Supreme Being: by its respect for human personality it provides the basis for democracy".[2]

5. Emphasis upon normative and social sciences. In the field of education, idealists place greater stress upon normative and social sciences than upon the natural and physical. The normative sciences are—ethics, logic and aesthetics. Of the social sciences the main ones are sociology and psychology. Idealists explain the universe on the basis of these sciences.

6. Normative description of the universe. Idealists have offered a normative and value-oriented explanation of the universe. For the idealist, facts alone are not sufficient explanation. The universe as a whole is explicable in terms of the ideals of truth, good and beauty .

7. Conceptualism. In its epistemology, idealism is conceptualism, for it believes that objects have no existence apart from the concepts related to them. An object and its qualities are not independent of the knowledge of the object. Knowledge influences the object and this knowledge is obtained, not through perception but indirectly, through the medium of concepts or ideas. Objects have no public reality, for they appear different to different individuals. All existence is related to consciousness.

8. Universe is knowable. Idealists believe that the universe can be comprehended through the mind, because both the mind and the universe are constituted of the same elements, intellect and spiritual essence. Hegel has gone so far as to identify

2. Rusk, R.R., *The Philosophical Bases of Education*, University of London Press, p. 154.

nature and mind by saying that the various categories of knowledge or mind are the different stages of the universe's development.

9. Greater emphasis upon the mental or spiritual aspect of the universe. The idealist conception of the universe does not either deny or neglect the physical aspect of it but it is based on the mental or spiritual aspect. It is this higher aspect of reality which grants a measure of meaning to the lower reality.

IDEALISM IN EDUCATION

Ever since knowledge dawned in human mind man has been thinking about problems ontological, epistemological, eschatological and axiological. The questions of philosophy in the beginning of human knowledge were everywhere mixed with psychological problems. Thus, psychology in the beginning was concerned with the nature of the mind and the processes of consciousness. As men lived in small groups and the society was generally confined to a particular village, city or group of villages, the solutions offered were simple. There was hardly any distinction between social and political problems as the political institutions were developed as a means to social welfare. Therefore, most of the ancient thinkers did not distinguish between social philosophy and political philosophy As the life was simple and social stratification and differentiation was not complex the thinkers offered solutions working in more than one field of knowledge. Most of the thinkers were teachers and men of education who used to pass their life completely free from worldly affairs. The state and the society generally extended support to these scholars and they were generally respected and followed. The job of instruction and education of the younger generation was generally entrusted to these men of letters. The state supported finance but not interfered in the process of education. These great teachers formed their own personal institutions where their disciples collected to hear their learned discourses and learn through their lives. In this way, society was generally governed by the teachings of these great scholars though the administrative machinery was almost everywhere in the hands of the state.

The most important contributions of the idealistic philosophers in the field of education have been made by Plato, John Amos Comenius, Jean Jacques Rousseau, John Henrick Pestalozzi, Johann Friedrich, Friedrich August Froebel and R.R. Rusk.

CONTRIBUTION OF PLATO

According to Plato, man's mind is always active. Man is attracted towards all things that he sees in his surroundings, and he runs after them. Educator should take advantage of this propensity in the child and educate him, He should pay attention to the objects which surround the child. Such objects should be beautiful so that the child is naturally attracted to them and his curiosity is aroused; The process of education advances through this constant interaction between these objects and the mind. A beautiful environment provides the right stimulus by which the mind develops. For this reason the child should be kept in a beautiful environment. In fact, the human individual requires such an environment not only in infancy but throughout his entire life, because, according to Plato, the process of education is never complete. It continues throughout one's life. Plato has laid the greatest stress on mental development in education. He conceives of the state as an advanced mind. Education aims not merely at providing information but at training the individual in his duties and rights as a citizen. Just as the state evolves from the mind, the mind itself passes through all those stages of development through which the state passes. In Plato's opinion, the aim of education is human perfection, and with this end in view, he suggests a curriculum which comprehends all subjects.

Curriculum

Plato has divided curriculum into three parts:

1. *Bodily development.* Plato's philosophy believes bodily development to be of utmost importance in education, but this bodily development is achieved not merely through exercise and gymnastic activity but also through a regulated and controlled diet. The educator must guide and train the educand to attend to his food. He must be a kind of doctor who advises a particular kind of diet after acquainting himself with the weaknesses of the educand's body. This must be done in order to get rid of these debilities and finally to lead to complete development of the body.

2. *Educational impressions.* But it must be remembered that bodily development is only a means to mental development, because a healthy mind resides only in a healthy body. Although much importance is attached to bodily development, even greater importance is attached to mental development. Being under the influence of Pythagoras, Plato recommended the teaching of mathematics as of supreme importance. The first step in the teaching of mathematics is the teaching of arithmetic. Geometry and algebra should then be taught. Plato believed that the teaching of mathematics can remove many mental defects. In addition to mathematics, Plato considered the teaching of astronomy as of great significance, as part of higher education.

3. *Training in music.* In order to achieve balance in education, Plato stressed the value of musical training as a supplement to training in gymnastics. Exercise is the source of bodily development while music helps in the development of the soul. But music and literature taught to the student must be capable of building character. Plato suggested that the child's curriculum should be purged of all literature and musical epics which tended to generate such qualities as cowardice, weakness, selfishness, egoism, etc. He was critical of the epics of Homer and other contemporary poets on this ground. Plato considered balance in human life to be of the greatest importance, because in the absence of such a balance, man should neither fulfil his social obligations nor enjoy his own private life to the full.

Hence it can be concluded that Plato suggested a balanced curriculum for education.

Role of Educator

In Plato's plan of education, the educator is considered to have the greatest importance. He is like the torch-bearer who leads a man, lying in a dark cave, out of the darkness into the bright light of the outside world. His task is to bring the educand out of the darkness of the cave into the light of the day. He is, thus, the guide.

In his methods of teaching Plato believes imitation to be of the greatest importance, for he realizes that the child learns a great deal through imitation. He will acquire the behaviour of the people among whom he is made to live. Hence, keeping in mind the status of the child, he should be made to live among people from whom he can learn good habits and avoid bad ones.

Education According to Classes

Plato's plan of education does not envisage uniform education for one and all. He accepted the concept of social stratification, and suggested that since different individuals had to perform different tasks in society, they should also be educated differently, in order to train each one in his own respective sphere. He believed that different individuals are made of different metals. Those made of gold should take up administration and government, while those made of silver were best suited for trade and defence. Others made of iron and the baser hietals should become labourers and agriculturists. The state must make different arrangements for the education of these different kinds of people, although Plato implicitly agrees that education of governing classes is of the greatest importance. The education of the other classes in society does not concern him very much.

Faced with the problem of determining the classes of each individual, Plato suggested various kinds of tests to be conducted at different age levels. In the first place, primary education will be given to all between the ages of seven and twenty, following which a test shall be administered to everyone. Those who fail the test are to be sent to labour in the various occupations and productive trades. The successful candidates will be sent to the armed forces where training will be imparted to them for the next few years. This will again be followed by a test, the failures will be compelled to remain in the armed forces while the successful ones will be sent to join the government. Then this governing class will be subjected to further education in science. Later on, one from among the governing class will be elected as the philosopher administrator whose task it will be to look after government and education of the state. This individual will occupy the highest position in the land, his word will be the law of the land. Apart from this supreme individual, all other members of the governing class will continue to receive education throughout their lives, most of this education consisting of teachings in philosophy. It is thus evident that Plato granted the highest place to philosophy in his educational scheme.

Evaluation

As has been pointed out earlier, Rousseau was correct when he commented that Plato's *Republic* is the finest text-book on education. But it must be admitted that Plato's scheme of education suffers from certain defects and shortcomings, which have been enumerated below:

1. Little education of the productive class. In any society the labouring or productive class is invariably the largest in size. In Plato's scheme of education, this class is granted only primary education, which implies that higher education of all kinds is intended only for the soldiers and the governing classes, assuming that the labouring class has no need for such an education. Plato's dictum was that the productive class actually required no more than primary education.

2. Absence of variety. Plato's educational plan pays no attention to the individual differences between one individual and another. He suggested the same kind of education to be given to an entire class of people, according to a uniform curriculum. This will inevitably lead to deadening monotony and lack of variety, which kills all future progress.

3. Stress on philosophy. Some people get the impression that Plato's insistence on philosophy is exaggerated, and that it could only lead to an increase in the number of contemplative individuals at the expense of more practical members. But it must be remembered that Plato has stressed the importance of both bodily and mental development and in this respect, he has achieved a remarkable harmony of both.

4. Neglect of literary education. Plato's curriculum also neglects training in literature by stressing the importance of training in mathematics.

In spite of the above defects, Plato's concept of education has influenced educational philosophy in almost all ages. In particular his influence can be seen in the idealist philosophy of education. And, many of the finest teachers still consider Plato as their only true guide.

CONTRIBUTION OF RUSK

Rusk's idealism establishes a synthesis between man and nature, and also stresses the superiority of man over animal beings. In fact, the chief difference in human and animal education is due to the special qualities of man. In Rusk's words, "Those powers and their products are peculiar to man, and differentiate him from other animals, they lie beyond the range of the positive sciences—biological and even psychological; they raise problems which only philosophy can hope to solve, and make the only satisfactory basis of education a philosophical one." Education is not an end in itself, but only a means to an end, for through the medium of education, parents acquaint their own ideals. It is through education that the state creates ideal citizens. Morality is spread by religious institutions through education. Where the idealists are concerned, they want to use education to spread democratic conceptions in society. They also want to attach more purpose to education and make it more utilitarian. On the one hand they believe in knowledge for its own sake, but on the other they also want to use such knowledge for progress in life. They believe in the importance of ideals. Man's life changes due to his ideals. Literary men, artists, scientists and philosophers develop according to their own ideals. Accordingly, then, the idealist aims at creating an ideal social organisation in the society and the race, a social organization essentially democratic in nature, which attaches the greatest importance to the human personality.

JOHN AMOS COMENIUS (1592-1670)

According to Comenius, God is the ideal of education. Education includes knowledge concerning the world and its relationship with man. Thus, Comenius was influenced by the religious aims of education. However, he also opened the gates of secular ideals of education. Education, according to him, starts in the lap of the mother. The mother makes a significant contribution to the first six years of the child development. The development of his tendencies in the next six years very much depends upon the school. In the next six years more intelligent students may be allowed to study in the Latin schools. Those who successfully pass through it may study at the university for another six years. The method of education, according to Comenius, should adhere to the rules of child's nature. His interests should be developed and intellectual development should be realised through the use of his senses. Perception should be given emphasis in learning.

According to Comenius there are three sources of knowledge—inner knowledge, observation and idea. The means of attainment of knowledge are: senses, intelligence and talent. The three aims of education are:

1. To give knowledge to man for success in life.
2. To give wisdom for moral and character-development.
3. To create devotion to God in man.

From the point of view of teaching methods, Comenius has laid down the following nine principles meant for the reform of the educational system of his time:

1. Whatever is to be taught to the child should be told in direct and clear words.
2. The thing to be taught should have practical utility.
3. Education should not be complex.
4. The purpose of whatever is to be taught should be clearly stated.
5. General rules should be explained before-hand.
6. It is necessary to teach everything or all aspects of a subject in a proper order, proper place and proper relationship.
7. All subjects should be taught in a proper order.
8. The subject should not be left unless the child understands it properly.

The above principles were summarised in the following rules for the development of the child:

1. Proceed from concrete to abstract.
2. If possible, present mutual co-relation.
3. Adopt result method.
4. Prompt the interest of the child.
5. It is necessary to proceed towards 'to prove' instead of 'to assure', 'to see' instead of 'to discuss' and 'to know' instead of 'to believe'.

School Management

Comenius has classified schools according to different stages of the development of the child. Thus school may be organised for infants, children, adolescents and the adults. Infancy schools may admit infants from birth to six years of age. Childhood schools may admit children from six years to twelve years to be taught through mother tongue. Adolescence schools provide education to adolescents from 12 to 18 years of age through Latin. These are also called Latin schools. Beyond 18 years of age the educand may be admitted to schools for adulthood. The functions of all these categories of schools are:

1. Teaching of language.
2. To develop faculties through the study of science and art.
3. To develop morality.
4. To create true devotion in God.

Establishment of New System of Education

The following characteristics show that Comenius established a new system of education in 17th century:

1. Practical. Children should be taught practical things having utility in their life and at the same time they should understand them as well.

2. Self-experience. The child should understand the reality by his self-experience, should explore things himself and should not depend on others.

3. Mother-tongue. The medium of education should be mother-tongue. Only then education will be enjoyable, easy and useful.

4. Nopressure. No pressure should be exerted on child. If the child does not take interest in studies, it means there is some defect in the teaching method of the teacher.

5. No punishment. The child should not be given corporal punishment, if he is unable to read.

6. Equal opportunities. Boys and girls should be given equal opportunities for education.

7. Physical development. It is necessary to make proper arrangement for the physical development of children. Provision of games only is not sufficient.

8. Greek and Latin. It is necessary to teach Greek and Latin through the mother-tongue. But these languages should be taught only to those who have interest in them.

9. Scientific methods. Education is a science. All subjects should be taught by scientific methods. By finding natural law and order it is necessary to base education on them. Object-knowledge should be given first and then word-knowledge. In order to develop the mind of children properly, it is better to discuss about the things before telling them the rule.

10. Psychological education. First easy and then difficult things should be taught. Proceed from concrete to abstract with objects so that they can understand them well. The children should take interest in analysis and should not study books only.

Evaluation

Though it is undeniable that reforms suggested by Comenius made alround improvement in the existing system of education, criticisms have been advanced by educationists upon the philosophy of education given by Comenius. The most important evaluation has been advanced as follows:

1. He considered the child as inheritor of human-race but could not present an educational system accordingly. He forgot ancient culture in his zeal for scientific study. He thought it necessary to teach the works of contemporary authors only.

2. Comparison is useful only when it is explained. In his principles he takes inspiration from nature and compares man to trees and birds. But he forgets human nature. He begins to give importance to nature, without man. Reality lies in proof.

3. On the basis of Divine-voice, he imagined that man should learn everything, but did not estimate 'knowledge' and 'human-power' properly. This made his educational system defective. Later on, in his old age Comenius admitted that his books did not fulfil the need of the time.

4. It is not proper to give the essence of 'worldly knowledge' to the children.

5. It is not proper to explain general rules first.

6. Comenius was of the view that the essence of language should be taught to the child, but this is not suitable because there are many words in the language which we do not know nor is there any need of knowing.

In spite of the above mentioned criticism, it should be remembered that Comenius has been compared to Copernicus and Newton in science so far as his contribution to education is concerned.

JOHN HENRICK PESTALOZZI (1746-1827)

According to Pestalozzi education depends on the inner development of the child. Therefore it should not be imposed from outside. The principles of education should be discovered through observation and experiment in the field of education. The success of the teacher depends upon teaching according to the interests of the child. Childhood is the most important period in a person's education. Education is the birth right of every individual. It aims at the all-round development of his capacities and abilities. The teacher should not only know various subjects but should also be conversant with best teaching methods.

JOHANN FRIEDRICH HERBART (1776-1841)

The ideal of education, according to Herbart, is the development of moral character in the educand. Moral education is helped by the education in history, literature, science and mathematics. The child's interest is the most important basis of his education. As long as he does not take interest, education cannot realise any significant aim in him. Various subjects of teaching are correlated. Preparation is the first step in teaching. After it teaching proceeds by presentation, comparison, generalisation and application. Thus in aims and ideals, methods of teaching, curriculum and school organisation Herbart presented an idealistic system of education.

FRIEDRICH AUGUST FROEBEL

Froebel has been considered to be the most idealistic philosopher of education. He believed that right since birth man possesses dormant capacities and abilities. The sole function of education is to arouse these dormant capacities and abilities and leave them to complete development. Therefore, education should be based upon the natural principles of inner development. As God is the source of creation, therefore there may be one common element among all living beings. Hence, the child should realise integrated development of his powers. According to Froebel self activity is the chief method of child's education. Therefore, his creativity must be encouraged. The school is a mini-society and social environment is very much important for the development of the child. These ideas of Froebel have been found to be particularly important in the field of primary education.

SIR T. PERCY NUNN (1870-1944)

Among contemporary idealistic philosophers of education the most important name is T. P. Nunn. He believed that out of society the man's personality was flawless. The society contributed both positively and negatively to the development of man's personality. Social environment has a far reaching effect upon the individual's development. This development must be natural and individualistic.

It requires self-realisation. Therefore, the chief aim of education is self-realisation or development of personality. It is the duty of the society and the state to provide proper environment for the development of the child.

According to T. P. Nunn, man's mind may be classified into horme and mneme. While horme is a drive or urge, mneme is the power of conservation. While the former keeps us active, moving, organising and planning, the latter conserves our experiences. Thus mneme is closely relative to memory and includes it. It conserves all the experiences including those memorised. Heredity is the unchangeable impact of past generations as engrains. There should be harmony between heredity and environment since both determine the development of the individuals. Thus both horme and mneme are important for the child's education.

The first eight years of the child should be educated by kindergarten and montessory methods. Primary education continues from the eight years of age to 13 years. After it five years are to be devoted to secondary education which is the pivot of educational system. In the adolescence stage boys and girls are developed as men and women respectively. Therefore, one's future depends upon his adolescent education.

As has been already pointed out, the aim of education according to Nunn, is self-realisation. This realisation, however, is both individual and social since man's personality is equally determined by heredity and environment. It is in the environment that the individual traits develop. On the other hand, it is the individual who is the vanguard of all progress and advancement in the society. These views of T. P. Nunn have been echoed among almost all contemporary idealist philosophers of education in West and East. One may find parallel statements in the philosophy of education of contemporary Indian thinkers including Vivekanand, Sri Aurobindo, M. K. Gandhi, Radhakrishnan and R. N. Tagore.

According to T. P. Nunn the curriculum should be balanced and integrated. The school should impart knowledge of culture and civilisation, both national and human. The aim and function of education is to develop inner traits of the educand. This requires study of humanities, social sciences, art and literature as much as that of science. Besides, music, science and mathematics are equally relevant. Knowledge and practice of all these subjects is required for an all-round development of the educand.

As has been already pointed out, with Rousseau, T. P. Nunn believes that man is free at birth. He requires freedom for natural growth. However, freedom should not hamper man's development. Real freedom is realised in the harmony of heredity and environment. It is not unrestrained behaviour but included self-control. Therefore, along with freedom, discipline is equally important in the educational system. Discipline includes prevention of unrestrained expression of inner tendencies. Discipline, however, cannot be imposed from outside since this hampers natural development of the child. Like all other contemporary thinkers T. P. Nunn declares that real freedom is discipline and real discipline is self-discipline. Very young children, however, may be given instruction about behaviour. The most important element in the growth of discipline, however, is the example set by the teacher.

AIMS AND IDEALS OF EDUCATION

Idealism has influenced every sphere of education. In the first place we will glance at the impact of idealism on the aims of education. Since idealism believes human personality to be the most important, it wants education to aim at the development of human personality culminating in self-realization. In the words of Home, "The end of ends, the goal of goals, according to Idealism, is the increasing realization of the Absolute Idea for the individual, society and the race". Further explaining this aim of education, Rusk has commented, "We may accept that the aim of education is the enhancement or enrichment of personality, the differentiating feature of which is the embodiment of universal values".[3] These universal values are expressed as the beauty, goodness and truth, and the aim of education is to concretise these values in the child's life. Thus the idealists cherish the following aims and ideals of education:

1. Development of personality. As has been already pointed out, the most important aim of education, according to the idealist thinkers, both ancient and modern, Eastern and Western, is the development of personality. This has been called man-making by Vivekanand. Explaining this ideal of education, Heraman Harell Home says, "The forces that make men and women I find to be heredity, environment and will. Education is not a fourth elemental force, but it does its work in co-operation with these three. Education, through public-opinion influences and may cometo control, the force of heredity, it is itself a part of the physical and social environment, it assists in the formation of will. By consciously directing, through education and otherwise, these forces shall in time have the true superman of our modern dreams, as well as the ideal people of Plato's Republic. But unlike Plato and Shaw, we shall have to work through, not without, the family as an institution".[4]

The idealists believe that man is God's finest and ultimate creation. That is why development of the human personality has been accepted as the aim of education, and stress has been laid on the teaching of humanitarian subjects such a literature, art, religion, ethics, etc. Through education the cultural and social heritage of the community must be maintained and transmitted to the following generations. Some other idealists believe that the aim of education is to guide the individual to self-realization, for this also includes the development of the personality. Such development, in fact, is the development of those divine qualities which are inherent in human beings but which are dormant at his birth. The educator's task is to manifest these qualities. And for this reason every human being has an equal right to education.

2. Self-realisation. As has been already pointed out, according to idealists the aim of education is self-realisation. This is the individualist aim of education emphasised by the idealist.

3. Development of will power. Self-realisation requires development of will power. H.H. Horne has given eight points for the realisation of this ideal:

(i) The training of the will should be indirect, by activity rather than idea.

---

3. Rusk Robert R., *The Philosophical Bases of Education*, p. 194,
4. Herman Harrell Horne, *Idealism in Education, Preface*, p. 10, Macmillan.

(ii) The object lesson method according to time and context should be used.

(iii) The power of will should be increased by self-suggestion, knowledge and practice.

(iv) Practice is the only way to acquire will power.

(v) Proper discipline leads to will power.

(vi) The educands should be acquainted of facts concerning nature and society.

(vii) Development of moral character by ethical instruction.

(viii) Freedom to make choice in most of the matters concerning the individual.

4. Synthesis of Man and Nature. Another aspect of the idealistic conception of education is the synthesis between nature and human beings. Adams has suggested that education must aim at achieving an understanding of nature in human beings and educating them to achieve harmony with it. This can be done by acquainting the educand with the permanent laws which guide and control natural phenomena. These laws of nature are the causes of all natural activity. Only through such knowledge can the educand arrive at a harmony with all that lies around him.

5. Cultural Development. Greatest significance is attached to the cultural environment created by religion, morality, art, literature, mathematics, science, etc. That is why the idealist tendency is to stress the teaching of humanities so that the cultural and social heritage is maintained intact and allowed to grow. Education is also concerned with enabling the individual to make his own contribution to the cultural development of the community. The ideals of beauty, goodness and truth are the spiritual ideals of the human race, and the child has to be trained to achieve them in reality. Education must transform the child into a true human being by educating him to manifest the divine qualities which are invested in him. The idealists argue that there is system in every part of the universe, and hence the individual must also be taught to create some system in his life through intellectual and spiritual guidance. For this it is essential to develop every aspect of his life—the physical, moral, ethical, intellectual, spiritual and the aesthetic. Failure to develop anyone of these would create an imbalance in the individual's personality. In the words of Froebel, "The object of education is the realisation of a faithful, pure, inviolable and hence holy life. Education should lead and guide man to clearness concerning himself, and in himself, to face with nature, and to unity with God".

6. Exploration of Universal Values. Idealism places more emphasis upon more universal objects of education. Ross puts it thus, The function of education is to help us in our exploration of the ultimate universal values so that the truth of the universe may become our truth and give power to our life. Education must aim at adapting not only to the physical environment but to every kind of environment".[5] Rusk points out, "The purpose of education is to enable the child to reconcile himself to reality in all its manifestations, not merely to adapt himself to a natural environment". From among all these various kinds of environment,

5. Ross, *The Philosophical Bases of Education*, p. 196.

the cultural environment is considered to be the most important because man's cultural characteristics are his most distinctive qualities.

IDEALISM AND CURRICULUM

Explaining the idealist bases of curriculum as the imparting of spiritual and cultural heritage to the child along with his self and personality development, Herman H. Home writes, "It is better to centre education in ideals for children and the race rather than in children themselves. After all children are immature, dependent and plastic members of the race. They are often irrational in their individuality". As Socrates said in effect to the sophists, "Not man but reason is the measure of all things, not individuality but universality; not percepts, but concepts. Ideals are the norms for all human experience, including that of children. After all, it is still true that obedience to just law is a virtue, that following physical laws leads to health, that truth is something to be discovered, rather than made, that conformity is a large element even in creativity, that repression is a necessary phase of expression. Under the influence of paidocentrism (what a hybrid), self-expression may easily become self-explosion".

Idealists insist on emphasis being placed on the study of humanities such as literature, art, religion, morality, etc., along with the teaching of science. All the elements necessary for attaining God are included in the curriculum suggested by idealistic followers of Plato, who laid down that education must aim to realize the ideals of truth, beauty and goodness. Hence, he has suggested the inclusion of all those subjects or disciplines which help in the realization of these ideals. Most significant among man's activities are the intellectual, the aesthetic and the moral. The teaching of language, literature, history, geography, mathematics and science will encourage intellectual activity while the aesthetic impulse can be reinforced through art and poetry. Moral activities can be taught and instilled in the educand through the teaching of religion, ethics, etc. This curriculum is determined on the basis of the goals to be realized through education and by the criterion that it must reflect the experience, culture and glory of the human race. Man's experiences relate not only to his physical or natural environment but also to his social experiences, knowledge of which can be obtained through a study of the natural and the social sciences.

James Ross, the educationist, has classified human activity in two groups—physical actions and spiritual activity. Physical activity includes the entire range of actions relating to bodily welfare and to motor skills. The teaching of these must also be a part of education and they can be taught through physiology, exercise, medicine, hygiene, etc. Spiritual activity comprehends all intellectual, ethical, aesthetic and religious activity, all of which can be taught through history, geography, science, mathematics, language, ethics, art and religion. Herbart, the idealist philosopher of education, grants these subjects the main place in the curriculum because these subjects can contribute more than any other to the spiritual progress of man. But this is the shortcoming of the idealistic philosophy because it does not attach any significance to the teaching of science. Herbart points out that the part that literature and history can play in the spiritual development of man, cannot be played by science. For that reason, scientific subjects such as the natural sciences, mathematics and even history and geography are granted a secondary role.

T. P. Nunn, another educationist, has glanced at the idealistic conception of the educational curriculum, and has remarked, "The school is to consolidate the nation's spiritual strength, to maintain its historic continuity, to secure its achievements, and to guarantee its future".[6] In order to achieve all these goals, education in the school should consider two kinds of activities. In the first group fall such activities which create conditions by which the individual and social life is ensured and maintained, and this can be done through physical health, customs, social organisations, ethical conduct, etiquette, religion, etc. Education must provide opportunities, therefore, for physical training, ethics, religion, etc. The second group of activities is the one which is more important outside the sphere of the school. In this group lie those activities which maintain the cultural life of the community because they are creative. In order to evolve skills for such activities, educationists advocate teaching of literature, art, music, various kinds of handicrafts and manual skills, sciences, mathematics, history, etc. Hence the curriculum must be so designed that it can help to acquaint the individual with his social and cultural heritage and also to enable him to make some positive contribution to this heritage. Nunn writes, "In the school curriculum all these activities should be represented. For these are the grand expression of the human spirit, and theirs are the forms in which the creative energies of every generation must be disciplined if the movement of civilization is to be worthily maintained".[7]

IDEALISM AND THE EDUCATOR

Idealistic pattern of education grants the highest place to the educator, and conceives of the educator and educand as two parts of an organic plan. The educator creates a specific environment for the educand's development and provides guidance so that the latter may progress towards perfection and a rounded personality. The most precise explanation of the educator's role is manifested in Froebel's kindergarten pattern of education, in which the school is treated as a garden, the educand as a delicate plant which requires nurturing and the educator as the cautious gardener. Although even in the absence of the gardener the plant will continue to grow and will inevitably follow the laws governing its nature, the gardener has a certain significance in that he has the skill to develop plants. He may be unable to change a rose into a cabbage, but he certainly can contribute his mite to the plant's development. His efforts help in achieving perfection in this development, a level of perfection which would otherwise have been impossible. The educator plays a parallel role in the school. He can guide the educand appropriately because he knows the rules which govern the latter's development. Through his guidance he can make this natural development into a process leading to perfection and beauty. Ross explains, "The naturalist maybe content with briars, but the idealist wants fine developing according to the laws of nature, to attain

6. Nunn, T. P., *Education: Its Data and First Principles*, London (1923), p. 221.
7. *Ibid.*

levels that would otherwise be denied to him".[8] Clearly, the idealists attach much more value to the educator than do the naturalists. Adams opined that both the educator and the educand are two parts of the intellectual universe both of which should be considered equally important. The educator inspires the educand to realize the ideals of truth, goodness and beauty, and guides him along the path to its realization.

IDEALISM AND EDUCATIONAL METHODS

Turning to methodology in education, idealists suggest that the method must be oriented to achieving the complete development of all the innate abilities of the child and to train him for self-realization. In Rivers' words, "The process of education in childhood consists, or should consist, in the direction of innate or instinctive tendencies towards an end in harmony with the highest good of society of which the child is an active member. Idealists believe in a harmony between individual and social objectives. The child must be provided with a liberal environment for his development and his education should be related to present experience. One finds, therefore, that many elements of the idealist methodology are common with those of the naturalist, realist and pragmatist methodology.

The idealist methodology in education lays special stress on the three following processes:

1. *Instruction.* The term instruction as used here implies educational instruction which is believed by Herbart to be essential to education. But instruction does not mean that the child's mind should be stuffed with various scraps of information. It implies a modification and a refinement of the child's mind. For this it is essential that the educator must provide sympathetic guidance. The idealists believe that training of all kinds must be provided in the school.

2. *Activity.* Like the naturalist methodology, the educational methods recommended by the idealists also are based on activity. The child must learn through doing. Although the child can learn much by asking questions after lectures in the school, creative activity is much more important. This creative activity should be natural, continuous and progressive. This helps in moving towards self-realization, because it encourages the child to manifest his innate tendencies. Through mental activity the child learns cheerfully and happily and this also helps in the development of his personality. Besides, by these means the child learns rapidly. Hence, idealists also stress that instruction should be active.

3. *Experience.* Idealist methodology also places considerable stress on experience. Every educand must base all his education on his own experience. The educator's task is not to stuff his own experience in the educand's mind but to provide the latter some insight into his own experience. The guidance given by the educator helps to manifest many frustrated and repressed tendencies and drives of the educand. Independence is an essential pre-requisite for experience. For this reason idealists believe freedom to be an essential part of education but it must be remembered that this freedom is not absolute, but controlled and guided.

It is evident from the foregoing account that idealists believe the experiences of both the educator and the educand to be of great importance. Both of them should be active and they should indulge in the mutual exchange of experience so

8. Ross, James, S., *Groundwork of Educational Theory*, p. 121.

that they can progress. The teaching method should be such that the child should recognise it as a mode of self-instruction.

IDEALISM AND DISCIPLINE

Discipline is a part of the question concerning educational methods and some people feel that idealists are in complete opposition to the naturalists for the latter believe in complete freedom while the former insist on discipline. The only grain of truth in this assumption is that idealists stress the value of discipline as part of the educative process, without, in any way, detracting from the importance of freedom and liberty. In fact, idealists interpret discipline as being based on independence, and they try to harmonize the two. Rigorous discipline is never accepted by the idealists. Discipline must always take the shape of self-discipline, because only then can it guide the educand along the path of self-realization. Education basically aims at training the child in true independence. It is argued that the child is not independent at birth. This independence is granted to him or acquired by him in the process of education because, in the absence of education, there is no self-realisation, and without self-realization there is no independence. Rousseau believed that the individual was born free but that later on he is bound in chains. On the contrary, Froebel expressed the conviction that man is born in chains, and that he has to steadily win this freedom for himself, for, no one can grant it to him. Independence is not a divine gift, because even God cannot give independence. True independence can be won only by oneself, by one's own acts. Through the medium of education the individual can break the chains which bind him at birth. The educator must develop in his educands the capability of reasoning and arriving at a decision by the use of which the educand can achieve his own development, naturally and by his own inspiration. Independence lies not in a revolt against the environment but in achieving harmony with it. Hence, the child must be trained for independence in the school. He should be taught to discipline himself and to contribute to the disciplined behaviour of others, besides himself. Through a steady development of this kind, the individual becomes the member of a group of self-disciplined individuals. It can thus be concluded that the idealists do not favour the notion of allowing the child to roam free of any restraint but prefer to guide his freedom. For this reason, the child's activities are controlled in the school. Physical punishment and external restraints are not the methods of achieving this. It is better realized through developing such qualities as self-resignation, obedience, humanity, politeness, etc. Once these qualities are evolved in the individual, he achieves a stage of self-discipline. Froebel denies any importance to any system of punishment. Instead, he believes that it is better to encourage self-control and self-guidance in the child through sympathy. He believes that the child should not be submitted to any external pressure. It is only through discipline that the child can realize the ideals of education, and once it has understood this, it can discipline itself. Idealists, therefore, believe in the efficacy of discipline through influence and impression, not through fear and coercion.

But, discipline can be created among the educands only when the educators themselves create and present good models of discipline. Their own conduct and behaviour should be conditioned by a knowledge of the child's interests and inclinations. In their own behaviour, they must present the highest ideal of self-discipline, for only then can any discipline be expected from the educand. Idealists have criticised the establishment of discipline through threats, repression and punishment. They believe that the entire natural, social and spiritual environment in which the child lives should be fashioned in such a way that it should encourage the desire for self-discipline in the child. Plato believed that the child in the school is restrained with the intention that he may be granted greater liberty gradually as he develops higher. As the individual develops to a level of higher responsibility, he should be granted successively more liberty.

CRITICAL EVALUATION

Though idealism may have been very much left aside in the contemporary field of education, it is undoubtedly the most ancient school which has influenced education throughout its history. Even now the following points may be noted concerning the influence of idealism in the contemporary field of education:

1. *Wider and higher aims.* As the nationalist aims of education are giving place to humanist aim, idealism has become more relevant to the modern educationist. The idealists present the highest and the widest aims and ideals of education summed up in such terms as self-realisation, man-making, development of personality, harmony of man and nature, realisation of truth, goodness and beauty and realisation of heaven upon earth. All these aims have been emphasised by contemporary philosophers of education in East and West.

2. *The ideal teacher.* In this age of science the model of ideal teacher is still presented by idealism. Whatever may be said about the need of practical education and the utilisation of scientific means, no teacher can influence the educands without some sort of idealism. Teaching involves communication which very much depends upon rapport between the teacher and the taught. This is possible only when the teacher considers the taught as a part of his self and thus becomes selfless in his profession. The ideal of character building cannot be achieved unless the teacher himself presents the model of ideal character.

3. *Integrated and multisided curriculum.* While other systems of philosophy of education lay emphasis upon science and technology, the idealists point out the eternal value of humanities, social sciences, art and literature. In fact, they lay emphasis upon an integrated curriculum which may include every branch of knowledge. Thus the idealist curriculum is the most liberal, the most dynamic, the most multisided and therefore, most conducive to the cultural development of the individual and society.

4. *Moral education.* Thinkers everywhere today lament at the general loss of moral character. Everywhere development of moral character is being considered as an urgent need, to save the world from future catastrophe. The idealists explain the aims and means of moral education.

5. *Self-discipline.* The idealist concept of freedom as self-discipline has come to stay. It prescribes central place to the child in the system of education and lays emphasis upon natural development. Natural development requires freedom but freedom cannot be enjoyed without self-discipline. Contemporary educationists unanimously accept the need of freedom and discipline and agree that self-discipline is the only way for proper development.

6. *Psychological methods.* Even the pragmatists agree that some sort of idealism is necessary for teaching, particularly that of humanities, art and literature. The idealists include instruction, activity and experience in their methods of teaching. The idealist method of teaching is most effective in religious and moral teaching. It is a solid ground for character building and realisation of intimate relations between the teacher and the taught.

In spite of the above mentioned contribution of idealism to education, today it is more and more being left in the background while pragmatism and realism are coming to the front. This is due to the following disadvantages of the idealist philosophy of education:

1. *Utopian aims.* Plato, the first idealist philosopher of education, presented a scheme which was through and through utopian in spite of its deep insight into human life here and there. In fact, in his idealistic flight the thinker often leaves the solid ground and presents aims and ideals which can be neither realised nor cherished.

2. *Theoretical methods.* The idealist method of teaching makes too much of memory, personal contact and brain faculties. They lay less emphasis upon the development of various types of interests and abilities which help the educand in playing important role in society.

3. *Lack of specialization.* The idealist curriculum is too wide and lacks specialisation which is a growing demand of modern education.

4. *Neglect of science and technology.* The idealist thinkers have laid emphasis upon culture in education and neglected science and technology. Therefore, today most of the educational institutions have rejected idealistic curriculum.

5. *Teacher centered.* While modern education is child-centred or educand-centred, the idealist system is teacher-centred. By expecting too much from the teacher it does not allow him to live as a human being with a multisided personality. Too much expectation from the teacher ultimately results in his criticism by the students and society. The role of teacher today is very much different from his role in ancient times. Education today is a life-long but limited part of life. It goes on even without the teacher. Various audio-visual means are replacing the all important role of the teacher. Therefore, neither the modern teacher nor the taught accept the ancient idealist concept and status of the teacher.

From the perusal of the above mentioned advantages and disadvantages of the idealist philosophy of education it is clear that though some sort of idealism must stay in every field of education, the aims and ideals, the methods, the curriculum and the school management, etc., the ideal of education cannot be realised without the help of naturalism, pragmatism and realism.

5

REALISM

Realism is the theory which holds that the existence of objects is real. For this reason it is also sometimes called objectivism. Both realism and objectivism are metaphysical theories concerned with the existence of things. In epistemology realism holds that in the process of knowledge things are independent of the existence and influence of the knower. Hence the main tenet of this theory in the epistemological field is that object and its qualities are independent of and uninfluenced by the knower and the process of knowledge.

Chief Tenets of Realism

As a general rule the chief tenets of realism are the following:

(1) Existence of objects is independent of knowledge. According to the naive realists objects exist irrespective of our knowledge of them. Scientific realism accepts this notion but according to it thoughts concerning the objects are based on the mind.

(2) Qualities are inherent in known objects. According to the naive realists the qualities that are experienced in the objects are part and parcel of the object while the scientific realist distinguishes between primary and secondary qualities, maintaining that primary qualities belong to the object while the secondary are attributed to the object by the mind in the process of knowledge.

(3) Knowledge does not affect the object or its qualities. According to the naive realists the objects or its qualities do not suffer by becoming the subjects of knowledge but according to the scientific realists this theory does not hold true for secondary qualities.

(4) Knowledge of objects is direct. According to the naive realists, knowledge of the object is direct and perceptual. According to representationism, this is true of simple thoughts, for in complex thought knowledge is indirect since complex thoughts are compounded of simple ones.

(5) Objects are common. According to the analytical realists objects are common while according to the representationists objects are commonly available only for the purposes of primary or elementary thought. Scientific realists hold that the same object may be experienced differently by different individuals.

(6) Relation between object and thought Naive realism holds that there is relation between object and its thought, but the scientific realist rejects this theory.

MAIN TYPES OF REALISM

The main types of realism are the following:

(1) Naive realism. This is a theory propounded by commonsense according to which objects are independent of mind whether they are known or not. Object possesses its own qualities. Knowledge does not affect the object. The object is precisely what it is seen to be. Objects are known directly and objects are common for all.

(2) Representationism. This theory is the product of Locke's mind. It states that the object's existence is independent of knowledge but metaphysical thought depends upon the mind. Primarily, objective, individual and secondary qualities are inherent in the object. Knowledge does not impress upon the object but it can influence metaphysical thought. Thoughts are the representations of objects. Knowledge of objects is direct in the case of simple thoughts but indirect in the case of complex ones. In simple thoughts objects are common or universal but not so in complex thinking.

(3) Neo realism. This is a novel approach to the Platonic theory of reality. In this theory it is believed that the total object is not the subject of knowledge but its aspects are, and they are independent of knowledge. The qualities of the object are its own and knowledge does not affect them. An object is what it is manifestly seen to be. Knowledge of the aspects of an object is direct while logical entities are universal.

(4) Critical realism. The theory was first propounded in America at the turn of the century and is critical in nature. It also believes that the existence of objects does not depend upon knowledge in any way. The object is possessed of qualities and is directly known. Objects may or may not be universal. Critical realism does not hold that the object is precisely what it is seen to be or that it is seen to be exactly what it is. When the object becomes object of knowledge it is influenced by knowledge. Knowledge can be direct as well as indirect. The relation between the knower and known is not direct but takes place through the medium of thought, which is the subject matter of knowledge. Different people can have different knowledge of an identical object.

These different theories of realism have been arranged in order of their historical appearance and none of them has been found to satisfy completely. Each and every one has been objected to and found wanting in some respect.

IDEALISM AND REALISM

In the varied fields of epistemology, metaphysics and evolution, idealism and realism present two almost completely differing theories. They differ in the following respects:

(1) Difference in epistemology. Idealism and realism differ in the following respects on the various questions of epistemology:

(*i*) According to idealism objects have no existence apart from their ideas, while according to realism, objects have an existence independent of any knowledge of them.

(*ii*) Idealism maintains that qualities are imposed on the object by the mind while realism holds that qualities are a part of the object.

(*iii*) The idealistic tenet is that knowledge influences the object and its qualities while the realist theory is that objects cannot be affected in this way.

(*iv*) According to idealism objects are known indirectly through the medium of their ideas but realism holds that objects are known directly.

(*v*) In idealism it is believed that different objects appear differently to different people but in realism it is believed that objects are universal.

(*vi*) According to idealism objects are not what they appear to be since their knowledge is indirect but realism maintains that objects are precisely what they appear to be.

(2) Metaphysical differences. From the metaphysical standpoint realism and idealism differ in the following respects:

(*i*) According to the idealists the universe exists within the mind while the realists are of the opinion that the natural world is independent of the mind.

(*iii*) The idealists believe in some kind of synthesis between man and nature while the realists deny the existence of any such synthesis.

(*iii*) Idealism states that man is the centre of the universe while realism does not attach the same importance to man with reference to universe.

(*iv*) Idealists are idealistic while the realists are realistic.

(3) Difference in cosmology. Realism and idealism differ in the following respects on questions regarding cosmology:

(*i*) According to idealism the mechanistic explanation of the universe is not adequate while realists propound this mechanistic explanation .

(*ii*) Idealism holds that creation of the universe is teleological while the realists do not believe in there being any purpose in creation.

(*iii*) In explaining creation the idealists lay the stress on normative and social sciences while the realists rely more heavily on the natural sciences in their explanation of creation.

(*iv*) Idealism puts forth a value judgement of the creation while realism is more factual in this analysis.

(*v*) According to the idealists the world is known through the mind while realists do not attach so much importance to the mind in understanding the universe.

(*vi*) Idealism stresses the mental and spiritual in its explanation of the world and realism the material and physical.

From the above analysis of idealism and realism it should be fairly obvious that the two theories are almost contradictory and mutually exclusive. In evaluating the two it must be said that idealism seems more appropriate for understanding the values of human life, which is, in fact, the aim of all our knowledge and science. A more comprehensive standpoint, on the other hand, will make it clear that both idealism and realism view the universe from different standpoints, and hence the difference in their respective metaphysics, epistemology and cosmology. To a liberal, dynamic philosopher with broad vision the two will appear to be complementary. In their respective ways both show glimpses of truth and according to one's standpoint one may be as satisfied with one as one may be with the other. It depends on one's mental make up as to which will appeal to one. Nevertheless, it must be said that idealism, on the whole, is a philosophy that is more mature, refined, optimistic, comprehensive and it elevates the lot of mankind. Nothing can be gained by denigrating realism but there can be no denying superiority of idealism.

HISTORICAL BACKGROUND

The following may be considered landmarks in the field of realistic thinking in education:

1. Erasmus (1446-1537). According to Erasmus knowledge is of two kinds: Object knowledge and world knowledge. Of these the world knowledge comes first and then comes object knowledge. However, object knowledge is more important than world knowledge. In the curriculum Greek, Latin and Grammar should be taught first of all. This helps in gaining proper object knowledge after which teaching in other subjects may be started.

2. Rabelais (1483-1533). Rabelais supported social, moral, religious and physical education in place of classical, linguistic and literary education. He pleaded for free thinking. According to him books should be not only mastered but also practised. The teaching should be made interesting. This is also true in physical education. The aim of education is to make practical life better.

3. John Milton (1608-1674). Milton's philosophy of education is available in his book entitled, *Tractate on Education.* According to Milton the aim of education is to know God, to love Him and to be one with Him. Milton presented a plan of education for the child from 12 to 21 years of age. First of all, Latin, Grammar, Arithmetic, Geometry and morality should be taught. After it education may be imparted in agriculture, physiology, handicraft, natural philosophy, geography, etc. Poetry, literature, languages, economics, politics, history, etc., may be taught as supplementary studies. Milton gives more importance to ideas than words, to practical efficiency than ostentatious achievements. He defined education in these words, "I call, therefore, a complete and generous education that which fits a man to perform justly, skillfully and magnanimously all the offices, both private and public of peace and war".

4. Michael de Montaigne (1533-1592). Montaigne represented socialistic realism which aimed at making child a worldly man. Socialistic realism supported utilitarian viewpoint in education. It criticised bookish knowledge and supported the idea to make knowledge practical. Montaigne was a humanist and a naturalist. He was a realist and a socialist. In fact, he was a socialistic realist. The aim of knowledge, according to him, is to enhance knowledge and reasoning power. Nothing should be admitted without understanding. It is improper to take abnormal interest in goods. Knowledge must be practical. The child should be trained for worldly activities. Virtues should be created since these are the bases of enjoyment of the world. The function of philosophy is not only to tell about thinking but about the livelihood. It gives us a knowledge of virtues. Moral knowledge should be gathered from the biographies of great persons.

5. Richard Mulcaster (1531-1621). Mulcaster represented sensuous or empirical realism. According to empirical realism real education emphasises training of senses and not the memory. Education is a natural process and should be based in nature. Philosophy of education should be scientific and not imaginary. Word knowledge should follow the perception of the object. New practical ways should be adopted. According to Mulcaster the aim of education is to develop physical and mental power. Child is the centre of education. Mother tongue should be the medium of education. The teachers should have a sound knowledge of the method of teaching.

6. Francis Bacon (1561-1626). Bacon was also a supporter of empirical realism. He condemned bookish education and tried to make it practical. According to him practical knowledge may be gained through the study of Nature. Subjects such as philosophy, literature and language should be considered secondary. Knowledge can be gained by inductive method. This is particularly true in the field of science. Bacon is known as a great supporter of the inductive method in science.

7. Ratke (1571-1635). Ratke was also a supporter of empirical realism. He favoured education through mother tongue. He maintained that one thing should be taught at one time.

Teaching should be done in free environment. Learning should be discouraged. Object knowledge should be acquired by direct experience and experiment.

8. Comenius (1592-1670). Comenius presented far more clear ideas than other realist philosophers. He laid emphasis upon mother tongue, graded curriculum, suitable text-books, practical application of teaching and four stages of educational structure.

9. Johann Friedrich Herbart (1776-1841). The aim of education according to Herbart, is the multisided development of interests. The child should be made interested in his social environment. The aim of education is character development. This, however, cannot be achieved by preaching but by presenting moral example before the children.

10. Herbert Spencer (1820-1903). Herbert Spencer was a naturalist as well as a realist. Complete living is the aim of education and also the aim of life. This may be realised by doing the following activities:

1. Self-preservation, i.e., care of health.
2. Earning a living (Preparation for vocation).
3. Fulfilling duties regarding race-preservation.
4. Fulfilling duties of a citizen.
5. Utilization of leisure.
6. All these activities should be done scientifically.

AIMS OF EDUCATION

The realistic aim of education is a happy and integrated life. According to the American educationist Franklin Bobit, happiness in life may be achieved by fulfilment of human responsibilities and obligations such as:

1. Activities concerned with language,
2. Activities concerned with hygiene,
3. Citizenship activities,
4. Ordinary social activities,
5. Leisure activities,
6. Activities of mental health,
7. Religious activities,
8. Activities concerning race-preservation,
9. Vocational behaviour activities,
10. Vocational activities.

The child should be provided complete knowledge of society. He should know the social circumstances, social organisation and natural environment. Learning is the art of leading practical life. This requires scientific attitude. Scientific attitude is a rational attitude. It is objective and sensuous. The aim of education is. to enable the child to acquire knowledge of definite and real objects and to analyse it through reason.

In the sphere of education, realism made its appearance as the revolt against theoretical and verbal education. From the earliest ages educationists have been trying to relate education to the social and natural environment, but very often this truth was forgotten and the process of education was allowed to become very theoretical and merely verbal. At all such times, realism has appeared as the reaction to this tendency. At the root of realism were two factors — the disutility of ancient and medieval ideals, and the development of the scientific tendency. By the sixteenth century an awareness had broken upon men that ancient ideals could not satisfy their needs because they were impractical. In Europe, during the Renaissance, there was a reaction to old Monasticism and Scholasticism. It came to be believed that men must aim at evolving humane qualities, and for this it was felt that a study of the literature in Greek and Latin was essential. After the Renaissance, the next tendency which became prominent was Humanism in which the Greek and Latin literatures came to be called humanistic because of their unique contribution to the progress of mankind. Individuals in favour of these literatures came to be called Humanists and their ideas on education gave rise to the concept of Humanitarian education.

But very soon it was realised that the only thing which could be derived from Greek and Roman literature was a definite style and grammar. When Cicero's style became the object and aim of education, humanitarian education was converted to Ciceroism. An unnecessary emphasis upon the study of dead languages and bookish language within the school drew education far away from real life, and bore little relation to the life outside it.

After the period of humanism came the period of Reformation. This, too, did not go beyond obeying a set of rules and concepts, but it gave a tremendous fillip to research by showing a deep inclination towards reason and intelligence which encouraged free thinking. It was the unprecedented growth of science. A revolution in the sphere of knowledge was created by the researches of Copernicus, Galileo, Newton, Kepler, Harvey, Bacon and others. In this manner, realism came into existence as the result of the growth of science and an inclination to search for the truth. According to the realists, education should be made to conform to the social and individual needs of the child so that he may lead a happy and contented life in the future. Whatever the other ideals of education, its primary purpose was to prepare the child for real life, and the criterion of successful education lay in its ability to prepare the child for adult life. One of the major problems which the individual has to face in adult life is the problem of earning one's livelihood. Hence, education must take care that it enables a man to earn his livelihood. And when the emphasis came to be laid on livelihood, it was only natural that the realist pattern of education should stress the need for teaching scientific subjects rather than artistic or literary subjects. In this, efforts are made to harmonise the child's education with real life. The environment of the school should be such that it creates qualities which are required in the life outside the school. Ancient and medieval education was both bookish and exclusively mental. According to the realists, the first function of education was to develop the qualities of determination, reason and intelligence so that he should facilely solve the problems of life. For this reason realists favour the empirical methods of teaching in which all education is done through actual experience. The realist thinkers also favour education through the medium of the mother-tongue through the medium of demonstrations, tours and actual experiments. This brings education nearer to life, and also stimulates the use of one's own intelligence instead of making demands only upon the educand's memory. In this manner, it can be concluded that the realists want education to keep in mind the social and individual needs of the educands.

CURRICULUM

According to the realists the child should be allowed to choose subjects according to his ability from detailed curriculum. He should be taught what is useful in his life. Learning according to one's abilities results in success in practical life. Subjects should be related to one another. They should be planned according to the needs of the society. Education should enable the student to adjust to changing social circumstances. Phrases such as, 'knowledge for the sake of knowledge', 'art for the sake of art', etc., are meaningless. The curriculum should have utility. Subjects such as literature, art, music, dance, etc., are unnecessary. The curriculum should lay emphasis upon science subjects — physics, chemistry, biology, astrology, etc.

METHODS OF TEACHING

Realist thinkers emphasise objectivity, knowledge of scientific facts and the knowledge of the real. Students should be helped to know objectively. This requires knowledge through sense organs. Words are symbols to convey experience. They help in communication of knowledge. Practical verification is the test of all knowledge. Propositions which cannot be verified are nonsense. Facts are related to the present. The teacher should enable the student to know the world. He should not give personal opinions but clarify the facts. In fact, the facts should themselves be revealed without any distortion. Thus, the realists support fact-centred method of teaching.

According to the realist the knowledge of the real involves two laws: Law of aggregation and the law of conversion of simplicity. There is continuity in nature. In concept formation the feelings should not be allowed to interfere. In the law of conversions of simplicity, it has been pointed out that space and time are divided for the sake of convenience. The whole is the aggregate of parts. The parts do not loose their existence in the whole. Therefore, the proper method of teaching is to begin with the part and reach the whole. Knowledge should be analysed into principles, and principles into hypothesis. Facts should be analysed into propositions. Thus, the method of teaching should involve analysis and rational classification.

Realist approach to education is child-centred. The method of teaching should change according to the requirement of the child. The intellect of the child should be developed to enable him to know the facts. Experimentation should be the basis of facts. Knowledge is uniform in nature. The teacher should have firm faith in science. He should have a scientific attitude and develop the same in the educand. He should himself investigate and encourage the educands to do so. He should know the experimental method and train the educands in it. He Should understand the needs of the student and fulfil them. He should render a clear, lucid and systematic understanding of scientific facts to the student. He should keep his personal opinion apart from objective teaching. He should keep an eye upon child psychology and adolescence psychology and mould his methods of teaching accordingly. He should make a selection of subject matter according to the interests of the student.

SCHOOL ORGANISATION

According to the realist the school should be organised on the basis of needs of society. Educational institutions should be opened according to local needs and not by political pressure. Science teaching must be done in every school as academic and literary subjects alone do not fulfil the needs of society. Science gives us an understanding of the real world.

Educational institutions may have co-education since the two sexes have to adjust in society. Living together is the best way to learn this adjustment. Sex education may also be imparted to boys and girls in order to check population growth in future. Population education may also form a part of curriculum. The school should minor the society and encourage all types of activities required in society. It is a miniature society and it should present a realistic picture of the world outside it.

DISCIPLINE

The school should be organised in such a way that the child should learn self-discipline. He should learn to control his feelings and desires and to perform his duties. Discipline is adjustment to objectivity. It is required to enable the child to adjust to his environment. It helps the child in concentrating on his studies. Every student is a part of the world and he should learn to adjust in his circumstances. Discipline, however, is not withdrawal. The students should remain in close touch with the harsh realities of life.

CRITICAL EVALUATION

Like other systems of philosophy of education realism has its advantages and disadvantages. Its impact can be seen everywhere. The realist philosophers influence practical education. In seventeenth century academies for the teaching of natural sciences developed everywhere in Europe and later on in America in 18th century. Technical and vocational education has become a common feature of education everywhere. Thus, the following may be considered to be the contribution of realism to education:

1. **Education in technical and vocational subject.** Every society needs technocrats and people trained in different vocations. Therefore, in every country of the world today the plan of education is based upon the needs of such persons in the development of the nation.

2. **Practical bias.** The realist insisted upon the practical nature of education. Modern education is empirical, experimental and practical.

3. **Practical aims.** Even in the field of ideals of education practical aims such as national development, earning a livelihood, personality development or realisation of happiness are being emphasised. These aims conform to real social aspirations.

4. **Widening of scope.** Realists have widened the scope of education to include scientific and technical subjects as well as social sciences and humanities.

5. **Scientific teaching methods.** Modern teaching methods are more scientific. Help is taken from audio-visual means of education particularly in the teaching of science subjects. Laboratory training is a must for science teaching. More stress is laid on inductive method. The universities are encouraging research in sciences and humanities.

6. **Objective attitude.** Today's education is objective. Personal opinions and feelings are ignored while objective facts are emphasised.

7. **Sense training.** Modern education is empirical, particularly in primary and nursery stages. Stress is laid on sense training so that the child may use his different senses with maximum efficiency in order to directly gain knowledge of the world around him.

8. **Realistic school organisation.** Modern school is organised to be a mini- society. Discipline means self-control and adjustment to facts. The students are required to develop all the traits of personality required in social life. The programmes in the school are geared to make him a responsible member of society.

In spite of the above mentioned advantages and favourable influences of realism on education, there have been certain disadvantages and limitations in realistic philosophy of education. Of these the most important are as follows:

1. Too much emphasis on objectivity. The terms objective and subjective are relative. Absolute objectivity is impossible. No scientist claims absolute objectivity. Knowledge as well as ignorance, both are subjective as well as objective. Realist's exclusive emphasis on objectivity ignores so much content of knowledge. It neglects imagination, feeling, emotion and sentiments which are also important facts of individual and social life. This leads to negligence of values which, of course, are not facts.

2. Too much emphasis on facts. Facts and values are interwoven in the fabric of individual and social life. By their exclusive emphasis upon facts the realists tend to ignore values. The theory that values are social facts has led to immoral and corrupt implications. In a sense, values are *sui-generis.* They are self-evident. No real human life is possible without values. The realistic attitude often becomes factual but not value-oriented. Practice, of course, is useful but theory has also its value. Facts and ideas, both are part of knowledge.

3. Positivism and **meliorism.** Positivism pleads that science alone is the real knowledge. According to meliorism we can make this world better only through science. Both these have some grain of truth but they have their limitations as well. Science cannot substitute philosophy, art and literature. Liberal education should find a place for all these. Some persons have better talents in philosophy, art and literature. Therefore, it is wrong to make science compulsory at all stages of education. Not only academic subjects but even some sort of training in ethics and religion are necessary for a happy life. Exclusive emphasis upon science makes education one-sided.

The above criticism is no condemnation. The contribution of realism is undeniable. The above discussion only shows its limitations. As has been already pointed out earlier, every type of philosophy has its positive and negative contribution to education. This is as much true of realism as of idealism, naturalism and other types of philosophies of education.

6

NATURALISM: JEAN JACQUES ROUSSEAU

In the history of philosophy of education naturalism is also as old as idealism. The term naturalism, by its ordinary meaning, means the ism laying emphasis upon nature in every field of education. Thus, the naturalist philosopher derives the aims and ideals, the means, the methods of teaching and the principles of curriculum and school management from the Nature. The most ancient form of naturalism was presented by Democritus (460-360 BC) in the form of atomistic naturalism. In Greece, Democritus explained the composition of universe in terms of innumerable, individual and indestructible atoms. This materialistic explanation of the world was the ground of naturalism in education. This theory was partly amended by Epicurus (341-270 BC). This atomistic naturalism was the beginning of naturalism in the West. This, however, is not the basis of modern naturalism as a philosophy of education.

PHILOSOPHICAL PRESUPPOSITIONS

In metaphysics, the ultimate reality, according to naturalism, is the Nature and Nature is material. In epistemology, the naturalists are empiricists. They believe that knowledge is acquired through sense organs and with the help of the brain. They do not accept the rationalist's position that all knowledge is innate. In modern western philosophy John Locke, Bishop Berkeley and David Hume, the British philosophers were empiricists. They believed in the possibility of direct knowledge. In axiology, the naturalists believe in living according to Nature as the best type of life. 'Follow Nature' is their slogan. Be natural is their motto. They are pluralists since Nature has made all persons different.

THREE PHILOSOPHICAL FORMS OF NATURALISM

From the standpoint of philosophical principles, the following three forms of naturalism are distinguished:

1. Naturalism of physical world. This principle seeks to explain human actions, individual experiences, emotions and feelings on the basis of physical sciences. It seeks to explain the entire universe in the light of the principles of physical sciences. It has little or no influence in the sphere of education, because all that it has done is to place knowledge of science above every kind of knowledge. It points out that not only is science one form of knowledge, but that it is the only form of valid knowledge. It is a concept of positivism, and it holds that even philosophical knowledge is worthless.

2. Mechanical positivism. According to this principle, the entire universe is a machine made of matter and is possessed of a self driving energy that ensures its functioning. This is materialism, for it suggests that matter is the only reality, and anything that exists is a form of matter. The human being is conceived of as nothing more than an active machine which is activated by certain environmental influences. The impact of this kind of positivism led to the emergence of the behavioural school in psychology which explained all human behaviour in terms of stimulus and response. Behaviourists do not believe in the existence of any consciousness distinguished from the material element. All processes of the mental faculty such as imagination, memory, thinking, etc., are explained in physiological terms. This school also makes no distinction between human and animal, because both can be explained in terms of stimulus and response. Behaviourism thus seeks to explain the entire range of human activity as a mechanical process. As naturalism it has had a tremendous impact on education.

3. Biological naturalism. It is naturalism in this form, as biological naturalism, which has had the greatest impact upon education. It has elaborated the theory of the natural man, and has explained that the evolution of man and animal is a single process. It refuses to admit the spiritual nature of man and expounds that his nature is the heritage he has received from his ancestors. That is why it traces many similarities between human and animal behaviour. Biological naturalism contends that all the processes of Nature and the entire existence of the universe cannot be explained in terms of mechanical and physical processes, because in the biological world, evolution is a more important phenomenon. All living beings have an instinct to live and for this reason life evolves from lower forms to higher and more complex ones. One can find all the characteristics of evolution in man's life. The principles underlying evolution can explain the form that a human being will ultimately assume and the manner in which he will progress. At the animal level, the process of evolution stops at the material or physical level, but in the case of human beings it is also manifested in the mental, moral and spiritual levels. This instinctive evolution is found not only in individual human beings but also in groups of human beings, because these groups also evolve to a stage of greater complexity. But this evolution is also governed by the same principles which govern the individual's evolution. In this process of evolution, the principles of struggle for existence and survival of the fittest have been considered the most important by Charles Darwin, because in his opinion the principle of self-preservation is the strongest law of nature.

HISTORICAL BACKGROUND

As has been pointed out earlier, naturalism, like other isms, started in ancient Greece and ancient India. Democritus (460 BC), Leucippus (793-57 BC), Thales (640- 546 BC), Epicurus (341 -270 BC) and Lucretius (96-55 BC) were prominent naturalists in ancient Greece. In ancient India the philosophers known as *Charvakas* were naturalists. In medieval period no significant naturalists prospered since religion had a wide influence upon thinkers. From the sixteenth to eighteenth century, the most important naturalist thinkers were Rousseau (1712-1788), Bacon (1561-1626) and Hobbes(1588-1679). Herbert Spencer (1820-1903 AD) presented a naturalist philosophy of education in contemporary times. Before an exposition of the views of modern naturalists, a review of its influence in education will be useful.

As a philosophy, naturalism has influenced education by determining the aims and objectives of education, apart from explaining the methods of education and means or agencies of education, through an explanation of human nature. In the sphere of education, naturalism is neither the positivism of the physical world nor mechanical positivism or even biological naturalism. It is an entirely different concept which seeks to base education on the experience of the child, and thus is a repudiation of all text-book teaching. In the eighteenth century Rousseau launched a bitter offensive against all traditional forms of formal education, and instead advocated the basing of all education on education according to nature. Ever since then, so much stress has been placed on studying the nature of the child, that it has led to a veritable revolution in the field of education because it has motivated considerable research in this sphere and applied the principles discovered through this research. Nineteenth century saw comprehensive educational reforms all over Europe, and the appearance of a tendency to make all education scientific. Naturalism adopts a scientific posture in as much that it wants the educational process to follow the natural inclination of the child, and it is thus opposed to all traditional and static methods of education. It stresses the value of dynamic methods. It seeks to base all education on psychology. Adam has pointed out that naturalism is a word obscurely applied to those principles of training which do not depend upon books but instead upon the laws of the natural life of the educand. Hence all those systems which oppose the use of text-books and prefer to centre education on the child can be called naturalistic. This principle is opposed to making education complex, for its motto is "Follow Nature". It is against artificiality of any kind. Naturalism is the inevitable reaction in education when education had been practically killed by the oppressive weight of tradition, stern discipline, rules of the school, dry curriculum, the formal behaviour of the teacher, etc.

JEAN JACQUES ROUSSEAU (1712-1778)

As has been already pointed out, in modern times Rousseau was undoubtedly, the most important naturalist philosopher of education. His writings were published since 1750 AD onwards. Some of his famous works are: (1) *The Progress of Arts and Sciences,* (2) *Social Contract,* (3) *New Heloise:* and (4) *Emile.* Of these the most important are *Emile* and *Social Contract. Emile* is a novel in which the author has described the education of Emile, an imaginary child. The author described the methods of bringing the child in contact with Nature and removing social evils. The child is left under the guidance of an ideal teacher away from school and society. The teacher teaches the child in a natural environment. The book *Emile* consists of five parts respectively devoted to infancy, childhood, adolescence, youth and the imaginary wife of Emile named Sofia.

Rousseau was particularly impressed by the poverty and suffering of the people. He hated society for the evils and wanted to reform it. He realised, "Everything is good as it comes from the hands of the author of the nature but everything degenerates in the hands of man". Thus Rousseau, on the one hand, opposed society and praised Nature on the other hand. His book *Social Contract* portrays his ideas concerning society and politics. He gave the slogan 'Return to Nature. His work *Emile* aroused reactions everywhere, favourable as well as unfavourable. France and Switzerland banned this book. It was burnt at so many places. Rousseau had to leave France for England in 1766. After 11 years he returned to France and wrote his last book entitled *Confessions.* He died in 1778. His thoughts influenced French revolution. He was acclaimed as a great revolutionary and reformer.

Rousseau's naturalist philosophy shows three forms: Social naturalism, Psychological naturalism and Physical naturalism. In his social naturalism he devices education as a method to develop society. According to him one cannot become a man and citizen at the same time. Every new culture is born out of the old. The past mistakes or evils must be removed though old ideals may be honoured. As a bitter critic of society Rousseau condemned old traditions opposing new reforms. He said, "Whatever is generally banned today you should do just the opposite, then you will find the right path". Rousseau's social naturalism may be found in his book *Social Contract.* His aim is man making and not the making of social man and citizen. In man making the man should follow his own inner feelings and natural tendencies. The child should be left to behave naturally. He learns in the contact of plants, animals, birds and natural objects. Society and man spoil the child. From moral and physical point of view the city is opposed to human good. The people should organise government to fulfil their needs. Wealth should not be concentrated in few hands. Thus, Rousseau pleaded for liberty and equality. According to him education means, "natural development of organs and powders of the child".

Negative Education

According to Rousseau, the first education ought to be purely negative. It consists not at all in teaching virtue or truth but in shielding the heart from vices and mind from errors. Thus Rousseau was against imparting any education to the child. According to him, "In childhood the aim of education is not to utilise time but to loose it". Elsewhere he said, "A twelve-year old child should know nothing. The teacher should pay attention to the child only and not to knowledge".

In Rousseau's time the children were given moral and religious education through various types of books in order to prepare them for adult life. Explaining his new system of education Rousseau said, "Give me a twelve-year old child who does not knowr anything. By 15 years of age, I will teach him so much as other children read in 15 years of early life. The only difference will be that your student remembers only knowledge and my student will be able to use it in practical life".

Thus, Rousseau precisely reversed the old order. As he said, "Take the reverse of the accepted practice and you will almost always do right". This was what he called, negative education.

Criticising the educational system of his time Rousseau said, "What must we think then, of that barbarous education which sacrifices the present to an uncertain future, which loads a child with chains of every sort and begins by making him miserable in order to prepare for him long in advance, some pretended happiness, which it is probable, he will never enjoy". This was positive education emphasising the mind and trying to make the child an adult. Negative education, on the other hand, strengthens the sense organs and the power of reasoning. As Rousseau said, "Nature wants that the child should remain a child before he becomes an adult. By changing this sequence we shall get raw fruits which shall soon perish. The child has his own ways of seeing, thinking and experiencing. We should not impose our own methods on him. It will be a folly"[1]. We do not understand the child and assume our ideas as his ideas.[2] Elsewhere he said, "I want that some wise man should tell us the art of counselling the child. This art will be valuable for us. The teachers have not learnt even its elementary rule".[3]

Thus, negative education is self education. It is the education of sense organs and body. This may be more possible in the playground rather than in the classroom. As Rousseau said, "We give too much importance to words. We produce by chattering education chatterers only. If you are all the time teaching morals to the child, you will make him a fool. If your mind is always giving instructions to the child, then his mind will become useless. Whatever the child learns in playground is four times more useful than what he learns in the classroom". According to Rousseau man's development may be classified into the following four stages:

1. *Infancy*, from birth to 5 years of age.
2. *Childhood*, from 5 years to 12 years of age.
3. *Adolescence*, from 12 years to 15 years of age.
4. *Youth*, from 15 years to 20 years of age.

Rousseau has suggested suitable education in all these stages in his book *Emile*.

Aims of Education

In the opinion of Rousseau, education aimed at the natural development of the child's inner faculties and powers. Education should help the child to remain alive. Life implies not merely the taking of breath but working. To live is to work, to develop and to properly utilise the various parts of the body, the sense organs and the various other powers of the body. In his book *Emile*, Rousseau seeks to train Emile in the profession of living so that he may become a human being before becoming a soldier, a churchman or a magistrate. Education, thus, in Rousseau's opinion, must aim at making the child a real human being.

1. Emile, p. 75.
2. Ibid., p. 185,
3. Ibid., p. 114

But the aims of education change at different stages of the child's development, because at each stage something different needs stress. The following are the various aims of education according to each level of the child's development:

1. Infancy. This stage begins at birth and continues up to five years of age. The chief objective during these five years is bodily development, the development and strengthening of every part of the body. This is essential if the child is to grow up healthy and strong. It forms the basis of subsequent healthy development of the mind. Rousseau expressed the opinion, "All wickedness comes from weakness. The child should be made strong so that he will do nothing which is bad". When the child is allowed to freely engage in playing and exercising his body, he remains active and has no time to indulge in undesirable activities. Nothing need be done to develop his instincts other than to give him complete liberty. If such freedom is given, he naturally develops his own instincts.

2. Childhood. This stage lasts from the fifth year to the twelfth, and it is the period of developing the child's sense organs. This development is achieved through experience and observation. Hence the child should be made to observe and experience those things in his environment which will assist the development of his sense organs.

3. Adolescence. For Emile, adolescence was believed to last from the twelfth to the fifteenth year. The child has, by this time, achieved the development of his body and his sense organs, and is, therefore, prepared, for systematic education. At this stage, education aims at developing the adolescent personality through hard work, guidance and study. During adolescence the individual should be given knowledge of various kinds so that he is enabled to fulfil his needs.

4. Youth. The individual passes through his youth between his fifteenth and twentieth year and undergoes development of emotions and sentiments. Rousseau pointed out, "We have formed his body, his senses and intelligence, it remains to give him a heart". Development of the sentiments will lead to development of moral and social qualities, but it is essential to pay attention to the development of religious emotions also. Summing up, the aim of education is to achieve the bodily, sensory, mental, social and moral development of the individual.

Curriculum of Education

It is possible to arrive at Rousseau's concept of a curriculum from an analysis of the various stages of development described in his *Emile*. Even in framing the curriculum, Rousseau paid attention to these four stages in development, and it will be better to consider the curriculum in the same fashion.

1. Infancy. Rousseau was very critical of the contemporary curriculum laid down for the education of infants, because he stressed the fact that infants should be treated as infants and not as adults in the miniature. The child is not a young adult, because his instincts and tendencies are dissimilar to those of the adult. For this reason, it is imperative to first understand child psychology and then to frame a curriculum. Instead of giving him controlled information of various subjects at this stage, it is far more important to pay attention to the development of his body and his senses. Before thinking of making the child a successful engineer or doctor, it is desirable to make him a healthy and self-sufficient young animal. In this age, the child can be taught a great deal through normal conversation carried on in the child's mother tongue. This will develop his linguistic ability. It is better not to try and instill any kind of habits in the child at this stage. Rousseau stated, "The only habit the child should be allowed to contract is that of having no habits".

2. Childhood. Even in childhood, Rousseau objected to the use of any textbooks for education, because he wanted to keep Emile away from books of any kind up to the twelfth year. He thought it necessary to give the child a chance to learn everything through direct experience and observation. Education of this kind is based on the concept of negative education which suggests that the child's mind should not be stuffed with information of different kinds. Instead he should be given liberty to learn through experience, because experience develops the sense organs which in turn lead to mental development, reason and development of the power of argument and reasoning. When the child is free to play, move, act at his own will during his childhood, he goes through a variety of experiences and learns all kinds of activities. During childhood, the child should not be given any verbal lessons on history, geography or even language. It is not desirable even to do any moral preaching. Rousseau opined that the child will learn his morality by the natural consequences of his own actions. Hence, up to the childhood stage no curriculum of any kind is required.

3. Adolescence. Having arrived at the appropriate level of bodily and sensory development, the child can now be exposed to teaching according to a formal curriculum consisting of education in natural science, language, mathematics, woodwork, music, painting, social life and some kind of professional training. Even here, Rousseau opined, more stress should be laid on the use of the sense organs than books. The very object of training in all these various subjects is the training and development of the sense organs. The study of science will enhance the child's curiosity and his inclination towards research, invention and self-education. Painting helps to train the muscles and eyes. Handicrafts help in developing the ability to work, apart from the mental development which is part of the process. Passing through various phases of social life, the individual learns that men depend upon each other, and thereby the child learns to assume and fulfil social responsibility. Rousseau gave it as his opinion that books do not give knowledge, but only train one to talk. Hence it is better if the curriculum for adolescence is based on active work than on books. During this period the adolescent must get adequate opportunity and time for hard work, education and study.

4. Youth. In the curriculum for youth, special stress has been laid on moral and religious education. But even moral education is to be derived through actual experience rather than through formal lectures. The youth leams a moral lesson when the sight of a physically handicapped person arouses in him the emotions of pity, sympathy and love. Religious education also follow s the same pattern, but it can be assisted by the teaching of history, mythological stones and religious stories. The youth derives many lessons from these stories. Apart from moral and religious education, Rousseau gave appropriate importance to education in bodily health, music and sex.

Educational Method

Pointing out the importance of experience in education Rousseau said, "To be alive does not mean to breathe, but it means to work and to develop our organs, senses and other powers. That man is not happy who has a long life but happy is one who has gained experiences of life". As the method generally pursued in education in his time was mainly oral and theoretical, Rousseau criticised the prevalent teaching methods. He said, "I want that some wise man should tell us the art of counselling the child. This art will be valuable for us. The teachers have not learnt even its elementary rule" Rousseau wanted to adopt playway method in education in place of verbal teaching. He maintained, "Education should be practical rather than oral. The child will not have to read through books, he will have to stop reading words". Then, what should be the proper method of teaching the child? For Rousseau education to the child should be provided by play. "Thus, real education is self education. The infant himself learns to develop by utilisation of his sense organs and reacting to the environment".

Principles of Education

Rousseau is a naturalist in his methodology of education just as much as he is a naturalist in the curriculum of education. He has stressed the importance of the two following principles governing the process of education:

1. Learning through self-experience. Rousseau wanted to educate Emile through experience and not through books. He was opposed to bookish education, because he contended that books try to teach one to talk about those things which one does not, in fact, know. That is why he wanted to keep Emile away from books for twelve years, so much so that he did not want Emile even to know what a book is. Rousseau has praised only one book, *Robinson Crusoe,* because it presents the natural needs of human beings in such a simple manner that the child can easily comprehend them. From this book the child can also learn the manner in which these needs are to be satisfied.

2. Learning through doing. Rousseau opposed the rote method of learning on the ground that knowledge acquired through actual doing or actual experience is far more permanent than knowledge acquired through words He wanted the child's power of reasoning and not his power of memorising things to be developed. That is why Rousseau was so severely critical of the existing methods of education. He wanted the child to become educated through his own observation, experience and analysis. Instead of stuffing the child's mind with his own know ledge, the educator's task is to arouse the child's curiosity so that the child is inspired to find out things for himself, thus developing his own mind. Science is best taught through curiosity and the desire to experiment and research. Rousseau's insistence on these elements was later manifested in the evolution of the Heuristic method.

If the child is to give moral education to himself he must be active. Long lectures bore the child, and instead of contributing to his education, only hinder it because they blunt the child's appetite for new things. Hence, instead of delivering long lectures to the child, it is better to give him the opportunity to act for himself. In education, the object is more important than the word. It is undesirable to fashion a method of education and to mould the child accordingly.

Discipline

Rousseau, being a naturalist, wanted complete freedom as the first step towards inducing discipline in the child. He wanted a total absence of any restraints on the child, because he felt that they hindered the development of discipline. It is better to leave the child free in free environment so that he can develop his natural powers. Rousseau's plan also did not include any arrangement for punishment, because he felt that punishment should be the natural outcome of their own mistakes. This is the naturalist conception of punishment. In this theory it is assumed that the child has no know ledge of good and bad, but he suffers pain when he makes a mistake and pleasure when he does something right. Hence, he gets the reward of his actions. This is the natural pattern of punishment and it is this which will instill discipline in the child. This is natural discipline, which implied obedience of natural laws, because neglect or violation of these laws invariably leads to pain and suffering. Hence, it is not necessary to lecture to the child. He is naturally possessed of a fine character, and this character is defiled by long lectures. He will learn better discipline, if he is left to himself.

School Organisation

The title given above may be a little misleading because Rousseau objected to the system of school education. He contended that the child is born innocent and pure, that he is only defiled and distorted by the defective environment of the school. In fact, the only suitable environment of every kind is defective and impure. It is better to separate the child from his parents, to take him away from school, and leave him by himself in a natural environment. The educator's only task is to look after the child, because in natural surroundings the child will himself look after the development of his natural abilities. Even if schools are created, they can be utilised by stressing the natural surroundings instead of insisting on creating a social atmosphere. In the predominantly natural surroundings the child will be able to develop naturally.

HERBERT SPENCER (1820-1903)

Herbert Spencer published his book *Education* in 1861. This book shows his naturalist philosophy of education. Like Rousseau he criticised the curriculums and methods of teaching of the schools of his times. He pointed out that they were too much theoretical.

Aims and Ideals

The aim of education, according to Herbert Spencer, is to prepare the child for complete living. The aim of life is complete living and is a means to know the techniques of this art. Complete living is a happy life. It requires development of body and mind. This development is acquired by full utilisation of natural resources and the use of organised powers.

Responsibilities of Man

The aims and ideals of education follow from the five responsibilities of man:

1. Self-preservation. The first and foremost responsibility of man is self-preservation. This is not individual but social. The individuals should help each other in realising this ideal. Self-preservation means the preservation of both the body and the mind. To realise this ideal the child should be given practical knowledge of physiology and hygiene. The knowledge itself however, is not sufficient. It requires practice of its implications. This practice is the function of education. Thus, self-preservation is the most primary aim of education. It goes without saying that this aim is naturalist.

2. Earning a living. In youth self-preservation requires earning a living. This is realised by means of education. Education develops one's capacity for earning a living. Its utility lies in voctiori. Science particularly helps in this process. Not only in work and vocation but also in our daily life the knowledge of science is required in construction of houses, agriculture, etc. Different sciences such as geology, chemistry, astrology, physics, etc., prepare us for various vocations in life. Therefore, Spencer prescribes education in all the sciences. Different science subjects should be taught according to the talents of different children. Science experts should be consulted for this purpose Spencer prescribes teaching of all science subjects to the children. This, however, is far from possible. Therefore, educationists have not accepted such a wide prescription of science in the curriculum. However, earning a living remains the aim of education in the present tune.

3. Up-bringing of children. After getting employment one marries and begets children. These children should be brought up for complete living. In order to realise this aim the boys and girls should be taught subjects which make them successful parents in future. This aim of education has also been generally accepted by educationists nowadays.

4. Citizenship. An important area of man's responsibility is citizenship. As a citizen the individual has to perform duties prescribed by the state. Therefore, in almost all the states since ancient times the children were taught things concerning citizenship. In order to develop citizenship, Spencer prescribes scientific study of history. He criticises non-scientific approach in history. According to him history should be taught with reference to the principles of political science. Its importance consists in the growth of liberalism and international understanding.

5. Use of leisure time. As mechanisation and scientific progress was realised, man found more leisure to utilise. One of the important responsibilities of man is worthy use of leisure time. Education helps in this process. For example, leisure time may be devoted to painting, music, sculpture, poetry and also recreation by natural scenes. These arts are developed through education. However, Spencer insists that even leisure time utilisation depends on scientific approach. Even success in music and other arts is not possible without the knowledge of physiology and mechanics. Therefore, Spencer prescribes the combination of innate powers and science. However, this too much insistence on science has not been accepted by modern educationists. It is not accepted that excellence in literature and arts requires a foundation in science, nor is science accepted to be more valuable than arts. In fact, by his too much emphasis on science Herbert Spencer leaves the ideal of complete living. In order to realise the aim of complete living literature, fine arts and science, all should be given proper place in the curriculum. It is wrong to say, as Spencer did, that science is more useful than language. It is again wrong to say that science develops memory and thinking. The value of science is unquestionable but to say that it develops moral values like truth, self-reliance and perseverance is to confuse science with ethics. What we lack today is not science but ethics. In fact, too much subordination of culture to science has led to the present crisis in human culture.

Principles of Teaching

Though not original but Herbert Spencer's principles of teaching admirably sum up the fundamental maxims to be followed by the teacher. These principles are as follows:

1. From easy to difficult. Both curriculum construction and teaching method should proceed from easy to difficult as this is the law of the mind.

2. From known to unknown. For association and integration of the newly achieved information both the curriculum and teaching method should proceed from known to unknown. While this will help in the assimilation of new knowledge, it will also facilitate interest and memory.

3. From indefinite to definite. In the development of man he proceeds from indefinite to definite. This maxim is the foundation of the educational process. The teacher teaches only because his knowledge is definite while the knowledge of the child is indefinite. The child develops from vague to clear knowledge. Therefore, the teacher should all the time proceed from indefinite to definite knowledge. As the knowledge grows, the area of definiteness increases. In the field of indefinite the scientists are always struggling to achieve definite knowledge.

4. Concrete to abstract. In the process of mental development the child first perceives and then ideates. Concept formation depends upon knowledge through sense organs. We first know concrete things and then arrive at abstract concepts. Therefore, it is a set principle of curriculum formation and teaching methods that one should start with concrete experiences and gradually reach abstract equations, concepts and formula, etc.

5. Principle of Stages of human development. Since ancient times to present day it has been an accepted principle of curriculum formation and teaching methods that these should vary according to the different stages of human development. The man passes through the stages of infancy, childhood, adolescence, adult and old age in his development. In all these stages his physical and mental powers constantly change. Therefore, the curriculum and the teaching method should be according to the stage of human development. While this will sustain interest, it will make education a success. In the construction of curriculum and teaching methods the environment should also be given new consideration along with stages of human development.

6. From experimental to rational knowledge. Like Rousseau Herbert Spencer was also against bookish education. According to him, the child should be allowed to experiment with things around him. This experimentation will develop his talent and give him experience. This will prepare him to imbibe and retain rational knowledge given in books.

7. Principle of interesting teaching method. Interest is intimately related to attention and memory. Therefore, the teacher should always make his method interesting according to the individuality and development of the educands. Audiovisual aids may be utilised to create interest, particularly in science subjects.

Moral Teaching

Herbert Spencer followed Rousseau in the case of moral teaching. Like Rousseau he prescribed the formula of return to nature as the basis of moral teaching. He criticised the cruel and immoral practices concerning punishment to the child in the family. He pointed out that the child's conduct can develop only when the parents and family provide proper atmosphere. According to Spencer natural consequence is the best punishment. Therefore, the child should be allowed to learn by natural consequences. This point, however, cannot be stressed too far. It may be remembered that the child cannot be left free to make all sorts of experiments, such as playing with knife and fire. In such cases he should be forewarned as he does not know the consequences of so many actions.

Physical Education

In order to realise the aim of complete living, Herbert Spencer prescribed physical education. His physical education is based on science. He points out four different defects in the prevailing physical education system. Firstly, the children are not given full food, secondly, they do not get sufficient clothes. Thirdly, they do not get enough physical exercises. Fourthly, they are asked to do too much mental work. Spencer insists upon provision of balanced food and sufficient clothes according to laws of physiology. The physical and mental work should be balanced with the viewpoint of efficiency and good health. Good health alone leads to joy of life and success. Therefore, it is the duty of the parents and teachers to provide physical education for good health.

Critical Evaluation

The above mentioned philosophy of Herbert Spencer made the following changes in the field of education:

1. Aim. Herbert Spencer, like Rousseau, made the aim of education more practical.

2. Curriculum. Due to the influence of Spencer science was given an important place in the curriculum of schools. Science was included in secondary school in different countries. Similarly, it was included in the curriculum of primary school.

It was included in the curriculum in Protestant universities. Science academies were opened at several places. Gradually, all the universities in different European countries started science departments and awarded bachelor and doctorate degree in science.

In spite of the above useful impact of Spencer on education the following drawbacks in his philosophy of education have been pointed out by the critics:

1. As Spencer did not study education, one hardly finds any originality in his views.
2. Spencer preached reform but without any scientific basis.
3. Spencer exclusively stressed the teaching of science from primary to university stage. He even proposed for a scientific form to be given to every subject of study. He neglected the value of literature, art and history.
4. Spencer was against traditional methods of study. He made education more practical. However, he neglected the importance of language in education.
5. According to Dewey educational aim as preparation for future is too limited. It is vitiated by utilitarian bias.

AIMS OF EDUCATION

Concerning the aims of education, naturalists adopt a biological and evolutionist attitude. Even among the different forms of naturalism one finds a variation in the objectives assigned to education. Mechanical naturalism suggests that education should aim at the efficiency and perfection of the human machine. But this concept does not represent completely the naturalist school. Biological evolution uses education to ensure the proper adjustment or adaptation of the child to his environment. McDougall points out that education aims at the transformation, synthesis and sublimation of instincts. Darwinists argue that education must train the individual to struggle successfully for his own survival. Lamarck and his followers agree with the concept of biological evolution, because for them also the aim of education is to adapt to the environment. On the other hand, Herbert Spencer believed education to be a preparation and a training for the complete life. Bernard Shaw believed that education must aim not only at the individual's development but also at making the individual capable of stimulating and sustaining social development, for this will add to the social heritage of the succeeding generations. T. P. Nunn prefers to use education as a means of making the individual capable of developing his own individuality and of contributing to society. Naturalists of the nineteenth and twentieth centuries believe that education should achieve a synthesis and adjustment between individual and society and also between man and nature. Rousseau believed that education should develop the child according to his natural ability. And it is accepted today that education should conform to the child s abilities. To quote Rousseau's words, "Now of the three factors in education, nature is wholly beyond our control; things are only partly in our power; the education of men is the only one controlled by us; and even here our power is largely illusory, for who can hope to direct every word and deed of all with whom the child has to do.

What is the goal? As we have just shown it is the goal of nature since all three modes of education must work together, the two that we can control must follow the lead of that which is beyond our control".[4] The naturalist approach to the aims of education is rather narrow in that it fails to include the spiritual aspect of man s nature. Its inclusion would almost naturally remove the distance between idealism and naturalism and this is what is being attempted now.

NATURALISM AND CURRICULA

As a system of philosophy, naturalism has been exceptionally susceptible to the development of science, and by virtue of this influence it has attached much importance to evolutionary theory, empirical teaching and scientific analysis, etc. As a result of the significance ascribed to scientific study naturalists want to introduce physical and social sciences at every level of education because they believe these to be more important than the humanities. Language and mathematics for the naturalists, are tools for the learning of science and both should be taught only so long as they assist the learning of science. Literature, in any case should not completely absorb the students' interest and attention. Curricula should be so constructed as to encourage the educand to take an interest in science and to gain knowledge which is factual and objective.

Granting that the present is more important than the future, the naturalists have not fallen into the mistake of neglecting the past, because the past contains many valuable suggestions for the educand. For this reason, naturalists believe in the value of historical study. Such a study will enable them to construct a new social structure and thus plan for the future.

Since evolutionists believe man to have developed or evolved, from the animal stage, and since they also believe that there is no gap or discontinuity in the transition from the animal to the human, they want education to develop the instincts and emotions.

On the subject of curriculum, naturalists have expressed theories which differ from each other to some extent. Comenius wanted the educand to study every subject, without making any selection. Locke refitted this notion by demonstrating that every individual cannot be made to study the same subject, because of certain natural handicaps. Hence, much emphasis was laid upon modifying the curriculum to suit the needs of the individual. Herbert Spencer arranged the curriculum with science as its nucleus and tried to synthesise the other subjects to science. The arts were given a secondary place in his programme because he believed that one must first create the basic elements before refining or making them sophisticated. In fact, he wanted to synthesise all subjects to the study of science, arriving at a conception of liberal education arranged around science. T. H. Huxley, another naturalist, attached greater importance to the cultural aspects of life than to the study of science.

Thus, his conception of a liberal education differed materially from that of Spencer. In contrast, modern naturalists do not stress the importance of any one subject against that of any other, although more importance is attached to

---

4. Jean Jacques Rousseau, *Emile*, Barbara Foxley, Translator. New York E. P. Dutton & Co, Inc. Every man's Library, 1911.

the sciences. Yet, the arts are not neglected, but given an important place in the curriculum so that it may acquire a definitely wide base.

EDUCATIONAL METHODS

Naturalist education is paidocentric. The child occupies the central place in it. The child, in order to develop, should be left on its own. The society or the state should not interfere in his contact with nature. This will allow the growth of the child in natural circumstances. Therefore, the most important method of teaching, according to the naturalist, is to leave the child free to learn from nature. Naturalism was responsible for a violent denunciation of the traditional methods of education. It opposed all kinds of negative techniques and the stress on rote learning. Instead, it favoured teaching by more positive methods. Being empirical, it preferred to educate the child by giving him actual experience of all that he is to learn. Locke believed that training of the sense organs or sensory training, should be the first stage in the child's education. Naturalists considered experience to be more important than books, for they propounded the principle of do and learn. They felt that the child learns much from natural consequences, and therefore it is best that the child be left to do as he is inclined, so that he may follow the dictates of his own nature.

Much emphasis is laid upon direct experience. It is argued that the child learns more by direct experience of nature, men and objects than through books. By the same reasoning, teaching of science can be more effective if it is done through practical work in the laboratory, just as geometry is better learnt by calculating the configuration of actual objects and spaces than through hypothetical problems posed in the text-books. Geography can be taught better through tours of places of geographical interest than through maps and charts. The same holds true of the teaching of history. Hence, the naturalistic educational methods depend more upon direct experience and personal observation than upon text-books.

Naturalist thinkers suggest the following two methods of education:

1. Positive method. In this the educator tries to inform the child about various subjects. This is the traditional method which the naturalist rejects as old fashioned and ineffective.

2. Negative method. Concerning the negative methods of education, Rousseau has commented, "I call a negative education one that tends to perfect the organs that are the instruments of knowledge before giving them this knowledge directly and that endeavours to prepare the way for reason by the proper exercise of the senses". Hence negative education consists in training the child to use his sense organs and motor organs instead of filling his mind with bits and pieces of information. By using the various bodily powers at his disposal, the child will generate much knowledge for himself.

The play way method of education is very popular with naturalists because, during play, the child gets the opportunity to manifest his dormant powers. He is often faced with situations which compel him to use these powers. Irrespective of the definition of play — as recapitulation of man's ancient activities, as a rehearsal for the rough and tumble of future life, as safety valve for letting off excess energy it is undoubtedly the most natural and facile way of developing the child's natural inclinations. That games provide an outlet for man's creative power is true not only of the child's games but also of games played in adult life.

Artificiality of any kind is another thing which the naturalists find objectionable. The atmosphere in the class and the school should be informal, and the time-table should not be rigorously adhered to. Apart from the subjects taught as part of the prescribed syllabus, the child must be encouraged to take active part in various extra curricular programmes. And, in fact, the child should not be burdened by or compelled to submit to any definite teaching method at all. Left to himself the child is perfectly capable of evolving an educational technique which suits him best. If the educator wants to know what this method is, he should observe the child, since through such observation he can learn what the child wants, in which direction he is inclined, in what things he evinces interest. Consequently, the teacher will be enabled to mould his own technique to suit the child.

THE TEACHER

Naturalism opposes the traditional concepts of education in which the educator inflicted any and all kinds of punishment on the child in order to make it progress in the desired direction. Naturalists believe that the period of infancy is important in itself, not merely as a stepping stone to adult life. That explains their extreme emphasis upon the playway technique of education. They opine that the child should be encouraged to enjoy his infancy and childhood as much as he can, with the least possible interference from the teacher. Consequently, the teacher does not occupy as high and respected a position as he does under the idealistic tradition. One example of this is Neil's Summerhill School in which the educator mixed with the educands, played and practically lived with them Even the matter of discipline was in the hands of the educands who selected a cabinet of five educands for this purpose. This cabinet was even empowered to expel an educand from the school, if it felt the necessity for such an extreme step. Neil's only function was to remove the various difficulties of the educands, after discussing everything with them. Hence, in this school, the educator was no more than just one of the members of the school.

Naturalists suggest that the educator should be a guide and a friend, and that in his behaviour with the child, the educator should try to recollect his own childhood and infancy. The child is naturally inclined to laughter and happiness. Hence the educator should be jolly and not grave, for undue seriousness of manner and behaviour depresses the child. The educator's role is primarily negative inasmuch as he is required to protect the child's inherent goodness from bad influences originating in the environment. He is responsible for creating an environment in which the child can experience the greatest amount of freedom. He must study the child's psychology and intervene in his activity only when some obstacle bars the way to the child's progress.

Hence, the aim of education is, thus, to provide the child with opportunities for completely unrestricted self-expression. The role of educator, therefore, is only to protect the child from repressions, mental conflicts and mental disorders of all kind. Naturalism warns the educator against unnecessary seriousness, the desire to assert his authority, physical punishment, etc., since all these measures have a detrimental influence upon the child's development. The educator must think in terms of what he must avoid doing rather than think of things he must do. He can do even better and become literally a child in dealing with children. But his guidance is apparent when he can give a positive and confident opinion on controversial matters, and for this he must be possessed of unbounded self-confidence. He can also guide the children in their search for new things, and can train them in new techniques of doing things so that in later life they should become capable of doing things on their own. The role of the teacher is most clearly defined by Ross in the following words, "His (educator's) place, if any, is behind the scenes; he is an observer of the child's development rather than a giver of information, ideas, ideals and will power, or a moulder of character. These the child will forge for himself, he knows better than any educator what he should learn, when and how he should learn it. His education is the free development of his interests and motives rather than an artificial effort made on him by an educator. "It is evident, therefore, that the educator should never have recourse to any kind of pressure or force, even to the use of his own authority. His task is simply to provide the theatre for the child's acting, to collect the materials required, to provide the child with an opportunity to do as he likes, to create an ideal environment. As a result of the impact of naturalism, many of the latest techniques of education, such as the Montessori system, Dalton plan, Project method, etc., all grant to the teacher a similar status.

Compared to naturalistic philosophy, the idealistic school grants a more responsible position to the teacher. Adams expressed the opinion that the educator himself has been through the same situations as the educand is experiencing at present. He is no less a part of the intellectual world than anyone else. Both the educator and the educand are two elements of the organic structure of the universe, and both have their own status and role in God's plan. The educator teaches and guides him along the path of perfection.

The educator's role in the naturalist organisation of education is clarified by the example of Froebel's kindergarten system. In this system, the school is conceived to be a garden, the educand to be a delicate plant and the educator the careful, responsible and cautious gardener. The plant grows by itself, it seeks its own nourishment, and its development is governed by natural laws. It is impossible to turn one plant into a plant of another kind. This is beyond the abilities of even the greatest gardener. His only function is to make sure that the plant and the weed grows according to its own nature, and that this development is not hindered.

Up to this point, the idealistic conception does not differ very much from the naturalistic conception. But, as Ross has commented, the naturalist may be satisfied with wild flowers, but the idealist can be satisfied only by the finest of roses. The idealist places greater stress on the aims of education, and believes this aim to be self-realisation or perfection. Hence, under the idealistic pattern of education, the educator allows the educand to follow the natural pattern of growth, but he reserves the right to guide the educand towards perfection. It is implied that such perfection cannot be achieved without the educator's guidance, and hence the educator does not remain merely a friend, but becomes a guide and a sage.

DISCIPLINE

As in the case of curriculum and educational methods, the naturalist philosophers oppose the traditional concepts of discipline. And more than anything else, they oppose the method of physical punishment for they believe that this gives rise to undesirable conflict in the child. Rousseau has written, "Children should never receive punishment. Freedom and not power is the greatest good". If the child makes a mistake he will get his reward from nature itself, and thus he will learn to distinguish between the right and the wrong through the consequences of his own actions. For this reason the child should be given every liberty. To the naturalist, liberty does not imply freedom to interfere with the activity of others. The child can never be independent in this sense because he is controlled by many rules and laws which unconsciously or consciously operate in his mind. Only external and obvious discipline should be done away with. All the work of school administration and organisation should be left to the educand, for then he will learn to make the rules and to obey them.

Respect of discipline is sought to be instilled in the child's mind through natural consequences. Spencer writes, "When a child falls, or runs its head against the table, it suffers a pain, the remembrance of which tends to make it more careful; and by repetition of such experiences, it is eventually disciplined into proper guidance of its movement". But, there is a limit to learning through this method. In fact, very often the child is not able to reason out the relation between his various actions and the total consequences. As a result, he repeats even the harmful activity many times. And, hence, in such a situation, as Dewey has hinted, it becomes necessary to scold the child, to caution it, or even to punish it. As T.H. Huxley observes, "Nature's discipline is not even a word and a blow, and the blow first, but the blow without a word. It is left to you to find out why your ears are boxed".[5] Hence, it is not enough to abandon the child to learn for itself through these natural consequences of his actions. They do play a significant role in his training, but it is necessary to caution him at times. He should be warned against certain kinds of activities. The system of reward and punishment has been found effective everywhere. But it must be remembered that the value of the naturalist concept lies in that it hints at the shortcomings of excessive external discipline, although there is no doubt that the theory is definitely one-sided.

SCHOOL ORGANISATION

Naturalism distinguishes between formal and informal agencies. While the formal agency of education is the school and other educational institutions, the

---

5. Quoted by Ross. J.S.: *Ground Work of Educational Theory*, George G. Harrap & Co., London, (1949), pp. 94-95.

informal agencies include family, society, community and state, etc. Of these the informal agency, family starts the education of the child. The state influences the formal agencies of education. The school management, according to naturalists, should be liberal, free and based upon natural laws. According to the naturalist philosophers nature itself is a school where the child is taught according to natural principles. The school should be organised in such a way so that the child may get natural atmosphere for his growth. The naturalists cherish democratic values. The social environment of the school should be based upon the principles of liberty, equality and fraternity. The teacher's role should be reduced to minimum. The students should themselves govern the school. They should receive training in leadership. The time-table of the school should be flexible because a rigid time-table hampers freedom. The naturalist school organisation may be found in Dalton plan where classes are changed into laboratories and there is no definite time-table in the school. The school buildings should have proper arrangement of light and air. Rousseau recommended organisation of schools according to the nature of children and the stages of development of the educands.

CONTRIBUTION OF NATURALISM TO EDUCATION

Like other systems of philosophy of education, naturalism has also made important contribution to education. It made education paidocentric, psychological, free, self-dependent, related to nature and society, based upon developmental psychology, democratic, multisided and natural to the stages of development. These points may now be discussed in detail.

1. Paidocentric education. In the naturalistic conception of education, the child is in the forefront while all other things such as the educator, the books, the curriculum, the school, etc., are all in the background. Sir John Adams called this the conception of paidocentric education. Naturalism stresses the fact that education should be guided by the nature of the child, that the natural inclination of the child is always good. Rousseau said, "Everything is good as it comes from the hands of the Author of Nature but everything degenerates in the hands of man". It is, therefore, argued that the child is naturally invested with all goodness, and all that is necessary is to protect him from a defective environment. He must be provided with the kind of environment which will encourage him to develop his innate goodness, his natural sense of the beautiful. He must be enabled to avoid the ugly, to manifest the natural truth inside him so that he can combat the falsity which is thrust upon him by the defective environment. In this process, the educator can perform only the function of the guide. Naturalists are not inclined to transform the child's nature through education or to apply to him the standards of the adult. Education according to them, is not the preparation for life but life itself. Children should live like children, because infancy has its own significance, and it is not merely a stepping stone to adulthood. The child is not to be prepared and made ready for his future, but instead to be allowed to enjoy the present. Munro opines that Rousseau was the first to state the principle, that, "Education finds its purpose, its process and its means wholly within the child life and the child experience" In this manner, it can be summarised that education is the process of living a natural life and moving towards evolution, because the child has within himself the germs of evolution.

2. Emphasis upon psychology. The influence of naturalism was the cause of the psychological tendency gaining so much prominence in the field of education. By stressing the fact of the child's nature, it emphasised the importance of natural development. And, in order to determine what is natural and what is abnormal in child development, the naturalists turned to the psychologists. Thus it came to be understood that education must study the child and observe him. Many psychological researches have established that the child is not a young adult, that he has a distinct psychology which differs from adult psychology. It has been established that the child's mental activities of thinking, memory, imagination, recall, learning, etc., all differ from similar activities in the adult. Hence, naturalism stressed the value of psychology for education. Rousseau is often credited with introducing the psychological tendency in education for he was the first to point out that education should follow the child's nature, which must first be understood. Although Thomas Fuller had stressed even before Rousseau the importance of studying the educand more than books, it was the latter whose theorising in this sphere took practical shape. Rousseau's ideas were put into practice by Pestalozzi, Herbert, Froebel and other educationists. The introduction of psychology into the sphere of education led to considerable research in child psychology, and the entire process finally culminated in the emergence of a distinct branch of psychology called educational psychology.

William McDougall has made valuable contribution to the literature on and knowledge of child psychology by his analysis of the child's instincts and his definition of the process of character formation, determination and sentiment formation in the child. Thorndike and other psychologists contributed great wealth of knowledge in the sphere of manual skill and other aspects of child learning. By comparing and examining the various stages in the evolution of the child, it was found that child psychology differed considerably in infancy, childhood and adolescence. As a consequence, great stress was placed on adopting different techniques of teaching at each one of these stages. Apart from this, education was further influenced by the discovery that children differed from each other to a very great extent in respect of their physical and mental capabilities, their nature and emotions, etc. It was considered desirable to make education flexible so that it could accommodate all such variations and still contribute to the healthy development of the child.

But probably the greatest impact on education was that of the psychoanalysts. Freud put forward many novel theses about child psychology. Other psychoanalysts were responsible for many interesting and illuminating books on child psychology, and these were avidly read by educators the world over. In the main, the influence of psychoanalysis can be seen in the knowledge it provides of the harmful effects of repression and the fresh attitudes to sex, authority, the child's attitude to authority. Besides, this branch of psychology also warned educators against, the harmful effects of threats, physical punishment and asserting oneself. Ross is of the opinion that the greatest benefit derived from psychoanalysis is that it has helped to explain the causes of juvenile delinquency and also suggested ways and means of curing it.

3. Emphasis upon free choice. Naturalists contend that a predetermined pattern of education must never be foisted upon the child even when the pattern is entirely scientific. Education must give the child an opportunity of making a free choice in everything that he wants to study or play or even the manner in which he wants to behave. No external restraints should be placed on this free choice. Some naturalists even object to the very institution of school education, because they fear that the school is an obstacle in their normal and independent development. They also believe that the atmosphere in the home is freer than the school environment but they are contradicted by others more conscious of the constant interruptions made by parents in the child's activities. Apart from this naturalists, in general, are opposed to all educands in one class being taught in the same manner, or by the same method of education. They even object to the introduction of any kind of time-table. One example of a completely unrestrained environment is to be found in Summerhill School established by A. S. Neil. It was taken for granted at this institution that the child was not expected to be fit for school, but that the school had to prepare itself for the child. Liberty was the first principle in the child's education, so much so that the children could play through the entire day if they were so inclined. They were given no religious education because a child is not naturally religiously inclined. No adult values were forced upon the children who were also taught none of the principles of culture. Naturalists also believe that the child should not be made cultured unless he realises the need for culture. It was, therefore, thought better to leave the child in his more primitive condition. The liberty granted to the children even extended to their being allowed to roam naked if they so wished. It was found that no moral difficulty was raised due to the sex instinct, and it was decided that a healthy attitude to sex could only be generated through co-education. Neil was of the opinion that undesirable behaviour is due to moral and unnatural repression, and that no undesirable incidents take place due to co-education if the environment is completely free and liberal.

4. Place of the teacher. Naturalism grants to the teacher the place of the friend and the guide, not of the administrator, for he is not to interfere in the child's activities, nor to make any attempt at influencing him. He is there merely to observe them, not to give them any information or to fill their minds with facts or to form their characters. It is for the child to decide what he wants to learn. He will learn from experience what he should learn and when, what he should do and what he should avoid. His interests and instincts should be given an opportunity to manifest themselves freely. All this does not imply that the teacher has no role at all in education, for he has a definite role inasmuch as he is the one who will provide the educative material, create the opportunities for learning, create the ideal environment and thus contribute to the child's development. For example, in the Montessori method of education, the child is given many kinds of equipment to play with, while the teacher looks on and observes. Naturalism, thus, favours the concept of self-education. Norman Mancken has gone one step further and suggested that children can even educate each other. Nothing should be done with a view to turning the child's mind in any particular direction. He is not to be taught to read or write, to make use of the various parts of his body, or be taught moral lessons, but merely to be left to himself so that he can develop independently. This is what Rousseau implied by his concept of the educator's negative effort in the process of education. Negative effort did not imply that the teacher was merely to pass his time, but to observe the child, avoid any interference in his activities, to prevent or protect him from defects, to protect him from a defective environment. The educator must be perfectly aware of all that he has not to do, but at the same time this negative attitude is to be supplemented by the positive one of love and sympathy. He can love the child only when he himself has been a child, that is, he has not completely forgotten his childhood. He should have the inclination to laugh and play like the child, to forget that he is an adult, to mix with the children and become one of them himself. Only then can he give anything to them.

At times, one finds children developing some bad tendencies and it becomes necessary to guide them. But even this should be done in the form of an informal conversation with the child. In such a dialogue the educator understands the difficulties of the educand, shows his love and sympathy and encourages the educand to solve them himself. He makes the educand aware of the difficulties he is likely to face. Neil called this re-education. He saw in his own school that mam of the children often sought opportunities for such informal dialogues. Whenever the children showed any disinclination for such dialogues, they were immediately abandoned.

5. Direct experience of things. Naturalists believe Rousseau's dictum, "Give your scholar no verbal lesson; he should be taught by experience alone". Hence, the naturalist lays stress on teaching through direct experience. The child will learn more by coming into contact through the objects surrounding him than through books. He should be allowed to examine these objects. Similarly the teaching of science should not take the form of verbal lectures, but actual performance of experiments in the laboratory. Geometry should be taught not by the problems written in books but by the actual measurement of the areas of the school and the height and other dimensions of the school buildings and other objects. If geography is to be taught, the educand should be taken to the various parts of the country, and not taught only through maps and charts produced on the blackboard. Thus naturalists insist that the educand must learn from the things that exist in the school, not through the lectures of the educator.

6. Direct experience of social life. What is true of the natural environment of the child, is also equally true of the social environment in which he lives. He should leam the various duties, obligations and responsibilities of social life not through lectures of the educator but through the natural society of the school, of which the educand is a member. Here, left to himself, he will learn to do those things which should be done and leave alone those which should be avoided. In Neil's Summerhill School the children themselves decided upon the form of behaviour which others found objectionable or which hindered their adjustment, and thus learnt to avoid it. This formed the basis of the child's social education. The concept of co-education is also favoured by the naturalists because then the society within the school resembles more closely the society outside school. Besides, it has been contended that unnatural attitudes to sex are the inevitable result of segregated education of boys and girls. This is a very controversial subject and many educationists fail to agree with the naturalists, although in many cases the results of experiments in coeducation favoured the naturalists' thesis. It can undoubtedly be said, however, that the child's experience of the social life within the school, forms the basis of his later social and moral life.

7. Self-government. Another characteristic feature of the naturalist conception of education is the insistence on self-government. Neil's Summerhill School experimented in this direction also by allowing the educands to form their own government. They created a cabinet of five educands whose function it was to reflect on various difficulties, to give decisions in cases of indiscipline and even to inflict punishment for such acts. These five cabinet members met every Saturday night, and one of them was elected to the chair. All problems were then discussed. The cabinet even had the authority to expel an educand from the school, if it so decided, although in fact this right was never exercised. Neil states that this arrangement led to the development of highly democratic qualities in his educands, and it was felt that this weekly meeting had a much greater influence and impact than an entire week of traditional teaching. And, in fact, no one can doubt that such an arrangement of self-government is very beneficial for training educands in democratic living. The condition of self-government does impose certain restrictions on the educand's activities, but because it is imposed through his own rules and regulations, it takes the form of self-government and self-discipline. All kinds of self-control can be learnt through self-government, and it has none of the drawbacks of the method of external control. There is undoubtedly no better way of teaching public morality. And it is only self-government which teaches cultured behaviour and co-operation.

8. Playway of education. Of the many methods of education, naturalists prefer the playway. In this technique, all that the child learns is through a sense of playing or indulging in sport. Psychologists contend that the child best manifests his instincts and tendencies in an independent game, and his development can also be achieved through sport. Whatever the objectives of play—the recapitulation of man's primitive activities, the preparation for future life, or a kind of safety valve for an individual's excessive energy—it is undoubtedly the most natural method of teaching. Playing affords education not only during childhood, for people learn many things through playing even in adult life. It also provides an opportunity for constructive activity. Games are an important medium of constructive or creative education. Naturalists have, therefore, placed adequate stress on the value of games a fact which even modern educationists accept without reservation. Nowadays the playway of education is adopted for the education of infants and children, and thus they acquire all the advantages of a naturalist education. Montessori education, for example, is a good instance of this because in this method of teaching the child learns even reading and writing through play. Scouting is another activity in which the child's taught many things through the medium of play. In Neil's Summerhill School, more stress was placed on character than on learning. Children were free to play from morning till evening. There was no system of examination, and books had less importance in the school than most other kinds of activities. Some lessons were taught, but attendance was never compulsory because most of the work, in any case, was done outside the classroom. On the other hand, educands favoured the craftsrooms much more, where they were taught to make things out of wood, plastecine and metal. Educands and educators sat together to write plays. It was found that drama writing is an important means of developing the creative imagination.

9. Development of the child according to its nature. Naturalists stressed the fact that the child must develop according to his own nature, and educational pattern must be modified to suit the various needs of children, because children differ from each other on account of their innate individual differences.

10. Importance of developmental psychology. By stressing the value of studying child development, naturalists made contributions to the progress of developmental psychology which scientifically studies the various stages of man's development.

11. Comprehensive curriculum. Naturalists have favoured the adoption of a multi-faceted and comprehensive curriculum, which reflects, apart from the scientific, sociological and psychological tendencies, the holistic tendency in education. The holistic approach is, in fact, a synthesis of the scientific, sociological and psychological tendencies. Schools make use of all kinds of modern audio-visual aids, and arrange for teaching of sciences and the various arts. Extra curricular programmes and activities are also believed to be of considerable importance.

12. Development of democratic qualities. Naturalism is opposed to repression and vigorous discipline of any kind. It seeks to replace the traditional by the modern, the dogmatic by the liberal and the progressive. It consequently helps in the development of such democratic qualities as liberty, equality and fraternity. It favours a complete rejection of the traditional modes of teaching and instead advocates greater dependence upon self-government.

13. Development of child psychology. Naturalists played a significant role in the development of child psychology as a result of their insistence on education being oriented to the child's nature. As a result of this development in child psychology, it was discovered that the child is not a young adult, but a distinct kind of human being possessed of a different psychology. Naturalists insist that the child is born good, and that education must seek only to protect him from evil.

14. Support of residential schools. Under the naturalist mode of teaching, the educator has the negative role of protecting the educand from evil. For this reason naturalists favour residential schools because the educand's environment can be controlled much better if the educand lives in hostels attached to the school. They also favour the pattern of co-education because this develops more natural attitudes in boys and girls.

15. Revolution in all fields of education. Finally, it can be said that naturalists were responsible for some of the most revolutionary ideas in all spheres of education. As has already been pointed out, naturalists vigorously opposed all traditional thinking on child psychology, educational techniques, curriculum, administration, co-education, etc. Although all their ideas are not found acceptable today, many of the principles propounded by the naturalists are still being applied. For example, such educational principles as learning through activity, going from the simple to the complex, from the concrete to the abstract, from the definite to the indefinite, from the easy to the difficult, and from the known to the unknown, are all principles which were originally propounded by the naturalists. And all these have been established as correct. Modern educationists now agree that the aim of education is not to provide education but to encourage spontaneous development. The significance and efficacy of broad based and comprehensive curricula have been almost universally accepted. Frustration and repression are held to be harmful everywhere. And the role of the teacher is now universally seen as the guide and not the administrator.

CRITICISM OF NATURALISM

The contribution that naturalism made to education is evident from the foregoing account but there are certain elements in it which other educationists find difficult to accept. As a consequence, all such difficulties were used to criticise naturalism on the following grounds:

1. Confused conception of the aims of education. Most educationists find it difficult to accept the aims of education propounded by naturalism. Evolutionists believe that the aim of education is biological development, while Spencer specifies it as self-preservation. Some evolutionists have ascribed more comprehensive aims to education but even these aims do not include everything.

2. Too much emphasis upon the present. In fact, the evolutionist places more emphasis upon the present than upon the future. It can be accepted that infancy is a significant period in life and that the child should be given every opportunity to enjoy it to the full. But if it is agreed that in later life this same individual will have to face the responsibility of earning his livelihood, creating a family and supporting it, it is only desirable that he should be educated and prepared for it. If he is to be a useful citizen of society, he has to be taught his responsibilities and how to fulfil them. The present has its importance, but up to a certain extent it is definitely a preparation for the future.

3. Many explanations of nature. The concept of nature differs from one realist to another. Some evolutionists interpret it in the sense of physical nature while others take it to mean human nature. And even among the latter there is often disagreement about what constitutes normality and abnormality in human nature. Very few, if any, evolutionists have placed any emphasis upon spiritual nature, and for that reason realism separates itself so much from idealism, although both want education to conform to human nature.

4. Defects in the theory of Instincts. Evolutionists believe that the child is possessed of some instincts, and they want education to aim at the development of these. But it is difficult to get the evolutionists to agree about the number and nature of these instincts. McDougall counted 14 instincts while L.L. Bernard made a list of 300 so-called instincts. Most of the instincts are common between man and animal, but the latter does not possess the instinct for religion. Besides, in the light of modern anthropological and sociological research, it is difficult to believe that anything is innate in human nature, after one has discounted the influence of the cultural environment. Dewey has gone so far as to say, "All that is human is learned". Modern psychology does not accept the theory of instinct and specifies that it is well nigh impossible to understand human nature after abstracting it from the cultural environment. Consequently, it is not easy to interpret what is meant by an education according to instinct.

5. Isolation of man from environment. Whenever the evolutionist or naturalist talks of adjustment or maturity, his argument often implies a total isolation from the physical or natural environment, as if this has no influence upon man. Such an attitude is not acceptable to other philosophers. It is generally believed that the human personality is the outcome of an interaction between heredity and environment. Without such an interaction with the environment no development is possible. Besides, as soon as the human being reacts with the environment, the latter itself undergoes immediate change.

6. Adaptation requires man's subordination to environment. It is accepted that man can change his environment to a very great extent, but he cannot be believed to be independent of it while interacting with it. Such an interaction demands some subordination from the individual. On the other hand, when adaptation is accepted as the aim of education by the evolutionists, it is often forgotten that struggle has its own significance and value in the process of growth.

7. Defects in the conception of evolution. The naturalist is an evolutionist but he often forgets that it is difficult to accept man's evolution from the animal stage because of man's language, intelligence and certain other characteristics which distinguish him from the animal. Besides, complete evidence has yet to be discovered to completely substantiate Darwin's theories. Evolutionists have also failed to explain the fact of mutation. Weisman's experiment indicated that although some change occurred in the living being of a particular species over a period of several generations, this change was not transferred to the chromosomes of that species. Besides, the biological explanation of evolution cannot be applied to social and spiritual development. This is what the evolutionists have frequently attempted. Social evolution differs from biological evolution in that it combines conflict with co-operation.

8. Limits of free development of the individual. Naturalist believes in the free development of the individual but the question is, is man really independent and can he exist when completely independent of nature and society? If nothing else, so much stress on the freedom of the individual can at least lead to uncontrolled egoism, which in itself is likely to bring many difficulties. And, in fact, in certain situations, much can be gained by becoming one's own individuality. In order to rise above the conflict between the individual and society, it is necessary to believe that man is not only individual, but also universal to a very great extent.

9. Defects of Hedonism. The application of naturalistic principles to ethics leads to the creation of Hedonism. Spencer established the school of evolutionary Hedonism, according which the aim of life is not the maximum good of the maximum number, but the preservation of life and or social health, implying social balance. Right and wrong are measured by the extent of happiness. In Spencer's own words, "The business of moral science is to deduce from the laws of life what kinds of action necessarily tend to produce happiness, and what kinds tend to produce unhappiness. Its deductions are to be recognised as laws of conduct, and are to be conformed to, irrespective of a direct estimation of happiness or misery". Many arguments have been given to refute this hedonistic principle. Since the biological and the moral worlds differ from each other, the rules of conduct cannot be derived from the history of social conduct. Happiness does not always promote health, neither does misery invariably destroy it. Happiness is not the sole motive of action, just as the longevity of life is not the moral aim of life. In ethics a concept is defined not by its origin but by its objective. Synthesis is not based on ideals. Morality, too, is not an adventitious element of moral consciousness. The concept of a perfect society denies the fundamental tenets of evolutionary theory. The objective of a secular policy is not moral. Many evolutionists have themselves refuted Hedonism as an ethical philosophy. As Rusk puts it, "According to this doctrine there is no moral law, no place for duty for duty's sake: self-sacrifice would be utter foolishness; one's own selfish satisfaction is the greatest good."

10. Defects in education through natural consequences. Naturalism wants to leave the child to the natural consequences of education, on the presumption that he will naturally learn the consequences of his own actions. For example, if he does not wear adequate clothes, he will learn to do so when he feels cold. This is accepted on the presumption that every violation of natural law will bring him pain and thus compel him to change his pattern of behaviour. It is neither proper nor very humane to accept this principle of natural consequences. As T. H. Huxley has commented, "Nature's discipline is not even a word and a blow, and the blow first; but the blow without the word. It is left to you to find out why your ears are boxed". Hence, it cannot be presumed that the child will realise the source of his discomfort when one of his actions leads to some painful consequence. And, besides, in human society such rigid conditions do not prevail. Many people commit mistakes without ever being punished for them. Hence, the child cannot be educated merely by natural results. He also cannot be allowed to completely take the initiative. In many cases it is necessary to warn him, in many cases to prevent him. It is desirable to explain certain casual relationships in order to prevent mistakes.

11. Negative principle. In fact, the evolutionist or naturalist theory is negative because it admits the propriety of an action as long as one can evade the consequences of that action. Can such a principle be applied to social activity? If it is, then it will negative the possibility of achieving any ideal

12. Negation of all human characteristics. Influenced by the concept of evolution, naturalists believe that man is nothing better than the next step after the animals, but man actually possesses many qualities which animals do not possess even in the rudimentary form. For example, man is not merely conscious but also self-conscious. Spearman put this truth in this way, "Psychology is no mere flower of biology but one of its greatest roots". Recall is a quality found in human beings. Many characteristics of the human mind differ from the nervous system of animals. Man is a rational animal, the only living being capable of thinking.

13. Many interpretations of naturalism. To begin with, the very term naturalism has been open to several interpretations. It is often accepted to be a reaction against dogmatism and artificiality, but it is also transformed into positivism, which has faith in science, and later on into Hedonism. Naturalists like Herbert Spencer, T. H. Huxley, T. P. Nunn, Glen Johnson, etc., differ from each other in their ideas to a very great extent. Many of Rousseau's concepts are also not palatable to the naturalists.

One cannot justifiably deny the contribution of naturalism to education, for it has influenced all spheres of it, the aims of education, methods, curricula, school administration, discipline, its significance, etc. It achieved the complete refutation of traditional and dogmatic concepts of education by basing child education on the principles of child psychology and developmental psychology. Although the emphasis laid on experimental teaching was justified, it soon gave way to evolutionary influences. Naturalism limited its interpretations of nature to a very narrow field by considering human nature to be nothing more than biological. Had it chosen to integrate with this the spiritual nature of man, the idealistic school would have had no quarrel with the naturalists. In more recent years, one finds that the gap between naturalism and idealism is rapidly filling up. Modern naturalism is more comprehensive, in that it has abandoned the purely biological explanation and has come nearer the idealistic conception.

7

PRAGMATISM: JOHN DEWEY AND BERTRAND RUSSELL

One of the most important schools of philosophy of education is pragmatism. It is also as old as idealism, naturalism and realism since it is more an attitude, than a philosophy. In the fifth century B. C. Heraclitus said, "One cannot step twice into the same river". Thus Reality is a flux, things are ever changing. Modern pragmatists agree with the Greek sophists. According to Protagores, "Man is the measure of all things". This maxim is the basis of modern humanism. Another famous sophist Gorgias used to say, "Nothing exists and if anything exists we can never know it". This agnosticism has led to relativism in pragmatic epistemology. In modern times Francis Bacon and Auguste Comte were pragmatists. John Dewey regards Bacon, as the prophet of a pragmatic conception of knowledge.[1] Auguste Comte created positive philosophy which formed the basis of pragmatic social philosophy. Pragmatists agree with Comte that the universe is composed of laws and relations and not substance. John Locke said, "Our business is not to know all things but those which concern our conduct" [2]. Immanual Kant used the word pragmatic in a different sense.

MEANING OF PRAGMATISM

According to Robert R. Rusk, the Oxford Dictionary first referred to the term 'pragmatic' in 1643 and the term 'pragmatism' in 1663.[3] According to *The Concise Oxford Dictionary* the term 'pragmatic' means dealing with matters according to their practical significance or immediate importance. The term, 'pragmatism', according to the same source, means, "Doctrine that evaluates any assertion solely by its practical consequences and its bearing on human interests".[4] The term pragmatism has been derived from the Greek term *pragma* which means use. Thus pragmatism is an ism according to which use is the criteria of reality.

1. John Dewey: *Reconstruction in Philosophy*, p. 38. London, University of London Press Ltd., 1921.
2. John Locke: *An Essay Concerning Human Understanding*, 1960, Introduction.
3. Robert R. Rusk: *Philosophical Bases of Education*, p. 68, footnote. London, University of London Press, 1956.
4. *The Concise Oxford Dictionary.* Sixth Edition, IIIrd Impression, 1976, p. 88.

In 1870 in Boston and Cambridge a study circle informally but frequently met for discussion. It was called The Metaphysical Club. As Charles Pierce points out, "It was there that the name and doctrine of pragmatism saw the light".[5] Thus historically speaking the doctrine of pragmatism in contemporary time was first referred by Charles Sanders Pierce in his famous essay of 1878 in the *Popular Science* monthly on "How to Make Our Ideas Clear". Pierce gave it its first clearcut formulation and later decided to use the label "Pragmaticism as one ugly enough to protect his views from unwanted associations going with pragmatism". In point of fact pragmatism is a name which has referred to many varieties of doctrines since Pierce took over from Kant the adjective 'pragmatic' to stress the relation of thought and knowledge to definite human purpose.

PRAGMATISM AND NATURALISM

1. Universality of scientific theories. According to naturalism the scientific conclusions are universal and objective. Pragmatism, however, does not admit any scientific principle to be universal and objective. According to William James, all the laws are determined by space and time, no law is independent of circumstances.

2. Explanation of the world. Pragmatists do not accept the mechanical and impersonal picture of the world drawn by the naturalist which has no place for human values. On the other hand, the pragmatists admit with the idealists that there is a spiritual order behind this mechanical physical world. In the pragmatic world-view, human efforts have been given a respectable place.

3. Opposed to monism. Both the idealists and naturalists are monists, while the pragmatists are pluralists. In the words of Robert R. Rusk, "Pragmatism joins issue with Naturalism and Idealism insofar as both the latter are monistic, seeking to explain nature, man and God by reduction to a single principle—Naturalism to life, Idealism to mind or spirit. Pragmatism regards this way of conceiving the universe as singularly unimaginative and lacking in verity". Thus, in the explanation of the world the pragmatists do not mention one but many elements. In comparison to the naturalists the pragmatists find idealistic standpoint more satisfactory in human life, but while idealists place the source of this satisfaction within man, the pragmatists attribute it to external success.

4. Opposed to abstraction. The naturalists establish a single element in the world through abstraction. The pragmatists, on the other hand, are against all abstractions. They give more importance to concrete things and facts. As William James has explained the pragmatist viewpoint, "He demands a universe with real possibilities, real indeterminations, real beginnings, real ends, real evils, real crises, catastrophes and escapes, a real God, and a real moral life".

5. Opposed to static reality. Explaining the distinction between naturalism and pragmatism concerning the nature of reality, William James has said, 'For Naturalism reality is readymade and complete from all eternity, while for Pragmatism it is still in the making, and awaits part of its complexion from the future". Thus, the Pragmatists believe that our aim is not so much to know the world as to make it. The life should not be rigid or static but dynamic and flexible.

---

5. Pierce: *Chance, Love and Logic* (MR Cohen, Editor), Harcourt, Brace and Co., 1923, p. 19.

It is clear that the pragmatist explanation of reality is nearer to modern human consciousness.

6. Value of moral ideals. The moral values have no place in the naturalist world-view. The pragmatist, on the other hand, considers moral values to be very important in human life. While the naturalist makes moral and aesthetic aims secondary, the pragmatist considers them primary'.

PRAGMATISM AND IDEALISM

As has been already pointed out, in comparison to naturalism Pragmatism is nearer to idealism. However, the two differ in the following respects:

1. Explanation of the world. The idealists explain nature, man and God in terms of one spiritual element. This has led to pragmatists' reaction in metaphysics. According to the pragmatists the world is neutral, neither spiritual nor physical. The presence of an eternal unchanging spiritual substance at the basis of the world is not admissible by logic or experience.

2. Number of reality. As regards the number of reality the idealists are monists while the pragmatists are pluralists. This pluralism is characteristic of pragmatists' explanation not only in philosophy but also in ethics, religion and other fields of life.

3. Change and status. The values, ideals and truths; according to idealists, are eternal and unchanging. According to Pragmatists, on the other hand, there is nothing eternal or unchanging. The world is a constant flux. The truths, values, ideals and postulates change according to space and time.

4. Value of reason. The idealist philosophers consider reason to be most valuable and interest as the source of moral dictates and cultural expressions. According to the pragmatists, on the other hand, reason is and ought to be the slave of passions. It has no other business but to follow will. Man's future depends on his will and his intellect and the will is based upon natural tendencies and not reasoning. Thus, reasoning has got the secondary place in pragmatist psychology.

5. Ends end means. While the idealists emphasise ends, the pragmatists give importance to means in education. This difference makes for the distinction in their contribution to education. While the idealists present aims and ideals, the pragmatists explain important means. However, even in the field of aims and ideals, while the idealists emphasise spiritual values, the pragmatists hold human values in highest regard.

6. Role of concept and action. The idealists are conceptualists. Idea is most important in their philosophy. To the pragmatists, on the other hand, action is more important than idea. This difference makes so much distinction among the two types of thinking concerning teaching methods, and curriculum.

7. Value of the world. Most of the idealist philosophies consider the objective world to be less real than the world of ideas. This has sometimes led to world negating attitude. On the other hand, according to the pragmatists, the physical world and mundane life are the ultimate valuable.

8. Static versus dynamic approach. Thus the idealist thinking is static while the pragmatist thinking is dynamic. The pragmatists present a progressive and evolutionary approach in education.

In spite of the above distinction between the idealism and the pragmatism, the two are nearer than pragmatism and naturalism.

JOHN DEWEY

John Dewey (1859-1952), greatest of the pragmatists and generally recognized as the most outstanding philosopher his country has yet produced, made significant contributions to virtually every field of philosophy as well as to such other areas of inquiry as education and psychology. Active for 70 years as a scholar, he was a prolific writer publishing approximately fifty books and more than eight hundred articles. Many of these have been translated into various foreign languages. New volumes are still coming out with more Dewey material, mainly correspondence; and books and articles on him are appearing at a rapidly increasing rate.

Some Dewey material is at present available only in Chinese. In February and March of 1919 he lectured at the Imperial University of Tokyo, and these lectures were published as *Reconstruction in Philosophy.* While in Japan he was invited to lecture in China also, he spent from May 1,1919 to July 1921 there, finding the developments there of extremely great interest. He lectured extensively in Peking, Nanking, and Shanghai, speaking in English from brief lecture notes; and his lectures were translated and recorded in full on the spot in Chinese by his former students. Dr. Hu Shih, for example, translated his Peking lectures. According to Dr. Hu Shih's account in John Dewey in China",[6] Dewey provided the translators and recorders with his typed lecture notes in advance of each lecture so that they could study them and think out suitable Chinese words and phrases before the lecture and its translation. The translation was checked against his notes before publication in newspapers and periodicals or later publication in book form. What was known as "Dewey's Five Major Series of Lectures" in Peking, some 58 lectures on Modern Tendencies in Education, Social and Political Philosophy, of Education, Ethics, and Types of Thinking, according to Hu Shih, went through ten large reprintings in book form before Dewey left China and continued to be reprinted for at least three decades before government authorities on the mainland put a stop to them. There were also series on such other topics as Democratic Developments in America, Experimental Logic, History of Philosophy, and (as an introduction to Russell's lectures there in 1920), Three Philosophers of the Modern Period: James, Bergson, and Russell.

Fortunately, the Institute for Advanced Projects, East-West Center, University of Hawaii, with Professor Robert W. Clopton as special consultant, had undertaken to translate these materials, and in the fall of 1964 Dr. Tsuin Chen Ou as the first of a team of translators began the work of translation. When this material was available it shed significant new light on various areas of Dewey's thought.

The Southern Illinois University Co-operative Research Project on Dewey Publications has discovered a number of previously unlisted publications by Dewey, and it has assembled the most complete collection in existence of works by and about him. Under the direction of its Editorial Board—Professors George E.

6. Charles A. Moore, ed., *Philosophy and Culture-East and West* (Honoululu, University of Hawaii Press, 1962), pp. 762-769.

Axtelle, Jo Ann Boydston, Joe R. Burnett (University of Illinois), S. Morris Eames, and Lewis E. Hahn— the project, with the co-operation of a number of other leading Dewey scholars, planned a definitive edition in forty or more volumes of all his published writings (books and articles).[7] The materials were to be arranged chronologically with careful textual editing but with a minimum of interpretive comment. The editorial and textual work connected with this pioneering venture for a major American philosopher extended over many years, but it was hoped that the first volume would be ready from the Southern Illinois University Press in 1967. Accompanying *The Work* was a one-volume *Readers' Guide* with interpretive essays by eminent Dewey scholars on the main subject areas of his thought and writings. It was expected that this volume should be completed by 1967 so that it might be used throughout the publication period of *The Work.*

Further evidence of the contemporary relevance of Dewey, especially in education broadly conceived, may be had in connection with the activities of the John Dewey Society for the Study of the Education and Culture. Organized at Atlantic City in February 1935, it existed to promote the study of the educational aims and educative methods of a democratic society. Regular meetings were scheduled in connection with the annual meetings of the National Society of College Teachers of Education. Much of the work of the society was carried on through its Commissions on Meetings and Communications, Monographs in Educational Theory, and Annual John Dewey Lectures. It helped launch the journal, Educational Theory, and it had a distinguished series of year-books going back to 1937 when William H. Kilpatrick edited the first one on *The Teacher and Society.* Among the other editors for this series were Harold D. Alberty, Christian O. Arndt. George E. Axtelle, Harold Benjamin, Theodore Brameld, Boyd H. Bode, John S. Brubacher, Samuel Everett, Hollis L. Caswell, H. Gordon Hullfish, Virgil Clift, Archibald Anderson, Ernest O. Melby, Harold Rugg, William Van Til, Harold G. Shane, Lindly J. Stiles and William W. Wattenberg. The Annual Dewey Lectures have included Ordway Tead, Oscar Handlin, Seymour Harris, Gardner Murphy, Loren Eiseley, R. Freeman Butts, and Huston Smith. Arthur G. Wirth was the current Chairman of the Society's Commission on Publications.

For one who has written so voluminously and who has made major contributions in so many different areas, no brief summary can be fully adequate. Selecting a few emphases, moreover, is especially dangerous in connection with the thought of one who commonly transcended conventional categories and boundaries and who habitually saw special topics in terms of larger contexts. And yet if one is to discuss this complex thinker as well as a group of others in a single chapter, a high degree of selectivity is required. One can only hope that many readers will be led to turn to extensive reading in his works, to supplement this review.

1. Analysis of reflective inquiry. Perhaps the most important single emphasis of John Dewey is his insistence upon applying reflective or critical inquiry to problems or indeterminate situations. What is involved in problem solving or thinking through a problem? What is critical inquiry? How does one apply intelligence to human affairs? Dewey's answer to these questions is set forth in

7. The Editorial Board had the assistance of a larger Advisory Committee under the chairmanship of Professor Willis More, Chairman of the Philosophy Department Southern Illinois University.

its simplest terms in *How We Think*; and a more sophisticated version is given in *Logic; The Theory of Inquiry.* In a sense the phases or steps in a complete act of reflective thinking afford an outline for each of his major works; and he had a lifelong concern with what is involved in reflective thinking.

(i) The first step in a complete act of reflective thinking is the appearance of the problem. This maybe marked by a, more or less, vague sense of something having gone wrong, a breakdown in habitual responses or modes of action. One of our beliefs is questioned, or acting upon it leads to a conflict or perplexity, (ii) The second step or phase is clarification of the problem. Through analysis and observation we gather sufficient data to formulate the difficulty or define the problem. If, for example, a belief is disputed questioning or analysis may indicate what precisely is in dispute, (iii) With the problem clearly stated we pass to the stage of appearance of suggested solutions or hypotheses as to how to solve the problem. Various ideas occur to us as to how it may be solved, (iv) The fourth stage is that of deductive elaboration. We reason out the implications of the various hypotheses. If we take the first hypothesis, we may expect such and such consequences; or we need to make additional observations or gather more information to see what may be expected. If we take the second one, we may expect such and such other consequences; and so on. On the basis of a survey of the implications of the various proposed solutions we decide which to test in action, (v) The fifth step is that of verification. Through observation or experiment we check out the hypotheses or hypotheses which looked most promising to us. If one of the hypotheses works out, the indeterminate situation is replaced by a determinate one in which stable lines of action are possible; instead of the problematic situation or perplexity we have a resolved or clarified one.

These steps or stages do not necessarily come one right after another in the sequence in which these have been listed here. For example, the first three stages may be telescoped in such a fashion that we do not get a clear indication of the stages, but in general, the more difficult the problem, the more likely the stages are to be clearly outlined before it is solved. Or, again, after we have reached the stage of deductive elaboration, we may discover that we need to go back and further clarify the problem or think of additional ways of trying to solve it.

Though this pattern is somewhat oversimplified, in fundamentals it is basically accurate. This is what is involved in problem solving activity whether it is a personal problem, an important social conflict, or a weighty scientific problem. When we solve a problem in this way, moreover, we have not merely a solution to our difficulty but also some descriptive or explanatory statements about how it was solved.

2. View of experience. Experience is one of the central concepts in Dewey's thought, occurring and recurring throughout his writing. Though he finally concluded that he might have done better to use another term, many of his most important works are concerned with clarifying it-for example, his Casus Lectures: *Experience and Nature:* or his *Art as Experience* or *Experience and Education.* For him experience constitutes the entire range of men's relations to, or transactions with the universe. We experience nature and things interacting in certain ways made up of experience.

A brief presentation of Dewey's views can perhaps best be summarized in terms of a contrast with what he calls the orthodox view of experience, that is accepted by both the traditional empiricists and their opponents.[8] Whereas the orthodox view treats experience primarily as a knowledge affair, Dewey speaks of it as intercourse between a living being and its physical and social environment. The traditionalists regard it as a subjective inner affair, separate and distinct from objective reality; but Dewey has always thought of experience as being of a piece with the objective world, which enters into the actions and sufferings of man and which, in turn, may be modified through human response. Instead of a gulf between disparate inner and outer realms of being, one may move freely from experience to that which surrounds, supports, and maintains it. The proponents of the orthodox view have been preoccupied with what is "given" in a bare present, whereas Dewey was more concerned with what might be done to change what is given or taken, in furtherance of human purposes. The older empiricists thought in terms of what has been or is given, looking toward the past if they passed beyond the present. For Dewey the salient trait of experience is its connection with a future. If change is what we are interested in, we look primarily toward the future, and not recollection but anticipation is central for the experimental form of experience.

One of the main differences between Dewey's and the orthodox view of experience, however, turns about the latter's particularism, its concern with sense data to the neglect of connections and continuities, and its supposition that relations and continuities are either foreign to experience or are dubious by-products of it. Dewey, like James, emphasized the relations. The contextual, situational, transactional, or field character of experience stands out in his account. The traditional view opposed experience thought in the sense of inference, but for Dewey experience is full of inference, as might be expected for one who sees the directional and relational character of experience. Where one seeks to control what is to come through employing present environmental supports to effect changes which would not otherwise occur, inference is of vital importance. From the standpoint of the future life-activity of the organism, environmental incidents are favourable or hostile; and if one is to eliminate the latter and insure the former, an imaginative forecast of the future is essential for guidance in this process.

The structure of experience, however, comes out most clearly on Dewey's view in aesthetic experience. There we have experience in full, vivified, clarified and intensified.

3. View of knowledge. Dewey rejects the traditional epistemology which sets up a knower outside the world and then asks about the possibility, extent and validity of knowledge in general. He laughingly suggests that we might equally well have a problem of digestion in general—its possibility, extent, and genuineness—by assuming that the stomach and the food-materials were inhabitants of different worlds. The significant problem is not how such a knower is somehow to mirror the antecedently real out but rather one how one set of experienced events is to be used as signs of what we shall experience under another set of conditions. The important

8. See "The Need for a Recovery of Philosophy" in John Dewey and others, *Creative Intelligence, Essays in the Pragmatic Attitude* (New York Henry Holt and Co., 1117), pp. 3-69.

distinction, moreover, is not between the knower as subject and the world known as object. Instead it is between different ways of being in the movement of things, between an unreflective physical way and a purposive, intelligent one.

On Dewey's view knowledge needs to be placed in the context of the problematic or indeterminate situation and reflective inquiry. Knowledge is more than immediate awareness or the presence of a set of sense data. Having qualities before us does not constitute knowing. Knowledge is always inferential, and the problem is how the processes of inference are to be guided to trustworthy or warranted conclusions. It involves operations of controlled observation, testing, and experimentation. It is a product of inquiry—the steps in a complete act of reflective thinking. Dewey liked Bacon's idea that knowledge is power and it may be tested by the promotion of social progress.

4. Conception of philosophy. In *"The Need for a Recovery of Philosophy"* Dewey declares that philosophy must cease to be "a device for dealing with the problems of philosophy" and become "a method, cultivated by philosophers, for dealing with the problems of men". But the problems of man as he sees them cover a range broad enough to include in one way or another most of the traditional problems as well as many others. The method involves treating philosophy as vision, imagination and reflection; and though the clarifying process may show that certain epistemological problems are pseudo-problems, the fact that they are raised may point to genuine cultural crises. If action at all levels needs to be informed with vision, imagination and reflection to bring clearly to mind future possibilities with reference to attaining the better and averting the worse, there is more than enough for philosophy to do.

Developing an adequate conception of the place of intelligence in human affairs is one important task for philosophy. How can intelligence which is a creation of a culture also be a creator or forming influence on that culture? How can it define the larger patterns of continuity between a stubborn past and an insistent future? How can philosophy adjust the body of traditional beliefs to scientific tendencies and political aspirations which are novel and incompatible? These are tasks which involve the application of reflective inquiry on the broadest scale possible, and in applying it we need to remember. Dewey reminds us in the little essay on *Philosophy and Civilization,* that in philosophy we are occupied with meaning rather than truth. This, of course, is not to deny either the crucial importance of truths as a sub-class of meanings or the relevance of existence to meanings. It is rather to suggest that imaginative sweep, values and significance are our primary concern.

In *Reconstruction in Philosophy* Dewey stresses the social function of philosophy, holding there that the task of philosophy is to clarify men's minds as to the social and moral issues of their day, to enlighten the moral forces which move mankind, and to contribute to the aspirations of men to attain a more ordered and intelligent happiness.

For Dewey, in general, philosophy is both a product of human culture and a process of criticizing or clarifying it, distinguishing meanings within and helping give it direction and form. In *Experience and Nature* he speaks of philosophy as criticism or criticism of criticism; as the "critical operation and function becomes aware of itself and its implications". It becomes a kind of theory of criticism-a consideration of alternating ways of critically evaluating values and beliefs. Meaning and values are focal in Dewey's conception of philosophy, and this aspect is not lost when he treats philosophy as general theory of criticism. For him we criticize for the sake of instituting and perpetuating more enduring and extensive values; and each of the various philosophical disciplines, metaphysics no less than the others, makes its distinctive contribution to this end.

5. Biologism. What is sometimes referred to as Dewey's biologism reflects: (a) his emphasis on the genetic point of view, and (b) his conviction that inquiry has a biological matrix. He was interested in how ideas originate and become more complex, in the parallels between human responses and lower levels, and in the continuity of different species of organic life from the lowest forms to man. To understand the present situation, he held, we inquire into its specific conditions as well as into its probable consequences.

Darwin and James helped Dewey to see the focal importance of the living creature adjusting or adapting to its environment and to view intelligence as a distinctive form of behaviour-one concerned with choosing appropriate means for the attainment of future ends. Whatever else mind may be, it is at least a means of controlling the environment in relation to ends of the life process. Within this framework the senses are not primarily gateways to knowledge but stimuli to action, and sensations are not so many pellets of knowledge but signals to redirect action, or signs of problems to be solved. In *The Influence of Darwin on Philosophy* Dewey suggests that the philosophic lesson of Darwin is that philosophy itself becomes a method of locating and interpreting the most serious of the conflicts that occur in life and a method of projecting ways of dealing with them.

6. Experimentalism. Dewey's experimentalism relates to his analysis of reflective inquiry for which hypotheses, prediction and experimentation are central. An experiment is a programme of action to determine consequences. It is a way of introducing intelligence into a situation. It is an intelligently guided procedure Rediscovering what adjustments an organism must make to its environment to ward off ill or secure goods. Experimentation for Dewey is relevant not merely on the individual biological level, but wherever planned reconstruction of a situation may help effect desired transformation, for example, in social planning or in education. The more important the issue at stake, the more clearly is experimentation seen to be preferable to such alternatives as authoritarianism, simple guesswork or merely waiting for events to run their course.

In some ways the best contrast with Dewey's experimentalism is the quest for certainty. Whereas Desecrates sought demonstrable proof or certainty through reason and Berkeley took sensory awareness as the bedrock of certainty, Dewey argued that what we are really after is not certainty of any sort but security in the face of a hostile environment. We are trying to stabilize responses or adjust successfully to a hostile environment.

7. Instrumentalism. Dewey's instrumentalism also stems from his analysis of reflective inquiry. Ideas are not copies, images or visions of external objects but rather tools or instruments to facilitate an organism's behaviour. They are instruments for operating on things or on stimuli. Things or objects are what we can do with them, and we can distinguish among them by the behaviour reactions they make possible.

Truth, accordingly, is adverbial. It is a way ideas work out in practice. It is a matter of whether hypotheses lead to predicted consequences, an affair of verified predictions or warranted assertions.

Dewey's instrumentalism encourages a new respect for instruments or means. The more we value ends or goals, on his view, the greater is our attention to the means which may bring them about. The separation of goods into natural and moral or into instrumental and intrinsic may have the harmful consequence of making moral and intrinsic goods more remote from daily living besides encouraging us to think that we can have the intrinsic without having to concern ourselves with the instrumental. Viewing any good as merely instrumental, moreover, is fairly sure not to do it justice.

8. Relativism. Dewey's relativism is to be opposed to absolutism and is a way of stressing the importance of context, situation, relationships. To take things out of relations is to deprive them of value and meaning. Absolutes are ruled out on his view, and unqualified generalisations are likely to be misleading. An economic policy or a plan of action is a good relative to a specific situation which makes it desirable. A knife may be good for sharpening pencil and bad for cutting a rope; but to speak of it without qualifications as good or bad is quite misleading.

9. Meliorism. In ethics, according to Dewey's account in *Reconstruction in Philosophy,* the emphasis should be placed on improving or bettering our present situation rather than upon good or bad in some absolute sense. The good, if one is to speak of the good rather than the better, is what will enable us to solve the problem or difficulty. Thus what is usually referred to as a moral end or standard becomes on this view a hypothesis as to how to overcome a moral problem. Since every problematic situation is unique, values are also unique; but if one is to specify an end, then growth, education, or problem solving would be that end. Instead of treating acquisition of skill and attainment of culture as ends, we should see them as marks of growth and means to its continuing difficulties or furthering growth.

In the *Quest for Certainty,* Dewey's Gifford Lectures, we find a somewhat different approach, stressing the construction of the good; and in this construction, it is argued, we have to test our likings, enjoyments and desires. We do this by checking on the conditions and the results of certain forms of enjoyment of liking; and this involves running through the steps in a complete act of reflective thinking. It is not simply a question of whether as a matter of fact we do or do not enjoy or like something but whether this enjoyment or liking meets the test of reflection. It is not merely enjoyed or desired but also desirable or enjoyable in the sense of being worthy of being desired or enjoyed? When we say that something is desirable we are claiming that future consequences will be such as to meet the test of reflection.

Further discussion of Dewey's views on valuation and some of the questions growing out of his view may be found in the *Theory of Valuation*[9] and in Ray Lepley, Editor, *Value: A Cooperative Inquiry*[10] in which Dewey, H. D. Aiken, C.E. Ayres, A.C. Garnett, G. R. Geiger, L. E. Hahn. B. E. Jessup, H. N. Lee, Ray Lepley, E. T. Mitchell, Charles Morris, D. H. Parkar, S. C. Pepper, and P.B. Rice re-examine fundamental issue of value.

10. Humanism. Dewey's humanism stems from his acceptance of the Beconian view that knowledge is tested by promotion of human intelligence based in good part on the experience of modern science for the sake of bettering the human situation. Supernaturalism and the usual dogmas of revealed religion have no place in Dewey's view. As he tells us in *A Common Faith,* the things of greatest value in civilization exist by the grace of the continuous human community in which we are a link and we have the responsibility of conserving, transmitting, rectifying and expanding our heritage of values in order that those who come after us may share it more generously and more securely. Our common faith draws its main stand from our attempt to carry out his responsibility.

Dewey's humanism is expressed also in his democratic outlook. As he saw it, democracy as a way of life is controlled by a working faith in the possibilities of human nature. Granted proper conditions, and Dewey devoted a lifetime to working for them, human intelligence can work out aims and methods by which experience can grow in richness. His faith in discussion, persuasion, education and conference techniques as opposed to force or coercion as a way of resolving differences was at one with his democracy or his faith in human nature. With free inquiry, free assembly and free communication of ideas, he was convinced, reflective inquiry is self-corrective.

11. Art as experience. On Dewey's view, as set forth in *Art as Experience,* there is an aesthetic quality to all experience and not merely to works of art. His account stresses the continuity between everyday experience and art. Wherever experience is vivified, clarified, intensified and unified, we have an aesthetic experience more meaningfully more coherently, and with greater vividness, clarity, and intensity, than daily life ordinarily manifests. The humdrum and the routine are the chief enemies of the aesthetic. Ordinarily, we simply recognize objects for this use, but if we can have full perception of them, take in their full quality for its own sake, then we have an experience in a distinctive sense.

If any experience has the potentiality of becoming something appreciated for its own quality, moreover, human intelligence has the responsibility of applying aesthetic principles, not merely in art, but to our houses, our machine products, our cities, our highways and our general environment.

12. Education and experience. Most of the major theses in Dewey's general philosophy find expression in his philosophy of education. Reflective inquiry is as central for education, on his view, as for any other phase of life or experience. Indeed, for him education is a problem solving process, and we learn by doing, by

9. In *International Encyclopaedia of Unified Science* (Chicago: University of Chicago Press, 1939), II. No. 4.
10. *Op. Cit.* New York, University Press, 1949.

having an opportunity to react in real life situation. In education not indoctrination, but inquiry is focal. Not simply amassing facts but learning to apply intelligence to problem solving has top priority. Education must be experimental without being simply improvisation.

The reconstructive purpose is as much at work in education as anywhere else in experience. As he says in *Democracy and Education,* "Education is a constant reorganizing and reconstructing of experience". Present experiences must be so guided as to make future experiences more meaningful and worthwhile. Though the values and the knowledge of the past are transmitted, this must be done in such a fashion as to broaden, deepen and otherwise improve them. Criticism and not simply passive acceptance is demanded.

Dewey equates education and growth. As teachers we start with the child where he now is, with his present stock of interests and knowledge and seek to help him expand and enrich both his interests and his knowledge and grow as a person in his community and his society. He learns to work responsibly for his own development and for social conditions which will encourage a similar development for all other members of his society. Education must not be simply a means to something else. It should not be merely preparation for the future. As a process of growth it should have its own enjoyable and intrinsically rewarding features at the same time that it helps further continued education, and, on Dewey's view, the test of our social institutions may be found in their effect in furthering continued education or growth.

Dewey himself had considerable reservations over some features of "progressive education", but he continued to emphasize some of the strengths of the newer education as compared with the traditional outlook. His humanism and meliorism are richly exemplified in his account of the theory and practice of education. His philosophy of education stresses the social nature of education, its intimate and multiple relations to democracy, and its cultural significance.

AIMS OF EDUCATION

According to Dewey the aim of education is the development of child's powers and abilities. It is impossible to lay down any definite principle for a particular kind of development, because this development will differ from one child to the next, in conformity with the unique abilities of the individual. The educator should guide the child according to the abilities and powers he observes in it. It is better, in Dewey's opinion, to leave the question of educational objectives unanswered. If a definite aim is ascribed to education, it may do very great harm by compelling the teacher to guide the educand in a particular direction, not in keeping with the innate abilities of the child. In general, the aim of education is to create an atmosphere in which the child gets an opportunity to be active in and contribute to the social awakening of the human race. From the pragmatic standpoint, education aims at creating social efficiency in the child. Man is a social being who must develop within the confines of society, outside which he cannot develop at all. For this reason, education must aim at creating social efficiency and skill.

Pragmatic education aims at instilling democratic values and ideals in the individual, at creating a democratic society in which there is no distinction between one individual and another, each individual is completely independent and willing to cooperate with others. Every individual must be given the freedom to develop his own desires and achieve his ambitions. Every individual must be equal to every other member of society. Such a society can be created only when there is no fundamental difference between the individual and collective interest. Hence, education should create cooperation and harmony among individuals, instilling democratic values in school-going children. In fact, the school itself is a miniature form of a democratic society in which the child undergoes various forms of development, of which moral education and development is the most important. Morality can be developed through active participation, because such participation in the activities of the school trains the child in shouldering responsibility. This develops the individual's character and grants him social skill. Equality of opportunity in the school helps to develop boys and girls according to their own individual traits and inclinations.

Pragmatic education is basically practical inasmuch as it aims at preparing the individual for future life in such a manner that he can fulfil his requirements and achieve contentment. Future life in the pragmatic sense implies not merely individual life but also social life. Dewey was critical of the contemporary modes of education because they tend to drive the child away from democratic life by giving advantages to a small section of society. It also lays more stress on book or formal teaching than is really desirable. This mode of teaching compels the educand to listen long lectures which blunt his own mental powers Hence, Dewey laid the foundations of a progressive education in the form of a Progressive School which aimed at establishing democratic values and developing the child's personality.

CURRICULUM

Dewey believed that the educational process has two aspects — psychological and social.

(*a*) **Psychological.** The curriculum and the method of education should be determined by the child's instincts and abilities. The child should be educated according to his interest and inclination. Education should be attempted only after discovering the interests of the child, and these should be used as the basis for determining the curricula for the various stages of education.

(*b*) **Social.** All education has its beginnings in the individual's participation in the social consciousness of the race. Hence it is necessary to create an atmosphere in the school which will allow the child to take an active part in the social awakening of his group. This improves his conduct and develops his personality and abilities.

Dewey has stressed the following four principles as underlying the formation of educational curricula :

1. Utility. The curriculum imposed on the child must have some utility, meaning thereby that the curriculum should be based on the child's interests and inclinations during various stages of his development. In general, the child evinces four major interests — the desire to talk and exchange ideas, discovery, creation and artistic expression. The curriculum should be conditioned by these four elements, and designed to include the teaching of reading and writing, counting, manual skill, science, music and other arts. It is not desirable to introduce the child to all these subjects at once, but to teach a subject only when it is desired at a particular stage of mental development.

2. Flexibility. It is better for the curriculum to be flexible and not predetermined and rigid. It must be capable of accommodating the changes in the child's interests and inclinations.

3. Experiential. The curriculum should be related to the child's contemporary experiences, and these can be multiplied and reinforced by presenting different kinds of activities in the guise of problems which inspire the child to attempt a solution. In this way, the variety of his experiences can be increased. As far as possible, the teaching of each subject should be related to the content of the child's experiences.

4. Close to life. As far as possible, the curriculum should include only those subjects which can be related to the child's pattern of life at that particular stage. This proximity to life can help in creating a distinctive unity in the knowledge imparted to him and thereby some harmony can be created in the teaching of history, geography, mathematics and language, etc. Dewey was very critical of the contemporary method of dividing knowledge into separate compartments, because he felt that such fragmentation of knowledge was unnatural. As far as possible the various subjects in the curriculum should be harmonized.

EDUCATIONAL METHOD

Dewey, himself a successful educational psychologist, has presented many novels and useful ideas on educational methods in his two books, '*How We Think?* and *Interest and Efforts in Education* . The most well-known principle enunciated by him is the theory of learning by doing, in which the child learns best when he himself performs actions related to particular subjects. The educator is not to stuff the child's mind with information he himself has gathered throughout his life, but to guide the child to those activities by which the child can develop his own natural abilities and qualities. The child should be acquainted with facts while he is engaged in activity relating to those facts. Besides, the child should be confronted with practical difficulties and problems which he should try to solve. Problem solving is a good technique because it adds to the child's experience.

Dewey is of the opinion that there should be integration between the child's life his activities and the subjects he studies. All subjects to be taught to the child should be arranged around his activities in such a manner that he acquires knowledge in the process of doing activities to which he is accustomed. Dewey's principle was later on adopted by Mahatma Gandhi in his plan of basic education.

The next question that arises is that of designing the method of teaching according to the child's interests. Dewey considers interest and effort to be of supreme importance in the process of education. The educator must understand the child's interest before organising the activities which are useful for the child. Given the opportunity to formulate programmes on their own, children will be able to make programmes according to their own interests. It is better if this effort is free of any fear or compulsion, because only then can the children make a programme independently. Once this is done, all school activity takes on the form of self willed activity. Dewey's ideas on educational methods later on led to the evolution of the project method in which the child was made to indulge in those activities which helped in the development of enthusiasm, self-confidence, self-reliance and originality.

In a democratic educational pattern, the child should be made to participate in collective activity which can help in evolving a cooperative and social spirit.

This method of education is apparently very suitable inasmuch as it meets the requirement of educational psychology. But in fact it has one inherent shortcoming that if the education of the child is fashioned exclusively according to the child's natural inclination he will remain ignorant of many subjects. Besides, even his knowledge of other subjects will remain disorganised, objections which are accepted by Dewey himself.

SCHOOL ORGANISATION

Dewey has commented in detail upon the organisation of schools as follows:

Role of the Educator

Pragmatic education grants considerable importance to the educator, who is conceived as a servant of society. His task is to create in the school an environment which will help in the development of the child's social personality and enable the child to become a responsible democratic citizen. Dewey considers the educator to be so important that he goes so far as to call him God's representative on earth.

In dietermining the educator's own behaviour in the school, Dewey accepts democratic principles and educational psychology as suitable guides for shaping the educator's conduct. In order to realise the values of equality and independence in the school, the educator should not treat himself as superior to the children. He must also consciously abstain from, imposing his own ideas, interests, views and tendencies on the children. He must confine his own activity to an observation of the child's own natural inclinations and personality traits, to engaging the child in suitable activities which will help in developing these traits. Hence, it is essential for the educator to pay constant attention to the individual differences of the children. If this is done, administration of the school becomes easier. The educator must also try and engage the children in activities which compel them to think and reason out things for themselves.

Discipline

If the educator conducts himself on the lines suggested above, discipline in the school becomes easy. Difficulties arise only when discipline takes the form of an external force employed to restrain the child from expressing his natural desires. This is the traditional concept of discipline, which was severely criticised by Dewey. He argued that discipline depends not only upon the child's own personality but also upon the social environment in which he is placed. True discipline takes the form of social control and this is evolved when the child engages in collective activity in the school. It is therefore desirable to create an atmosphere in the school which encourages the children to live in mutual harmony and cooperation. Discipline and regularity of habit can be induced in children by making them act in consonance with each other in trying to achieve a single objective. This objective may be social, moral, intellectual or purely physical. School programmes go a long way in creating the child's character. It is therefore better to provide the child with a social environment and a mode which inspire him to self-discipline rather than to subject him to long lectures. By methods such as these the child can be turned into a really social being. A peaceful atmosphere is undoubtedly conducive to good and rapid work, but peace is only a means, not an end in itself. The educator's real task is to engage the children in work which suits their natural inclination. If, in the process, the children come into conflict with each other, it is not desirable to scold them and compel them to be peaceful. Self-discipline is a better weapon, and this can be taught through responsibility. When the educand is faced with the responsibility of looking after most of the work of the college or school he automatically evolves self-discipline.

Participation in social activity is an essential part of educational training, in Dewey's opinion. The school itself is a rudimentary form of society. If the child is encouraged to take part in all collective activities in the school, he will not only be able to maintain discipline in the school, he will also be simultaneously trained for many activities he must perform in social life. Thus he will also learn to lead a disciplined life as an adult.

CRITICISM

Although Dewey's views on educational principles were enthusiastically received, they were also subjected to criticism on the following grounds:

1. Difficulties of not accepting truth to be permanent Pragmatist philosophy does not treat truth as permanent and objective. Instead, as Dewey explains, all truth is relative to time and space. No philosophy is always true or correct. It has its utility only in a particular set of circumstances. And utility is the final criterion of truth. In actual practice, of course, Dewey's philosophy is fairly useful, but when his own principles are applied to his own theories, the latter also become relative to time and space and thus have only a limited utility. Hence, the principle of pragmatism itself becomes only relatively true because it does not accept truth as something permanent.

2. Materialistic bias. Pragmatism was born out of reaction to idealism, and consequently it manifests a distinctly materialistic bias, in contradiction of the spiritual bias of idealist philosophy, At the same time, Dewey wants to realize democratic ideals of freedom, equality and fraternity through education. But it is difficult to understand how this can be done unless he accepts an idealistic basis for his system of education. If worldly success is the only criterion of truth, few if any people will concern themselves with moral superiority, since the latter has no obvious relationship with material success.

3. Absence of any aim of education. The achievement of democratic ideals through education seems to be implicit in Dewey's educational philosophy, because he rarely ascribes particular aim to education in explicit terms. For him, education is life itself, and it is not possible to determine any objective for it. Most scholars disagree with this opinion because they believe that education can progress only when it has some definite aim and objective. There is always some definite purpose in sending the educand to school. And even though school resembles society in many ways, it has a distinct existence within the larger framework of society. Hence, the aims of education must be defined.

4. Excessive emphasis upon individual differences. Modern educational psychology accepts in principle that the curriculum of education must take into account the individual differences of children and that children must be educated according to their individual and unique interests and inclinations both in respect of curriculum and also of the method of teaching. While in theory this is quite acceptable, any attempts to apply it in practice lead to immediate complications. It is almost, if not completely impossible to provide a separate educational plan for every individual child in a school. It is for this reason that all schools nowadays provide a uniform pattern of education imparted in the same manner. Besides, the teacher may have to educate the educand in a subject in which the latter is not all interested. Thus, it is not possible to eliminate many complex and difficult subjects from the curriculum only because the student is not interested in them.

5. Limitations in learning through doing. There is no doubt that the child should learn by actually doing things, as Dewey suggested yet the theory has its limitations. Many facts known to an individual are acquired from another person. It is almost impossible for one individual to experience every fact known to him. Thus, the educand should also try to benefit from the experience of his teacher, educator and colleagues. The educator must also supplement the educand's efforts at self-education with guidance and communication of his own experience.

DEWEY'S INFLUENCE ON MODERN EDUCATION

Many of Dewey's ideas have had great impact on modern education. Some important facts in this connection are:

1. Impact on the aims of education. Nowadays, one of the important aims of education is the teaching of democratic values. Dewey insisted on developing social qualities in the child. In modern schools these aims of education have been accepted as valid.

2. Impact on educational methods. The greatest impact of Dewey's ideas is seen in the methods of education in more recent times. Dewey suggested that education should be based on the child's own experience, and also that the method of teaching should vary according to the interests and inclinations of each individual child. These ideas influenced modern teaching techniques and led to active teaching in schools. One such school is the Activity School. The project method is also a result of Dewey's ideas. Even in the other schools, attention is paid to the principles of child psychology which guide the educator in creating an atmosphere suitable for developing social consciousness in the educand.

3. Impact on curriculum. The impact of Dewey's ideas on the subject of curriculum led to the introduction of manual skill subjects into modern curricula. Special importance is now being attached to various kinds of games, objects, the use of certain tools and implements, etc. In selecting the subjects to be taught, attention is now paid to the individual interests and abilities of the child.

4. Impact on discipline. As a result of Dewey's theorising on the subject of discipline, now the educand is entrusted with much of the work done in the school. In this manner the educand is trained in self-control and democratic citizenship. Apart from this, once the educand has to face responsibility, he is compelled to think scientifically and reason out things for himself.

5. Universal education. Dewey's thinking and ideal also led to faith in universal and compulsory education. Education aims at the development of personality. Hence every individual must be given the opportunity to develop his personality through education. The current stress on the scientific and social tendency owes much to Dewey's influence. He pointed out that education was social necessity, in that it was not merely a preparation for life, but life itself. It aimed at the development of both the individual as well as society. This leads to the comprehensive development of the individual.

BERTRAND RUSSELL (1872-1970)

In contemporary times the philosophy of education of Bertrand Russell is a fine example of pragmatic approach to education. Among his most important works may be mentioned:

(1) *Principles of Social Reconstruction*, 1916.
(2) *The A.B.C. of Atoms*, 1923.
(3) *The A.B.C. of Relativity*, 1925.
(4) *On Education*, 1926.
(5) *The Analysis of Matter.*
(6) *Principia Mathematica*, 1927.
(7) *The Outlines of Philosophy*, 1928.
(8) *Sceptical Essays*, 1928.
(9) *Marriage and Morals*, 1929.
(10) *The Conquest of Happiness*, 1930.
(11) *The Scientific Outlook*, 1931.
(12) *Education and the Social Order*, 1932.
(13) *Freedom and Organization*, 1934.
(14) *Power: A new Social Analysis*, 1928.
(15) *An Enquiry into Meaning and Truth*, 1940.
(16) *A History of Western Philosophy*, 1946.
(17) *Human Knowledge, Its Scope and Limits*, 1948.
(18) *Authority and Individual*, 1949
(19) *Now Hopes for a Changing World*, 1951.
(20) *The Impact of Science on Society*, 1952.

Philosophical Ideas

Russell's philosophy has been called *Logical Atomism.* For the first time Russell propounded his mature views on Logical Atomism in a series of Lectures, delivered in London, in the year 1918. Later on, the University of Minnesotta published them under the title, *The Philosophy of Logical Atomism.* Russell was an eminent mathematician. He developed his philosophy of Logical Atomism as a consequence of his deep and penetrating studies in the philosophy of mathematics. By atom Russell meant that point in analysis where further analysis is not possible. In other words, logical atom is the irreducible element of logical analysis. Thus, Russell tries to find irreducible elements through logical analysis instead of physical or chemical analyses. Explaining the reasons for naming his philosophy Logical Atomism, Russell writes, "The reason that I call my doctrine logical atomism is because the atoms that I wish to arrive at as the sort of last residue in analysis are logical atoms and not physical atoms".

The philosophers subscribing to the viewpoint of Logical Atomism believe that logical analysis is a method of discovery. According to Bertrand Russell, we can learn about the fundamental elements of the universe by using the technique of logical analysis. The fundamental task before philosophy is the discovery of the basic elements of the universe and this is possible through analysis of the gross objects. The philosophers like Hegel, F.H. Bradley and B. Bosanquet do not accept the technique of logical analysis to be valid. According to them an object upon analysis ceases to be what it originally was; it is transformed into something else. For example, if we analyze man into his limbs, this would be distortion. The man can exist as a totality only; his limbs have no existence apart from this totality. Therefore, according to them, we can understand things as a unity; apart from this unity they are not real but merely appearance. Russell, however, rejects this line of argument and firmly believes in the efficacy of the logical analysis to reveal reality. It is, according to him, a most appropriate means of discovery. It may not be practically a very fertile method in philosophic inquiry; but undoubtedly, there is no theoretic difficulty or problem in its application to philosophy. The logical analysis is different from the physical or chemical analysis. David Hume also used the analytic method in his philosophy, but his method was psychological and not logical. In psychological analysis we analyze memories, thoughts, emotions and such psychological processes, whereas in logical analysis the objects of analysis are concepts and propositions. The main object of logical analysis is the discovery of the fundamental elements of the universe and from this it follows that logical atomist philosophy postulates the reality of the universe and the existence of facts therein.

After the First World War Russell published his famous work *Principles of Social Reconstruction* in 1916. In this book he maintained that expression of creative tendencies of the individual and society is the aim of human life. Creativity can be expressed in a democracy and free atmosphere. It is the opposite of possessive tendencies which are the major source of evil in social institutions. Russell maintained that family, marriage, education, religion, state and other human institutions should be guided by creative tendencies and not possessive tendencies. Happiness is the result of expression of creativity. Therefore, Russell suggested reconstruction of social institutions and social organisation in such a way as to realise maximum expression of creativity.

Aim of Education

The aim of education, according to Russell, is to create individuals who are creative and may realise a creative society. Such a system will be democratic. According to Russell, one cannot progress without education. Therefore, with Dewey and other American educationists, Russell supported democratic system of education. He appreciated American system of education as an ideal system. The aim of education is to develop the child in such a way as to express his creative tendencies. In this process the educand should develop vitality, courage, sensitiveness and intelligence. The educated persons must have openness of mind. Observation, patience, industry and faith in the possibility of knowledge are necessary for everyone who wants to learn. The above-mentioned four qualities are necessary for the development of character and personality.

General Principles of Education

The child's education should start at the age of six years. At this stage the aim of education should be to satisfy curiosity and to develop the natural skills of the child. The most important traits required for the educand are curiosity, freedom from prejudice, faith in the possibility of knowledge, preservance, intense, durable and voluntary attention, patience and realism in ideas, words and action. Education must be interesting according to the educands stage of development. The teacher should act as a friend, philosopher and guide.

Nursery Schools

The responsibility of the early development of the child may be entrusted to nursery schools. Nursery education must be free and compulsory. The teacher at this stage should be well versed in psychology and medicine so that he may help in the physical development of the child. Kindergarten and Montessori schools are ideal for nursery education.

Pre-Primary Education

At this stage care should be taken to provide education according to the individual peculiarities of the children. The children should develop the ability of reading and writing. This should be creative during the first five years. Mental exercises such as the study of mathematics may be postponed up to the age of seven years. Before it a knowledge of geography and history and general knowledge may be given. The teaching of history and geography should start at the age of five years. Children may be allowed to develop skill in art and languages. Teaching of science and mathematics should start between the age of 12 and 14.

Arithmetic, Algebra, Geometry, Physics, Chemistry and Biology may form part of the curriculum during this period. Classical languages should be taught between 12 and 11 years of age.

Education between 14 and 18 years

Russell has classified curriculum into:

1. Classical languages,
2. Mathematics and Science,
3. Modern Humanities.

Science and Mathematics are correlative, however, they may be taught separately. By the age of 18 the child must learn at least one of these special groups.

Teaching Method

The teaching method should be based upon interest of the child. Educational standards must be maintained. The teacher should himself have sound knowledge of the subject. He should be well prepared and motivate students to learn. Along with interesting subjects the students must learn uninteresting subjects in science and mathematics. The teacher should try to make these subjects interesting. The educand should actively participate in the learning process. Learning by doing is an important method. Individual work should be given more importance than class work. The students may be given guidance and opportunities for developing their individual potentialities. Academic, physical and social development should go together. The school should be treated as a miniature society and the students may be asked to develop interest in all sorts of subjects, social, political, religious and secular. They should be taught to think independently. Their aim should be the search of truth. Free exchange of ideas should be developed.

School Organisation

There may be day schools and residential schools, since both have their own merits and demerits. These schools should be organised on democratic basis. Either of these two type of schools may be selected for the child on the basis of his circumstances, health, age, household conditions, nature and interests. The parents should select a suitable school for the child after careful consideration.

University Education

University education should be allowed only to the able and willing students. The aim of university education is firstly to expand knowledge and research and secondly to prepare trained men and women for various vocations. Admissions to the universities may be given according to merit. The teachers should encourage the students to study books giving necessary knowledge and also catering individual tastes, interests and abilities. The teacher should guide the students in their studies and evaluate their abilities. The teachers themselves should be free from financial worries. They should get sufficient leave for enrichment of their knowledge. Research work is an important aim of universities. The universities are research workshops. The research work should aim at welfare of humanity and progress of the world.

FUNDAMENTAL PRINCIPLES OF PRAGMATISM

The following are the fundamental principles of pragmatism in the field of education:

1. Pluralism. Philosophically, the pragmatists are pluralists. According to them there are as many worlds as human beings. The ultimate reality is not one but many. Everyone searches truth and aim of life according to his experiences. The truth changes according to different spatio-temporal circumstances.

2. Emphasis on change. The pragmatists emphasise change. The world is a process, a constant flux. Truth is always in the making. The world is ever progressing and evolving. Therefore, everything here is changing.

3. Utilitarianism. Pragmatists are utilitarians. Utility is the test of all truth and reality. A useful principle is true. Utility means fulfilment of human purposes. The results decide the good and evil of anything, idea, beliefs and acts. If the results are good, these are good, if bad these are evil. Beliefs and theories are determined by circumstances. Utility means satisfaction of human needs.

4. Changing aims and values. The aims and values of life change in different times and climes. The old aims and values, therefore, cannot be accepted as they are. Human life and the world is a laboratory in which the aims and values are developed. Everyone should seek aims and values according to his tendencies and abilities.

5. Individualism. Pragmatists are individualists. They put maximum premium upon freedom in human life. Liberty goes with equality and fraternity. Everyone should adjust to his environment.

6. Emphasis on social aspects. Since man is a social animal, therefore, he develops in social circumstances. His success is success in society. The aim of education is make him successful by developing his social personality.

7. Experimentalism. Pragmatists are experimentalists. They give more importance to action than ideas. Activity is the means to attain the end of knowledge. Therefore, one should learn by doing constant experimentation which is required in every field of life. According to William James, "Pragmatism is a temper of mind, an attitude; it is also a theory of the nature of ideas and truth, and finally it is a theory about reality".

FORMS OF PRAGMATISM

According to H. H. Home, "The main principle of pragmatism is that the theories that work are true". As E. S. Brightman maintains, "Primarily, pragmatism is a criterion of truth." According to them everyone should discover his truth according to his experience and commonsense. The following four types of pragmatism are distinguished according to emphasis:

1. Humanistic pragmatism. This type of pragmatism is particularly found in social sciences. According to it the satisfaction of human nature is the criterion of utility. All truths are human truths. As the British humanist philosopher F.C.S. Schiller pointed out, "Some London squires are circular". Contradiction in this statement disappears when we know that the term squire here means the meeting of roads and not the geometrical figure known by this name. Similar instances may be multiplied in different social sciences. In philosophy, in religion and even in science man is the aim of all thinking and everything else is a means to achieve human satisfaction.

2. Experimental pragmatism. Modern science is based upon experimental method. The fact which can be ascertained by experiment is true. In other words, whatever works in the real world is the truth. The truth of a theory in science can be ascertained by its workability. No truth is final, truth is known only to the extent it is useful in practice. The pragmatists use this criterion of truth in every field of life. The field of experiment, however, is widest in the field of science. In science, experiment is the only basis for arriving at conclusion in a controversial matter. The human problems can be solved only through experiment. This is true even in the field of religion. In his famous book *Varieties of Religious Experience* William James has advised that everyone should discover his God, mode of worship and man-God relationship by experiments in his own life. No other proof is required for a belief. By experiment in a field of life, one may know what to believe and what not to believe, what to do and what not to do. Whatever is proved by experience is true.

3. Nominalistic pragmatism. When we make any experiment we attend to the result. Our aim is examination of the material. Some hypothesis about the results invariably precedes every experiment. According to nominalistic pragmatism, the results of an experiment are always particular and concrete, never general and abstract. According to medieval European nominalistic philosophy, a universal is only a name. While only particulars are existing, the universals have no concrete existence. For example, while we find existing human individuals, we do not find humanity outside these individuals. In the words of E. S. Brightman,[4]"This kind of pragmatism is closely affiliated with sense experience as criterion for the particulars that we meet are mostly sense data, including their relations". In the field of education emphasis is laid on concrete particular things and their experiences in comparison to verbal knowledge.

4. Biological pragmatism. According to John Dewey, "The pragmatic test is found in the function of thought in adapting the human organism to its environment". Experimentalism of John Dewey is based upon this biological pragmatism according to which the ultimate aim of all knowledge is harmony of the man with the environment. Education develops social skill which facilitates one's life. The school is a miniature society which prepares the child for fixture life. From the biological point of view, man is a psycho-somatic being. Everyday we begin our work by means of set habits. Suppose some day we receive a letter which raises a problem requiring immediate decision the success of thinking in this function depends upon the best answer to the problem.

PRAGMATISM IN EDUCATION

Pragmatism emerged as the twentieth century revolution against the nineteenth century rationalism, dogmatism, universalism and monism, etc. On the basis of their philosophy, pragmatists refuted the doctrines of other thinkers in the sphere of education and presented their own novel propositions. Some of the more important pragmatic concepts are the following:

1. Importance of human effort. Pragmatists believe that education depends upon the active participation of the child. The entire form of the universe is based on human effort and man is the architect of his own destiny.

2. Faith in the future. The pragmatic thinker is convinced of the brilliant and prosperous future of the human race. He believes that by making continuous and dedicated effort in the sphere of education, man can create a better adjusted and more powerful generation.

3. Empiricism. It is suggested that, at every stage of education, the educator and the educand should refer every fact to his own experience and interpret it in that light. Only then can the new piece of information become a part of his life. Hence, only vocal or verbal education is not enough. It cannot be sufficient until it is based on and related to experience. For this reason, pragmatists believe that the child should be given oral instruction, but this instruction should be supplemented by experience in the fields related to each particular subject.

4. Experimentation. Pragmatic philosophy believes in continuous experimentation in every aspect of the educator-educand relationship and in every sphere of education. These experiments will reveal many new facts which can be useful in modifying the curricula, educational methods, aims of education, etc. Seen from this viewpoint, the school itself is a laboratory in which the educator is continuously experimenting. This approach of the pragmatic thinkers has given immense encouragement to educational psychology and child psychology, both of which have experienced remarkable progress.

5. Dualism. Concerning the aims, methods, curricula, etc., of education, pragmatism adopts a dualistic approach. It demands that every educator is to base his education on his own experience and philosophy, while every educand is required to acquire an education in keeping with his own specific inclinations, interests and abilities.

6. Stress on practical success. The only criterion of the propriety of teaching methods, aims and curricula is the individual's success in later life. Only those principles of education are correct which take the educand to success. Our only aim is to satisfy our natural desires and to develop life. All that assists in this process is true and good, and knowledge of this truth can be obtained only through experience and experimentation.

7. Humanitarianism. Pragmatism aims to create humanitarian values in every sphere of education, the methods of teaching, aims, curricula, etc. Education of all kinds should aim at evolving human values.

8. Democracy. Pragmatists are fundamentally democratic because democratic society is the best means of achieving humanitarian ideals. They want to utilise education to create democratic values and ideals in educands, so that they can be trained to occupy a responsible place in a democratic society.

9. Emphasis on human personality. Pragmatists attach the greatest importance to the human personality, because they consider it the most significant element in the process of education. Education must be paidocentric, based on the natural activities and inclinations of the child. Besides, it must aim to make the child capable of adapting to the social environment.

10. Social function of education. Brubacher points out that the pragmatic conception of education is based on two basic principles, the first that education has a social function and the second that it must provide experience to the child. Knowledge for its own sake is a principle which the pragmatist does not accept. For him, knowledge must have some purpose, the purpose of adaptation which must take place in the social context. In the school the educand must be trained to become used to a democratic pattern of life. Pragmatists stress the importance of social values. Society is composed of man's social experience. One important mode of education is for the educand to participate in social experience. The school itself is only a miniature society, which should be organised on democratic principles of society. If this is done, then the child can acquire many democratic qualities in the process of his education, and these qualities will facilitate his social life later on. In such a society, these social qualities can be easily acquired because a democratic society stresses the importance of equality, liberty and fraternity. Prejudices relating to caste, language, religion, region, etc., can and should be eliminated by creating a we-feeling in the school. The organisation of the school, the administrative system, the curriculum, in fact, everything pertaining to the school should be so evolved as to prepare the educand for a democratic social life.

11. Comprehensive education. Pragmatists believe that the aim of education is a comprehensive practical education, a concept of education which is based on the philosophy of liberal education. The aim of education is to achieve the educand's intellectual, moral, aesthetic, physical and spiritual, in fact, every kind of development. Neither knowledge nor ideals, in themselves are the ends. They are only means to satisfy certain human needs, just as education is intended to facilitate human life. Not only the ideals of goodness, beauty and truth, even spirituality and religion are means of developing life. Hence, education must be comprehensive and it must aim at developing the educand's personality in order to help him achieve a better social adjustment.

THE AIMS OF EDUCATION

The various characteristics of the pragmatic concept of education clearly indicate the aims of education as conceived of by pragmatists. Pragmatic thinking is opposed to all kinds of dogmatism, blind faith, narrow mindedness, etc. It objects to imposing some particular ideal on the child against his wish. Besides, it is not prepared to accept an ideal as correct or good merely because it has been so accepted in the past and because some famous educationists have propounded it. Pragmatism favours frequent experimentation in the field of education in order to determine more modern ideals which accord with present-day social life. In the words of Brubacher, "The progressive education has no fixed aims or values in advance. Educational aims, no matter how well authenticated by the past, are not to be projected indefinitely into the future. In a world rendered precarious and contingent by a compound of the novel and the customary, educational aims must be held subject to revision as one advances into the future. If education has any general aim in the light of which their successive revisions can take place, it is only that of pupil's growth. But growth itself has no end beyond further growth. In other words, education is its own end". It is apparent, thus, that pragmatists accept growth or development as the aim of education. The various ramifications of this aim are not discussed in detail, for they are to be discovered in the future. The pragmatist refuses to lay down any aim or ideal which can be permanently valid, its validity unchallenged by changes in time and space. All the aims of education must be concerned with the present and the future, and must be subject to modification. As John Dewey puts it, "Education, as such has no aims; education is an abstract idea. Only persons have aims. And the aims of persons are indefinitely varied, differing with different children, changing as children and their teachers grow. Stated aims, such as we are about to make, will do more harm than good unless they are taken only as suggestions as to how to look ahead for consequences, to observe conditions and to choose means in the liberating and directing of children's energies". Obviously, then, the aims of education are mere suggestions, not to be taken literally. They are to be taken as guides by the educator so that he is assisted in his task of educating the child. He is primarily concerned with training the educand in facing those situations which are likely to arise in his future life. In providing such a training, the educator is to take advantage of any aim that helps his effort. John Dewey believes that in fact these aims are to be determined by the educator himself. Despite this, he points out, that the educational aim must possess the following three elements in order to be a good or proper aim:

1. Such aims are based on the educand's actions and needs.
2. They elicit the educand's co-operation.
3. They are specific and temporary, not permanent and general.

Keeping in mind the above directive principles, it is easy to arrive at the aims of education. But this does not imply that the pragmatic thinkers have not adduced any aim of education themselves. If one glances at the criterion of good educational objectives one can see that by thinking along the lines suggested by it, the pragmatist does arrive at some conclusions. Dewey points out, "Education is all one with growing even as growing is all one with living". Thus, the aim of life is growing, and hence education aims at growing. Put differently, it implies, that education aims at the comprehensive development of the educand. Despite this, such imprecision and lack of definiteness has led to confusion in educational circles in America. Commenting on this, Bode points out, "The chief defect in American education today is the lack of a programme, a sense of direction. It has no adequate mission or social gospel". Although this is one criticism of the pragmatic conception of education, it does apply in its totality because the pragmatic aims of education imply that education must aim at realizing democratic values in life. The United States of America is the representative of democratic societies in the world, and it is vigorously engaged in protecting democratic values against the constant onslaught of communist thinking. Hence, pragmatic thinking in America indicates that education aims at creating a democratic environment in society which can instill in the educand a respect for democratic institutions. Kilpatrick, the finest exponent of Dewey's philosophy of education in America, is correct in saying, "Our school rooms must become living democracies, that in a democracy it is self-directing personalities that we try to build, the kind that can carry forward life even more successfully in a developing world, and that the progressive development of a better life for all men is the basis out of which morality and moral conduct arise". It is evident that pragmatism favours the democratic ideals of education.

CURRICULUM

As has already been pointed out, pragmatists favour an educational curricula which permits the educand to develop all his qualities and obtain all knowledge that he can use fruitfully in future life. They have suggested the perusal of the following guidelines in determining a curriculum:

1. Principle of utility. Pragmatists are utilitarians who believe that utility lies in facilitating human adjustment and adaptation. The greater the satisfaction of human needs, the greater is the utility of the object achieving such satisfaction. The more it helps the child to adapt in his later life, the greater is the utility of his education. Hence the curriculum must make it easy for the child to later on take up some profession. For this reason, technical and scientific education forms an important part of the pragmatic curriculum. Pragmatists suggest that girls should be taught home science and boys trained in agriculture and the sciences. Apart from this, great stress is laid on physical training because it is essential for physical development. Putting it briefly, pragmatists favour the inclusion of all those subjects which will help the educand in adapting to his circumstances in later life. That is why it is suggested that the curriculum should include history, geography, mathematics, hygiene, etc. No uselesss subject which cannot assist in the child's adaptation, should be included in the curriculum. The aim of education is human progress which can be achieved through various kinds of knowledge. Only those subjects the knowledge of which can assist in this progress should be taught.

2. Principle of child's interest. The child's own interest plays a significant part in the process of learning. Generally, children evince four kinds of interests-talking, searching or discovering, creative activity and artistic manifestation. In order to shape the curriculum according to these interests, it must be made to include reading, counting, handicraft, painting, etc. As the child develops, his interests also undergo change and modification, and therefore it is desirable that the curriculum at different stages of education should accord with the interests manifested by the educand at that stage.

3. Principle of child's experience. Being empiricists, the pragmatic thinkers insist on teaching through providing the child with actual experience rather than rote learning. Thus, teaching through books should be supplemented by programmes which provide practical experience of various kinds. In this connection, Dewey has pointed out, "Abandon the notion of subject matter as something fixed and ready made in itself, outside the child's experience; create thinking of the child's experiences as something hard and fast; see it as something fluent, embryonic, vital; and we realise that the child and the curriculum are simply two limits which define a single process.... The studies represent the possibilities of development in the child's immediate crude experience". Thus, the pragmatic conception of a curriculum is dynamic. It is desirable to create such a community and environment in the school which will enable the child to learn the technique of self-discipline and evolve qualities of citizenship in it.

4. Principle of integration. Pragmatists believe that knowledge and intelligence are same all over the world, and that is why integration is of special importance in education. In the school, the different subjects should not be completely segregated from each other, because the subjects themselves are not important. What is more important is the human activity they encourage. The educand should be encouraged to acquire knowledge of many subjects and therefore the teaching of various subjects should not be separated, but integrated into a single unit.

THE EDUCATOR

The pragmatic methodology of education is based on psychological facts, and in direct contrast to the naturalist method, it grants far greater importance to the educator. Like the idealists, the pragmatist believes the educator to be a guide and a counsellor who educates the child in self-discipline and active participation. In fact, the educator is the most important element in the school's social environment. By coming into contact with the educator, the educand can develop a set of very desirable and useful social habits, attitudes and interests. The educator can help this process by constantly observing the educand and devising new ways and means of solving the various problems that afflict the child. In this, he should also concentrate on motivating the educand himself use his intelligence to solve such problems. It is essential for the educator to present a good model in his own behaviour to create an atmosphere of co-operation and brotherhood. On the one hand, he must examine the child's habits and the characteristics of its personality, while on the other he must try to discover the conditions under which the child can be usefully influenced. The intelligent and devoted educator is forever studying the methods by which various subjects can be successfully taught to the educand. He realizes that many things unconsciously influence the educand in the school. Since this influence comes from the child's natural action and reaction to the environment in the school, the educator must aim at creating a desirable social environment and at evolving proper educational techniques.

EDUCATIONAL METHODS

The pragmatic methods of education are based on psychology and sociology, subject to the conditions that they give adequate scope for active participation by the educand and also that the method adopted must be dynamic and changeable. Both these conditions are laid down by the pragmatists because they believe in teaching through actual experience. One of the methods evolved by them is the Project method. Pragmatic thinkers point out that the success of any educational philosophy lies in its ability to raise the standard of teaching. They are critical of the traditional methods of teaching, because they believe in constant experimentation. They revolt against the traditional belief that the educand should sit at the educator's feet and learn anything that is thrown at him by the education. For the pragmatist, education lies not in learning what the educator teaches, but in developing the ability of independent cogitation. And this is possible only when the method of teaching is purposeful and is fashioned by the child's interests, desires and inclinations.

Pragmatism refuses to distinguish between theory and practice. True education lies not in knowing but in doing, and the child learns by active Work, either in group activity or individual activity. This is known as the method of learning by doing. The educand has to learn not from the educator's experience but by his own experience, and this experience cannot be replaced by books, schools or any other institution. The first element in any educational method is the educand's own effort. Once he motivates himself to learn something, he needs no encouragement to gain knowledge. This does not imply that verbal teaching is meaningless. All that is implied is that the teacher must create a set of circumstances in which the child is inspired to face the situation. The educator must also provide the child with the means of facing the situation and solving any problems inherent in it.

The principle of integration is of major importance in pragmatic theory. It is believed that knowledge should not be fragmented. The process of learning should be an integrated one, because it is natural for human beings to create a unity in their experience. Man forever tries to create a unity in the myriad impressions which impinge upon him. The educator must take care that the child achieves a synthesis of all the information that he gathers in the process of education. One of the methods of achieving this is purposeful teaching. All these qualities can be seen in the Project method invented by Kilpatrick, Dewey's follower. In Kilpatrick's own words, "A project is a whole-hearted purposeful activity proceeding in a social environment". In the project method the educand is presented with a problem in the form of a project. He makes his best effort to try to put this project into practice. And, because it is posed in the form of a problem, the child is inspired to solve the problem. Most of the problems of day-to-day life, and the solution of such problems requires more than mere mental activity. The educand is compelled to bring into play all his other faculties, in order to solve the problem. During the task the environment is entirely natural. As far as possible the educand is made aware of the importance of the project. As the problem changes, the form of the project also changes. In the early stages of growth the child is faced with simpler problems, which grow more complex as he grows older and improves his ability to face it. Some of these educational projects relate to handicrafts, linguistic difficulties, problems concerning scientific subjects, problems of history and geography, trade and industry, etc. The first step in the project method is to determine the objective, and then to consider the various ways in which it can be achieved. The next step is to formulate a project for achieving it. Following this the project is put into actual practice and finally the success or failure of the project is evaluated. All that remains is to prepare a complete detailed report of the project. The merits of this method lie in the fact that it involves active participation and hence it takes the educand along the path of self-development and self-discipline. Being psychological in nature, it helps to evolve social and civic qualities in the individual and thus leads to success in adult life. The project method has been particularly successful in the case of curricular programmes. On the whole, this method of education is natural, purposeful and highly motivating.

DISCIPLINE

Even in general, discipline is an important factor in school life and administration, but under the pragmatic pattern of education it assumes special importance.

Pragmatists believe that the child must benefit from his social environment, and this he obviously cannot do, in the absence of discipline. According to the pragmatist theory, discipline is primarily social, and it emerges through active participation in group activity and purposeful activity. In the words of Dewey, "Out of doing things that are to produce results and out of doing in a social and cooperative way, there is born a discipline of its own kind and type". This is self-discipline, the foundation of the educand's character. In the school, the educand must be permitted to perform those activities which help him to develop such qualities as self-reliance, independence, sociability, co-operation, sympathy, etc.

Freedom is an important element in the pragmatist conception of discipline, for it is assumed that the aim of education is to generate democratic qualities in the educand. Of these democratic qualities, the first and most important is liberty. Consequently, it is only desirable that the educand be given as much freedom as is possible. In democratic countries, educators try to protect this freedom as much as they can. They realise that if this freedom is taken away from them, schools and colleges will never be used as the means of social progress. This freedom is the root of all true discipline, because this discipline is never imposed from outside. It is self-discipline. That is why the pragmatist believes in an intimate relationship between freedom and discipline. The aim of discipline is to create in the educand a social consciousness which will prevent him from indulging in anti-social activity. He is also inspired by this self-discipline to engage in those activities which lead to the fulfilment of his social obligations. The school's only responsibility is to equip the educand with all those qualities, such as responsibility, inspiration, insight, etc., by the use of which he can assume the role of a responsible democratic citizen. Discipline certainly does not mean a simple obedience of rules or commands imposed from outside. When such commands issue from the individual's own mind, the obedience of them amounts to self-discipline. Blind obedience is, in fact, a negation of democracy. All that the educator has to do to create discipline is to evoke a sense of social responsibility in the child, not to compel the child to submit to external pressure. Social responsibility helps the educand to become disciplined and this discipline helps him in successfully performing all personal and social tasks. This is the psychological justification of discipline. The pragmatic educationist constantly experiments in order to discover new ways to creating real discipline in the school. As a result of such untiring effort, many new methods have been evolved.

CRITICAL EVALUATION

Though the contribution of pragmatism in the field of education is undeniable, the following criticisms have been levelled against it:

1. Biological bias. The pragmatist philosophy of education suffers from biological bias. As reason has been subordinated to passions, there is a likelihood of uncontrolled expression of passions.

2. Limitation of the theory of truth. According to the pragmatist expression, that idea is true which explains our problem. The truth of any idea does not depend on the fact of its conformity with reality. The true ideas, according to the pragmatist, are workable. According to the realist, on the other hand, the true is that which correctly represents the facts. For example, the proposition that the sun shines is true as it is a fact. Thus the criterion of a concept is its factuality. It should correspond to facts. What the pragmatists call truth is the impact of truth according to the realists. Now, if the criterion of truth supported by pragmatists is applied to their philosophy, it will be held true only if its followers succeed. However, success may also be found in the case of idealist and realist. Again, the pragmatist's theory of truth is not accepted everywhere and this failure is an argument against its truth. Now, if some one points out that it may be true in fixture, this criterion will not be pragmatist since it will have to be submitted that the present success is not a necessary attribute of truth. John Dewey has admitted the influence of circumstances. Then, the pragmatist theory will also change. Such a view will fail to provide any theory of truth. As H.H. Horne has pointed out, "The truth that does not change is so because it correctly represents a situation". Thus pragmatist theory of truth is self-contradictory. It will lead to conflicting theories and criteria everywhere. So many examples confirming this truth may be cited in different fields of knowledge. While pragmatist approach may encourage original thinking about so many problems in a brilliant student, it will confuse the average and below average student since he wants a definite answer to his question. Again, sometimes even wrong theories succeed at least for the time being. In such cases, they may be taken as right and correct.

3. Eternity and permanence. Pragmatist denies any eternity and permanence to anything. He rejects the idealist worldview and everything eternal along with it. At least in the field of aims and ideals of education some sort of permanence is necessary.

4. Lack of purpose. Basing everything upon individual experimentation will result in lack of purpose everywhere. Most of the persons cannot derive any principle as they do not succeed much in any field of life. The pragmatic ideal may be more conducive to the creative persons but not to the average students.

5. Neglect of cultural ideals. The pragmatist's emphasis upon the physical and mundane world may sometimes lead to neglect of cultural ideals which is not acceptable in the field of education.

The above criticisms show that in order to arrive at an integral philosophy of education, the pragmatist philosophy should be synthesised with idealism, naturalism and realism.

8

EXISTENTIALISM

Ever since the inception of reflective thought, the problem of Being and Existence has loomed large in the minds of philosophers, saints and seers. In ancient Upanishads we find direct reference to this question in the form of an inquiry into the quintessence or the element in man which survives death and destruction, that is, which is unaffected by becoming or change. The philosophers of East as well as West, of the ancient as well as modern times have all been seriously preoccupied by the problem of Existence. In short, no philosopher can avoid considering the ontological problems and thus all philosophies are at bottom existentialists. Then, how is the modern existentialist different and why do we not call other philosophies existentialism? The reason is that modern existentialism is concerned, unlike other philosophies, more with the problem of becoming than the problem of being; more with particulars than universals; more with existence than essence. As the father of modern existentialism, S. Kierkegaard puts it, the chief concern of an existentialist Christian is not the knowledge of rules and principles of Christianity but "how am I to become a Christian". The non-Christian or atheist existentialists substitute the word "Authentic Being" for the term Christian. Thus the extentialists have emphasized "Action" and "Choice" instead of usual emphasis on knowledge and explanation, and replaced the question of what by how.

Attempts have been made to trace the beginning of existentialism in the Greek philosophy; in particular, the philosophy of Socrates. According to Dr. Radha Krishnan, "Existentialism is a new name for an ancient method' '. And, according to J. Blackham, Existentialism "appears to be reaffirming in modern idiom the protestant or the stoic form of individualism, which stands over against the empirical individualism of the Renaissance or of the modern or of Epicurus as well as over against the universal system of Rome, or of Moscow or of Plato.... It is a contemporary renewal of one of the necessary phases of human experience in a conflict in ideals which history has not yet resolved".

THE CHIEF CHARACTERISTICS OF EXISTENTIALISM

It is clear from the above account that in existentialism, human person and his freedom are given great importance. In it the ancient personal value stressed by Stoics and Epicureans and exemplified in Socrates' hemlock drinking have been reinterpreted. According to existentialism personal growth and development can take place through individual's own efforts and none can help him in this regard. Thus the practical problems of living are attached great value and importance. Briefly, the chief characteristics of existentialism are the following:

1. Criticism of Idealism. Existentialism has emerged and developed as a reaction against idealism. Existentialist philosophers are highly critical of idealism and conceptualism.

According to idealism human person is essentially an expression of some underlying spiritual or psychic element which is of universal character: that is all men are fundamentally same and share with each other the universal character. It is this common character which truly defines the man. Therefore, the human freedom is subject to the good of humanity in general. There is no arbitrariness or individual will accounting for human freedom. But the existentialists criticize idealist's contention about universal element and man's good being subject to general good. They regard the search for essence a mistaken pursuit and according to them it is not the essence but existence which is real.

2. Criticism of naturalism. The existentialist philosophers are also critical of the philosophy of Naturalism. According to naturalists, life is subject to physico-bio-chemical laws, which, in turn, are subject to the universal law of causation. According to the law of causation whatever happens is due to antecedent causes and there is no event which can appear suddenly without some or the other cause. Thus, if the law of causation is universally operative there can be no human freedom of action. Human acts are as mechanical as the actions of an animal. This, however, is anathema to the existentialists and they stoutly defend the freedom of man.. As a matter of fact, man is so free, according to J. P. Sartre, that he is fearful of his freedom.

3. Criticism of the scientific philosophy. Besides being critical of idealism and naturalism, the existentialist philosophers are also critical of scientific conceptualism. Science abstracts from the immediate data and brings them under some universal law or general rule, whereas, according to existentialists, all abstraction is false, reality is in the immediate data only. Furthermore, with the tremendous progress in science and technology, rapid industrialization and urbanization have taken place. This has given rise to crowded towns in which an individual is lost. Everything is done or happens on a large-scale and all personal values, individual likes and dislikes are altogether lost sight of. Today it is not the individual who chooses his end; rather all decisions are made by computers or statistical laws and data. Thus, science has made the value of man negligible. This is why the existentialists are opposed to scientific philosophy and culture. Indeed, the appeal of existentialist philosophy for artists and litterateurs is due mainly to the stout opposition to science by existentialism. It is the basic belief of existentialism that any true philosophy must be grounded in axiology or theory of values and not in epistemology or theory of knowledge.

4. Born of despair. As has been indicated above, on account of an unparalleled progress of science and technology, huge, industrial complexes and townships have sprung. Everywhere man is losing touch of nature. In big towns the problems and inner conflicts of man have multiplied phenomenally. The two world wars have completely shaken man's faith in world's fixture and philosophy. With the growing application of technology and consequent increase in the mechanisation of life, there is a growing despair in the minds and hearts of men. The worth of human efforts is decreasing and the life is becoming like a raft on the open sea which is carried hither and thither without any definite direction. Under these circumstances a sensitive mind finds himself lost and forlorn. The existentialists try to analyze and describe these human predicaments and find a way out of these. The existentialist is attacked on this count as indulging in gross exaggeration and raising false alarms. While it is very true that modern life is infested with hydra-headed problems and that intricacies of life overwhelm the spirit of man, giving up struggle in despair and cry in stiflement is no sensible solution of the current human predicament. Rather, any intensification of the feeling of despair and hopelessness would further complicate the matters. What is needed is an intelligent and sensible compromise with the hard and harsh facts of life. If man allows himself to be overwhelmed by misery, pain and apparent hopelessness of the situation, he would sink into apathy and cynicism. Thus he would not be able to improve his situation, on the contrary, every hope of any possible way out will recede. Psychologically, such an attitude is symptomatic of hypersensitiveness and hypochondria. Moreover, by advising man to feel fully unremittingly responsible for his life-situation, the sense of responsibility becomes abnormal and pathological. Such a man feels so intensely that he is led to commit suicide for small acts of omission and commission. As it is true elsewhere, it is true in this context that too much of anything is bad. The sense of responsibility and duty and the respect for human person are good things; but an exaggerated version of these can produce abnormal and pathological personality.

5. Value of human personality. From the observations made above about existentialism, it is obvious that existentialism recognizes the paramountcy of the human personality. As a matter of fact, for an existentialist "man" is the centre of the universe and nothing else is equal to it. Even Brahman, God, universe, etc., are subsidiary to "man". The basic feature of human person is his freedom—unfettered and unrestrained. Society and social institutions are for the sake of man and not vice versa, as is believed by idealists and others. There is no "general will" to which the "individual will" is subject. If any social law or principle is restrictive of human freedom it is invalid and unjust. Anything which obstructs the growth and development of the individual must be discarded. With this aim in view, existentialist writers, artists and thinkers have expressed their views uncompromisingly and waged great battles for securing these freedoms for man.

6. Importance of subjectivity. The Danish philosopher S. Kierkegaard has said that truth is subjective, truth is subjectivity: objectivity and abstraction are hallucinations. While scientists lay so exclusive a stress on the objectivity and consider any intrusions by subjective elements as wholly unwarranted and vicious, the existentialists are extremists who believe that only the immediate feeling or apprehension reveals the truth and that abstraction in any form or manners vitiates the truth and reality. The immediate experience or feeling about which existentialists talk is the direct experience by individuals of things like conflict, divisiveness, pain, anguish, anxiety, suffocation, etc. It is these conflicts and pains that tell a person the quality of his life and the business of philosophy is to analyze and describe these conflicts and trace their causes. Usually these conflicts are moral in nature and are indicative of inauthentic existence. The various existentialists have tried to describe in minute details the experiences like spiritual crisis, sexual crisis, marital crisis, etc. The existentialist thinking is beyond thinking and reasoning and is rooted in direct experiences and their ungarbled descriptions. A biographical account, if honest sincere and frank, usually helps in appreciating and understanding the truth of one's own situation. For example, a marital discord may be due to lack of respect for the other spouse and too much expectation of him or her. An honest account of such an experience may help relieve tensions in many purusers of this account by providing them insight into their own problems. Everyone by probing into the depths of one's subjectivity can discover the truth of one's being and discover his authentic role in life. This is a creative process which gives rise to fresh insights. The man, when he encounters his existence first hand, stands alone. It is only when one is alone that one comes to grips with his true self. This ability to be alone, to stand by oneself, is the true freedom and this again is the basis of all morality. According to existentialists the origin of values is not in the social situation but in the personal insight.

7. No construction of philosophical system. From the ancient times philosophers have cogitated and pondered over problems of God, Soul, Space, Time, physical world, its origin and evolution, etc. They have tried to present philosophies which embraced all these problems and developed a theoretical system. However, the existentialists distrust system making and theorization. According to them, the true aim of philosophy is action and not theory. Therefore they do not cogitate over traditional problems.

8. Emphasis on the problem of the relation of individual and world. Lastly, a problem which is thought to be crucial by the existentialists is the relation between individual and world. The traditional explanations to this problem are not satisfactory according to existentialists. If we, after Hegel, believe in the one universal element called Absolute whose manifestation everything is, the individual has no value *perse* and is not free. According to Hegel the acceptance of necessity is the true freedom. This robs individual of all freedom and his unique quality. Such a view is repugnant to the existentialists; they, therefore, are consistently and consensusly anti-Hegelian. According to existentialists man cannot be considered subject to any law, rule or principle, be it a universal natural, social or political law. They are uncompromising free-willists and are extremely wary of any external encroachment upon human freedom. The rule does not verify and authenticate the case; on the contrary, the case does verify the rule. The validity of art is in the artistic impulse and expression and not in any aesthetic theory. The worth of man is underivable from any universal element. The existentialist's account of man is neither mystical nor philosophical. Man and world both are unbound and free. Briefly, the existentialists consider man to be the centre of all value and activity. That is why their view is also called anthropocentrism.

9. Emphasis on the problem of inner conflict. The central problem of the modern highly complex world is not ideological but practical. It is neither relevant nor important today to win followers for a particular ideology or theory but to inspire in men a sense of responsibility and freedom. If there is this sense, the process of communication is facilitated. The world peace cannot be accomplished by raising slogans. We require for this purpose individuals who are free, who communicate freely and, above all, who respect theirs as well as other's personalities. A *fortiori* the peace is possible if and only if there is peace in each heart; if each man is free from inner conflicts, if each can be free from the desire to subject others to his will. That is why existentialists attach so great importance to the problem of inner conflict. The traditional philosophies do not consider these problems philosophically worthwhile; but for existentialists these are extremely crucial and fundamental. The source of modern philosophical issues is the feeling of alienation from world, society as well as self. If we regard the existence and thought disparate, the problems arising out of this severance between reason and existence cannot be rationally solved. These can be resolved in practice only.

A true harmony is not a harmony of ideas or thoughts but a harmony of desires. A true philosophy is not a philosophy of substance but rather a philosophy of existents, a philosophy of immediate experiences. The true nature of this philosophy is not thinking about the being but participating in its movement, that is, commitment. The existentialist philosophy does not have any definite aim because, life being movement and flow which is not mere mechanical change but a creative advance, it is not possible to tie down life to any particular aim. Life cannot be aimless or having an aim but only inauthentic and authentic. An authentic existence is the only aim that life has but this is not some future state but a present quality of life. An authentic life can be personal only. The existentialism condemns both historicism and the scientific philosophy. With the exception of Karl Jaspers no other existentialist philosopher attaches much importance to history or science.

The existentialist philosophy is not a creation of any single philosopher. We find the existentialist writings scattered in the works of many philosophers, the important ones of which are Friedrich Nietzsche, Soren Kierkegaard, Gabriel Marcel, Martin Heidegger, Jean Paul Sartre, Karl Jaspers, Abbagnamo, Bardyaev and Albert Camus, etc. These philosophers have elaborated various themes and cardinal features of existentialist philosophy. There is of course no consensus among existentialists as to what is the essential nature of existentialism. J. P. Sartre calls his philosophy existentialist in a peculiar sense, while G. Marcel and K. Jaspers do not at all consider Sartre an existentialist philosopher. Kierkegaard and Marcel are both religious and subjectivist whereas the philosophy of Heidegger is objectivist. Some existentialist thinkers are theist while others are atheist. Whereas Kierkegaard, Jaspers and Marcel are theist, Heidegger, Sartre and Nietzsche are atheist. Nietzsche is severely critical of Christianity and considers the morality of Christianity to be the morality of slaves.

THE AIM OF EDUCATION

The aim of education, according to existentialism, is the realisation of inner truth. Contemporary mechanical and industrial life has alienated modern man. He is full of anxities, frustrations, fears and guilts. He is lonely though in the crowd. His individuality is being corrupt. The education should make him realise his subjective consciousness. The existential aim of education is humanitarian and humanist. It aims at self-realisation. It provides knowledge of self-existence.

CHILD-CENTRED EDUCATION

Existential education is child-centred. It gives lull freedom to the child. The teacher should help the child to know himself and recognise his being. Freedom is required for natural development. Education should convert imperfection into perfection. Education should be according to the individual's needs and abilities of the child. The relation of the child to himself should be strengthened by education.

CURRICULUM

Existentialist's approach to education is almost an inversion of the realist approach. In the field of curriculum while the realists exclusively emphasise science, the existentialists find out that science and objective education severs our relation with ourselves. Science cannot help in inner realisation and achievement of peace. This, however, does not mean that science education should be ignored. It only means that besides science the curriculum must include humanities, ethics and religion. In keeping with this viewpoint contemporary engineering colleges have included some philosophy, ethics and social studies, in their curriculum. Without this synthetic approach to curriculum the aim of character formation and personality development will be defeated.

THE TEACHER

According to the existentialists the teacher creates an educational situation in which the student may establish contact with himself, become conscious of it and achieve self-realisation. This requires existential approach in the teacher himself. He should also have an experience of self-realisation so that he may be capable of guiding the students in this process.

RELIGIOUS AND MORAL EDUCATION

The existentialists particularly lay emphasis upon religious and moral education. Religion allows a person to develop himself. Religious education gives him an understanding of his existence in the cosmos. It shows the religious path of self-realisation. It also makes him capable of utilising faith in self-development. Moral education is closely related to religious education.

Both develop the inner self and help in the realisation of the infinite within the finite.

CRITICAL EVALUATION

Existentialism developed as a reaction against the contemporary social, economic and political situation in which man has lost his self. This philosophy has widely influenced art and literature. In politics it has stood against war. Its followers are active pacifists. In the field of education the contribution of existentialism is as follows:

1. Total development. The existentialists have aimed at total development of personality through education. Education should aim at the whole man. It should aim at character formation and self-realisation.

2. Subjective knowledge. The present age of science has made too much of objective knowledge, so much so that the term subjective has come to mean unreal, non-sense, ignorant and irrelevant. The existentialists rightly point out that subjective knowledge is even more important than objective knowledge. They rightly hold that truth is subjectivity. It is a human value and values are not facts. Reduction of values to facts has led to widespread loss of faith in values. Therefore, along with the teaching of science and mathematics, the humanities, art and literature should also be given suitable place in curriculum at every stage of education. Most of the ills of the modern man are due to over-objective attitude. This requires a subjectivist correction in the light of existentialist ideas.

3. Importance of environment. The present industrial, economic, political and social environment is valueless. Therefore, it helps confusion and corruption, tensions and conflicts. The existentialists seek to provide an environment proper to self-development and self-consciousness. This environment in the school requires contribution from humanities, arts and literature. These will help in the development of individuality in the educand so that he may cease to become a cog in the social wheel. Rather he should develop to be a self-conscious and sensitive individual.

In spite of the above mentioned contribution of existentialism its disadvantages are obvious since, as a philosophy also it has never provided a balanced thought. Some of the existentialist theories, in spite of all their genius, verge upon pathological symptoms. Such is the philosophy of Kierkegaard, the father of modern existentialism. If truth is not objective, it is not merely subjective. Existentialist revolt against intellectualism has its merits but also its serious limitations. Existential methods may be useful in moral and religious education but it cannot work in the education of science and technology. Therefore, the following limitations of existential philosophy of education may be noted:

1. Existential aim of education is as much one-sided as that of any other 'ism'.

2. Exclusive emphasis on humanities, art and literature is as much one-sided as emphasis upon science.

3. In their enthusiasm for self-realisation, the existentialists forget that a very important aim of education is earning a living. For that purpose the utilitarian aim of education has its advantages.

4. The existentialist method of teaching may be useful in moral and religious education but it will not work in the teaching of science and technology.

5. From a perusal of the advantages and limitations of existential approach in the field of education, it is clear that it serves as a corrective to contemporary gaps of education. However, it is far from being satisfactory as a complete philosophy of education.

9

LOGICAL POSITIVISM

Logical Positivism is the most recent trend in philosophy. Though its parallels may be found in all times and ages in philosophy in the form of anti-speculation tendencies, it is only in the 20th Century that this philosophy has been fully elaborated and has come to dominate the philosophic scene. In the 20th Century, logical positivism came into existence with the establishment of Vienna Circle. The Vienna Circle was a group of philosophers or scientists with philosophic inkling who met off and on under the Chairmanship of Moritz Schlick, who, at that time, was holding the chair of philosophy in the University of Vienna. The common thread binding this group together was a thorough dissatisfaction, with the current philosophy, which, according to them, was non-scientific, speculative and non-empirical. They wanted to cry halt to all speculation and give a new turn to the philosophy by basing it upon science and experience. G. Weinberg in his books *Examination of Logical Positivism* has said that "the official programme on which the Viennese Circle was first organized had two principal aims: to provide secure foundation for sciences and to demonstrate the meaninglessness of metaphysics". Thus the aim of the founders of Vienna Circle was to show that only a philosophy based on experience and scientific methodology has any validity and that the speculative philosophy of the past was merely will-of-the-wisp and lacked all validity and veracity. They wanted to usher in a new era in philosophy wherein all speculation would be abandoned.

In the beginning, the activities of the Vienna Circle amounted to the activities of a private club and were not like an open movement, that is, during the incipient stages the philosophers of Viennese Circle debated and discussed the various issues amongst them and had not as yet formulated any positive philosophic programme. In order to propagate and disseminate their views, the members of the Vienna Circle published a pamphlet *"The Vienna Circle, Its Scientific Outlook"* wherein they put forward their point of view and programme. Indeed, it was the manifesto of the logical positivism. In the early twenties, the logical positivism has had most impact on the philosophers of Vienna and Cambridge universities; but soon the movement of logical positivism swept the whole world. The philosopher whose views had maximum impact on the Vienna Circle philosophers in turning them away from metaphysics and formulating a philosophy sans Metaphysics was Ludwig Wittgenstein. Wittgenstein's *Tractatus Logico Philosophicus* had paved way for anti-speculation philosophy. He had asserted that the traditional philosophical problems were merely verbal tricks and that philosophy must fight this "bewitchment of intelligence". The period between 1930 and 193 9 was a golden age of Vienna Circle; during this period logical positivism was riding the high crest of philosophic tidal wave. It was a young movement and had all the enthusiasm and zeal of the youth. Many top intellectuals of the world joined the movement in these years. In 1930, the eminent Polish logician Alfred Tarske was invited to deliver his discourses on mathematics. Rudolf Carnap was greatly impressed by these lectures and he propounded his logical principles on these lines. Though logical positivism has made sufficient progress since then, the Vienna Circle had begun disintegrating during Second World War. In 1934, Professor H. Hahn died of heart failure. In 1936, Professor Schlick was murdered by his student. After Schlick the mainstay of the Vienna Circle was gone. The best known members of this group were M. Schlick, R. Carnap, F. Weismann, O. Neurath, Feigl, F. Kaufmann, H. Hahn, K. Menger and Kurt Godel.

THE AIMS OF LOGICAL POSITIVISTS

If we make a close examination of logical positivism, we find in it two strains; one positivist and the other negativist. On the positivist side, the aim of these philosophers was to make the foundations of the science, to rid it of the pseudo concepts of metaphysics and to lay its foundations on strictly empirical principles. On the negativist side their aim was to prove the futility and barrenness of the traditional philosophy and condemn metaphysics as meaningless, invalid and misleading.

According to logical positivists, it is sheer waste of time and energy to indulge in speculation because that which transcends experience has no meaning, no sense. Only those statements, theories or principles have meaning and relevance which are about something within our experience and which can be validated or invalidated by reference to the facts of experience. And inasmuch as the theories and principles of Metaphysics are not based upon any experience, they are meaningless. Metaphysics, which literally means after-experience, is *exhypothesis* concerned with something that transcends experience. And as only empirical facts can be the subject matter of science and can have any validity or meaning, the subject-matter of Metaphysics, if any, is therefore, beyond the realm of sense or meaning. That is why, the logical positivists are so fond of debunking Metaphysics as "nonsense". What they mean is not that Metaphysics is a folly or foolish but that it has no relevance because it is nonsense (non experiential or not about sense experience). If philosophy cannot deal with transcendental spheres without losing sense and with regard to facts of experience it stands nowhere before science, then what can be the proper function of philosophers. Some thinkers are of the opinion that the proper business of philosophy is to harmonize or synthesize the scientific knowledge. The science deals with particular aspects of the Reality. In order to gain a general or total viewpoint, we need philosophy. Thus, philosophy is the science of sciences. However, this view is unacceptable to logical positivists. According to them, the conceptions of harmony, synthesis, totality, etc., belong to the sphere of literature and poetry.

Explaining the proper function of philosophy Rudolf Carnap writes: "The proper function of philosophy is to analyze the statements asserted by scientists and study their kinds and relations". Thus the logical positivists deprived philosophy of its traditional function of being surveyor of all knowledge and determiner of what should constitute valid knowledge and to reveal to man the hidden laws of the universe. They have restricted philosophy to a narrow and technical function of evaluating the scientific assertions. According to logical positivists philosophy is to science what grammar is to language. As the knowledge of grammar does not enable us to create the language but equips us only with the rules which any linguistic expression must follow, similarly, philosophy frames the rules whereby it can be determined if a particular scientific assertion is correct or incorrect.

THE CONCEPTION OF MEANING

In his first book *Tractatus Logico Philosophicus*, Wittgenstein developed his conception of meaning through the logical analysis of language and experience.

According to Wittgenstein philosophy is nothing but analysis and discussion of language. The language is nothing but a symbolic expression of the facts of experience. The language is comprised of two types of expressions or statements: the simple and compound. The entire fabric of language is analyzable in compound statements, which, in turn, are analyzable in simple statements. Thus, language is nothing but 'The totality of propositions". A simple or atomic proposition is a mirror or reflection of the reality. According to Wittgenstein, "A proposition is a picture of reality". Since language represents the facts of experience, the relationship between facts and the linguistic expressions thereof must indeed be very close. It is the fact which makes a proposition true or false. If the proposition is correspondent to the facts it is time; otherwise false. Wittgenstein is here reviving the correspondence theory of truth, according to which a proposition is true if and only if it asserts what the facts indeed are. For example, if we say that a ripe Dusseri mango is sweet, what we are asserting is according to the nature of Dusseri, that is, our statement of Dusseri mango corresponds to the fact. On the contrary if we say "King of Nepal is a Moslem" our statement is untrue because King of Nepal happens to be a Hindu.

Thus, we learn that a compound proposition can be so translated or analyzed as to give us simple proposition and that each simple proposition is a symbolic expression for a single fact. Since a simple proposition stands for some simple fact, the truth of the proposition can be determined by comparing the two. A momentous and crucial fact which follows from this analysis is that each linguistic expression is, directly or indirectly, overtly or covertly, connected with some or the other fact of experience. Therefore, if there is any linguistic expression which masquerades as a proposition but on analysis fails to show any connection with any fact of experience, then that linguistic expression is not a proposition but a pseudo-proposition. A pseudo-proposition is not merely not connected with any fact but it is impossible to think that it can be so connected. This is the basic difference between pseudo-propositions and false-propositions. This difference can be best explained by examples. Let us have two following propositions: (1) "Aspirin causes headache" and (2) "God exists". Now (1) is false because aspirin is a pain remover but aspirin and headache are facts, whereas (2) is neither true nor false but meaningless because there is and cannot be a fact which will answer to or correspond with our idea of god. Thus a pseua-proposition is neither true nor false because the criterion of truth has no relevance to it.

The precise and scientific explanation of Wittgenstein's conception of the meaning is in the following words: "The sense of a proposition is the method of its verification". That is, a proposition is a proposition if and only if some empirical facts are to be found which may confirm or disconfirm the proposition in question. Those propositions which can neither be confirmed nor disconfirmed by the empirical evidence are meaningless. It is a mistake to call them propositions.

EUMINATTON OF METAPHYSICS

It was the British philosopher David Hume who was the first philosopher to have maintained that Metaphysics was impossible because its principles were neither tautologies nor were based on experience. Taking the empirical foundations laid by Locke and Berkeley to their logical conclusion Hume had argued that there can be no basis for inferring something unseen from the seen. If we observed no causal necessity or regularity in nature, we could not be justified in believing it to be there. Thus, Metaphysics is unwarranted because it has no basis in experience. Kant had also declared that the science of Metaphysics is impossible. However, it was left to logical positivists to lead an organized revolt against Metaphysics and to make their viewpoint heard and respected in philosophical circles. According to A.J. Ayer the futility of metaphysics becomes transparent if we remember that "The fundamental postulate of metaphysics is that there is super-phenomenal reality". And whatsoever the super-phenomenal reality may or may not be, one thing is quite clear; namely, that the statements pertaining to "this reality" cannot be analyzed into simple propositions or protocol statements. Such being these are unverifiable. Being unverifiable they make no sense. Like couplets, stanzas or cantos of poetry they may have great impact upon our feelings; they may be highly edifiable, but seen on the touchstone of meaningful propositions they lack credibility. Thus, metaphysics has no relevance to knowledge.

Though in his *Philosophical Investigations* Wittgenstein is not uncompromisingly critical of metaphysics, in his earlier work referred to above he is vehemently opposed to metaphysics. According to him the metaphysical language is confusing and its problems unreal. The metaphysical problems are due to conscious or unconscious abuse of the language. According to him it is the business of philosophy to remove the veil of secrecy and show that metaphysical problems are unreal. As a phobic, if one understands the irrationality of his fear, he immediately gets rid of his phobia, in the same way if we see through the subterfuges of linguistic manipulation in the creation of metaphysical problems we would instantly cease to regard them as problems, Wittgenstein believes that word is invariably linked with some or the other sense-experimental fact. Therefore, if we find that there are certain alleged linguistic expressions which have no connection with empirical facts, then these expressions must be pseudo. Therefore, Wittgenstein refuses to consider metaphysical statements to be propositions, because, these, by definition, transcend experience and hence cannot be verified. Though since ages philosophers have been making metaphysical assertions, none of them has ever tried to offer any empirical evidence in their favour. As they cannot be subjected to either logical or empirical proof, these must be rejected as meaningless expressions.

The metaphysicians claim that though metaphysics is not based upon any external experience, it is nonetheless based upon internal experience.

Wittgenstein does recognize that there are internal experiences but these cannot be known unless we express them. When we express them they are linked with some objective reality and should, therefore, be verifiable. But the statements of metaphysicians are unverifiable, therefore they cannot be claimed to be based upon any experience whatever.

The basic contention of Wittgenstein is that all logical propositions are correspondent to facts, that is, these stand for some or the other objective fact. The metaphysical statements, on the other hand, are devoid of all objective reference and are, therefore, logically sterile. These propositions are not made up of simple propositions but are supposedly based on spiritual experiences and facts; therefore these are unanalyzable and consequently unverifiable.

LANGUAGE

As has been earlier referred to there was some change in the viewpoint when Wittgenstein wrote his second book—The *Philosophical Investigations.* Unlike Tractatus, in which he had defined meaning as the mode of verification, now he defines meaning in terms of a game or play. To imagine a language; according to him, is to imagine a form of life. Thus, language is a style of life and the activity of man is a game. The terms used in a language have some special meaning. If a word has no special meaning it is senseless. For example, the words "sky" and "flower" each has meaning and refers to some thing particular; but the word "sky flower" is devoid of meaning because no special meaning is inherent in it. It refers to nothing.

Applying the analogy of "sky flower" to the philosophical problems, Wittgenstein asserts that though sky and flower each has meaning, yet the syntax of two "Sky flower" fails to convey any meaning. In the same manner, the words used in asserting metaphysical problem may each have meaning but the assertion taken as a whole may be syntactically defective and therefore has no meaning. A simple example would explain the point. The metaphysical assertion: "All reality is ideal" has no meaning though each word in it is meaningful. We can only talk of this or that real object or fact but to say "All reality" makes no sense because there is nothing corresponding to all reality as we have objects corresponding to a red rose, a philosophy book, etc. In order to resolve metaphysical puzzles the philosophical usages should be, according to Wittgenstein, re-interpreted as commonsense usages of daily life. "What we do is to bring words back from their metaphysical to their every day use." In an ideal language, according to Wittgenstein, only the words which are symbols for some real state of affairs are used. The philosophical problems crop up when we deviate from this principle and use words having no referents. The philosophical language usually is immaturish and imperfect. This is the reason for the lack of clarity in the philosophic assertions. Wittgenstein disregards grammar. The grammar sometimes misleads and systematically misleading expressions produce in us illusion of a problem and we feel restless. Once we let reality juncture and dispel the illusion our problem vanishes into thin air. The one-sidedness of philosophy is responsible for the puzzles of philosophy. In *Philosophical Investigations*, Wittgenstein says that "philosophy is a battle against the bewitchment of intelligence by language". The role of philosophy is to protect us against falling into illusions due to grammatical similarities. For example, a noun is a name of something and it follows that to every name there must correspond an objective fact. This may lead us to believe that since God is a noun, there must be some person, place or thing which is called God. By avoiding these errors we find almost all metaphysical problems disappear. They are dissolved like a dream dissolving on waking.

Though the writings of Wittgenstein had great impact on the logical positivists and linguistic philosophers, the conclusions drawn by him through rigorous analysis are not universally acceptable. Indeed, they have been severely criticized. Undoubtedly the views of Wittgenstein brought about a revolutionary change in philosophical thinking and his theories proved very fertile in as much as through their criticism new insights were achieved. The verification theory of meaning propounded by Wittgenstein has been shown to be built upon the foundations of shifting sand. Among its numerous criticisms the most crucial is that the criterion by which the meaning is to be tested is itself untested. For example, "This is a table" ' can be verified by visual, tactual and other means but there is no way to verify that to verify the meaning by these means is a meaningful proposition. To this criticism, Wittgenstein replies that "My propositions are elucidatory in this way; he who understands me finally recognizes them as senseless, when he has climbed through them, on them, over them. (He must, so to speak, throw away the ladder, after he has climbed upon it.) He must surmount these propositions, then he sees the word rightly". The principle of verification, if strictly adopted as a criterion of meaning, would render many a scientific proposition meaningless. For example, "There are atoms" is not verifiable in the ordinary sense. We know the existence of atoms inferentially and direct observation of these is as yet not possible. Therefore, adherence to the strict verification criterion would rule out science as senseless.

The crucial errors into which Wittgenstein slipped was that he failed to make distinction between science and philosophy and treated them as similar, whereas science and philosophy are unlike both in subject matter and methodology.

Wittgenstein greatly under-valued philosophy. He accorded to the physical world the status of ultimately as real, but, as a matter of fact, the world of values is as much real as the physical world. The values are not capable of analysis. Philosophy has made significant contribution towards understanding and development of values. Wittgenstein utterly ignored this aspect of philosophy. He did so on account of his over-reliance on the physical world as being ultimately real.

THE NEW ROLE OF PHILOSOPHY

The elimination of Metaphysics is not the only task before logical positivists. In fact, they are equally, if not more, interested in filling up the vacuum created by the rejection of metaphysics by a new role (the logic of science). According to Carnap, it is "to analyze the statements asserted by scientists, study the kinds and relations and analyze terms as components of those statements and theories as ordered systems of those statements". The linguistic analysis of the scientific statement has been called "logic of science" by Carnap. According to him only sciences can give us the knowledge about facts. Philosophy has no technique and methodology to assess and determine the facts. Philosophy, therefore, must not try to evaluate facts but accept them on the basis of scientific knowledge. This is why Philosophy should address itself exclusively to the task of analyzing the language of science. The logic of science performs two following functions:

1. Logical syntax 2. Semantics.

1. Logical Syntax

In logical syntax we study the forms of linguistic expressions. Inasmuch as logical syntax is concerned with the forms and not the contents of linguistic expressions or propositions, it is also called formal logic. In the study of the logical syntax we are not concerned with the content or meaning of the propositions but with the reduction of complex forms into elementary forms and the elementary forms into their constituents. It also inquires into the logical relations of consistency and inconsistency, dependence and independence among different propositions. Logical syntax helps us to reach the basic statements of various sciences and realize the logical relations among these.

In his book *Logical Syntax of the Language*, Carnap has split up language in two divisions: the primary and the secondary. He has separately treated the rules of *the two.*

Primary Language or Language I

Defining Language I, Carnap says, "Language I is restricted so as to admit only the definition of those concepts and the formulation of those propositions which fulfil some requirements of constructivism ".

Although the scope of Language I is limited it does not follow that it has definite sentences. The real reason for the limitation of Language I is that it "consists primarily in the fact that only definite number of properties occur in it". On account of this limitation it is called definite language. Language I has been classified into two categories by Carnap:

1. Universal and 2. Existential.

Besides, there are five types of preliminary statements:

1. Sentential Calculus; 2. Sentential Operators;
3. Identity; 4. Arithmetic;
5. K-Operator.

As there are two sentences, there are two types of operators as well viz.:

1. Universal and 2. Existential.

These can be limited or unlimited. They are expressed with the help of symbols which may be defined or undefined.

Besides, in Language I there is reference to the rules of inference and judgement. The logical syntax of Language I is formulated on the basis of these rules.

Language II

Contrary to language I the scope of Language II is wide. According to Carnap, "Language II is very comprehensive, it makes available sufficient sentential forms for the formulation of everything that occurs in classical mathematics and in classical physics. Whereas Language I is limited in scope, the Language II is comprehensive in scope. Language I is, however, employed in Language II as a sub-class. Though the Language II is more clear and accurate than the Language

I, the Language I's sentences and symbols are appropriate to the Language II. Inasmuch as it is comprehensive, the Language II "contains indefinite concepts".

The General Syntax

Besides linguistic syntaxes, Carnap has also referred to the rules of general syntax. Whereas the rules of linguistic syntax are applicable to a particular language, the rules of general syntax refer to all languages, oral as well as gestural. Carnap has related the general syntax with the philosophical discourse. According to him, in theory there are two types of questions:

1. Questions relating to Subject matter.
2. Questions relating to Logic.

The contextual questions pertain to metaphysical, ontological and physical inquiries and the logical questions pertain to Epistemology and Logic.

2. Semantics

Rudolf Camap has propounded his view on Semantics in his three books: *Introduction to Semantics, Formalization of Logic* and *Meaning and Necessity.* In semantics the concepts of meaning and truth are studied and the various theories thereof examined. Semantics considers the relation of linguistic expressions to objects designated by them. The Semantical analysis of the scientific language reveals that a word may represent a particular object (e.g., table) or a certain property (e.g., sweetness) or a relation between two things (e.g., friendship) or a physical function (e.g., breathing). It also reveals the fact of synonymity[7], that is, two words may stand for the same object or same property.

In language there are three distinct elements:.

1. The speaker;
2. The expression uttered and
3. The designatum.

And a language system makes use of three types of rules: (i) Syntactical rules; (ii) Semantical rules; and (iii) Pragmatic rules. The science dealing with these rules is called Semiotic,

In Semantics, Carnap splits language in two parts; the object Language and the Metalanguage. The object language is that which is the subject matter of our discussion and analysis. In Metalanguage we say something about the object language. For example, if the teaching of Hindi is done through the medium of English, Hindi is the object Language and English the Metalanguage. The simple most unit of a language is sign. A series of signs is known as expression. Furthermore, signs are also of two types: sign event and sign-design. The semantics, too, is of two types: descriptive semantics and pure syntax. The descriptive semantics studies the historical changes in the forms of semantical signs and expressions. The pure syntax analyzes the methods and techniques of Semantics. A concatenation of signs results in a formula. A concatenation is the serial order of the signs. The different patterns of concatenation give rise to different forms of sentential syntax. The various syntactic arrangements or systems have their peculiar logic. If we know the pattern of arrangement in any concatenation, we can formulate the rules of its syntax. The peculiar concatenation of signs determines the terms, operators, sequence and sentential calculus and the techniques thereof. The pure syntax examines the techniques of semantics and this is known as calculus. The semantic technique frames rules for determining the necessary and sufficient truth of every type of sentence. Besides formulating the semantical rules, Carnap has also developed a number of metalanguage systems. He has shown that a metalanguage has four elements-(i) The Logical; (ii) The Sentential Syntax; (iii) Translation; and (iv) Semantical. These elements in a metalanguage are interdependent. The semantics is not a science, according to Carnap, because it does not help us to gather facts about the physical world. It is only an instrument for acquisition of knowledge. It determines and regulates modern logic. The modern logic has two chief constituents — the sentential syntax and semantics. According to Carnap the apparatus of modern logic is applicable to and useful not only in philosophy but sciences as well.

The views given above have been propounded in *Formalization of Logic* and *Introduction to Semantics* two of the three books mentioned above. In his third book *Meaning and Necessity* Carnap has analyzed in depth and detail the semantic aspects of meaning. The other feature of this work is the theory of forms. In it the concepts of necessity, chance, possibility and impossibility have been examined in detail. This part is known as Logic.

In his book *Logical Foundation of Probability* Carnap has considered the problems of probability and induction. According to him there is a close relationship between the two. Indeed, the inductive logic is the logic of probability. The probability is a type of relationship obtaining betwixt two propositions. The concept of probability plays crucial role in statistical science.

THE VALUES

According to Rudolf Carnap it is not possible to present any comprehensive theory of values. This is so because values depend upon human interests and desires. Carnap divides values in two classes —(1) The Relative values and (2) The Absolute values.

The Relative valued are born of experience. They are the outcome of desires, interests, likes and dislikes. A man acts according to his values because these help him achieve the desired ends or goals. The acts done in accordance with absolute values are automatically good. They are not derived from experience.

According to Camap all values are meaningless. All statements regarding values are incomplete because they have neither logical nor scientific evidence in support of these. The belief of certain philosophers that values are universal is mistaken. The values are nothing but the outcome of human desires and interests which, in the long run, assume the status of law. For example, the moral rule that telling lies is bad is an outcome of the experience of man that life is impossible in a society where lying is permissible, because in that event it will be impossible to believe anyone. Therefore, it is the interest of man which dictates the moral rule "Lying is bad."

Camap has formulated three principles of morality. His ethics can be best described as Scientific Humanism. The three principles of morality proposed by Camap are:

(1) There is no transcedental being who may be regarded to be the destroyer or the preserver of man. It follows, therefore, that for the development and progress of man the self-help or personal efforts by man are indispensable.
(2) Man can effect such modifications in the changing circumstances of man that he can gain freedom from pain and disease. These constructive efforts can bring about definite improvement in personal and social life of man.
(3) The science is the best instrument for the betterment of human life.

Camap has made definitive contribution to the realm of knowledge by his linguistic analysis and logical studies. Besides, he has also purged philosophy of many redundancies. However, like other logical positivists Camap has been more successful in condemning philosophy than in presenting a positive philosophy.

The view of Camap that philosophy has no independent status and that it is dependent upon science is utterly false. As a matter of fact, it has an independent status and is in no way dependent upon science. Without the foundations provided by philosophy it is impossible to raise the structure of science, therefore it is science which is subject to philosophy and not vice versa. The dictum "Philosophy is science of sciences", expresses a fundamental truth.

The explanation of values by Camap is based on a misconception. As a matter of fact values are not just the expression of human desires and interests. The values are the fundamental principles underlying the facts. In order to know the bases of a fact we should know its values.

Camap has gone into very fine details of logical principles but has, in the process, rendered them extremely intricate and complex. He has made his logical and linguistic theories too complicated to be of value.

EDUCATIONAL IMPIICAHONS

Logical positivism is a philosophical system and not a theory of education. In philosophy its contribution is particularly notable in the field of epistemology. Therefore, its implications are particularly important in teaching methods and the methods of communicating knowledge in education. The following are the important implications of logical positivism in the field of education.

1. Aims of education. Logical positivists insist upon meaningful propositions so that some meaning may be conveyed. Therefore, according to them, the aim of education is to distinguish between sense and nonsense, knowledge and ignorance, meaningful and meaningless propositions. It aims at propagation of scientific knowledge. It seeks to base the entire educational process on intelligence and reasoning. It lays emphasis upon objective knowledge as against subjectivity. Thus, its aim is precisely the opposite of existentialism. Knowledge, according to it, is empirical. The educational system should be based upon reliable and verified knowledge. Verification is through the practical consequences. Thus, logical positivists advise the use of utilitarian criterion in knowledge. Education aims at creating critical and scientific attitude. This is possible by training in language.

2. Educational method. The educational method, particularly emphasised by logical positivism, is both logical and positive. The teacher should himself analyse propositions in knowledge and check their verification. His approach should be strictly scientific and objective. He should adopt educational methods verified by educationists. He should test hypotheses and assumptions in every field of knowledge. He should develop the power of reasoning. He should train the student in logical thinking. He should have a sense of purpose everywhere and reject everything which cannot be verified.

3. Curriculum. The logical positivist rejects metaphysics, religion and all such knowledge which may not be verified. Language and grammar, besides logic, find central place in logical positivist curriculum. The training in analysis of language is necessary for every student. It is only analysis which leads to clarity of thought. Religious, moral and spiritual education have no place in positivist curriculum. Sciences occupy a prestigious place in it. It rejects self-criticism everywhere. All criticism must be objective. Science and scientific research, both theoretical and practical, should be encouraged by the universities. The students should develop constructive imagination.

4. School organisation. Logical positivists believe in scientific humanism. The school should be managed by the students as much as by the teachers. The school organisation should be based upon functional efficiency, utilitarianism and humanism. Humanism considers every thing relative and nothing absolute. So, innovations should be encouraged in place of confirmity and traditions. Educational process should be confined to the realm of knowledge. Only objective knowledge should be propagated. Only logical definitions should be accepted. Only valid interpretations should find currency.

In the final analysis the contribution of logical positivism is the evolution of philosophy of language and a principle of verification. Logical positivists develop a scientific theory of truth. They reject everything which may not be verified. The task of philosophy, according to logical positivist, is to work as a science of sciences. Thus, logical positivists act as catalysts. They down right reject all confused and unverified beliefs, hypotheses and propositions.

Logical positivist's method is not only useful in the field of philosophy but also in the field of sciences. The scientists present a theory after prolonged observation and experimentation, gathering the data, classification, generalisation and verification. The presentation of theory, however, should be strictly according to the rules laid down by logic and grammar. Without this method scientific knowledge will not be valid and no valid implications may be deduced from it. This training is necessary for all the students. This is also necessary for all the teachers and researchers, Thus, logical positivists have sought to remove confusions and indefiniteness in every field of knowledge. They are against all verbosity and verbal tricks. The movement started as an examination of empirical principles. It condemned the traditional role of philosophy and allotted new functions to it. It made philosophy concur to science According to it what grammar is to language that philosophy is to science.

10

SOCIALISM, FASCISM, MARXISM AND COMMUNISM

SOCIALISM

Characteristics of Socialism

(1) *Social Justice.* Socialism aims at social justice.
(2) *Equality.* Socialism aims at equality.
(3) *Classless Society.* Socialism aims at establishing a classless society, free from exploitation, oppression and disparity.
(4) *Fellow Feeling.* Socialism aims at establishing a society based on mutual co-operation and fellow feeling.
(5) *Public Ownership.* Socialism pre-supposes public ownership of the means of production.
(6) *Abolition of Capitalism.* Socialism aims at abolishing the capitalist system.
(7) *Abolition of Class Conflict.* Socialism aims at abolishing conflicting classes in the society.
(8) *Active Participation.* Socialism aims at the active participation of the individual in the productive process of society.
(9) *Developing Necessary Attitude.* Socialism aims at developing necessary skills and favourable attitude towards work.
(10) *State Control.* Socialism stands for total state control in affairs of life.

Impact on Education

Various Committees and Commissions in India have suggested educational measures conforming to Socialist Pattern of Society. The Kothari Commission has observed, "One of the important social objectives of education is to equalise opportunity, enabling the backward or under-privileged classes and individuals to use education as a lever for the improvement of their condition. Every society that values social justice and is anxious to improve the lot of common man and cultivate all available talent, must ensure progressive equality of opportunity to all sections of population. This is the only guarantee for the building up of an egalitarian and human society in which the exploitation of the weak will be minimised". The impact of socialism on education is as follows:

1. Teaching of socialism. It is the responsibility of educational institutions to bring about adequate awareness regarding socialism among the teachers and students. Such knowledge will enable the young people to chart the course of nation towards the goal of socialism. A school can convey positive attitudes and values regarding socialism to students through the following:

(1) Direct teaching of socialism.

(2) Living the values and attitudes to be learned through the organization of various activities.

(3) Teachers becoming models embodying the desired values and attitudes.

2. Common school system. The so-called public schools provide good education only to microscopic minority of rich children. It goes against the principles of socialism. The Kothari Commission advocated the abolition of this system and suggested a system of common schools throughout the country which will be open to all children, irrespective of caste, creed, community, religion, economic conditions or social status. It observed, "On grounds of social justice as well as for the furtherance of democracy it is essential to make special efforts to equalise educational opportunities between these groups". However, due to various reasons this has not been possible in India. The public school system of education still thrives in our country. In fact, it is becoming popular day-by-day.

3. Nationalisation of textbooks. Textbooks at the school stage have been nationalised as an impact of socialism. Their contents are oriented and regulated according to the national policy and ethos. Efforts are being made to keep price range of textbooks within the easy reach of the parents.

Means of Providing Equality of Opportunity in Education

(1) *Tuition Free Education.* School education should be completely free from tuition fee.

(2) *Free Textbooks at the Primary Stage.* At the primary stage, a programme of providing free textbooks should be given high priority and introduced immediately.

(3) *Book Banks.* A programme of book-banks should be developed in secondary schools and in institutions of higher education.

(4) *Grants for Purchase of Books.* The top 10 per cent of the students in educational institutions should be given small grants annually for the purchase of books which need not necessarily be textbooks.

4. Adequate scholarships. The Education Commission has suggested the following programme of scholarships at different stages:

(i) *Scholarships at the Primary Stage.* At the end of the lower primary stage, no 'promising' child should be prevented from continuing his studies. The target should be to provide scholarships for 25 per cent of the enrolment at the higher primary stage.

(ii) *Scholarships at the Secondary Stage.* The target should be to provide scholarships for 10 per cent of the enrolment.

(iii) *Scholarships at the University Stage.* Scholarships should be available to at least 25 per cent of enrolment at the undergraduate stage. Scholarships should cover at least 50 per cent of the enrolment at the post-graduate stage.

5. Kinds of scholarships

(i) *Scholarships for those who have to stay in hostels.* These should cover all direct and indirect costs of education, i.e., tuition fees, books, supplies, etc., and living costs.

(ii) *National Scholarships.* As against the present provision of one per cent, the target to be reached should be to cover 10 per cent of such students.

(iii) *Scholarships for Study Abroad.* A national programme for award of scholarship is needed to enable some of our talented persons to go abroad for further education or training in research.

(iv) *Loan Scholarships.* A comprehensive programme of National Loan Scholarship should be undertaken. A National Loan Scholarship Board may be set up for administering this programme.

6. Transport facilities. Adequate transport facilities may be provided in the rural areas so that students are encouraged to attend educational institutions.

7. Day-study centres and lodging houses. At the secondary and university stages a large number of day-study centres should be provided for students who do not have adequate facilities for study at home. Lodging houses may also be provided where students can stay throughout the day, and even at night, but go home for food.

8. 'Earn while learn' facilities. Facilities for students to earn and pay a part of their expenses should be provided on as large-scale as possible.

9. Special Facilities for girls. Special facilities may be provided to the girls.

10. Education of the backward sections of society. Special investigations may be earned out, regarding important aspects of spread of education amongst the tribals and their effects. The Education Commission recommends, "The education of the backward classes in general and of the tribal people in particular is major programme of equalization and of social and national integration. No expenditure is too great for the purpose".

11. Egalitarian admission policy. There is a great need to introduce an egalitarian element in admissions to institutions so that students coming from rural areas are not handicapped due to language or some other factors.

12. Special Assistance to Backward Areas or States. At the national level, it should be regarded the responsibility of the Government of India to secure equalization of educational development in the different states. The necessary programmes for this, include special assistance to the less advanced states.

13. Meeting the Needs of Slow Learners. In the ordinary classes, where instruction is traditionally geared to the need of the average child, the dull children have to work under a great hardship. They need individual attention, special, remedial help and a modified curriculum to suit their rate of learning. In some educationally advanced countries, special schools have been established for this category of children. Such a feasibility may be explored in India in big cities. Special classes in ordinary schools can also be held very profitably. Such a treatment is likely to be better for their emotional and social development also. Guidance and counselling services have an important role to play in the education of such children.

14. Common school system. A common school system of public education should be evolved in place of the present system which divides the management of school between a large number of agencies whose functioning is inadequately coordinated. An adequate level of quality and efficiency should be maintained so that no parent would ordinarily feel any need to send his child to the institutions outside the system. Such a step will be helpful towards eliminating the segregation that now takes place between the schools for the poor and the underprivileged classes and those for the rich and the privileged ones.

15. State schools. The state should itself open a large number of state schools for the spread of education.

16. Suitable legislation. The state should take suitable steps to exercise control on private enterprise which thrives on high fees charged from the students. The public schools run by such organizations should not be allowed to perpetuate class differences.

FASCISM

Meaning

Derived from the Italian word Fascio (a bundle of wood), fascism expresses unity, discipline and strength. This term was applied to the regimes of Mussolini and Hitler which were established in 1922 and 1933 in Italy and Germany respectively. Aggressive nationalist, undemocratic, communal, anti-communist regimes, movements and parties are usually called fascist. Fascism is a reactionary and counter-revolutionary theory. Its object is to safeguard the crisis-ridden capitalist socio-economic and political order. It is opposed to democracy, human rights, socialism and any kind of revolutionary change.

Fascism in Europe

The first Fascist state was established on the 28th October, 1922, when armed members of Fascist party, dressed in black, held a 'March on Rome' in Italy under the leadership of Mussolini.

Fascism in Germany

German Fascism evolved under the leadership of Nazi Party, led by Hitler, formed in 1920 on the basis of an attractive and radical 25-point programme.

Educational Implications

1. Objectives. The primary objective of fascism is to cultivate in the young an emotional and intellectual commitment to the racial superiority. The individual's education must develop in him an intense spirit of nationalism. My country, right or wrong, should he the dominating factor and slogan guiding all educational activities including the aims and objectives of education.

2. Curriculum. Fascism attaches great importance to the inclusion of subjects relating to physical education. Hitler held the view that as a certain racial quality is the pre-supposition of the intellectual efficiency, so all education must first of all develop physical health. The Fascists decry physical weakness as crime against the state. They believe that the genetic constitution of the body owes much from physical education.

3. Methods of teaching. Fascism discourages questioning and independent thinking on the part of the students Students are required to listen to their teachers passively.

4. Discipline. There are rigid and strict rules and regulations to be followed by the students. They are treated like dumb-driven cattle. They are required to sacrifice their individuality for the sake of state.

5. Teachers. The primary duty of a teacher under fascism is to prepare children in such a manner that they would profess faith in the service of their nation.

MARXISM

What is Marxism?

Marxism has been regarded as a body of social doctrine worked out by Karl Marx (1818-1883), a revolutionary author, thinker and philosopher of his age. He was assisted by his colleague and friend Frederick Engles.

Main Characteristics of Marxism

1. Revolutionary programme. In the contemporary world, Marxism makes its claims as a scientific philosophy, revolutionary programme, progressive movement, and the socio-economic, political, cultural and moral basis of the social systems of more than a thousand million people. During the course of its history of 130 years or so, Marxism had to face many challenges from within and without, guided many revolutionary movements and aroused hopes in millions of people. It provided a scientific outlook towards the universe, society, history, man, etc. The revolutionary power of this ideology and of the revolutionary mass movements based on it, has divided the world into two blocks the capitalist or liberal block, and the socialist block.

2. Anti-capitalism. Marx did not appeal to the conscience of the capitalists to improve the conditions of the working class. He did not appeal to the reason of the capitalist class. He did not entrust the state with the welfare functions to improve the conditions of working class. On the contrary, he gave a revolutionary message of changing the society— "Workers of the world unite, you have nothing to lose but your chains and you have a world to win".

3. Philosophy of socio-political change. The most important aspect of the development of Marxism is its philosophy of socio-political change.

4. Materialistic concept of history. Marx found the paradigm of actual social and human development and translated it into materialist terms. Materialistic conception of history was the Hegelian idealistic conception turned upside down or back upon its feet. Marx rejected idealism and replaced it with materialism. His method is known as dialectic materialism and it is the philosophical basis of Marxism. It is called-dialectical materialism because its approach to the phenomena of Nature, its method of studying and apprehending them is dialectical, while its interpretations of the phenomena of Nature, its conceptions of these phenomena, its theory is materialistic.

5. Proletarian revolution. Marx wrote in *Communist Manifesto,* "All previous historical movements were movements of minorities, or in the interest of minorities. The proletarian movement is the self-conscious independent movement of the immense majority, in the interests of the immense majority. The proletariat, the lowest stratum of our present society, cannot stir, cannot raise itself up, without the whole super-incumbent strata of official society being sprang into the air. The proletariat revolution will be social revolution, as the proletariat represent the interests of the society as a whole. Thus, Marxism is a theory of revolutionary change. Capture of political power by the working class is a beginning and, after it, the dictatorship of proletariat should be established and massive task of social and economic transformation should start, so that the way for a classless society may be paved.

Criticism of Marxism

1. Revolutionary. Development and change in society can be brought through reforms rather than through revolution.

2. Destructive. Revolution is destructive and it implies violence.

3. Dictatorship. After the revolution, instead of the dictatorship of the proletariat, dictatorship over proletariat is established and it destroys the liberties available in an open society, and gives birth to a closed society.

4. Class Conflict. Classes are not abolished by revolution and even after the revolution class-struggle continues.

5. National Loss. During the revolution, one generation has to pay a very heavy price and it is illogical that a generation should sacrifice itself for the sake of the coming generation.

6. No withering away of state. In socialist societies there are no chances of the withering away of the state.

Implications of Marxism in Education

1. Formation of character. According to Marxism, the character formation of the child should be guided by the objectives of the classless society which was the ultimate end or objective of communism.

2. Production-oriented education. According to Marx, education should be combined with productive work. He appreciated the work of a British factory owner, Robert Owen, for initiating this idea in his factory at New Lanark, Scotland in 1799. He observed, "From the factory system budded, as Robert Owen has shown us in detail the germ of education of the future, an education that will, in the case of every child over a given age, combine productive labour with instruction and gymnastics, not only as one of the methods of adding to the efficiency of production, but as the only method of producing fully developed human beings".

About "socially useful work" the views of Gandhi and Marx are quite similar. Brubacher has stated in this context, "Gandhi not only strongly opposed a purely literary education because it unfitted youth for the manual work in which most of them would be engaged during rest of their lives, but he believed education through economic work to be a great moral source as well". According to Marx, the teaching of practical life activities is essential and these activities must be social as well as useful.

3. Study of history. Marx stressed the importance of studying history scientifically. It is not to be confined to any particular region, but it must have a universal appeal. History is not a catalogue of past events but useful for the present flowing into the future.

4. Study of economics. Marx emphasized the study of social sciences including economics for understanding the social and economic conditions of life. The significance and importance of "class struggle" may be fully understood through the study of social sciences.

5. Stress on group work. Marxian education mitigates competition and substitutes it by group activities of different kinds. In Russian schools as well as in daily life, competition is eliminated and a cooperative spirit is promoted. Marxism insists that man will develop his full nature by participation in social life. The child is made to feel that he is a unit in society and has a duty to the society.

Marx has made an important contribution in propounding a philosophy of great significance. Moreover, it is very difficult to give a concrete shape to his ideas in the field of education. As C.E.M. Joad said, "Marx's writings, despite the great influence they have exercised over the working classes, are by no means free from difficulty, and there is considerable controversy as to the correct interpretation which should be placed upon them".

COMMUNISM

Meaning

According to Websters *New World Dictionary,* communism means, "1. a theory or system based on the ownership of all property by the community as a whole. 2. (a) a hypothetical stage of socialism, as formulated by Marx, Engels, Lenin, etc., to be characterised by a classless and stateless society and the equal distribution of economic groups, (b) the form of government in the USSR, China, etc., professing to be working toward this state, 3. (a) a political movement for establishing a communist system, (b) the doctrines, methods, etc., of the communist parties". From this definition of communism its following characteristics may be derived:

(1) Communism is a theory based on community ownership of property. Therefore, it is against the capitalist system of individual ownership of property.

(2) Communism envisages a classless and stateless society.

(3) Communism asks for an equal distribution of economic goods.

The Communist Manifesto

In the above mentioned definition of communism it has been pointed out that it is a philosophy propounded by Karl Marx and Engels and later own developed by Lenin. Therefore, it will be only in the fitness of things to go through the fundamentals of communism as laid down in *The Manifesto of the Communist Party,* published first in German language in 1872. It was written by Karl Marx and Frederick Engels. Its Russian Edition was published in 1882 and English Edition was published in 1888. Distinguishing the programme of the communist party from the programme of other political parties Marx and Engles wrote, "The Communists are distinguished from the other working class parties by this only:

(1) In the national struggles of the proletarians of the different countries, they point out and bring to the front the common interests of the entire proletariat, independently of all nationality. (2) In the various stages of development which the struggles of the working class against the bourgeoisie has to pass through, they always and everywhere represent the interests of the movements as a whole. In the words of C.E.M. Joad, "Communism seeks to lay down principles upon which transition from capitalism to socialism is to be accomplished and its two essential doctrines are class war and the revolutionary, that is the absolute transference of power to the proletariat". According to Gettel, communism is a philosophy of history based upon the materialistic theory of human development. The following characteristics of communism were laid down by Marx and Engels in *The Manifesto of the Communist Party:*

1. Progressive ideal. Laying down the outline of the progressive political ideal of the communist party, Marx and Engels wrote, "The Communists, therefore, are on the one hand, practically, the most advanced and resolute section of the working-class parties of every country, that section which pushes forward all others: on the other hand, theoretically, they have over the great mass of the proletariat the advantage of clearly understanding the line of march, the conditions, and the ultimate general results of the proletarian movement".

2. Immediate aim. According to Marx and Engels, "The immediate aim of the communists is the same as that of all the other proletarian parties: formation of the proletariat into a class, overthrow of the bourgeois supremacy, conquest of political power by the proletariat".

3. Abolition of private property. According to Karl Marx and Engels, capital is not a personal but social power. Therefore, it should be converted into common property. In the words of Karl Marx and Engels, "We Communists have been reproached with the desire of abolishing the right of personally acquiring property as the fruit of a man's own labour, which property is alleged to be the groundwork of all personal freedom, activity and independence . . .". When, therefore, capital is converted into common property, into the property of all members of society, personal property is not thereby transformed into social property. The social distinguishing feature of communism is not the abolition of property generally, but the abolition of bourgeois property. Modern bourgeois private property is the final and most complete expression of the system of producing and appropriating products, that is based on class antagonism, on the exploitation of the many by the few.

4. Abolition of exploitation. Therefore, communism deprives no man of the power to appropriate the products of society ; all that it does is to deprive him of the power to subjugate the labour of others by means of such appropriation. This has been called expropriation of expropriators.

5. Abolition of the family. The most important charge against the communist view of human society is their concept of abolition of the family. Explaining this idea, Marx and Engels have written, "On what foundation is the present family, the bourgeois family, based on capital, on private gain"? In its completely developed form this family exists only among the bourgeois. But this state of things finds its complement in the practical absence of the family among the proletarians and in public prostitution. The bourgeois family will vanish as a matter of course when its complement vanishes, and both will vanish with the vanishing of capital. Do you charge us with wanting to stop the exploitation of children by their parents? To this crime we plead guilty. But, you will say, we destroy the most hallowed of relations, when we replace home education by social.

6. Role of education. The communists do not approve the present capitalist system of education. They advocate their own system of education which is free from the influence of the ruling class. Criticising the current capitalist system of education Marx and Engels wrote, "The bourgeois clap-trap about the family and education, about the hallowed co-relation of parent and child, becomes all the more disgusting, the more, by the action of modern industry, all family ties among the proletarians are tom asunder, and their children transformed into simple articles of commerce and instruments of labour".

7. Ideal of human unity. Marx and Engels rejected nationalism and called for a unity of the working men of all countries which will gradually abolish the boundaries of nations and establish one human world. Explaining his ideal Karl Marx and Frederick Engels wrote, "The working men have no country. We cannot take from them what they have not got. Since the proletariat must first of all acquire political supremacy, must rise to be the leading class of the nation, must constitute itself the nation, it is, so far, itself national, though not in the bourgeois sense of the word".

National differences and antagonisms between peoples are daily more and more vanishing, owing to the development of the bourgeoisie, the freedom of commerce, to the world-market, to uniformity in the mode of production and in the conditions of life corresponding thereto.

The supremacy of the proletariat will cause them to vanish still faster. United action of the leading civilised countries at least, is one of the first condition for the emancipation of the proletariat.

In proportion as the exploitation of one individual by another is put to an end the exploitation of one nation by another will also be put to an end. In proportion as the antagonism between classes within the nation vanishes, the hostility of one nation to another will come to an end.

8. Revolution. For the total change and transformation of society from the capitalist society to communist society Marx and Engels have suggested communist revolution. This revolution will be developed according to local circumstances in every country but Marx and Engels have also laid down some fundamental characteristics which will be common in communist revolution in every country. As they put it, "Nevertheless in the most advanced countries, the following will be pretty generally applicable:

(1) Abolition of property in land and application of all rents of land to public purposes.

(2) A heavy progressive or graduated income tax.

(3) Abolition of all right of inheritance.

(4) Confiscation of the property of all emigrants and rebels.

(5) Centralization of credit in the hands of the state, by means of a national bank with state capital and an exclusive monopoly.

(6) Centralization of the means of communication and transport in the hands of the state.

(7) Extension of factories and instruments of production owned by the state; the bringing into cultivation of wastelands, and the improvement of the society generally in accordance with a common plan.

(8) Equal liability of all to labour. Establishment of industrial armies, especially for agriculture.

(9) Combination of agriculture with manufacturing industries, gradual abolition of the distinction between town and country by a more equable distribution of the population over the country.

(10) Free education for all children in public schools. Abolition of children's factory labour in its present form. Combination of education with industrial production, etc.

9. Classless society. The most significant characteristic of communist society is that it is a classless society. In the absence of classes, the state will also wither away. As Marx and Engels put it, "When, in the course of development, class distinctions have disappeared, and all production has been concentrated in the hands of a vast association of the whole nation, the public power will lose its political character. Political power, properly so-called, is merely the organized power of one class for oppressing another. If the proletariat during its contest with the bourgeoisie is compelled by the force of circumstances, to organize itself as a class, as such, sweeps away by force the old conditions of production, then it will, along with these conditions, have swept away the conditions for the existence of class antagonisms and of classes generally, and will thereby have abolished its own supremacy as a class".

11

HUMANISM

Humanism is the philosophy according to which man is central in the scheme of things. Man is the only worthy object of knowledge. Humanism is the criterion to solve the controversies arising in human life. Ever since reason dawned in man, thoughtful persons have been in search of some one or the other criterion of reality to solve the controversies arising in human life. Such have been the attempts of Socrates, Plato, Aristotle and other ancient Greek philosophers. Philosophical thinking in ancient times everywhere was not distinguished from the religious thought. But gradually philosophers extricated themselves from religious dogmas and established philosophical thinking on independent grounds. Such were the rationalists, the empiricists, the realists and the idealists and other modern philosophers. In contemporary world of philosophy, philosophical thought was very much influenced by the developments in physical and social sciences with the result that new criteria of reality were accepted by the philosophers. The unprecedented progress in the means of transport and communication have today made the world small and brought human beings very near to each other. Human problems, therefore, have become central in all serious thinking. This has created a favourable climate for the rise of humanism.

Like other trends of thought the roots of humanism can be traced in the old Greek philosophy and in the ancient thought of India. In the West, Protegoras of Greece declared that man is the measure of all things. After Protegoras, the humanist idea could be seen in the thought of sophist philosophers and the ideas of Plato and Socrates. But this humanist trend received maximum encouragement by the Naturalist and Materialist philosophies. Charles Darwin's *Theory of Evolution* established that there is no deep gulf between man and animal in Nature. After Darwin, the idea of evolution was utilised in almost every field of human thinking and so many theories were established. Today, it has been generally accepted that animal and man are two different stages in the same process of evolution.

Humanism: Its Meaning and Implications

The English word humanism has been derived from the Latin term 'Homo' which means human being. Thus, literally speaking, humanism is the philosophy in which man occupies a central place. Etymological meaning, however, is not the sufficient meaning of a term, it includes its historical usage as well. The use of a term in the historical tradition gradually unveils the different aspects of its meaning. Thus, in order to understand the full implication of the term humanism one must take into account its historical evolution. In this historical evolution whatever has been found to be useful for human welfare has been attached with the concept of humanism such as the idea of social welfare, scientific attitude, progress of democratic institutions, etc.

Essentials of Humanism

The above discussion makes it clear that humanism is obviously against all types of super naturalism or super-humanism. It cannot consider any man to be essentially greater than other human beings. In it the term human welfare means the welfare of ordinary human beings. It does not aim at superman but only at man. Its central standpoint is faith in the dignity of man. Since man is the creature of this earth, humanism is this — worldly and against all types of other — worldly theories. The humanist ethics is not governed by any religious faith other than faith in human dignity. So far as human welfare has been advanced by science, the humanist respects science but if science becomes an impediment in his progress he would not hesitate in criticising it and fixing its limitations. The Western humanists have been lagging behind in this particular function though today many Western thinkers have started pointing out to the evils and dangers of a cult of science. Since each human being is important for the humanist, humanism is against all distinctions among human beings on the basis of country, nation, race, class, caste, sex, religion, economic status, scholarship and abilities. As a human being no human being is lower than the other. Thus humanism supports the idea of world citizenship. But as has been already pointed out, the concept of humanism does not negate other human loyalties but fulfils them because unity in diversity is the basis of the richness of the human culture.

Every philosophy holds some particular concepts in metaphysics, epistemology and axiology. As the philosophy differs so do its conceptions in these fields. According to humanism, man is the essence of reality. There is no other super human ontological reality beyond him. He is the proper object of knowledge and whatever human faculties help us in knowing any thing are faculties of knowledge. All truth is human truth and there is no truth beyond man. In axiology humanism seeks to realize a world in which the human values may be achieved to their maximum limit. For this purpose we will have to, first of all, satisfy the physical needs because in their absence no mental or spiritual development is possible. But since man is more than the animal, the bread and butter, clothes and house are not sufficient for his welfare. After the satisfaction of the physical needs the humanist, should plan for mental and spiritual progress. Man is an animal, but he is a cultural animal. Without the cultural evolution he cannot realize his humanity. Therefore, after the satisfaction of the basic physical needs, the humanist seeks to achieve progress in the fields of literature, art, thinking and other fields of cultural evolution.

Humanist Sociology

In the field of sociology the humanist approach has led to the thinking that every where the social scientist has to find social factors governing human behaviour aiming at the reform and welfare of the human individual. For example, in the field of criminology, an important branch of sociology, the social scientists have been busy in finding out the causes of crime and the possible ways of reforming the criminal. Thus, the humanist trend has led to the search for social reforms in the field of different social institutions.

Humanist Psychology

In the field of psychology the humanist trend is particularly clear in the branches known as fields of applied psychology. Thus, in industrial psychology, the psychologist aims at finding out the of all-round welfare of the human beings working under industrial conditions. His aim is not only search into conditions for realising maximum production but achieving circumstances where the worker may develop as a human being. Thus, the psychologists help him in labour welfare, a branch of human welfare in general. Similarly, in the fields of abnormal psychology and psychiatry the psychologists aim at the understanding ofhuman beings suffering from psychological ailments and finding out ways to cure them so that they might enjoy their normal life and behave as normal human beings. Thus, the aim here is not merely curative but seeks welfare. The application of psychology, consequently, is growing gradually in different fields of industry, law, medicine and above all in education. In the field of education the psychologist is everywhere in search of ways and means to improve educands as human beings. Thus, in the field of education today the humanist approach is the guiding principle.

Aims and Ideals of Education

According to humanism education aims at man-making. It should be secular, rational and scientific. It should aim at the realisation of humanist values in the individual and society. According to it the education aims at complete development of human personality. It enables man to solve individual and social problems. Its purpose is to increase efficiency and happiness of human beings. It supports democratic philosophy of education since the values of liberty, equality and fraternity are fundamental human values. Thus, the educational institutions should be based upon democratic principles. It seeks to realise peace upon the earth. The humanist tendency is rationalist and integral. It is positivist since it supports meliorism. Science alone can provide more leisure for cultural development. The individual and society are intimately related. Therefore, the children should develop team spirit and cooperation through play-way method. Community programmes should make community living easy and spontaneous. The society should be made conductive to all-round human progress.

The humanist trend integrates psychological, sociological and eclectic tendencies in education. It makes human nature the basis of education. It emphasises the value of individual differences in education. It makes education child centred.

While on the one hand the aim of education is the propagation of knowledge, social control, social development and preservation of social heritage, it also seeks to integrate all these. Thus, it is an integral approach to education. Its aim of education is integral.

This aim of education is based upon integral psychology. Man, according to the humanists, is a self having body as well as intellect. All these should be integrated.

2. Curriculum. The humanist curriculum is liberal and extensive. Along with science it has arts and humanities and also moral, religious and spiritual subjects. In fact, all types of knowledge are included in humanist curriculum.

Method of Teaching

The humanist method of teaching is based on psychology. The teacher educates according to the principles of child psychology, developmental psychology and educational psychology. Besides, the theoretical instruction methods for development of social virtues are emphasised.

Education is provided through the mother-tongue since it encourages originality and creativity. National and international languages are also taught at higher stages since the humanist seeks to encourage human communications on national and international stage.

School Organisation

The school organisation should be democratic in which the management, the teachers and the students should together govern all the activities. The school should be organised in such a way as to encourage responsibility, liberty, equality and fraternity. The school administration should be liberal and democratic. Discipline should be self-discipline. Peaceful relations should be encouraged so that the boys and girls may help in the establishment of peace upon earth. The rules and regulations should be rational and secular. Humanism is against narrow nationalism. It synthesises nationalism and internationalism. Of these it even subordinates nationalism to internationalism. Humanists believe in the principle of unity through diversity. The universities should encourage development of all the aspects of culture. Regional universities should encourage preservation of regional culture but also its synthesis in the national culture. Again, national universities should not only help in the preservation of national culture, but also encourage mixing of students from different nations and thus create an international humanist cultural atmosphere. Examples of humanist universities in India are Santiniketan of Rabindra Nath and Sri Aurobindo International University at Pondicherry.

The above educational implications of humanism reveal that it is the best blue print for the planning of future education. It is the solid basis for development of values and culture. It is an integral approach to aims and ideals, means, curriculum and organisation of education. In fact, humanism may be called the future philosophy of education acceptable and required everywhere.

12

SECULARISM

DEFINITION OF SECULARISM

The word 'secularism' was first used in the nineteenth century by George Jacob Holydake. He derived it from the Latin word 'Seculum' meaning "this present age" He used it in the context of social and ethical values or systems. Thus, secularism came to be known as a social and ethical system. The following principles were evolved by Holydake to mark this system:

(i) Primary emphasis on the material and cultural improvement of human beings.

(ii) Respect for and search for all truth, whatever be its source, which can be tested in experience leading to human betterment.

(iii) Concern for this age or world and its improvement.

(iv) An independent rational morality, which does not base itself on faith in divine commandment.

Bradlaugh observed that secularism was hostile to religion and maintained that either secularism or religion should survive.

1. Chambers Dictionary. According to Chambers Dictionary secularism is, "the belief that the state, moral, education, etc., should be independent of religion."

2. Oxford Dictionary. Oxford Dictionary defines secularism as, "the doctrine that the morality should be based solely in regard to the well-being of mankind in the present life, to the exclusion of all considerations drawn from belief in God."

3. Webster's Dictionary. Webster's Dictionary states that secularism is, "the belief that religion and ecclesiastical affairs should not enter into the functions of the state".

The limited sense of the word secularism is often placed in contrast with religion. Thus Webster gives us an alternative definition of secularism: "A system of doctrines and practices that rejects any form of religious faith and worship".

4. Brubacher. Secularism has "no religious point of view while it has a theory of moral education". "If the secularist has any religion at all it is likely that scientific doctrine constitutes the presuppositions of that religion and that scientists are its high priests".

EDUCATION COMMISSION (1964-1966)

The adoption of a secularist policy means that no religious community will be favoured or discriminated against. The instruction in religious dogmas will not be provided in state schools. But the secularist policy is not an irreligious or anti-religious policy. It does not belittle the importance of religions. It gives to every citizen the fullest freedom of religious belief and worship. It promotes not only religious toleration but also an active reverence for all religions. We have to make a distinction between 'religious education' and 'education about religions'. The former is largely concerned with the teaching of tenets and practices of a particular religion in a particular form, and it would not be practicable to provide this type of religious education in respect of any religion to pupils belonging to different faiths. But it is necessary for a multi-religious democratic State to promote a tolerant study of all religions so that its citizens can understand each other better and live amicably together.

The Education Commission (1964-66) has recommended: "We suggest that a syllabus giving well chosen information about each of the major religions should be included as a part of the course in citizenship or as a part of general education to be introduced in schools and colleges up to the first degree. It should highlight the fundamental similarities in the great religions of the world and the emphasis they place on the cultivation of certain broadly comparable moral and spiritual values". The Commission further observed: "There will be natural points of correlation between the moral values sought to be inculcated and the teachings of the great religions. All religions stress certain fundamental qualities of character, such as honesty and truthfulness, consideration for others, reverence for old age, kindness to animals, and the compassion for the needy and the suffering. In the literature of every religion, the story of parable figures prominently as a means of impressing an ethical value on the followers. The narration of such stories by the teachers at the right moment in the programme of moral education would be most effective, particularly in the lower classes. At a later stage, accounts of the lives of great religious and spiritual leaders will find a natural place.... Similarly, the celebration of festivals and different religions will afford opportunity for the narration of incidents from the life history of the leaders of these religions. In the last two years of the secondary school, a place should be found for the study of the essential teachings of the great religions".

CONSTITUTIONAL PROVISIONS

After obtaining her independence India adopted secularism as a way of life. Our Constitution guarantees the fullest freedom of religious belief and worship. It has laid down the following provisions in connection with religious and moral education in educational institutions.

Article 19 (1). "Subject to public order, morality and health and to other provisions of this part, all persons are equally entitled to freedom to conscience and the right freely to profess, practise and propagate religion."

Article 21. "No person may be compelled to pay any taxes, the proceeds of which are specifically appropriated in payment of expenses for the promotion or maintenance of any particular religion or religious denomination."

Article 22 (1). "No religious instructions shall be provided in any educational institution wholly maintained out of State funds."

Provided that nothing in this clause shall apply to an educational institution which is administered but has been established under an endowment or trust which requires that religious instructions shall be imparted in such institutions.

(2) "No person attending any educational institution recognised by the State or receiving aid out of State funds shall be required to take part in any religious institution or to attend any religious worship that may be conducted in such institution or in any premises attached thereto unless such person, or if such person is a minor his guardian has given his consent thereto."

Article 30 (1). "All minorities whether based on religion or language, shall have the right to establish and administer educational institutions of their choice."

(2) "The State shall not, in granting aid to educational institutions, discriminate against any educational institution on the ground that it is under the management of a minority, whether based on religion or language."

RECOMMENDATIONS OF THE SECONDARY EDUCATION COMMISSION

The Secondary Education Commission (1949) observed that healthy trends in regard to religion or moral behaviour spring from three sources: (1) The influence of the home, (2) the influence of the school, through the conduct and behaviour of the teachers themselves and life in the school community as a whole, and (3) the influence exercised by the public of the locality. No amount of instruction can supersede or supplant these three essential factors.

The following steps were suggested:

(1) Morning assembly with all teachers and students present should be utilized for this purpose. A general non-denominational prayer may be offered.

(2) Inspiring talks on moral instruction may be given by suitable persons selected by headmaster. Such talks should dwell on the lives of the great personages of all times and of all climes.

(3) In view of the provision of the Constitution of the Secular State, religious instructions cannot be given in schools except on a voluntary basis and outside the regular school hours; such instructions should be given to the children of the particular faith and with the consent of the parents and the management concerned. In making this recommendation we wish to emphasize that all unhealthy trends of disunity, rancour, religious hatred and bigotry should be discouraged in schools.

CHARACTERISTICS OF SECULAR EDUCATION

Secular education is identified because of the following characteristics:

1. Moral outlook. Secular education results in development of moral outlook. It is the foundation for development of character and moral development. It inculcates in students humanity, truthfulness, tolerance, honesty, courtesy, sympathy, spirit of service and sacrifice which form a noble character of man and develop his personality.

2. Development of wider attitude. Secular education makes a man dynamic and enlightened. It develops in him a wider attitude towards life, and he takes interest in social service by sacrificing his selfish motives. Education makes him courageous enough to face the problems of life and solve them to the best of his efforts and intelligence.

3. Pluralistic outlook. Secular education leads to the emergence of a healthy pluralistic outlook which fosters the growth of science, art, philosophy and even religion. A pluralistic outlook is the very essence of democracy.

4. Democratic value. Secular education helps man in developing democratic qualities like liberty, equality, fraternity and co-operative living. True secularism stresses the dignity of the individual and the sacredness of human personality. Secular education helps to establish and incorporate democratic process. Every person is treated as an end and never as means only.

5. Cultural development. Secular education helps in promotion of cultural development. It preserves and reinforces culture. Secularism and culture go hand in hand and influence each other. Secularism is the dynamic aspect of culture.

6. Scientific spirit. Secular education helps in fostering scientific spirit. It releases the individual from the bonds of blind faith. Scientific spirit implies a spirit of free enquiry, a spirit of looking at things objectively and rationally, freedom from an obsession with the past, and a more humble attitude towards our own history and achievements. Secular education promotes scientific values of rationality, objectivity and open-mindedness.

7. Synthesis of spiritual and material. Secular education glorifies material needs and promotes reverence for earthly life, without rejecting spiritual values. Secularism is based on fundamental human values. It looks upon science not merely as a means of material progress but as a quest for truth and a search for harmony with nature. It helps to strike a healthy balance between the spiritual and the material.

8. Humanitarianism. Secular education leads to humanitarianism. It stands for peace, good-will and understanding. It helps in fostering the brotherhood of man and the unity of the world. Absence of secular education causes exploitation, corruption, disaster, selfishness, aggression and hatred, chaos and disorder. Betterment of society depends upon secular based education. It raises man to a high level. It encourages the policy of Tive and let live'. It provides the basis for true humanitarianism. It helps in replacing hatred by love, selfishness by self-sacrifice and violence by non-violence. Secular education leads to happiness, order and contentment in the society by cultivating faith in truth, beauty and goodness.

EDUCATION FOR SECULARISM IN INDIA

India's present educational system promotes secular attitudes and values through its broad-based aims, curricula, enlightened teachers and appropriate activities, all emphasizing open-mindedness, progressivism, rationality, freedom from bigotry and superstition, and equal respect for all religions. The following traits characterise education for secularism in India:

1. Aims. The aims and objectives of such a system are secular. They seek to develop India as a rational, democratic, progressive and modern welfare state. The philosophy of humanism guides such educational objectives. The well-being of all the citizens of the country is the goal towards which India's educational energies are directed.

2. Organization of educational institutions. The organization of most of Indian educational institutions is based on secular principles. It is necessary to observe secular, democratic, rational criteria in appointments, promotions, admissions, and all such matters.

3. Curricula. The educational curricula at all levels in India lay special emphasis on the promotion of secular values. Lessons in textbooks are free from religious bigotry and prejudice while the good ideas and values emphasized in different religions are presented in appropriate forms. The co-curricular activities aim at promoting harmony and co-operation among different groups and respect for each other's culture in the students. It is not permitted to condemn or unduly praise any one particular religion or cultural system or institution. It is the usual practice in all schools, colleges and universities to celebrate fairs, festivals, birth anniversaries, etc., relating to different religions. While imparting moral education equal importance is given to different faiths.

4. Science teaching. Secularism stands for scientific rationalism. It stresses logical thinking and abhors superstitions and irrational things. Therefore, Indian education today puts much emphasis upon science teaching. Science is taught in a practical manner at all levels of schooling, so that it might influence the attitudes and values of the pupils. The spirit of science with emphasis on inquiry, experimentation, proof and critical outlook, permeates the teaching of other subjects also.

5. Teachers. In the education for secularism in India the teachers today are expected to treat their pupils in an impartial manner. They eschew all caste, community and class considerations in dealing with students and colleagues. Equal respect is given to all students and to all religious groups. Every conscientious teacher behaves in a truly democratic and fair manner.

Thus, the present Indian secular educational system is trying to create a social climate in the country in which secular values are sought to be promoted effectively and enthusiastically.

DIFFICULTIES IN SECULAR EDUCATIONAL SYSTEM

In a country like India, in which traditional institutions like religion, caste, untouchability, and dowry have been prevailing for thousands of years, the building up of a secular state is a very challenging task. Despite the best intentions of our Constitution makers and great leaders, it is difficult to establish and promote a really functional climate of secularism in India. The main difficulties in secular educational system are as follow:

1. Traditional bias and narrow outlook. In our country today denominational schools are allowed to function with a lot of freedom. There are D.A.V. Schools, Jain Schools, Vaish Schools, Ahir Schools, Kayastha Pathshalas, Shia Schools, Catholic Schools, Rajput Schools, etc. In these institutions the children of the respective communities or castes are admitted on preferential basis, and also the teachers of the same communities are preferred. This creates a serious difficulty in the functioning of Indian education as an integrative and secular force in Indian society.

2. Too much emphasis on theoretical learning. Our educational system presents many things only in theory. Very little effort is made to change the values and attitudes of education. Many highly educated people do not hesitate to demand big dowries. They are too much fastidious about gotras and sub-castes in deciding marriage. They ill-treat women-folk and do not show respect to other religions. The lack of tolerance and courtesy on the part of educated persons towards villagers, women, poor people, minority community members, old people, etc., in buses, trains and at other public places reveals that our present education has failed to change our values system in a desired manner.

3. Neglect of religious and cultural celebrations. Schools and colleges observe holidays on the days of important religious fairs, festivals and birthdays. The result is that the students do not get enough opportunities to understand or imbibe secular values.

4. Neglect of group activities. Educational institutions do not encourage group activities. Group activities and group methods of teaching and learning are neglected. This is a serious difficulty in the promotion of secular and free ideas and values.

13

ANCIENT INDIAN PHILOSOPHY OF EDUCATION

The aim of Indian education was initially laid down by the Vedas. According to Vedic worldview the world is pervaded by divinity and the aim of every living being is to achieve liberation. This is possible by following one's own dharma. Thus, according to the Vedas the aim of education is liberation. According to a famous statement, 'That is knowledge which gives liberation', therefore, A S. Altekar has rightly pointed out, "The knowledge, is a third eye of man, which gives him insight into all affairs and teaches him how to act. In the spiritual sphere it leads to our salvation, in the mundane sphere it leads to all-round progress and prosperity. The illumination given to us by the education shatters illusions, removes difficulties and enables us to realize the true values of life".

PHILOSOPHY OF VEDIC AND UPANISHADIC EDUCATION

The cause of liberation and bondage, according to Vedic thinker, is the mind or chitta. Therefore, liberation is possible only through the control of the mind. This was known as the technique of chitta-vrattinirodh. The Indian philosophers developed a whole technique for the control of the mind. Equanimity of the mind leads to self-realization. This self is neither individual nor social self but Brahman which is the essence of the individual and the society. The Vedic axiology does not distinguish between the social and the individual values since according to it both are part of the fundamental universal values.

The ancient Indian education was even more developed by the Upanishads. While in the field of religion the Upanishads were more introvert and monistic, they continued the tradition of the Vedas. This tradition was oral. In the words of Radha Kumud Mukerjee, "For thousands of years, even up to the time of Kumarila (8th century A.D.) it was considered a sacrilege to reduce the Veda to writing, for learning was not reading but realization, and knowledge was to be in the blood, as an organic part of one's self. Another point to be noted in this connection is that sabda or sound by itself has its own potency and value, apart from its sense, and its intrinsic attributes, its rhythm, and vibrations should be captured, Sabda is Brahma."

According to ancient Indian philosophy knowledge may be gained by three steps, Shravan or hearing, Manan or meditation and Nididhyasan or realization.

Shravan or hearing was further categorised into six types—(i) *upakrama*, a formal ceremony performed preceding the study of Veda, (ii) *abhyasa*, recitation of the texts, (iii) *apurvata*, a ready grasp of the meaning, (iv) *phala*, a comprehension of the outcome, (v) *arthavada*, the reading of elucidatory books, and (vi) *upapatti*, attainment of final conclusion.

TYPES OF EDUCATIONAL INSTITUTIONS

Describing the condition of education in ancient India, P.N. Prabhu has said, "Education in ancient India was free from any external control like that of the State or Government or any party politics. It was one of the king's duties to see that the learned pundits pursued their studies and their duty of imparting knowledge without interference from any source whatever. So also education did not suffer from any communal interest or prejudices in India". There were three types of educational institutions:

1. Gurukula. This, as the name indicates, was the family of the teacher and his residence where the students used to stay during the period of study. Gradually, the Gurukula were extended to include a number of buildings. However, the institution was built up around the family of teacher. The primary duty of the student was to serve the teacher and his family. The students were like sons of the teacher and the whole institution lived like a family.

2. Parishad. These were bigger educational institutions where several teachers used to teach different subjects. This may be compared to a college.

3. Sammelan. Sammelan literally means getting together for a particular purpose. In this type of educational institutions scholars gathered at one place for discussions and competitions, generally on the invitation of the king.

DISCIPLINE

The Vedic system of education very much emphasized the importance of discipline in the attainment of knowledge. This, however, was self-discipline. In fact, it was self control which was realized by observance of rules of the Brahmacharya Ashrama. These rules will be discussed in details in sequence. The Parishads or the local academies were initiated by the king. Therefore, the scholars and aspirants of knowledge gathered at the Parishad with perfect academic order. There was hardly any need for insisting upon rules and regulations as these were laid down by scriptures. No one questioned the scripture's command concerning discipline. Therefore, discipline was self-imposed as a part of self-culture.

EDUCATION IN THE ASHRAMA SYSTEM

Education, according to Vedic system, is the sole aim of Brahmacharya Ashrama. All the details concerning education have been given in the context of Brahmachaiya Ashrama.

Meaning of Ashrama

According to *Sanskrit Hindi Dictionary* of V.S. Apte the term ashrama means stages, monastery, duties, etc. Writing in *Encyclopaedia of Religion and Ethics,* the German scholar Paul Deussen gives two meanings to the word ashram: (1) That place where people labour or make efforts, (2) To labour or make efforts. The word ashrama comes from the Sanskrit root srama giving the meaning of making an effort. In this way Ashrama literally means a step in the journey of life. In the words ofP.V. Kane, "The word ashrama is derived from srama, to exert, to labour and etymologically means a stage in which one exerts oneself". According to Hindu ethics, the final aim of life is liberation. And every ashrama is a step in the long journey to that aim. "The whole of the life of a human individual is for the Hindu," says P.H. Valvalker, "a kind of schooling and self-discipline". In the Shanti Parva of *Mahabharata,* Saint Vedavyasa has described ashrama as a four rung ladder which takes one in the direction of Brahman. Vedavyasa says, *Chatushpadi hi nihsreni brahman yesha Pratishthita, etamaruhya nihshreni brahmaloke mahiyate.*

In this way, in each ashrama the person prepares himself for every succeeding ashrama state. Literally, an ashrama is a halting place. The ashrama system is a means of systematic development for the better life. Dr. P.M. Modi has tried to prove that in the beginning there were only three ashramas and that Vanprastha and Sanyasa were considered as one ashrama. He has cited instances in his favour from *Chhandogya Upanishad and Manu Smriti.* It is in *Jabala Upanishad* that one finds the mention of four ashramas for the first time. This scheme of the stages of life during the period preceding Dharmashastras was rather indefinite. They were made definite for the first time by Dharmashastras. The Dharmashastras maintained clearly that each individual should normally pass through the four stages of life known as ashramas. In the second chapter of *Manu Smriti,* the author has described in details the characteristics and the activities of Brahmacharaya Ashrama. The third chapter describes the duties of Grihastha Ashrama. The fourth chapter describes this ashrama in four varnas. The Vanprastha Ashrama has been discussed in chapter sixth. This chapter also discusses the last ashrama known as Sanyasa. Thus, according to Dharmashastras, the stages of human individual's life are four: *Brahmachaiya, Grihastha, Vanprastha and Sanyasa.* Of these, at last three have been described by Upanishads before Dharmashastras. According to P. V. Kane, "The word ashrama does not occur in the Samhitas or Brahmanas. But this cannot be stretched to mean that the stages of life denoted by this word in the Sutras were unknown throughout the Vedic period".

Number of Ashramas

From the times of the most ancient Dharmasutras the number of ashramas has been four, though there are slight differences in the nomenclature and in their sequence. According to *Ap. Dh. Sutra,* "There are four ashramas, viz. (staying in) the teacher's house, the stage of householder, stage of being a muni, the stage of being a forest dweller". According to *Gaut. Dharmasutra,* there are four ashramas; brahmachari, grihastha, bhikshu and vaikhanasa. According to *Vas. Dh. Sutra,* there are four ashramas, brahmachari, grihastha, vanaprastha and parivraj aka. According to *Manu Smriti* there are four ashramas, the last being called Yati and also sanyasa. According to *Manu Smriti* the span of human life is 100 years though all do not live to that age. In fact, it is the maximum age one can expect to reach. This has been divided into four parts so that one may lead an all-round integral life. It is not necessary that each of these stages should be lived for 25 years it may be more or less. However, normally the span of each ashrama was prescribed as 25 years. According to *Manu Smriti* the first part of man's life is Brahmacharya in which he learns at his teacher's house and after he has finished his study, in the second part of his life he marries and becomes a householder, discharges his debts to his ancestors by begetting sons and to the Gods by performing yajnas. Then, when he sees that his head has grey hair and that there are wrinkles on his body he resorts to the forest, i.e., becomes a vanaprastha. After spending the third part of his life in the forest for some time he spends the rest of his life as a sanyasin. Similar rules have been laid down by other Dharmashastras with, of course, minor differences here and there. For example, according to *Baudhayana Dharmashastra,* the stage of sanyasa starts after the 70th year.

Interpretation of this Scheme

The abovementioned scheme of four ashramas was interpreted from three different points of view, as follows:

1. Samuchchaya (orderly co-ordination). According to this view a person can resort to the four ashramas one after another in order and that he may not drop any one or more and pass on to the next nor may he resort to the householder's life after becoming a sanyasin. This view was primarily supported by Manu. This view lays emphasis upon the householder since the other ashramas depend upon it. Most of the Dharmashastras push the last two ashramas in the background so much so that according to some of them these are forbidden in the Kali age.

2. Vikalpa (option). According to this view there is an option after Brahmacharya, i.e., a man may become a parivrajaka immediately after he finishes his study or immediately after the householder's way of life. This view has been supported by *Vashistha Dharmashastra, Yajnavalkya Smriti* and other.

3. Buddha (annulment or contradiction). According to this view there is really one ashrama and that is that of the householder. The first stage is a mere preparation for this ashrama while the other last two ashramas are inferior to it. This view was supported by Gautama and Baudhayana. According to Gautama, there is only one ashrama. According to Baudhayana the ashramas other than that of householder do not beget off-spring and are therefore not much important. It was due to the influence of this viewpoint that almost all the Dharmashastras praise the ashrama of householder as the highest. This is particularly important from the point of view of provision for social development, progress, stability and justice.

In spite of the above three views about the following of the ashrama system, the general view believes that all the four ashramas have their value and details about the activities and duties of all these ashramas have been prescribed by Dharmashastras. Some have clearly pointed out that there is no distinction due to a superiority among the four ashramas. Other maintained that the householder's life was the rule and other ashramas were for the blind and other incapable persons. This view has been vehemently opposed by others.

Brahmacharya Ashrama

The first of the four ashramas is Brahmacharya Ashrama. It starts with the *Upanayana* ceremony. Brahmacharya means the leading of the life like a Brahman. In this ashrama, the student or Brahmachari lived up to 25 years of age with his teacher studying the Vedas and leading a life of self-control. The education and control of the Brahmacharya prepared a person for future life. Certain rules and observances are prescribed for all Brahmacharins. They are of two kinds, some are prescribed for a very short time and some have to be observed for all the years of studenthood. The first kind of observances were generally concerned with studies. The second kind of observances, i.e., those which have to be observed throughout this period were concerned with the daily routine and general discipline of the persons in this stage of life. Of the two the later were definitely more important. These are principally *achamana, gurususrusa, vaksamyma* (silence), *samidhadana.* The smritis have laid down detailed rules about these observances. The rules centre principally around *agniparicharya* (worshipping fire), *bhiksha* (begging for food), *sandhyopasana*, study of Veda and its methods and duration, avoidance of certain foods and drinks and other matters like singing, etc., *gurususrusa* (including honouring him and his family and other elders) and the special vratas of the Brahmachari. The rules about different aspects of the students life also fall in the category of the rules about Brahmacharya Ashrama.

ASPECTS OF VEDIC EDUCATION

Teacher as a Pivot

The pivot of the whole educational system of ancient India was the teacher variously called acharya, guru, upaddhyaya. In *Manu* and other *Smritis* there is some divergence about the greatness of the acharya. According to *Manu Smriti* the father (janaka) and the teacher are called father (Pita) but the father who imparts the sacred Veda is superior to the father who gives birth, since the birth in spiritual learning is for a Brahmin of eternal benefit, here and hereafter. But in another place, Manu says that an acharya is ten times superior to an upaddhyaya, the father is superior to a hundred acharyas. According to Gautama, the acharya is the highest among all gurus while according to some the mother is the highest. According to *Yajnavalkya Smriti* the mother is higher than the acharya.

The Dharmashastras define the acharya as one who performs the upanayana of the student and imparts the whole Veda to him. The nirukta defines acharya as follows: he makes the student understand the proper course of conduct, or he collects wealth from the student or gathers together the meaning of words, or he increases the intelligence of the student. According to *Ap. Dh. Sutra,* "The acharya is so-called since the student gathers his duties from him". According to *Manu Smriti,* the teacher, after performing upanayana, teaches his pupil the rules about *saucha* (bodily purity), *achara* (rules of conduct in every day life), the offering of fuel-stick in fire and *sandhya* or adoration. Though the words *acharya*, guru and upaddhyaya are very often used as synonyms, ancient writers made a distinction between them. According to *Manu Smriti*, an upaddhyaya is one who teaches to a student a portion of the Veda or the Vedaftgas (subsidiary lores of the Veda) as a means of his own livelihood and a guru is one who performs the samsakars and who maintains the child. This latter definition shows that guru means the father here. According to *Yajnavalkya Smriti*, the guru is one who performs the samsakars and imparts the Veda. This corroborates the statement made above that originally the father himself taught the Veda to his son. The word guru is often used in the sense of any elderly person, male or female who is entitled to respect. According to *Manu Smriti* whoever confers on another the benefit of knowledge, whether great or small, is the latter's guru. All these praises of the guru by the Dharmashastras shows that they held knowledge as the highest value and insisted upon the sense of gratitude in every one who achieved knowledge. Faith in the teacher was a necessary qualification for the achievement of knowledge. It is undeniable that this glorification of the teacher may have left to some of them loosing their needs but in contrast to the modern western philosophy of education it has its advantages. In fact, both these extremes are unjust, the former to the educand and the latter to the educator. In a just system of education both should be given a proper place.

The Dharmashastras have not praised the teacher without any reason. They have insisted upon very high qualifications for being a teacher. They have warned about the dangers of entrusting the job of a teacher to persons not worthy of it. According to *Ap. Dh. Sutra*, he whom a teacher devoid of learning, initiates enters from darkness into darkness and he also (an acharya) who is himself unlearned (enters into darkness). It further provides that one should desire a performer of one's upanayana who is endowed with learning and whose family is hereditarily learned and who is serene in mind and that one should study Vedic lore under him up to the end (of Brahmacharya) as long as the teacher does not fall off from the path of dharma. Similar qualifications have been laid down by other Dharmashastras. The teacher had to be a Brahmana, learned in Veda, knowing Dharma, pure, coming from a good family and having an ideal character. In educational system also the Dharmashastras have insisted upon the varna hierarchy. It has been generally maintained that Brahmana should be the teacher. According to *Vayupuran*, as to acharya in upanayana must be a Brahmana; as to the study of Veda one should ordinarily learn the Veda from a Brahmana teacher; in times of difficulty (i.e., when a Brahmana is not available) one may learn the Veda from a kshatriya or vaisya teacher; but in such circumstances the only service that a Brahmana student rendered to the guru would be following after the non-Brahmana teacher; he had not to render bodily service (such as shampooing or washing the feet, etc.). The *Mit.* on *Yajnavalkya Smriti* remarks that a kshatriya or vaisya should teach a Brahmana only when urged by him and not at his sweet will. Manu allowed only teaching to a kshatriya, but did not allow him to make it a means of his livelihood. In fact, the Indian thinkers prescribed a social structure with definite division of labour and permitted only exceptions in certain cases. They very much insisted upon keeping the social structure in tact and not violating it. This rigidity had obviously resulted in so many disadvantages but it also facilitated continuity, regularity and order in social system.

Method of Instruction

The method of instruction of education was generally oral. The first thing that was taught to the boy was the *pranava* and the *vyahrtis* and the *Gayatri.* Then the boy was to be taught other parts of the Veda. Detailed instructions were laid down about the method of teaching. According to *Manu Smriti,* the student should sip water *(achamana)* when about to begin Vedic study, should face the north, should fold both hands together (and place them on his knee), should wear light (pure) clothes, should at the beginning and end of Vedic study, clasp the feet of the teacher with crossed hands and should touch the right foot of the teacher with his own right and left foot with the left hand, should repeat 'om' at the beginning and at the end of Vedic study. The teacher should say to the pupil 'repeat' and should stop from teaching with the words 'let there be a pause. ' The study of Veda was the first duty of every twice born person *(dvijati).* According to *Manu Smriti,* the whole Vedas together with Upanishads were to be learnt by every dvijati. According to *Yajnavalhya Smriti,* it is Veda alone that confers the highest bliss upon dvijatis by enabling them to understand and perform sacrifices, austerities and auspicious acts (like samsakars). Since the literature was very wide, concessions had to be made to the shortness of human life and the weakness of the human mind. Therefore, generally it was prescribed that one should study the Shakha of the Veda which his ancestors studied and should perform religious rites according to it. As the study of the Veda was a duty enjoined upon a Brahmana, so teaching Veda to another was a duty. This exclusive glorification of the Brahmins very much led to what N.K. Dutt describes as the "pride of scholasticism" among the professed scholars. And it has been rightly pointed out by S. Cromwell Crawford, "Compounded with racial and sacerdotal pride, the pride of scholasticism elevated barriers between Brahmins and non-Brahmins. In this way, the good effect of the strictness of Brahmacharya in specialising learning and in enforcing high moral discipline was neutralised by the increased rigidness and hauteur of caste, which is one of the many factors making India a land of contrasts".

EDUCATOR'S DUTIES

It should not be supposed that the Dharmashastras, while insisting upon educands' respect towards the educator, used less strict words while insisting upon educators' duty towards the educand. In fact, the educational relationship was a two-way relationship. It was reciprocal. According *to Apastamb Dharmasutra,* "Loving him like his own son, and full of attention, he shall teach him the sacred science, without hiding anything in the whole law. And he shall not use him for his own purpose to the detriment of his studies, except in times of distress. The pupil who, attending to (teacher), accuses his (principal and first) teacher of ignorance, remains no (longer) a pupil. A teacher also, who neglects the instruction (of his pupil), does no (longer) remain a teacher". The purport of education was the moral and intellectual growth of the students. These two elements were never separated. Indeed, the later was contingent upon the former. According to the Sacred Law, only the person who is pure may be instructed in the Veda. Neither (the study of) the Vedas, nor liberality, nor sacrifices, nor any (self-imposed) restraint, nor austerities, ever procure the attainment (of rewards) to a man whose heart is contaminated (by sensuality). Moral culture not only preceded intellectual culture, but was the weightier of the two. A Brahmana, who completely governs himself, though he knows the Savitri only, is better than he who knows the three Vedas, (but) does not control himself.

ABSENCE OF SOCIAL JUSTICE

The absence of social justice in education is particularly observed in case of partiality towards the education of all the vamas other than Brahmin and also of the women. These were given a secondary place. Literary education among women was in a languishing state. Therefore, there was no question of co-education. Not much material is available about the education of Kshatriyas, Vaishyas and Sudras. The entire education system was entrusted to Brahmanas. Summing up the state of education in Dharmashastras, P.V. Kane has written, "The salient features of the educational system outlined in the Dharmashastras works are the high and honourable position assigned to the teacher, the close personal contact of the pupil with the teacher and individual attention, the pupil's stay with the teacher as a member of his family, oral instruction and the absence of books, stem discipline and control of emotions and the will, cheapness as no fees were stipulated for".

CRITICAL EVALUATION

The institution of education as prescribed by Dharmashastras can be favourably compared with any other system of education in the West, ancient or modern. Given the high character and scholarship of the teacher, it was the most ideal system of education. However, its defects are equally obvious. Summarising these defects, P.V. Kane, has admitted, "The defects of the Indian system were that it was too literary, there was too much memorising, boys under it had hardly any instruction in useful manual arts and crafts, the studies were not brought in contact with practical life". The discipline was rigorous and joyless. Many of these defects were due to the exigencies of the caste system which assigned particular avocations to particular, castes. Kane, however, rightly adds, "We cannot and should not compare the system with the systems of education prevalent in the 20th century, when several subjects such as literature, music and the fine arts, handicrafts, mathematics, science, history and geography are taught in the schools to all boys and when it has been recognized that education is a prime concern of the State".

14

Swami Dayananda

Aims of Education

The ultimate aim of education according to Dayananda is to get liberation. In his *Satyartha Prakash,* Dayananda has written, that the individual who can realize the form of knowledge and ignorance simultaneously can win liberation by achieving freedom from ignorance, from the cycle of birth and rebirth. Being an idealist, Dayananda has laid special emphasis upon education as a means of character development. Development of character is based on achieving knowledge, because in the absence of knowledge character cannot be formed. Knowledge brings happiness in the present world as well as in the next. The aim of education is to give true knowledge to the individual and thus enable him to conduct himself properly. On this subject, Dayananda has written in *Vyavahara Bhanu* that man can never get happiness through ignorance, and therefore, in order to get salvation one must try to acquire knowledge.

Emphasis on Practice

It is clear from the foregoing account that Dayananda laid great emphasis upon the practical aspect of education also, not merely on the spiritual aspect alone. One of the chief aims of education is to develop morality and good conduct. For this, Dayananda believes that abstinence or self denial is essential. Another objective of education is to provide real knowledge. In his *Satyartha Prakash* Dayananda has pointed out, that parents and teachers must guide their children and their educand and tell them to adopt the actions dictated by their religion and also to discard those activities exercised by the same religion. Besides, all those who gain knowledge must propagate that knowledge. Dayananda did not neglect the social aspect of education when pointing out the objectives. Education aims not merely at the development of individuals but also at the creation of individuals who can successfully fulfil their obligations in society. Dayananda was also in favour of universal education including even the most backward sections of Hindu society, even those traditionally prevented from receiving education, for religious reasons. He believed that the educated individual is a successful and useful member of society. Dayananda said that blessed are those men and woman whose minds are constantly anxious to get the satisfaction of knowledge, those who are devoid of egotism and vanity, full of gentleness, sweetness, beautiful expression, those who are engaged in destroying the pains and sufferings of others by bestowing knowledge and truth upon them, those who put an end to the darkness of others, those who are constantly in doing good and benefiting others.

Universal and Compulsory Education

Dayananda was in favour of universal and compulsory education in the country. He favoured the education of every man, woman and child, irrespective of the caste or creed to which he or she belonged. He held the state responsible for ensuring that every parent sent his or her child for education. Obviously, Dayananda was in agreement with the democratic ideal of education. He even insisted that the State must punish those who deprived their children of education. In this manner Dayananda refuted the medieval practice of denying education to certain sections of society.

Child Education

Dayananda gave it as his opinion that the child's earliest education should take place at home. His opinion is borne out by many modern educationists. In his *Satyartha Prakash*, Dayananda has commented on child education, and pointed out that parents must give the best possible education to the children so that they may progress on the path of civilization. They should never be permitted to indulge in any bad activity. When the child learns to speak, his mother should guide him in correct pronunciation so that he may enunciate his words and sentences with the correct intonation of seniors and equated people so that he may learn, apart from proper speech, how to behave correctly in the presence of revered people.

Diversified Multi-Faceted Curriculum

Expressing his opinion on the subject of a proper curriculum for the education of individuals, Dayananda suggested a more or less common pattern for everyone. He opposed the traditional bias against allowing women to study the Vedas on the ground that ignorance of Vedas would handicap their pronunciation of Sanskrit mantras and thus make it impossible for them to participate in religious ceremonies, like the yagya. In addition to a common educational programme for children of all the four castes, Dayananda paid special attention to specific education to conform to the requirements of each caste. He did not favour the principle of allowing the educand to read any and all religious texts. He felt it would be better to subject these texts to various tests prescribed in the shastras, and only those should be prescribed which pass these tests. Education should begin with the teaching of Panini's *Grammar of Sanskrit*, paying special attention to accurate and precise pronunciation. This should be followed by teaching of the mantras of *Astadhyayi*.

Contribution to Educational Philosophy

Thus, it is clear that Dayananda favoured a diversified education, combining general education with religious as well as professional training. The need for religious education is felt in the sphere of character building, because character cannot be developed without it. And for this purpose, Dayananda established a number *of Arya Samajas* and *Gurukulas* all over the country, particularly in the north. The *Arya Samaj* is an organizing institution which looks after the Vedic colleges and schools. A Dayananda Anglo Vedic College was established at Lahore in 1886, and a *Gurukula* at Kangri in 1902, which has now become an independent university. In addition to these institutions, Dayananda also established *Gurukulas* at Jawalapur and Vrindavan. For girls he established Gurukulas at Dehradun, Baroda, Sasni, and at other places. Nowadays, one finds similar colleges and schools in almost every district and big town, operated by the Dayananda Anglo Vedic Trust, which seeks to propagate the ideas of Dayananda. Thus, not only did the organisation support the idea of universal education, he also established an organization in the form *of Arya Samaj* which is trying to spread education in every part of the country.

Dayananda's educational philosophy is based on Vedic philosophy, although his interpretation of Vedic philosophy is unique. When he first preached his lesson, there was the greatest need to protect Hindu religion and philosophy from the insulates of Muslim and Christian religions. He saved Hindu society from fragmentation, and gave to women a new place in Hindu society. He protected the ancient Hindu values from the influence of Muslim and Christian cultures and tried to maintain the traditional modes of thinking. His ideas on education have great significance for contemporary educational philosophy.

15

ANNIE BESANT

In his article *Indian Unrest* (London, 1910), Sir Valentine Chirol wrote, "No Hindu has done so much to organize and consolidate the movement of revival as Mrs. Annie Besant, who in her Central Hindu College at Banaras, and her Theosophical Institution at Adyar, Madras, has openly proclaimed her faith in the superiority of the whole Hindu system to the arrogant civilization of the West. Is it surprising that Hindus should turn their backs upon our civilization, when an Englishwoman of highly trained intellectual power comes and tells them that it is they who possess and have from all times possessed the key to supreme wisdom—that their gods, their philosophy, their morality are in a higher plane of thought than the West has ever reached"?

Thus Annie Besant had two chief lines of approach to the re-awakening of India and the achievement of Independence: (1) the Religious (2) the Educational. She gave lectures and supported the Independence movement. She criticised the British openly regarding their policies in India. The British, in India as well as in England, opposed her strongly for her critical views.

Annie Besant was the founder of the All India Women's Conference. This attracted many Indian women and became a strong force for Women's Education, Child Marriage Bill, the Sharda Act, and many other reforms affecting women and children. Annie Besant started many of the reforms that have given women the equality of status and rights which they enjoy today in India. She brought about a revival in the study and application of Hindu philosophy and culture at a time when these were fading. To quote in her own words, "I set myself toward showing the insufficiency of materialism as an answer to the problems of life and the immense superiority of Hinduism as a philosophy encasing an all-embracing reverence, and a science of Yoga. All these were an open road to the invisible, to the ancient Rishis of India and the East, to the saints of Christendom, to the wisdom which included all religions and excluded none."

Annie Besant lived and worked in India during the period when Rabindra Nath Tagore, Sri Aurobindo Ghosh and Mahatma Gandhi were carrying on their revolutionary ideas and ideals in the social, educational, religious and political fields. She supported their causes and furthered their aims by her great work and noble example. She had a great zeal and missionary endeavour for social reform, educational expansion and India's freedom.

In India her publications include the following:
(1) Education as a National Duty (Benaras, 1903)
(2) The Education of Indian Girls (Benaras, 1906)
(3) Principles of Education (Madras, 1915)
(4) Education for the New Era (London, 1919)
(5) Theosophical Education Report (Madras, 1917)
(6) Some Lessons from the Mahabharata (Benaras, 1899)
(7) Sri Ramchandra, the Ideal King (Benaras and London, 1901)
(8) Hindu Ideals (Benaras and London, 1904)
(9) Sanatan Dharma: An Advanced Textbook of Hindu Religion & Ethics (Benaras, 1904)
(10) The Universal Textbook of Religion and Morals (Adyar 1914-1915, 3 Vols.)
(11) Lectures on Political Science (Adyar, 1919)
(12) Legends and Tales (London, 1883)
(13) Civilization's Deadlock and the Keys (London, 1924)
(14) Kamala Lectures: Indian Ideals in Education and Philosophy, Religion and Art (Calcutta, 1925)
(15) World Problems of Today (London, 1924)
(16) India Bound or Free (London and New York, 1925).

Annie Besant died in 1933. She left an indelible mark on Indian education, the fight for women's rights as well as on India's aspirations for freedom.

PRINCIPLES OF THEOSOPHY

True religion, according to Annie Besant, consists not only in one's feelings towards God but also in performing duties towards our fellowmen. A morally good man who in an atheist is in a far higher state of being than the man who believes in God and is selfish, cruel and unjust.

Theosophy as a great religion has two parts—a spirit and a body (1) Knowledge of God (2) Dogma and rites. Knowledge of God is called Brahma Vidya and belongs equally to all great religions of the world—Hinduism, Christianity, Islamic Sufism, Judaism. No man is a true theosophist unless he has a direct knowledge of God. Thus he may arrive at through any religion, or by his own earnest efforts to seek the truth.

Thus Theosophy emphasizes two principles: (a) The Unity of God who is the Universal source of all existence and (b) Universal brotherhood of man.

Ethics of Theosophy

This consists of the highest and purest teachings of world's noblest saints, prophets and founders of religions. All that is sweet and most lofty in the world's religions and all that is most inspiring and ennobling in the philosophies of all countries and religions of the world form the ethics of theosophy. If man lives by the highest principles that he can grasp, he becomes capable of appreciating the sublime. The theosophist looks up to the examples of Christ, Buddha, Rama and all great religious leaders. He strives to become like them.

IDEAS ON EDUCATION

Annie Besant's educational philosophy is based on the Theosophical Ideal of Education according to which each child should receive an education suited to develop his particular and individual faculties. He should be imparted education which will make him useful as a citizen in his community and his country.

Aims of Education

According to Annie Besant education should draw out the child's capacities, and develop and train them so that he becomes a healthy and useful member of a civilized society.

The object of theosophical education are as follows:

(i) To train the body in health, vigour and grace, so that it may express the emotions with beauty, and the mind with accuracy and strength.

(ii) To train the emotions to love all that is beautiful.

(iii) To sympathise with joys and sorrows of others and to inspire to serve others until we love our elders as our parents, our equals as our brothers and sisters, and youngsters as our children.

(iv) To find joy in sacrificing for great causes for the helpless and compassion for those who suffer.

(v) To train and discipline the mind in right thinking, right judgment and memory.

(vi) To subdue body, emotion and mind to spirit.

(vii) Education should make man a good citizen of free and spiritual commonwealth of humanity.

Annie Besant divided the entire period of education in life, into three parts. These are as follows:

First Period: 1-7 Years

(1) The physical height and development of the child's body should be the chief concern of parents and the teacher. The child's entire future depends on the care bestowed on the child during the first seven years of his life. In later years nothing can fully make up for insufficient food or insufficient light, exercise and sleep, during this period.

(2) This is also the period for cultivating observation, for training the senses into alertness, accuracy and grasp, for training hand and finger, skills of memory especially the word-memory which is very quick and retentive in childhood. Nursery rhymes remain in the memory for life. Rhymes and poems employing succession of events, names or dates learnt in childhood, are never forgotten.

(3) No abstract reasoning processes should be forced upon the child during this period. His attention should be directed to observation of sequences of facts but not the logical processes. The brain cells are not sufficiently interrelated to make any train of reasoning intelligible. There is no benefit in memorising logical sequences which are not understood by the child.

Second Period: 7-14 Years

During this period education should be chiefly directed to the development and training of the emotions, and thus to the building of character. Histories consisting largely of biographical stories of great men of varied types, saints, heroes, martyrs, political, artistic, literary leaders in every department of human life. These should inspire enthusiasm and shape the ideals of developing boys and girls. In this way character will be built and the channels of right emotions will be prepared. Thus the great emotional rush which follows the attainment of puberty will find channels ready to receive it, to rentier it uplifting and beneficent, instead of degrading and mischievous.

Third Period: 14-21 Years

This period should be the time of intellectual development of hard and strenuous mental labour. The reasoning faculty should be thoroughly trained by logic and mathematics. Specialization in some areas should prepare the youth for his future career.

Curriculum. Annie Besant prescribed the following curriculum for different periods:

(i) First Period: 1-7 Years. Tales of noble deeds and heroism, emphasis on health, physical dexterity and skills; nursery rhymes, cultivation of word-memory, observation of sequences of facts, love of beauty, arousing of sympathy for the poor and helpless.

(ii) Second Period: 7-14 Years. History and Biography, Geography, Physiology, Physics, Chemistry and Geology should be taught. Practical and laboratory work in the sciences should be included. Algebra, Geometry and Arithmetic should occupy an important place in the curriculum.

(iii) Third Period: 14-21 Years. This is the period of the rapid intellectual development. Therefore, Logic and Mathematics should be taught intensively. The sense of duty to one's fellowmen should be taught through Civics and Social studies. Sciences such as Biology, Philosophy and Psychology should be mastered. Literature, Philosophy, Economics should occupy an important place. Various aspects of the Arts should also be included in the curriculum. Specialization in some chosen field should prepare the student for his future career in life.

Religious Teaching should begin with easy stories in the child's early stages of education and pass on to metaphysics in the later years in all of the three stages, being adapted to the intelligence and understanding of the student.

Physical Training should be all-pervading. It should be adapted in theory and practice to the physical development and needs of the growing pupil in all the above-mentioned three stages.

All Round Education

Explaining her scheme of all-round education Annie Besant writes, "I look forward to a time when every child shall receive, in the national schools, the elements of a literary, scientific, artistic and technical education. No boy or girl should leave the school ignorant of our literature, or of the wonders of science. He should delight in beauty. He should also learn some definite means of bread-winning, let it be tailoring, cooker or carpentry or any trade or profession. Every pair of hands should be able to do at least some one thing well by which an honest living may be earned".

DR. ANNIE BESANT'S CONTRIBUTION TO EDUCATION

1. Patriotism. Dr. Besant loved India. Her respect and understanding of India's religions and philosophies was profound. She wrote many books and pamphlets on Hinduism, as well as text-books for students in Physics, Chemistry, Biology and stories from the Mahabharata as well as narratives of heroic deeds for children to read.

2. Nationalism. Dr. Besant's support of India's national aspirations led her to encourage and support many innovative educational efforts. She founded many schools and colleges. The Central Hindu School and College was founded by her in 1898 at Benaras. It later became the Benaras Hindu University. She also founded the Theosophical Institute at Adyar, Madras.

3. Multisided efforts. Not only did Dr. Besant start the Central Hindu School and College at Benaras, she organized its debating clubs and many sports organizations. She was an excellent teacher and educational administrator. She set high standards for other teachers and organizers around her. She was admired and loved by her students and colleagues for her dedication and efficiency in educational endeavours.

4. Against Child-Marriage. Annie Besant took a firm stand against Child-Marriage which was widely prevalent in India at that time. Students were discouraged from marrying while they were still studying. They and their parents were made to realize that the students were not mature enough to assume adult responsibilities.

5. Social Reform. She gave speeches on nationalism, freedom and social reforms in schools and colleges as well as in public. This made the students realize their responsibilities to live and work for a tree India.

6. Women's education. Annie Besant was an ardent promotor of women's education in India. She organized many groups to strive for the furtherance of girls' schools and colleges in many parts of India where facilities did not exist, and girls and women were neglected. She worked to raise the status of girls and women through education.

7. Growth of educational institutions. Due to Annie Besant's pioneering work in education, many communities, Parsi, Muslim, Arya Samaj, Dev Samaj, Brahmo Samaj and other started schools for their youth on modern lines. She inspired a great deal of enthusiasm for education in India at a time when the British neglected educational betterment and expansion to fit the needs of the country, in their schemes.

8. Vocational Education. Dr. Besant was a strong advocate of vocational education in schools. By the end of schooling, every pupil should have learnt some trade or craft: carpentry, cooking, tailoring, or any useful skill or vocation, to enable him to earn a living, at any stage in his educational career.

9. Anti Racism. Annie Besant strongly believed and preached that there is no such thing as racial superiority. She maintained that the white races and the so-called higher castes of people are not in any way superior to other people. Therefore, domination by races and castes of people over other is totally unjustified. All people in the world are endowed with intelligence and ability, regardless of race or caste. All have a right to educational opportunity and the amenities of life. There should be free schools established for universal, free and compulsory education in India. No one should be denied the right to education and the right to upward mobility.

16

M. K. GANDHI

AIMS AND IDEALS OF EDUCATION

1. Drawing out the Basic. Elaborating his views about the aims of education, Gandhiji has said, "By education I mean an all round drawing out of the best in child and man, body, mind and spirit. Literacy is not the end of education, not even the beginning. It is one of the means whereby man and woman can be educated. Literacy in itself is no education".

2. Livelihood. Gandhiji was highly critical of the educational policy implemented by British government. In his opinion the aim of education is self-dependence, and education must enable every girl and boy to develop the ability to depend upon himself or herself. The ability to earn one's livelihood is part of this independence or self-reliance. As he himself puts it, "This education ought to be for them a kind of insurance against unemployment". That is why Gandhiji placed so much emphasis upon industrial training in his own plan for basic education which was intended to acquaint the child with real life. He wanted the educator to become the means of producing ideal citizens. Seeing the endemic poverty of the nation, he suggested that education in India should be based on industrial training and the development of manual skill and handicrafts.

3. Character Formation. Like Rousseau Gandhiji also believes in paidocentric education, that is, education which centres around the child. He impressed upon people that the cultural aspect of education was far more important than its literary aspect, because it is through the cultural aspect that the child learns conduct and ideas and develops his character and ideals. As he puts it, "True education is that which draws out and stimulates the spiritual, intellectual and physical faculties of the children". Hence, the aim of education is the complete development of the child, its physical, mental and spiritual aspects. For him character formation was more important than literacy. He was once asked what his education would aim at after the country won its independence. He answered without hesitation that it would be designed to develop the character of the people. And, in character, Gandhiji addressed the importance of thought, word and deed, non-violence and truth. He, like many before him, felt that abstinence was an essential weapon for the educand. He was a supporter of the ancient Indian ideals of education. He in fact felt that the words educand and Brahmachari should be treated as synonymous. And for him, abstinence meant a persistent effort to reach God in the least possible time.

4. Complete Development. It is clear from the foregoing account that Gandhiji viewed education from a comprehensive or broadminded standpoint. Any education that develops only one aspect of a child's personality can be dubbed narrow and one sided. And it is just such an education which has been the bane of our culture. Education must aim at developing the child's personality instead of limiting itself to providing the child with bits and pieces of information. Not only must education guide the individual towards self-knowledge, it must instill in him all those qualities which go to the making up of a good and responsible citizen. Gandhiji has made a distinction between the immediate and long-term aims of education, suggesting that such aims as getting certificates of merits or degrees or obtaining education for livelihood should be considered the immediate aims. But the final aim of education can only be self-knowledge. Thus, Gandhiji states that education must make the individual to live and earn his daily bread, to be the means of his sustenance. As he himself puts it, "I value individual freedom, but you must not forget that man is essentially a social being. He has risen to his present status by learning to adjust his individuality to the requirements of social progress". His faith in religion is at the base of his liberal attitude to education. Realization of good is, in fact, the end or the goal of all human activity and sendee to humanity its finest means. It is only natural that such a faith should lead him to stress the social objectives of education more than the personal or individual ones.

5. Synthesis of individual and social aims. In this way Gandhiji synthesized the individual and social aims of education. He did not restrict education to the achievement of any one single aim. He looked to the process of education from various perspectives. Therefore, he assigned different aims to education at different times, so much so that sometimes they looked mutually contradictory and even self- defeating. A closer examination of all these statements of Gandhiji, however, shows that these aims of education are complementary to each other.

6. All round growth. In the history of education different educationists have defined the ideals of education in different ways. Most educationists have, however, felt that the aim of education is integral development of human personality. Such was also the ideal of education formulated by Gandhiji. Like Vivekananda, Gandhiji maintained that character formation and manual skill were equally important. On the one hand, he wanted the child to earn while he learns. On the other hand, he also wanted the child to develop his character. According to him the criterion of an individual's cultural development is not the width of his knowledge but his inner growth. Culture according to him is not an adjunct of the mind but a characteristic of the soul. The aim of education is the development of such a culture. Gandhiji's plan of education laid stress upon all types of education—physical, mental, moral, aesthetic and religious.

7. Self-Reliance. As has been already pointed out, Gandhiji aimed at self-reliance through education. Therefore, he visualised a craft-centred education. Explaining his scheme of Basic Education as an insurance against unemployment in India, Gandhiji said, "The child at the age of 14, that is, after finishing a seven- year course should be discharged as an earning unit. Even now the poor people's children automatically lend a helping hand to their parents—the feeling at the back of their minds being what shall they give men to eat, if I do not work with them? That is an education in itself. Even so the State takes charge of the child at seven and returns it to the family as an earning unit. You impart education and simultaneously cut at the root of unemployment". Recommending this scheme of education in the report on national education the Kothari Commission declared, "We recommend that work-experience should be introduced as an integral part of all education—general or vocational. We define work-experience as participation in productive work in school, in the home, in a workshop, on a farm, in a factory or in any other productive situation".

8. Democrative Ideals. Like his contemporary Indian educationists, Gandhiji aimed at the evolution of democratic ideals through education. His basic plan of education amply demonstrates this fact. He aimed at an education for ideal citizenship. Education, according to him, should make children ideal members of a democratic society. The school, according to Gandhiji, is itself a small democratic society in which such democratic values are imparted to the children as wide outlook, tolerance and good neighbourhood. In the miniature society of the school the child learns the virtues of sympathy, service, love, brotherhood, equality and liberty, etc. These qualities are transferred from one generation to another through education. The welfare of the individual and the Nation are complementary to each other. Therefore, if the country has to progress, the future generation should develop the virtues of democratic citizenship. As Gandhiji said, "A nation cannot advance without the units of which it is composed advancing, and conversely, no individual can advance without the nation of which it is a part also advancing".

9. Moral and Spiritual. All knowledge is useless without a good character in his speeches to the students at various institutions. Gandhiji laid emphasis upon the moral and spiritual aims of education. Emphasising the moral aim of education, Gandhiji said, "The end of all knowledge must be the building up of character". Character building is the moral ideal of education. According to Gandhiji that is most important in a man's life. His ideals in this connection were as much in agreement with the ancient Indian thinkers as with contemporary Western thinkers like Emerson, Ruskin, etc., Gandhiji very much admired the Indian *Gurukula* system of education and the ideal of *Brahmacharya.* According to ancient Indian ideal, education aims at liberation. This was also the aim of Gujarat Vidyapeeth established by Gandhiji in 1929. Gandhiji, however, defined liberation in a very wide sense, including political, social and economic liberation of all the members of society. Real freedom is spiritual freedom. To attain this freedom is the task of education. Again, education equally aims at intellectual, economic and political uplift, though its chief aim is moral and spiritual. Condemning the widespread indiscipline among the students Gandhiji asked them to follow the ideal of *Brahmacharya.*

10. God-Realization. According to Indian philosophy the ultimate end of all knowledge is God-realization. This God-realization again, is the meaning of self-realization which has been considered to be the ideal of education by most of the educational philosophers in East and West. Agreeing with this line of thinking Gandhiji maintained that a student should live a life of *Sanyasi.* God-realization and self-realization are mutually complementary, the one leads to the other. This spiritual ideal of education does not negate mundane or immediate ideals but fulfils them. In the words of Gandhiji, "Self-realization is in itself an all comprehensive ideal". This ideal includes other ideals of education. With Sri Aurobindo, Gandhiji believed that the ultimate aim of education is spiritual. He also agreed that spiritual growth includes physical and mental, individual and social development. Thus, he synthesized different ideals of education. In this scheme of Basic Education, he planned for an education suitable to present-day Indian society. He pondered over the difficulties of the present-day Indian society and tried to find out their solution through education. His educational philosophy is based upon ancient Indian idealism. While he did not restrict the scope of physical education his attention was mainly directed towards spiritual growth.

EDUCATION FOR SARVODAYA

Gandhiji was very much aware of the needs of the country and considered Basic Education as the only type of education which may lead to success. His chief aim in planning for education in India was to fulfil the needs of the country. India is a country of villages. Most of the villagers in India cannot afford to pay for their children's education. In addition to it they require their children's assistance in their occupations. Therefore, Gandhiji planned for Basic Education which may not be a burden upon the parents and through which the children may be able to earn to meet the expenses of education themselves, laid stress upon the importance of dignity of labour and manual skill. He was convinced that an education which prepares the young men for white-collar jobs can hardly be suitable for an agriculture community. It is hence that he so much emphasized the learning of craft in his plan of Basic Education. In spite of all this idealism Gandhiji's approach everywhere was pragmatic. He was an experimenter in every field of life. Before devising his plan of Basic Education he experimented upon its different aspects. For him all human truths were relative. God was the only absolute. Therefore he tested every thing before suggesting it for the education of the child. He postulated that the child should himself gather knowledge from the environment and put it in actual use in life. Like the pragmatists and instrumentalists Gandhiji stressed the importance of interest and activity and the need for variety in the subjects taught to the educand.

Sarvodaya Society

The social philosophy of M.K. Gandhi may be termed as 'Sarvodaya'. This was the foundation of his philosophy of education. Sarvodaya aims at all round development of all, without distinction of caste, creed, sex and nationality. Gandhiji wanted to establish a welfare state in India which he called 'Ram Rajya'.

The ideal of Sarvodaya does not aim at the maximum number but maximum good of all without exceptions. While Marx aimed at the welfare of the proletariat, Gandhiji aimed even at the welfare of the capitalist. According to Vinoba Bhave the important characteristics of the Sarvodaya Society are the abolition of all monopoly, emphasis on social welfare and equal, moral, social and economic importance of honest work. There is no place for any type of exploitation in Sarvodaya Society. No one may be forced to do a certain type of work, so much so that even the wealth of the capitalist cannot be forcibly snatched away. Centralization, according to Gandhiji, is the chief source of social evils. Sarvodaya requires decentralization. Gandhiji aimed at political, economic, social and all other types of decentralization. In the political field decentralization requires establishment of village panchayats. In the economic field it requires that wealth and money should not be allowed to be concentrated in few hands but should be distributed among all the people. Social decentralization means the abolition of all types of untouchability and social distinctions.

Nai Talim

In order to achieve the abovementioned aims of Sarvodaya in India, Gandhiji presented his plan of Basic Education. He called it Nai Talim (New education) because it sought to build up a new society in the country. He realized that what the country needs today is not so much higher education as the education of the masses. Therefore, he did not lay so much emphasis upon higher education.

The Basic Education sought to fulfil the needs of the educands in a Sarvodaya Society. It is hence that Gandhiji planned for craft centred education with mother tongue as the medium. Literacy, according to him, is not an end but only a mean of education. Education ultimately aims at the development of both mind and body and the capacity of earning one's livelihood. The syllabi for the new education were framed in such a way so as to eliminate narrow nationalism and emphasize the ideal of Sarvodaya. World history was taught along with Indian history. Similarly, the syllabus included the study of fundamental universal ethics. The cost of education was brought down by compulsory manual labour and education was tried to be made self-sufficient as far as possible.

Social Revolution

Pointing out the value of basic education for bringing about a silent social revolution in the country, Gandhiji said, "It will provide a healthy and moral basis of relationship between the city and the village and thus go a long way towards eradicating some of the worst evils of the present social insecurity and poisoned relationship between the classes. It will check the progressive decay of our villages and lay the foundation of a just social order in which there is no unnatural division between the 'haves' and the 'have-nots' and everybody is assured of a living wage and the right of freedom. And all this would be accomplished without the horrors of a bloody class war or a social capital expenditure such as would be involved in the mechanisation of a vast continent like India. Nor would it entail a helpless dependence on foreign imported machinery or technical skill. Lastly, by obviating the necessity for highly specialized talent, it would place the destiny of the masses, as it were in their own hands.

Non-violent Education

As has been already pointed out, Gandhiji emphasized the principle of non-violence in every field of life. He considered non-violence as the characteristic human quality. He said, "Non-violence is the law of our species as violence is the law of brutes". Even truth was subordinate to non-violence. Gandhiji said," One had better not speak it (truth) if one cannot do so in a gentle way". To those who doubted the value of non-violence to be the principle of human social organization, Gandhiji pointed out,"The fact that there are so many men still alive in the world shows that it is based not on force of arms but on the force of truth and love". This principle of non-violence, Gandhiji used in every aspect of education, so much so that his theory of education may be called non-violent education. Explaining his idea he wrote, "If India has resolved to eschew violence, this system of education becomes an integral part of the discipline she has to go through. We are told that English spend millions on education. America also does so. But we forget that all wealth is obtained through exploitation. They have reduced the art of exploitation to a science, and might well give their boys the costly education they do. We cannot, will not think in terms of exploitation, and we have no alternative but this plan of education which is based on non-violence". Thus, according to Gandhiji, India can play her role in the community of nations only by adopting the gospel of non-violence. To quote Gandhiji again, "Good brought about through force destroyed individuality. Only when the change was effected through the persuasive power of non-violent non-cooperation (i.e., love), could the foundation of individuality be preserved and real, abiding progress be assured for the world".

WARDHA SCHEME

This principle of non-violence was the basis of Gandhiji's scheme of Basic Education. Through this scheme he wanted to develop those qualities in future citizens of India which he considered necessary for building a non-violent society. His system of education wanted to root out exploitation and centralization in society and create a non-violent social order. In 1937, Gandhiji evolved a scheme popularly known as the Wardha Scheme of Basic National Education. This Wardha scheme was based on same principles of education which were listed by Gandhiji in a paper in 1932 in Yervada Jail. These postulates were as follows:

(1) Boys and girls should be taught together.

(2) Their time should be mostly spent on manual work under the supervision of the teacher. Manual work should be considered as part of education.

(3) Work should be entrusted to each boy and girl after ascertaining his or her inclinations.

(4) The child should know the why and the wherefore of every process.

(5) General knowledge should be imparted to the child as soon as it is able to understand things. This knowledge should precede literary education.

(6) The hand of the child be trained to draw geometrical figures before he learns to write, that is good handwriting should be taught from the beginning.
(7) The child should learn to read before he is able to write, i.e., he should learn to recognize letters as if they were pictures and then draw their figures.
(8) By this method and by word of mouth, the child should acquire much knowledge before he is eight years old.
(9) Children should not be compelled to learn anything.
(10) The child should be interested in whatever he learns.
(11) The process of teaching should be conducted in a play-way, for play is an essential part of education.
(12) All education should be imparted through the mother-tongue of the child.
(13) Every Indian child should learn Hindi-Urdu, i.e., Hindustani as a national language before his literary training commences.
(14) The second stage of the child's education begins when he is eleven and lasts up to sixteen.
(15) Manual labour has a place in education during this period also. The time for literary training should be increased according to need.
(16) The child should learn some vocation as preparation for his future life.
(17) He should acquire a general knowledge of World History, Geography, Botany, Astronomy, Arithmetic, Geometry and Algebra.
(18) A boy or a girl of sixteen years should know sewing and cooking.
(19) In the third stage which begins at sixteen and ends at twenty-five, a young man or woman should receive education according to his or her desires and circumstances.
(20) The education commencing at the age of nine should be self-supporting. The student, while he is learning, should be engaged in such a vocation that its produce may meet the expense of the school.
(21) Production should, no doubt, begin right from the start. But it may not be enough to meet the expenses during the initial years.
(22) Teachers cannot possibly have big salaries, but they must get enough to maintain themselves. They should be animated by a spirit of service. They must have a good character.
(23) Huge and costly buildings are not necessary for education.
(24) English can and should have a place in the syllabus only as a language. Just as Hindi is our *lingua franca* English is a language of international intercourse and commerce.

On 23rd October, 1937, a conference was organized at Wardha to finalise the basic system of education. This conference resolved that the children should be provided free education for seven years. Mother tongue should be the medium of education. Every educand must be taught some basic craft. The expenses of education should be met by the sale of the production in the school. In order to implement these recommendations a committee was formed under the chairmanship of Dr. Zakir Hussain. This committee highlighted the basic principles, aims and organization of B asic Education in its first report on 2nd December, 1937. In its second report in 1940 this committee reviewed the curriculum of Basic Education. Its recommendations were accepted by Indian National Congress in its Session at Haripura. After Zakir Hussain Committee, another committee was formed under the chairmanship of B.G. Kher to review basic education. This committee connected it to Sargeant scheme. In the final form, the basic principles of Gandhiji's scheme of primary education were: compulsory free education, education through craft, education through mother tongue, self-reliance, education connected with the life of the educand and finally inculcation of the ideals of democratic citizenship. A booklet was published by Government of India to popularise Gandhijian system of education entitled *Understanding of Basic Education.* This booklet thus summarised the scheme of basic education, "Activities involving personal and community cleanliness are the foremost in a basic school. Education for the young is not stuffing impractical idea into the minds of children. It is essentially training them in good habits, the daily experiences that every child has to undergo as regular morning evacuation, cleaning the teeth, nose and eyes, bathing, physical exercise, washing clothes and other daily activities can be exploited for teaching as well as the inculcation of good habits"

MEANS OF EDUCATION

The scheme of Basic Education clarifies the means of education according to M.K. Gandhi. The most important means of education in basic scheme was craft. About this means of education Gandhiji said, "The principal idea is to impart the whole education of body and the mind and the soul through the handicraft that is taught to the children. You have to draw out all that is in the child through teaching all the processes of the handicraft, and all your lessons in History, Geography, Arithmetic will be related to the craft". Thus some handicraft was necessary to be the centre of the child's education. Besides, other crafts recommended were: weaving, carpentry, agriculture, gardening and other handicrafts and rural crafts. It was pointed out that the following criteria should be followed in deciding about the basic craft:

(1) Craft fulfilling individual and social means.

(2) Craft based upon local requirements.

(3) Craft in tune with the local conditions.

(4) Craft favourable to the interest, aptitude and ability of the child.

(5) Less expensive and simple craft!

(6) Craft leading to all round development of personality.

At the back of craft as the means of education were the psychological principles of education through activity as is visible in the Western playway of education, project methods, etc. Besides, this means of education was economically useful as the basic craft could be utilized by the educand to earn his livelihood. It was also supposed to create a tendency for physical labour in the educands. According to Gandhiji, "Labour is the source of all wealth. All higher castes live on the exploitation of the lower castes. Wealth is inevitably reduced and large scale poverty occasioned". Thus, craft was means to inculcate the lesson of physical labour.

Another important element in the means of education in basic scheme was synthesis between the actual problems of life and education, between different subjects of the curriculum and finally between theoretical education and practical ability. In order to implement the principle of synthesis in basic education it was insisted that the teachers and educands should together formulate yearly projects divided into quarterly, monthly, weekly and daily projects. After this planning, the means such as raw material and necessary tools should be gathered. Efforts should be made to fulfil the schedule of the projects. Each project must be evaluated monthly or quarterly as the case may be. In the end the teachers should note their experiences in order to profit by them in future.

TYPES OF EDUCATION

Our discussion of the Gandhian scheme of education so far shows his emphasis upon primary education and the education of the child. He, however, equally devoted his thought to the adult education also known as social education. He realized that in order to bring about a Sarvodaya Society in India, the views of the adults should be changed. Therefore, he made adult education programme a vital element of his political movement. Thousands of volunteers were trained in adult education at Sabarmati and Sevagram Ashrams. They spread in thousands of villages and hundreds of urban centres to educate the adult males and females in night schools. The help of thousands of regular teachers in so many educational institutions was also utilized for this purpose.

An important characteristic of Gandhian philosophy is the aim of Sarvodaya. Therefore, he planned different types of education for the country. Besides basic education and social education he thought seriously over rural education and education for women.

MEDIUM OF EDUCATION

A staunch votary of mother tongue as the medium of education, Gandhiji said, "I must cling to my mother tongue as to my mother's breast, in spite of its shortcomings. It alone can give me the life giving milk". He was vehemently against English as the medium of education in this country. He said, "To inflict English on children is to stunt their natural growth and perhaps to kill originality in them". He pointed out to many modern western countries including U.S.S.R. who have made tremendous scientific progress without any help of English language. He maintained that our insistence on English is a remnant of our long slavery to the British. He was never prepared to accept this submission to foreign yoke. He maintained that the national language alone can be the vehicle of creating a common culture and rich literature. He was very much conversant with the language problem in India. He wanted to keep the country united particularly from the point of view of language. Therefore, he devised a common national language Hindustani which may be written in both Devanagari and Persian script. According to him there is no difference in Hindi and Urdu.

CHARACTERISTICS OF GANDHIAN EDUCATIONAL PLAN

M.K. Gandhi viewed the process of education from many different angles and saw that it must achieve something more than one objective. That is why he ascribed to it many different aims. At times a superficial study of these aims may give the impression that they are mutually contradictory or self-defeating, but a deeper examination will show that they complement each other. Even a cursory glancing through the history of education will show abundantly that different educationists have ascribed different aims to education. For some it is training for livelihood and sustenance, for others it is self-realization, for yet others the individual aims take precedence over the social objectives of education while some educationists favour the social aspects. Most educationists, however, have felt that education must strive for human perfection. Cultural development is another aim that has been ascribed to education. Idealists emphasize the idealistic aspect more than the realistic while naturalists and realists stress the realistic forms of education. Gandhiji's philosophy of education aims at harmonizing all these contradictory viewpoints. His Wardha plan of education laid great stress upon training in self-reliance, because he felt that the highest criterion of an educational system was its ability in putting an end to unemployment. For him both character formation and manual skill were Important. Education should also be accompanied by earning money, and that is why he felt that the educator's salary should be paid out of goods produced by the educands. He believed that character building was as important as, if not more than, collecting information. The criterion of an individual's cultural development is not the extent of his knowledge but the qualities he manifests. In the cultural aspect of education, he placed emphasis upon the behaviour and thinking of educands. Culture, according to him, is not an adjunct of the mind but a quality of the soul, and cultural development an important objective of education. Education is the means to the child's physical, mental and spiritual development. His plan of education gave importance to physical, moral, aesthethic and religious education along with the teaching of mathematics and literary skills. In addition to this he stressed that handwriting should be neat and clean.

Gandhiji's educational plan exhibits all the major qualities found in the Western educational patterns. For this reason, the following points must be kept in mind in attempting an evaluation of his plan:

1. Naturalism. Gandhiji's educational philosophy gives due recognition to biological naturalism because it lays stress on man's complete development. Like Rousseau, Gandhiji revolted against the existing pattern of education and suggested the establishment of a new system of education. He laid more stress on the child's environment than on books. He wanted to give an indigenous touch to education, and make it capable of achieving independence and naturalness. But, at the same time, he did not neglect discipline. His education is centered around the child, not around textbooks.

2. Idealism. On the one hand one finds a strong element of realism in Gandhiji ' s philosophy of education, but on the other it also exhibits some signs of idealism. There is no denying that he was always an idealist because he always was a religious individual. He felt that the aim of man's life was realization of God, and that is why he stressed the importance of moral and religious education. He preached that one must indulge in service, sacrifice and contemplation in order to achieve selfrealization. Gandhiji's educational philosophy shows all the finest elements of idealism, and while he does not restrict the scope of physical education, his attention is mainly given to spiritual training. He wanted to use education as a means of developing a harmonized personality in the child. Like Pestalozzi, he wanted to make the child the centre of educational progress and like Herbart he felt that the aim of education was building up a moral character. He attached the greatest importance to the childs interests and inclinations. He agreed with Froebel that the child, at birth, is full of many undeveloped abilities and it is for education to develop these.

3. Pragmatism. Despite his inclination towards idealism, Gandhiji always attended to the practical and pragmatic aspect of education. That is why he entitled his autobiography *My Experiments with Truth.* He was an experimenter in every sphere of his life. Before arriving at a settled opinion about education he preferred to experiment in all its spheres. He accepted no truth as absolute. For him God was the only absolute entity. In keeping with the pragmatic tradition, he also believed that the child should gather for himself all the knowledge from the environment and select from it that which he could put to use in later life. The pattern of education suggested by him compares in many respects with that suggested by the pragmatists. Both stress the importance of interests and activity, and the need for variety in the subjects taught to the educand. Like Dewey, Gandhiji also felt that the child should learn through actual work. Besides, he also agreed with Dewey that education should seek to establish the democratic values in life. In short, he wanted to relate education to life as far as possible.

4. Educational system is **based on psychological facts.** Although Gandhiji was not a professional psychologist, he had gained remarkable insight into human psychology through his acute observation of life around him. By virtue of this qualification, he could attempt to make his educational system completely psychological. He, too, objected to the attempts at stuffing the child's mind with too many facts. He felt that education should aim at arousing curiosity and providing motivation to the child so that he should himself achieve his own physical, mental and spiritual development. He insisted on the importance of acquiring manual skills, but he felt that this training should be supplemented by knowledge of other objects so as to achieve physical, mental, moral, psychological and spiritual development also. He was very much in favour of the eduands' indulging in games and sports and gymnastic activity, because he felt that physical development is an essential prerequisite of mental development. In his own Ashram children were given opportunities of physical development by participating in the work done there. He also felt that education should not be allowed to become mechanical but should be acquired through play.

5. Importance of impressions and actions. Gandhiji's opinion that impressions of early childhood have a tremendous impact on later development is in agreement with the modern psychologists. He was aware that the impressions once imprinted on the child's flexible mind are difficult to wipe out later on. In his infancy and childhood, the child learns a very great deal by imitating his parents, and for this reason it is desirable that the impressions made on his mind should be beneficial. Psychologists also agree with Gandhiji's theory that there should be learning through doing. Most educationists agree that learning through doing helps in the complete development of the child and that this also enables him to earn his livelihood later on in life.

6. Sociological importance of Gandhiji's plan. Gandhiji's plan of education is not only psychologically valid but it has sociological significance also. While thinking of his plan of education, Gandhiji was not concerned with one or two individuals, but with the vast multitude of illiterate men and women who make up the country's population. He wanted to use education as the medium of establishing in the country a non-violent social system from which exploitation of all kinds would be absent. He was a vigorous opponent of exploitation and he realized that it could not be eradicated without education. He advocated discipline as an essential part of freedom and liberty. He wanted that education should help the individual to become an ideal democratic citizen. He opposed the teaching of all those subjects in schools which had no real link with life. He stressed the importance of social service, labour, agriculture, handicrafts, hygiene, collective living, etc., and pointed out that they were more important than any curriculum. Sarvodaya was as much his guiding principle in education as it was in the field of politics. This concept of a Sarvodaya Society was based on traditional Indian and modern democratic values.

From the economic standpoint also, Gandhiji's educational plan appears to be appropriate for India's economy. Gandhiji felt that the principles of truth and nonviolence could be as effective in the field of economic activity as they were elsewhere. He opposed exploitation in all its various forms and pointed out that exploitation had its origin in the individual's desire to get his work done by someone else instead of doing it himself and the desire to take charge of fruits of another's labour and effort. Gandhiji advised that the only way of putting an end to exploitation is for every individual to do his own work. He suggested that the educand should himself do his own work and all work connected with the school. He should learn to respect labour and should not feel that manual labour is in any way worse than or inferior to mental labour. India being an agricultural country in which the villagers have small pieces of land to cultivate, it would be better if these people developed various kinds of cottage industries. Only then can the villagers become self-sufficient.

7. Education conforming to the country's needs. Whatever the arguments one may advance against Gandhiji's plan of education, one cannot question his sincerity, because it is only too obvious that in presenting it, he was perfectly aware of the needs of his countrymen. He considered this the only kind of education which can be successful in this country. Most villagers cannot afford to pay for their children's education and in addition most of them require their children's assistance in their own occupations. Hence, their children should receive an education which can enable them to share their parent's burden. And this is possible only when the system of education lays stress on the importance of labour and manual skills. There can be no arguing the fact that the existing pattern of education in the countiy only prepares the young men for white-collar jobs. But this type of education can hardly suit the needs of an agricultural community. In the second place, Gandhiji wanted the educand to be engaged in gainful work the product of which could be sold to pay for his education. This may appear to be impractical on the face of it, but it is inspired by the idea that the child's education should not add to the parents' burden. The only other alternative is free education, and this is hindered by the psychological fact that anything gained free has little value for the recipient. Besides, free education does harm to the educand's character. Gandhiji favoured the idea that education as well as the educand should be independent of everyone else. There are definitely many difficulties in translating this plan into action. But on the theoretical level, one cannot question the justice of his thesis that education should be independent and self-reliant. There is no doubt that it is difficult to turn manual skill and physical labour into a game, and that it almost necessarily becomes monotonous and mechanical, but this does not prove that the idea itself is wrong. Gandhiji considered not only what the child studied but also what he would do later on. The existing problem of educated unemployed has been created only because the present system of education has no aim and purpose. Besides, Gandhiji wanted that the individual should become independent during his education, or at least that he should learn some skill which would enable him to find employment immediately after completing his education.

8. Teaching Methods. The teaching methods in the Gandhi an scheme of education can be deduced from his Basic Education. As has been pointed out, Gandhiji pleaded that the child should be educated through a basic craft. He should first be taught a basic craft from among the different types of it and other subjects such as Arithmetic, Language, Geography, History and Civics should be taught in association with the basic craft. In his educational institutions children were busy in craft activities for hours. There was no provision of rigid time-table or ringing of the bell after every hour. There was no compulsion to work in the class-room. The child was left free to select a craft according to his natural interests, abilities and according to his learning. This method of teaching has been justified by Western educationists Rousseau insisted upon the value of total freedom in teaching methods. Herbart admitted the value of synthesis in education.

As has already been pointed out, an important characteristic of the teaching method in Gandhian scheme was synthesis. Projects were drawn for the year, quarter, month, week and the day. They were carried on according to schedule and reviewed periodically. The teacher profited by this review. He gathered experiences to make better projects and implement them more successfully. This method was natural, saved time, was interesting, synthesized knowledge and action, helped in transfer of learning and led to the development of high moral character. It was based upon the educational principle of proceeding from gross to subtle. It required experienced and able teachers who could synthesize the educand and his environment and the different parts of the curriculum. They should be trained for this purpose.

This teaching method of Gandhiji's scheme of education has its advantages as well as disadvantages. It was pointed out that it converted schools into mini-factories and prolonged hours of engagement in crafts hardly left any leisure to the children for recreation and extra-curricular activities. Gandhi thought that the sale proceeds of the products of basic crafts in an educational institution will be sufficient to meet the salaries of the teachers. This, however, could never be realized. It was based on false expectations. However, no body can doubt Gandhiji's intensive insight into the teaching methods of the children and adults so much clear in his plans of basic education and adult education.

EDUCATION FOR DIFFERENT SECTIONS OF SOCIETY

We have already pointed out Gandhian scheme for education of different sections of society according to age. He planned equally well for the education of children, as well as the adults. On the basis of sex, society is divided into two broad sections, male and female. Gandhiji planned for the education of both these sections. Regeneration of Indian women was a part of the political movement of M.K. Gandhi. Therefore, he had to speak and write about the education of women of India. In the basic scheme of education and in his plans of adult education Gandhiji did not make any distinction on the basis of sex. He recommended same primary and adult education both for the male and female. He was, however, not very much in favour of co-education. He allowed co-education up to the age of 8 years and then after 16 years of age. He, however, pleaded for separate educational institutions for boys and girls in adolescent age. The selection of co-educational or otherwise institutions was finally left to the discretion of the parents. Gandhiji maintained that family alone can create suitable tendencies for the success of co-education in educational institutions. He strongly supported all types of education both for male and female.

Society is again divided into progressive and backward sections both socially as well economically. As a champion of the uplift of backward classes in the country Gandhiji devised elaborate plans for the education of scheduled tribes and scheduled castes in India. These plans were mainly based upon local circumstances. They aimed at the unity of the nation without distinction of caste, language, religion, region or community, etc. Thus, Gandhiji planned for education suitable for all the sections of society. This was a necessary corrollary to his social ideal of Sarvodaya. His scheme of education not only aimed at character building but also social, political and economic uplift of all the sections of the society.

17

RABINDRA NATH TAGORE

EDUCATION AS SELF-REALIZATION

Rabindra Nath Tagore believed that the aim of education is self-realization. lie was a poet and a saint, who had, through his imagination and insight, realized the universal soul in himself and in nature. He believed that this realization was the goal of education. Because the universal soul is the root of our own soul, man's aim in life is to reach that universal soul of which all human beings are parts. The evolution of nature is consciously or unconsciously driving us towards this universal soul, a process which can be assisted by education. Even if it is not assisted the progress towards the universal soul will continue, but then individuals will be deprived of self-realization. It is thus evident that Rabindra Nath's educational philosophy is an adjunct of his general philosophy of life. In fact, he did not find any dichotomy between thought, life and philosophy. Besides, he believed that every human being is one who has potentialities of progressing towards the Super human being, the universal soul. His conception of the universal soul bore clear imprint of the Gita and Upanishadic philosophies. Although Rabindra Nath was clearly aware of the ideas of Western thinkers on education, he based his own ideas on the ancient Indian thought. Indian tradition believes that man's soul and the universal soul are one, and that self-realization amounts to realization of integration with God.

Principles of Self-Education

Self-education is based on self-realization, and the process of self-realization is as permanent as that of education. What is most important in this is that the educand must have faith in himself and in the universal self, underlying his own individual soul. All those actions which provide a natural sense of satisfaction and contentment will promote the educative process. This contentment is the reaction of the soul, and hence not the same as mere satisfaction and pleasure. In following Rabindra Nath's concept of self-education, the educand had to follow the three following principles:

1. Independence. Rabindra Nath believed in complete freedom of every kind for the educand—the freedom of intellect, decision, heart, knowledge, action and worship. But in order to attain this freedom the educand had to practise equanimity, harmony and balance. Through this practice the educand can learn to distinguish between the true and the false, the natural and the artificial, the relevant and the irrelevant, permanent and temporary, universal and individual, liberal andnarrow, etc. Consequently, after making this distinction the educand can bring about a harmony and synthesis in the true, natural, relevant, permanent and real elements that he has acquired. Once the educand has acquired this ability he can turn to self-guidance, for which he is now competent. He can himself distinguish between the elements likely to impede his progress and those which may help him. Rabindra Nath interprets independence as normalcy or the fact of being natural. In other words, when intelligence, feeling and determination are naturally distributed, it can be said to be a state of freedom. This independence is not to be confused with the absence of control, because it is self-control, it implies acting according to one's own rational impulse. Once this level of freedom has been achieved, there is no danger of the individual straying from his path, because his senses, intelligence, emotional feelings and all other powers are directed by his ego.

2. Perfection. The second active principle underlying self-education is that of perfection. Perfection here implies that the educand must try to develop every aspect of his personality and all the abilities and powers with which he has been endowed by Nature. Hence, the aim of education is not merely passing examinations, acquiring degrees and certificates of merit and ultimately achieving economic self-sufficiency through pursuing some profession. The sole aim of education is development of the child's personality which is possible only when every aspect of the personality is given equal importance, when no part of the personality is neglected and no part is exclusively stressed.

3. Universality. Development of the individual remains imperfect and incomplete until he acquires an abiding faith in the universal soul, a part of which exists inside himself. And for this, it is necessary to identify one's own soul with the universal soul. Thus, education exists not in simple development but it inheres in literally a rebirth in which the individual rises above the limitations of his individual personality and loses this individuality in the universality of the universal soul. One can search for this universal soul not only within oneself, but in every element of Nature and of one's environment. This search is assisted by knowledge, worship and action. Once this realization of the universal soul is achieved, it becomes easier to progress further.

It is evident from the foregoing account that the aim of Rabindra Nath's pattern of education is independence, perfection and universality. In the process of education, the educator creates an environment in which the child's personality undergoes a free, perfect and unrestricted development.

AIMS OF EDUCATIONS

According to Rabindra Nath, the aim of education is self-realization. He is a poet and a saint who through his imagination and insight, realized the universal soul within himself and in Nature. According to him this realization by every one is the goal of education. Self-realization, according to Rabindra Nath, means the realization of the universal soul in one's self. Man's aim of life is to achieve this status. It is a process which cannot be realized without education. In the absence of education the individual will be deprived of self-realization. Rabindra Nath does not find any dichotomy between thought and life, philosophy and education. He believes that every one is potentially divine and every one can realize his potentiality. His philosophy is very much influenced by the 'Gita' and the 'Upanishads'. He is, however, well aware of the educational ideas prevalent in the West. Therefore, like Vivekananda, he synthesizes the ancient Vedantic traditions with the modern Western scientific attitude in formulating the goal of education.

1. Integral Development. Defining the aim of education, Rabindra Nath says, "The fundamental purpose of education is not merely to enrich ourselves through the fullness of knowledge, but also to establish the bond of love and friendship between man and man". This is the humanistic aim of education in Tagore's philosophy. His approach to ultimate reality is integral. He believes in an inner harmony between man and Nature and God. In man, again, the physical, the mental and the spiritual aspects are equally important and internally related. Therefore, like Sri Aurobindo, Rabindra Nath believes in a multisided education with physical, intellectual, moral and religious aims.

2. Physical Development. Like Vivekananda, Rabindra Nath condemned the prevalent system of education which partially exercised the intellect only to the entire neglect of the body. According to Rabindra Nath, "Education of the body in the real sense, does not exist in play and exercise but in applying the body systematically to some useful work". Thus, one of the aims of education according to Rabindra Nath, is physical development. It is hence that he so much emphasizes games in school education. Pointing out the value of physical activities in the child's education he says. "Even if they learnt nothing, they would have had ample time for play, climbing trees, diving into ponds, plucking and tearing flowers, perpetrating thousand and one mischiefs on Mother Nature, they would have obtained the nourishment of the body, happiness of mind and the satisfaction of the natural impulses of childhood". Thus physical fitness is the first cardinal principle in the child's development. This is realized through his intimate contact with Nature. As a poet Tagore very well realizes the life giving values of Nature's contact with man. About the child's contact with the Nature he says, "I speak in very moderate terms: Seven years—till then let child has nothing to do with clothes and shame. Till then let Nature alone conduct the indispensable education of the savage". This is particularly important for the educational institutions in our society. Almost all contemporary Indian philosophers of education, including Gandhiji, Vivekananda, Dayananda and Sri Aurobindo, besides Tagore, lay emphasis upon the importance of setting educational institutions in natural environment so that the educand may learn by their touch with Nature.

3. Mental Development. Besides the physical aim of education, Tagore equally lays emphasis upon the mental aim of education. Like Vivekananda, he is critical of the prevalent system of education which laid sole emphasis upon bookish learning. Presenting this attitude he says, "We touch the world not with our mind, but with our books. This is deplorable. Intellectualism takes us away from Nature and creates a gulf between man and man." To quote Rabindra Nath, "We know the people of books, not those of the world, the former are interesting to us, but the latter tiresome". In fact, the intellectual aim of education, according to Rabindra Nath, is the development of the intellectual faculties which should be developed through education. These are: the power of thinking and the power of imagination. Both these are necessary for real manhood. Rabindra Nath criticizes the prevalent system of education which puts too much stress on memory and two little on imagination and thinking. He suggests, "Ever since childhood, instead of putting all the burden on the memory, the power of thinking and the power of imagination should also be given opportunities for free exercise".

4. Harmony with Environment In the end, the aim of education according to Rabindra Nath, is the harmony of the educand with the environment. The educand should know his environment and create harmony with it. To quote Rabindra Nath, "True education consists in knowing the use of any useful material that has been collected, to know its real nature and to build along with life a real shelter for life". This is particularly true about the rural education. Education should facilitate the educand's assimilation of his national culture. Through education, the educand should imbibe his cultural heritage and should be able to use it in his interaction With the environment. Explaining this aim of education, Rabindra Nath says, "If we believe that the chief aim of education in India is to be initiated into this unique pursuit of India, then we must constantly remember that neither the education of the senses, nor the education of the intellect, but the education of the feeling receive the place of honour in our schools... . Our true education is possible only in the forest, through intimate contact with Nature and purifying austere pursuits".

5. Earning Livelihood. Thus, about the aim of education, Tagore's approach is realistic. He, however, does not favour the utilitarian aim of education. This is his objection against the imposition of British system of education upon India. He says, "Knowledge has two departments: one pure knowledge, the other utilitarian knowledge. Whatever is worth knowing is knowledge. It should be known equally by men and women, not for practical utility, but for the sake of knowing.... The desire to know is the law of human nature". But Rabindra Nath does not ignore the earning of livelihood aim of education. He appreciates the practical bias in Western system of education. Though he does not want to make education an instrument for earning bread alone but he admits that bread earning is a necessary part of any sound goal of education. Therefore, he says, "From the very beginning, such education should be imparted to them (village folks) that they may know well what mass welfare means and may become practically efficient in all respects for earning their livelihood". While he is critical of the British system of education which wanted to create clerks out of the Indian educated people, he emphasized that the real aim of education is to develop men and women who may be able to fulfil the needs of the country. In his own words, "One of the main aims of education is to prepare the individual for the service of the country".

6. Multisided Aim. The above discussion concerning the means of education according to Rabindra Nath, make it clear that his is a multisided attack on this problem. He is against any one sided aim of education. He is humanist. A humanistic aim of education requires a multisided approach.

CRITICAL EVALUATION

1. Education for Human Re-generation. Thus Rabindra Nath's philosophy of education aims at developing a system of education for human re-generation. Man is in the centre of all his thinking, his philosophy, religion, literature, poetry, social activities and educational programmes. He is a humanist in the real sense of the term, not a naturalistic humanist but an integral humanist in the Indian tradition. He is not rationalist but believes in something higher than reasons in man. He does not think science alone to be capable of delivering the human goods but wants to synthesize it with Vedanta. He is a nationalist and at the same time an internationalist. To him the ultimate God is the universal man and only aim of all the man's activities was the realization of this God. Human regeneration is his sole aim and only ideal. His educational system is a means to achieve this aim. He, therefore, bases his educational system on essential human virtues such as freedom, purity, sympathy, perfection and world brotherhood.

2. Corrective to Prevalent Defects. Like other contemporary Indian thinkers of his time Tagore objected to the prevalent system of education due to its origination in a foreign country. He protested against emphasis on foreign language resulting in the alienation of the educated people from the general society. He tried to build up educational centres where these defects may be removed. He deliberated on different problems of Indian society particularly that of the rural people and tried to remove them through education. His educational system was a synthesis of East and West, Ancient and Modern, Science and Vedanta. It is hence that man like Jawaharlal Nehru considered Vishva-Bharati as the true representative of India.

18

SWAMI VIVEKANANDA

In the Neo-Vedanta humanistic tradition of contemporary Indian thought, Vivekananda presented a philosophy of education for man-making. Among the contemporary Indian philosophers of education he is one of those who revolted against the imposition of British system of education in India. He was severely critical of the pattern of education introduced by the British in India. He felt that the current system of education did not confirm to India's culture. He pointed out that such an education only brings about an external change without any profound inner force.

CRITICISM OF PREVALENT EDUCATIONAL SYSTEM

Against the contemporary educational system the chief objection raised by Vivekananda was that it turned men into slaves, capable of slavery and nothing else. About the prevailing university education, he remarked that it was not better than an efficient machine for rapidly turning out clerks. It deprived people of their faith and belief. The English educated people believed that *Gita* was false and the *Vedas* were no more significant than rural folk lore. Criticising this system of education Vivekananda compared it to the person who wanted to turn his ass into a horse, was advised to thrash the ass in order to achieve this transformation and killed his ass in this process. Vivekananda also criticised the contemporary system of education from the humanistic viewpoint. He was a humanist and pleaded for education for manmaking. Such was not the education propounded by the British. Therefore, Vivekananda condemned it. He remarked, "It is not a man-making education, it is merely and entirely a negative education. A negative education or any training that is based on negation, is worse than death. The child is taken to school, and the first thing he learns is that his father is a fool, the second thing that his grandfather is lunatic, the third thing that all his teachers are hypocrites, the fourth, that all the sacred books are lies. By the time he is sixteen he is a mass of negation, lifeless and boneless. And the result is that fifty years of such education has not produced one original man in the three presidencies. Every man of originality that has been produced has been educated elsewhere, and not in this country, or they have gone to the old universities once more to cleanse themselves of superstitions".

AIMS OF EDUCATION

1. Self-development. In contrast to the contemporary system of education Vivekananda advocated education for self-development. He said, "By education I do not mean the present system, but something in the line of positive teaching. Mere book learning won't do. We want that education by which character is formed, strength of mind is increased, the intellect is expanded and by which one can stand on one's own feet. What we want are Western science coupled with Vedanta, '*Brahmacharya*' as the guiding motto, and also '*Shraddha*' and faith in one's own self These words by Vivekananda represent the characteristic Indian definition of education. Education according to most of the Western educationists aims at man's adjustment with the environment. According to the Indian philosophical tradition, on the other hand, education is the realization of the knowledge inherent in man. True knowledge does not come from outside, it is discovered with the individual, in the self which is the source of all knowledge. To quote Vivekananda again, "All knowledge that the world has ever received comes from the mind; the infinite library of the universe is in your mind. The external world is only the suggestion, the occasion, which sets you to study your mind. The falling of the apple gave suggestion to Newton, and he studied his own mind. He rearranged all the precious links of thought in his mind and discovered a new link among them which we call the Law of Gravitation". Thus, according to Vivekananda, the function of education is the uncovering of the knowledge hidden in our mind. Education is the process of self--development. In the words of Vivekananda, "You cannot teach a child any more than you can grow a plant. The plant develops its own nature". A person's education is not judged by the number of books he has read but by the thickness of the cover of ignorance on his mind. The thicker is this cover, the greater is the ignorance. As the light of knowledge dawns this cover of ignorance gradually shatters. The teacher's job is to uncover knowledge by his guidance. His guidance makes the mind active and the educand himself unveils the knowledge lying within him.

2. Fulfilment of Swadharma. Vivekananda supported the idea of Swadharma in education. Every one has to grow like himself. No one has to copy others. It is hence that he condemned the imposition of foreign education. He asked, "Getting by heart the thoughts of others in a foreign language and stuffing your brain with them and taking some university degree, you can pride yourself as educated. Is this education"? True improvement is self-inspired. There should be no external pressure of any type on the child. External pressure only creates destructive reactions leading to obstinacy and indiscipline. In an atmosphere of freedom, love and sympathy alone, the child will develop courage and self-reliance. He should not be unnecessarily checked in his activities. The educator should not constantly tell him to do this or that. Such negative directions tend to blunt his intelligence and mental development. He should be talked to stand on his own, to be himself. This is so since as Vivekananda suggests, "If you do not allow once to become a lion, he will become a fox". Therefore, education should be modified to suit the individual child. Each child should be given opportunities to develop according to his own inner nature.

3. Freedom of Growth. Thus Vivekananda is against any type of external pressure upon the child. He is a staunch champion of freedom in education. Freedom is the first requirement for self-development. The child should be given freedom to grow, according to his own nature. In the words of Vivekananda, "You cannot teach a child an more than you can grow a plant. All you can do is on the negative side—you can only help. You can take away the obstacles, but knowledge comes out of its own nature. Loosen the soil a little, so that it may come out easily. Put a hedge around it, see that it is not killed by anything, and there your work stops. You cannot do anything else. The rest is a manifestation from within its own nature". The teacher should not exert any type of pressure on the child. The child should be helped in solving his problems himself. The teachers should have an attitude of service and worship. Education ultimately aims at realization. It is a means to the establishment of a fraternity of mankind.

4. Character Formation. Character is the solid foundation for self-development. The aim of education as self-development, therefore, leads to the aim of education for character. Defining character, Vivekananda said, "The character of any man is but the aggregate of his tendencies, the sum total of the bent of his mind. As pleasure and pain pass before his soul, they leave upon it different pictures and the result of these combined impressions is what is called a man's character". The aim of education is character building. This depends upon the ideals cherished by the individual. The educator should present high ideals before the educands. The best way to develop a character is the personal example of high character set by the teacher. Laying emphasis upon this point Vivekananda said, "Without the personal life of the teacher there would be no education. One would live from his very boyhood with one whose character is like a blazing fire, and should have before him a living example of the highest leaching.... The charge of imparting knowledge should again fall upon the shoulders of 'tyagis'. In ancient Indian system of education the teachers used to present high ideals", before the pupils, who in their turn imitated these ideals according to their capacities. Following things are required for character formation:

(i) *Hard Work.* Character formation, according to Vivekananda, requires hard work. This is not possible by those who have a wish for all types of enjoyments. Struggle is the best teacher in character building. Activity and *purushartha* are the signs of life. Inactivity shows absence of vitality. While living in all types of comforts and escaping from all types of labour, no one can build up high character.

(ii) *Moral and Spiritual Values.* Besides hard work, character formation requires traits such as purity, thirst for knowledge, perseverance, faith, humility, submission and veneration, etc. These qualities may be developed by the teacher's example and the pupil's efforts. According to Vivekananda, "Without faith, humility, submission and veneration in our hearts towards the teacher, there cannot be any growth in us. In those countries which have neglected to keep up this kind of relation, the teacher has become a mere lecturer, the teacher expecting his five dollars and the person taught expecting his brain to be filled with the teacher's words and each going his own way after this much is done. The true teacher is he who can immediately come down to the level of the student, and transfer his soul to the student's soul and see through and understand through his mind.

(iii) *Gurukula System*. Such a relationship between the teacher and the taught is possible only in a Gurukula system of education. Therefore, Vivekananda favoured the ancient Indian Gurukula system of education. In these Gurukulas the pupils served the teacher, who in his turn, helped the pupils everywhere to achieve knowledge. There was hardly any economic relationship between the teacher and the taught, which is the curse of the present system of education.

(iv) *Formation of Good Habits.* Character is intimately connected with habits. Habits express character. Good habits make for good character. While the contemporary psychologists admit the value of habits in one's life, Vivekananda has pointed out the value of habits not only in this life but in lives to come. A bad habit may be broken by developing the opposite good habit. If a man constantly thinks that he will be courageous and progressive, he may develop confidence for breaking bad habits. It is not the teacher nor the guardian who may reform the habit of a person but only he himself. Man is caught in the net of his own *karmas* from which he alone can get out, no one else can directly help him. Our own self in us is our best guide in the struggle that is life.

(v) *Learning through Mistakes.* The child should be allowed to commit mistakes in the process of character formation. He will learn much by his mistakes. Errors are the stepping stones to our progress in character. This progress requires courage and strong will. Strong will is the sign of great character. Will makes men great. Therefore, there is no occasion to be discouraged or to weep, one should exercise his will and he will see that things which he considered to be impossible become easy and possible. Vivekananda himself was an ideal teacher. His words worked like magic upon men and women. This is possible only in the case of a teacher who has himself risen high. Presenting his own example, Vivekananda asked the people to build up their character and manifest their real nature which is the Effulgent, the Resplendent, the Ever Pure.

MEANS OF EDUCATION

1. Love. The best means of education, according to Vivekananda is love. Education should be based upon love. Love is best inspiration in character building. The child should be taught through love. This is love for men, for human beings. The only motive in imparting education should be love for the educand, for the man in him. That is why Vivekananda's philosophy of education is known as education for man-making. The teacher's aim should be neither money making nor attainment of fame but only bestowing human love. The spiritual force works through love. This love within the educator is the real source of his influence upon the educand. This may be amply clear by the example of the relationship of Vivekananda with his Guru Ram Krishna. It was the force of spiritual love in Ram Krishna which helped Vivekananda in God realization. It is this which makes the educator to take the educand from untruth to truth, darkness to light, death to immortality.

2. Help. The task of the educator is to help the educand in manifesting and expressing his abilities and capacities. Educator should help the individual to recognize his cultural heritage and to use it in his struggle of life. The educator can guide the educand because he himself has the experience of treading on this path and knows how to face its difficulties. Vivekananda has not only presented high ideals of education but also developed a sound system by which these ideals may be achieved.

3. Guidance. Education is not a bed of roses. Every educand has to face problems peculiarly his own. He solves them by his own efforts and with the guidance of the teacher. The skilled teacher guides the pupil through these difficulties and takes him forward. This requires a sufficient knowledge of human psychology because most of our problems are psychological in nature. The teacher should teach the educand to concentrate his attention, only then can the problems be solved. The greater the attention, the more is the effort effective.

4. Concentration. Concentration, according to ancient Indian thought, is the key to true knowledge. Therefore, Vivekananda has placed much emphasis upon focusing of attention. It is only after years of concentration that a man becomes a scholar and a great scientist. The educands should be distinguished according to their abilities, every one of them has to develop concentration. Again, while teaching concentration the educator should keep in mind the varying abilities of concentration is spontaneous and easy, for others it is difficult and requires long training. Hence, the educator must organize his teaching in such a way that he may be helpful to each educand separately. He should attend to every one's difficulties and try to solve them as much as possible. Thus, Vivekananda supported the ancient Indian means of achieving concentration.

5. Brahmacharya. Again, according to ancient Indian thinkers, Brahmacharya or abstinence is the first means of achieving concentration. It gives irmtal and spiritual powers of the highest kind. It transforms sex drive into a spiritual force. *Brahmacharya* implies purity of thought, deed and action. It helps to improve and sharpen various psychological processes such as learning, remembering, thinking, etc. It helps in achieving power of memory and improve the powers of the mind. Vivekananda therefore strongly emphasized the need for the students to observe *Brahmacharya.* This leads to both mental and physical advantages. Firstly, it takes effective care of all distractions. Secondly, it improves the body and the mind so that they may become effective means of knowledge.

6. Discussion and Contemplation. In addition to concentration the other means of education are discussion and contemplation. It is only through these that the educand may remove his difficulties. Discussion should be carried out in an informal atmosphere. Contemplation should be practised in a calm and quiet atmosphere with the mind fully alive. In the end the educational process requires faith and reverence of the educand in the teacher and his teachings. Without faith and reverence no true knowledge can be achieved. It is faith and reverence which are sound foundation for all character development and self-education. The faith and reverence, however, depend not only upon the educand but also upon the high examples presented by the teacher. In the educational process, therefore, the teacher also occupies a very high place.

MEDIUM OF EDUCAHON

1. Mother tongue. In teaching languages Vivekananda laid particular stress upon teaching through the mother tongue. Here he is supported by all other contemporary Indian philosophers of education.

2. Common language. Besides mother tongue, there should be a common language which is necessary to keep the country united. This may be taught in addition to the regional languages.

3. Sanskrit. The teaching of Sanskrit forms an important part of the curriculum envisaged by Vivekananda. Sanskrit is the source of all Indian languages and a repository of all inherited knowledge. It is, therefore, absolutely necessary that every Indian should know Sanskrit. Vivekananda appreciated the greatness of Sanskrit in eloquent words when he said that this language granted power, ability and prestige to the nation and that our awareness of our cultural heritage and past greatness depends very much upon our knowledge of this language. He felt that in the absence of this knowledge, it will be impossible to understand Indian culture. If the society has to develop and progress it is necessary that men and women should know this language which is the store house of ancient heritage, besides the knowledge of the mother tongue.

TYPES OF EDUCATION

Vivekananda elaborately discussed the teaching methods in physical, moral and religious education. This discussion gives an idea, of types of education as well as methods of teaching.

1. Physical Education. Vivekananda laid particular stress on the value of physical education in curriculum. He said, "You will be nearer to Heaven through football than through the study of *Gita.* You will understand *Gita* better by your biceps, your muscles a little stronger. You will understand the *Upanishads* better and the glory of the Atman, when your body stands firm on your feet and you feel yourself as man". Self-realization or character building is impossible in the absence of physical education. One must know the secret of making the body strong through physical education, for a complete education it is necessary to develop both mind and the body. Vivekananda himself took physical exercise every day. He glorified power and opposed weakness in any form. Power was happiness and weakness a never ending burden. It is hence that he so such emphasized the importance of physical education particularly for young men and women.

2. Moral and religious education. Laying emphasis upon religious education Vivekananda said, "Religion is the innermost core of education. I do not mean my own or any one else's opinion about religion. Religion is as the rice and everything else, like the curries. Taking only curries causes indigestion, and so is the case with taking rice alone". Therefore, religious education is a vital part of a sound curriculum. This religious education is necessary in order to counter effect the evil influence of modern materialism. It is only by synthesis of religion and science that men may reap the advantages of both. As has been already pointed out, religious education in itself is never sufficient. It should not be the whole of curriculum but only a part of it. This religion, again, is not any particular dogma or sectarian philosophy, in fact, it is what Tailor called religion of man. It is hence that Vivekananda did not distinguish between secular and religious education. He thought that the former may be given by the latter. He said, "We have to give them secular education. We have to follow the plan laid down by our ancestors, that is, to bring all the ideals slowly down among the masses. Raise them slowly up, raise them to equality. Impart... secular knowledge through religion".

(*i*) *High Ideals.* The best way of imparting religious education is to present the high ideals of saints and religious men before the students. They should be taught to worship saints to follow their ideals. Among the great souls, Vivekananda pointed out to Ram Chandra, Krishna, Mahavir and Ram Krishna. In the ideal of Shri Krishna he laid more emphasis on his personality as the author of *Gita.* He said, "Keep aside for the present the Vrindavan aspect of Shri Krishna, and spread far and wide the worship of Shri Krishna roaring out the *Gita* with the voice of a lion, and bring into daily use the worship of *Shakti* the Divine Mother, the source of all power. We now mostly need the ideal of the hero with the tremendous spirit of *rajas* thrilling through his veins from head to foot, the hero who will dare and die to know the truth, the hero whose armour is renunciation, whose sword is wisdom; we want the spirit of the brave warrior in the battle field".

(*ii*) *Courage.* Thus, Vivekananda wanted men and women to develop qualities according to their particular sex and their role in society. He asked young men to develop manly qualities. Even in religious practices he considered courage to be a higher quality. Religion is not mere ritualism. It is a progress towards high ideals in the face of extreme difficulties.

(*iii*) *Service and Devotion.* Besides courage, Vivekananda prescribed service and devotion in religious education. For this purpose he eulogised the ideal of Hanuman who was a living example of service, devotion and courage. He deplores the dramatic imitation of *Ras Lila* because it is against the interest of the country at present. Purity is the real basis of the country at present. Even in music Vivekananda advised young men to adopt manly music so that it may infuse bravery and courage. This, however, does not mean that Vivekananda rejected any particular type of religious practice. He only wanted to adopt religious practices according to the needs of the times. India, according to him, today needs a religion which should be harmonious with science and teach patriotism, service and sacrifice. Then alone religious education may be useful to the nation. Religion influences total man. It encourages all types of qualities, soft as well as virile. Vivekananda emphasized the inculcation of the latter type of virtues. He exhorted young men by saying, "Never allow weakness to overtake your mind. Remember Mahavir, remember the Divine Mother, and you will see that all weakness, all cowardice will vanish at once".

(*iv*) *Self-confidence.* It goes without saying that such a moral and religious education will develop self-confidence among young men and women. Self-confidence, according to Vivekananda, is the real religion. It includes world brotherhood and love of humanity, because a person having self-confidence means having confidence in humanity. Thus, Vivekananda[5]s religion was humanistic. Religion is the source of all powers. It is again, the source of all good. Thus, for Vivekananda, ethics and religion are one and the same. God is always on the side of goodness. To fight for goodness is therefore service to God. Weakness is the source of all evils. It is at the root of all violence, hatred and enmity. If a man sees his own self everywhere he need not fear any one. Fearlessness and power are eternal truths, the real nature of the self.

(*v*) *Realisation of Truth.* Thus, Vivekananda pleaded for realization of truth through religious practices. Long before Gandhiji identified truth with God, Vivekananda called truth God. The seeker after truth should search for it in every aspect of life. Truth is power, untruth is weakness. Knowledge is truth, ignorance is untruth. Thus, truth increases power, courage and energy. It is light giving. It is, therefore, necessary for the individual as well as collective welfare.

(*vi*) *Achievement of Power.* Thus Vivekananda worshipped power. This power, however, was not physical or biological as that of Nietzche. It was spiritual power. Rising high in the tradition of Vedanta, Vivekananda never allowed his feet to leave the solid ground. His teachings influenced the West where materialism was rampant. This was due to the reason that his teachings were based upon universal truths. Modern man is not prepared to leave the world. He wants to enjoy it. Vivekananda, therefore, gave a practical garb to his religion. India in his time was groaning under slavery. Vivekananda, therefore, asked Indian men and women to shed all types of weakness and to march forward courageously. According to him we have to speak less and work more, achieve power first than anything else. To quote Vivekananda, "First of all our young men must be strong. Religion will come afterwards".

(*vii*) *Study of Scriptures.* In the curriculum for religious education, Vivekananda considered *Gita, Upanishads* and the *Vedas* as the most important. The study of these scriptures will fill young men and women with courage. These are the eternal sources of the life force of Indian culture. These are the bases of our spiritual education. Vivekananda, however, was not in favour of preaching any particular religious dogmas. Religion for him was self-realization. Temples, mosques, churches and synagogues do not make religion. Religion is divinization. It is not intellectual development but transformation of total man. It is nothing if it does not teach us service and sacrifice. It is the basis for character formation. It should lead to man-making. In tune with his Guru Ram Krishna, Vivekananda pleaded for unity of world religions. He considered all religions to be equal. A true religion cannot be limited to a particular place or time. The religious books, teachers and institutions are eternal Their ancient forms are worshipped and their modern forms are respected. Thus, in his moral and religious education Vivekananda pleaded for the education of unity of world religions.

3. Education for weaker section of society. Vivekananda respected human individuality everywhere and pleaded for freedom for everyone. "Each soul", according to him, "is potentially divine. The goal is to manifest external and internal. Do this, either by work, or worship, or psychic centre or philosophy by one or more or all of these—and before. This is the whole of religion. Doctrines or dogmas, or rituals or books, temples or forms are secondary details". It was due to his devotion for the poor and backward people that Vivekananda wanted to make education an instrument for the uplift of the masses. Like Gandhiji after him, Vivekananda, throughout his life, worked for the uplift of backward classes. He pleaded for universal education so that these backward people may fall in line with others. He said, "A nation is advanced in proportion as education and intelligence is spread among the masses. The chief causes of India's ruin have been the monopolizing of the whole education and intelligence of the land among the handful of men. If we are to rise again, we shall have to do it by spreading education among masses". Thus, education should spread to every household in the country, to factories, playing grounds and agricultural fields. If the children do not come to the school the teacher should reach them. Two or three educated men should team up, collect all the paraphernalia of education and should go to the village to impart education to the children. Thus, Vivekananda favoured education for different sections of society, rich and poor, young and old, male and female.

4. Education for women. In the education for women Vivekananda laid particular stress on chastity and fearlessness. He conceived an ideal institution for women known as Math where literature and religion may be taught. Pointing out to the curricula in this institution he said, "Other matters such as sewing, culinary art, rules of domestic work and upbringing of children will also be taught while *'Japa'* worship and meditation, etc., shall form an indispensable part of the teaching. The duty of the teaching in school ought to devolve in every respect on educated widows and *'Brahmacharinis'*. It is good to avoid in this country any association of men with women's schools". Thus, he presented a comprehensive curricula for women so that they may develop high character, courage and confidence. He presented the ideal of Sita and lamented that modern Indian women are imitating Western ideals which had led to all round degeneration. Like males he advised females also to observe *Brahmacharya* which is a solid foundation for any type of education. He was extremely sorry for the lowly condition of Indian women. He considered women to be the incarnation of power and asked men to respect them in every way. He pointed out that unless Indian women secure a respectable place in this country, the nation can never march forward. The regeneration of Indian women, according to him, depends upon proper education. Women's education should be in the hands of women. Clarifying his scheme in this connection he said, "After five or six years' training in this 'Math', the guardians of the girls may many them. If deemed fit for 'Yoga' and religious life, with the permission of their guardians they will be allowed to stay in this Math, taking the vow of celibacy. These celibate nuns will in time be the teachers and preachers of the Math. In villages and towns they will open centres and strive for the spread of female education. Through such devout preachers of character there will be the real spread of female education in this country.... Spirituality, sacrifice and self-control will be the motto of the pupils of this Math, and service or 'Seva Dharma' the vow of their life.... If the life of the women of this country be moulded in such fashion, then only will there be the re-appearance of such ideal characters of Sita, Savitri and Gargi".

CRITICAL EVALUATION

Our discussion about Vivekananda's concept of the aims and ideals of education, its process and curriculum has made it amply clear that he was a humanist in the true sense of the term. He said, "Look upon every man, woman and every one as God. Blessed you are that this privilege was given to you when other had it not. Do it only as a worship. The only God to worship is the human soul in the human body. Of course, all animals are temples too, but man is the highest, the Taj Mahal of temples. If I cannot worship in that, no other temple will be of any advantage". Vivekananda's humanism, however, was different from naturalistic humanism. It is in this background that his education for man-making should be understood. Man, according to him, is the highest of all living beings so much so that according to Vivekananda even the angels will have to come down again and again for salvation through a human body.

The educational ideals advocated by Vivekananda have been supported by most of the modern Western educationists. Education today is defined as the process of all-round development of the child. Such a development can take place only from within while the external environment provides occasion for such development. The teacher has to provide the environment so that the child may become aware of the treasure of knowledge lying buried in his mind. Modern psychologists point out that in every individual there are certain dormant powers which have to be developed through education. The teacher's real job is to see that there should be no impediments in the child's path to self-development. He is like a gardener who prepares grounds for the growth of his plants, protects them and nourishes them so that the plant may grow properly. Similarly, the teacher takes care of the child, provides him a suitable environment and looks after his proper growth. Thus, though education comes from within the teacher is an indispensable part of it. While the motivation comes from within the teacher activates it. He encourages the child to use his mind, body and sense organs. Thus, Vivekananda presented a positive system of education. He wrote, "Education is the manifestation of the perfection already in man. I look upon religion as the innermost core of education". In his philosophy of education Vivekananda synthesized spiritual and material values. He felt that India needed a system of education based on the ancient Vedanta but at the same time worthy of making individual earn his livelihood so that the country may progress. He maintained that no profession is bad provided it is done with a sense of service and self-sacrifice. It is the absence of this dignity of labour which is responsible for the degraded condition of this country. Long before M.K. Gandhi, Vivekananda pleaded for the worship of God in poor. He said, "So long as the millions lie in hunger and ignorance, I hold every man a traitor who having been educated at their expense pays not the least heed, to them". He asked young men to change the situation. He pleaded for universal, compulsory and free education. He asked the educator to reach every village and every hutment so that the country from awake from ignorance.

19

SRI AUROBINDO

OBJECTIVES OF EDUCATION

Defining the objectives of education Sri Aurobindo said, "It must be an education that for the individual will make its one central object the growth of the soul and its powers and possibilities, for the nation will keep first in view the preservation, strengthening and enrichment of the nation-soul and its dharma and raise both into powers of the life and ascending mind and soul of humanity. And at no time will it lose sight of man's highest object, the awakening and development of this spiritual being".[1]

Sri Aurobindo was not only one of the greatest philosopher and yogi of his time but also one of the greatest political leader, social reformer and educationist of his era. He was a great patriot whose first concern was always the good of motherland. Therefore, he presented a national system of education which may be adopted for the educational reconstruction in India and at the same time develop the Indians as world citizens and the fore-runners of the advent of the supramental race upon earth. Sri Aurobindo's philosophy not only gives an important place to individual and nation but also to humanity. In these three principles, the higher determines the lower. Therefore, the national scheme of education will be not only from the point of view of the needs of the country but also from the standpoint of the needs of humanity. It is so since the highest principle governing the life of individual and nation is the humanity itself It is as a human being first and last that the individual has to grow. It is as a member of a community of nations that a nation has to grow and develop. It is the forgetting of this central truth in the life of the individual and nation that has been the source of all evil and error. Again, Sri Aurobindo everywhere considers fulfilment of Swadharma as the law of life. Each individual in a nation has to fullfil his Swadharma. The purpose of education in a nation is to prepare the individual to serve their roles according to their status in society. Individual differences are the basis of modern system of education. Nature has bestowed different human beings with different capacities and powers. Therefore, the educationist has to develop in the child whatever has been already endowed to him by God. The child is, "A soul with a lean, a nature and capacities

1. Sri Aurobindo, *Sri Aurobindo and The Mother on Education*, Part I, p. 3.

of his own, who must be helped to find them, to find himself, to grow into their maturity, into a fullness of physical and vital energy and utmost breadth, depth and height of his emotional his intellectual and his spiritual being".[2] Thus, each human being is a self developing soul.[3] Parents and teachers have to help him in this development. In the words of N.C. Dowsett, the concept of education in Sri Aurobindo's philosophy is summarised thus, "The meaning of the word education is to educe the inner, hidden, latent, dormant, potential secret within every human being, secret because it is not of the senses but of the inner truth of being and because it is that most unknown pan of the being which has yet to evolve to its full stature".[4]

THE TRUE EDUCATION

Defining true education, Sri Aurobindo wrote, "There are three things which have to be taken into account in true and living education, the man, the individual in his commonness and in his uniqueness, the nation or people and universal humanity. It follows that that alone will be true and living education which helps to bring out to full advantage, makes ready for the full purpose and scope of human life all that is in the individual man, and which at the same time helps him to enter into his right relation with the life, mind and soul of the people to which he belongs and with that great total life, mind and soul of humanity of which he himself is a unit and his people or nation a living, a separate and yet inseparable member".[5] Thus, the true education should take into account not only the individual but also the nation and the humanity. It has to prepare the mind and soul of the individual and also of the nation to serve humanity. It has to unfold the individual potentialities, uniqueness and commonness. At the same time it has to develop a right relation of the individual with the life, mind and soul of the community and humanity. In the words of Sri Aurobindo, the true national education is that, "which helps to bring out to full advantage, makes ready for the full purpose and scope of human life all that is in the individual man and which at the same time, helps him to enter into right relation with the life, mind and soul of humanity of which he himself is a unit and his people or nation a living, a separate and yet inseparable member".[6]

Besides Swadharma, the role of a nation is determined by Swabhava. Swadeshi, was the avowed principle in Sri Aurobindo's political philosophy. Each nation, according to him, has to grow and develop in tune with its peculiar Swabhav and Swadharma. This principle has been advocated by Indian thinkers since ancient times. Indian philosophy always considered everything as an instrument of spiritual growth. It may be called *spiritual instrumentalism* in contrast to the biological instrumentalism of John Dewey. Thus, the nation has to develop its mental, ethical and aesthetic being to make it a fit instrument for the growth of

2. Sri Aurobindo, B.C.L., 1971, Volume 15, p. 605.
3. *Ibid.*, pp. 27-28.
4. Dowsett, N.C., *Psychology for Future Education,* Aurobindo Ashram Pondicherry (1977). p. 9.
5. *Sri Aurobindo and The Mother on Education,* Part I, p. 1.
6. Sri Aurobindo, B.C.L., 1972, Volume 17, p. 198.

the soul. This is the highest purushartha. India, according to Sri Aurobindo, is a nation which has to fulfil a spiritual role in the community of nations. Its ideal for the humanity also is spiritual. Therefore, Sri Aurobindo has everywhere called for the spiritual growth of humanity.

Rational Education

This, however, does not mean that Sri Aurobindo finds no place for reason in education. In his philosophy everywhere Sri Aurobindo has supported reason like any staunch rationalist and lauded its role as the law giver to the irrational elements, the passions, the sensibilities and the sense organs. A true and living education is also a rational education though it goes beyond reason for the spiritual growth of man. A rational education, according to Sri Aurobindo, includes the following three things:

1. To teach men how to observe and know rightly the facts on which they have to form a judgment.
2. To train them to think fruitfully and soundly.
3. To fit them to use their knowledge and their thought effectively for their own and the common good.[7]

Meeting of East and West

Brought up in the West Sri Aurobindo had the first hand knowledge of the Western system of education. Like Vivekananda and Tagore he was also conversant with the advantages of European system of education. Though one of the greatest admirers of ancient Indian thoughts, Sri Aurobindo was a votary of the synthesis of whatever is good in East and West. This synthesis is visible everywhere in his thought. Therefore, while presenting a scheme for Indian education, he advocated synthesis of ancient Indian educational ideals along with the Western methods and techniques. As he said, "The first problem in a national system of education is to give an education as comprehensive as the European and more thorough, without the evils of strain and cramming. This can only be done by studying the instruments of knowledge and finding a system of teaching which shall be natural; easy and effective. It is only by strengthening and sharpening these instruments of their utmost capacity that they can be made effective for the increased work which modern conditions require. The muscles of the mind must be thoroughly trained by simple and easy means; then, and not till then, great feasts of intellectual strength can be required of them".[8]

Integral Education

True education, according to Sri Aurobindo, is not only spiritual but also rational, vital and physical. In other words, it is an integral education. This integral education has been explained by Sri Aurobindo's closest collaborator the Mother, in these words, "Education to be complete must have five principal aspects relating to the

7. Sri Aurobindo, B.C.L., 1971, Vol. 15, p. 186.
8. *Sri Aurobindo and The Mother on Education*, Part I, p. 7.

five principal activities of the human being: the physical, the vital, the mental, the psychic and the spiritual. Usually these phases of education succeed each other in a chronological order following the growth of the individual. This, however, does not mean that one should replace another but that all must continue, completing each other, till the end of life".[9] Sri Aurobindo's scheme of education is integral in two senses. Firstly, it is integral in the sense of including all the aspects of the individual being, physical, vital, mental, psychic and spiritual. Secondly, it is integral in the sense of being an education not only for the evolution of the individual alone but also of the nation and finally of the humanity. In his *Essays On Gita* Sri Aurobindo initially presented the concept of integral education as outbringing ail the facets of an individual personality. The ultimate aim of education is the evolution of total humanity which includes the evolution of the nation which in its turn depends upon the evolution of the individual. In this scheme of evolution the principle of growth is unity in diversity. This unity again, maintains and helps the evolution of diversity. Thus each individual in nation and each nation in humanity has to develop a system of education according to its own Swabhav and fulfilling its Swadharma.

Supramental Education

The education again, is ultimately supramental education, that which leads to our evolution towards the supramental. This supramental evolution, however, will necessarily pass through and only after the evolution of the physical, the vital, the mental and the psychic. Physical education is the education of the body. It includes the order, discipline, plasticity and receptivity of the body. Its principal aspects are: 1. Control and discipline of functions, 2. A total, methodical and harmonious development of all the parts and movements of the body, and 3. Rectification of defects and deformities, if there are any.[10] The vital education is indispensible, though difficult. It is so since the nature of vital has been often misunderstood. In the words of The Mother, the vital education involves two principal aspects, "The first is to develop and utilise the sense organs, the second is to become conscious and gradually master of one's character and in the end to achieve its transformation". [11] Thus vital education includes sense training and the development of character. This character again will be developed according to individual differences. It requires redirection and transformation of the instincts and emotions, drives and propensities. Describing the mental education the mother has laid down the following five phases:

1. Development of the power of concentration, the capacity of attention.
2. Development of the capacities of expansion, wideness, complexity and richness.
3. Organisation of ideas around a central idea or a higher ideal or a supremely luminous idea that will serve as a guide in life.
4. Thought control, rejection of undesirable thoughts so that one may, in the end, think only what one wants' and when one wants.

9. *Sri Aurobindo and The Mother on Education*, Part I. p. 8.
10. *Ibid.*, p. 10.
11. *Ibid.*, p. 11.

5. Development of mental silence, perfect calm and a more and more total receptivity to inspirations coming from the higher regions of the being.

While the physical, vital and mental education are the means to develop the personality, the psychic education alone leads to the future evolution of man. Sri Aurobindo's system of education does not aim only at the adjustment and normal development of the human personality but its total growth and transformation. The idea of psychic education has not been developed in any existing philosophy of education. It is so since psychic element was never considered and understood by the Western educationists. In India also in spite of the importance of psychic element found in Yoga, its nature has been seldom understood. The core of the psychic education is the achievement of our identification with the psychic principles in us. This may be reached by psychological, religious or mechanical methods. Every one will have to find out the method best suitable to him and his aspiration. The psychic education requires sincere and steady aspiration, a persistent and dynamic will, concentration, revelation and experience. In the words of The Mother "Only one thing is absolutely indispensable: the will to discover and realise"[12] This is in fact the field of occult and yoga.

Thus the supramental education requires the above steps as a prelude to its realisation. It is only after one gets through the physical, vital, mental and psychic education and realises a certain transformation that one can enter into supramental education. To quote The Mother again, "Then will begin also a new education which can be called the supramental education; it will, by its all-powerful action, work not only upon the consciousness of individual being, but upon the very substance of which they are built and upon the environment in which they live".[13] The idea of supramental education like that of the psychic education is Aurobindo's significant contribution to the field of education. This is more important at the present juncture when most of the educationists are realising the need for an educational system aiming at man-making. According to Sri Aurobindo, humanity today has already reached what has been called by him a subjective stage. The future evolution has to be above the mental level. This will require a great insight and persistent efforts. The different types of education already discussed should not be given successively but simultaneously. The focus should be all the time on the inner growth. As the educand advances he should be taught to identify his real self and to find out the law of his being. The principles of this new type of education have been explained by Sri Aurobindo and the Mother in their different works.

AIMS OF EDUCATION

The aims of education in the educational philosophy of Sri Aurobindo are as follows:

1. Perfection. Sri Aurobindo was a perfectionist. He was never satisfied with partial remedies. It is hence that he left the political arena to pursue a more perfect method of realisation of perfection of human race. It is hence that he presents his integral yoga as a solution not only of the individual needs but also of the

12. *Sri Aurobindo and The Mother on Education*, Part I. p. 14.
13. *Sri Aurobindo and The Mother on Education*, Part I. p. 16.

social and political problems facing nations and humanity. This perfectionism is the strength and this again is the weakness of Sri Aurobindo's philosophy of education. In tune with the Indian concept of human nature Sri Aurobindo considered the individual as, "A growing soul with a being, a nature and capacities of his own".[14] The aim of education therefore was to realise these capacities and grow, "into a fullness of physical and vital energy and utmost breadth, depth and height of his emotional, his intellectual and his spiritual being".[15]

2. Harmony. Harmony is the key to understand Sri Aurobindo's thought eveiywhere. Those who complain about the difficulty in understanding his writings lack this inherent urge to harmony. On the other hand, those who seek harmony easily understand Sri Aurobindo's works. In his philosophy of education, as in his metaphysics, epistemology, political philosophy and social philosophy, Sri Aurobindo searches after the principle of harmony in the individual, community and humanity and aims at its realisation. He seeks to achieve harmony of the individual by the growth and evolution of his different aspects such as physical, vital, mental and psychic, etc. For this he proposes a scheme of physical, vital, mental, moral, religious and spiritual education. He also seeks harmony of different individuals in a community. Compatibility and not uniformity is the law of collective harmony. The roles of the male and female, the different types of individuals in a community are not identical but diverse and therefore complementary. Thus Sri Aurobindo proposes an educational system in which details must be planned according to individual differences. This is particularly true about the women's education, education of backward classes and the education of below normal, abnormal and supernormal children.

3. Evolution. The edifice of Sri Aurobindo's philosophy is based upon his theory of evolution. It stands and falls with the truth of evolution. Evolution, however, has been felt and realised by almost all the thinkers of our age. Therefore, Sri Aurobindo aims at the evolution of the individual, nation and humanity through education. This evolution will be continued as spiral. It is hence that Sri Aurobindo aims at nothing less than supramental education. Evolution involves not only growth but also transformation, not only adjustment but a more intimate harmony. In the words of N.C. Dowsett, Sri Aurobindo's education aims, "To educate the true individual potential within each student, to help him to manifest that within him which is uniquely his, so he may find that as a perfection to be offered to life as his individual contribution to a collective perfection which is the evolving spirit of man and the true heritage to which he aspires".[16] This evolution can be achieved by man's opening and uniting with the universal divine. In other words this requires divine perfection.

4. Humanisation. Education, according to Sri Aurobindo, as according to Vivekananda, aims at man-making. The individual and the nation have to grow as members of one humanity. Sri Aurobindo's system of national education

14. Sri Aurobindo, B.C.L. 1970, Volume 13, pp. 499-500.
15. Sri Aurobindo, B.C.L. 1971, Volume 13, pp. 605.
16. Dowsett, N.C., *The Psychology for Future Education*, Aurobindo Asliram Pondicherry (1977), p. 13.

ultimately aims at evolution of humanity. Describing the aim of Sri Aurobindo's international university at Pondicherry The Mother declared, "It is in answer to this pressing need that Sri Aurobindo conceived the scheme of his international university, so that the elite of humanity may be made ready who would be able to work for the progressive unification of the race and who at the same time would be prepared to embody the new force descending upon earth to transform it".[17]

5. Harmony of the individual and collectivity. While most of the thinkers in social-political field have either laid emphasis upon the individual or the collectivity, Sri Aurobindo aims at realisation of harmony between individuals and also between nations. His scheme of education therefore is truly international. It is not only for India but also for the world. Explaining this ideal of Sri Aurobindo's scheme, The Mother said, "For all world organisation, to be real and to be able to live, must be based upon mutual respect and understanding between nation and nation as well as between individual and individual. It is only in the collective order and organisation, in a collaboration based upon mutual goodwill that lies the possibily of man being lilted out of the painful chaos where he is now. It is with this aim and in this spirit that all human problems will be studied at the university centre; and their solution will be given in the light of the supramental knowledge which Sri Aurobindo has revealed in his writings".[18]

6. Building the innate powers. The central aim of education according to Sri Aurobindo is, "The building of the powers of the human mind and spirit—the evoking of knowledge and will and of the power to use knowledge, character, culture that at least if not more".[19] The child is born with certain innate powers of the body, the vital, the mind and the spirit. The aim of the school and the teacher is to develop these powers to their perfection. For this a programme of sense training, body building, character formation, development of logical and other mental faculties, religious education and finally a training in integral yoga is necessary. Moral development and aesthetic development should go side by side.

7. Cultivation of values. The present crisis of man is due to the chaos of values. Old values have been challenged while new values have not firmly taken their place. In his social philosophy Sri Aurobindo has particularly discussed this problem.[20] The values to be cultivated should be physical, mental as well as spiritual. Character formation very much depends on value. The supreme value in Sri Aurobindo's thought is harmony. Other values are: spirituality, divinity, evolution, ascent, transformation, etc. All these must be cherished and developed. But the most important value required for all growth is sincerity. Once that is developed, the rest follows. Right emotions and Sanskars, Swabhav and nature are the foundation of Sri Aurobindo's scheme of education. Sri Aurobindo not only aims at moral status but also going beyond it, rising above virtue and vice. This is the supramental status aimed at both by the individual and collectivity in Sri Aurobindo's thought.

17. *Ibid.*, pp. 25-26.
18. *Ibid*, p. 28.
19. Sri Aurobindo, B.C.L., 1972, Volume, 17, p. 194.
20. Sharnia, R.N., *Social Philosophy of Sri Aurobindo*, 1981, Vineet Publications, Meerut, Chapt. I.

The Educational Model

While Sri Aurobindo outlined a national system of education, a model to realise his scheme was developed by The Mother in the form of Sri Aurobindo international university at Pondicherry.[21] It was developed as a new centre of education to experiment for the realisation of the aims outlined by Sri Aurobindo. The curriculum, the teaching methods, the system of education and all the other details were formed with this central aim. The fundamental principle underlying the model was freedom since freedom is the only essential spiritual principle working any where. As has been already pointed out, this ideal control of education not only aimed at revelation of Sri Aurobindo's aim in India but also in humanity. All the aims of education outlined earlier were practised here. Children were admitted from a very early age. They gathered from all the parts of the country as well as from different countries in the world to make it a true representative of world cultures. The natural scenery, dress, games, sports, industries, food, art, etc., were developed on the principle of unity and diversity. An effort was made to realise a cultural synthesis. Students of different nations were placed at different places with their own groups so that while they may develop international culture, no rigid time-table, classes, curriculum, teaching method or system of evaluation and examination was insisted. This was left upon individual choice of the educand himself.

The idea was to give full freedom to the individual growth of the educand. The experiment fared very well but did not grow elsewhere due to obvious difficulties in such experiments. However, it is undoubtedly a model for a new system of education which may be hoped to develop in India and also in parts of the world.

THE SCHOOL

The ultimate ideal of the school is man-making. It prepares the educand to work first as a human being and then as a member of a nation and finally as an individual. The circles of moral responsibility and loyalties proceed from wider to narrower and not vice-versa. The man has to develop first as a human being then as a citizen and finally as an individual. Most of the present confusion of values is due to an inversion of this order.

Sri Aurobindo believes in three ultimate principles, individuality, commonality and essentiality. These, in other words, are the educand, the society and the humanity. Integral evolution, according to him, must include evolution of all these three elements. Thus the individuality and commonality should develop together. This is the purpose of the school. The school should treat all children as equal and provide sufficient scope for the development of their individual variations without insisting upon similarities. In his lecture at Baroda College Sri Aurobindo observed that the colleges and universities should educate through their academic as well as social-activities.[22] Thus the college should have its bearing upon the community around it.[23] The school cannot be isolated from society. It cannot give

21. Sri Aurobindo, B.C.L., 1972, Volume. 17.
22. Sri Aurobindo, B.C.L., 1972, Volume III, p. 131.
23. *Ibid*, p. 132.

total education in isolation. Its teachings have to be practised in the society outside it. The university merely gives some materials to the educand which he may use.

In the integral school four types of rooms are required to carry on various activities: 1. Rooms of silence, 2. Rooms of collaboration, 3. Rooms of consultation,

Lecture rooms.[24] Thus the school will develop different types of activities such as silence, collaboration, consultation and lectures. It will provide play, activity, discovery, innovation and finally development of the powers of the body, mind and spirit of the educand. In brief, the integral school will provide opportunities for integral development.

THE TEACHER

Like the ancient Indian system of education, Sri Aurobindo has assigned a very important place to the teacher. He has however not made him central as in the ancient Indian scheme. The central place, as in the Western systems of education, has been occupied by the educand. His philosophy of education, therefore, is paidocentric. However, the teacher remains the philosopher and the guide. The Guru does not have absolute authority. He aims at turning the disciple's eye towards the beacon light of his own Godhead. In fact, the real teacher is within the educand. He is the God. He is the ultimate guide and yet the teacher plays an important role in arousing the educand towards God within. He has not to impose his opinions or demand passive surrender from the educand. He has to create an atmosphere so that the educand may grow freely. Sri Aurobindo accepts the role of a gardener in the teacher as maintained by many Western educational philosophers. The teacher acts as an aid, a means and a channel. His relationship with the educand is very close. In the ancient Indian tradition, Sri Aurobindo emphasises an inner relationship between the educator and the educand. For this the teacher should develop certain innate qualities.

Describing as to who is a teacher, The Mother has laid down the following qualifications, "Teachers who do not possess a perfect calm, an unfailing endurance, an unshakeable quietness who are full of self-conceit will reach nowhere.

One must be a saint and a hero to become a good teacher.

One must be a great yogi to become a good teacher.

One must have the perfect attitude in order to be able to exact from one's pupils a perfect attitude.

You cannot ask of a person what you do not do yourself. It is a rule.

You must then look within you at the difference between what is and what should be, and this difference will give you the measure of your failure in the class.[25]

In brief, the teacher should be an integral yogi. He should be able to eliminate his ego, master his mind, develop an insight into human nature and to progress in impersonalisation. He should be absolutely disciplined and having an integrated personality. The most important thing in a teacher is not the knowledge but the attitude. An intellectual excellence is not sufficient without a development of other

24. Joshi, Kirit *Nav Chetana*, Mothers International School (1977), pp. 5-7.
25. *Sri Aurobindo and The Mother On Education*, Part II, pp. 4-5.

aspects of personality. The teacher should have the capacity to project himself to the educand so that he may have an understanding of the needs of the educand. The schools aim not only on the progress of the educand but also of the educator. In the words of the Mother, "The school must be an occasion of progress for the teacher as well as for the student. Each must have the freedom to develop himself freely. One never applies a method well unless one has discovered it oneself."[26] In practice the central trait of the teacher is the inner calm. He should exercise influence not by scolding but by moral control. In the words of the Mother, 'I must tell you that if a professor wants to be respected, he must be respectable."[27]

Personality Traits of the Teacher

In order to fulfil his role, the teacher should take it seriously and honestly. He should develop his personality more than the ordinary man so that he may be able to influence others. He should be a representative of divine on earth. He should be in close touch with the divine consciousness. He should be a representative of the supreme knowledge, the supreme truth and the supreme law. Then alone his influence will work. The Mother has prescribed the following personality traits for a true teacher:

1. Complete self-control not only to the extent of not showing any anger, but remaining absolutely quiet and undisturbed under all circumstances.
2. In the matter of self-confidence, he must also have the sense of the relativity of his importance.
3. Above all, he must have the knowledge that the teacher himself must always progress if he wants his students to progress, must not remain satisfied either with what he is or with what he knows.
4. Must not have any sense of essential superiority over his students nor preference of attachment whatsoever for one or another.
5. Must know that all are equal spiritually and instead of mere tolerance must have a global comprehension or understanding.
6. "The business of both parent and teacher is to enable and to help the child to educate himself, to develop his own intellectual, moral, aesthetic and practical capacities and to grow freely as an organic being, not to be kneaded and pressured into form like an inert plastic material."[28]

THE CURRICULUM

As has been already pointed out, the essential principle of Sri Aurobindo's philosophy of education is freedom. Unity is never demanded at the cost of diversity. On the other hand, diversity creates a rich unity. Therefore, no rigid scheme of curriculum has been prescribed. However, hints are scattered in Sri Aurobindo's works about different criteria of curriculum. The earliest permissible age for starting regular study according to Sri Aurobindo is seven or eight years. At this age the child is sufficiently grown up to take up regular study. The proper medium for early

26. *Ibid.*, p. 7.
27. *Ibid.*, p. 8-9.
28. *Ibid.*, p. 8.

education of the child is the mother tongue. It is only after the mother tongue that the child can learn other languages. As has been already pointed out, the following criteria for planning curriculum are found in Sri Aurobindo's writings:

1. Human nature. The curriculum should aim at developing whatever is already given in seed form in the child. Education can only lead to the perfection of the instruments which are already present in the educand. Nothing can be taught or imposed from outside. In the words of The Mother, "Fundamentally the only thing you must do assiduously is to teach them to know themselves, and to choose their own destiny, the way they want to follow".[29]

2. Individual differences. The curriculum should be planned according to individual differences. The mind has to be consulted in its own growth. The aim of the teacher is to help the growing soul in drawing out his best and to make it perfect for a noble use.[30]

3. From near to the far. Another principle governing the planning of curriculum is to proceed from near to the far, from that which is to that which shall be.[31]

4. Modern and uptodate. Sri Aurobindo was not a reactionary or a conservative. He was a modern thinker with a love for modernity and uptodate knowledge. Therefore, he prescribed that the education must be uptodate in form and substance and modern in life and spirit.[32]

5. Universal knowledge. The curriculum should include whatever is universally true. That is the basis of all scientific knowledge and philosophy. Truth and knowledge are one and not confined to any country. Therefore, according to Sri Aurobindo, education should be universal without any nationality or borders.[33]

6. Successive teaching. Sri Aurobindo disagrees with some educationists who wish to introduce every subject simultaneously to the child. He prescribes that the subjects should be taught successively. New subjects should be introduced after the earlier are mastered. Thus few subjects should be taught at a time.

7. Co-curricular activities. The school should provide not only academic but also co-curricular activities.

8. Five-fold curriculum. As has been already pointed out, integral education is five-fold. It includes the physical, the vital, the mental, the psychic and the spiritual education. Therefore, the curriculum must be five-fold according to these five types of education. Of these the education of the mind involves the most detailed curriculum. It requires different curriculum for the development of the different powers of the mind such as observation, memory, judgment, comparison, contrast, analogy, reasoning and imagination, etc. Sense training requires curriculum involving all the five senses.

9. Multisidedness. Integral education is multisided. It aims at allround growth. Therefore its curriculum involves music, poetry, art, painting and sculpture,

---

29. *Ibid.*, p. 1.
30. Sri Aurobindo, B.C.L., 1972, Volume, 17, p. 205.
31. *Ibid.*
32. *Ibid.*, p. 194.
33. *Ibid.*, p. 193.

besides the academic subjects. These are necessary for the aesthetic development of the child. These aim at contemplation and understanding of beauty and just arrangement of the tastes, habits and character of the educand. According to Sri Aurobindo, in contrast to many other educationists music, art and poetry purify, control, deepen and harmonise the movements of the soul . [34] In his work entitled *The National Value of Art,* Sri Aurobindo points out three uses of art. Firstly, it is purely aesthetic, secondly, it is intellectual and educative and thirdly, it is spiritual. The aesthetic development purifies conduct and disciplines the animal instincts and lower feelings of the heart. The artistic sense helps in the formation of morals and purification of the emotion.[35] Thus art has both intellectual and spiritual value. It is subtle and delicate and makes the mind subtle and delicate.[36]

10. Provision for the genius. The curriculum must provide for the genius. According to Sri Aurobindo,"What we call genius is part of the development of the human range of being and its achievements especially in things of the mind and their will can carry us half way to the divine".[37] The curriculum should cater for the perfection of the different powers of the genius.

11. Moral and religious education. Curriculum for moral education should aim at refining the emotions and forming the proper habits and associations. Religious teaching like moral teaching does not involve so much of curriculum as teaching by example and provision of right atmosphere. In the words of Sri Aurobindo, "Whether distinct teaching in any form of religion is imparted or not the essence of religion, to live for God, for humanity, for country, for others and for oneself must be made the ideal in every school".[38]

Thus the aim of the curriculum according to Sri Aurobindo, is the actualisation of the potentialities of the educand. The material is the basis and spiritual is the summit of education. The curriculum gradually becomes more and more abstract leading to the realisation of higher experiences. Same curriculum may be followed by male and female. The schools may be co-educational. Sufficient emphasis should be laid upon aesthetic, moral and religious teaching. The curriculum should not be fixed but flexible and evolutionary. A variety of choice and opportunities must be prescribed for maintaining the freedom of growth. The integral curriculum should find a due place for every subject and every discipline.

A TENTATIVE EDUCATIONAL PLAN

Norman C. Dowsett has presented the following tentative educational plan developed by International Centre of Education, Pondicherry, based upon educational philosophy of Sri Aurobindo.[39]

1. The Play school (1-3 years)

   Provision of love, security, wonder, discovery and adventure.

34. Sri Aurobindo, B.C.L., 1972, Volume 17, pp. 244-46.
35. *Ibid* pp. 24-42.
36. *Ibid.*, p. 245.
37. *Ibid.*, pp. 207-8.
38. Sri Aurobindo, B.C.L., 1972, Volume 17, p. 212.
39. Dowsett N.C., *Psychology for Future Education*, Aurobindo Ashram, Pondicherry (1977), pp. 218-29.

2. Pre-School discipline of the physical mind (3-5 years)
   a. order
   b. activities, physical exercises and games.
3. Prime-School of fulfilment of the vital mind (5-7 ½ yrs)
   a. body awareness—discipline of the physical mind to continue.
   b. fulfilment of vital energies — The vital should be fulfilled through art, drawing, painting, sculpture dance, drama, music, etc.
4. High school of the freedom of the mental mind I phase (7½ - 10½ years) use of the instruments of knowledge.
5. High school of the freedom of the mental mind II phase (1014-14 years) integration of the progressive series of creative energies.
6. Graduation school of psychic education (14-17): years appreciation of individuality, progressive understanding of his inner potential and his contribution to the group, society, nation and the world.
7. College of spiritual education (17-21 years) spiritual realisation, integration of all that has been achieved.

THE IDEAL CHILD

Sri Aurobindo's system of education is paidocentric. It aims at the creation of ideal children. The ideal children are absolutely sincere and constantly progressive. They are forbidden fighting any where. They are always truthful. The Mother has given the following description of an ideal child.[40]

1. Good-Tempered. He does not become angry when things seem to go against him or decisions are not in his favour.

2. Game. Whatever he does it to the best of his capacity and keeps on doing in the face of almost certain failure. He always thinks straight and acts straight.

3. Truthful. He never fears to say the truth whatever may be the consequences.

4. Patient. He does not get disheartened if he has to wait a long time to see the results of his effort.

5. Enduring. He never slackens his effort however long it has to last.

6. Poised. He keeps equanimity in success as well as in failure.

7. Courageous. He always goes on fighting for the final victory though he may meet with many defeats.

8. Cheerful. He knows how to smile and keep a happy heart in all circumstances.

9. Modest. He does not become conceited over his success, neither does he feel himself superior to his comrades.

10. Generous. He appreciates the merits of others and is always ready to help another to succeed.

11. Courteous. On the field he does not jeer at errors, he does not cheer at the opponent's defeat; he treates them as guests, not enemies. In school he is considerate to the authorities, the fellow students, and the teachers. In life he is respectful to others; he treats them as he would be treated.

40. *Sri Aurobindo and The Mother on Education*, Part II, pp. 28-29.

12. Obedient. On the field he observes the regulations. In life he respects the rules which help to promote harmony.

13. Fair. On the field he competes in a clean, hard fought but friendly way; he helps an injured opponent. In school he does not waste his time nor that of the teachers. He is always honest. In life he sees impartially both sides of a question.

Thus Sri Aurobindo's integral education gives highest place to the children. They are considered as divine force, the leaders of the future gnostic race on the earth. All the hopes for man's future lie upon the proper development of the younger generation. There is no gap between the teacher, the Guru and the children. Integral education considers the inner relationship and rapport as the first condition of all education. It is in this spirit that the Mother said to the children of the Ashram, "My children, we are united towards the same goal and the same accomplishment for a work unique and new, that the divine Grace has given us to accomplish. I hope that more and more you will understand the exceptional importance of this work and that you will sense in yourself the sublime joy that the accomplishment will give you. The divine force is with you, feel its presence more and more and be very careful never to betray it. Feel, wish, act, that you may be new beings for the realisation of a new world and for this my blessings shall be always with you".[41]

Thus the children are highly respected. The job of the teacher is not utilitarian or for earning his bread but for man-making. It is in the spirit of offering of one's action to God that the teachers can create the spirit of sacrifice in the children. Sri Aurobindo's integral education is based upon faith in human nature. As against the explanation of human nature offered by most of the Western thinkers including Hobbes, Sri Aurobindo, like many other religious savants, considers man as divine. It was in this spirit that the Mother said to the children of the Ashram, "Be courageous, enduring, vigilant; above all be sincere, with perfect honesty. Then you will be able to face all difficulties. And victory will be yours" [42]

TEACHING METHODS

Thus the teaching methods in integral education of Sri Aurobindo are based on the one hand on faith in the inner goodness and evolutionary nature of the educand and on the other hand on the psychological principles involved in teaching. Sri Aurobindo's explanations and suggestions are everywhere psychological. Without going into the details he has aways kept his eye focussed on the tendencies working within him. Therefore his suggestions are very valuable.

Teaching Children

Sri Aurobindo and The Mother gave particular attention to the methods of teaching children. In this connection the following suggestions are offered:[43]

1. The teachers should have sufficient documentation of what they know. They should be able to answer all questions.

41. *Ibid.*, Part III, p. 22.
42. *Ibid.*, p. 23.
43. *Ibid.*, pp. 19-21.

2. They should have at least the knowledge if not the experience of true intellectual and intuitive attitude. This knowledge can be attained through mental silence.
3. He is the best teacher who has the capacity and not only knowledge of the different fields of evolution.
4. Thus the professors must be sincere in discipline and experience. They should not be propagandists.
5. To start with, "The children, as soon as they have the capacity to think (it begins at 7 years but towards 14 years it is very clear) should be given small indications at 7 and a complete explanation at 14, of how to do it, and that it is the unique method to enter into relation with the profounds, that all the rest is a mental approximation, more or less inapt of something that can be known directly".[44]

Teaching Very Small Children

About the teaching of very small children, The Mother has laid down the following principles for the teachers:[45]

Never to deceive oneself.
Never to be angry.
Always to be understanding.
Never try to impose on them.

Never scold but always try to understand. With Rousseau Sri Aurobindo believes that the child is naturally good but gradually corrupted by bad environment. In an adverse environment the child looses all contact with the self in him. Therefore, the Mother has insisted that the most necessary thing to be taught to the child is to follow the inner psychic consciousness. As she said, "That is why I insist on that and I say that from the very earliest age children must be taught that there is a reality within themselves, within the earth, within the universe and that he himself, the earth and the universe, exist only as a function of this truth and if it did not exist, he would not last, even the short time he lasts and that everything would dissolve as soon as it is created.[46]

This, however, does not require philosophical explanations. The child is not prepared for mental understanding of the self. He should be made to realise the inner consciousness. His education, therefore, should be by projects and playway methods. The child responds to the psychic vibrations. He is most impressed by affection and feelings. Therefore, integral education rules out all harsh treatment, scolding or being angry towards the children. One must have sufficient patience with them. The habits for cleanliness and hygiene should start very early. This, however, does not require creating fear of illness in the child. The Mother has warned, 'Fear is the worst incentive to education and the surest way of attracting what is feared"[47] This warning is timely not only for early education but for secondary and university education in our country.

44. *Ibid.*, p. 20.
45. *Ibid.*, p. 21.
46. *Ibid.*, p. 23.
47. *Ibid.*, p. 26.

How to Teach

Sri Aurobindo, in his exposition of teaching methods, keeps his eye focussed on the truth alone. He is neither prejudiced in favour nor against the ancient Indian teaching methods or the Western ways of teaching. As he said, "The past hangs about our necks with all its prejudices and errors and will not leave us; it enters into our most radical attempts to return to the guidance of the all-wise Mother. We must have the courage to take up clearer knowledge and apply it fearlessly in the interests of posterity".[48]

Successive Teaching

Accepting that every child has multiple tendencies and abilities requiring teaching of various subjects, Sri Aurobindo favours successive teaching as against simultaneous introduction of so many subjects in early education. Among the different subjects to be taught to the child, the basic subjects should be introduced first so that a sound foundation for education is made. As Sri Aurobindo points out, "The old system was to teach one or two subjects well and thoroughly and then proceed to others and certainly it was a more rational system than the modern. If it did not impart so much varied information, it built up a deeper, nobler and more real culture".[49] Thus different subjects should be studied one by one. The same principle is applicable to the teaching of text-books. Each chapter should be studied thoroughly and in succession. In the words of The Mother, "One should leave a chapter when it has been fully grasped then only take up the next one and so on. If a chapter is finished, it is finished: and if it is not finished it is not finished".[50] The child's education should start at the age of 7 or 8 for, according to Sri Aurobindo, "That is the earliest permissible age for the commencement of any regular kind of study".[51] At this age the child is capable of concentration and interest. Therefore, the first thing to be created in the child is interest in the subject.

Education through Practical Experience

Thus, like all other modern educators, Sri Aurobindo pleads for introduction of different subjects to the child through practical experience. First of all he should acquire mastery of the mother tongue as the medium of the education, because that is the required sound basis for regular instruction. Elaborating the needs of practical foundation of child's education, Sri Aurobindo gives valuable suggestions for the teaching of different subjects appealing to the imagination, the dramatic faculty, love for the narrative, hero worship, urge to enquiry and other natural characteristics of the child. To quote his advise, "Almost every child has an imagination, an instinct for words, a dramatic faculty, a wealth of idea and fancy. These should be interested in the literature and history of the nation. Instead of stupid and dry spelling and reading books, looked on as a dreary and ungrateful task, he should be introduced by rapidly progressive stages to the most

48. *Ibid*, p. 11.
49. Sri Aurobindo, B.C.L., 1972, Volume 17, p. 213.
50. *Sri Aurobindo and The Mother on Education*, Part II, p. 17.
51. *Ibid.*

interesting parts of his own literature and the life around him and behind him, and they should be put before him in such a way as to attract and appeal to the qualities of which I have spoken. All other study at this period should be devoted to the perfection of the mental functions and the moral character. A foundation should be laid at this time for the study of history, science, philosophy, but not in an obtrusive and formal manner. Every child is a lover of interesting narrative, a hero-worshipper and a patriot. Appeal to these qualities in him and through them let him master without knowing it the living and human parts of his nations's history. Every child is an inquirer, an investigator, analyser, a merciless anatomist. Appeal to those qualities in him and let him acquire without knowing it, the necessary fundamental knowledge of the scientist. Every child has an insatiable intellectual curiosity and turn for metaphysical inquiry. Use it to draw him on slowly to an understanding of the world and himself Every child has the gift of imitation and a touch of imaginative power. Use it to give him the ground work of the faculty of the artist".[52]

Three Principles of Teaching

Now, before trying to understand methods of teaching of different instruments of the educand one should remember the following three principles of teaching laid down by Sri Aurobindo:

1. The first principle is that nothing can be taught.
2. The second principle is that the mind should be constantly consulted in its growth.
3. The third principle is to work from the near to the far, from that which is to that which shall be.[53]

Integral Teaching

Integral teaching involves training of all the aspects of the educand's mind and personality. Starting with sense training it develops the memory and judgement, the observation and comparison, analogy, reasoning, imagination, language, grammar and meaning of the logical faculty, etc. All these characteristics are present in every child. In the words of Sri Aurobindo, "Every child is an inquirer, an investigator, analyser, a merciless anatomist".[54] The first thing to do is to arouse the curiosity, imagination and natural interest of the child so that he may spontaneously enquire, understand and learn. As Sri Aurobindo advises the teachers, "The first work is to interest the child in life, work and knowledge, to develop his instruments of knowledge with the utmost thoroughness, to give him mastery of the medium he must use. Afterwards the rapidity with which he will learn will make up for any delay in taking up regular studies and it will be found that... he will learn many tilings thoroughly well".[55]

52. *Ibid.*, pp. 11-12.
53. Sri Aurobindo, B.C.L., 1972, Volume, 17, p. 204.
54. *Ibid.*, p. 215.
55. *Ibid.*

Obervation

Sense training starts with observation. The child has a natural urge to observe the nature around. It is hence that most of the educationists have advised that early education should start with child's observation of nature under the guidance of the teacher. Explaining this method of teaching Sri Aurobindo said, "We may take the instance of a flower. Instead of looking casually at it and getting a casual impression of scent, form and colour, he should be encouraged to know the flower to fix in his mind the exact shade, the precise intensity of the scent, the beauty of curve and design in the form. His touch should assure itself of the texture and its peculiarities. Next, the flower should be taken to pieces and its structure examined with the same carefulness of observation. All this should be done not as a task, but as an object by skillfully arranged questions suited to the learner which will draw him on to observe and investigate one thing after the other until he has almost unconsciously mastered the whole".[56]

The observation is not confined to the flowers and leaves. The child will also leam by the observation of stars, earth, stones, insects, animals and things made by human beings. The example of observation given above is particularly useful in the teaching of botany. To quote Sri Aurobindo, "The observation and comparison of flowers, leaves, plants, trees will lay the foundations of botanical knowledge without loading the mind with names and that dry set acquisition of information which is the beginning of cramming and detested by the healthy human mind when it is fresh from nature and unspoiled by unnatural habits".[57] Elaborating further use of observation method of teaching other subjects, Sri Aurobindo said, "In the same way by the observation of the stars, astronomy, by the observation of earth, stones, etc., geology, by the observation of insects and animals, entomology and zoology may be founded. A little later chemistry may be started by interesting observation of experiments without any formal teaching or heaping on the mind of formulas and book knowledge".[58]

Training of Memory and Judgement

As in the case of sense training so also in the case of training of the mind Sri Aurobindo wants to make them spontaneous and unconscious. He is against all mechanical, burdensome and unintelligent way of memory training. He is against any use of rote memory. Memory training should involve nothing of similarities and differences in things observed. According to Sri Aurobindo, "A similar but different flower should be put in the hands and he should be encouraged to note it with the same care, but with the avowed object of noting the similarities and differences. By this practice daily repeated the memory will naturally be trained."[59] This in its turn will train the faculty of judgement. To quote Sri Aurobindo again, "At every step the boy will have to decide what is the right idea, measurement,

56. *Sri Aurobindo and The Mother on Education*, Part II, p. 13.
57. *Ibid.*, p. 14.
58. *Ibid.*
59. *Ibid.*, p. 14.

appreciation of colour, sound, scent, etc., and what is the wrong. Often the judgments and distinctions made will have to be exceedingly subtle and delicate. At first many errors will be made, but the learner should be taught to trust his judgement without being attached to its results. It will be found that the judgment will soon begin to respond to the calls made on it, clear itself of all errors and begin to judge correctly and minutely. The best way is to accustom the boy to compare his judgments with those of others. When he is wrong, it should at first be pointed out to him how far he was right and why he went wrong; afterwards he should be encouraged to note these things for himself. Every time he is right, his attention should be prominently and encouragingly called to it so that he may get confidence".[60] The training of memory and judgement is the basis of every scientific teaching. In the opinion of Sri Aurobindo, "There is no scientific subject the perfect and natural mastery of which cannot be prepared in early childhood by this training of the faculties to observe, compare, remember and judge various classes".[61] Judgement gives the ability to choose between right and wrong. It is therefore a prelude to every decision about values.

Training of Logical Faculty

Training of judgement very much depends upon the training of logical faculty. According to Sri Aurobindo, training of logical reasoning requires the following three elements:[62]

1. the correctness of the facts,
2. the completeness as well the accuracy of the data,
3. the elimination of other possible or impossible conclusions from the same facts.

The young child should be trained to take interest in drawing inferences from the facts. For this purpose he should proceed, "From the example to the rule and from the accumulating harmony of rules to the formal science of the subject"[63] The reasoning should proceed from concrete to abstract, since this is the law of training of mental faculties, the sound should be acknowledged before the sense. Explaining his principle in this connection Sri Aurobindo has remarked, "The true knowledge takes its base on things, arthas, and only when it has mastered the thing, proceeds to formalise its information".[64]

Training of Imagination

Several subjects including literature, particularly, require a training of imagination. This is the first requirement of any excellence in any creative art. As Sri Aurobindo has given an important place to art and literature in his plan of education, he insists upon the child's training in imagination. According to him, "This is a most important and indispensable instrument".[65] For the training of

60. *Ibid.*, p. 15.
61. Sri Aurobindo B.C.L., 1972, Volume, XVII, p.223.
62. *Ibid.*, p. 226.
63. *Ibid.*, pp. 226-27.
64. *Sri Aurobindo and The Mother on Education*, Part II, p. 16.
65. *Ibid.*

imagination Sri Aurobindo recommends, "It may be divided into three functions, the forming of mental images, the power of creating thoughts, images and imitations or new combinations of existing thoughts and images, the appreciation of the soul in things, beauty, charm, greatness, hidden suggestiveness, the emotion and spiritual life that pervades the world".[66]

Training of Language

Explaining his principle for training of language, Sri Aurobindo finds out that first the child should know the things and then the ideas. He laments that most of the dealings with language show an absence of fine sense of words. He suggests, "The mind should be accustomed first to notice the word thoroughly, its form, sound and sense; then to compare the form with other similar forms in the points of similarity and difference, thus forming the foundation of the grammatical sense; then to distinguish between the fine shades of sense of similar words and the formation and rhythm of different sentences, thus forming the foundation of the literary and the syntactical faculties".[67] All this should be done informally. One should avoid set rules of teaching and memorising. Sri Aurobindo is everywhere against mechanical processes. The teaching should first arouse the interest of the child and then depend upon spontaneous use of his abilities. The child should be allowed absolute freedom in his progress.

Free Progress System

The followers of Sri Aurobindo have developed a free progress system of education, whose salient features are as follows:[68]

1. The structure is oriented towards individual needs, interests and abilities.
2. The aspiration, experience of freedom, self-education and experimentation relating inner needs with the curricular provisions, discovering the higher lines of life and the art to encompass.
3. Each student is free to study any subject he chooses at any given time under a sympathetic guidance.
4. Promotion of individual endeavour.
5. Weekly announcement of time-table and lectures to be delivered.
6. Promotion of discussion between teachers and taught and between taught and taught.
7. Projects are announced in each subject and the students select according to their choice.

No Set Distinction

In his system of education, Sri Aurobindo does not make any distinction on the basis of sex. The education for man and woman should be similar in all respect. Clarifying this rejection of sex distinctions in education, The Mother said, "What we claim is this, that in similar conditions, with the same education and

66. *Ibid.*
67. *Ibid.*
68. Joshi Kirit, *Nav Chetna*, Mothers International School, New Delhi (1977), pp. 5-7.

the same possibilities, there is no reason to make a categorical distinction, final and imperative between what we call men and women, for us human beings are the expression of a single soul".[69] In his interpretation of his Indian social system Sri Aurobindo laid emphasis upon equality of sexes. He lamented that later on the women were subjugated to men leading to degeneration of society. He proposes that the women should be everywhere treated as equals to men. He is against Indian psychological dictum that male and female should avoid each other's company. He, on the other hand, maintains, "There is no impossibility of friendship between man and woman pure of this element (sex), such friendships can exist and have always existed. All that is needed is that the lower vital should not look in it through the back door or be permitted to enter".[70] Therefore, no distinctions are made between boys and girls in Mother's International School or Sri Aurobindo International University at Pondicherry. The most unique feature of the education at these two institutions is the prescription of physical exercises both for boys and girls. Clarifying this policy the Mother said, "In all cases, as well as for boys as for girls, the exercises must be graded according to the strength and capacity of each one. If a weak student tries at once to do hard and heavy exercises, he may suffer for his foolishness. But with a wise and progressive training girls as well as boys can participate in all kinds of sports, increase their strength and health".[71] According to Sri Aurobindo both men and women are equally capable to evolve toward perfection to reach gnostic age.

DISCIPLINE AND FREEDOM

The Mother has rightly said, "No big creation is possible without discipline"?[72] Defining discipline in terms of the highest principle Sri Aurobindo maintained that it is 'To act according to a standard of truth or a rule or law of action or in obedience to a superior authority or the highest principle discovered by the reason or intelligent will".[73] Thus discipline is a controlled life. The physical, the vital and the mental sources are guided by spirituality. It is against unbridled indulgence in fancies, impulses and desires. It is obedience of the inner sense. Partly, it is also obedience of authority.

Kinds of Discipline

Discipline, according to Sri Aurobindo, is: Individual discipline, Group discipline and finally Discipline towards the Divine. These distinctions have been made on the basis of the authority functioning in imposition of discipline. Individual discipline is imposed by the individual himself Group discipline is imposed by the group or the majority or the leader in it. Discipline towards the Divine means, rigorous perusal of the dictates of the Divine. However, these three types of discipline are essentially the same since underlying the individual, group and the

69. *Sri Aurobindo and The Mother on Women*, 1978, p. 17.
70. Sri Aurobindo, B.C.L., 1970, Volume 23, p. 817.
71. *On Women*, 1978, p. 58.
72. *Sri Aurobindo and The Mother on Education*, Part II, p. 26.
73. Sri Aurobindo, B.C.L., 1970. Volume 23, p. 862.

universe there is only one Divine principle. Sri Aurobindo maintains that the three aspects of reality, viz., individuality, commonality and essentiality are in fact one.

Disciplinary Measures

The best way to impose discipline, according to Sri Aurobindo is the atmosphere and the example by the teacher. The following measures have been recommended by Sri Aurobindo and the Mother to inculcate discipline among the students:

1. Generally speaking, the discipline should start at the age of twelve.
2. The most important measure is the example of the teacher. The teacher should be punctual, properly dressed, calm, methodical, orderly, sympathetic and courteous. He should himself present high examples of sincerity, honesty, straightforwardness, courage, disinterestedness, unselfishness, patience, endurance, perseverance, peace and self control. He should first of all train his own emotions and morals. He should have a respect of the child. Nothing should be imposed from outside but suggested by examples. Examples are the best for the personal guidance and to exercise influence upon the educands. In the words of the Mother, "It is through example that education becomes effective. To say good words, give wise advice to a child has very little effect, if one does not show by one's living example the truth of what one teaches".[74]

The vibrations between the teacher and the taught should be favourable, there should be no use of force in discipline. According to The Mother, before the age of seven years the child is not conscious of himself and does not know why and how to do things. During this period he should be trained to acquire traits of a human being. From the age of seven years to fourteen years of age, the child should be taught to choose what he wishes to be. At 14, he should be clear at what he wants to do. After 14 years of age he should be left independent to pursue his course. He may be only advised now and then.

There can be no definite rules for the guidance of the students in the process of discipline. Sri Aurobindo recommends emphasis upon individual difference without any hammering of the child. He believes that, "Everyone has in him something divine, something his own, a chance of perfection and strength in however small a sphere which God offers him to take or refuse. The task is to find it, develop it and use it".[75]

Finally, discipline is ultimately spiritual. This requires psychic realisation. Sri Aurobindo suggests the following two ways for converting mental seeking into living spiritual experience".[76]

1. The concentration of the consciousness within especially in the main centres—in the heart (the cardiac centre in the middle of the chest) and the head.
2. To accord the nature—physical, vital and mental with the inner realisation so that one may not be divided into two discordant parts.

Among the several ways to accord the nature with the inner realisation, the following two have been particularly emphasised by Sri Aurobindo:

74. *Sri Aurobindo and the Mother on Education*, Part II, p. 27.
75. Sri Aurobindo, B.C.L., 1972, Volume, 17, p. 204.
76. Ibid., *Volume* 23, pp. 517-19.

1. To offer all the activities to the divine and call for the inner guidance—the inward soul is being opened, the psychic being comes for help, gradually the imperfections are being removed and the physical consciousness is being reshaped.
2. To stand back detached from the movements of the physical, vital and mental being—becoming aware of the inner opening of body, life and mind in the psychic entity.

Discipline and Freedom

From the above discussion, it is clear that according to Sri Aurobindo, freedom is the real discipline. This, however, is only spiritual freedom. In the realm of Spirit there is no chasm between discipline and freedom. Each one has to grow and expand according to his own principle. The inner voice in every educand is in fact the divine principle in him. Thus realisation of freedom is God realisation. As order is the prelude to liberty, similarly discipline is a precondition for realisation of freedom.

Code of Conduct

This, however, does not mean that there is no code of conduct at The Mother's International School or at Sri Aurobindo's International University. As the principal guide of both these institutions the Mother has laid down code of conduct for the educands. She is against any outward limitation of the child's liberty but she insists that once the choice for joining the above mentioned institutions has been made, there is no turning aside. She is against any use of compulsion or obligation. She however insists upon taking judgement and following them. She advises the educands to arrive at rational decisions and to follow them. She maintains that the class discipline must be followed. In her own words, "But if a student has decided to follow a class, it is an absolutely elementary discipline for him to follow it, he must go to the class regularly and behave decently there: otherwise he is quite unfit to go to school".[77] She was against any illusions about the abilities of the educands. She warned, "Do not mistake liberty for licence and freedom for bad manners. The thought must be pure and the aspiration ardent".[78] She laid down the following code of behaviour for the students:

1. The good manners should be always observed.
2. Everyone should always speak the truth.
3. Truth in speech demands truth in acts too.
4. It is forbidden for children to fight at school, in the street, in the playground and at home. "Always and everywhere it is forbidden for children to fight among themselves, for each time one gives a blow to someone, it is to one's own soul that one gives it."[79]
5. The child should always remember:
   The necessity of an absolute sincerity.
   The certitude of Truth's final victory.
   The possibility of constant progress with the will to achieve.[80]

---

77. *Sri Aurobindo and The Mother on Education,* Part III, p. 20.
78. *Ibid.,* p. 22.
79. *Ibid.,* p. 27.
80. *Sri Aurobindo and the Mother on Education,* Part III, p. 22.

EVALUATION AND EXAMINATION

Rejecting the so-called mental tests, the Mother said, "I find tests an obsolete and ineffective way of knowing if the students are intelligent, willing and attentive. A silly, mechanical mind can very well answer a test if the memory is good and these are certainly not the qualities required for a man of the future".[81] She not only rejects the mental test but also suggests alternatives. "To know if a student is good, needs, if the tests are abolished, a little more inner contact and psychological knowledge for the teacher. But our teachers are expected to do yoga, so this ought not to be difficult for them."[82]

Spontaneous Evaluation

In two words, the method of evaluation in Sri Aurobindo's system of education, may be called spontaneous evaluation. This depends upon the inner contact, keen observation and impartial outlook of the evaluator. The tests of progress are not the essay type examinations. In the words of Sri Aurobindo, "We must direct our school and university examinations to the testing of these active faculties and not of the memory".[83] Criticising the prevalent system of education conducted by the British in India, Sri Aurobindo pointed out that in it the students do not achieve the real purpose of education. He was against education only for earning livelihood. According to him the students are, "To learn in order to know, to study in order to have the knowledge of the secrets of nature and of life, to educate oneself in order to increase one's consciousness, to discipline oneself in order to be master of oneself, to overcome one's weakness, one's incapacity and ignorance, to prepare oneself in order to progress in life towards a goal that is nobler and vaster, more generous and more true...".[84]

To meet the above purpose, Sri Aurobindo's International Centre of Education, Pondicherry, has evolved "Free Progress System," based upon subjective evaluation by the teachers. Progress records ware to be filled by the students while the teacher has to note their comments. Clarifying this system of evaluation, the Mother told the teachers, "At the end of the year you will give notes to the students, not based on written test-papers, but on their behaviour, their concentration, their regularity, their promptness to understand and their openness of intelligence".[85]

Our discussion of the philosophy of education, as given by Sri Aurobindo, clearly points out that this is a new experiment in education. Its philosophical foundations and psychological credibility is sound. Its success, however, requires a large band of devoted, sincere and spiritual teachers, prepared to carry on the burden of education against all odds. So long as such a band is not available it is just an experiment.

81. *Ibid.*, Part, II, p. 30.
82. *Ibid.*, p. 31.
83. *Ibid.*
84. *Ibid.*
85. *Ibid.*

20

CONCLUDING REMARKS

In concluding our discussion of Western and Indian philosophies of education. We are summarising important identical trends with in East and West. This will help in arriving at a synthesis of Eastern and Western approaches in the field of philosophy of education.

IDEALISM

According to Adams, "Idealism in one form or other permeates the whole of the history of philosophy."[1] This is particularly true in the case of Indian philosophy of education. Explaining the idealist philosophy of education, Rusk said. "It bestows dignity and grandeur upon human life by emphasising the distinctiveness of man's nature, attributing to him powers, not possessed by animals, which issue in ideal-logical and aesthetic; it admits the existence of a Supreme Being; by its respect for human personality it provides the basis for democracy."[2]

All the notable Indian philosophers of education followed Neo-Vedanta philosophy, a contemporary version of ancient Indian idealism. Therefore they presented a teleological explanation of the world with harmony between man and Nature. They provided central place to man in the universe and presented axiological explanation of the world enigma. According to them, ideas and ideals are the acme of education. This idealist trend however, was not opposed to realism, positivism and pragmatism. Therefore a synthesis between all these is possible.

REALISM

The philosophy of realism in almost opposed to that of idealism. According to the realists the world is material in nature. The object and its qualities exist outside the mind and without any necessary relation with it. Thus realist metaphysics is materialism. Its epistemology is positivism and axiology pragmatism. In contemporary Indian philosophy of education one finds a meeting of the extremes of idealism and realism, due to their eclectic and integral approach to thought and life. This meeting of extremes may be found in the educational philosophy of Vivekananda, Dayananda, Sri Aurobindo, Rabindranath Tagore, Gandhi and

1. Adams J., *The Evolution of Educational Theory*, p. 28.
2. Rusk, R.R., *The Philosophical Bases of Education*, p. 154.

Radhakrishanan. In the aims and ideals of education they were idealists while their detailed plans of education were based upon realism and pragmatism.

PRAGMATISM

Pragmatism believes that man's first concern is to make this world worthy of human life. Pragmatism is this-worldly. It is against all other-worldly goals. It is pluralistic. It is utilitarian. It lays emphasis upon change as a necessary element of life. It is individualist though emphasising the social aspect of man. It is humanist and experimentalist. In the field of education, the pragmatist trend has led emphasis upon economic, cultural and ethical progress of the individuals so that they may develop characters of world-critizens. This is a sound basis for the creation of a better world in future. Programmes and schemes for social service at different stages of education find an important place in educational institutions today. From time to time, the boys and girls, render social service to the community outside the educational institutions so that they may develop a habit of genuine altruism and social service based upon the value of equality of all human beings.

Contemporary Indian philosophy of education had to be pragmatist since its avowed aim was to present a national system of education suitable for a free country. Contemporary Indian philosophers were very much conversant with the socio-economic problems of Indian masses, their poverty and illiteracy. Therefore, while drawing the details of their schemes of education they everywhere paid attention to making education a means of livelihood while being a means of integral development of human personality. The pragmatic approach is explicit in the advice of Vivekananda to the students to care more for body building than even spiritual development. M.K. Gandhi's scheme of basic education was everywhere guided by pragmatic spirit.

ECLECTICISM

Indian philosophers of education have looked to human personality from an eclectic perspective to discover the inner kernal which is often missed by social sciences. They emphasise the spiritual aspect of man as an integrating principle which alone can boost his future evolution. It is because of an eclectic theory of human nature that Sri Aurobindo, Radhakrishnan, Tagore, and Gandhi advocated an eclectic scheme of education including physical, moral and religious education. "The aim and principles of a true national education." said Sri Aurobindo, "is not certainly to ignore modern truth and knowledge but to take our foundations on our belief, our mind, our own spirit."[3]

Thus contemporary Indian philosophy of education has been characterised by eclecticism. This is because most of its spokesmen, including Aurobindo, Radhakrishnan, Vivekananda, Gandhi and Tagore had a wide and deep knowledge of western science, art, literature and culture and a first hand contact with the West. It is hence that they could compare Eastern thought with Western and reach at an eclectic viewpoint. Thus one finds a meeting of idealism and realism, ancient

3. Sri Aurobindo, *The Life Divine*, Vol. II, p. 726

Indian ideals and modern western principles, nationalism and internationalism, individualism and socialism in their writings. They drew their inspiration from ancient scriptures, Upanishads and Gita.

NATIONALISM

The most powerful expression of the nationalist tendency in education among contemporary Indian thinkers may be found in the educational theory of Swami Vivekananda and Sri Aurobindo. Both these thinkers called patriotism the highest religion. They almost worshiped their motherland. Their reformist schemes in education were inspired by love of the fellow countrymen. They asked the students to work hard and live for the country.

This nationalism however, was spiritual nationalism and therefore was in tune with internationalism. It is what Sri Aurobindo called 'Subjective Nationalism'. Therefore it was free from all the defects of aggressive nationalism seen in the West. In fact it was based upon the ancient Indian ideal of *Swadharma.* According to this ideal, everywhere, in man, nation and humanity the ideal is to follow the *Swadharma.* The humanity it self has a *Swadharma* accordihg to its nature. The idea of *Swadharma* includes respect for the other's *dharmamd* the understanding that for everyone his own *dharma* is the best.

HUMANISM

The most important trend in contemporary philosophy of education is humanism. The English word 'humanism' has been derived from the Latin term 'Homo' which means human being. Thus literally speaking, humanism is the philosophy in which man occupies a central place. In historical evolution, whatever has been found to be useful for human welfare has been attached to the concept of humanism such as the idea of social welfare, scientific attitude, progress of democratic institutions, etc. Like the West, humanism was born in India in ancient thought of the Upanishads. These Upanishads show humanistic trends. The metaphysical postulates in Bhagwad Gita are the same as found in the Upanishads. Indian philosophy after the Upanishads and the Gita had been a re-interpretation of the ancient philosophy according to changed circumstances and with difference of emphasis. Not only these orthodox systems but also the heterodox systems as well had their origin in the Upanishads. The contemporary Indian thinkers have developed their thinking on the basis of ancient Upanishadic thought. Thus Sri Aurobindo, Vivekananda, Rabindranath. Gandhi and Dayananda have presented Neo-Vedanta Philosophy according to contemporary conditions in India and in the context of development of thought in the West and East. All these philosophers, with minor differences among them, have maintained what can be called integral humanism, the philosophy of our age which alone supplies the philosophical framework for understanding the problems of education.

The humanist trend in contemporary Indian philosophy of education may be seen in Vivekananda's interpretation of the aim of education as man making. It is clear in Sri Aurobindo's ideal of superman as the aim of future education. It is explicit in Rabindranath Tagore's emphasis upon cosmopolitanism in education. Dayananda considered human welfare as the only ideal of the truth seeker, the teacher and the taught. Similar tendencies may be seen in the educational philosophy of other Indian thinkers.

SYNTHESIS OF RATIONALISM AND INTUITION

Dayananda, Sri Aurobindo, Vivekananda, Rabindranath Tagore and Radhakrishnan follow the ancient tradition according to which aims and ideals, goals and values are intuitive the means are supplied by reason. Swami Dayananda, the great revivalist thinker proposed and adhered to the rationalist principle in the propounding of his famous work *Satyartha Prakash.* He promised that he will not accept anything which is not supported by reason. In Indian, the fields of intuition and reason have been clearly defined and none of the two has been allowed to transgress another's field. Thus, in the field of educational values, for example, intuition is the primary means while reason has to follow the dictates of intuition. Contrary to the western rationalism which makes reason a slave of passions, the Indian thinkers make it subordinate to intuition and always superior to passions. The primary function of reason has been to control the infra-rational passions and tendencies. Upto the mental level reason is the highest law but as one rises above mind reason has to bow its head and acquiesce. Thus the rationalist trend in contemporary Indian philosophy of education is a part of the fundamental integral approach. In the educational philosophy of J.L. Nehru and M.N. Roy, of course, one finds a tendency towards western type of rationalism, but at places they have also agreed about the value of intuition and other sources of human knowledge.

INTEGRALISM

Contemporary Indian philosophers of education Sir Aurobindo, Vivekananda, Rabindranath, Gandhi and Dayananda depict an integral approach in philosophy. "The work of philosophy," says Sri Aurobindo, "is to arrange the data given by the various means of knowledge, excluding none, and put them into a synthetic relation to one truth, the one supreme and universal reality."[4] Thus, these philosophers believe in a monistic, idealistic and integral philosophy. There is one spirit underlying matter, life and mind in the world. This spirit is the reality while man, nature and God are its triple manifestation. In the words of Radhakrishnan, "It is the basis and background of our being, the universality that cannot be reduced to this or that formula."[5] This spirit evolves in the form of the universe. This evolution is not linear, dialectical or emergent but spiral. To quote Bhagwan Das, "The words 'evolution' and 'involution' embody, with instinctive correctness, the idea that these processes are forth and back, circling and cycling in a spiral."[6]

To realise this spirit Indian philosophers have utilised intuitive method. This is spiritual intuition, distinct from physical, mental or vital intuitions. According

4. Aurobindo, S., *The Renaissance in India*, p. 72
5. Radhakrishnan, S., *An Idealist View of Life*, p. 205
6. Bhagwan Das, *The science of the self* p. 44.

to Bhagwan Das, "It is the immediate condition or rather awareness of the self by the self, eternal self-consciousness."[7] In the words of Radhakrishnan, "The deepest things of life are known only through intuitive apprehension."[8] Thus contemporary Indian philosophers have advocated the use of intuitive method in order to arrive at an integral philosophy of education.

Contemporary Indian philosophers have looked to human personality from an integral perspective. They have maintained an integral theory of human nature. It is because of this that Sri Aurobindo, Vivekananda, Rabindranath, Gandhi and Dayananda have advocated a multisided scheme of education including education for physical mental social, moral and religious development of the male and female. To formulate such a scheme of education, these philosophers borrowed both from ancient Indian wisdom and modern western scientific knowledge. This was the basis of the international universities founded by Rabindranath and Sri Aurobindo. In the words of Sri Aurobindo. "The aim and principles of a true national education are not certainly to ignore modern truth and knowledge but to take our foundations on our own belief, our own mind, our own spirit."[9]

7. *Ibid*, p. 137 footnote.
8. Radhakrishnan, S., *An Idealist View of Life.*, p. 142
9. Aurobindo, S., *Integral Education*, compiled by Dr. Indrasen, p. 4.

QUESTION BANK

PHILOSOPHY OF EDUCATION

Q. 1. Why should a teacher study educational philosophy? Would not educational psychology do?

Or

Discuss whether there is a need for a philosophy of education over and above a science of education.

Q. 2. Discuss and elucidate, "All educational questions are ultimately questions of philosophy" —Ross.

Or

"Education is the dynamic side of philosophy." Discuss.

Or

"Education may be regarded as the practical side of philosophy and philosophy as the intellectual aspect of education." How far do you agree with this statement? Give reasons.

Or

'Both philosophy and education go hand in hand. Education depends on philosophy for its guidance and philosophy depends on education for its own formulation." Discuss.

Q. 3. What is Philosophy of Education? Discuss its scope and nature.

Q. 4. Point out the fields of Education in which a teacher needs philosophy.

Q. 5. Discuss the Methodology of Philosophy of Education.

Q. 6. Explain the need of Philosophy of Education in Modern Times.

Q 7. "Idealism in one form or another permeates the history of education the world over." Discuss and explain important characteristics of idealism.

Q. 8. Discuss idealist aims and ideals in education.

Q. 9. Write short note on Idealist Curriculum.

Q. 10. What is the role of an educator according to idealism? Explain idealist educational methods.

Q. 11. Write short note on Idealist Concept of Discipline.

Q. 12. Point out the influence of Idealism in the contemporary field of education. Show the disadvantages of Idealism.

Q. 13. Trace the history of Naturalism in education. Point out its philosophical presuppositions and philosophical forms.

Q. 14. Write short note on Naturalist Educational Methods.

Q. 15. What is the role of a teacher according to Naturalism? Discuss its concept of discipline and school organization.

Q. 16. Analyze the contribution of Naturalism to education. What criticisms have been levelled against it?

Q. 17. Explain the fundamental principles and forms of Pragmatism.

Q. 18. Evaluate the contribution of Pragmatism to education.

Q. 19. Explain the aim of education and principle of curriculum according to Pragmatism.

Q. 20. What is the role of education according to Pragmatism? Explain pragmatic educational methods and discipline.

Q. 21. Write a short note on Criticism against Pragmatism.

Q. 22. Discuss Realist Philosophy of Education.

Q. 23. Discuss educational implication of Logical positivism. Assess its contribution to philosophy of education.

Q. 24. What is Existentialism? What are its chief characteristics? Explain Existential philosophy of education.

Q. 25. What is Humanism? What are its essentials? Discuss its contribution to education.

Q. 26. Discuss Rousseau's contribution to Naturalist philosophy of education.

Q. 27. Write an essay on John Dewey's philosophy of education.

Q. 28. What criticisms have been levelled against Dewey's philosophy of education? Discuss his influence on modern education.

Q. 29. Discuss Bertrand Russell's philosophy of education.

Q. 30. Write short note on Vedic philosophy of education.

Q. 31. Explain the role and influence of teacher in Vedic philosophy of education.

Q. 32. How has Buddhism continued Brahmanical tradition in education? How does Buddhist philosophy of education differ from it? Summarize Buddhist contribution to education.

Q. 33. Discuss the condition of education under Muslim Rulers.

Q. 34. Discuss Dayananda's contribution to education.

Q. 35. Explain Annie Besant's philosophy of education and assess her contribution in education.

Q. 36. Critically discuss the Aims and Ideals of Gandhi's philosophy of education.

Q. 37. Write an essay on M.K. Gandhi's Education for Sarvodaya.

Q. 38. Discuss the characteristics of Gandhiji's educational plan. Give a critical evaluation.

Q. 39. Examine Rabindra Nath Tagore's philosophy of education and its influence on Indian education.

Or

Explain the philosophical thinking behind Tagore's scheme of education in Shanti Niketan. How has its character changed now? Why?

Q. 40. Discuss the aims of education according to R.N. Tagore.

Q. 41. How has Vivekananda criticised prevalent system of education? Discuss aims of education according to him.

Q. 42. Discuss the means, types and medium of education according to Vivekananda.

Q. 43. Discuss teaching methods in various types of education according to Vivekananda.

Q. 44. Discuss the nature of education envisaged by Sri Aurobindo.

Q. 45. Write a short note on Principles of Sri Aurobindo's New Education.

Q. 46. Explain Sri Aurobindo's concept of the School and the Teacher.

Q. 47. Discuss Sri Aurobindo's criteria for planning curricula. Give a tentative eudcational plan.

Q. 48. Describe Sri Aurobindo's methods and principles of teaching.

Q. 49. Elaborate the various elements of Integral Teaching according to Sri Aurobindo.

Q. 50. What are the characteristics of Socialism? Give the outline of an educational programme for realizing the objectives of Socialism.

Q. 51. What is Fascism? Explain how political ideologies influence educational aims, curriculum and methods with reference to Fascist approach.

Q. 52. What is Marxism? How has it influenced educational theory and practice?

Q. 53. Explain Secularism. Does it go against religious ideas in schools? Justify your answer.

Or

"Secularism acquaints the child with the basic principles of human values," Explain this statement.

Or

Define Secularism. Identify the characteristics of secular education.

Give a plan for secular education in India pointing out the difficulties in it.